THE HISTORY

OF THE

2/6th (RIFLE) BATTALION "THE KING'S"
(LIVERPOOL REGIMENT)
1914–1919

LIEUT.-COL. W. A. L. FLETCHER, D.S.O.

THE HISTORY

of the

2/6th (Rifle) Battalion "The King's" (Liverpool Regiment)

1914–1919

BY

Capt. C. E. WURTZBURG, M.C.

Adjutant, Nov. 1916–Nov. 1918

With a Foreword by

Major-General Sir R. W. R. BARNES, K.C.B., D.S.O.

Late G.O.C. 57th (West Lancs.) Division

To the Memory

OF

LIEUT.-COL. W. A. L. FLETCHER, D.S.O.

THE OFFICERS
WARRANT OFFICERS
NON-COMMISSIONED OFFICERS

AND

RIFLEMEN
WHO LAID DOWN THEIR LIVES
FOR THEIR
COUNTRY

———

Not fearing death, nor shrinking for distress,
But always resolute in most extremes.

FOREWORD

As I had the honour of commanding the 57th (West Lancashire) Division during the greater part of the time that the Division was fighting in France and Flanders in the Great War, included in which Division was the 2/6th Battalion " The King's " (Liverpool Regiment), I am very glad that the Author has given me the opportunity of recording in print my appreciation of the gallant and soldierly conduct of this fine battalion whilst under my command.

Captain Wurtzburg's work in writing this history of the battalion in which he served is, I am sure, of great value : to the survivors of the battalion, as a record of their achievements ; to the relatives of the fallen, as showing that their sacrifice was not in vain ; and to the historians of the future, who will obtain inspiration as to the realities of war from the experiences of this fighting unit.

The 2/6th " The King's " (Liverpool Regiment) took part with distinction in all the fighting of the Division from February, 1917, up to the Armistice. The battalion showed its offensive spirit in the third battle of Ypres, the breaking of the Drocourt— Quéant switch of the Hindenburg Line, the battle of Cambrai, and the capture of Lille ; and its steadiness in defence during the long periods of trench warfare, and especially in the terrible gas bombardment of Armentières.

The battalion was always to be depended upon, and its fine " tone " was, I think, largely owing to that good Commanding Officer and sportsman, the late Lieutenant-Colonel W. A. L. Fletcher, who imbued his battalion with his own personality, and than whom no man in the war more truly gave his life for his country.

In these present difficult times of peace we are all, I think, inclined to forget the great lesson of the war—that it is only by "comradeship" we can overcome these difficulties; and the records of the 2/6th "The King's" (Liverpool Regiment) should help to remind us that this battalion gained its name and achieved its object by the equal and united efforts of its Officers, Non-Commissioned Officers, and Riflemen.

Personally, I feel I cannot end these few lines without expressing my intense gratitude to all my old comrades of the battalion.

R. W. R. BARNES,
Major-General.

LIVERPOOL,
July, 1920.

PREFACE

SHORTLY after the Armistice Colonel Fletcher wrote to me asking if I would undertake to write a history of the battalion. All through the war I had cherished a vague idea of doing something of the kind, and with this view had devoted considerable care to the War Diary and to the preservation of other records. I was, therefore, only too pleased to accede to my old Commanding Officer's request, though I felt that I should experience—as, indeed, I have done—some considerable difficulty in dealing with periods during which I was away from the battalion. These cover the time from January, 1915, to March, 1916; the action of the battalion in the third battle of Ypres; and the major portion of the second battle of Cambrai, for which I have had to rely on information which has been readily supplied by those who were present.

The work of compilation has, I must admit, been arduous to a degree, and an active business life has necessitated the whole work being written in my evenings and at week-ends. To this fact, I think, the unevenness of the book may fairly be attributed, written as it had to be at odd times, bit by bit, and in the varying states of mind in which I found myself after my day's work at the office. It has, however, been a labour of love, and if the book does in any way fulfil the objects for which I mainly wrote it—first, to perpetuate the memory of our gallant comrades who laid down their lives for their country; and, secondly, to aid those who survived to recall to their recollection our days of service, and to hand down to their descendants some written record of their lives during those great years—I shall feel that my labours have been amply repaid.

I have received so much assistance in the preparation of the book that I am afraid it is impossible to make any adequate individual acknowledgments of my debt. My thanks, however, are particularly due to the following :—For continuous advice and valuable suggestions, to C. W. Wilson, J. L. Heyworth, T. Sutherland, and A. L. Reade (whose diary, placed freely at my disposal, has proved invaluable) ; for contributions, to R. Barker, N. L. and W. A. Corkill, W. M. Ewan, E. A. Garrod, H. M. Griffiths, J. K. Harris, J. L. Henderson, J. B. Herbert, F. C. Hildred, F. Hooper, V. J. Kneen, G. L. Lane, J. Longridge, R. E. Noon, J. Payne, W. Penrice, K. V. Stevenson, H. Taggart, C. W. Walter, and T. A. Williams ; for compilation of addresses, to J. McCoy ; for map work, to A. S. Brown and J. T. Hazell ; for photographs and drawings (the reproduction of which, on grounds of economy, had drastically to be curtailed), to W. T. Barrow, J. Beavan, W. A. Belk, C. S. Freeman, E. Fryer, T. H. Louden, F. V. Smith, and A. E. Williams ; and for unfailing courtesy and ready assistance, to the War Office and No. 1 Infantry Record Office, Preston.

To my father, E. A. Wurtzburg, I owe a great debt for assistance of every description, the value of which I cannot adequately express. He has, further, revised all the proofs.

I should also like to record the help rendered by my publishers, Messrs. Gale & Polden, Ltd. ; throughout the long period that has elapsed since the work was first commenced their interest and assistance have never flagged.

In conclusion, I must add that financial responsibility for the production of the book was generously accepted by a small body of gentlemen who shall be nameless, but in the absence of whom it is certain that the work could never have been undertaken.

C. E. W.

3, LAWN ROAD,
  HAMPSTEAD, N.W. 3.
    August, 1920.

CONTENTS

APPENDICES

ILLUSTRATIONS

MAPS

Battalion Cap Badge, Title, and Distinguishing Patch

Photo by

THE BATTALION, WO

KING, FEBRUARY, 1917.

Gale & Polden, Ltd., Aldershot.

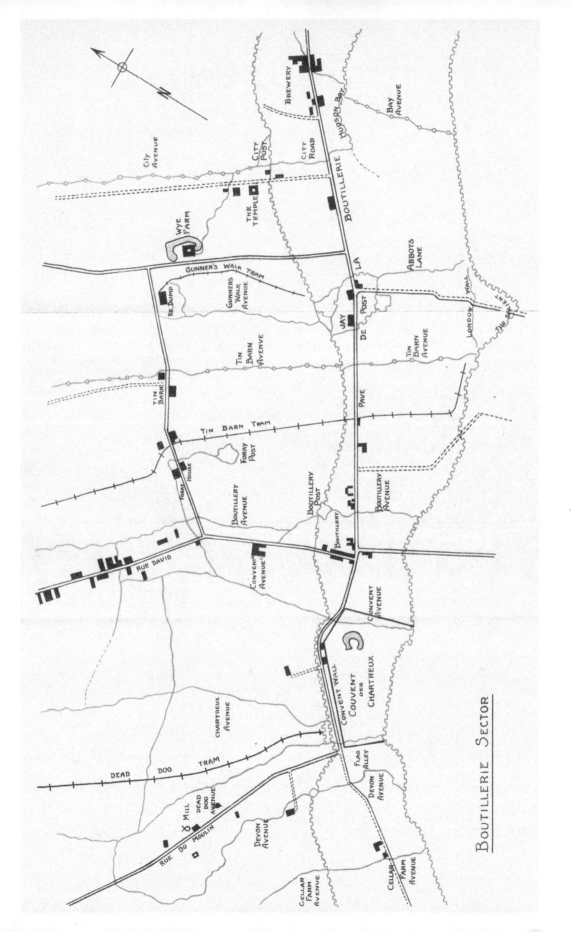

BOUTILLERIE SECTOR

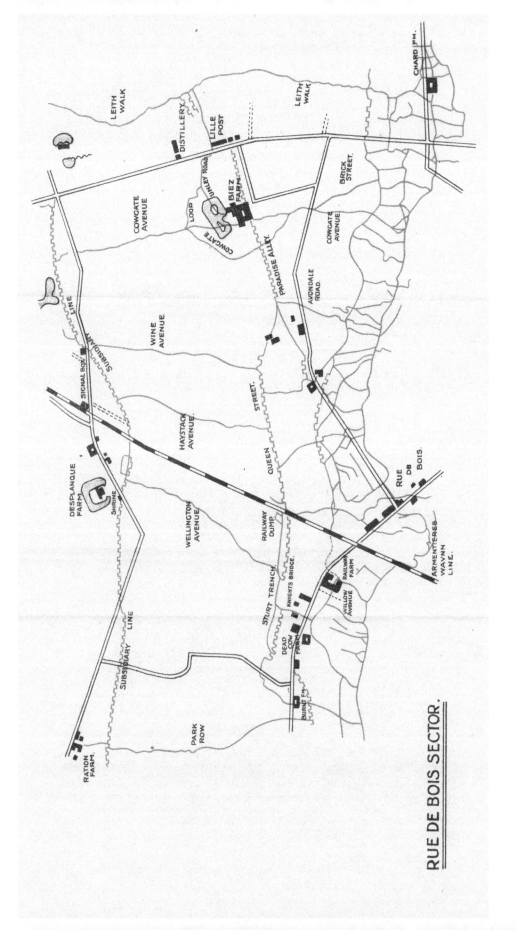

RUE DE BOIS SECTOR.

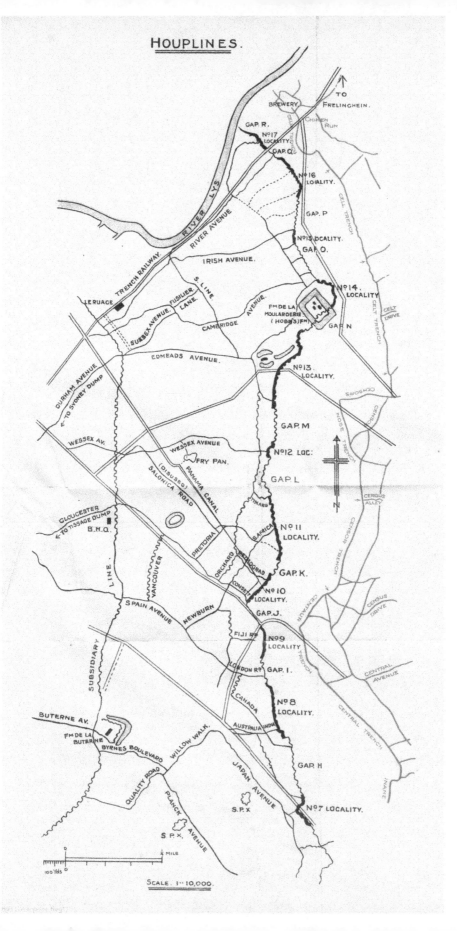

HOUPLINES.

PONT BALLOT SALIENT HOUPLINES.
AREA RAIDED 21·6·17.

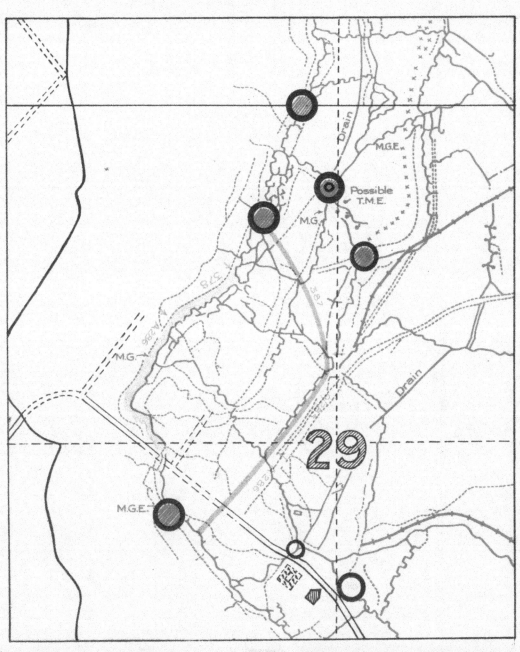

SCALE : $\frac{1}{5000}$

18 PR. ZERO TO ZERO + 2 MIN:
How.

18 PR. HOW.

L.T.M.B.

M.T.M.B.

I.M.9.8.

Sheet. 36. N.W. 2.

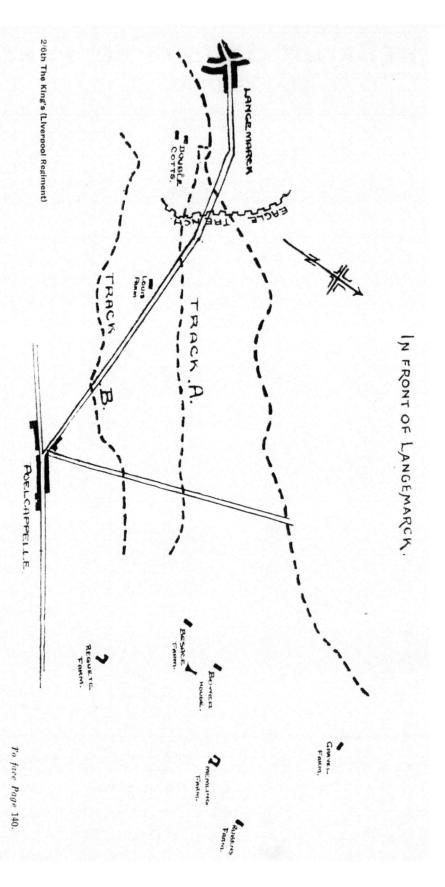

IN FRONT OF LANGEMARCK.

LANGEMARCK

DOUBLE COTTS.

EAGLE TRENCH

LOUIS FARM

TRACK A.

TRACK B.

POELCAPPELLE

BESACE FARM.

BOWER HOUSE.

REQUETE FARM.

MEALING FARM.

GRAVEL FARM.

RUBENS FARM.

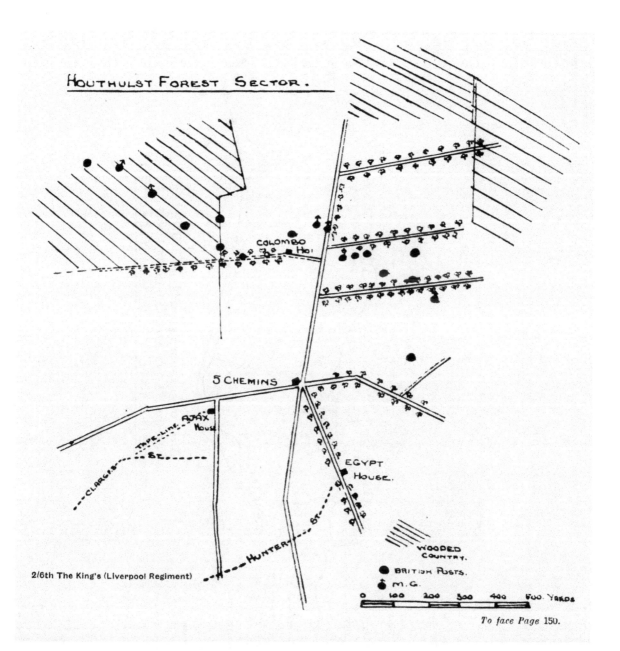

HOUTHULST FOREST SECTOR.

COLOMBO HO!

5 CHEMINS

AJAX HOUSE

TAPE-LINE

CLARGES ST.

EGYPT HOUSE.

HUNTER ST.

2/6th The King's (Liverpool Regiment)

WOODED COUNTRY.

● BRITISH POSTS.

M.G.

0   100   200   300   400   500 YARDS

To face Page 150.

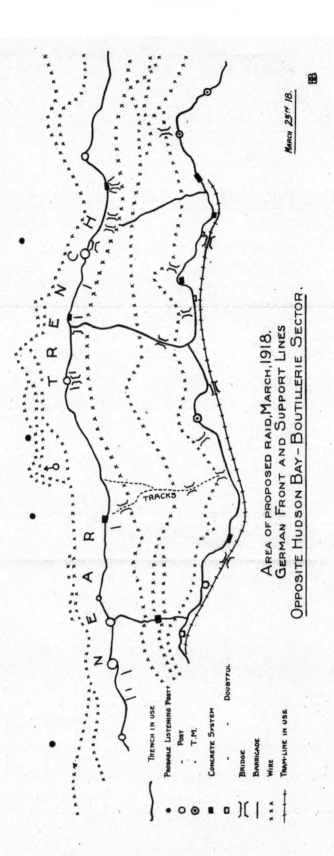

HUDSON BAY

BAY AVENUE

BORROW DITCH
VERY NARROW IN FRONT OF FRONT LINE
BUT BROAD · · · SUPPORT LINE

MARCH 25th 18.

TRACKS

AREA OF PROPOSED RAID, MARCH, 1918.
GERMAN FRONT AND SUPPORT LINES
OPPOSITE HUDSON BAY – BOUTILLERIE SECTOR.

TRENCH IN USE
PROBABLE LISTENING POST+
POST
T.M.
CONCRETE SYSTEM
DOUBTFUL
BRIDGE
BARRICADE
WIRE
TRAM-LINE IN USE

% The King's (Liverpool Regt)

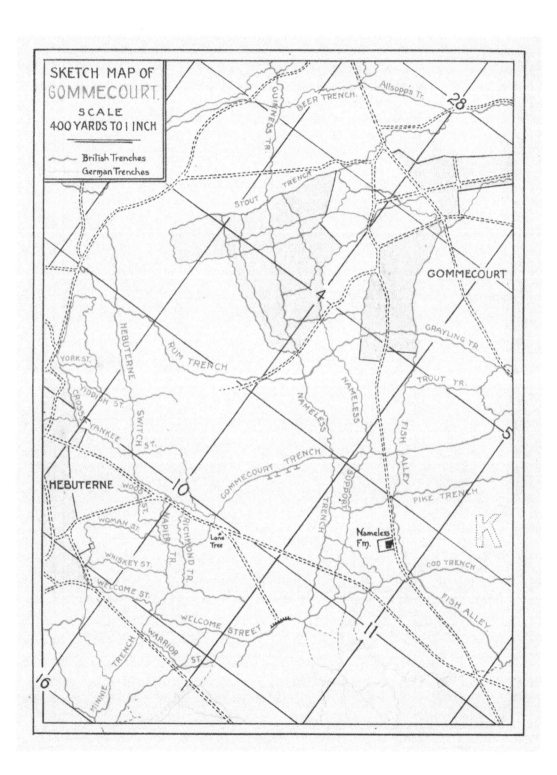

SKETCH MAP OF
GOMMECOURT.
SCALE
400 YARDS TO 1 INCH

British Trenches
German Trenches

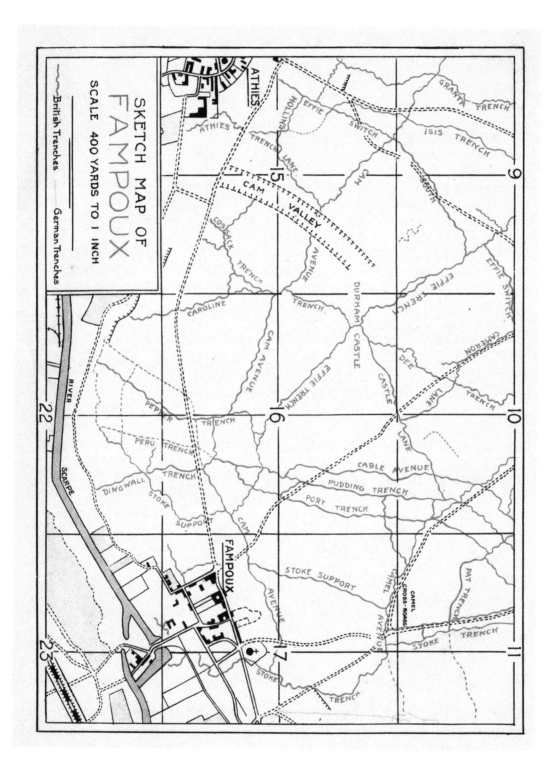

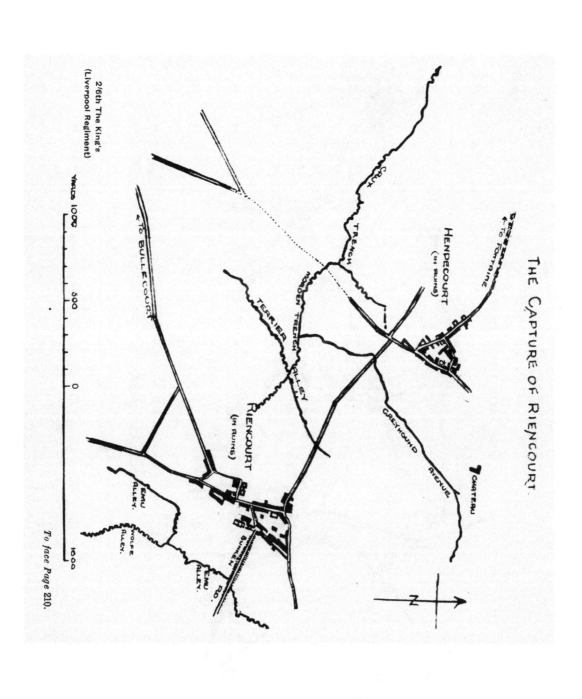

THE CAPTURE OF RIENCOURT.

HENDECOURT
(IN RUINS)

→ TO FONTAINE

CROIX
TRENCH

NORDEN TRENCH

TERRIER ALLEY

RIENCOURT
(IN RUINS)

GREYHOUND AVENUE

→ CHATEAU

← TO BULLECOURT

EMU ALLEY.

WOLFE ALLEY.

EMU ALLEY.

SUNKEN RD.

N

2/6th The King's
(Liverpool Regiment)

YARDS 1000   500   0   1000

To face Page 210.

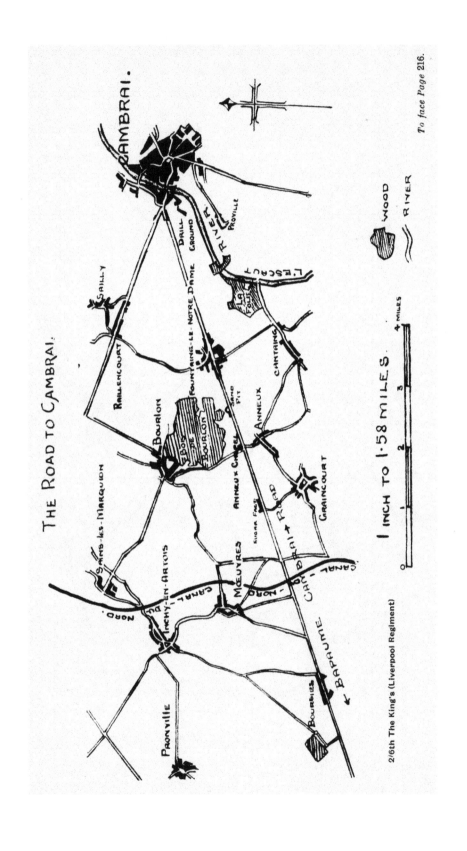

THE ROAD TO CAMBRAI.

1 INCH TO 1·58 MILES.

CAMBRAI.

WOOD
RIVER

To face Page 216.

2/6th The King's (Liverpool Regiment)

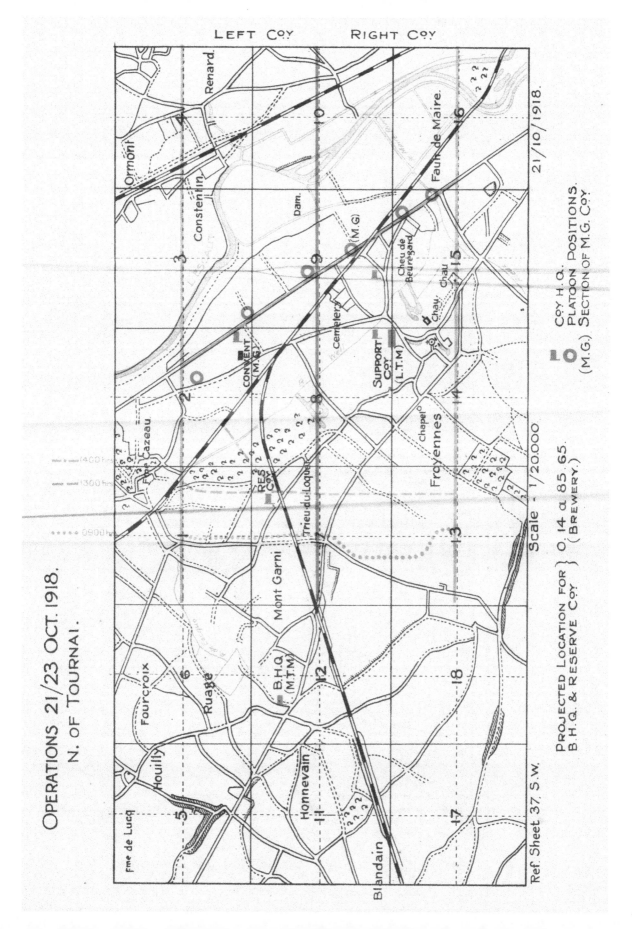

OPERATIONS 21/23 OCT. 1918.
N. OF TOURNAI.

LEFT COY   RIGHT COY

21/10/1918.

Scale - 1/20.000.

Ref: Sheet 37. S.W.

⊙ COY H.Q.
○ PLATOON POSITIONS.
■ SECTION OF M.G. COY.
(M.G.)

PROJECTED LOCATION FOR } O. 14 a 85. 65.
B.H.Q. & RESERVE COY } (BREWERY.)

HAZEBROUCK

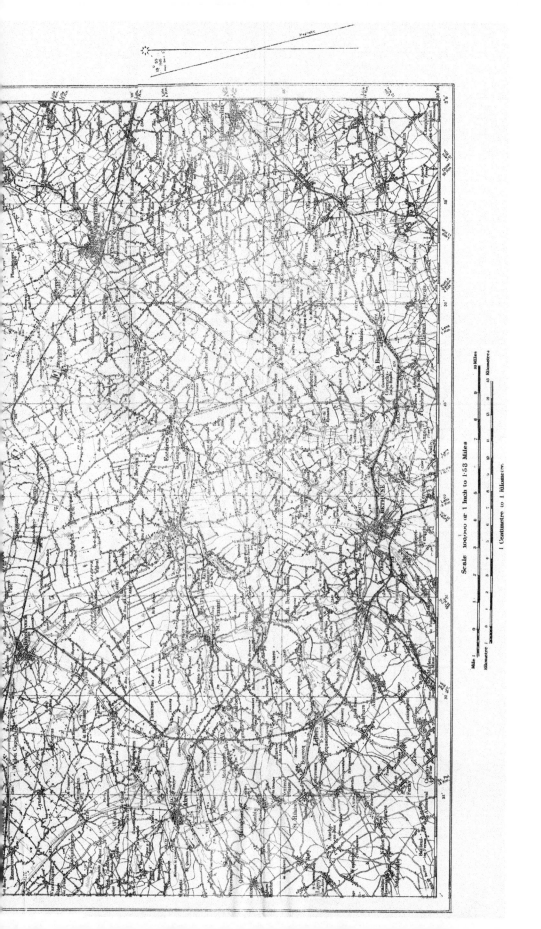

Scale 100/000 or 1 Inch to 1·58 Miles

Mile 1

Kilometre 1

1 Centimetre to 1 Kilometre.

LENS

Mile 1. 0 1 2 3 4 5 6 7 8 9 10 Miles

Scale 100,000 or 1 Inch to 1·58 Miles

Kilometre 1. 0 1 2 3 4 5 6 7 8 9 10 11 12 13 14 15 Kilometres

1 Centimetre to 1 Kilometre.

Magnetic

ARRAS

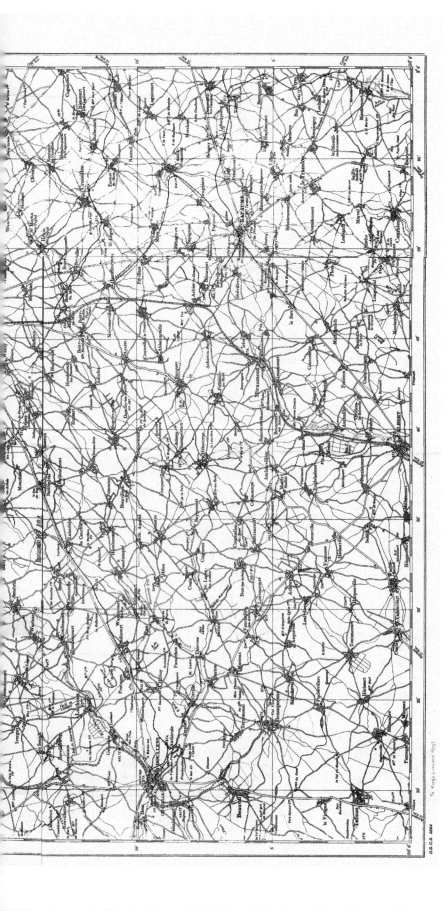

— CAMBRAI AREA —

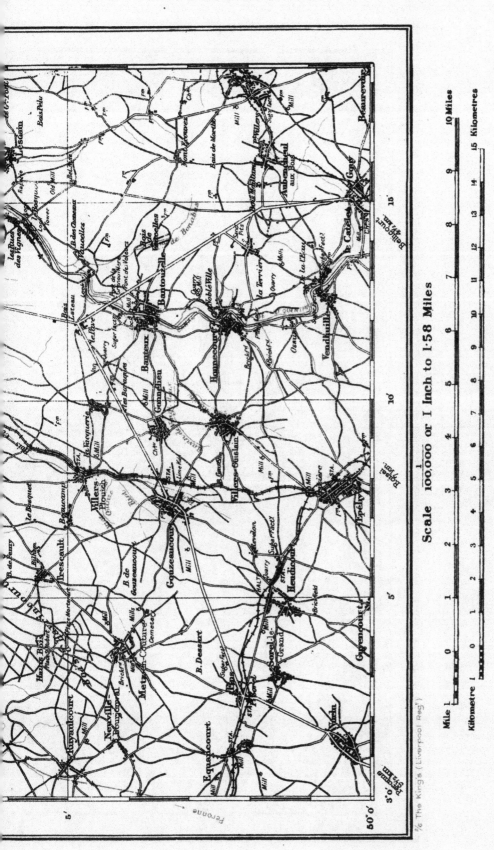

Scale $\frac{1}{100,000}$ or 1 Inch to 1·58 Miles

1 Centimetre to 1 Kilometre

Mile 1   0   1   2   3   4   5   6   7   8   9   10 Miles

Kilometre 1   0   1   2   3   4   5   6   7   8   9   10   11   12   13   14   15 Kilometres

– LILLE AND TOURNAI –

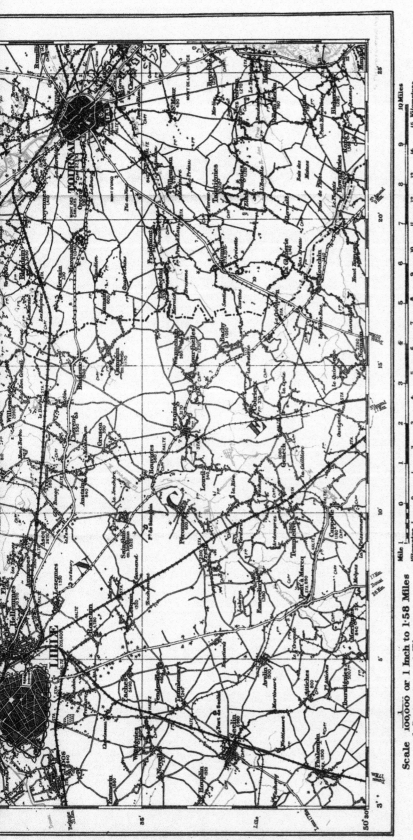

Scale 100,000 or 1 Inch to 1·58 Miles
1 Centimetre to 1 Kilometre

THE HISTORY

OF THE

2/6th (Rifle) Bn. "THE KING'S" (Liverpool Regiment)

CHAPTER I

FORMATION OF THE BATTALION—THE DEPOT—BLACKPOOL—CANTERBURY—MARGATE—UPSTREET CAMP—CANTERBURY—GORE STREET CAMP

OWING to the rush in the early days of the war, when recruits were many and records few, the actual date of the formation of the 2/6th (Rifle) Battalion " The King's " (Liverpool Regiment) is obscure, but from general evidence we can assume the date to have been September 10th, 1914. Certain it is that recruiting for the Second Line opened on that date.

Before going further it may be worth setting forth the reasons which prompted the War Office to create ours and similar battalions.

The Territorial Force was planned for Home Defence, and presumably it was considered that there would be time and opportunity to train recruits to replace the casualties and normal wastage of war. The wholesale volunteering of battalions for Foreign Service altered the situation completely, and it became necessary to create Reserve Battalions. Their duty was twofold : first, to replace the battalion that went abroad and relieve

B

it of its function as a defensive force ; and, secondly, to supply it with the necessary drafts.

Consequently enlisting for the Reserve Battalion included both men for Home and Foreign Service, and it was not until the following spring that the success of the Territorial Battalions abroad prompted the authorities to go one step further, and make the Second Line Battalions, as they were then called, into Overseas Battalions. To make this possible, Home Service men were transferred to Home Defence units, known as Provisional Battalions, while Third Line Depots were created for training drafts for the battalions on active service.

A clear understanding as to the position is necessary, so that the reason why we remained in England till February, 1917, may be grasped. Owing to the call on us for drafts throughout 1915 and early 1916, our strength was much reduced. The Third Line Depots, however, owing to the falling off in recruiting, were never strong enough to repair the wastage of the First Line Battalion already overseas, much less bring us up to strength. The necessary troops had, therefore, to be raised from broken-up divisions in England, and it was from one of these in 1916 that we were to receive the necessary men to complete our strength. However, the terrible casualties of the Battle of the Somme diverted to France as reinforcements the men that we were to have had (some of them found their way to us in 1917 at St. Hilaire), and we found ourselves with a couple of hundred " Derby men " in their place, with a promise that we should go overseas as soon as these were trained.

However, to return to September, 1914, the early destinies of the Reserve Battalion were placed in the hands of Captain J. Howard Temple, who, with Captain H. K. Wilson and Captain Broad, had been sent back to the Depot from the original 6th Battalion to organize the new unit, and they could not have been placed in better hands. During the first two days about 200 men were enlisted, and the work that devolved on the head

2

of Captain Temple may be better imagined than described. The staff at his disposal were Colour-Sergeants Taggart, Firth, Ramsay, Staff-Sergeant Miller, and Sergeants Blackburn, Cormack, Pender, Lee, and Leask. In addition some budding officers with O.T.C. experience helped to fill the gap, and the work of training and organization proceeded apace, though most of the staff for a considerable period had to sleep and eat at the Depot.

As the numbers increased the men were formed into eight companies, and from the ranks men with some experience were picked out and appointed Acting Lance-Corporals, amongst these being Heyworth, Batson, Higginbottom, H. Lewis, Hockenhull, Hinde, C. E. Peck, Brunner, Pryce, and Beeston.

Those early days are amusing to look back upon. We came daily to the drill-shed for training in every form of costume that can be imagined—some men in everyday clothes of a clerk, some in shooting coats and grey trousers, others in khaki bought at their own expense, and so on. Bowler hats were early discouraged, but except for that there were no restrictions as to dress.

Little by little khaki began to appear and our regulation black puttees, though the regimental " walking out " uniforms had for some time to be used as a temporary arrangement, which made us look a motley crowd.

" Bugles " were soon formed, and behind these we marched gaily to the Old Farm Field in Sefton Park for drill, and to Allerton or Arrowe Hall for field days. In those early irresponsible days life proceeded easily ; the " King's Regulations " and the " Manual of Military Law " were volumes unknown except to a very few. Keenness and enthusiasm were the keynotes of our life. Some-one murmured the word " inoculation," and forthwith we trooped in gay crowds to the Medical Officer to undergo that much-discussed but very innocent operation. The 1/6th Battalion wanted men to complete their numbers : the draft could have been made up ten times over. How proudly we marched through the streets of Liverpool! How we envied the New Army Battalions—the

" blue-eyed boys " of the War Office—who called themselves " Regulars," and on whom everything seemed to be lavished. Beyond frequent inspections, we got no serious assistance for two and a half years, and equipment was doled out but sparingly up till the last moment. The reason of this apparent neglect was probably sound and in accordance with policy, but it was none the less heart-breaking at times.

With the beginning of November things began to move apace. Colonel G. A. Wilson, V.D., was appointed Commanding Officer, and to this fact we can attribute the smartness and *esprit de corps* that distinguished the battalion up till the end of its history. The sound principles on which Colonel Wilson proceeded to train his battalion produced the best and most lasting results, and, without wishing in any way to overstep the mark, one may say that few, if any, battalions were brought from the early chaotic state to a well-organized and self-contained machine in such a short time as our own. It was not only, however, in his scheme of training that Colonel Wilson was so successful, but also in his choice of officers. He gathered round him officers of many kinds : not only young and enthusiastic members of School and University O.T.Cs., but older men also—some without military experience, it is true, but with that broader outlook and ability that more mature years bring with them ; others, again, who had much military experience to their credit, and—precious above all —experience of war itself. Of the latter, Captain W. A. L. Fletcher, D.S.O., Captain C. W. Wilson, Captain G. L. Fletcher, and Captain G. P. Rogers had all served with distinction in the Boer War, and, be a war great or be it small, the knowledge that comes from actual shells and bullets is worth the having.

Captain W. A. L. Fletcher, who came as Adjutant, requires further mention. One of the greatest oarsmen Oxford ever produced, a great traveller and big game shot, he represented the very finest type of Englishman, and his presence with the battalion first as Adjutant and later as Commanding Officer, was an asset

4

impossible to estimate. Strong and self-reliant, capable and far-seeing, he had a natural genius for military science, while for personal gallantry the deed that won him the D.S.O. when a subaltern in South Africa was more than sufficient testimony. From the day he joined till the day of his death, in 1919, his thoughts were centred on the success and the welfare of the battalion with the most whole-hearted devotion.

The organization of the battalion into eight companies, which had been roughly sketched out, was now completed, the Commanders being respectively—Captains Wilson, G. L. Fletcher, W. R. Clarke, Rogers, Lawrence, A. T. Miller, Herschell, and Wurtzburg. Colour-Sergeant-Instructor Kelly was appointed regimental sergeant-major provisionally, and Regimental Sergeant-Major Barnett, of the 1/6th "The King's" (Liverpool Regiment), was gazetted Lieutenant and Quartermaster.

Training proceeded on the normal lines of arms drill (with twenty old D.P. rifles circulated in turn), outposts, guards, musketry (including miniature range practice), route marching, and physical training. The foundations were also laid of the scout and signal sections.

On November 4th a draft of 240 men left for Redhill to join the 1/6th Battalion, and a very fine body of men they were. In addition, four officers were dispatched—2nd-Lieutenants G. Hughes, T. E. Rome, E. H. Tyson, and N. B. Ronald. We also received a draft of men in exchange, composed of those too young or unfit for active service, with a sprinkling of those unwilling to undertake foreign service obligations.

On November 10th the battalion proceeded to Blackpool with the remaining reserve units of the Liverpool Regiment, under the command of Colonel Wilson as Acting Brigadier. Captain Broad remained as O.C. Depot. The route to Exchange Station was thronged with people to wish us good-bye and God-speed. The battalion was now entering its first real stage on the road to active service. We arrived at Blackpool to find the sun shining

5

brightly, and all were as cheerful as could be. The men were billeted with subsistence, at a heavy cost, in streets at North Shore, the officers being quartered at Stretton Private Hotel on the front.

Military life now assumed a more stern aspect. Early morning parades on the cold and breezy front, hours of drill on the sands or on the bleak and wind-swept slopes of Norbreck Hill, were somewhat more severe than our easy training at Liverpool. However, we meant to get efficient, and though we worked all day and every day, including Saturday afternoons, with lectures in the evening, life at Blackpool was happy enough, and the local attractions all the more alluring by reason of our hard work and fine condition.

We found ourselves forming, with the Reserve Battalions of the 5th, 7th, and 8th Liverpools, the Reserve Liverpool Infantry Brigade, under the command of Colonel S. H. Harrison, an old " King's " officer—a most courteous and kindly Irishman, and a very keen and enthusiastic soldier. Our Divisional Commander, Brigadier-General F. A. Adam, C.B., lately commanding the British brigade at Malta, had been appointed to command a division ear- marked for immediate service in France, but had most unluckily been injured in an accident while riding. A most capable and efficient soldier he was, and his misfortune was the good fortune of our division.

On November 28th we were inspected by our Brigadier at Singleton Hall, the owner of which kindly lent his grounds for the purpose, and we were complimented on our bearing and steadi- ness. This was our first introduction to the intricacies of the " Manual of Ceremonial."

Christmas leave was our great anxiety at this time, and, after having been at first disappointed, we were at length allowed to go in batches to our homes. From Christmas till the move down south we were actively employed—guards on the pierheads, piquets on the North and South Shores, drill, and, later, musketry with real rifles at Fleetwood. The battalion was now organized into four companies in accordance with " Infantry Training, 1914," which were respectively commanded by Major H. K. Wilson (" A " Company), Captain C. W. Wilson (" D " Company), Captain G. L. Fletcher (" C " Company), and Captain Lawrence (" B " Company). Colour-sergeants were divided into company sergeant-majors and company quartermaster-sergeants to meet the new organization ; and R. Smith was appointed regimental sergeant-major, Kelly being made company sergeant-major of " B " Company.

Many more officers meanwhile had joined—so many, in fact, that we were for a time over strength. Captain Wurtzburg was attached as Acting Staff Officer at Brigade, and was subsequently gazetted as a Brigade Major.

On January 12th a draft of 210 men were dispatched to Canterbury, many N.C.Os. gladly giving up their temporary stripes to join the draft. That was ever the spirit. Two days later General Sir R. Pole Carew, Inspector-General, Territorial Force, inspected us on the South Shore field, and expressed himself much pleased with our steadiness on parade.

Transport, consisting of requisitioned civilian vehicles, had recently arrived, and Lieutenant L. G. May was appointed as Transport Officer. His men were not long in appearing clad in riding breeches and spurs, and lent a slightly military aspect to their antique civilian carts.

Route marching formed a considerable part of the training programme, and on January 20th the battalion marched to Garstang and back, a distance of thirty-three and three-quarter miles. It was congratulated by General Adam on being " so hard and fit that it can perform a long march in such good order." On February 1st a more ambitious scheme of marching to Liverpool and back was entered upon. Rifles had arrived that morning, and were issued on parade, string being provided in lieu of slings. The first day's march was to Preston, where we billeted for the night. The next day it rained steadily, and we were glad enough to reach Ormskirk, where the popular reception was such that the orderly-room was deluged with requests from people asking if they could not entertain at any rate one man. The spirit of Ormskirk was, indeed, conspicuous all along the route, and the arrival on the Exchange flags the next day produced a rousing reception. After breaking away for the rest of the day, the battalion set off for the return march the following day, and completed its 100-mile march in splendid form, only a few men having become casualties, and these because of ill-fitting boots. " Rip," the battalion dog, led by the Commanding Officer's groom, attracted no little attention during the march.

Forms of recreation at Blackpool were manifold, the town going out of its way to entertain the troops. The Salford Harriers put up a military run of seven miles, and this was won by Rifleman J. N. C. Davies in 45 minutes 18 seconds.

On February 8th the battalion moved down to Canterbury to replace the 1/6th Battalion, and at Blackpool we left behind many friends and a high reputation, of which the battalion may well be proud. Captain Lawrence left us at this point, *anno domini* having proved too much even for his dauntless spirit.

At Canterbury we found the band and 170 details of the 1/6th, the former being a great asset under the able direction of Sergeant Hodgson. Billets were different from those at Blackpool. We now had at the most two or three men to a billet, and we also had army rations. However, the " occupiers " were most kindly and made us very welcome, though they were apt to resent the rigorous daily inspection—apparently a novelty to them. Our transport was further augmented by some quaint vehicles and still quainter mules discarded by our predecessors, also one or two pack ponies. The mules were productive of considerable amusement. On March 15th, after this brief stay in Canterbury—due to the congestion of troops—we marched down to Margate, and were given billets in Cliffonville. We were the only battalion of the

8

"THE KING'S" (LIVERPOOL REGIMENT)

Division in Margate, the rest of our Brigade being at Canterbury. That we were popular at Margate, and that Margate was popular with us, need hardly be added. The behaviour of the battalion fully justified the continued and generous attention which we received from the authorities and people of the town.

We had now left the reserve training area of the north, and were in the zone of possible invasion. The First Line Division had gone overseas piecemeal, and their Divisional and Brigade Staffs now took charge of us. Major-General J. B. Forster, C.B., commanded our Division, which was a unit of the Central Force, commanded by General Sir Ian Hamilton ; while our Brigade was commanded by Brigadier-General A. R. Gilbert, D.S.O., with Major Fulton, of the Worcesters, as Brigade Major, and Captain Beazley, of the 1/6th, as Staff Captain.

Soon after our arrival in Margate, Major Temple, to our great regret, left us, being seconded to the Navy for special service, with the rank of Commander. He had been the principal pioneer of our battalion, and had done all that industry and money could do to further our interests. Though detached from us, we are glad to think he followed our movements and furthered our schemes by every means in his power.

We now entered on a series of inspections by many Generals, including Lieutenant-General Hon. Sir Frederick Stopford, Commanding the Second Army, Central Force, in Dane Park, when he was good enough to say that we were one of the best units he had seen.

Equipment now began to arrive, and Japanese rifles, which we could really fire, and we began to feel that we were becoming a fighting, and not merely an ornamental, battalion. We were responsible for the Margate defences, and alarms, practice or otherwise, occurred at most inconvenient moments with most unpleasant frequency. Many are the stories connected with these alarms, but lack of space prevents their narration. Easter Monday morning, in particular, saw us marching hurriedly to

Broadstairs at 5.30 a.m., where the remainder of the Brigade met us from Canterbury. This was believed to have been a genuine alarm, but it ended in nothing. Zeppelins were the only form of enemy we saw, and they dropped no bombs on Margate while we were there.

Musketry parties were now busy at Sandwich, where they were billeted in the Golf Club-house; and a Vickers' machine-gun was received, which enabled Lieutenant Bowring to teach his most efficient section with something more satisfying than a wooden dummy.

In the middle of April those who had not signed the form in which the obligation to serve overseas was accepted were separated, and formed, with others, the 43rd Provisional Battalion for Home Defence. This left us only 700 strong, but the defence of Margate and the entrenching in connection with it passed from our hands, and left us more time for training. It may be worth recalling that some of the men who elected to join a Home Service Battalion actually proceeded overseas, by reason of the Military Service Act, before we did.

On May 17th the Third Line Depots were formed, and a nucleus of officers and N.C.Os. were dispatched to Weeton Camp, near Blackpool, to organize our new unit. Amongst the former were Captain G. L. Fletcher to command and Captain A. T. Miller to act as Adjutant. Captain Clarke also left us to take command of the Depot at Liverpool. Captain Moon soon after was appointed to command " B " Company, vacated by Captain Miller, which had been temporarily commanded by Lieutenant R. L. Dobell, who was attached to us for a short time. " C " Company was given to Captain Parker on Captain G. L. Fletcher's departure.

About this time the Central Force was amalgamated with the Eastern Command, and we came under the orders of that Command for operations. General C. L. Woollcombe, C.B., lost little time in coming to inspect us, and confirmed the good reports already made by inspecting officers.

"THE KING'S" (LIVERPOOL REGIMENT)

Two serious changes now occurred in our Battalion Headquarters Staff. Lieutenant Barnett, while acting as umpire at a big field day, was knocked down and sustained a fracture of the skull. He was away for some time, returning eventually as Captain and Adjutant; his place as Quartermaster, after it had been held as a temporary measure by Lieutenant Kelk, being taken by Sutherland, till then orderly-room sergeant, who more than filled the post he took over. In addition, Colonel Wilson on June 20th resigned command owing to pressure of business which demanded his personal attention. As has already been said, he had laid the best foundations that a battalion could wish for. A keen " rifleman " himself, he had never been content with anything but the best. If he worked us hard, if he was stern and exacting, he always himself set the example, and the spirit of leadership with which he inspired Officers and N.C.Os. remained with the battalion till its last days.

Training at Margate was carried out with zeal and energy of no mean order. As a rule the battalion formed up in companies in line opposite Lancaster House, to the strains of the band. After that the programme varied between route marches round Thanet, Minster and Sarre generally figuring somewhere on the route; field days on Thanet Golf Course; battalion drill—always a prominent and important feature in our training; bayonet fighting, under Sergeant Bowling; bombing with tiny bags filled with sand; or general training in a field at the North Foreland end of Margate. A cold ration was usually taken, and the battalion returned about 8 p.m., and, after marching past the Commanding Officer by companies, dismissed for the day, and found its way severally to " Bobbie's " or other popular cafés for tea. Night operations occurred weekly, and resulted in many amusing contretemps.

Church parades were carried out with full military ceremonial, and the sight of the battalion marching back on a gorgeous Sunday morning, with the band playing at its head, was a sight to be remembered, and evoked the unstinted admiration of the

11

people and visitors of Margate. The parade ended with " Officers, take post," after which the companies moved off under their senior warrant officer or N.C.O.

Upstreet Camp, some miles along the Canterbury Road, was in the meantime being prepared, and our advanced party was busy putting up tents and other necessities.

If we had been worked hard at Margate, we had certainly had a good time. Sea bathing, concerts, Sunday afternoons on the promenade with our band playing in the Oval, and other pleasurable forms of recreation abounded. Mention must also be made of two most successful singing competitions organized under the auspices of the Mayor and Corporation, for which the proprietors of the Winter Gardens very generously provided their magnificent hall free of charge. Some 3,000 people were present, and the success of these concerts, not only for the prizewinners, but for all present, was undoubted. The reports in the local press are eloquent on the subject, as they were, in fact, on the " unfailing kindness, courtesy, and general behaviour " of the 2/6th (Rifle) Battalion (as we were now styled) of " The King's " (Liverpool Regiment).

On July 13th we marched to Upstreet Camp, set close to the Thanet Marshes, a pleasant spot in summer, but a quagmire in the autumn, as we found out later to our cost.

While in camp at Upstreet, except for occasional field operations towards Reculvers and one memorable Brigade field day at Whitstable, the battalion was engaged practically continuously digging trenches, wiring, and revetting in the vicinity of Upstreet and St. Nicholas. The effect of the three months' hard manual labour on the physique of the battalion was very marked, the men growing and broadening out almost beyond recognition. There was considerable movement of men at this period. On August 3rd Captain Wilson conducted 96 men overseas, and on August 6th 112 men were received from the Third Line. Officers were also proceeding at intervals overseas, and others recruiting from hospital were also attached to us for varying periods of time. In November our establishment was reduced to twenty-three officers, and all the remainder were dispatched to the Third Line.

On August 8th Major W. A. L. Fletcher, D.S.O., was gazetted Lieutenant-Colonel, and took over the command of the battalion. Captain Gilling had meanwhile assumed command of " A " Company.

By October 10th we were more than pleased to vacate our camp, where we were wellnigh drowned and frozen, and moved to billets at Canterbury once more. Our move was made more dignified by the presence of regulation transport, which had been received at Upstreet Camp, in place of our miscellaneous collection of almost prehistoric civilian vehicles.

Headquarters at Canterbury were at Dagmar House in Dane John, the men being billeted in all the neighbouring streets, Wincheap, York, Oxford, Guildford, and Martyrsfield Roads being the chief. A number of mules were received, of varying dispositions, the most notorious rejoicing in the name of " Lusitania."

The end of 1915 found us plodding steadily on with the now somewhat monotonous round of general training, the only excitement being an occasional Zeppelin scare or a more serious " stand to." The latter, during the earlier days of 1916, kept us for nearly a week in a state of readiness to move at half an hour's notice. Transport vehicles were kept fully loaded, and meals were served from field kitchens, while trains stood waiting with steam up in the station.

During the first three months of 1916 fourteen drafts of " Derby " recruits were received, numbering in all 319 men. Some of these men we thought were rather old at first, but they turned out splendidly. These drafts were distributed into squads under specially selected instructors, whence they were drafted as they became qualified into the companies to which they had been posted. The care and attention lavished on these men were productive of excellent results, as the records of many of them can testify. A Brigade N.C.Os.' class was also held during this period at Old Park, and was conducted by Captain Barnett.

Training, owing to the weather, was apt to be confined to the " vicinity of billets " or the Presbyterian Hall. Dane John was generally tenanted by signallers or other specialists. We also had occasional field days at Bridge, and withheld stoutly the attacking Germans who had invariably landed at St. Margaret's Bay.

In February our first Lewis guns were received, and the number went on increasing from that time till about the spring of 1918, when we reached a total of twenty-eight. Rumours of the separation of machine gunners into a new machine gun corps had been for some time afloat, and on May 2nd twenty-two men of the battalion were discharged and re-enlisted in the Machine Gun Corps. The quick promotion which practically all these obtained is a proof of the good tone of the battalion and of the magnificent instruction which the men had received under Lieutenant Bowring. A draft of 150 men had been sent just prior to this to the Third Line *en route* for overseas, but the majority reappeared shortly after. A party, under Captain Gilling, was detached at Birchington for some time, working on the defences, and a small observation post for hostile aircraft was stationed at Wootton, and a party was also kept at the R.F.C. ground, Bekesbourne.

On April 19th the battalion was inspected at Sturry by General Right Hon. Sir Arthur Paget, who expressed himself favourably impressed ; and on May 8th the Commanding Officer went to France for a tour in the line, bringing back many valuable hints. He spent his time in front of Gommecourt, a spot that was to be very familiar to us later on.

Musketry was now resumed at Sandwich in intensely hot weather, the march—some sixteen miles—proving too much for some of the men who had not experienced that training in march discipline with which the older members of the battalion were acquainted. The balance of the battalion not so employed were

14

inspected, with the rest of the 57th Division (we had ceased to be the 2/1st West Lancashire Division and 2/1st Liverpool Infantry Brigade, the latter now being designated the 171st Infantry Brigade), at Westbere by Sir John French, who had recently been appointed Commander-in-Chief Home Forces. He endeavoured to explain our continued presence in England, which was in no way connected with inefficiency, but was due to the lack at the moment of any adequate force of trained troops for Home Defence.

The continued rumours of early foreign service, however, still buoyed us up, in spite of their failure to materialize, and it speaks wonders for the battalion that they endured two and a half years of training in England, with every kind of alteration in policy, without losing to any extent their cheerfulness and their keenness

Canterbury, with its church parades in the Cathedral, with its general training at the Parsonage Farm, its company training and battalion operations, its company concerts and its comfortable billets, was now about to join Blackpool and Margate among the memories of the past.

Advanced parties were now at Gore Street, where a joint camp was being constructed for the 2/5th K.L.R. and ourselves. Excellently situated on a branch from the main road between Monkton and Minster, it was only some four miles from our old camp at Upstreet. Standing, however, on higher ground, it looked over the Thanet Marshes, and so escaped the disadvantages of damp and mist which belong to such low-lying ground. The tents were also particularly good. The only disadvantage was a lack of space, the area, limited as it was, being further cramped by the presence of the Wessex Field Ambulance, a pleasant party though they were.

Digging operations now recommenced, in addition to the usual round of general and specialist training. A visit by Sir Francis Howard with an Ordnance inspector who murmured of " foreign service " filled us with the highest hopes. Our equipment was condemned, and likewise our rifles, which had replaced the

15

HISTORY OF THE 2/6TH (RIFLE) BATTALION

Japanese weapons some months previously. Apparently we were to have everything we wanted, proceed to Aldershot for final training, and then to France. Before we left Gore Street some very successful sports were organized in conjunction with the 2/5th K.L.R. and many amusing sideshows were added. A practice night alarm for hostile aircraft caused some merriment when Captain Moon was seen hurrying to report attired in a service cap, nightshirt, British warm, and a pair of gum-boots. One memorable field day must be recorded, which was known for long after as the Battle of Pluck's Gutter, the scene of operations.

The command of " C " Company passed to Captain Eccles about this time. He had relieved Lieutenant May as Transport Officer when the latter joined the Home Service unit, but had handed over this duty shortly after to Lieutenant Hutchinson.

On July 15th, after vast preparations—we had made no considerable move for eighteen months—we entrained at Canterbury, after a long and tiring march, for Aldershot, getting a magnificent send off from our Canterbury friends, not to mention ample supplies of fruit from the manager of the Queen's Hotel, Margate.

With what high hopes we set off on our journey! Now at last we felt that the final stage in our education had been reached. Aldershot and Salisbury Plain were the universities of the military student, whence he was launched into the vortex of war complete with all the necessary knowledge. That we had now at last been admitted to this select academy must mean that our days in England were strictly numbered. Alas for our hopes!

16

COL. G. A. WILSON, V.D.

CHAPTER II

PREPARATION FOR OVERSEAS—BOURLEY CAMP—INKERMAN
BARRACKS, WOKING

ON arrival at Aldershot we detrained at the military siding and marched off over the switchback road across the edge of Laffan's Plain to Bourley Bottom, some two miles from the town in the direction of Fleet. The camp, which was on the site of one of the usual summer camping grounds, was from the picturesque point of view delightfully situated. It lay in the centre of a ring of low, wooded hills which sheltered it from all wind, and the white tents stood out in pleasing contrast to the surrounding browns and greens of the background. As a place of habitation, however, it could not compare with Gore Street ; the canvas was poor, and the general arrangements by no means so modern. More-over, by its very situation the camp was damp, and in continued bad weather would probably have proved unhealthy. However, we had come there with a purpose—viz., to complete as quickly as possible our military knowledge—and we were in no mood to cavil at details.

From the moment of our arrival we realized that every moment would be precious. A musketry course had to be fired, and the outline of a tactical training programme had already been issued. Musketry commenced on July 17th, two days after arrival, and we fired on alternate days on Cæsar's Camp ranges, hardly a mile away, and on Ash ranges, a good six miles away. As firing was always to commence at 7 a.m. when not prevented by an early morning mist, as frequently happened, we used to rise very early for Ash ranges, and the " butt party " still earlier. Away we would tramp over the rough road to Aldershot, through the silent streets, past the many barracks when " Reveillé " was just sounding, and so out of the town again towards the Fox Hills and our destination at Ash ranges.

Throughout the musketry course the weather was brilliant, but the heat tremendous. Home we would come after a cold ration for lunch, and sing ourselves hoarse as we marched through Aldershot. Many were the comments passed on our singing powers, and truly the men sang well, and marched even better. Our musketry also proved good, and we came out top of our Brigade and second in the Division.

On August 6th Lieutenant-Colonel H. D. Spencely, T.D., Honorary Colonel of the battalion, came and paid us a visit, to our great delight, and we think that he was more than satisfied with what he saw.

We were now embarked on a series of the field operations of which brigade training mainly consists. Each day saw us marching off towards the Long Valley, for ever famous in military annals, there to practise attack formations, advance and rear guards, outposts, fire control, and so forth. Some days we joined battle with the other battalions of the Brigade, one against three or two against two. Norris and Eelmoor Bridges frequently figured somewhere in the scheme of operations, or, again, Cocked Hat Wood or Outridden Copse. Many of the battles were of the most determined description, and casualties were caused, if not by enemy action, at any rate by order of the supervising staff, which consisted frequently of several distinguished soldiers, including General Sir Archibald Hunter, G.O.C.-in-C. Aldershot Command, and Sir Francis Howard, Inspector-General of Troops for overseas. The work was hard and the conditions variable. Sometimes the dust stirred up seemed almost too choking to be endured; at other times one waded through mud and slush well over the boots, to the great detriment of black puttees. Sandy Lane, the euphemistic name for the track to our camp, was notorious for its depth of mud, which the constant passing of vehicles churned up into a paste of most vile consistency.

18

Many were the amusing incidents of these training days, but one cannot detail them here. Still, they helped us to carry through the long days of strenuous physical exercise.

A pleasant respite, however, was ahead. On August 19th the whole battalion, less a small party left to guard the camp, proceeded to Liverpool for its "last leave," reassembling on August 24th on St. George's Plateau for the return. Great was the enthusiasm that welcomed the battalion and again sent it on its way.

On August 18th fifteen men, too young for foreign service, had been dispatched to the 5th Territorial Force Reserve Battalion K.L.R. at Oswestry, and on August 22nd we said good-bye to nine more machine gunners who were transferred to Grantham. Moreover, a light trench mortar battery was in course of formation in each brigade, and to this we contributed Lieutenant H. E. Barrow to command, 2nd-Lieutenant D. G. Leonard, and twenty-three men. The battery proceeded on September 3rd to Pirbright, returning again after some range practice on September 10th, when they occupied a corner of our camp. Later in September they finally left us for Pirbright, and we saw them no more till we met in the trenches in France.

Another important part of our training took place in the trenches constructed in the vicinity of the Foresters Public-House (or "P.H.," as the maps described it, and as, in fact, it was generally called), which was situated about two miles north of our camp on the far side of the race-course. Here an elaborate set of trenches had been dug, and these the battalions occupied in turn for varying periods not exceeding thirty-six hours, relieving each other in the approved fashion, and carrying on in the trenches as far as possible as they would do in France. An enemy was generally provided in the enemy front line opposite, and silent raids occurred at uncertain intervals. Major Geddes, the Brigade Major, and 2nd-Lieutenant Bevir, the Brigade Bombing Officer, even worked a gas attack on us ; but as the sentry thought it was only smoke from an adjacent rubbish destructor the efforts of our enthusiastic staff fell somewhat flat. That these practices were valuable no one can doubt ; added to which we learnt something of night-working parties, ration carrying, patrolling, laying of telephones, S.O.S. alarms, and so on ; but it must be admitted that nights in the Foresters P.H. Trenches were vastly more uncomfortable than those in any trench sector we held in France in similar weather. Apart from mere practice in trench routine, we carried out some elaborate attacks across these trenches in the " wave " method then in vogue, such an operation on September 19th being performed under the eye of Sir John French, who made some flattering comments on the Division.

Three days before this we had a practice alarm, followed by a concentration of the whole Division in the Long Valley, where our Divisional Commander, Major-General Forster, carried out his final inspection before giving up command. On September 23rd the Division had the honour of being inspected by His Majesty the King. It was a brilliant day, and the scene was one that will long live in the memory of those who took part in it. The Division was drawn up in review order on the Review Ground facing the Pavilion, and after a Royal Salute the King rode round the ranks. It was a pretty severe test of discipline and steadiness, but, as a regular officer was heard to remark in the Aldershot Club that evening, " the men were magnificent, and the march past first rate. You would have thought it was a regular division." The battalion gained great credit for their share in the march past, though the pace set by the band was almost too quick even for riflemen. After this Commanding Officers were introduced to His Majesty, and we set off for home, feeling more than satisfied with our turn out, our discipline, and our drill.

We had all this while been confident of our early departure for overseas. We had had our last leave and been inspected by the King, we had lent our rifles to a draft of men from the Home Counties Division to enable them to complete their musketry before joining us, and we had all been recently inoculated and vaccinated. How near we were then to going abroad only those in the secret know, but gradually the suspicion spread that our time had not yet come, and it proved only too true. Our draft, or what we called " our draft," proceeded overseas direct, and we learned to our dismay that we were shortly to proceed to Woking for winter quarters. It was a terrible disappointment. Everyone had felt that at last the promised day was come, and here were our hopes dashed to the ground once more. The battalion behaved splendidly, however, and only those who knew the men intimately realized how severe was the blow. For two long years had we been training, and now, when our hopes were all but realized, we found ourselves condemned once more to the old grind and the old routine for an indefinite period. Men were almost ashamed to go on leave and face the heartless gibes of those who did not know the facts ; but they settled down again to the old tasks with grim determination, feeling that one day they would really be allowed to go, and that the more efficient they made themselves, and the quicker they trained the promised drafts of raw men, the sooner would their ambition be realized.

Our stay at Aldershot, although it had not proved the final prelude to our move overseas, had not been without its value. During the long period of training in the different stations where we had been buartered work had to a certain extent suffered either from lack of facilities or from the special attention that had to be paid to drafts, and also from the changes necessitated by the latters' departure. Consequently an undue proportion of time had perforce been devoted to certain special aspects of training, such as physical drill, rifle exercises, bombing, and so forth ; little scope being provided, except occasionally, for the more practical side of training of which field operations mainly consist. During the period at Aldershot we had for the first time worked daily not only as a self-contained unit with all the specialists co-operating according to their particular functions, but also as part of an active field force, represented by not only the whole Brigade, but by the various arms of the service, which nominally work in unison during active operations. The experience gained was therefore very valuable, and the instruction in trench routine gave every man some inkling, at any rate, of what the real life in the line was like.

On September 27th the battalion set off on a fine, sunny day to march to Woking, a halt being made about 12.30 p.m. in a pleasant wood for dinner, which had been cooking in field kitchens as we marched along. We arrived at our destination in comfortable time for tea. Inkerman Barracks in normal times must be a very pleasant spot. They stand well on high ground above Woking and close to the hamlet of St. John's, and are well laid out. Unfortunately, owing to a lack of space we shared these barracks with the 2/5th K.L.R., and in addition a squadron of Bedfordshire Yeomanry and a company of A.S.C. were also accommodated in the outbuildings. We had half the barracks, together with the guard-room and the orderly-room at the entrance to the barrack square, while the officers had the officers' quarters. The 2/5th K.L.R. had the other half of the barracks and most of the married quarters for their officers. We had also one or two of these small cottages. The mess we shared jointly.

For training there was a large field next the barracks, and some rough ground behind, where final assault courses were constructed. There were several pieces of common land in the near vicinity, and some four miles away was the splendid piece of country known as Chobham Common. On the whole, therefore, we were well off ; while the barrack square was admirably suited for close order drill, there being just room to move a whole battalion *en masse*.

The barracks were very dirty when we took them over, but before long they became spotless under the keen eye of the Commanding Officer at his weekly inspection. The men were accommodated in large dormitories, the majority on beds ; and though the rooms were apt to be somewhat cold and draughty, there was no

22

real cause of complaint. There was a Y.M.C.A. hut in the barrack square, and another one nearer Woking.

The morning after our arrival the Commanding Officer read out the message from His Majesty the King, in which he expressed himself most satisfied with the appearance of the Division at the review, and his confidence that when the time came the men would fight as Lancashire men always fought. He added, however, that he would reserve his final message until definite orders were received to proceed overseas. On October 3rd General Broadwood inspected the battalion in the barrack square, and all officers were introduced to him. We now commenced a further General Musketry Course at Pirbright Ranges, the weather being on the whole good, though intensely cold.

The promised drafts now began to arrive, and between October 10th and 23rd 229 men arrived, bringing the strength of the battalion up to 1,116 men. On their first arrival the new-comers created no very favourable impression, but by the time that we proceeded overseas they had grown and broadened out almost beyond recognition. After considerable discussion all the drafts of the Division were sent to Training Reserve Battalions at Aldershot for six weeks—an arrangement which certainly had some points in its favour, but in the light of experience probably more against it.

On October 6th the Signal Section competed in an efficiency competition, open to all battalions in the Aldershot Command, and finished a good winner over a large number of competitors. This was the prelude to further victories in similar competitions won by the battalion, to which we shall refer later.

On October 14th an elaborate mine explosion took place at Frith Hill under the most realistic conditions, including an occupation of the crater by a large force from the adjoining model trench system. The proceedings were admirably stage-managed, and were witnessed by a most imposing display of General and other Officers from all parts of the country. The detonation was expected to be such that even as far as Woking all windows had to be left open for fear of damage from concussion. However, so heavy was the charge, and apparently so light the soil, that, so far from anything very spectacular occurring, a small quantity of earth was flung almost silently into the air, and the greater portion of it fell back into the place from which it had been dislodged. In spite of this misfortune, the occupation party dashed forward, and, regardless of the heavy fire from the enemy trenches, consolidated the position and constructed wire entanglements with great vigour and determination.

As another form of instruction suitable for men about to proceed overseas, we commenced, under R.E. supervision, deep dug-outs on Dawney's Hill. These were worked in the first instance by the 2/5th K.L.R. and ourselves in continuous forty-eight hour shifts. Other men were meantime engaged in such exercises as construction and capture of a strong post, wiring and revetting, throwing live bombs (each man throwing one by day and one by night), and instruction in gas-helmet drill, including the standard tests; and in addition there was the usual rapid loading, bayonet fighting, and drill.

On November 3rd Captain Barnett was examined by a Medical Board and found to be permanently disabled by the injury to his head which had been caused by the accident previously mentioned. He proceeded, accordingly, the next day on leave, pending the *Gazette* notifying the relinquishment of his commission; and Captain Wurtzburg took over his duties, being subsequently gazetted Adjutant.

To any battalion, however well trained, Captain Barnett, by reason of his vast experience of every side of military training, would have been invaluable. It is therefore quite impossible to over-estimate the benefit that a young battalion like ours derived from his knowledge and efficiency. The Commanding Officer had just previously left us for a few weeks to undergo a slight surgical operation, and the Command had devolved on Major C. W. Wilson,

24

in the absence of Major H. K. Wilson, who was attending the Senior Officers' Course at Aldershot.

On November 15th a draft of four officers—Lieutenant Ormrod, 2nd-Lieutenants McCormick, E. E. Paul, and Moseley—from the 6th Battalion Lancashire Fusiliers arrived, and their arrival was most timely. We were being absolutely swamped with courses of every possible description ; in addition, we had to maintain and relieve regularly an officer with the deep dug-out party ; there were numerous courts of inquiry and courts-martial on foot, and the result, of course, was that the shortage of officers had become acute. Moreover, to stimulate efficiency, the Divisional Commander had devised four competitions—route marching by a battalion ; bayonet fighting and physical training, each by a company ; and wiring by a platoon. Preliminary Brigade competitions were held, and we were selected to compete in the Division for the first three events.

On November 21st the Division organized a concentration march and billeting scheme for our Brigade, involving a march of some eight miles to Chertsey. Coming as this did only two days before the final of the Divisional Route Marching Competition it was rather a severe handicap. However, on November 24th the whole battalion (except about half a dozen men required to guard our quarters), accompanied by a full regimental transport, set off on a fifteen mile march, which was to be done in five hours. Marks were given for accurate timing in passing the starting and finishing posts, for appearance of the men at the end of the march, for march discipline, and for correct contents of vehicles and packs. Hidden judges watched us at different parts of the march ; others checked our halts, ten minutes every hour ; and the contents of one platoon's packs were duly examined. The battalion marched magnificently, and although a cooker horse dropped a shoe and had to be shod by the cold shoer and regain the column without trotting, and although during the latter part of the march the road was inches deep in sand along a steep gradient, the last vehicle was clear of the finishing point with five seconds to spare. Our casualties were only two or three men, and but for the concentration march would never have occurred. After some discussion over the case of another battalion, who, contrary to the rules of the competition, had marched all the way headed by a band who did not wear packs, we were declared the winners, which we should have been in any case had we not forfeited a large number of points. We lost these because one man had no boot-laces in his pack ; he remembered afterwards that they were in his pocket after all ; and another man was also apparently deficient of some small article of kit. However, the battalion had every reason to be proud of itself, and the result certainly served to remind the Divisional Headquarters that other battalions existed besides the two Brigades in their close vicinity at Blackdown. " B " Company trained for the bayonet fighting, and, under Captain Moon, put up a display on November 29th, before the Chief Instructor of the London District School, which astonished him, and in due course they were declared the winners. " D " Company, under Captain Parker, also produced a splendid exhibition of physical training, and were proclaimed joint winners with the company of another battalion. In these last two competitions Company Sergeant-Major-Instructor McLelland, A.G.S., deserved the very greatest credit ; he had been indefatigable in his exertions, and his methods proved most efficient.

For the continued successes of the battalion we were awarded a richly deserved twenty-four hours off parade.

All this time the specialists were receiving what may be described as intensive training. Apart from the ordinary work under their own instructors, they attended lectures and demonstrations of various descriptions with the object of increasing their efficiency and familiarizing them with the conditions under which they would have to work. The snipers in particular received great attention, and were not infrequently proceeding to Aldershot in connection with training. A splendid model miniature range was also constructed by them in one of the huts in the barrack square.

On December 11th Captain Moon left us to join the Portuguese Expeditionary Force as an interpreter; and on Christmas Eve Major C. W. Wilson proceeded overseas for a tour of instruction in the Ypres Salient. On Boxing Day the battalion proceeded on a final three days' last leave, receiving an even warmer welcome and send-off than before from the good people of Liverpool, who realized that the departure of the battalion for the front was imminent at last.

From Christmas till our actual departure was a period of intense activity. Travelling Medical Boards came and examined our " Category men," who were dispatched to various units according to their medical fitness; others were earmarked, by reason of special knowledge, for munition works, and so forth. Nominal rolls had to be completed and checked, casualty forms filled up for every man, the N.C.O. establishment completed, and a hundred other items of detail to be foreseen and provided for.

On February 4th we had a further welcome addition of officers— 2nd-Lieutenants Royle, Goulding, Evans, and Rothwell, all of whom had seen considerable active service with the 1/6th K.L.R., and Lieutenant Parkinson and 2nd-Lieutenants Dugdale and Rule, from the " King's Own." Of the latter, Lieutenant Parkinson was a fully qualified R.F.C. pilot resting after a " crash."

On February 17th Major Turner, now convalescent after a serious wound received while serving with the 1/6th K.L.R., arrived as O. i/c Details, and began to take stock of everything; and on January 22nd the battalion appeared for the first time in khaki puttees, a sure sign that a real move overseas was intended. All the animals were examined and " duds " replaced, and all vehicles completed in all items of equipment. The distinguishing patch first approved at Aldershot, and originally consisting of a small rectangle of black and green cloth in two equal triangular sections (later divided by a thin red strip), was now abolished, and we found our new mark was a green diamond worn on each sleeve between the elbow and the shoulder.

In spite of our manifold activities, we managed to have some really good entertainments, to which our newly formed orchestra, Rifleman Kessen, the conjurer, and another rifleman, a superb banjo artiste (unfortunately, in a low medical category), added talent of the highest order ; and the Divisional Band,—the old 6th it was—which had been selected from all the bands to accompany the Division overseas, came from time to time to give us the benefit of their music.

On February 3rd, 1917, we were inspected at Woking by H.R.H. the Duke of Connaught, who in a short speech wished us all God-speed.

On February 12th the transport and Lewis gunners, with their respective officers, under the command of Major H. K. Wilson, entrained at Brookwood at 9.30 a.m. for Southampton. The Battalion was to proceed on February 14th viâ Folkestone. The long years of training were over ; the memories of Blackpool, Margate, Canterbury, Bourley were fast fading away. Only the future concerned us now. All that could be done by training had been done, and it now rested with each individual whether the battalion maintained its reputation and assisted the Division to justify the confidence placed in it by His Majesty the King, who had sent us the following most gracious message :—

" OFFICERS, NON-COMMISSIONED OFFICERS AND MEN OF THE 57TH DIVISION,

" On the eve of your departure for active service I send you my heartfelt good wishes.

" West Lancashire Regiments have earned a high reputation on the field of battle, and from the impression I formed on the

" THE KING'S " (LIVERPOOL REGIMENT)

occasion of my inspection of your Division last September, I am confident that you, too, will equally uphold the traditions of the fine regiments whose names you bear.

" Your period of training has been long and arduous, but the time has now come for you to prove at the front the results of your instruction, and with your comrades now in the field to maintain the unceasing efforts necessary to bring this war to a victorious ending.

" Good luck and God speed.

" GEORGE R.I."

" *February 2nd, 1917.*"

CHAPTER III

OVERSEAS—STRAZEELE—FLEURBAIX—BAC ST. MAUR—RUE DU
BOIS—RUE MARLE—RUE DORMOIRE

FEBRUARY 13TH. It seems impossible to believe that to-morrow the battalion really embarks for France; that the long period of training and waiting has at last come to an end, and that to-morrow we embark on the enterprise for which we all joined up, and for which some of us have now been waiting two and a half years. The sceptics of the battalion even now throw doubts on it. Admitted that the Transport and Lewis gunners have gone; admitted that the entraining orders are issued for to-night; admitted that everything is packed and ready. We have been fooled before, and likely enough this is only a ruse of the War Office to give another fillip to our flagging spirits, such as they administered in the summer when the move seemed almost a certainty; so much so, in fact, that we all enjoyed a " last leave " and returned ready for the front, only to commence the dull round of general training once more.

The barracks present an air of subdued excitement. Men stand about in groups discussing soberly the prospect of active service, each wondering in his innermost soul how he will acquit himself in the unknown trials that are before him. After all, England is a comfortable place. Life proceeds quietly and peacefully in spite of the bugle calls, the shouts of N.C.Os., the almost inhuman activity of the " physical jerks expert," and the endless exhortations of the officers. May not one in a few days be looking back on all this with bitter regret, and wondering sadly why we were so anxious to quit it and to plunge into the dangers and discomforts

30

of war; the real war, that is to say, not the war of " blanks " and umpires, from which one returns punctually for tea, and grouses if the battalion should be half an hour late ?

The only really active people are the O. i/c Details and his myrmidons. Major Turner is seen hurrying across the barrack square, hot on the trail of some deficient item of barrack equipment. The Quartermaster smiles to himself as he looks forward to the day when " destroyed by enemy action " will be the conclusive answer to all inquiries into deficiencies.

Slowly the day drags on. For fear that anything should be late, everything has been finished hours too soon. One last visit is paid to our old haunts and our old friends, and now it is time to collect our kit and get ready for the parade—" *the* parade," we call it, because it is different from all others. Never since the days of 1914 have we paraded with such alacrity and " dressed " with such zeal. Weird rites prescribed by King's Regulations for regiments proceeding on active service are about to be performed. The moon shines brightly, as befits this solemn ceremony. Two sergeants, not proceeding with the battalion, are standing by while the roll is called, and woe betide the absentee with such witnesses to proclaim his guilt! Surely no one, having waited so long, will now miss the chance, but yet something seems to be wrong. Company Sergeant-Majors and the Regimental Sergeant-Major are in solemn conclave with the Orderly Sergeants. Two men are missing. Reference is promptly made to the Adjutant, who is standing by, and more discussion follows. It is all right, no one has missed his chance, but the Commanding Officer's and Adjutant's servants are proceeding by taxi to the station in charge of some kit.

And now it is time to move off. As companies in turn form fours and move out of the barrack gate, it is odd to feel that we shall never again execute this familiar movement on this well-remembered spot. Quietly, in the dead of night, we move down on the frosty road to Brookwood Station. The battalion is to go in two trains, with a short interval between, the second train under the orders of Major C. W. Wilson. At Brookwood the ladies of the district are dispensing hot drinks and buns. Modern conditions have taken away the glamour of war. No longer do we leave for the fight amid a crowd of cheering people, with flags flying and bugles blowing. The ladies of Brookwood, and our unlucky pals who could not bluff the doctor, are the only ones to see us depart, but their send-off leaves nothing to be desired.

The run to Folkestone was only a matter of a couple of hours, and the early morning light saw us detraining at the Jetty Station. Here the arrangements were excellent The R.T.O. was full of information, and guides appeared to conduct the troops to the Rest Camp. This was a crescent of pre-war lodging-houses and an hotel, all railed in. As the companies marched through the gate, the guides took them to their destined houses, where breakfast was served. The officers were conducted to the hotel and similarly provided for. The hour of parade for embarkation was simultaneously communicated to officers and men.

There were several hours to wait even after a shave and a breakfast, but the time passed quickly enough. After all, it was our last sight of England, perhaps for all time, and we were not in quite so much of a hurry as a week before. At 12.30 p.m. we marched on board s.s. *Victoria*, one of the regular cross-Channel boats. Besides ourselves there were innumerable officers and men returning from leave, who glanced with casual interest at the obviously new crowd going out for the first time. The Commanding Officer was O.C. Ship, and consequently entitled to a cabin, where wonderful instructions dealing with action in event of submarine attack, etc., were to be found. There was also an amusing notebook in which Os.C. Ships were asked to make their comments on the ship. The names of many distinguished Generals were to be found among the signatures, and some of the remarks were highly entertaining.

THE BATTALION - BLACKPOOL, 1914.

GROUP—CANTERBURY, 1916.

" THE KING'S " (LIVERPOOL REGIMENT)

The day was fine and cold, with a strong wind blowing, and although it was not exactly calm, few showed any serious signs of sea sickness. Two other transports and a couple of torpedo-boat destroyers made up the party. Boulogne was reached about 2 p.m., but owing to the speed of the other vessels we were last in. A long wait followed, and eventually we had to cross over another ship to get to the quay, a tiresome process in full kit. We had intended to have a very orderly landing, but the efforts of the Commanding Officer to get the men formed up were frustrated by the Assistant Military Landing Officer, who would not allow any halt until we were clear of all the quays and over the bridges into the town. An unpleasant and fatiguing " follow my leader " round trucks and over metals, dodging engines and motor lorries, resulted, during which process the whole battalion got well mixed up. Eventually, however, after considerable excitement, we formed up in close column of companies, and proceeded to march to Ostrehove Camp.

No one who took part in that march will ever forget it. It was not a long one, two or three miles at the most, but the last part of it was up a hill of the very steepest description. This is bad enough in itself at any time when you are carrying a heavy pack and all the rest of the impedimenta that adorn the " P.B.I.," but when, owing to burst water-pipes, the road is covered with very smooth ice for yards at a stretch, the march becomes laborious and painful to a degree.

Arrived at the top of the hill, we looked round hopefully for the promised rest camp. The sight was indeed depressing. A few dejected and battered-looking tents, one or two marquees struggling with the gale, and an odd hut or two, were the only signs of human habitation on this bleak and wretched moor. The temperature was several degrees below freezing, the wind swept over us in an icy gale, and daylight was rapidly failing. So this was active service, and how warm and comfortable those barracks at Woking were, and how strange that once we thought them cold and bare !

Little time, however, was allowed for reflections. The Camp Warden was there to introduce us to the amenities of the place, and companies and platoons were soon struggling off to try to find shelter from the wind. Blankets had to be drawn and rations issued, and as darkness fell parties were still hurrying about in every direction, endeavouring to get things straight for the night. Presently our indefatigable Quartermaster arrived, having forced a lorry driver, apparently at the point of his revolver, to bring the mechanical transport up to the camp; but how it got up, and still more how it ever got back, are among the unsolved mysteries of the war.

It now appeared that we had to entrain at Boulogne at 8 a.m. the next morning, and an early rise and breakfast were arranged. Few were sorry that our stay on this frozen mountain was to be short; most of us, indeed, regretted that we had ever to come there at all. Very early next morning all were astir. The misery of shaving with freezing water on an icy cold morning was a new experience, and no more pleasant on this than on the many subsequent occasions when it occurred. The officers were more fortunate; they had luckily secured a wooden hut, and also a good breakfast at the Church Army Hut, a veritable oasis in the desert.

After some heated moments while the Commanding Officer inspected the men, who looked rather different from the spotless battalion of Woking—how distant, by the way, that place seemed! —the battalion proceeded down the hill. The descent, if less arduous than the ascent, was certainly more perilous. Even the " higher command " could not always control its feet, and the battalion descended in various postures, mostly in a sitting or prone position; while the clatter of equipment, the crash of falling rifles, and the curses of the victims, aroused the local inhabitants, who regarded us with unseemly mirth.

On arrival at the station we found, to our surprise, that our train was in. It was of the usual kind, " Chevaux 8, Hommes 40," new to us then, but familiar to all the world now. Into this the

34

battalion was sorted, the officers having a first-class carriage of an old-world aspect. Then we began to wait, a practice in which we were all greatly skilled, and about 9.30 a.m. we started off.

Before leaving England we had been issued with two wonderful pamphlets on embarkation and landing, containing, amongst other details, some remarkable returns of great length and complexity which had to be given to various railway, embarkation, and landing officials. The compilation of these returns had wellnigh deprived the Orderly-Room Sergeant of his wits, and but for the fact that he was to join that mysterious body called " 3rd Echelon," we might have felt inclined to abandon the returns in order to save his reason. However, done they were. The next thing was to get rid of them. This proved even more difficult than their compilation ; in fact, in the end we had to admit defeat. Every official wearing " tabs," a " brassard," or in any other way disclosing an official capacity, was offered these returns. Persuasion, threats, entreaties, demands were tried in turn without success. As a last resource, just as the train was moving off, they were thrust into the hands of the R.T.O. at Boulogne, who, however, hastily returned them, muttering that they were as dead as the dodo, and retaliated by presenting us with a Movement Order and a sheaf of papers dealing with the manifold responsibilities of O.C. Train.

The journey up from the Base has been so often described that it requires no particular notice here. It is a long and stately process. The train, when it moves at all, which is only occasionally and for short periods, makes a great deal of fuss about it ; but if you should happen to be wandering about on the permanent way, in spite of orders to the contrary, you can always walk after it and climb on board once more. For the new-comer there was much of interest. On the outskirts of Boulogne the train passed huge dumps of war material of every possible description—guns, ammunition, wagons, trucks, stores, etc., with which gangs of " P.B." men, " Chinks," and other miscellaneous persons were coping in a leisurely fashion. As the train proceeded, the scenery of Northern France began to unfold itself. It is not very interesting—flat for the most part and agricultural, but full of differences from our own English country. The lack of hedges, the strange advertisements, the women at the level-crossings with their quaint horns, all struck a fresh note, especially for those who had never crossed the Channel before, even in the days of peace.

At 8.30 p.m., long after it was dark, the train drew into Bailleul Station, where the Staff Captain, Captain Beazley, was awaiting our arrival. Instantly everyone was galvanized into life. Huge flares illumined the darkness, and officers and N.C.Os. rushed about rousing their men, who were wildly searching in the dark recesses of their cattle-trucks for missing articles of kit. As usual, in a short time apparent chaos resolved itself into order, and the battalion moved off on its eight-mile march to billets under the guidance of an Australian, who was quite distressingly frank about his ignorance of the route. It was a trying march. The experience of the last two days, including twelve hours cramped up in trucks, had not been a very good preliminary to a three hours' tramp. Never had one's kit weighed so heavily. The " tin hat " between the pack straps seemed to increase the weight terribly. The road through the silent streets of Bailleul was cobbled, but as soon as the town was cleared a good country road with a pleasant surface took its place. Slowly the column moved along, and it was nearly midnight before we reached the forked roads where some of the companies had to branch off to their billets. The guide went with them, as the Quartermaster, who had passed us with the stores in a lorry, knew about the billets in Strazeele village. The guide, however, proved a broken reed, and much marching and counter-marching took place, and many an angry conversation with irate householders, before the tired companies at last got to rest in their respective billets—empty barns of a draughty nature. Headquarters proceeded to Strazeele, and eventually settled into billets where, in one case at any rate, a kindly hostess was waiting up with ample supplies of excellent coffee.

About six o'clock the next morning Major Wilson awoke the Adjutant to say that the transport had arrived, and where was it to go ? On this question the Adjutant was entirely devoid of information, having seen nothing of the village in the blackness of the previous night. However, on further inquiry the Major found the field that had been selected, and soon the transport were settled in it, and the battalion was now collected and ready for any emergency.

Strazeele is (or was) a typical little village, consisting of two main streets forming a cross, a few straggling houses wandering off from these, two chief avenues, a church, a mairie, and innumerable estaminets. The surrounding country is slightly undulating arable land dotted with small farms, in which the various companies were billeted. The frost held for the first two days, but then the thaw set in with the thin rain and thick mud so strongly identified with Northern France and Flanders.

Beyond getting things straight, little training was attempted except the fitting of small box respirators and instruction in their use, which was duly carried out. Then each man had to pass through tear gas to test his respirator. When the Commanding Officer's turn came, Lieutenant James, the Gas Officer, to make assurance doubly sure, produced such a powerful mixture that Colonel Fletcher suffered severely, and his return to the orderly-room caused a rapid exodus of the staff with streaming eyes. The only other item of interest was the valiant attempt of a fatigue party, working night and day, to bury a dead horse in ground which, owing to the recent frost, was as hard as iron, which caused an interchange of very emphatic telegrams between Brigade and Battalion Headquarters.

Orders were now received for the Brigade to move on February 20th to the Sailly area, the battalion to pass the starting-point at 8.35 a.m. This meant early breakfasts and early preparations generally ; but this, our first move on active service, proved a severe test of our training. However, after some vigorous criticisms from those in authority, we managed to take our places to time in the Brigade column, and set off for the new area in a steady drizzle. On the way we passed the Corps Commander, Lieutenant-General Sir A. J. Godley, commanding 2nd Anzac Corps.

After leaving Merville we were warned against gas shelling. This, together with the screens which now became conspicuous at all points of the road open to observation from the enemy's positions, served to remind us that we were now at last personally interested in the war, and had ceased to be mere onlookers.

In due course we arrived at La Rue de la Lys, a little distance short of Sailly, where we were to spend the night. Our billeting officer had meantime got lost ; we overshot the mark and nearly reached Sailly itself, but fortunately discovered our error in time. We turned about by the military cemetery, where the first name to catch the eye was that of a sergeant who had been with us in Margate.

The billets consisted of a group of farmhouses, which with difficulty accommodated the battalion. Intermittent rumbling of artillery could now be heard quite distinctly, and you really felt that the war was getting nearer, and that any day now you might be taking an active part in it. That night we felt this still more keenly, as the New Zealand Division, whom we were to relieve, were celebrating their departure by a battalion raid, and the farmhouses shook and echoed to the roar of the guns as the barrage opened on the Germans. At all times a barrage is rather awe-inspiring, but when heard for the first time without warning on a winter's night by raw troops, the effect produced is distinctly sobering.

At 8.15 a.m. the next morning (February 17th, 1917) the battalion was on the road again, this time for Fleurbaix, just behind the line. The column was pursued by a Brigade motor-cyclist, demanding the names of two nominees for commissions.

38

" THE KING'S " (LIVERPOOL REGIMENT)

The reply that none were suitable only produced a further and more peremptory demand, and names had to be supplied. This was the beginning of that inevitable process which, more quickly even than the tax levied on the battalion by the enemy, robbed you of your best N.C.Os. as fast as you trained them.

The final stages of the march revealed clearly that we were now in the region where more than an occasional shell descended. The people of Strazeele had proudly pointed to isolated bullet marks and so forth, relics of the fighting of 1914, but here there were real shell holes and houses that had been hit obviously by something more effective than a bullet. Fleurbaix itself was a ruined village, though some of the surrounding farms were intact and flourishing. The church was a mere skeleton, and whole sides of some of the streets were in a state of collapse. Windows were few and far between, and the spaces usually covered with glass were now mostly filled with canvas, or in a few privileged places with oilsilk, which lets in the light. According to the local report, the enemy shelled the place heavily at regular intervals, gas shell being particularly plentiful in the previous bombardment. We hoped secretly that the next bombardment would be deferred for a while, and inspected our box respirators carefully before turning in that night.

As soon as the battalion reached the village the Commanding Officer and Adjutant reported to the New Zealand Brigade Head-quarters, under whose orders we were to come for that night. There we met the Colonel of the 2nd Battalion Wellington Regi-ment, the battalion holding the line, who had come down to meet Colonel Fletcher. After a few preliminaries it was decided that the Commanding Officer and Adjutant should proceed up the line forthwith (it was then about noon), and the Company Com-manders, for whom guides were provided, should come up after lunch. We were somewhat surprised to hear that we could go up on horseback, so after getting rid of spare kit and seizing tin helmets and box respirators we set off.

As we cleared the village evidences of hostile activity became more apparent, and our own 18-pounders were found in barns on either side of the road, their front being screened with hangings painted to resemble a brick house wall. The country looked depressing enough—flat as could be, and intersected with sluggish ditches full of dirty water and fringed with stunted willows. Remains of farms and flapping canvas screens stood about, looking strangely gaunt in this empty wilderness. The grass was rank and overgrown, while here and there lay remnants of trenches and great strips of rusty barbed wire, the defences of Fleurbaix. Suddenly our guide pointed to a notice, "Steel helmets will be worn forward of this point," which served to remind one, if a reminder had been necessary with shell-holes all around, that the German was within a distance measurable in yards.

After a few minutes' ride a large farm, to which had been added huts and also some defences, appeared in view. This, our guide informed us, was Elbow Farm, where the reserve company was located; likewise the best water supply and the gum-boot store. Still we went on till we came to a forked road with a large sand-bag wall. This was Sand-bag Corner, and here we left our horses. The enemy, it appeared, was a bit free with overhead machine-gun fire at night, and this screen had been put up to limit the flight of the bullets. A few minutes brought us to Wye Farm, in front of which was a large pond, and round this we skirted on duck-boards. On the right lay the military cemetery, where several figures were lying wrapped in blankets. We had met the walking wounded from the night's raid as we marched to Fleurbaix. These silent figures were those whose luck had not brought a "Blighty," but a more permanent rest in a foreign land.

The Headquarters at Wye Farm were in a sense commodious, but hardly of a description to inspire much confidence in a new arrival. Imagine an ordinary block of farm buildings with barn and cowshed attached. Knock holes in the roof till all the tiles and most of the beams are down; put one layer of sand-bags to protect the ceiling of the first floor in the house itself, and add sand-bag walls where walls of the usual description have ceased to exist, and you will have a fair idea of the Battalion Headquarters. There was one small sand-bag "bivvy" leading out of the orderly-room, late a stable for a couple of horses; and the regimental aid post was situated in a small brick outbuilding beyond the cemetery. In front of the house was a double duck-board track, which wandered round the corner into the farm-yard behind. The Officers' Mess consisted of a low room with a fine fireplace; and the Commanding Officer's sleeping room was of reasonable size, and contained R.E. bunks for the Commanding Officer and Second-in-Command. Here we were introduced to the Second-in-Command, the Adjutant, and other Headquarters' officers of the battalion we were relieving; and then, under the guidance of the Adjutant, we set off to have a look at the line. All the way from Fleurbaix, and, in fact, the whole time we were going round the sector, the enemy preserved an entire and complete silence, due perhaps to the inoffensive nature of our particular opponents, or more probably to their rather harrowing and costly experience of the night before.

City Avenue, the communication trench we were to use, had one branch, which started from Wye Farm through a hole in the wall at the back of the farm. As in most communication trenches in that part of the world, the track rests on "A" frames to keep it above water level. Down this track we moved, experiencing for the first time the impression of the endless duck-board beneath one's feet and a few yards of trench, with an occasional glimpse of bushes or rank weeds, as the only prospect before the eye. The air was damp, and strange stale odours filled the nostrils. Everything was symptomatic of death and decay. Water and mud predominated, and everything looked dreary and unkempt to the last degree.

The support line round Hudson Bay looked fairly bright, with quite reasonable "bivvies," but the mud was there; and now

41

empty tins and refuse of every sort began to add to the wretched aspect of the place.

As we neared the front line in the left sector—we were now in Bay Avenue—water and mud became still more plentiful, the ground even more bare, and the general sense of desolation even more pronounced. Suddenly we found ourselves in the front line— a sand-bag breastwork, looking old and weather-beaten, with a duck-walk running along it and a sudden descent of two or three feet to a continuous chain of pools of green and stagnant water. A few sand-bag " bivvies " among the traverses, an occasional roof consisting of a single sheet of corrugated iron—here was " home " for the next eight days. Whichever way you looked along the line you saw the same endless bays and traverses, most of them more or less fallen in ; the same pools of evil-smelling water ; the same stretches of shell-churned ground ; the same old litter of tins and débris. If you turned your gaze backwards towards Wye Farm, in search of something less desolate and inhuman, the scene was hardly more inspiring. Overgrown bushes, stunted willows and mud ill concealed by discoloured grass, were all that met the eye ; and the landscape was only broken by the irregular lines of trenches which showed up in the distance like Brobdingnagian mole runs.

We visited the scene of the raiding party's exit from the line, and the smears of recent blood on the duck-boards and the pieces of field-dressing lying about similarly stained told their own story. We also heard how our advance party, who left us in Woking, had been initiated during the last few days into the mysteries of trench warfare. We then returned to Battalion Headquarters, where all the details of trench routine were gone into and ex- plained with great clearness and precision.

No one could have been more kind and helpful than those New Zealanders, from the Commanding Officer downwards. They knew we were totally inexperienced, and they did everything possible to instruct us in the short time available. Their name became a synonym in the battalion for gallantry and courtesy, both of which qualities we had full opportunity of estimating.

As the weather was misty, and showed every sign of remaining so, it was arranged that the relief should take place on the next day (February 22nd) in daylight, commencing at 7.30 a.m. In the afternoon Company Commanders and selected N.C.Os. arrived to visit their areas, and their New Zealand opposite numbers proved as helpful and instructive as the Battalion Headquarters staff had been.

That night in Fleurbaix was quiet enough, and it was hard to realize how close we were to the war. The village, in fact, was only a mile or two from the British front line. As one looked from the windows, Véry lights could be seen shooting up into the sky, while the rattle of desultory machine-gun fire rang clear in the stillness of the night. Billets, on the whole, were good, the houses we used being but slightly damaged ; but the draughts through the broken panes, and the subdued light caused by opaque coverings, did not make for comfort, as that word was understood by those whose idea of billets was a snug room in Blackpool or Margate.

Next morning (February 22nd) revealed a scene of great activity. Relief day is always a busy one, but when the process has not yet become so familiar as to be almost a second nature there is considerable excitement, and not a little confusion, before things begin to straighten out. Our guides, one for each platoon, duly arrived, and at 7.30 a.m. Captain Gilling and his heavily laden company were moving off. To the uninitiated it might seem that the Army Authorities had given the infantry soldier under ordinary circumstances, as much permanent equipment as one man could well carry. But it is a trifle compared with the loads carried on a relief. It is true that greater experience enabled one to devise means for reducing the distance over which these extra items had to be borne ; but on this occasion, owing to the request of the New Zealanders to reduce horse transport as far as possible in case visibility improved, the men struggled off under fearful burdens. In the peaceful days of trench warfare a relief was almost tantamount to a household removal. There were valises, mess boxes, orderly-room boxes, Lewis guns, carriers for Lewis-gun drums, Véry pistols, periscopes, gum-boots, wire-cutters, rations, fuel, and a thousand and one other things to be taken up. The rate of movement decreases in proportion to the load, and consequently one mile per hour became the average pace. Companies proceeded in an order determined by the distance each had to cover. " A " Company led off, as they were bound for the right sector of the front line, viâ Elbow Farm and Tin Barn Avenue. Captain Steward and " B " Company followed, heading for the left sector of the front line past Wye Farm and up City Avenue and Bay Avenue. Captain Eccles and " C " Company only had to go to Jay Post, as the support line was in close proximity to Battalion Headquarters ; while Major Charles Wilson and " D " Company had to go no farther than Elbow Farm, where life " in reserve " was comparatively peaceful— " comparatively " only, because all the fatigues and working parties generally fall to the lot of the reserve company, which means that the night is spent in tramping about and toiling. Headquarters proceeded last. They are not required till the relief is well advanced, and the Headquarters of the battalion being relieved can begin to dribble out and make room for them.

Reports of " relief complete " soon began to arrive, and the last company was through in a remarkably short time, a fact which the New Zealanders commented on with pleasure. Nothing is more annoying for an outgoing unit than to be held up by a bad relief. The last words of wisdom were spoken, trench stores signed for, and the other little formalities completed. With a cheery " Good luck !" and a hearty handshake they were off, and our Commanding Officer found himself for the first time in sole charge of a sector As soon as our friends were clear, he, with his usual energy, was

44

calling for his runner, and was off round the line to see how " A " and " B " Companies were getting on. With their wonted consideration, the New Zealanders had left an officer and N.C.O. for the first twenty-four hours with each company, knowing that the first night in the trenches is rather a strain, and the helping hand of the experienced was a great asset. Many were the problems which were exercising the minds of the Company Commanders as the Commanding Officer visited them in turn. Endless questions of detail presented themselves, which had first to be learnt and understood by oneself, and the information then passed on to the company—a far more laborious and difficult task.

Only a few hours of daylight remained, and there was still much to be done. The lists of things contained in the Trench Standing Orders, " What every Platoon Commander should know," " What every Section Commander should know," and so forth, were enough to distract the most phlegmatic mind, especially when nobody knew the answers to half the questions. The ideal— that is, when everyone knows and understands the answers to all these vital questions—is never attained except in a sector in which every member of the battalion knows them by heart, and at present no one had the requisite knowledge. To add to the difficulties, you constantly lost your way and wandered aimlessly in half derelict trenches, searching in vain for (say) No. 2 Post, where Sergeant X., only recently promoted to that exalted rank, was certain to be in need of advice and assistance. Eventually, giving up for the time all hope of finding this elusive post, you decide to return to Company Headquarters, where the Company Sergeant-Major is anxiously working out patrols, ration parties, and duties of every description, only to find your own Headquarters even more cunningly concealed than the much-sought No. 2 Post. In vain you consult the elegant sketch map of the trenches, that pretty but fallacious document which shows the way so clearly, but omits any reference to *disused* trenches, which often look in such good condition as to lead you astray and lure you by gradual stages into a forlorn wilderness of abandoned saps. It is all very trying.

The sector itself—La Boutillerie, as it was called—requires little description beyond what has already been given and what can be seen on the map. Its two outstanding features were the Salient, a triangular piece of trench said to have been dug in one night during the days before trench warfare became stabilized, and Jay Post, a wonderful deep dug-out of magnificent proportions, which was but slightly used, as the enemy, in spite of our elaborate camouflage, had all its exits accurately registered.

That night, and in fact all the time the battalion was in this sector, the Germans were amazingly quiet. It is true that the vicinity of Battalion Headquarters, the road leading up to it, and the principal communication trenches, were liberally be-spattered with machine-gun bullets. This was apt to " put the wind up " those whose duties compelled them to move about at night, and caused many curses to be heaped on the head of " Parapet Joe," as the chief offender was called, from the skill with which he could traverse along our front line parapet, with its many variations in level, even on the darkest night. An occasional " minnie " also descended on the front line with a loud report ; and the Brewery, where the pump was, and where the observers had an observation post along with the gunners, received spas-modic attention from " whizz-bangs." At first people in the front line talked in whispers, although generally speaking the enemy was 400 yards away ; but common sense, and the war experience of some of the officers who had been out with the 1/6th Battalion, soon put an end to that and many other little absurdities. The main stumbling-block at night was the tendency of people, con-trary to orders, to take refuge in shelters and " bivvies." The order forbidding this caused considerable heartburning, though its sound sense was clear enough.

The weather, after being muggy and wet, had now turned bitterly cold again, and nights in the trenches under arctic conditions are never pleasant, and for the new-comer very trying. Accordingly, we were not sorry to be informed that our time in the line was to be of only four days' duration, and almost before we had realized we were in the line, officers and N.C.Os. of the 2/7th K.L.R. were arriving on tours of exploration. On the last night we had our first casualties, a "minnie" falling right on to a post, killing three men and wounding two. The fortune of war is very curious: some men go for months, and even years, unscathed through dangers of every description; others, like these three, are killed on their first tour of duty in one of the quietest sectors in France. We buried them next day in the cemetery by Battalion Headquarters, and it was melancholy to realize that the dissolution of our happy band had now commenced in grim earnest, and was likely to proceed more rapidly in the days to come.

At 7.30 a.m. (February 26th, 1917) the relief commenced, and in due course the companies were finding their way back to billets at Fleurbaix, feeling themselves twice the men they were but a few days before. They knew now what the real trenches were; previously their knowledge had been limited to those poor imitations at the Foresters Public-House at Aldershot.

Before completing the impressions of our first tour in the line, we cannot omit one thing from our account of this sector; not that the phenomenon is peculiar to these trenches or any other particular sector—in fact, till the more persistent use of gas sounded their death knell, they were to be found everywhere, "they" being, of course, rats. Now at home, in small numbers and well under the control enforced by long-established civilization, rats present no particular terrors or inconvenience except, perhaps, to a sensitive female. But in the trenches, where food was abundant and engines of destruction, at least as far as rats were concerned, few, they waxed plentiful, and their audacity increased with their size and their numbers. Not content with running all over the duck-boards, and all but refusing to step aside

47

and let you pass, they ran riot in your dug-out, gnawed your clothes, devoured your food, scampered all over you as you slept, and in one notorious case caused grave inconvenience to a Medical Officer by removing bodily his set of false teeth. In the front line they climbed on the sleeping soldier and gnawed through his haversack to reach his iron ration. In the " bivvy " they nibbled holes in a man's socks as he lay on the ground. In fact, so bold were they that you could fire two or three rounds at a rat and hit all round him before he would condescend to move at all, and then he would only twitch his whiskers and remove himself in a leisurely fashion to some less disturbed spot. The services of Mr. Browning's " Pied Piper " would have been invaluable to us. There were, to be sure, various trench cats and an occasional dog, but they had other and better means of subsistence and took little heed of the rats. So the latter flourished, and, though curious diseases broke out among them, their lot must have been a happy one till the gas shells began to fall in every sector, and then their numbers dwindled rapidly, and in many parts they " ceased to be," at any rate for the moment.

Our second visit to Fleurbaix, for our first had been but a fleeting one, enabled us to get a more comprehensive view of our surroundings. The destruction in the village proved more considerable than had at first been realized, and though civilians abounded, the place had a weary and depressed air, which was hardly to be wondered at. Everything looked so sadly out of repair; little attempt had been made, or was indeed possible, to make good the ravages of war. Streets where there was little traffic were grass grown, gardens were rank with weeds, fences and railings were broken down, and débris of bricks and mortar littered the ground. Work on improving billets was at once put in hand, and things left unfinished by the 2/7th K.L.R. were completed and improved, in accordance with one of the unwritten laws of trench life—viz., " Always leave a place better than you find it." The 2/8th K.L.R., working with the 2/5th K.L.R.,

THE OFFICERS—MARGATE, 1915.

occupied in turn billets opposite ours ; and in rear of the village in quite a decent house were Brigade Headquarters, pleasantly adjacent to a couple of 60-pounders !

Being now Battalion in Brigade Reserve, we were initiated at once into one of the special functions of that privileged position, the reconnoitring of emergency routes. This necessary but tedious performance is complicated by the very hazy details usually supplied, and the tendency of the local inhabitants to remove guide posts and to put wire fences across the tracks.

Although the battalion remained in Fleurbaix till March 6th as Brigade and Divisional Reserve, it must not be imagined that the time was an idle one. Even in so-called " rest periods " the infantry are never allowed much peace, while in reserve in the vicinity of the front line there is more than enough for all to do. To begin with, the troops found, to their disgust, that general training was not confined to England, and for those not otherwise employed the usual physical training and bayonet fighting, rapid loading, wiring, and all the other inventions of the training enthusiast, appeared once more on the scene. All the same, the proximity of the enemy added interest to the bayonet fighting and other exercises, for no one knew but that skill in those arts, and of the very highest order, might be demanded of every man at the shortest notice. The natural tendency to dirtiness and slovenly appearance produced by a time in muddy trenches had also to be checked, and the battalion soon realized that the best soldiers in action are generally the best turned-out behind the line.

Apart from training in arms and discipline, the majority of the battalion were heavily engaged, under R.E. supervision, in digging or cleaning out drains and channels in rear of the line. This most necessary but unpleasant and tedious work fills the soul of the fighting man with burning indignation ; and though warnings to that effect had often been uttered, it took practical experience to prove that more than half an infantryman's work consists of digging. It is curious to note that, essential as is proficiency in the use of the spade, no real instruction in the subject is ever given at Officers' or N.C.Os'. Schools, though to watch an untrained digger and a trained one working side by side is a revelation. In Major Bishop, R.E., we found a man full of knowledge and withal of consideration and tact. Everyone liked him, and while he commanded the Field Company with which we worked, though misunderstandings sometimes arose and mistakes occurred, as was inevitable, our relations with him were always most cordial, and it was with deep regret that we heard of his death at Passchendaele later in the year. His place was, luckily, filled by another good man.

There is nothing particularly amusing, still less heroic, about a night working party. As soon as the light begins to fail the parties fall in, wearing gum-boots and skeleton equipment, with the rifle slung across the back. Each man carries a pick or shovel, or, if it is a wiring party, rolls of wire slung on a stick between two men. Off they go, their footsteps, owing to the rubber soles, sounding rather ghostly as they tramp along the *pavé*. Rapidly darkness falls, and, except for the subdued sound of their feet, the gentle " swish " of water in the water-bottles, and the occasional " clang " as someone stumbles and hits his spade against his rifle, there is little in their progress to attract attention. Presently the party halts, and a voice from the darkness inquires : " Is that ' A ' working party, 2/6th K.L.R. ?" The answer is in the affirmative, and the party is allotted its task.

An occasional Véry light shows up the men in silhouette, their rifles and equipment lying in a row out of the way of the earth they are throwing up, but ready to hand in case of emergency. Presently a machine gun begins to speak and slowly traverses in their direction. The work continues, but attention is centred on the stream of bullets which may suddenly spray right across the party. Here it comes, and down they all go on their stomachs as the bullets hiss and crack above them. It ceases as suddenly as it began, and work proceeds again. Another moment and there is a swift, rushing sound, followed at once by a loud report, then by another and yet another in quick succession. Those nearest hastily take cover, for a " whizz-bang " at close quarters can be very destructive. The stretcher-bearers accompanying the party listen for the call, " Stretcher-bearers forward," but no one calls, and work begins again. About midnight it is finished. Plastered with mud—thick, stinking mud—the men collect their equipment, spades and picks are checked (it is so easy to leave some behind, just put down for a moment and forgotten) and off they go, listening eagerly for the order, " Smoke if you like," back to Fleurbaix, where hot tea awaits them ; " and so to bed," as Mr. Pepys says.

Another interesting experience was our first visit to the Divisional Baths. This entailed a pleasant march in light order to Sailly, where bathing apparatus had been erected in a disused factory. The apparatus consisted of showers and tubs. As each man passed in he handed over all his personal effects and received a numbered disc in exchange. He then proceeded to undress, and while he was bathing his uniform was " stoved." As soon as the bather had dried himself he was presented with a clean set of underclothing, and his soiled linen was removed. This was really an excellent system, but it suffered from one serious drawback. A man gave up a good shirt and perhaps his own home-knitted socks. The quality, not to mention the size, of the articles issued in return did not always correspond to those handed in. This was apt to be a frequent source of complaint, but, taking all things into consideration, it did not appear that any other system was feasible. For the officers there were half a dozen hip-baths, surrounded by duck-boards, with which, in fact, the whole floor of the baths was covered ; and though the Commanding Officer possessed a rubber saucer-bath, which he lent freely to the other officers, a complete immersion in hot water was a pleasure too keen to be resisted, and the comfort of it almost indescribable.

One rather interesting little ceremony was performed at Fleur-baix. This was the presentation by our billet lady at Headquarters to each of the battalion runners of a rosary specially blessed by the priest. She assured them that so long as they wore these rosaries no harm could befall them, and it is interesting to note that only two out of the ten died : one of them, Manick, was killed in 1918 while serving with another battalion ; the other, Turnock, died as a prisoner-of-war, having been captured while serving with another unit. Manick, it is said, had sent his rosary home a few days before he was killed.

At 7.30 a.m. on March 6th " Gipsy," the new code name for our battalion, commenced to relieve " Giddy," the *nom de guerre* of the 2/7th K.L.R. The order of march this time was " C," " D," " B," " A " ; " C " on the right and " D " on the left in the front line, " B " in support, and " A " in reserve. An innovation, always adopted in future, was made by the dispatch of signallers into the line ahead of the battalion, thus ensuring the proper take-over of signal stations throughout the sector in the ample time at their disposal. Taking over a complicated exchange at Headquarters and smaller switch-boards at the Company Headquarters, involving as it does a clear understanding of which line is which and where it is laid, where the test boxes are, and so forth, is a business that requires care and takes time. The irritating and even disastrous results that might arise from mistakes or erroneous information can easily be imagined.

Nothing eventful happened during the relief, but Headquarters were interested to learn that the Germans had shelled Wye Farm, putting one shell, in fact, right through the roof just above where Colonel Slater was sleeping. The New Zealanders had warned us that the place looked like an empty ruin from the enemy's position, and that only charcoal or coke should be used during the day, so as to prevent smoke: Whether these precautions had been relaxed. or whether the enemy was merely being spiteful, was not clear ; but at any rate the work of making shell-proof " bivvies " which had already commenced, was hurried on, and " baby elephants," the smaller corrugated iron semi-circular shelters, began to arrive and were inserted into some of the rooms, together with a liberal supply of sand-bags.

The weather was again positively arctic, and everyone looked half frozen. No one, therefore, was particularly displeased when orders were issued at 11 p.m. on March 7th that " Gilt "—*i.e.*, the 2/8th K.L.R.—would relieve us, commencing at 8 a.m. the next morning. The 2/8th K.L.R. were in the trenches on our right, and the scheme was that they should thin out their posts and with the surplus troops take over the most vital positions in our sector. This thinning-out process was taking place all up and down the line, men being drawn from quiet sectors to increase the number available for the great offensive planned for 1917. Profound secrecy was to be maintained, and strict orders were issued that no troops should move in daylight along routes where they might be detected. Nature, however, took the matter into her own hands, and thoughtfully provided a blizzard throughout the whole period of the relief.

The orders for the relief were somewhat complicated. Two platoons of " C " Company were to move out at once, the other two to remain and be relieved in the positions they held. " D " Company could release one platoon and retain three ; " B " Company released two platoons less one section, and " A " Company the same. Plenty of guides were provided, each supplied with a note as to the location and name of his post, and the relief proceeded steadily and without a hitch. Wye Farm, from being a Battalion Headquarters, sank to the more humble position of a telephone exchange, with one section to guard it.

An interesting item in the orders was paragraph 9, which stated that on March 9th the battalion would proceed to Bac St. Maur into billets, and that 2nd-Lieutenant Clarke was to proceed there at once as billeting officer. The battalion gradually percolated to Fleurbaix as the relief proceeded, and the Quartermaster and his satellites were busy there packing up and making ready for the move on the morrow. The Quartermaster's Stores and transport lines were already quite close to Bac St. Maur, and many were the inquiries as to the sort of billets we were likely to get.

For the following morning orders were issued on the zero principle, companies and platoons being ordered to fall in at so many minutes after zero, which was 9.30 a.m. It was an experiment in timing, and was not used again except for active operations. Intervals of 50 yards between platoons and 200 yards between companies had to be observed, while a space of 50 yards had also to be maintained between every group of three vehicles. These precautions were valuable, not only in the case of hostile artillery fire, but also to prevent congestion and blocks on the narrow French roadways. Never, even in rest areas, did a battalion move in that solid stream of which we used to be so proud in England. Long distances between battalions and shorter distances between companies was the invariable rule, though it gave a battalion a somewhat disjointed appearance and, if horses for any reason were not available, made communications between the companies rather a tedious performance on the march.

The distance to Bac St. Maur was only a matter of two or three miles, and we were soon there. The village consisted of two long rows of ugly houses and factories on either side of the main Lille—Armentières—Estaires road. Most of the houses were small and poor-looking, such as you find in little industrial villages ; and the *pavé* road, much in need of repair owing to the continuous stream of lorries, by no means added to the beauty of the place, which indeed looked dreary enough. However, it seemed pretty peaceful, and the war seemed removed to a far greater distance than the few miles traversed really warranted. After the usual discussion over billets—for everyone thinks another company has done better than his own in the allotment—the battalion settled down very comfortably, and prepared to carry out the work usually assigned to a Brigade in Divisional Reserve—viz., providing working parties. Of these there were two distinct kinds : one was for the improvement of the line of strong posts in front of Fleurbaix, which rejoiced in such names as " Croix Marèchal," " Command Post," " Ferret Post," etc., where the only excitement was an occasional shower of " whizz-bangs " ; the other was working on the dumps at Strazeele, which meant starting by motor transport at 6 a.m.—or rather being ready to start then, as the lorry was anything up to two hours late. For the rest of the men there was general training, and the companies were changed about daily.

A pleasant addition to Bac St. Maur was the Divisional theatre bought by our Division from the Australians. It was a large army hut, suitably fitted with stage, etc., and here the Divisional Concert Party, " The Dons," used to perform with great skill.

We were much worried at this time with anti-gas instructions. Not only did the Divisional Gas Officer, whom we had not seen since our first arrival at Strazeele, begin to realize our existence once more and come to inspect respirators, but countless instructions came out containing a perfect maze of directions. The whole of the front was divided into zones—" Gas Alert," " Precautionary," etc.—and notice boards were posted on the roads warning the wayfarer as to which zone he was entering. Further, when the wind was " dangerous," boards revealed that fact to all and sundry, and harrowing accounts were circulated as to the swiftness with which the German gas penetrated into back areas.

The Quartermaster's stores and transport lines were quite pleasantly situated on a side road about ten minutes' walk from the battalion. The former consisted of two or three small Armstrong huts, where the Quartermaster and Transport Officer lived in considerable comfort and entertained freely. All the animals were in good covered standings, and the billets for the drivers and the grooms were conveniently adjacent. The transport section always distinguished themselves by their taste for beautifying their surroundings, and in their spare moments Lieutenant Hutchinson and Sergeant Lloyd had many an anxious discussion as to the most suitable site for a row of whitewashed stones, collected with great trouble from the neighbourhood.

One thing which impressed us during our stay in Bac St. Maur was the very pronounced salient in which we were living. At night this was very marked, as in whichever direction you turned Véry lights could be seen in your rear. So striking, in fact, was this that a soldier of another battalion, somewhat the worse for drink, came up to Lieutenant Sutherland one evening, and, pointing to those Véry lights rising well behind our backs, inquired in a confidential manner : " Can you tell me, sir, if that is the same war as we are taking part in ?"

On March 17th our first draft of officers, three in number, arrived—2nd-Lieutenants McWilliam, Fell, and Hodgkinson. Of these McWilliam had been badly wounded in 1915 while serving as a sergeant in the 1/6th K.L.R. As against this access of strength we had to set the loss of a sergeant and a number of men who had to be sent as bridge guard to Estaires, and whose return, when we had ceased to be in Divisional Reserve for some months, was only effected after a very lengthy correspondence. Sergeant Webster was also dispatched on traffic control duty, at which work he remained till the end.

We had thought in England that we knew something about men being employed on extra-regimental duty, but the few we had so employed there was a trifle to the host supplied by us in France. Corps, Divisional and Brigade clerks, area sanitary men, Divisional Baths employees, cooks and servants at Formation Headquarters, traffic control, A.S.C. loaders, men loaned to trench-mortar and machine-gun companies, gum-boot store-keepers, tramway men, men employed at Corps Rest Camps, N.C.O. instructors at schools, and Heaven knows what else, continued to be a steady drain on the battalion. Vacancies for courses, too, came pouring in ; and when you consider the number of cooks, transport drivers, clerks, police, storemen, etc., who are required for every battalion's own use, it will be clear enough that the number left in platoons and sections for ordinary duty was very small.

Our time in reserve was now drawing to a close, and it appeared that on March 29th we were due to relieve the 2/5th South Lancashire Regiment in the Rue du Bois sector north of (and next but one to) La Boutillerie, the Fleurbaix trenches. The usual procedure followed. We (*i.e.*, the Commanding Officer and Adjutant) set off one morning and rode along the road to Erquinghem, where we turned off to the right and called at La Rolanderie, a pleasant farmhouse with some extra Nissen huts, the Headquarters of the 172nd Brigade, the present tenants of the sector. From there, after the usual discussion about the enemy and the disadvantages and peculiarities of our new sector, we proceeded viâ Gris Pot and La Vesée to a junction of roads a few hundred yards south of the latter place. Here the horses were left, and inadvertently our tin helmets, which were hanging from our saddles, and we proceeded on foot. The country was flat and depressing. Tattered screens stood here and there masking the roads. An occasional section of guns hidden in old houses ; a runner or two riding along the *pavé* on that invention of the devil an army cycle ; an artillery officer and his signallers making for a forward observation post—those were the only signs of life. All the houses were untenanted, which was to be regretted, as piquant advertisements testified to the excellence of Pierre Les Cornez beer !

In the background behind the German front line the slopes of the famous Aubers Ridge, the barrier that blocked the road to Lille, rose steadily to a height of more than fifty metres, almost a mountain-range in this flat country, giving the enemy a very fine view of all our activities. Passing Billet and Ration Farms, which bristled with R.E. material and salvage, we crossed a duck-board bridge and struck the subsidiary line of the Bois Grenier sector on the immediate right of the Rue du Bois. We plodded steadily along the duck-board track till Desolanque Farm (or Deplanque Farm, as its real name is : the official map is wrong), the usual ruin surrounded by a rectangular moat, appeared in view. The subsidiary line ran about fifty yards in front of this, and close up against it, in a long concrete dug-out, were the Battalion Headquarters that we were seeking. Down the steps into this dug-out we descended with more haste than dignity, as the enemy selected this particular moment to send a shower of " whizz-bangs " into the farm, just skimming the top of the dug-out. In the narrow stairway we met the Commanding Officer, full of wrath. " Whizz-bangs " generally meant that too many people were wandering about in the vicinity of the farm, and strict orders had been issued to prevent this. It is extraordinary how insensible to danger the average man soon becomes, and the most reasonable orders for the protection of life are ignored or disregarded unless very strictly enforced.

The Headquarters consisted of a very long concrete passage with five small rooms opening on to it—the mess, two sleeping rooms, a signal office, and the Adjutant's office and sleeping room combined. All the rooms were small and required artificial light, and a general feeling of chilly damp prevailed everywhere. We arranged ourselves as best we could in the mess ; but we were all crowded together in a space far too small for the number of occupants, and the table was covered with maps, defence schemes, aeroplane photographs, and the usual litter of a trench headquarters, not to mention box respirators, tin helmets, and other impedimenta which are hastily doffed on entering a dug-out.

It appeared that the artillery observers had decided that the Germans were registering, and a sketch map that was produced showed the area which it was presumed they intended to raid. Colonel Bates, of the 2/5th South Lancashire Regiment, was rather contemptuous of the whole thing, and ascribed the apparent registration to mere casual shooting on various targets. But, at

any rate, the matter had to be attended to, although the expected
raid never took place. The line was held with three companies
in the front and support lines, and two in the subsidiary line, the
additional company being supplied by another battalion. The
total frontage was about 2,800 yards, and to cover this a system
of "gaps" and "localities" had been arranged—*i.e.*, a series
of posts covering vital points of the line. The "gaps" were
ordinary but unoccupied trenches, often derelict; but they were
usually wired and made difficult to penetrate.

Before leaving the 2/5th South Lancashire Regiment we were
introduced to Major Brookes, M.C., A/286 Battery R.F.A., and
from that moment commenced a long and lasting friendship
with a most gallant and capable officer in whom every man (and
all knew him) placed the utmost confidence. In the trying days
ahead in Houplines at its worst Major Brookes was daily round
the line; and though his battery was continually shelled by guns
of every calibre, he always managed to do all we asked him, and
never failed to let the enemy have even more than his daily quota
of 18-pounder shells.

At 8 p.m. on March 28th Lieutenant F. C. Bowring, Sergeant
Machell, and the company Lewis gunners set off for the trenches.
In view of a possible hostile raid, it was thought advisable that
they should relieve in daylight, and be in a position to make their
presence really felt on the relief night in the event of the Germans
choosing that time for a raid. The route to be taken was viâ
Erquinghem, Armentières, and Rue Marle Level Crossings, and
then straight down past Crown Prince House to the subsidiary
line, where they were to spend the night, taking over their posts
at dawn the following day.

It was a long and tiring march of many miles from Bac St. Maur,
and one which was considered too long for the battalion to undertake at one stretch on relief night, and it was therefore arranged
that a long tea halt should be made in Armentières. The Commanding Officer decided to spend the afternoon of the relief day

(March 29th) in the trenches with the Company Commanders;
while Major Wilson was to meet the battalion in Armentières,
where he and the Quartermaster were making the necessary
arrangements for housing and tea; and the Adjutant brought up
the battalion. Coming through Chapelle d'Armentières on their
way back from the trenches, a question arose between the Commanding Officer and the Company Commanders as to the location
of some place on the map. As it was raining and they wanted to
examine the map, they adjourned to a ruined house for a few
minutes. The point at issue being settled, and time getting on,
they hurried out of the house and on down the street. They had
not gone thirty yards when a shell entered the house they had
just vacated and blew the place to smithereens. How often in
this and in every other war a few minutes have made the difference
between life and death!

The school at 57, Rue de Lille, had been selected for the tea
halt, a place eminently suited for the purpose, and fairly safe from
possible interference by the enemy. It was a fine building built
round a playground, with the front facing the Rue de Lille, and
one side of the school facing the Rue Gambetta. It had obviously been repeatedly hit by shells of various sizes, but the
Germans had not shelled Armentières itself for some time; and
although the concentration of the whole of the battalion in such
a small space caused some misgivings, the scheme worked excellently, and nothing untoward occurred. Field kitchens arrived
with the companies, and as soon as tea was well under way the
officers repaired in turns to the " Au Bœuf," an excellent restaurant
—one of the few still doing business in the town.

At 7 p.m. the head of the battalion arrived at Sand-bag Corner,
a junction of roads with a great sand-bag barricade on the way to
Chapelle d'Armentières, where guides awaited us. The companies were to hold in the order " D," " A " (now commanded by
Captain Wyatt) ," C " from the right, with " B " Company in
reserve in the subsidiary line, which " B " Company, 2/7th K.L.R.,

proceeding viâ Gris Pot and La Vesée, had already taken over, as extra company in the subsidiary line, from a company of the 2/4th South Lancashire Regiment. For the first time the men wore their packs detached from their equipment on kicking-straps, this again being due to the possibility of a raid; and in future this was the order for all reliefs, the manifold advantages being very obvious. The last part of the route up to the subsidiary line was along a lane full of shell-holes, but the frequent illumination produced by German Véry lights made the going fairly simple. Transport came right up to Battalion Headquarters, and dumps were formed accordingly in the subsidiary line for Headquarters and for each company. The relief proceeded quietly and without incident, and its speed was naturally increased by the possibility, owing to their number, of having " up " and " down " communication trenches—Wine Avenue and Leith Walk the former; Park Row, Wellington Avenue, and Cowgate the latter. At 12.40 a.m. on March 30th relief was reported complete, and our friends of the 2/5th South Lancashire Regiment proceeded joyfully to Crown Prince House and the reserve billets in the Rue Marle.

The tour, in spite of the gloomy forebodings of the gunners, proved quiet enough. For the first night or two strong fighting patrols lay up in No Man's Land in the hope of catching the enemy raiding party. The Germans, however, showed no signs of any hostile intent, and after a day or two the various precautions that had been adopted were discarded.

The left sector came in for a considerable amount of shelling, particularly in the vicinity of Captain Eccles's Headquarters and also the Ferme de Biez in rear of it, which our observers used to haunt. However, there was plenty of room in the sector for shells to fall without doing any serious harm, and our casualties were, fortunately, very low in consequence. In the right company's front a stream came in under the front line and wandered across the sector. Strict orders had been issued that the water was not to be used for drinking or cooking, inasmuch as it came

from the enemy's line.   Walking round one day, Captain McHugh,
our newly arrived and most delightful Irish Medical Officer, took
a sample for analysis through curiosity.   It was interesting to
learn that a strong arsenic result was obtained.

A small incident that occurred during this tour, while we were
still fresh and inexperienced, and which caused considerable
merriment at the time, may be worth recounting here.   In the
apex of the salient C.S.M. Barker, of " D " Company, had found
a rifle-grenade machine—simply the barrel of a rifle mounted
on a fixed stand, at a point within comfortable range of the enemy
trench.   Now, Barker had in the training days in England been
Bombing Sergeant, and was anxious to give a practical demonstration of the skill he had acquired in the handling of these
treacherous and dangerous weapons.   Moreover, O.C. " D " Company was determined to show his company that " live and let
live " was not to be their motto, so his support in the venture
was assured.   " I will come down to-night, corporal, and send a
few over," remarked Barker in an off-hand manner to Corporal
Wright, whose section held the post of honour at the salient.
Accordingly that same night Barker, with a small host of supporters, including Lieutenant Ormrod, the Trench Officer, F. G.
Roberts, the Trench Sergeant, Riflemen Forster, Alpine, and
Liderth from the next post, and Moody and Heath (runners) was
to be seen in the vicinity of the lethal weapon.   All took such
cover as they could while Barker loaded the machine with a
" Newton Pippin " and prepared to do his worst.   " Look out ! "
Bang !   With a thin whistling sound the grenade wended its
way towards the enemy.   Tense silence.   A second later an uninteresting report over the way.   Hardly had that noise subsided
than a sinister " pop " was heard.   " What was that ? Keep
low ! "   A rushing, hissing noise approached, becoming rapidly
louder.   Clang ! Clang ! as " pineapple " after " pineapple "
burst in and among the party, covering the prostrate soldiers with
mud as they flattened themselves against the ground.   A swift

62

crawling, creeping, shuffling, and the party were hurrying away blindly trying to escape from " those damned things !" For the remainder of the night the shoot was " off."

However, O.C. " D " Company was reluctant to leave the initiative with the enemy. It is true that we might have known that he had the spot registered from his previous experience, and that we laughed heartily over the whole thing. Still, something had to be done. Suddenly O.C. " D " Company remembered that at 6 a.m. the next morning the Light Trench Mortar Battery were to do a shoot, supported by 18-pounders if required. Here was the chance of showing the Germans that " D " Company were not easily worsted. It was arranged that a " Newton " should be mounted once more. Watches were quietly synchronized with the unsuspecting Light Trench Mortar Battery. At five seconds before 6 a.m. the " Newton " was fired. Instantly came the German retaliation as before, but hardly had the " pineapples " started when our Light Trench Mortar Battery opened with great vigour. This annoyed the enemy, who were expecting another easy victory, and the aid of their artillery was invoked. To this our 18-pounders replied, and before long a regular artillery duel was in full swing. This was more than the Germans bargained for, and they soon stopped. " D " Company were avenged !

At night we used to get magnificent views of distant barrages, especially towards the south. It was a wonderful sight, like summer lightning, only more vivid and impressive ; while every now and again the uniform colour of yellowish light would be shot with a sudden streak of vivid red as a dump exploded or some conflagration broke out. It was fascinating to watch the endless dance of flickering light against the blackness of the sky. One minute the whole heaven was lit up, the next moment all was dark ; or perhaps a series of small flashes appeared, darting up now here, now there. If the barrage was far away, no sound would be heard, though if you entered a dug-out facing in that direction you would be conscious of a dull rumbling that warned you this was no mere pyrotechnic display, but the most nerve-wracking feature of modern war, an intense bombardment.

During this time we learnt with regret that General Gilbert, who had commanded in turn for many years first the original and then the Second Line Liverpool Infantry Brigade, was return-ing to England on account of age, being relieved by Brigadier-General R. N. Bray, C.M.G., D.S.O., of The Duke of Wellington's Regiment. General Gilbert's dignified kindness had made him most popular with all ranks, and we would gladly have con-tinued under his leadership, come what might. He arrived one morning with his successor, and after the usual introductions they were proceeding round the line when a curious thing happened. Going along the front line just short of Chard's Farm, they must have been spotted. Fortunately, however, General Gilbert stopped a few moments in a part of the trench hidden from observation to point out certain features of the ground. As they resumed their walk along the trench to the farm, it suddenly became the centre of a regular storm of " whizz-bangs," obviously timed to greet their arrival, which had so happily been delayed.

Another visitor was Major Derry, D.S.O., of the Welch Regi-ment, who had just succeeded the late Major Thompson as G.S.O.2. Major Thompson had been practically cut in two by a " whizz-bang " while talking to Colonel Cohen, of the 2/5th K.L.R., outside the latter's Headquarters in the Bois Grenier sector. We had seen little of Major Thompson, but what we had seen we liked. Major Derry, with his cheery laugh and complete disregard of personal danger, soon became highly popular among us.

On the evening of March 6th the 2/7th K.L.R. relieved us, commencing at 8 p.m. with the right front company. " B " Company in the subsidiary line was to remain as extra company, merely moving along to the positions held during our tour of duty by " B " Company 2/7th K.L.R. Soon after midnight the battalion was clear of the trenches and heading for Rue Marle,

Photo by

Gale & Polden, Ltd., Aldershot.

THE KING'S INSPECTION—REVIEW GROUND, LAFFAN'S PLAIN, 1916.

where the reserve billets were situated. At the top of the long straight stretch past Crown Prince House " D " Company turned to the right, and were billeted in houses on the left of the road ; " A " and " C " turned to the left, " A " Company being next to Rue Marle Church, a bright red brick edifice with a brick spire, looking as if it had only been finished the day before ; while " C " Company were in houses several hundred yards farther down the same road.

Nothing of much importance happened while the battalion was in reserve at Rue Marle. One company was always detailed as inlying piquet, and spent its time training in the vicinity of its billets. The other companies were up nightly, carrying medium trench mortar ammunition up into the trenches in preparation for the raid to be carried out by the composite company of 172nd Brigade—" Paynter's party," as it was called, after their Brigadier.

One morning the Corps and Divisional Commanders arrived at Crown Prince House and immediately demanded a map showing the Fleury Switch. Every conceivable map was produced, but in vain ; nor had anyone the faintest idea what the switch was to which they so repeatedly referred. In the end the A.D.C. to the Corps Commander sped back to the car (left round the corner out of sight), and in due course produced the precious map, and the party proceeded on their way restored to a more amiable frame of mind.

On the night of March 11th " D " Company relieved " B " Company in the subsidiary line. A night or so before a German aeroplane had made a determined effort to do them serious harm by dropping a number of heavy bombs in their immediate vicinity. Oddly enough, that night, as the Adjutant and Lewis Gun Officer were undressing in their bedroom, which faced the line, they suddenly noticed that the shutters were not drawn. A rush was made for the candle, which was hastily extinguished. At that moment there was a deafening report, and we felt that here was the reward for our carelessness. However, it was soon realized that the noise was not shelling, but the above-mentioned bombing, the hum of the aeroplane being clearly audible; but after depositing its load it departed, and peace reigned once more. No casualties were caused, and quite a number of " D " Company were sleeping so soundly that they knew nothing of the matter till the following morning.

It was always a remarkable thing to us who lived there that Crown Prince House was not shelled. It was a large house in full view of the enemy, standing quite isolated at the side of a long straight road. It must have been very tempting to the German gunners, who liked to see the red dust rise from a direct hit on a house. There was no sort of cellar accommodation worth mentioning. Signals had the only cellar, and that was but half underground. We used to encourage one another by saying that the Germans could not shell the house without committing *lèse majesté* (the Crown Prince was reputed once to have made his Headquarters there), though some very recent shell-holes at the entrance seemed to prove that they were prepared occasionally to risk being guilty of that serious offence. As a matter of fact, the Headquarters of a South Lancashire Battalion were soon afterwards shelled out of the house, and a very unpleasant proceeding they found it.

The only other excitement was the sudden arrival of a shell in Armentières; not by the railway-station, a place not infrequently shelled in retaliation for a 12-inch railway mounting gun which used to come up there occasionally, but right into the town, and only just over the Rue de Lille. This single shell caused quite a sensation, but as nothing more happened we concluded that the enemy had let off a gun by mistake.

On March 13th after dinner the battalion (less " D " Company) moved off to billets in the Rue Dormoire, the 2/5th South Lancashire Regiment moving in at the same moment. In spite of all precautions, the congestion of traffic was very great for a short time, but was soon straightened out. We crossed Rue Marle Level Crossing, then left-handed up the Boulevard Faidherbe, and so round to the Armentières Level Crossing. The route after that was the main road through Erquinghem, about a mile beyond which lay our new area. Headquarters was situated in a fine old seventeenth-century farmhouse, built round the usual quadrangle, with its usual vast heap of manure. Two sides were flanked by a moat which you crossed by a brick bridge, entering the farm through an archway. Opposite the entrance, and on the other side of the road, was a large open field with a duck-board track running across it, which led to two blocks of Nissen huts, occupied by " C " and " D " Companies, the latter not expected to arrive from the subsidiary line before midnight ; though, owing to confusion over the transport for the Lewis gunners, this estimate proved highly optimistic. Continuing down the lane past Battalion Headquarters—and an unpleasant lane it was, full of the most appalling holes and ruts, and deep in liquid mud which concealed many a sharp stone and pitfall—you eventually arrived at a group of farms. Here " A " and " B " Companies were accommodated in large barns in which great tiers of bunks had been erected. These were promptly nicknamed the " birdcage."

Reconnoitring of emergency routes and schemes for the reinforcing of divisions in front or on the flanks again came to the fore. Though all was quiet in our neighbourhood, considerable activity was apparent at night north of the Lys opposite the Messines Ridge, where bursting shrapnel and coloured lights were eloquent of raids in progress. Working parties (of a minimum strength of a platoon) and training became once more the order of the day. Rifle-grenade practice with " Newtons " was very popular, even after Lance-Corporal Cathels and a rifleman had been injured by the bursting of the breech of a rifle.

CHAPTER IV

ARMENTIÈRES UP TO GAS ATTACK

ON April 19th we received orders to reconnoitre the Boutillerie sector, held by the 2/5th King's Own Royal Lancaster Regiment, with a view to early relief; and the Commanding Officer, Adjutant, and Company Commanders proceeded the same day to Foray House, the " King's Own " Headquarters. This sector was a combination of the old Boutillerie trenches, held by us in February, and the trenches on our immediate right. There had been several British and enemy raids since then, and the damage caused had been considerable. The difficulty of maintaining 2,800 yards of front in a decent state of repair throughout its whole length had further impaired the condition of the trenches, and we were not surprised to find serious signs of decay on every hand. Our first experience, moreover, of walking quite considerable distances—*i.e.*, several hundred yards—without finding a trace of the defenders proved very instructive, and showed us what to expect for the future. The next day (April 20th, 1917) these orders were cancelled, and we were now informed that on the 26th we were to take over the Houplines sector in front of Armentières from the Australians. We set out once more on a tour of exploration. We rode to the Australian Brigade Headquarters in the Rue Jesuit, and thence on foot along the Houplines road to Tissage Dump, where the trenches began.

Those who now saw Armentières for the first time might well be impressed by the feeling of desolation which prevailed. The silent, shuttered houses, the empty streets, the ruins and the débris were familiar from the villages which had been already visited, but nowhere hitherto had the picture been on so large a scale as here. Armentières had been a bright and busy town before the war, with a population of some 30,000 people. Large spinning factories, fine houses and handsome shops abounded. Many of the streets, it is true, still contained quite a number of inhabitants ; but as you made your way down the Rue Jesuit towards the line, fewer and fewer grew the signs of any civil population, and more and more battered became the houses. It is a long walk to Tissage Dump. On the left you soon passed Barbed-Wire Square, then quite a pleasant grass-grown square with young trees just beginning to bud. In the far corner a wonderful green and blue tiled house had apparently been the residence of a lady fortune-teller. The next landmark was the level-crossing, beside which a huge church bell was suspended on a wooden frame to give warning against gas. The road a little farther on swung round first to the right, past some very dilapidated workmen's cottages of a curious blue tint; and then to the left, where stood L'Octroi d'Houplines, the familiar little wooden erection to be found on the outskirts of every French town. This had been hit by a shell ; it was a corner of ill repute, and the board bearing its title hung at an acute angle, being only supported by a fastening at one end. On the left of the road, next to the factory belonging to an English firm, stood Von Kluck's house, alleged to have been once the Headquarters of that famous General, and now used as the A.D.S., which for many months escaped a direct hit, while neighbouring houses were all but obliterated. A strip of open country followed ; on the left, a wilderness of ruins and marshland, with a glimpse of 18-pounders cleverly concealed ; on the right, loop-holed screening with a considerable view of the country beyond.

Nouvel Houplines (often thought to be Houplines itself, which was close to the river) consisted of two main streets forming an acute angle. At the junction stood Tissage Dump, where R.E. material for the line was stored. In the adjoining houses were a pioneer workshop, an observation post, the canteen, and the regimental aid post. The trench tram line (a continuation of the ordinary tram line from Armentières) divided here, one line running up alongside Gloucester Avenue to the trenches, the other following round to Durham Castle and other dumps. Several tall factory chimneys were grouped about this spot, all used as observation posts, and rejoicing in colonial names difficult to pronounce. Most of them bore signs of shell fire, one having been pierced right through close to its base, another having a large piece taken right out of its side.

The entrance to Gloucester Avenue—or " Gloster Ave," as the signboard called it—was really very picturesque, the trench descending gradually below ground level through what had once been a garden. On either side was abundant foliage, which later became prettily covered with flowers and presented a picture that might well have been the setting for the opening scene of " The Arcadians."

We began our walk up Gloucester Avenue, noting the trench running off to Spain Avenue, another fine communication trench. The way was up a gradual incline. At the top a network of narrow trenches appeared, and through these we made our way into the subsidiary line to Battalion Headquarters, a group of " bivvies " and short trenches entered under a small overhead traverse. On the immediate left stood a small elephant back, which combined the dual functions of mess and Adjutant's office, and opposite this was the cook-house. To the left was a double concrete dug-out, where " Signals " dwelt, and up a little short trench a minute concrete " bivvy " for the Commanding Officer.

In the mess we found the Commanding Officer of the 38th Battalion A.I.F. awaiting us, and he explained that our present place of rest was the old right Battalion Headquarters, while the left was in more commodious but less conveniently situated quarters in the spacious cellars of Cambridge House, some way along the subsidiary line. Half the Australians' Headquarters lived in one place and half in the other, and, though the two were connected by telephone, the disadvantages of the separation were obvious.

The Company Commanders now proceeded to their respective areas, while the Commanding Officer and Adjutant took a general survey of the line under the guidance of the Australian Colonel. The first impression was certainly most unfavourable. The principle of gaps and localities was maintained here, and constant shell fire, combined with lack of any means of repair, gave the sector a most dilapidated and depressing appearance, which was intensified by a great superfluity of water and a number of useless and derelict trenches running in all directions. Lateral communication, too, as so often happens in a combined sector, was extremely bad. After lunch at Cambridge House, the Commanding Officer and Adjutant proceeded on a tour of the left sector. This was notoriously the weak point, the left being bounded by the River Lys, which in winter rendered an area of several hundred yards along the bank quite impassable, though in summer this same area was perfectly passable, and to a large extent undefended. From the support line an excellent view could be obtained, the ground falling steeply away from there to a flat stretch called the Cricket Field, and then sloping upwards to a raised plateau on which Frelinghien stood, and on the hither side of which was built our front line. The sector, we found, was full of notices warning you that the spot you stood on was under direct observation from the Germans, which caused you to move round the traverses with alacrity. Most of these notices, we found, were obsolete, but on the left company's front, parts of the front line were certainly exposed, and till these spots were blinded casualties occurred from snipers. Generally speaking, the line appeared fairly quiet that afternoon, only intermittent shelling of a very desultory nature occurring. To our disgust, however, we learnt that gas cylinders were installed along practically the whole length of the front line, and the absence of heavy shelling was accordingly noted with some pleasure.

The relief took place on March 26th, the Lewis gunners entering the line the previous evening, and, in addition, one signaller per station, two battalion runners, all snipers, of whom one N.C.O. and three men were to take over the observation post, and one officer and one N.C.O. per platoon. On the morning of the 26th the Sniping Officer and Sergeant, the Medical Officer's orderly, the Bombing Officer and Corporal, all Company Sergeant-Majors, the Regimental Sergeant-Major, and two runners, together with the balance of the signallers under the Signalling Officer, made their way up to the trenches. This was the usual advance party for a new sector, and the arrangement undoubtedly quickened the relief, while in addition increased knowledge of a sector was acquired from the extra length of time spent with members of the outgoing unit.

Guides were to meet the companies at Houplines Level Crossing, commencing at 7 p.m. The following were the dispositions and routes : " D " Company, right front sector viâ Spain Avenue ; " C " Company, right centre viâ Gloucester Avenue ; " B " Company, up Durham and Edmeads Avenue to left centre ; while " A " Company went up Durham and along the subsidiary line to Irish Avenue and thence to left sector. Each company was responsible for its own supports and reserves, the latter consisting usually of a few cooks and ration carriers. Headquarters were accommodated in " bivvies " in the subsidiary line round Battalion Headquarters, and a few details at Cambridge House. The relief was completed at 11.40 p.m., and the Australians moved off for a rest and training preliminary to the Battle of Messines. They were a very cheery crowd and extremely obliging, and rendered the relief a very agreeable task. The code word was dispatched by telephone to Brigade, and we commenced our first tour in a sector that we were destined to occupy, turn and turn about with the 2/7th K.L.R., for four and a half months.

"THE KING'S" (LIVERPOOL REGIMENT)

As the period was such a long one, a more detailed description may be attempted than has been thought necessary in regard to other sectors held from time to time by the battalion. There were three main communication trenches leading into the line, all previously referred to. Spain and Gloucester Avenues, both starting from Tissage Dump, cut the subsidiary line on the right and right centre respectively. Durham Avenue started from Nouvel Houplines a few yards from Tissage Dump and to the north of it, and joined the subsidiary line close to Cambridge House. There was also the road from Nouvel Houplines to Frelinghien which ran past the north end of the subsidiary and support lines, but was under observation by day and unhealthy by night. On the extreme right, and just beyond our boundary, was Buterne Avenue, a deep traversed trench over which we had a right of way. It wandered about distressingly, and eventually ended in a small side street near Barbed Wire Square. Farther to the right and well on into the Epinette sector was Lunatic Lane, which eventually became an open track and led into the outskirts of Armentières by the Asylum.

The subsidiary line was marked on the right by a large civilian cemetery, through which the trench passed. It was full of graves with wooden crosses and artificial flowers such as are usually to be found in a French burial-ground. From there to the Battalion Headquarters the trench was traversed, but there was little parados. "Bivvies" of small breadth and height abounded, and there were one or two concrete dug-outs, usually full of water. A ditch, with a railing in front of it, marked the approach to Battalion Headquarters, after which the trench narrowed into two small alley-ways where Gloucester Avenue joined the subsidiary line, and thence ran down steeply to a road from Nouvel Houplines to Quesnoy. Here the tram line crossed the subsidiary line and ran across country to the right company front. The open road was masked by a big screen. At this point the subsidiary line was built on a somewhat higher level, and contained big bays

73

and long traverses, protected in rear by a parados, behind which was a traffic trench, in which a number of " bivvies " had been constructed.

Continuing your course, you came to Wessex Avenue, the finest communication trench in the sector, though but little used. The line now became a long, straight trench with a high parapet, with duck-boards along the side of the bank and also at the bottom. Beside the lower track was a green ditch. At the end of this stretch was a bridge across the Panama Canal, which ran back in a south-easterly direction to the support line in the right company sector. In design it was merely a deep drain, but it was duck-boarded and a handy short-cut diagonally across the sector. It was seldom used in daylight, in the hope, which was probably justified, that the enemy would regard it merely as a drain. Durham, Edmeads, and Sussex Avenues all met at this point ; and a few yards in the rear stood Cambridge House. The last part of the line was full of " bivvies," and just before the end, Irish Avenue, the left-hand communication trench of the sector, led off to the front line. At the end the ground fell away steeply to some marshland beside the banks of the Lys. The only other means of communication with the front line, except the communication trenches above mentioned and a few overland tracks, was the road which ran from the junction of Wessex Avenue and the subsidiary line to Edmeads Farm. This was only passable at night, but it was an excellent short-cut, though subject to bursts of machine-gun fire and " whizz-bangs."

The description of the trenches forward of the subsidiary line is a far more formidable undertaking. We will commence with the right, as being the simplest and also, generally speaking, the most healthy. The subsidiary line was followed to the right almost as far as the cemetery. Just before reaching it a communication trench was found leading off (if you were lucky and knew the way) to the left under an overhead traverse, and guarded by a sentry. The latter in the early days informed you, in a bored fashion, that the wind was dangerous or the reverse, and criticized your box-respirator if not in the alert position. Following the trench in its windings for a short distance, Vancouver Avenue branched off to the left. This was only half finished, though you could with much floundering get through it to Gloucester Avenue; in reality, however, it was quite useless. A hundred yards or so farther on you suddenly came on a corrugated iron sentry-box, with a small weather-cock and a shell case suspended from a stick beside it, where the gas sentry over the right company Headquarters was stationed. Here in an open space you found two or three log huts of small dimensions, with one or two orthodox " bivvies." You then passed over a bridge, and, ducking your head to avoid a sheet of corrugated iron, under which cooking operations were usually going on, you entered a low edifice, which was lighted, it may be mentioned, with two small windows of real glass. Here you might find O.C. " D " Company sitting at the table, endeavouring to compose one of the innumerable reports that the higher powers delighted to collect. Two or three bunks adorned the walls ; and a form on either side of the table, a Véry pistol, a tin of cigarettes, some recent pamphlets, and odd pieces of officers' equipment, made up the furniture. You could stand up more or less erect, and the place was really quite comfortable, but hardly shell-proof.

Beyond Company Headquarters the communication trench showed the strongest inclination to close in. It was extremely narrow, and but for the overhead struts would very soon have become impassable. Newburn Lane led off to the left, certainly more of a lane than a trench, through which you could reach the Orchard, a regular target for German gunners, and a place to be avoided at certain times of the day. Farther down the communication trench was a slit on the left where Light Trench Mortar Battery men lived. Just below here the trench suddenly came to an end, and you crossed a little stream running along a diminutive valley. The tram line also came in sight, wandering away along an old road through tangled bushes and weeds to the front line. It was badly smashed in places, and was never used as far forward as this. The trench began again up the far side of the tiny valley—London Road, as it was now called—and here stood two graves marking the resting-place of two unknown soldiers. The going was sticky and the trench much battered. Later on grass and green things generally were conspicuous on either side of the trench, but now everything looked bare and muddy—just yellow clay, shell-holes, mud banks, and trenches more or less derelict. Suddenly you heard voices, and without quite realizing it you found you were in the front line.

A broad breastwork formed the means of defence, occasional bays being held, but the majority being unoccupied and full of loose barbed wire. Everything betokened the effects of shell fire where men were too few to do more than just repair their own particular posts. Derelict " bivvies," odd broken duck-boards half covered with slime, sheets of corrugated iron riddled with holes, bits of old ground sheets, and fragments of equipment, lay about in all directions. Everything presented that damp, yellow aspect peculiar to clay soil. The traverses, sodden with water, were bursting down the hurdles or wire netting with which they were revetted, while the empty bays were falling in of their own accord, or presented a crushed and crumbling appearance, the result of the direct burst of a shell or " minnie."

As you rounded the traverse of an occupied bay the following picture met your eye. Imagine a narrow trench about 12 feet long by 4 feet wide, with a firestep running along the entire length some 12 inches from the ground. Near the centre of the trench stands a rifleman in skeleton equipment, gazing into the bottom mirror of a box periscope which is fastened by a spike to the parapet, its top covered by dirty canvas to match the surrounding sand-bags. By the sentry's side is a rifle, and close at hand are the empty shell-case gong and strombos horn, in case of gas. Next to him sits his relief, similarly attired, all men

76

invariably wearing equipment in the front line. The relief sentry is passing the time in cleaning some clips of ammunition from an open small-arms ammunition box. The corporal and two men are filling sand-bags, which will be required at dusk. Another rifle-man sits at the far end, sleeping peacefully and dreaming of something (we hope) remote from the war. He was the last sentry. Two boxes let into the parados contain Véry lights and bombs ; the Véry pistol hangs from a peg in the parapet. Five rifles with swords fixed stand in a row against the side of the trench; while a shelf holds some mess-tin lids, two water-bottles, some bread, and a tin of bully beef. Two sand-bags for salvage and rubbish hang at the end of the bay. Round the corner two " bivvies "—mere hovels about three foot high, wet and slimy— complete the " home comforts " of this cheerful abode. From one of the " bivvies " protrude two pairs of muddy boots and four legs covered with clay-stained puttees. Their owners are enjoying a well-earned rest, having spent most of the night prowling about in No Man's Land.

Taking the next communication trench, Gloucester Avenue, we could make our way up to the front line to a point not far distant from the top of London Road ; or, better still, we could branch off along Pretoria to the right-centre company's support line. Gloucester Avenue was a good winding trench cut through what had once been cornfields. Pretoria was even better, and brought you out close to the point where the Panama Canal joined the support line. By the end of the canal were two deep con-crete dug-outs, both small and damp, and in one of these the signallers and in the other the Company Commander were to be found. In the latter, as you carefully descended the steps, you would have been able at once to recognize, not only from the orderly appearance of the spot, but from the number of parcels from Fortnum and Mason, that Captain Eccles dwelt there ; and, sure enough, there he was, looking as if he had just stepped out of a band-box, with Company Sergeant-Major

Heyworth sitting by his side working at the company card index.

After making your way along the support line round interminable traverses, you squeezed your way up Timaru to the front line. Thence you went along past Wessex Avenue, which requires no further description, to the end of Locality 12. From here a path led up to the support line—Gap " M " being impassable—and from the support line by another path to the left centre company's front line—quite a decent stretch of bays and traverses with a wilderness of ruined trenches in their rear. Half-way along this sector you turned up a miserable ruin of a trench to Captain Steward's Headquarters, a concrete dug-out set like an oasis in a desert of derelict trenches. In spite of the neighbourhood, Captain Steward would appear perfectly groomed and with a cheerful smile, though denouncing the Germans for making him so uncomfortable. Another dug-out adjoining was used by his subalterns.

To visit the left sector it was now necessary to go right down Edmeads Avenue and then up Sussex Avenue, whence you could go to Hobbs Farm along Cambridge or along Fusilier Avenue to Captain Wyatt's Headquarters at Goodwood. The latter was another of these concrete dug-outs, and the owner, whether Captain Wyatt or any other Company Commander, generally had some severe remarks to make about the enemy, who gave the left sector but little rest. To reach " A " Company's front line you went along the support line to Irish Avenue, which from there back to the subsidiary line was good enough, but forward of the support line was hardly better than a track, and, except for some canvas, pretty well exposed to view from all points of the enemy front line. The whole of the left front line, in fact, from Edmeads Farm past Hobbs Farm, the ruins of which had almost been obliterated, was a maze of battered and derelict trenches, only entered by the inquisitive or by some luckless individual who had lost his way. The left company front was built into the side

78

of a small ridge, and possessed no general parados, though most of the posts were self-contained. It ended some two or three hundred yards from the Lys, though from the enemy point of view it probably appeared to go much farther. It was very much knocked about, and it was hard work to maintain even a semblance of respectability.

Such is a brief outline of the Houplines sector. Its main features were its size, its maze of useless and ruined trenches, and its lack of lateral communication. There was not a single dug-out that would have stood the direct hit of a 5·9, and only a few that one would have cared to be in when hit by a " whizz-bang."

The day after relief (April 27th) was spent quietly enough. We had not yet got used to the presence of so many gas cylinders in the front line, and were not anxious to provoke unnecessary retaliation. The Germans were also very quiet. Some shrapnel, a few " whizz-bangs," six " pineapples," and two medium " minnies " made up his total expenditure for the hours of daylight. Sniping from the Chicken Run on to " A " Company's front line was, however, fairly persistent, but no casualties occurred that day. " A " Company of the 2/7th K.L.R. moved into the subsidiary line that evening as a more permanent garrison, and occupied the line between Battalion Headquarters and Cambridge House.

At midnight a gas attack from the whole front of our Brigade and that of the Brigade north of the Lys had been planned, but was cancelled at the last minute, as the wind proved unfavourable. However, the right battalion was not warned in time, and released their cylinders. We much regretted that ours could not be released too, as the clearing of the line had been arranged, and already several cylinders were leaking badly. But on the night of March 29th, after many " alarums and excursions," our two flank companies and the Brigade north of the Lys let off their gas, while projectors were flung into Frelinghien at the same time. It was a very bright night, and the whitish cloud could be seen rolling across No Man's Land. The wind was rather light, and the Germans must therefore have obtained sufficient warning. A number of coloured lights shot up into the air, bells rang, and rapid rifle and machine-gun fire commenced, which caused the inquisitive to expose as little of their heads above the parapet as was feasible. " Whizz-bangs " and " minnies " began to rain on the front line, where the special R.Es. working the cylinders and the garrison of infantry had a somewhat uneasy time. Our orders were to send an officers' patrol to inspect the damage in the enemy's front line. Fortunately, however, this futile and dangerous performance was countermanded, as No Man's Land was itself full of the gas, which the wind hardly carried beyond our trenches, and three of the R.Es. and four of our men were gassed, and a corporal was killed. Otherwise no one was hit during the retaliation. In due course the R.Es. withdrew in motor lorries and the rest of the men returned to the front line, where the sickly smell of gas was strongly in evidence.

Now that most of the cylinders were empty we paid less regard to the enemy, and determined to try to damp the ardour of the sniper, who had already shot two of our men through the head. Every effort from the front line to spot the fellow had failed, but the observation post in the support line had detected him, though the distance from there to the Germans made it futile to try a shot with a rifle. Major Brookes's assistance was accordingly invoked. A telephone line was run out to the observation post, and a trial round was fired with an 18-pounder. This was sufficiently near for the purpose, but unfortunately was too much for the sniper, who promptly retired. However, a few rounds of " battery fire " were delivered, and the area in the immediate neighbourhood of the sniper's lair was greatly disturbed. We knew he was not hit, but *he* knew that we had spotted him, and from that moment his activities ceased.

The next day, April 30th, a great aeroplane fight took place

Photo by

Gale & Polden Ltd., Aldershot.

THE OFFICERS—WOKING, FEBRUARY, 1917.

high over our line. The day was perfect, and it was a wonderful sight to see the aeroplanes twisting and doubling and hear the thin rattle of their machine guns. Suddenly one of the enemy's machines commenced to fall, with a tell-tale streak of smoke trailing behind him. In a moment the grey smoke became a vivid red, and the burning machine came roaring down, crackling and spluttering as the ammunition went off in the flames. For a few minutes it seemed that it must come down right on the top of Battalion Headquarters, but eventually it crashed about two hundred yards away on the open stretch between Battalion Headquarters and Spain Avenue. Both the occupants must have been dead before the machine reached the ground; the pilot was burned beyond recognition in the machine; the observer, an artillery officer, fell out about fifty feet from the ground, and among his papers we found a secret correction card for artillery shooting with aeroplane observation. All attempts to salve anything from the machine proved fruitless. It burned and smouldered for more than twenty-four hours, and its proximity was rendered dangerous by the exploding ammunition.

The question of our billets now began to exercise our minds. The 2/7th K.L.R., in spite of remonstrances, had been located at first in a row of houses close to the Houplines Level Crossing. In that position they had been continually shelled, and the powers that be had finally decided to move them back to a more salubrious locality. This we were very glad to hear, because, other things being equal, billets that are not regular targets for enemy artillery are distinctly preferable. Casualties in billets are always more trying than elsewhere, as they generally seem so gratuitous.

In the Houplines sector more than in any other our snipers and observers had found plenty of scope for the exercise of their special talents. The battalion observation post was in an upper room of a small house in the Rue Solferino, a narrow street which ran off the main road close to Tissage Dump. The Germans had kindly put a " dud " 5·9 through the gable end, thereby providing an excellent view point. The official apparatus installed in this spot was a telescope working on a pivot which was fixed to a quadrant. The observer sat on a chair raised on a rough platform to the necessary height, while next to him sat another man to make the necessary written notes of observations. In addition to a blanket to screen the shell-hole, the observation post was supplied with maps and compass, and also a telephone to Battalion Headquarters and the battery immediately in rear. A fine view of the enemy trenches and the ground in rear was obtainable from this observation post. In addition, there were three sniping posts in the front line, from which subsequently P. G. Jones, Maddocks, Matchett, and Corkill all secured definite " hits "; while for additional observation purposes there was a natural observation post half-way up Irish Avenue, about level with the support line, from which much valuable information of a more local description was obtained.

On May 1st the activity of the hostile artillery began to give evidence of registration on the left half of the battalion front, and support lines, important trench junctions, and communication trenches received direct hits or bursts sufficiently near to be suggestive. That night, as had been anticipated, it being the German Labour Day, sounds of shouting were clearly heard from the enemy lines, while a regular " Brock's benefit " was kept up for a considerable time. Next day the registration was even more marked, so early on the morning of May 4th 2nd-Lieutenant Hodgkinson and a small party of stout-hearted men from " D " Company (Walmsley, Mann, Moore, Evans, Woods, and Bissell) crept out to try to kidnap a German sentry. They worked their way up to a post in Centaur Trench opposite the Pont Ballot salient, and got right under the parapet without being detected. Hodgkinson was, in fact, just climbing into the trench to effect the capture when, most unluckily, the relief arrived, and one of them spotted the blackened face of Rifleman Mann peering over the parapet. Dawn had broken and the game was up. Bombs were

82

hurled in among the Germans, the fellow who had spotted Mann receiving a back-hander from a Mills grenade in the face, and the party raced for home under a hail of machine-gun bullets, rifle grenades, and "pineapples." No casualties were sustained, and, as the G.O.C. Division remarked, " it was a bold and useful bit of work," which only failed through sheer bad luck.

At 10 p.m. the 2/7th K.L.R. began to arrive, and at 12.40 a.m., relief being complete, the various companies and platoons were making for Tissage Dump, where transport awaited the Lewis guns and trench stores. " C " Company moved into the subsidiary line.

Two companies were billeted in large houses in the Rue Jesuit adjoining Brigade Headquarters. These must have been fine residences once, and even the ravages of war had not been able entirely to destroy their architectural pretensions. What was of more importance, they were very strongly built and had good cellar accommodation.

The other two companies were at 57, Rue de Lille, where the battalion had spent the evening *en route* for the Rue du Bois. Battalion Headquarters were in a good house, No. 3, Rue Bayard, a turning off the Rue de Lille. You entered through a gateway into a paved courtyard, surrounded by various domestic offices, and thence up a few steps into a roomy building with a delightful garden behind. The dining-room contained a book-case full of beautifully bound volumes. The Quartermaster's Stores were situated in a large house in the Rue de Lille, opposite which the truck-lines for the trenches started. Mule-drawn trolleys as far as Tissage Dump, and from there smaller trucks man-handled, were the methods of transport employed. The transport lines remained at Bac St. Maur. For the men there were several good estaminets dotted about the town ; while a good meal for officers could be obtained at the " Au Bœuf," an ordinary French provincial restaurant, while the more fastidious frequented " Lucienne's," opposite the church of Notre Dâme. There was also " Madame Burberry's " shop, where most items of clothing and field kit were on sale.

The period in reserve was not without incident. To begin with, General Headquarters' pamphlet S.S. 143, " The Training of Platoons for Offensive Action," had just been issued. It contained a scheme for the employment of a platoon as a small force of all arms—one section Lewis gunners, one rifle grenadiers, one bombers, and one riflemen, with a platoon headquarters consisting of the officer, platoon sergeant, runner, and signaller. Each battalion was now ordered to tell off one platoon for special instruction in this latest scheme. This was not particularly difficult, except that the average strength of a platoon and its four sections never approached the strength of the " War Establishment " platoon for whose instruction these illuminating pamphlets were always designed. The selection of ground proved far more difficult, but an open space in the vicinity of the Nieppe Bridge, where some old practice trenches stood, afforded reasonable facilities at a moderate distance from the billets. The Second-in-Command, Major H. K. Wilson, undertook to find a site, and ultimately decided upon what seemed suitable for the purpose. Unfortunately, the site selected had also been chosen as the position for certain silent batteries and defensive machine-gun companies, who watched Major Wilson making notes in his note-book and arrested him as a suspected person. Major Wilson persuaded the machine gunners to accompany him to Battalion Headquarters, whence, after he had been identified, they retired, feeling no doubt that they had at least done their duty. The incident caused considerable merriment, but to no one more than to the officer chiefly concerned.

The shelling of Armentières by the enemy had recently become a daily and nightly operation. Our gradual increase of guns of major calibre hidden among the houses—there were two 8-inch howitzers in a garden in the Rue Bayard—was quite sufficient to attract hostile notice. Apart from Armentières itself, the enemy had also been busy shelling many back areas, and in retaliation the Second Army decided on a general back area shoot, commencing at 7.30 p.m. on April 7th, and all ranks were warned to keep under cover.

The shoot duly commenced, but in spite of the din we heard what sounded uncommonly like a barrage on the 2/7th K.L.R. front. However, we imagined, as at first did they, that this was the anticipated retaliation. At 7.45 p.m. a false gas alarm occurred, but at 8 p.m. the order came for the battalion to stand-to. The raid for which we thought the Germans had been registering had actually come off, and, as ill-luck would have it, at the same moment as our area shoot. At 10.15 p.m. we were ordered to send up a company to reinforce the 2/7th K.L.R., and " D " Company duly moved off, returning at dawn the next morning without casualties. A further barrage at 10 p.m. caused a second stand-to, but the fire died away in a short time, and normal conditions were finally re-established.

On May 8th " A " Company relieved " C " Company in the subsidiary line, and full particulars of the raids were obtainable. The enemy had certainly put up a very fine barrage, but fortunately " C " Company had escaped casualties, though Captain Eccles, returning from Battalion Headquarters, had a narrow escape, and had been forced on one occasion to make a somewhat hasty descent into a muddy ditch.

Preparations now commenced for the relief, an operation which became easier every time the battalion returned to the old sector. On May 11th the Lewis gunners moved in, and the trollies were soon busy trundling up and down the Houplines road, which became more unhealthy every day. Shelling was, in fact, much more frequent and general by day, though our nights also were regularly disturbed by the scream and crash of the shells landing in the houses. The area round the Pont de Nieppe attracted special attention, and many civilians were killed or wounded. The gas-works, where a number of guns were concentrated, the churches of Notre Dâme and St. Vaast, the Rue Sadi Carnot, the railway station, and other places, also came in for their share of attention, till really one began to think that perhaps the trenches were preferable to the billets.

On May 10th a Padre was attached to us, the Rev. M. T. Eland, and it was arranged that he should share Captain McHugh's elegant quarters at Tissage Dump. This was a reasonably intact house, containing, amongst other choice bits of furniture collected from the neighbouring houses, some beautiful plush-covered chairs. The area just beyond Tissage Dump itself used to come in for a good deal of shelling, but McHugh slept unconcernedly on the first floor, and paid little attention to the noise of falling débris and the hum of flying splinters. It was a handy place of call for visitors, often rather breathless in consequence of having traversed the last part of the Houplines road in what the text-books call " a series of short rushes."

Just before the relief the enemy expended more than his usual quantity of ammunition on Armentières, and we were not sorry when he desisted shortly before the march to the trenches was scheduled to commence. The relief itself was carried out without any interference on the part of the foe. The companies had been moved round, and the order from right to left was " A," " B," " C," " D." To our disgust, we found that great quantities of gas were in process of being installed in our sector, projectors being located near the cemetery and on the extreme left. Every night large carrying parties of the Irish came struggling up the trenches ; and for the benefit of those who have never had personal experience, it may be stated that gas cylinders are no light weight and are awkward things to handle, apart from the extremely unpleasant nature of their contents should a flying piece of shell happen to cause a leak. One very wet night, when the duck-boards, slippery with the rain, made the task more than usually distressing, Captain Eccles was passing down Wessex Avenue on his nightly tour of inspection. Suddenly the sounds of highly-coloured language from the direction of the Fry Pan attracted his attention. Now, it was quite easy to turn into the Fry Pan unwittingly, and even in daylight very far from easy to find your way out again. An unfortunate carrying party, loaded with cylinders, were found by Captain Eccles just completing their third tour round this circular redoubt—an occupation which, when the frequent low overhead traverses were concealed by the blackness of the night, would warrant the employment of any form of bad language. Great apprehension existed in the minds of the authorities, and not without reason, lest the enemy should detect what was going on. Cylinders and gas were never allowed to be alluded to as such either in the front line or on the telephone. They were called "eggs," and incidentally by the men many other names not fit for publication. In addition to this, companies had to send out covering parties into No Man's Land to prevent the approach of any inquisitive German. Lying flat on your stomach in wet mud and grass on a drenching night, and for two hours at a stretch, is most dispiriting work, especially if you have to live in your soaking garments for the next eight days, with the added joy of expecting that you may be in the front line when the gas is being released. Fortunately, during these operations the enemy remained exceedingly quiet. Artillery destructive shoots drew no response; and a rifle grenade and light trench mortar battery shoot on Cell Trench, and wire-cutting in front of Centaur Trench by medium trench mortar batteries, produced no effect on him whatever.

The damage done by the raid barrage was found to be considerable. A trench which had been laboriously constructed from the left-centre Company Headquarters to the detached post at Hobbs Farm, previously only accessible viâ Cambridge Avenue, had been completely obliterated. It appeared to have been in the 100 per cent. zone of the barrage line, and though to save time one did go along it, one risked constant exposure.

The observers now began to notice considerable movement in and behind the enemy's line. Men were seen wearing packs, others popped their heads over the parapet, and transport was heard at night. A relief was suspected, and on May 17th the suspicion was more than confirmed by the unusual activity of the Germans. Their attitude became suddenly aggressive. " Pineapples " became unpleasantly frequent on the left company sector, and a sniper reappeared in the old loophole in the Chicken Run, which had not been used for fifteen days. Fortunately, the larger " minnie," which commenced operations just before our last tour ended, showed no signs of activity ; it was probably part of a " travelling circus " brought up for the raid. Anyhow, " pineapples," small though they may be, are noisy and destructive, and made the left company sector very unpopular. There was also a long-range light " minnie " which carried nearly to the subsidiary line. Artillery activity, though spasmodic, was considerable on some days. The left-hand communication trenches—Edmeads and, more particularly, Irish Avenues— were heavily shelled, direct hits being not infrequent, and parties were always being sent to clear away the fallen earth. On other days a few rounds on Houplines and two or three bursts of shrapnel over the cemetery were the only signs of activity.

On May 20th Colonel Fletcher went on leave, and Major H. K. Wilson assumed command of the battalion.

On the night of May 20th we made an attempt to get into Centaur Trench, but the party was detected, and had to retire hastily under a shower of grenades. At 2 a.m. the next morning the enemy returned the compliment by trying to cut off a bombing post situated between Edmeads and Hobbs Farms. The operation commenced with a sudden shower of stick grenades, and a couple of men were seen trying to get through the wire into the derelict trenches in " N " Gap. Bombs were thrown and rapid fire opened, and Rifleman " Gink " Bailey distinguished himself by standing on the parapet and slanging the Germans to the full extent of his very adequate Irish-American vocabulary. The Germans, disliking this, or at any rate not appreciating their general reception, withdrew, and a patrol was immediately dispatched, which located a dead German on the wire. He proved to belong to the 14th Bavarian I.R. Shrapnel was called for on the enemy's front line to welcome their return, after which the night settled down to its normal state once more.

As the spring advanced the trenches lost a great deal of their barren unloveliness. What had been mud or greyish-looking grass now became a deep and luxuriant carpet of bright fresh green, with many a wild flower peeping out here and there. The trees, which so far had been but gaunt skeletons, began to cover their nakedness with fresh foliage. The sides of Gloucester Avenue were gay with poppies and white daisies ; Sussex Avenue became an ideal country footpath, dotted with may-trees ; and even that forbidding-looking spot the Orchard assumed quite a cheerful aspect. Round Cambridge House the lilacs blossomed out, both purple and white. Roses bloomed in the old gardens near Tissage Dump, and later on a small crop of strawberries and currants was gathered there. A stroll round the line in the early morning was a real pleasure. Just as the dawn was breaking you could wander anywhere. Not a shot would be fired and the guns were silent. As the sun climbed higher in the heavens, the pleasant smell of fresh, moist earth filled the nostrils, instead of the stale stench of which one had grown so sick. Dew-spangled grasses and fern overhanging the trench brushed your face as you passed along. In the rapidly clearing mist that heralded the hot day even the ugliest features of the line seemed to take on a certain softening outline, a certain grace in harmony with the country-side. High over No Man's Land you could see the fluttering lark, and all the air was resonant with its trilling notes. The call of the cuckoo sounded from the trees, and the chatter of sparrows and finches in the overgrown hedges filled the air with a merry sound, while but a few hours previously the nightingale had been pouring out its full-throated melody. " Oh, to be in England now that April's here !" How we re-echoed Browning's wish, with the substitution for " April " of the month of June, at which we had now arrived! How true the words seemed, how deep their significance! Beautiful as Nature was around us, rejoiced as we were at this delightful contrast to the hideousness of strife, yet it increased the bitterness and made one feel more keenly than ever the loathsome misery of war. How one pictured to oneself the peaceful beauty of the English countryside, so like this in outward appearance, and yet so different in reality! How one longed for the war to be over, to wander once more in the fields on a summer's morn, with the black clouds of war cleared away for good, and not merely lifted for a few precious moments!

Boom! The " morning hate " has begun. With a start we come back from our pleasant dreams. Another stifling day is before us, and the never-ending struggle with its monotony, its destruction, its every detestable feature, claims us once more for its own.

One of the special delights of the Commanding Officer was crawling about exposed parts of the sector by day. It was not only his anxiety to acquire an accurate knowledge of his sector, though that was certainly one reason ; he wanted to find out where every derelict trench led to, what secrets lay hidden in those areas of abandoned chaos in which the sector abounded, and no one could ever have known his sector better than did Colonel Fletcher. But apart from all this, his old big-game hunting instincts were aroused. This time he was not tracking the shy koodoo or the skulking lion, but matching his brains and his woodcraft against the ever-watchful German. Major Geddes more than once accompanied him on these excursions, as he crawled and wriggled on his stomach from place to place, now lying up to use telescope and field-glasses, now tracing out all the intricacies of our own or the enemy trenches. Home the pair would come at last, with the perspiration streaming down their faces. " Well, that is the best afternoon I have had since the war started !" the

Commanding Officer would exclaim, as he sat mopping his face and drinking large cups of tea.

The gas attack had originally been fixed for the night of May 20th–21st. The targets selected for the projectors were Census Support Line, Les 4 Hallots Farm, and Battalion Headquarters at Census Farm. The inclusion of the latter target caused some people certain misgivings, as they had a suspicion—afterwards confirmed from a captured German map—that our own Headquarters were not unknown to the enemy. The usual invasion of our sector by " N " and " L " Special Companies, R.E., took place on the night in question. Extra telephones had been rigged up, and in addition cryptic messages about " presentations of medals " and " indents for bicycles " came frequently over the 'phone. At the last moment the wind veered round, as it frequently did at night. It was too late to cancel the orders by message, so a special signal rocket was fired from Headquarters. It was a red, green and red rocket. The first one lighted refused to move at all; but the second, a parachute light, went up with a roar for about twenty feet, and then sailed off along the subsidiary line. Fortunately, it was successful in stopping the discharge of the gas. We took a more than usual interest in this discharge, as it appeared that we could not be relieved till it took place. However, in the end, when we had been in ten days, the attack was definitely postponed for twenty-four hours to allow the relief to be effected. On the early morning of May 22nd 2nd-Lieutenants Hodgkinson and Little with patrols attempted entries into the German line at Cell Trench, opposite Hobbs Farm and at Centaur Trench respectively. Both were spotted and heavily bombed, Little being slightly wounded, but not sufficiently for evacuation. Lieutenant Alcock two days previously had been hit in the eye by a splinter from a " pineapple," and had retired temporarily to a Base hospital.

In spite of rather depressing accounts from the 2/7th K.L.R. as to shelling in the vicinity of billets, we were glad to find, on

May 22nd, that the relief, twice postponed, was really to take place. Dug-outs or " bivvies " are not particularly comfortable—some, indeed, very much the reverse. You get tired of stooping, of working by the light of one miserable candle, of eating at odd times and of sleeping at odd hours. The daily and nightly tours round the line become more than usually wearisome. Duck-boards seem to get more treacherous, angle irons and stray bits of barbed wire seem to project still farther from the sides of trenches ; while for the man in the post—and everyone else's position is bliss compared with his—the time must have been trying indeed. Not that it was particularly dangerous, though even in quiet sectors most posts have their highly unpleasant periods ; but it was infinitely uncomfortable and trying to the last degree. Besides, there was the pleasant hope that the wind would surely be favourable for one night at least out of the next eight, and then the 2/7th K.L.R., and not we, would experience the delights of a gas discharge, to the accompaniment of the applause of the enemy, which was usually of a vigorous nature. However, the relief took place at last without any hitch, and the early hours of May 23rd found us back in our old billets in Armentières. The routine was the same as last time—working parties, one platoon for special training, and the remainder general training. The new extension for the box-respirator was also fitted, and in addition we received twenty horse respirators, to which even the mules raised no violent objection. The opportunity was also taken to have all the swords sharpened. Two officers at a time were attached for instruction to A/286 Battery, R.F.A., and as the latter's quarters were situated in a comfortable orchard, the two days allowed passed pleasantly enough.

On May 26th " B " Company, who had remained in the subsidiary line, were relieved by " D " Company. Early the next morning sounds were heard suggestive of a gas attack. The great bell at Houplines Level Crossing was tolling. Runners flew off to rouse the companies. Officers appeared at doorways, clothed

in pyjamas, gum-boots, and box-respirators; while Lieutenant
James, the Gas Officer, sniffed the early morning air like a war-
horse scenting battle. Each person in turn thought he smelt
chlorine—or was it phosgene? In every case it turned out to
be the smell of a stale cigar, the proximity of the refuse-bin, or
something else equally harmless. Gas there was none, and at
length, after conversation with the Brigade, it was discovered
that a few gas shells had fallen near the sentry at the level-crossing,
and thus produced an alarm. So back we all went, cursing, to
bed, everyone feeling a bit resentful that after we had been thus
disturbed no gas had come after all.

On May 29th the gas stored in Houplines was at length released.
The only part that we took in the proceedings was the posting
of six stretcher-bearers at the top of Irish Avenue, an unpleasant
spot, though fortunately they sustained no casualties.

During these days in billets the presence of the Battalion
Orchestra made itself felt, with excellent results. The instruments
had been brought over for us by the Division. It was a considerable item for regimental baggage, consisting as it did of ten
instruments. Sergeant Lawton, battalion sanitary N.C.O., was
in charge of the orchestra, and played the trombone when his
duties permitted. Rifleman Garrod, the first violin, was a player
of exceptional merit from the Liverpool Philharmonic Orchestra.
As a soloist he was particularly fine. The remaining members of
the party, all well above the average, were—violins, Lewin,
Hardacre, and Lance-Corporal Hume; viola, Edmondson; 'cellos,
Kaye and Kennedy; bass, Lance-Corporal Buckley; trombone,
Williams; drums, Burden; and librarian (self-styled and self-
appointed), Rifleman King. Lance-Corporal Bell, from the
Quartermaster's Stores, occasionally performed on the oboe.
Rifleman Collins, an excellent violinist, had been left behind,
unfortunately, in England suffering from influenza.

By arrangement with the other units of the Brigade, our contribution to the recently formed Brigade Pioneer Company was

reduced by the strength of the orchestra. In return for this, the latter was always loaned to another battalion while we were in the line, and also for special occasions when we were out. In addition, it used to play for our own mess on guest nights, and very delightful it was; and also occasionally for the Divisional Concert Party's performances, and for the Brigade and Divisional Commanders. It was in great demand everywhere, and there can be no doubt that the results more than justified the employment of the personnel thus utilized. Another invaluable asset was Rifleman Kessen, a very prince of conjurers. He seemed to have an infinity of excellent tricks, and he fooled you under your very nose in the most baffling fashion.

On May 31st the battalion once more relieved the 2/7th K.L.R. The arrangement of companies—" A," " B," " D," " C " from the right—was due to the forthcoming raid, to be carried out by parties from " A " and " B " Companies on Centaur Trench, opposite the Pont Ballot salient. This necessitated " A " and " B " Companies being as near the proposed area as possible. Colonel Fletcher arrived in the line from leave at midnight, and with characteristic energy proceeded at once on a tour of inspection.

This spell in the line was one of exceptional activity. To begin with, there was the impending raid, which, being our first, occupied nine-tenths of our thoughts. There were innumerable special patrols to examine the wire and the approaches to the points of entry; the artillery wire-cutting operations had to be settled; the incessant visits to observation posts and the selection of forming-up places, raid headquarters, regimental aid posts, etc., to be arranged for. In addition to all this, the Battle of Messines took place during the tour. Immediately after that came orders for following up the enemy, if he voluntarily evacuated his trenches; and before we were half through that came schemes for the defence of Armentières in the event of an attack by the Germans. But we must take things in order.

The morning after relief (June 1st, 1917) the enemy dropped

a "pineapple" into a Lewis-gun post of "C" Company, killing three men and wounding two. His activity in this direction was now so great that steps had to be taken to cope with it. Two light trench mortars were permanently established in the front line, and for every "pineapple" we returned a number of Stokes shells. The teams did not have a pleasant time of it, as the Germans made every endeavour to knock them out; but they stuck to it gallantly, and by the end of the time their efforts had become singularly effective, although the enemy later retaliated by producing a medium "minnie."

A slight scare was caused by the alleged appearance of a German near "C" Company's cook-house, at the left extremity of the subsidiary line, and patrols spent several nights down by the river trying to catch the supposed intruder. Whether there was anything in the rumour or not was never satisfactorily settled, but it would have been perfectly simple for him to get there. Between our left and the river there was a gap of a couple of hundred yards, which after weeks of fine weather had become dry and hard, and, as subsequent investigations after the Armistice proved, there was ample cover for a whole battalion to come up unseen. Moreover, the German raids on the left sector must have revealed to them the absence of any serious opposition in that part of the line. In fact, the liability of the battalion to be outflanked on the left was the subject of a strong memorandum from Colonel Fletcher, but nothing was done except that some wire was erected later, and a Lewis gun post located in the cellar of a ruined house close to the river and in line with our support line. The presence of fresh earth on a footbridge crossing a branch of the Lys, which was discovered by the patrol, certainly gave some colour to the story of "C" Company's cook.

June 4th, 5th, and 6th produced barrages on the Messines Ridge; they took place each afternoon, and lasted for about an hour. It was understood that barely half of the guns to be employed on the day were in action, but it was a wonderfully awe-inspiring

95

sight to watch the effect of the mass of shells crashing down on the slopes of the ridge. The heavies in Armentières and our own 18-pounders took part in these preliminary barrages, with the result that the shelling of Armentières by the enemy became intense, and particularly in the vicinity of battery positions, which constant firing had now revealed to the enemy, and produced the most severe counter-battery work on his part. Our trenches, too, received marked attention. The enemy seems always to have been suspicious of an attack on Frelinghien, and he set to work on the left and left-centre company sectors with great determination. Shells of a calibre not usually employed in ordinary trench warfare began to plough up our communication trenches, Irish Avenue especially. Cambridge House was frequently shelled intensely, and, in fact, there was no part of our sector that did not receive considerable attention daily. The wire-cutting on the right provoked the enemy terribly, and each time it was carried out severe retaliation took place. Houplines road was now shelled regularly with great bursts of 5.9's and heavy shrapnel. One 4·2 battery kept up such an incessant fire into the vicinity of Tissage Dump that we used to call it the "rising tide," the noise of the stream of shells as they passed over sounding not unlike the steady onrush of the sea.

Quesnoy, nearly opposite to us, we used to bombard heavily, and some part of it was usually on fire. Frelinghien was frequently almost hidden in red dust, while Wytschaete Ridge for long periods at a stretch looked as if it were enveloped in a sandstorm. Every night north of the Lys one or both sides were raiding, and the rumble of barrages, the red bursts of shrapnel, and the stream of coloured rockets continued well on into the daylight.

At 3.10 a.m. on June 7th the Battle of Messines opened with the most tremendous mine explosions and the most magnificent barrage that can be imagined. It was a lovely morning, and there was not a cloud in the sky. With a stupendous roar and upheaval

Photo by

Gale & Polden, Ltd., Aldershot.

SERGEANTS' MESS—WOKING, FEBRUARY, 1917.

that baffles description the mines exploded. Simultaneously the whole weight of the artillery gathered together for the occasion, and hidden away in every conceivable place, opened on the enemy. From their trenches lights of many colours shot into the air, mutely appealing for assistance from their gunners. These were not long in replying, but our counter-battery work, which had left them in false security during the preliminary barrages, was dealing faithfully with them now. For a few moments the ridge stood out clear and distinct. Then clouds of smoke and dust shut out the view, and it was only by the alteration in the sound that we knew that the barrage was creeping forward, and we waited anxiously for the telegrams announcing the result.

During the first few hours we were unmolested. A 4·2 battery opened on Houplines ten minutes before zero, but switched as soon as the barrage opened. About 7 a.m., however, "whizz-bangs" came down in a regular barrage on the front line, and then high explosives up and down the subsidiary line for about a couple of hours. Between two and six in the afternoon the enemy concentrated on Tissage Dump, putting over 300 high explosive shells into that locality during the four hours. Aeroplanes were very busy, and a German machine dropped two bombs about fifty yards from Battalion Headquarters. The enemy balloons were in a state of great excitement, being hauled down whenever a plane appeared, till at last one of them apparently got tired of this, broke away, and sailed off out of sight. One thing that greatly interested us was that both this day and the next the enemy shelled his own front line opposite the Brewery. Up to the end of this tour the Germans continued intensely active, the left sector and Irish Avenue receiving the lion's share of the shelling.

One very necessary piece of work was completed before we quitted the trenches—the cutting of the grass in front of the parapet. It was now so high and so close to the parapet that it entirely obstructed the view through the periscope, and made it quite possible for a man to work his way unseen right up to the trenches. Sickles had to be obtained and parties went out nightly to " cut the hay crop." To do this just in front of the posts alone would, of course, have revealed their exact position to any inquisitive airman, and a strip had therefore to be cut along the whole length of the front line.

At 9.30 p.m. on June 9th the leading company of the 2/7th K.L.R. began to arrive. At the last moment, owing to the continued harassing fire of the Germans on to the Houplines road, we decided to proceed out by Lunatic Lane in the right battalion sector. This was a long and winding communication trench which so far had sustained little damage. It brought you out by the Lunatic Asylum, and from there you went up the Rue Gambetta and so on to the Rue de Lille. " C " Company remained in the subsidiary line.

On arrival in billets we were somewhat astonished to learn that we were under orders to move at one hour's notice, and that guides to bring up reinforcing troops were always to be kept in readiness at Battalion Headquarters. The retirement of the enemy, after the Battle of Messines, from his remaining trenches north of the River Lys had caused the Higher Command to think that a partial retirement might be effected opposite our front also. Consequently some most elaborate schemes to meet this emergency had been issued, and we were now in the throes of trying to draw up, in conjunction with the 2/7th K.L.R., a scheme of movement in the event of the enemy's voluntary withdrawal. We were therefore not a little surprised to find signs that an attack by the Germans might now be expected. The mental effort required to concentrate your attention simultaneously on an advance and a defence—and both had to be fully provided for—and at the same time to attend to the all-absorbing orders and arrangements for the raid, proved somewhat exhausting. For clearness' sake we will take them one by one, but it should be remembered that three sets of orders, and in addition a salvage scheme (a kind of corollary to the advance orders), were all drawn up at the same time, and the difficulty of remembering which you were working on at any particular moment was by no means imaginary.

Operation Order No. 22, dated June 15th, 1917, began with the words : " In the event of the enemy voluntarily evacuating his present front line system opposite the battalion frontage, companies will be ready to move forward and occupy the sectors of the enemy line with minimum of delay." The orders ran into fifteen headings with seven appendices and, it need hardly be added, three pages of subsequent amendments, dated July 1st. As the orders, fortunately, were never put into operation, it will be sufficient to deal with them quite briefly. Each company was allotted an area in the enemy front line, and on the word "floreat" fighting patrols, consisting of one officer and twenty-four men, were expected to dash across No Man's Land " at ten minutes' notice." The difficulty of this initial part of the proceedings did not at first occur to the higher authorities, but some weeks later the time allowed was suddenly increased to six hours !

A consolidating platoon, armed with picks, shovels, sand-bags, etc, followed as a carrying party ; and, finally, Company Head-quarters moved into the German front line, and Battalion Head-quarters moved up to Edmeads Farm. The Brigade Pioneer Company, assisted by working parties from the reserve battalion, were responsible for digging communication trenches from Fiji Road on the right and Hobbs Farm on the left, to the enemy's front line. The Reserve Battalion Headquarters and two remaining companies moved up to the subsidiary line.

To assist in these operations advanced dumps, containing vast quantities of R.E. stores and bombs and small-arms ammunition, were gradually accumulated in the vicinity of the front line, to the great delight of the Germans, who shelled them cheerfully. An elaborate system of flags and identification marks was also evolved. In addition to this, it being now presumed that we had to all intents and purposes occupied the German trenches, the collection of salvage from our old trenches became a matter of considerable moment, and comprehensive orders were issued for that work also ; but these we may pass over.

To change for a moment from the offensive to the defensive, it was also considered possible that the enemy was likely to make an attack on Armentières, in the hope of obtaining a good head-line, " Capture of Armentières," for his newspapers, which might divert attention from the rumour that Messines had fallen.   Moreover, his possession of Armentières would have made our tenure of Messines Ridge extremely uncomfortable, if not impossible. Consequently, an extensive system of routes for reinforcing troops was worked out, and guides instructed for this purpose.   Men not required to carry bombs and R.E. material to the front line dumps were now collecting similar material in Armentières itself. Others were busily engaged wiring up the streets, building machine-gun emplacements, and generally trying to make up in a few weeks for the total neglect of the old defences, which during the last two years had decayed to a degree almost beyond repair.   A Major was appointed O.C. Armentières Defences, and the place began to hum with life and movement.   Throughout the proceedings the foe kept up continual shelling with every description of gun, and made life in the town anything but comfortable.   The swimming-baths, which had been so acceptable, had to be abandoned owing to the fact that they only had a glass roof, and shells came perilously near it.   Training was confined to the vicinity of billets, or more often to the cellars.   The destruction of the big brewery near Pont de Nieppe, whence came our beer supply, so needed in those scorching hot days, helped to complete our unhappiness.   The baths near Erquinghem were also destroyed, thanks to the action of the Heavy Artillery Commander, who had placed some 60-pounders just in front of them.   The sight of the soldier bathers, in every kind of dress or undress, running wildly across the fields in the company of the French laundry-maids certainly produced considerable merriment ; but the price paid for this piece of humour, the entire demolition of

100

the only bathing-place reasonably handy, was thought to be excessive.

The only people who really appreciated the spell out of the line were the raiding party. Captain Steward, Captain Parker, Lieutenant Clarke, 2nd-Lieutenant Moseley, and 100 men were comfortably installed close to Croix du Bac in the quarters of the old Divisional Reinforcement Camp, which had recently been moved to Steenwerck, the present railhead. Division Headquarters had removed from the White Chateau at Sailly, and were now in Croix du Bac ; and a field close to their offices was secured for the training-ground. Here a replica of the enemy trenches was made with tapes and turned sods, care being taken to add sufficient " duds " to mislead the aerial photographer should he chance to wander over. Aeroplane photos were studied till the head nearly swam to ensure that the reproduced line corresponded as exactly as possible with the original. Throughout these proceedings Captain Glyn, G.S.O.3, was most helpful in procuring photographs and maps. The choice of the sector to be raided was limited by the necessity of having reasonable approaches to our own front line, and these the right sector alone provided. Moreover, the old road passing through the Pont Ballot salient made a fine natural guide, and was selected as such for the right flank. Centaur Trench and support, with their two communication trenches, Centaur Lane and Centaur Row, formed roughly speaking the area of operations. There were three parties— Captain Parker and twenty men of " D " Company, who were to enter on the right ; Lieutenant Clarke and sixteen men of " A " Company in the centre, though Clarke himself was to remain on the parapet with a 'phone to our own front line to Captain Steward, O.C. Raid ; and 2nd-Lieutenant Moseley and thirty-one men of " B " Company, who were to enter on the left. The route up to the gap in the wire was to be indicated by tapes. Bridges were to be laid and the parties formed up in No Man's Land between sign-boards by zero minus three minutes. The barrage was to lift and the raid commence at zero plus two minutes. The duty of the blocking parties, etc., was worked out to the smallest detail and rehearsed again and again.

The co-operation of medium trench mortar batteries, light trench mortar batteries, and machine guns was on a large scale both for barrage and neutralizing purposes. The artillery consisted of 18-pounders and 4·5 howitzers, fourteen pieces in all. All this time the Quartermaster was busy collecting revolvers, knobkerries, torches, and all the other minor but necessary articles of equipment, and many were the alarums and excursions.

During this period in billets the reorganized seniority of the Territorial Force was published, all temporary rank being cancelled. We suddenly found ourselves with no Majors and only four Captains, while several of our Company Commanders fell to 2nd-Lieutenants. The system of promotion to acting ranks was, however, at once instituted, and we resumed most of our original ranks, though Major Charles Wilson lost his majority, only one Major being allowed instead of two. About this time Captain Bowring took over command of " A " Company.

On June 12th " A " Company relieved " C " Company in the subsidiary line, and on the 15th the battalion relieved the 2/7th K.L.R. The route chosen was Buterne Avenue, the common communication trench between ourselves and the right battalion. Owing to the destructive shooting of the enemy, Irish Avenue had more or less ceased to exist ; and " C " Company, who once more found themselves in this unhealthy sector, had to use Cambridge Avenue and Regent Street, which made their relief a slow and tedious process. " B " Company was on the right, and then came " A " and " D " Companies. Owing to the raiding detachment being left out of the line, " D " Company had to be assisted by a loan of men from " C " Company; while " A " and " B " Companies were supplemented by various employed men— buglers, grooms, etc.—normally left out of the line.

102

" THE KING'S " (LIVERPOOL REGIMENT)

The sector was again full of gas, and the persistent efforts of the R.Es. to discharge it seriously hampered the patrolling that had to be carried out nightly in the vicinity of the area to be raided, and which was of vital importance. The real nature of the bridge over the ditches, which eventually proved to be a brick culvert, had long been in dispute, and Lieutenant Royle, the Intelligence Officer, spent every night while we were in Armentières with the Battalion scouts in No Man's Land up to and including the night of the raid. In spite of his multifarious duties as Intelligence Officer and his two daily summaries, he never spared himself in his efforts to make certain that the gaps were open and the routes beyond dispute. The enemy activity had meanwhile still further increased. Irish Avenue was reduced to a mere chain of shell-holes and débris, while every communication trench, and in fact every part of the sector, was well hammered. We were surprised and pleased to find how well the gas cylinders stood being knocked about.

On June 20th a practice disconnection of all telephones was ordered by the Division. The result as far as we were concerned was highly satisfactory, Battalion Headquarters getting a brief respite from those in authority. As regards the internal routine work it made no difference, as telephone messages had been reduced, at any rate during the daytime, to the lowest possible figure. The repeated warnings that the enemy could pick up messages, and later the presence of a Police Listening Set in the subsidiary line, had greatly cooled our enthusiasm for this form of communication. The daily report of conversations picked up by the Listening Set was, in fact, a source of much merriment, the angry remarks of Major Brookes one day to someone at his battery causing special amusement. We also received a rather futile complaint from the authorities, so to prevent a repetition of similar rebukes we made a suitable arrangement with the Listening Set personnel, who were located in a dug-out they had long coveted; and after that

103

our conversations, when picked up, were treated with more discretion.

The enemy evinced considerable nervousness at night, possibly owing to our active patrolling. On more than one occasion he bombed his own wire. His apparent unpreparedness when our raid took place was therefore the more surprising.

On the morning of June 20th a serious loss was sustained by the Division. Lieutenant-Colonel Short, C.M.G., the artillery Group Commander, had arranged to visit our Headquarters to discuss certain details in connection with the barrage for the raid. His departure from our Brigade Headquarters happened to synchronize with the arrival of General Broadwood, who decided to walk up with him. They stopped for a few minutes on a rather exposed bridge in Houplines to examine the lie of the land. Whether they were observed or whether it was simply bad luck will never be known, but the bridge at this moment received a direct hit from a 5·9, and both officers were badly wounded. Their orderlies at once carried the General to a place of comparative safety, but while this was being done a second shell arrived, killing the Group Commander on the spot. General Broadwood was taken straight to Estaires, but his wounds proved mortal, and he only lingered for a few hours. He was buried in the cemetery at Sailly. The whole affair was a most unhappy tragedy, and the loss of the General was keenly felt throughout the Division. Colonel Short had been indefatigable in his efforts to ensure adequate support to our raid, and his cheerful disposition and amusing stories had made him very popular at Battalion Headquarters.

June 21st was a busy day for all. The final preparations for the raid, which was to commence early in the morning of June 22nd, were now in full swing. The bridges had been brought up overnight, and were duly concealed in the front line. Raid Headquarters, the advanced regimental aid post, and all the other details, were now being finally completed. The raiding party were brought up in lorries to the Houplines Level Crossing after dark, each man with his face blackened and his label, bearing number and name, tied to the top button of his jacket. All other traces of identification had been removed. About 11 p.m. the party was moving down from the subsidiary line with many a handshake and a " Good luck, boys !" The men were all as keen as could be. The official report has been reproduced as it stands. It gives a faithful account of what happened. That the raid was not so successful as we had hoped—that is to say, that no identification was obtained—was due to several causes. First, Captain Parker himself and several of his party were knocked out at the very start by pressing too close on the barrage and being caught in a short burst of shrapnel. Next, Lieutenant Clarke's party ought to have had an officer actually in the trench with them ; the men were willing enough in all conscience, but lacked the controlling influence of the officer's presence. Then Lieutenant Moseley's party missed their way, owing to fresh guides having to be substituted at the last moment. Although we did not claim it as a successful raid, yet there is no doubt that the effect on the battalion was good, and the men who had taken part in it were keen to make another attempt. Colonel Fletcher's disappointment was great, as he had slaved from morning till night to make the raid a success. Captain Parker's wounds were more serious than had at first been realized, and at one time nearly proved fatal. His reception at the Casualty Clearing Station was typical of his luck. He was, of course, wearing a " Tommy's " jacket, and so by mistake was put into a " Tommies' " ward, and was welcomed on his arrival by the words : " Gawd, Bill, here comes a b—— nigger !"

P. G. Jones, a Battalion Scout, who fell on this occasion, was one of our best and keenest young soldiers, and very popular with everyone. His death was a real personal loss to all who knew him.

HISTORY OF THE 2/6TH (RIFLE) BATTALION

REPORT ON MINOR OPERATION CARRIED OUT IN HOUPLINES
SUB-SECTOR ON THE NIGHT OF JUNE 21ST–22ND, 1917.

" *Strength of Party.*—Three officers and 97 other ranks.

" *Point of Exit.*—C.29.a.35.80—C.23.b.96.34.

" *Points of Entry.*—C.29.a.48.17—C.29.a.62.41.

" *Time.*—1.6 a.m.   Entry reported by telephone.

" *Object.*—(*a*) To continue a harassing policy and prevent the enemy from withdrawing troops.

" (*b*) Killing and capturing as many of the enemy as possible.

" (*c*) Obtaining identification and gaining information regarding the enemy's system of defence.

" *Narrative.*—Minus five minutes zero : Bridges laid across ditch.

" Minus three minutes zero : All parties formed up across ditch.

" Zero : Barrage commenced exactly on time.   All parties commenced moving on objective.

" *Right* (*Parker's*) *Party.*—This party was so keen to get into enemy's trenches that they followed the barrage too closely, and in consequence suffered the following casualties :—

" The leading scout was killed, and the officer who was close behind him was wounded in the leg and neck and could not go on.   The N.C.O. in charge of the leading party was fatally wounded, and two of his men were incapacitated.   The N.C.O. in charge of the second party was hit, and one of his men was killed and another wounded.

" The remainder of the party carried on and entered the enemy trench as arranged.   The party who were detailed to work along the trench to the right found a concrete dug-out, fitted with iron doors, in the front-line trench as anticipated, at about C.28.a.48.10.   There was a light in the dug-out, and three men were seen inside wearing blue uniform with Red Cross brassards. They were summoned to come out, but refused, and a bomb was therefore thrown into the dug-out just before the men inside

106

had time to slam the iron door. The bomb exploded, and groans and cries were heard, and also a noise which sounded like a trap-door being shut. Our men tried to force the door open, but were unable to do so. The muzzle of a revolver was then put through a loophole in the iron door and six shots were fired.

" Efforts were again made to open the door, but proved unsuccessful. Whilst trying to force this door, fire was opened on our party from the traverse next beyond ; this was replied to, and the Huns ran away. Much valuable time was spent trying to get into the dug-out for the purpose of obtaining identification, and owing to this, and also the casualties already suffered, this party were unable to get on to their farthest objective.

" In the meantime the party working along the trench to the left were bombed by the enemy, and when they retaliated the enemy climbed out of the trench and disappeared to the rear.

" Progress was then continued along the trench, and a dug-out was found, but on examination it proved to be empty. Shortly after this some of the Centre Party were met and connection established.

" Just after the withdrawal signal had gone up—zero plus 22 minutes—two Germans were seen approaching the front line over the top from the direction of their support line. Shots were fired at them and they withdrew. It is not known whether either of them were shot.

" Parker's party then left the enemy trench, bringing with them a rifle and bayonet which were found in the trench.

" On the way back those men who had been hit on crossing No Man's Land were all brought in except one man, who could not be found. It is believed that this man was killed. On reaching our trenches it was found that another man was missing. He was last seen soon after leaving the enemy's trench.

" At zero plus 33 minutes the N.C.O. i/c Right Party observed one green light and one golden rain rocket fired apparently from the enemy's subsidiary line in C.23 or C.24.

" The trench is very deep and narrow, and no duck-boards were found.

" *Centre (Clarke's) Party.*—This party crossed No Man's Land in the order practised. They found the ground much torn up by shell-holes, over which it was impossible to proceed quickly. They found the gaps in the wire, but had to zig-zag a good deal to get through. There was a considerable quantity of cut wire lying about, which further delayed their progress. They entered the enemy's trench at about C.20.a.44.21 (*i.e.*, about 30 yards farther to the right than had been intended).

" 2nd-Lieutenant C. W. Clarke established telephone communication with O.C. Raid at zero plus 7½ minutes, and sent a message to the effect that his party ' had entered enemy's trench.'

" The trench was deep, and in getting in the leading man stumbled and lost his rifle, which he was unable to find in the darkness. Thereupon another bayonet man was brought up to take his place. The first party then proceeded along the trench to the right, and immediately found a dug-out, into which a bomb was thrown. After the bomb had exploded the dug-out was entered and two dead Germans found. An effort was made to tear a button off the tunic of one of those men, but it was on too tight. At this moment a scuffle was going on outside the dug-out with a Hun who had come running down the trench, shouting ' Surrender,' and our man inside the dug-out hurried out to see what was happening, and picked up a German rifle on his way. The Hun was placed in charge of two men, to be passed out of the trench as soon as the two men waiting on the parapet had been called to the spot. Whilst the two men were holding the prisoner, one of them was wounded and let go. The prisoner thereupon wrenched himself free from the other man and escaped to the left. One of our men chased him along the trench, but, going over strange ground, was unable to catch him ; he came to a communication trench (Centaur Lane), and, hearing footsteps, threw a bomb

108

into this trench. As by this time the withdrawal signal had gone up, he withdrew and joined his own party.

"In the meantime the rest of this party had started working along the trench to join up with the right party, which they did. This party was followed by a small party which had been detailed to proceed along Centaur Lane and block it. They expected to find this communication trench to the right of where they entered the front line, but owing to the fact that they had unconsciously entered the trench farther to the right than had been intended, this trench was not found until too late.

"A bomb store was found and blown up as the party were leaving the trench.

"This party had one casualty (referred to above), and he was brought back to our trenches.

"No S.O.S. signal was seen and no artillery fire was opened until this party were half-way back across No Man's Land.

"*Left (Moseley's) Party.*—Moseley's party failed to enter enemy's trench. The two scouts who had reconnoitred the gaps and knew the ground well were sick four days before the raid took place. The new scouts did not know the ground as well, possibly, as some of the other members of the raiding party; also their reconnaissance was made difficult by enemy working at their gaps, and having covering parties out; also they had not the same opportunity of rehearsal as they should have had in laying tapes, etc. In consequence, after passing through the first gap, a doubt arose as to direction owing to other members of the raiding party thinking that they knew best, with the result that several parties tried to get through impassable wire. The main party moved to the left eventually, followed by other parties, and lost direction. While this was going on one of the scouts found the proper gaps, dashed after the party, who reorganized, and the leading men reached enemy's trench when return signal went up. In this Rifleman Bamber was wounded; he was found by Rifleman F. Taylor, who bound up his wounds, and as he was not certain of his direction, he waited for daylight, and brought the wounded man in the same morning at 10 a.m. This party had three rows of wire to negotiate, the second and third rows consisting of heavy knife rests, etc., and, the grass being very long, gaps were not easy to find.

" *Casualties.*—Two killed ; Lieutenant Parker and six other ranks wounded ; one missing believed killed.

" *Action of the Enemy.*—There is no doubt the enemy had no idea he was going to be raided. His action was extremely weak and slow in beginning.

" It is very doubtful if he inflicted any casualties on us.

" His barrage did not start until about zero plus 10 minutes, and then increased in intensity by degrees. His fire was directed chiefly on our front line (the shells falling just short of and just over our trench) and partly on our support line and subsidiary lines.

" The enemy's resistance in his trenches was very weak. Several men were seen running away.

" *Summing up.*—The raid, unfortunately, failed in its chief objects, for no prisoners or identifications were obtained, though there is little doubt that four, and probably several more, Germans were killed or wounded. Had the left party succeeded in entering the enemy's trench, there is every probability that more damage would have been done, and identifications, if not prisoners, obtained.

" The support of the artillery was excellent, the wire had been well cut, and the barrage started precisely at the time arranged.

" The medium and light trench mortar batteries were also most effective, and completely stopped all enemy machine-gun fire.

" The machine-gun barrages were all that could be desired.

" The reconnaissance had been well done. Enemy posts were found where they had been expected. Suspected machine-gun emplacements were adequately dealt with either by artillery beforehand or by my trench mortars during operations.

"THE KING'S" (LIVERPOOL REGIMENT)

"Signal communication worked well. Three special lines had been laid to Raid Headquarters. The raiding party established telephone communication from near the enemy's trench with commendable speed.

(Sgd.) "W. A. L. FLETCHER, *Lieutenant-Colonel,*
"*Comdg. 2/6th (Rifle) Bn. Liverpool Regiment.*

"*June 24th,* 1917."

At 9.15 a.m. two men missing from the raid suddenly appeared in our line, one of them wounded. This showed how easy it was to get into our trenches unobserved. Artillery was very active against us all that day. In the course of two hours and a half Hobbs Farm and the detached post received over 120 rounds from a 4·2 battery, while at times it seemed as if our wire in that vicinity was the real target. Spain Avenue, the Orchard, Panama, Pretoria, were all singled out in turn; but probably this was merely a cloak for the German activities on the left.

The following night the Brigade north of the Lys carried out a raid, and the enemy seemed very uneasy opposite our left company front, sending up innumerable Véry lights, letting off bursts of rifle fire, and industriously bombing his own wire.

The early morning of June 23rd found the German 'planes extremely active. There was a flight of scarlet machines, which performed various evolutions for our benefit, and at intervals swooped down and fired into our trenches. Rifle grenades were fired at one very low-flying 'plane, and at another a light trench mortar shell with a shortened fuse and a full charge. The latter must certainly have surprised the pilot when it exploded in the air.

Every part of the left sector, front line, support, subsidiary, and communication trenches was heavily shelled for long periods throughout the day, while a regular box barrage was put round the detached post. Even the new drain between Irish and Cambridge was regularly bombarded. The wire in front of our trenches, never very good, was now reduced to a mass of shattered fragments, and the impression that a raid must be expected in the near future grew apace. Down to the day of the relief this extreme activity continued, and it was difficult to keep Edmeads, Wessex, and Cambridge clear of blocks. Irish was still being heavily hammered, but, except for occasional repairs to keep up appearances, we had long since ceased to use Irish as an avenue. 2nd-Lieutenants E. E. Paul and J. N. Blake were slightly wounded in Fry Pan. On the evening of June 26th the relief took place. We were fully expecting the raid, and precautions were taken accordingly to prevent any sort of congestion in communication trenches, all of which had now been accurately registered. However, it turned out a wet night and as black as pitch, and the relief was completed viâ Buterne Avenue at 12.37 a.m. without molestation. " B " Company remained in the subsidiary line.

We found Armentières, as indeed we had expected, hardly less noisy than the trenches. The Rue de Lille had become more of a storm centre than previously, and the Quartermaster's staff were frequently compelled to make a hasty descent to the cellar. The battalion mess, which had been held in a magnificent house opposite, its ceilings decorated with fat cherubs flying in a bright blue sky, was abandoned, as it seemed too risky to have all the officers congregated together in such a shelled area. The usual working and wiring parties, made none the pleasanter by the double journey up the Houplines road, and the same efforts to carry out training under difficulties were resumed. On the 29th " D " Company replaced " B " in the subsidiary line.

June had seen an increase in our monthly total of casualties. Four officers, of whom one was the Padre (at duty), had been wounded ; fourteen men had been killed and sixty-three wounded. In addition, 2nd-Lieutenants Dugdale and Rule were at the Base marked " T.B. " (*i.e.*, Temporary Base). Captain Gilling, who had for several months been attached to the R.E., had now been invalided to England. Our " effective strength " was reduced

The Imperial War Museum.

Official Photograph by permission of

RUE DE LILLE, ARMENTIÈRES.

"THE KING'S" (LIVERPOOL REGIMENT)

from 33 Officers and 744 other ranks to 28 officers and 656 other ranks ; and from the latter numbers had to be deducted Lieutenant Parkinson and a number of men with the Brigade Pioneer Company, Lieutenant Huntley at Brigade, and several parties of men otherwise employed, but whom we were not permitted to strike off our effective strength. Our total strength in France on June 30th was 36 officers and 800 other ranks, a disparity in totals which is eloquent of the number of "employed" on extra-regimental duties or on courses. Leave had not yet begun seriously to affect our numbers.

July 3rd found us back in the trenches in order "A," "D," "C" and "B" from the right. Relief was complete at 2.25 a.m. on July 12th. We found that the enemy was systematically destroying the left company sector, especially the communication trenches and the support line. The latter, standing as it did on the forward slope of a ridge, presented a splendid target, and it was impossible to keep pace with the damage being done. The constant bombardment of communication trenches threatened to isolate the left company altogether, and work was accordingly commenced on a new cut from Cambridge Avenue to the front line, called "Peter's Cat." The Heavy Artillery were also persuaded to do some serious shooting on the enemy main communication trenches, Celia Row and Celt Drive ; but though this may have annoyed him, it did not damp his enthusiasm in the least.

At 1.30 a.m. on July 11th the gas cylinders were opened and the projectors discharged simultaneously. The noise of the latter was tremendous, just like a mine explosion, while a huge black cloud of great density drifted away from the scene of discharge. Unfortunately, these projectors had been so long in the ground that a large number fell in No Man's Land ; two fell almost on the top of a post in "A" Company's front line, while one landed practically on the top of "A" Company's Headquarters. In spite of precautions, a number of gas casualties occurred, and the usual kind of correspondence followed between ourselves and the Higher Command. Only a case of " trench foot " could exceed a gas casualty in the excitement it caused.

The patrols which had again been ordered to follow the discharge were once more countermanded. It was most unlikely that they would have achieved anything but casualties, though it would have been interesting to know something of the results. Certainly an inspection of the enemy line after the Armistice revealed frequent remains of projectors. These, and detonated but unexploded medium trench mortar bombs, were to be found everywhere. The same day the enemy vented his wrath on us in no small measure, so we hoped we had done him some harm.

To give an idea of what patrolling was like in this sector, the following account may be quoted as an example. The narrative was written by a member of the patrol who took part in it :—
" The patrol, which left our trenches shortly after midnight, was composed of Riflemen Bolshaw, Matchett, and Corkill, with the section sleuth, Rifleman Dixon, in charge. The front line to the left of the head of Irish Avenue was only held to within about two hundred yards of the River Lys, the remainder of the trench from that point up to the river being rendered untenable by the marshy condition of the ground and the enemy command. Judging the Boche lines opposite to be similarly governed, it was obvious that this deserted area formed an excellent approach to Frelinghien. About this time a Boche withdrawal was expected opposite. The object of our patrol was to advance as far, and learn as much, as possible. The music encountered *en route* for the front line speedily dispelled any idea as to a Boche retirement. A relief was in progress at the time, and Fritz must have spotted it, for we ran into a veritable nightmare inferno. Rifle and machine-gun bullets whined and snipped, ' pineapples ' cracked, shells crashed, and ' minnies ' crumped ! Added attractions were a dense fog and the choking fumes of the explosions. Through it all the fitful glare of the Véry lights grew and waned, and the

114

tout ensemble created in me a stronger desire to enter No Man's Land than I had ever experienced before. There, at any rate, we would miss some of the ' hate ' floating around. With due caution we made our way along the deserted trenches to the bank of the Lys. We then struck out sharply to the right some distance and lay down to listen. Barely distinguishable amid the din, we could hear a knocking, rattling, and clanking to our immediate front. A surmise that a Boche wiring party was at work was confirmed a few minutes later by the location of its covering party at no great distance from us. Our batteries about then commenced to retaliate for the " strafe," and a breeze, till then absent, commenced to carry the fumes from the Boche shells back home. Fritz's nerves were evidently not at their best that night, for almost immediately the musical tinkle of his gas alarms rippled south down the sector, incidentally causing us no little amusement. Having discovered that, far from being absent from Frelinghien, the Boche was busy improving his position there, and further progress on our part being impossible, we emptied our rifles into the darkness in the direction of the wiring party and withdrew."

During this tour Captain Charles Wilson left us for the three months' Senior Officers' Course at Aldershot. There were not a few who imagined the war would be over before his return. Lieutenant Burton took over command of " D " Company.

On July 11th the battalion was relieved, and proceeded once more (less " B " Company) to Armentières. One company was now required nightly to press on with the new Peter's Cat Trench; and as this meant a long journey and a night in the trenches, it may be doubted whether the men welcomed the change from the line to the billets. If anything, the Germans were still more active with their artillery, and movement within the town was limited to what was absolutely necessary. The one pleasure of mounted officers was a gallop along the banks of the Lys from Armentières to Bac St. Maur. If you were energetic you could follow the towpath as far as Estaires. Between Armentières and Bac St. Maur there were some fine shell-holes, and the farm at the wooden bridge by the Jute Factory had been gutted. Bac St. Maur bridgehead was not infrequently shelled, and our old Battalion Headquarters was found to have received a direct hit. Shrapnel used to be put over the Bac St. Maur road even beyond Erquinghem, and the latter place itself used to be shelled intermittently. For the battalion as a whole there was little recreation, except that afforded by the estaminets and an occasional concert.

The morning after relief (July 12, 1917) a 12-inch shell landed in the Rue Gambetta next to the school where " C " Company were billeted ; and before there was time to do anything another one, most unluckily, crashed right in and down as far as the cellar, where it exploded with a terrific detonation. It was followed by a third, which fortunately missed the building, but produced a crater which filled the whole width of the street. The shell which entered " C " Company's billet unfortunately killed five men and wounded six. It was a pleasant greeting for Lieutenant Penrice and a draft of thirty men who had arrived the previous evening. " C " and " D " Companies were now moved more to the back of the town to a less exposed position. This move had been under consideration for some time, as the vicinity of the Rue de Lille was far from ideal. It was also decided to bring " A " Company from the Rue Jesuit into a more " salubrious " neighbourhood. Brigade Headquarters had already moved to the Rue Sadi Carnot by order of the Corps Commander, who visited them one day during a period of enemy activity ; and certainly their former situation was far from pleasant—a feature, however, in which it resembled most other parts of the town.

The Quartermaster, going down to make some arrangements, was unfortunately badly wounded by a 5·9 which burst just in front of the entrance to " A " Company's billet. His left thigh was damaged, and two pieces of shell entered his stomach, one lodging in the muscles of the back near his spine. He was hurriedly taken to the regimental aid post, where Captain McHugh did his best for him, and thence to the Advanced Surgical Centre, Estaires. No one thought he could possibly live, but, with his usual determination, he won through ; and though his health was badly impaired,* he became in due course an S.O.3 in the Air Force after the Army had finally thrown him out. For his services with the battalion he was Mentioned in Dispatches. His place was taken by Regimental Quartermaster-Sergeant Wallas, for whom we tried in vain to obtain a Quartermaster's commission.

At 11 p.m. on July 14th the sound of a heavy barrage disturbed us, and shortly after one company was ordered to stand-to. We thought the German raid had come off, but except for the heavy barrage nothing further happened. The next night " C " Company relieved " B " Company in the subsidiary line, and were probably not sorry to leave the " peace " of reserve billets for a while. The post of extra company in the subsidiary line was undoubtedly very popular. The area they occupied was seldom shelled, and work could only be done by them at night and in the vicinity of their posts. In the early hours of the morning, just as " B " Company had got clear of the line, the barrage fell once more, and after rolling the length of the front line from right to left formed a box barrage on the left company front. It was a really heavy barrage, and two working parties from our " A " Company, who were just stopping work in Peter's Cat and had begun to arrive in Cambridge Avenue, suddenly found themselves in the centre of a tornado of exploding high explosives. 2nd-Lieutenant McWilliam, who was in command of one of the parties, was, however, equal to the occasion, and with great gallantry got the parties under cover, and then proceeded to reinforce the front line. A number of Germans were seen coming across towards Cambridge Avenue, and were called on to surrender. This they

* He died in June 1920, to the great regret of all who knew him.

seemed quite prepared to do, but an N.C.O. suddenly appeared, and they all fled back together. One prisoner, however, was captured by Rifleman Mills.

The 2/7th were not sorry to see the arrival of our men in the front line. They had suffered heavy casualties, and their position had become none too pleasant, as the Germans had come round the left flank and they were being bombed from behind as well as in front. Colonel Slater and Captain Drakeford, his Adjutant, were in the left post of all when the raid commenced, and had a pretty lively experience. Our men and the men in the posts got in some useful shooting at the enemy as he fled back to Frelinghien by the river road, and a dozen dead Germans were found, in addition to the live prisoner. It proved on the examination of the latter to have been a big raid ; and had the enemy shown a little more enterprise, they might have made the position of that left company extremely dangerous. There is no doubt that the accidental presence of our working party, with McWilliam to make full use of it, proved of great service to the 2/7th K.L.R. In connection with the operations Rifleman Mills and Rifleman J. Bailey were awarded the M.M.

The Light Trench Mortar Battery suffered severely, their S.O.S. positions having apparently been well registered by the enemy, with the result that in more than one case the team was buried, together with their gun. " C " Company dug them out, and spent over six hours cleaning up this part of the line, so great was the damage done.

During this period in billets our new Divisional Commander, Major-General R. W. R. Barnes, C.B., D.S.O., called at Headquarters, and was introduced to the Commanding Officer and others present.

On July 19th the battalion once more relieved the 2/7th K.L.R., " C," " B," " D," "A " being now the order in the line. The repair of the damage done by the raid, the erection of a complicated wire entanglement on the left (which was carried out, under

118

"THE KING'S" (LIVERPOOL REGIMENT)

Major H. K. Wilson's supervision, with some difficulty, owing to the heavy shelling and machine-gun fire), and the preparations for a two-company raid to be carried out under Captain Eccles, were quite sufficient to occupy our attention. In addition, one company of Portuguese was attached to us for instruction, forty men being handed over to each company. The relief of these men by another company on the night of the 20th produced rather an amusing scene. It had been arranged that the old company should not leave till the new company had arrived; but some time before the latter were due, the junction of Gloucester Avenue and the subsidiary line was packed with Portuguese, about half of whom went out on their own initiative. Suddenly the Germans opened a regular barrage of gas shells on Houplines Level Crossing, and the wind blew the gas back to our subsidiary line. The commencement of the barrage divided the relieving company into two halves, and likewise the old company, one half of whom, going back without orders, had just passed the Level Crossing. All those on the far side, relieving and relieved troops alike, hurried back to their billets in Armentières. The relieving troops, and a few others who had been stopped by the barrage, rushed into the trenches and mingled with those waiting to go out, thus producing the most complete confusion, to which the necessity of wearing small box-respirators added the finishing touch. It was a matter of no small difficulty to get them sorted out, especially as our only means of communication with the Portuguese was in bad French, and they all talked at once. However, eventually we got things straightened out somehow, and order was once more established.

On July 22nd, 1917, to keep up a pretence that we were going to attack Frelinghien, a practice barrage was put down on that place at 5 p.m. At 5.30 p.m. the enemy replied with a far heavier bombardment of our left company sector, which in a few moments was entirely concealed from view by smoke and dust. A Portuguese Commanding Officer and Adjutant arrived that day for

119

instruction, and Battalion Headquarters was the centre of quite a heavy gas shell bombardment. Fortunately, the next day all the Portuguese were removed. It was not a sector calculated to give new troops a very favourable impression of the line. During that night the battalion north of the Lys dug dummy assembly trenches opposite Frelinghien, and the following day another bombardment was carried out. A second company of 2/7th K.L.R. was now brought into the subsidiary line, partly to enable more work to be done, partly in view of the continued threatening attitude of the Germans.

At 1.55 a.m. on the 26th we discharged two torpedoes in the enemy's wire on the left, and a dummy barrage was put down to divert attention from a 2/8th K.L.R. raid about to take place on our right. We ourselves were scheduled to do a two-company raid, under the command of Captain Eccles, in a short while, and took considerable interest in the reception accorded to the " Irish " raiding party. Our barrage was thin, and the enemy paid little attention to it, but his retaliation fell heavily on the 2/8th K.L.R.

The next two days brought intense artillery fire all over the sector, and on the 27th heavy " minnies " appeared and blew in Captain Burton's Headquarters with two direct hits, though, fortunately, he was not there at the time and no one was killed. The night of the 28th, the original night for relief, produced continuous shrapnel from about 9 p.m. to 3 a.m. all over the subsidiary line and communication trenches. About 3 a.m. an aeroplane bombed Houplines Level Crossing, and a deluge of heavy " minnies " descended on the left-centre company's line; but on the whole we congratulated ourselves on our luck, little dreaming of what was to happen on the real relief night, July 29th. The 2/7th K.L.R. came into the sector without a shell being fired. Colonel Slater and his Headquarters had just arrived, and the relief was progressing well, when, with a sudden rush and roar, a terrific bombardment of Armentières commenced. A regular semicircle of flashes could be seen running continuously round the rear of the enemy line. This was clearly no ordinary shoot, but a specially arranged show with artillery in proportion. The relief was promptly stopped, and all troops stood-to. Suddenly the S.O.S. went up from the right battalion, and our guns opened up. This, however, shortly afterwards proved to be a mistake, and as the German infantry made no move the relief continued. The din was terrific. Apart from the actual noise of the batteries firing and the unbroken rush and scream of shells overhead, the uproar in Armentières was tremendous as buildings were smashed and battered and the broken debris hurled about in all directions by this unceasing rain of shells. Lieutenant Evans rang up on the telephone from Rue Bayard, where he had gone to take over billets, and told us that the town was soaked with gas, and warned us not to come out at present. Fires now began to appear all over the town, but still the barrage did not slacken. At 12.15 a.m. it stopped, but began again with renewed firing at 12.45 a.m., though about 1.15 a.m. this was reduced to one or two areas and some general miscellaneous shooting, lasting until about 4 a.m., when it was further reduced to action by one or two heavy guns alone.

About 3 a.m. " B " Company began to thread its way down Buterne Avenue towards the town. They were caught by a heavy bombardment in the Houplines road, and had to take temporary shelter in odd cellars. " C " Company and Battalion Head-quarters followed, but escaped with nothing worse than casual shelling. " A " and " D " Companies remained in the subsidiary line, and very glad they were to do so.

Our arrival in the area of our billets was anything but cheerful. A large part of the Rue de Lille, including the Quartermaster's Stores, was in flames. The house next to Battalion Headquarters was practically gutted, and both the company billets were blazing merrily. The streets were littered with gas shells and the grey powder which they had scattered. The houses also were full of gas, nor were any of the gas-proof cellars better off. The first casualties were being loaded up into the ambulances, the men gasping, vomiting, choking, and with bloodshot, streaming eyes. Lieutenant Wyatt, who gallantly carried a wounded man across Armentières through the bombardment, was especially bad; and Quartermaster-Sergeant Jackson, who had been found wounded and unconscious in the street, was little better. Most of our advance party were in various stages of collapse, and the road to the advanced dressing station was already marked by a small stream of casualties. The civilians were in a terrible state. Gas protection for them consisted merely of one or two "P.H." helmets per family, and many of the poor creatures were now in agony from the gas poisoning. Efforts to rouse the Town Major proved of little use, and a search was instituted to try and discover some part of the town where the gas was less pronounced. It need hardly be said that the Commanding Officer was tireless in his efforts to relieve the situation, and in company with Major H. K. Wilson searched the town from one end to the other. It was on occasions such as these that the ordinary man got a glimpse of what the Commanding Officer really was. After a prolonged search, the schools between St. Vaast Church and the Convent were found to be clear, and thither the remains of the battalion were removed. The men, utterly tired out, fell fast asleep, but only to wake up and find that they were blind. This was " mustard gas," till then unheard of by us; and processions of blind men, led by one who could still see, became more and more frequent. We did contrive to make some tea, but the rest of the food was splashed with gas and was unusable; otherwise there was little to be done. The shelling of the Place de la Republique now began from a heavy battery, and the shells came perilously near the open courtyard where we sat under the cloisters that surround it. A thunderstorm broke suddenly, and probably did more to clear away the gas than anything else could have done. That night and the whole of the next day the Germans shelled the town fiercely. Splendid work was done by Lieutenant Penrice, who had just gone to the Transport in place of Hutchinson; by Lieutenant Clarke, who had gone to join a Brigade Training School in course of formation; and by the transport drivers, who worked with unceasing energy and courage.

By July 31st the following had been evacuated: Colonel Fletcher, Major H. K. Wilson, Captains Eccles and Steward, Lieutenants Alcock, Collinge, Evans, Royle, Rothwell, J. R. Paul, 2nd-Lieutenants E. E. Paul, Pegge, Little, and Wyatt, the new Padre, Weaver, and the new Medical Officer, Robinson. The Adjutant, who went on leave on the 29th, before the far-reaching effects of the gas had fully revealed themselves, went into hospital on his arrival in England. Company Sergeant-Major Heyworth had started with him but had been compelled to remain behind at the M.D.S., Fort Rompu, being quite blind and delirious. The stream of ambulances, lorries, general service waggons, and farm carts pouring into and out of Armentières, was a sight that will long be remembered. The whole of " B " Company and the whole of " C " Company, except 2nd-Lieutenant Fell and one man, became casualties. Of Battalion Headquarters there remained only one policeman and one store-keeper. The rest, including the Regimental Sergeant-Major, Regimental Quartermaster-Sergeant, orderly-room, medical, sanitary, and Quartermaster's staff, the cooks, the tailors, the bootmakers, and all the other details, were evacuated. The Battalion Orchestra, who were playing when the barrage opened, were badly gassed to a man, and their instruments destroyed. Captain Bowring suddenly found himself Commanding Officer, and his command consisted simply of " A " and " D " Companies and the transport. The total casualties, including the gassed, for July were: 17 officers wounded, of whom Lieutenant Collinge died from the effects of the gas, 12 men killed, and approximately 428 wounded. Of these a few died later, and more were invalided from the service, but a good many rejoined us in due course.

Before proceeding any further it will be as well to discuss briefly the cause of this disaster. In the first place, this was only the second concentrated bombardment with mustard gas that had occurred. The first had taken place at Ypres a month before, and caused extensive casualties, but the report of these did not reach us till the night of relief, when it came with the usual correspondence, which, owing to pressure of work, was not opened till after the disaster had happened. The significance of the new form of gas should certainly have been circulated earlier. With the dangers of ordinary gas we were familiar, and in any case no one could have lived for five minutes in the area most strongly affected without a respirator. The slightest breath of this new gas was like inhaling red-hot air and choked you immediately. After the first density of the gas had dispersed, the area became comparatively clear, and the insidious and silent evaporation, practically free from smell, caused no one inconvenience, and in some places was so slight as to be barely perceptible. It was this that affected the eyes, an entirely new phenomenon to us ; and the comparatively small number that suffered from serious internal gassing proves that the ordinary precautions were taken. Moreover, most of those badly gassed were actually caught in Armentières itself by the original barrage, which began at the rate of hundreds of shells in a minute. When it is remembered that as late as the spring of 1918, after mustard gas had long been recognized and widely advertised, and every possible precaution taken against it, a concentrated bombardment still produced casualties running into hundreds, it is not so very surprising that on the second occasion when it was used, and the first as far as we were concerned, only about fifty escaped out of the total troops in Armentières, consisting of two half battalions, some field and heavy batteries, and some Royal Engineer, Machine Gun Corps, and Trench Mortar sections. Of the civilian population, it is probable that scarcely one single person got off unscathed.

This bombardment was the climax of our long period in Houplines. We had been instructed to be as offensive as possible, in order to divert the attention of the enemy by our aggressive tactics from the operations scheduled to commence on July 31st, and now known as the Third Battle of Ypres. Little glory attaches to a " feint " attack, whether it be stationary or by movement ; but if successful it brings down upon you severe hostile attention, which has to be endured without any compensating chance of sharing in the glory of a great victory. That we succeeded in our allotted task, and that the 171st Infantry Brigade bore the brunt of it, we know not only from what our Army Commander said, but because the Intelligence showed that the Division kept two German Divisions pinned down opposite to it right till the end, and this notwithstanding the fact that the hostile artillery was about ten times as great as our own. The steady increase of destructive shooting on the area immediately north and south of the Lys, the regular " crashing " of all lines of communication, the intense shelling of Armentières, culminating in the great gas bombardment, prove conclusively that the enemy was daily expecting an attack on Frelinghien, for which he imagined a force was concentrating in Armentières. That our casualties were not greater was due to the scattered position of the posts holding such a large sector, and to our constant efforts to provide such protection as could best be constructed under the circumstances.

CHAPTER V

THE disorganization in the Brigade resulting from the gas bombardment was naturally very great. The 2/5th K.L.R. and ourselves were reduced by 50 per cent, not including Battalion Headquarters, and the relief of the battalion for reorganization was therefore imperative. Accordingly, on the evening of July 31st Captain Bowring, the Acting Commanding Officer, was instructed to move out to Bac St. Maur, the 2/5th King's Own Royal Lancaster Regiment taking the place of " A " and " B " Companies in the subsidiary line. The move was made by sections, owing to the continued shelling and the state of the roads, which had not yet been cleared of débris. It was effected without incident beyond a drenching from the heavy rain which came steadily down.

The work of tracing the casualties now began. Most of the battalion records were half buried in Armentières. These were unearthed, and Lance-Corporal Longridge tackled his new duties as Orderly-Room Sergeant with the greatest determination and ability. Salvage work was also carried out, and such remnants of the battalion's equipment as were left from the fires and the subsequent looting were collected at Bac St. Maur. Little time was allowed, however, at the moment for reorganization. On August 2nd " D " Company and one platoon of " A " Company were ordered into the subsidiary line of La Boutillerie to relieve a similar force of 4/5th Loyal North Lancashires. On August 4th

126

"THE KING'S" (LIVERPOOL REGIMENT)

" the Battalion (less garrison of subsidiary line) "—so reads Operation Order No. 33—relieved the 2/7th K.L.R. The " Battalion," in fact, consisted only of three platoons of " A " Company and a few odd men who formed Battalion Headquarters. This same force was inspected next day by General Barnes, the Divisional Commander, who paid a very warm tribute to the work that the battalion had done during the past two months.

By the time Major H. K. Wilson returned from hospital, August 6th, Captain Bowring, in spite of the enormous difficulty of the task, had got the reorganization of the battalion well under way, for which he deserved the very greatest credit, and for which, in fact, he eventually received a " Mention." In this work he had been greatly assisted by the remaining officers of the battalion, who discharged their various new duties with great zeal and ability.

About this time Lieutenant Freeman joined us as Transport Officer. For many years he had been with the A.S.C., and we were lucky to secure an officer with so much experience in the management of horse transport.

On August 7th the 2/7th K.L.R. relieved our small garrisons in Croix Marèchal, Elbow Farm, Chapel Farm, Smith's Villa, and Command Post ; and the battalion went into billets at Fleurbaix, where Captain Plumley, R.A.M.C., reported as Medical Officer.

About this time Captain Alexander, London Regiment, who had been Brigade Major for about a month, relieving Major Geddes, was unfortunately killed by a bomb splinter while sitting in the Brigade Headquarters at Fleurbaix. He had been badly gassed in Armentières, but refused to leave. His death was greatly lamented. Captain P. H. Hansen, V.C., M.C., acted as Brigade Major for a time, being in a short while relieved by Captain R. W. Patteson, M.C., Norfolk Regiment, who remained with us to the very end, and whose ability outrivalled, if possible, even his great personal popularity.

HISTORY OF THE 2/6TH (RIFLE) BATTALION

On the evening of August 8th " A " and " D " Companies were attached to the 2/5th K.L.R., and took over the Cordonnerie sector on the right of La Boutillerie, probably the most peaceful sector in all France. The trenches were well constructed and dry, and hostile activity was normally of a very mild description.

But the fear that the enemy might intend a limited offensive on this front had not yet subsided, and elaborate orders dealing with this situation were still being issued. Meanwhile Battalion Headquarters, on August 15th, returned to Bac St. Maur, where they had more than enough to keep them occupied, as the first draft, consisting of 111 men, had arrived the previous day. On August 16th Lieutenant-General Sir R. C. B. Haking, commanding XI. Corps, presented Riflemen Bailey and Mills with the Military Medal which they had been awarded in Armentières.

On August 18th " A " and " D " Companies rejoined at Bac St. Maur ; and the Company of the 2/5th K.L.R., who had been attached to us to strengthen the " battalion on Divisional Reserve," returned to their own unit. Drafts now came in apace. On August 18th drafts of 192, 61, and 131 men arrived. After these had been posted, the draft of 61 men proved to have been intended for the 2/8th K.L.R., and had to be given up. All these parties were inspected on August 21st by Brigadier-General Bray.

On the 24th the battalion moved into Fleurbaix, finding posts for the subsidiary line ; and during this period two more drafts, of 79 and 45 men respectively, joined the battalion. The end of August found our effective strength 756 men, the highest figure that we had achieved since the end of February.

On September 2nd the battalion—and it was a complete battalion now—relieved the 2/7th K.L.R. in La Boutillerie : " A " Company on the right, " B " in the centre, " D " on the left, and " C " in the subsidiary line. Headquarters were situated at Foray House. This latter spot had been heavily shelled on August 21st when the Portuguese held the line, the intention of

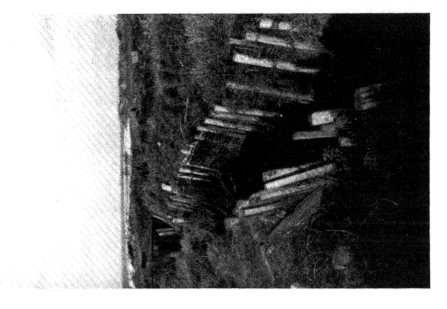

BOCHE FRONT LINE OPPOSITE LEFT SECTOR, HOUPLINES. FRELINGHIEN IN BACKGROUND AND RIVER LYS IN FLOOD.

HOUPLINES ROAD, LOOKING TOWARDS ARMENTIÈRES.

the Germans, according to the Portuguese official report, being "to disorganize the Battalion Staff for future operations"; which laudable object, the report naively added, "was attained by 10 a.m., at which time the orderly-room, kitchen mess, and orderlies' dug-outs were damaged." However, as far as we were concerned, the enemy took very little interest in us, and the time was exceptionally quiet. Moreover, the weather had turned fine and warm again, which made life pleasant as well as peaceful. The left sector occasionally received attention in the form of trench mortar shooting, which, we remembered, was characteristic of that corner of France, but it was not sufficient to cause any serious results.

On September 5th, to the great delight of the overworked remnant of officers, a draft of thirteen fresh ones arrived—Carr, Eupen, Harper, T. W. Jones, Lever, Novelle, Profit, Broad, Roberts, Robinson, Rycroft, Upward, and T. L. Williams. This was a great accession of power, as in the matter of men the battalion was already up to a good fighting strength. But there was still much to be done. Specialists had to be trained, N.C.Os. to be selected, and the general process of amalgamating and consolidating the new material so recently come together to be perfected. A new Quartermaster, Lieutenant Jackson, also reported for duty at this time.

The tour in the line ended on September 10th, when the 2/7th K.L.R. once more took over from us, and one platoon per company took charge of the four strong points in the subsidiary line. The only incident in the latter part of the tour was the attempt of a strong patrol of the enemy to round up a patrol of four men from our battalion. The effort was made with determination, and eventually our patrol had to scatter. All reached our line safely, but three of them were wounded in the fight.

On September 11th Colonel Fletcher returned from hospital, and the work of organizing and training the battalion was renewed with the greatest energy. Specialist classes both for officers and

N.C.Os. were soon hard at work ; while for the companies, now so very much changed in their personnel, general training, inspections, close order drill, and all other approved methods for increasing knowledge and morale were in full swing.

Meanwhile rumours of a move to a rest area had long been rife. The Division had now been doing trench duty continuously for seven months, and it was quite time that it was taken away for a general overhaul. During all those months we had been kept more or less continuously in the trenches, with no opportunity to improve on the lessons learnt, and nothing to inspire our men to increase their efficiency, beyond the regular round of eight days in reserve and eight days in the line. Already the ordinary wastage of trench warfare, not to mention the disaster of Armentières, had deprived us of many of our best N.C.Os. and men. We had, in fact, lost as many men as if we had been in a battle, but there was not that feeling of satisfaction, such as results from a successful push, to animate the remainder. However that may be, the theory that we were going out to rest grew steadily, and for once proved correct. The idea of a " rest " was not in itself particularly attractive, except that it meant freedom from shell fire, permission to give up wearing the box-respirator, and other little relaxations of that description. As a " rest " in the ordinarily accepted sense of the word, it had long since been discovered to be a fraud, being, in fact, a period of intense activity. Still, it was a change, and possibly meant that the Division would thereafter be required for work a little more stimulating than trench warfare.

On September 16th we were relieved by the 15th Welch, and proceeded to Neuf Berquin viâ Estaires, a distance of seven or eight miles, under a very hot sun. After a day's quiet training here, we handed over our billets to the 4/5th Loyal North Lancashire Regiment, and set off to L'Ecleme on September 18th. The Brigade marched as such, the battalion starting at 8.20 a.m., and passing the Brigade starting-point at 10 a.m. The route led round the southern outskirts of Merville, and thence via Calonne and Robecq. Our billets were in L'Ecleme, a little hamlet about a mile south-east of Busnes. The morning proved cloudy, which made marching pleasant ; and, thanks to our early start, we were in by midday.

Next day we were on the move again for our final destination, St. Hilaire. On the way we passed through the comparatively large town of Lillers, and then the village of Bourecq. The country, from being as flat as could be conceived, now became pleasantly undulating and very pretty, especially to eyes tired of the lifeless monotony of Northern France. St. Hilaire itself is a delightful little village, consisting of one long winding street with several little side streets running off it. Billets were, on the whole, good, and you felt at once the relief of being able to move without a box-respirator and steel helmet. Thoughts of war vanished for the moment ; the mind was occupied with the pleasant rural scenes and the air of quiet industry that pervaded the spot, so different from the wear and tear of war, and so infinitely refreshing.

At St. Hilaire the battalion spent a month, and from the first it became apparent that the " rest " was only a preparation for a " push." The first day was spent by the Commanding Officer in inspecting the battalion. This is a far more lengthy process than might be supposed, and it is surprising what a length of time can be spent on it without the inspector realizing that he has taken more than a few minutes.

The next day training areas, which had been duly allotted, were covered with the men performing various mysterious evolutions. Here you would see a whole company endeavouring to perform a wheel in close column, with the Company Sergeant-Major and Platoon Officers now urging on, now checking, the onrush of what from a distance is apt to look like a race crowd breaking on to the course. From another part of the field a sudden series of unearthly shouts betokens the efforts of a final assault party to inspire terror in the hearts of rows of disinterested sacks. Here, again, stand a group of men solemnly waving their arms in a slow and stately movement. There comes a sudden order, and in a trice the whole crowd are off, like a pack of hounds, to some neighbouring object and back again. "Physical jerks," if properly carried out, are full of variety.

In an adjoining field two rows of men are standing opposite each other, roaring orders to the full extent of their lungs. This is a rough and ready form of instruction in voice production, technically called "Communication" or "Shouting Drill." In retired corners little groups of men may be seen examining the intricacies of a Lewis gun or a field telephone. Theirs is a more peaceful form of existence during training, and one that is apt to lapse into story-telling, or even solo whist, if opportunity permits. But all the while the Commanding Officer and Adjutant (Captain Wilson, recently returned from his course in England), the Regimental Sergeant-Major, the Company Commanders, the Specialist Officers, and frequently the Brigadier and the Brigade Major, are hovering about, asking questions, correcting, suggesting, and generally supervising. Their assistance, it must be confessed, is often more readily given than desired ; but still that is part of the business. "Red hats" have little terror for us. We are not worried with that type of Staff Officer so frequently upbraided. Our Brigadier and Brigade Major, our Divisional Commander and General Staff, are in the main helpful and sympathetic.

In the midst of all this activity markers are called for, and a general sigh of relief goes up. Training continues, and everyone has an eye for the four men facing the Regimental Sergeant-Major. Here comes the Adjutant at last. " Get your company together, Captain X., and fall in on your marker as soon as you are ready." Work may have been proceeding languidly till now, and you might have thought the men were tired. Perhaps they were, but there is little sign of it now. Everyone is suddenly galvanized into intense activity. In a remarkably short time the battalion is formed up in mass, a few short orders are given, and the column winds its way back to St. Hilaire for dinner. The day's work is over. The afternoon is devoted to football matches and other forms of amusement; the evening to the estaminet. On Sundays the full ceremonial of Church Parade would be gone through, the band of the 6th (now the Divisional Band) supplying the music.

On September 21st a further draft of 130 men arrived, and the battalion was now stronger than it had ever been previously in France. This last draft came from the East Surreys, and a very fine lot of men they were. About this time General Bray met with an accident while riding, and Brigadier-General F. C. Longbourne, D.S.O., arrived to take over the Brigade. He was somewhat younger than General Bray, and of the very best type of officer—considerate, courteous, and capable. He was as popular as he was respected.

Training now became of a more specialized type, and it was obvious that we were destined in due course to take part in the Third Battle of Ypres, which was still raging with great fierceness, in spite of the almost insuperable difficulties of the ground and the weather. Attacks on strong posts by platoons and companies figured prominently in our training, and the general formations for attack by a battalion were the subject of continual study. Unfortunately, which is the best form of attack was (and probably still is) a matter of warm dispute on the part of the Higher Command. Some advocated two companies in front and two in support; others three in front and one behind. Others, again, supported " blobs," and another school " worms"; while a third body of opinion pronounced " leap-frogging " the only feasible scheme. The training in the attack, therefore, if lacking in continuity, was certainly not lacking in variety. Sheets of instructions poured in upon us in the most bewildering fashion, till even the most careful student was muddled beyond hope of recovery. Eventually all officers more or less abandoned any hope that they may have cherished of solving the higher mysteries of the attack, and devoted their whole attention to musketry, bayonet fighting, bombing, and so forth, trusting to the general efficiency obtained to solve the final problem as set by the enemy.

The commands of companies had now been arranged as follows : " A " Company, Captain McWilliam ; " B " Company, Lieutenant Penrice ; " C " Company, Captain Ormrod ; " D " Company, Captain Fell. Regimental Sergeant-Major Smith had returned from hospital, and Company Sergeant-Major Heyworth, who had been acting in his place, became Regimental Quartermaster-Sergeant.

On October 8th the Division had the honour of being inspected by the Commander-in-Chief, Sir Douglas Haig. Great preparations were made for this important event, but, unfortunately, the day proved of the wettest. We started at 8 a.m. and marched for about two hours in pouring rain along bad roads and worse field-tracks to some exposed ground above Estrée Blanche, where the whole Division was assembled. The position was swept by a biting wind, and there we stood for nearly two hours waiting for the Field-Marshal to arrive. After a general salute, he rode round the ranks, and then the usual march past took place. Everyone was soaked to the skin and half frozen, and right glad they were to get on the move again.

Field operations on a large scale now took place several times a week. They were conducted with such realism as modern resources can provide, and under the eyes of General Maxse, the Corps Commander, and other important personages. The former had a bright and breezy manner in dealing with the problems of training, and his presence generally produced considerable animation among those participating in the operations. From the point of view of the ordinary man in the ranks, these " stunts " are apt to be laborious and tiresome; but at the same time there is no doubt that only under these more or less realistic conditions can officers and N.C.Os. appreciate the value of the lessons learnt in theoretical training.

" THE KING'S " (LIVERPOOL REGIMENT)

The scene of operations on October 7th for the Divisional attack was the practice trenches behind Estrée Blanche, near Enguingatte. The march to the assembly positions through very pretty country was pleasant enough, although the weather was cold and dull. After forming up, the attack proceeded by waves, one of the orthodox methods at the time, preceded by a real trench mortar bombardment, and accompanied by a real contact aeroplane, for which flares had to be lit at various intervals. The operations ceased at four o'clock, and as the battle ended the rain began. From then till we got home it poured in torrents. We splashed along field-tracks and muddy lanes as darkness fell, and still it came down. As we entered our billets, about 8 p.m., we most of us felt that field days were a luxury we would willingly forego.

The period in rest was now fast drawing to a close. It had at its commencement seen the battalion strong indeed in numbers, but lacking in cohesion and unprepared for any continued action. The pleasant weeks at St. Hilaire, in spite of the vigorous training that had taken place, had proved restful to the old members of the battalion, and had given the new-comers a full opportunity of acclimatizing themselves to their new surroundings. Everyone was fit, and ready for anything that might come. Equipment was complete, specialists were replaced, and all gaps filled. It was well that it was so, as the change in store for the battalion was to be severe. Real hardships and real danger were ahead, which the battalion, as expected, proved itself fully capable of enduring.

The move commenced on October 19th, the battalion leaving the village about 8 a.m. to join the Brigade column. At St. Hilaire, as elsewhere in France, as well as in England, the battalion had become very popular with their hosts, and many a tear was shed and many a kindly " God-speed " uttered as we moved off. It was a good long march, about fifteen miles in all, and though the day was cool a few fell out. The new drafts, good men though they were, had not all yet appreciated the Commanding Officer's inflexible rules in the matter of march discipline. Our destination was the Renescure area, east-south-east of St. Omer, and the road lay through Wittes and Racquinghem. Lieutenant Goulding and a billeting party went on ahead to the Proven area; but the battalion halted for the night in a series of small farms standing in a piece of country not unlike the ground round Inkerman Barracks at Woking. The morning of the 20th saw us early afoot. At 8 a.m. we were formed up on the Arques—Eblinghem—Hazebrouck road, ready to embus. There is always a certain amount of amusement at embussing. To begin with, the buses almost invariably face in the opposite direction to what is expected. Moreover, they are frequently of all sizes and shapes, and thereby upset your most careful calculations. For a man wearing full marching order, plus a blanket wound round his pack, it is no easy matter to scale a lorry. A bus—that is, a real bus—presents less difficulty; but the stairs are awkward, and the constructional expert of the General Omnibus Company did not design his seats to accommodate people requiring at least twelve inches of spare seat behind the traveller before he can hope to sit down. The scene to the uninitiated would appear to be sheer chaos. Each vehicle is surrounded by a heaving and struggling mass; and when this has been dissipated, there are still men who have to be almost literally forced into vehicles which look hopelessly overcrowded already. The operation takes time, but eventually the long column moves off. With the violent motion caused by the lack of springs and bad *pavé* the human mass is gradually shaken into a more or less solid condition; and it is really rather remarkable that at the end of the journey anyone is sufficiently mobile to begin the process of debussing.

The trip was quite a long one, and it was after two o'clock when Poperinghe was passed and the column came to a final stop. Everywhere the " push " in progress was very evident. Poperinghe itself was seething with troops of all arms, and the general air of activity so conspicuous behind an " active " front was very marked.

"THE KING'S" (LIVERPOOL REGIMENT)

After the whole battalion had been extracted, like sardines from a tin, a march of two or three miles—a very trying performance with cramped limbs—brought us to Plurendon Camp, in the Proven area, recently vacated by the Welsh Guards; and a cheerless and bleak-looking spot it was, covered with old canvas tents. After the pleasant billets of St. Hilaire, we felt already a bit discouraged, but it was a perfect paradise compared with some of the places to which we were about to be introduced. The weather was also very unsettled, and the mud that the rain produced was quite up to the best traditions of Flanders. To add to our discomfort, the tea ration, which had been put on the mechanical transport, arrived very late owing to a breakdown. We did not move the next day, as we had expected, but on October 23rd proceeded in the morning to Proven Station. After despatching the " Life-boat Party," the nucleus of $33\frac{1}{3}$ per cent. of officers and men always left out by a battalion going into action, with a view to subsequent reorganization, and after about an hour in the train, we arrived at Elverdinghe about 1.30 p.m. A march of two miles followed, and then we entered Wolff Camp, in the Malakoff area. A more wretched and inhospitable spot it would be hard to find. Pitched in what had once been No Man's Land, it was an admirable representation of the tangled and disreputable desolation that one's imagination connects with such a place. The 2/5th Loyal North Lancashire Regiment had, moreover, failed to vacate the camp, and we had consequently to remain in the adjacent field for the time being, though the difference was little enough. The ground was broken and muddy beyond description. The only accommodation to be found consisted of tattered tents, through which the rain and wind drove at will—and there was no lack of either. A Y.M.C.A. tent, the sole refuge of the area, struggled manfully all day with a queue, often fifty yards long, of men waiting for tea and biscuits. Apart from this oasis, we were surrounded by a desert of hideous misery, but in spite of it all our spirits were high. Even for those not in the secret it was by now clear that

137

we were moving up to take our turn in the grim struggle in the morass, into which a continual barrage had long since converted the Passchendaele Ridge. At least we felt we had come for a purpose ; and if the usual routine were followed, we should be back in rest before long—those of us, at least, who had not " collected a Blighty," or a more permanent separation from the troubles of this world.

We were not allowed to be idle for very long. At 4.30 and 5 p.m. respectively working parties, 100 strong, moved up to the line, and the next morning a party of forty men went up to be similarly employed. Other parties were detailed to reconnoitre routes, a most necessary but difficult operation under the conditions. At 4 p.m. that day (October 26th) the battalion was suddenly ordered to move to Marsouin Farm, a camp nearer the line. As so often happens, the order synchronized with the approach of tea. The usual rush attended this sudden move, and resulted in the majority of the men missing their tea, a regrettable thing at ordinary times, but in view of the mental and physical strain about to be encountered particularly unfortunate.

Our Quartermaster left us at this point, his work being efficiently continued by Captain Bowring, summoned from the " nucleus party " for the purpose. Marsouin Farm proved to be the lowest form of habitation that can possibly be classified as a camp. " Bivvies " of the rudest description, " leans-to " of ground sheets or odd bits of corrugated iron, formed our quarters, all half immersed in mud of the thickest and vilest consistency. The biting air and heavy rainstorms combined to give the finishing touch to this execrable spot, which was calculated to inspire all ranks with as profound a contempt for death as was ever entertained by the most ardent believer in Valhalla. Similar " camps " were dotted about in the vicinity ; and an unending stream of guns, men, pack transport, and so forth, poured by continually, struggling and slipping on the crude roads or corduroy tracks which led up to the battle zone. Trolley trams and light trains wound their way forward, grunting and creaking under loads consisting of all the multifarious stores required in modern warfare. The surrounding country, if difficult to describe, was certainly of a uniform appearance. It consisted simply of endless mud and water. As far as the eye could reach there was the same yellowish waste of muddy misery, shell-hole touching shell-hole with never a break, save where a splintered and winding duck-board track, a primitive road of half-buried logs, or the spidery lines of a light railway, relieved the hopeless monotony. Across this wilderness of squalor and filth every fighting man had to pass to reach the enemy. Ammunition, rations, R.E. material, Red Cross stores, everything, in fact, had to be transported over this quagmire, and woe betide the luckless man who fell from the slippery safety of the duck-boards into its clutches ! All the while the guns on either side kept up their steady bombardment, now fierce and concentrated, now desultory and scattered.

On the evening of the 27th, at the usual short notice, the battalion was ordered forward to the reserve trenches. As has already been remarked, these sudden moves are very trying, and this one proved to be particularly so. The battalion was now leaving the last limits of what in such an area might be called civilization. Consequently rations, equipment, and ammunition had to be completed for the whole period in the desolate country into which we were now to penetrate. The scene that followed will not easily be forgotten. The march to Eagle Trench, which brought us into close proximity with the trench area, was made under considerable difficulties, owing to the large number of gas shells which were falling in the area. At one point on the duck-board track along which the battalion was winding its way in single file, Colonel Fletcher at its head, a large working party of another battalion was halted and blocking the way. This working party was held up in front by heavy enemy shell fire, which was falling on a road across which the track ran. After waiting some forty minutes, it was observed that the shell fire, which covered about

200 yards of the road, was being lifted at regular intervals of about fifteen minutes on to a different sector of the road, and after another fifteen minutes brought back to the former objective. Time was getting on, so Colonel Fletcher decided to try to rush his battalion through next time the bombardment lifted from the immediate neighbourhood of the track; and with this end in view arranged with the officer commanding the working party in front to get his men off the track to give the 2/6th K.L.R. a clear run through. It was known from a reconnaissance made the previous day that the track crossed the road and then the stream called the Steenbeck on the far side of it. The Commanding Officer calculated that he would just have time to get his battalion across the road and over the Steenbeck before the barrage returned to the track. Word was passed down the battalion from front to rear to be prepared to travel at the fastest possible speed, and at a correctly judged moment a move forward was ordered. The working party in front had meanwhile got off the track, so good progress could be made over the 200 yards which remained to be covered before the road was reached. When the head of the battalion arrived at the road, the unpleasant discovery was made that the bridge over the Steenbeck had been destroyed by the bombardment. An officer succeeded in crossing the stream by the trunk of a fallen tree, but on his return reported that the track on the other side had also been destroyed for a considerable distance, and that the place where it recommenced again could not be found in the darkness. The Commanding Officer came to an instant decision and ordered the column to turn to the left along the road in a north-easterly direction, with the intention of reaching another road which ran north-west through the village of Langemarck, from which place he expected to be able again to pick up the track which had to be followed. Unfortunately, the road on the side of the Steenbeck had been so churned up by shell fire that only very slow progress was possible ; in fact, one stretch of twenty yards was thigh deep in a stiff porridge-like mud, which,

for men loaded with Lewis guns and large supplies of ammunition, was extremely difficult to negotiate. It was a time of considerable anxiety, because the barrage was still proceeding about 300 yards south-east, and might come back at any moment, in which case the casualties could not fail to be heavy. However, good luck prevailed, and the tail end of the battalion had just got clear of the road before the bombardment lifted back on the section we had quitted.

Eagle Trench was reached and found to contain a good deal of gas, so all ranks had to be continually on the alert to adjust their box-respirators during the remainder of the night. Battalion Headquarters was established in an old German concrete pill-box, called " Double Cotts," in which the stench was almost unbearable. On the following night (November 28th—29th), we relieved the battalion in the front line and took over their positions, which consisted of a series of shell-holes, order of companies from right to left being as follows : " A " Company (Captain McWilliam), " B " Company less one platoon (Lieutenant Penrice), " C " Company plus one platoon of " B " Company (Captain Ormrod) ; support company, " D " Company (Captain Fell). Battalion Headquarters in a German pill-box called Louis Farm. About half-way between front line companies and Battalion Headquarters, on an almost imperceptible rise of ground, called " 19 Metre Hill," a transmitting station for lamp signals and also a relay post for runners were established.

The Higher Command had observed from aeroplane photographs that there were some new erections, which they thought were concrete pill-boxes, about 600 yards behind the enemy's front line; and the battalion was instructed to send a patrol out as soon as the front line had been taken over in order, if possible, to ascertain their nature. This reconnoitring patrol, detailed from " A " Company, under command of Lieutenant C. W. Clarke, and consisting of Sergeant Powell, Corporal Stubbs, and three riflemen (C. C. Smith, P. McGinn, and W. McGrath), succeeded in penetrating the enemy line as far as the objective they had been ordered to examine. Valuable information was obtained, but, unfortunately, on the return journey the patrol was observed by the enemy, who opened machine-gun fire, and both Lieutenant Clarke and Sergeant Powell were severely wounded, the former having his thigh broken. The remainder of the patrol displayed great gallantry in bringing in their wounded under heavy fire, for which act they were each subsequently awarded the Military Medal. Lieutenant Clarke was complimented by the Brigadier-General on his fine work, which was later on rewarded with the Military Cross. Among other gallant deeds performed this night was the recovery from No Man's Land of several British wounded who had fallen in an abortive attack on this front five days previously, and who had lain out in the shell-holes untended ever since. 2nd-Lieutenant T. Lever, of " C " Company, was particularly active in this good work, for which he also received the Military Cross.

At dawn on November 29th O.C. " B " Company despatched a message by runner to Battalion Headquarters, with advice to the effect that with daylight he had discovered that the company which he had relieved during the night had not handed over to him the positions of which they alleged they had been in occupation, but had in fact handed over positions some 300 yards farther back, and called these rear positions by the names of positions farther forward. The positions in question went by the names of Memling Farm and Rubens Farm, but the farm buildings had long since been utterly destroyed, and their places had been taken by a few scattered pill-boxes. Immediately on receipt of this message at Battalion Headquarters, Colonel Fletcher himself hurried up to the front line, and after a careful reconnaissance on the ground and study of the map confirmed the conclusions arrived at by O.C. " B " Company. He accordingly ordered O.C. " B " Company to have Memling and Rubens Farm reconnoitred, with the intention of occupying them, if so desired by the Higher Command, as soon as darkness fell ; and then himself returned to

Battalion Headquarters to report fully by runner to Brigade Headquarters. The latter ordered that the positions be captured without loss of time ; but, owing to difficulties of communication, this order did not reach Battalion Headquarters until night, when O.C. " B " Company was ordered to take the farms with two platoons. Meantime the reconnoitring party which had gone out by daylight had found the positions unoccupied ; and it is a matter of opinion whether the enemy observed them and jumped to the conclusion that the position might later be occupied, or whether they were held by the enemy as defensive positions at night only. The latter seems the most likely solution. Gallant attempts were immediately made by the platoons detailed (Nos. 7 and 8 Platoons), but they were met by heavy machine-gun fire, and found the pill-boxes were occupied in strength by the enemy. No. 7 Platoon, under Lieutenant Vaughan, made repeated attempts to reach the more distant objective (Rubens Farm), but after suffering heavy casualties was compelled to desist. Dawn was now approaching, and at 5.40 a.m. our artillery opened a barrage along the front, preliminary to an attack by the 58th Division on the immediate right of the battalion. This brought heavy retaliating artillery fire on our front, and No. 7 Platoon, which was still in the open attacking Rubens Farm, was practically wiped out, including Lieutenant Vaughan. It is evident the enemy were expecting the 57th Division also to attack, inasmuch as they maintained a heavy artillery bombardment for several hours, causing many casualties to the companies in the front line. The casualties, indeed, were so extensive that after a reconnaissance of the front by Captain Wilson under heavy fire, two platoons from the support company (" D " Company) were ordered up to strengthen the much-thinned front line. As soon as the bombardment had somewhat subsided, Lieutenant Penrice and Lieutenant Hodgkinson attempted to reach Memling Farm to see if it was still occupied, but they found that it was, and were very lucky to get back to our lines unscathed.

Apart from these particular incidents, the situation of the remainder of the battalion was far from comfortable. Sitting all day in a shell-hole half filled with water, surrounded by all the most ghastly features of war, and being shelled intensely the greater part of the time, was an experience that few would wish to repeat. The men bore it splendidly, and officers and N.C.Os. carried on their various duties with the greatest coolness. Captain McWilliam was, as always under trying conditions, most conspicuous, and, unfortunately, was very seriously wounded. For his general gallantry on this and many previous occasions he was awarded the Military Cross, which he had richly deserved.

On the night of October 30th-31st the battalion was relieved by the 2/7th K.L.R., and made its way back to Huddlestone Camp, near the canal, having suffered casualties to the extent of five officers and 122 other ranks.

Although our battalion did not actually participate in an attack (another Brigade of our Division carried out the first part of the projected operation; the rest was cancelled owing to the condition of the ground), we had our share of the horrors of the Third Battle of Ypres, confined though it was to an experience not new to us of taking the gruelling while someone else did the fighting. As an experience of the realities of war it was not without value, though it cost us dear. The misery of the countryside has already been indicated, and this was enhanced by the spectacle of the countless dead that littered the ground. So many were they that in places it was almost impossible to move without treading on them. Indeed, all that has been said and written elsewhere as to the conditions of this battle does not appear to have been exaggerated. The importance or necessity of the action in the main scheme of operations does not concern us here.

Those who took part in it will never erase from their minds its many ghastly features, among which the mud and the multitude of the dead will stand out pre-eminent. Of the former it must be said that the sodden condition of the ground, though it

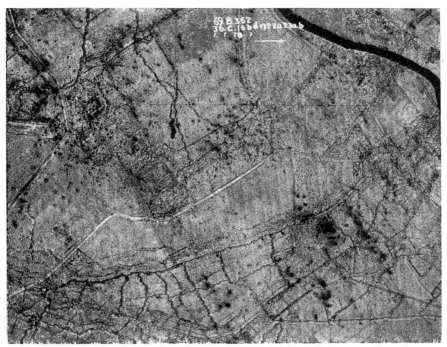

HOUPLINES. BRITISH AND GERMAN TRENCHES ON LEFT
COMPANY'S FRONT. RIVER LYS, HOBBS AND EDMEADS FARMS.
Aeroplane Photograph dated 1st January, 1918.

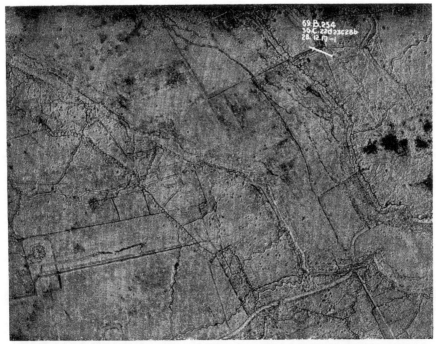

THE PONT BALLOT SALIENT, HOUPLINES. BRITISH AND GERMAN
TRENCH ON RIGHT AND RIGHT-CENTRE COMPANIES' FRONT.
Aeroplane Photograph dated 28th December, 1917.

stopped our advance, certainly prevented many casualties from shell fire ; but at the same time many a wounded man was sucked down into the horrible quagmire, and stretcher-bearers found their tasks in many cases quite beyond their powers. The enemy, too, seemed to take a fiendish delight in adding extra terrors to the work by sniping them with "whizz-bangs"; and Lieutenant Clarke had several of his bearers hit before his journey to the regimental aid post, which took some sixteen hours, was completed. His great patrol and Lieutenant Vaughan's gallant attempt which cost him his life are glorious memories of that grim period. If nothing else was learnt, the value of personal bravery, for the display of which the quiet routine of trench warfare had afforded but little scope, was now made clear to all; and not only by the performances of Clarke, Vaughan, and Lever and the gallant members of their parties, but also by the steady bearing of the battalion generally during those trying times. The courage and initiative displayed by the transport, and particularly by the specially organized pack-mule section, were worthy of the highest commendation.

Huddlestone Camp was just the ordinary collection of Nissen huts, but it represented to the tired and weary all the comforts of civilization. How long it seemed since we were last in any place that could be remotely described as civilized ! In point of fact it was four days, but the battalion during that time had achieved another stage in its education—and a big stage, too. We knew a good deal about trench warfare, and we knew something about being shelled, but we had never previously been at quite such close quarters with war in its fiercest aspect as we were in front of Langemarck.

The next morning (November 1st, 1917) we moved back still farther to Bridge Camp, arriving there at 11 a.m. We remained there till November 6th, cleaning up and making good deficiencies —of no inconsiderable nature after such experiences—and generally restoring mind and body by the normal routine of a soldier's

training. The same day we left our camp and marched to
Boesinghe, where we entrained about 1 p.m. for Audruicq, not
far from Calais, arriving about 10 p.m. Thence we marched to
Nordasques, which was understood to be our area ; but some confusion was abroad—our billeting party had gone one way, we
another, and so on. However, the hour was late, so we made the
best of it in Nordasques for the night, and moved to our proper
area, Louches, the following day (November 7th), which we
reached about 2.30 p.m.

This place proved a real " rest " area, and here we remained
for a very pleasant month reorganizing, refitting, and, above all,
resting. The day after our arrival the party in the " lifeboat,"
consisting of five officers and 71 men, rejoined, and on November
13th a draft of 76 men reported. At the end of November
our " effective strength " was up to 38 officers and 867 other
ranks.

This period at Louches requires little description, though it
was probably the most real " rest " the battalion ever enjoyed.
Training was of the more practical kind—" leap-frogging,"
counter-attack, consolidation, intensive digging, attack on strong
posts, and so forth. Among these were judiciously inserted the
usual drill, rifle exercises, physical training, and the like. Musketry was practised on a large scale at the Zouafques ranges.
Baths at Nielles also played a salutary if uninteresting part in
the life of the battalion ; while trips to Calais proved a great
attraction to officers and N.C.Os., that place being within easy
reach by means of a light railway. A Sergeants' Rest Billet was
instituted, and thither for short periods the sergeants in turn
betook themselves, free for the time being from all military cares.
It was a sign of the Commanding Officer's constant care for his
men, and the arrangement was strongly approved.

It was odd to find oneself once more living what was after all
the old life of home training areas. Here were no sudden alarms,
but just the ordinary regulation routine. Afternoons were free,

146

and football and musketry competitions soon blossomed into being.

While we were here Major H. K. Wilson, who had been long suffering from an injury to his ankle, the result of a collision with a lorry, proceeded to England on leave, and was there admitted to hospital. To our great regret, we saw him no more; he had been with us since the formation of the battalion. Another officer who left us at this time was Lieutenant Hodgkinson, a most gallant and popular officer, whom we were extremely sorry to lose. His venturous spirit led him to transfer to the R.F.C., where his career, we may be sure, was, if short, full of incident. He was, we understood, shot down near Valenciennes, and must have been a great loss to his Corps.

All good things come to an end in time—a law which fortunately applies also to their opposites—and 7.30 a.m. on December 8th found the battalion climbing once more into buses on the Crezeques—Autingues road to visit the area north of Ypres once more. After debussing we proceeded, two companies each, to two adjacent camps in the Proven area which rejoiced in the names of Privett and Portsdown, the latter being also the home of Battalion Headquarters. They were the usual camps of the area, no worse—possibly a little better—than the average. They consisted of Nissen huts. Training continued here for a few days prior to going into the line, which was visited by the Commanding Officer, accompanied by five officers, on December 12th for two days' instruction, from which they returned on December 14th.

The Adjutant, Captain Wurtzburg, reported from England for duty just before the battalion went into the line, and Captain C. W. Wilson in consequence gave up his duties as Adjutant and took over the appointment of Second-in-Command, with the subsequent acting rank of Major.

HISTORY OF THE 2/6TH (RIFLE) BATTALION

CHAPTER VI

PASSCHENDAELE (SECOND TIME)—ARMENTIÈRES—ST. HILAIRE
(SECOND TIME)—ARREWAGE—FLEURBAIX

On December 16th, at 8.45 in the morning, the battalion moved
off from camp to Proven Station, where we duly entrained for
Boesinghe, the transport moving to Birbeck Camp, near Elverdinghe. On arrival at Boesinghe a dispute arose with the 2/5th
K.L.R. as to the camp which each of us was to occupy, the orders
being conflicting. Eventually we agreed to take Canal Bank
Camp, and the 2/5th K.L.R. the more bleak and exposed Baboon
Camp, which from our point of view was a satisfactory arrangement. As this was the second time the battalion had been in
this area, there is no need to describe it further. It looked almost
as inhospitable as ever, though certain traces of civilization had
begun to appear. The enemy put a few shells in to the camp that
night, but did no serious damage. The next day (December 17th)
everyone was busy with preparations for going into the line.
Gum-boots and extra water-bottles had to be drawn from Baboon
Camp, and men had to be issued with " Tommy cookers," two
days' preserved rations, and spare socks. The weather was now
very cold, with occasional snow-storms, and offered a very poor
prospect of pleasant conditions in the line. At 3.30 p.m. " D "
Company moved, followed at quarter-hour intervals by " A "
(support) Company, and " B " and " C " in reserve. To Battalion
Headquarters the distance was about six miles, the whole route
being along a duck-board track, called Clarges Street. The scene
on either side of the track was the same—one unending chain of

148

shell-holes, as usual in this part of the world. It was a long and tedious march. A whole battalion strung out on a tortuous and slippery track, with countless short twists to avoid shell-holes and greater twists to prevent accurate shelling, moves very slowly. There was also a long footbridge over the Steenbeck to be nego- tiated, and the various side tracks running off from the main one confused the guides.

Two companies were taken round by an alternative way along the remains of the road from Koekuit to Les Cinque Chemins, our destination. This proved our salvation, as on reaching the end of Clarges Street, near Les Cinque Chemins, the leading guide of the two companies ahead of Battalion Head- quarters turned to the right along this same road, and promptly collided with " D " and " A " Companies coming up. But for this accident " B " and " C " with Battalion Headquarters, after many hours marching, might have arrived at Canal Bank Camp once more. The difficulty of finding one's way in the dark in these miserable districts baffles description. All landmarks are obliterated, and main roads are only recognizable under the most favourable conditions. Tracks lead off from the main way at frequent intervals, and there is nothing to show which is the correct way. The one thing usually certain is that one leads nowhere and the other the way you want to go. To discover which is which is rather a lengthy and tiresome business.

The sector was on the whole probably the most remarkable one ever held by the battalion. Representing as it did the high-water mark of a push, it was rather curiously organized. The front line (held by " D " Company) consisted of a number of shell-hole positions, movement along which was impossible in daylight, and three posts in the Houthulst Forest. These latter, as will appear, were mere wooden barricades of a very rough description and absolutely unbulletproof. No cover of any description, either from the weather or from the enemy, existed in any of these posts. There was one pill-box, Colombo House, in what was practically the front line, and, as usual, with its door facing the enemy. This acted as a kind of advance headquarters for the front-line company.

The next thing in the rear of these scattered posts was a pair of pill-boxes—Ajax House, Battalion Headquarters; and an unnamed one adjoining, which was shared by the front and support company headquarters, " D " and " A " Companies. Ajax House was a magnificent pill-box with a side door ; the other one was smaller, and with a door facing the Germans.

Behind Battalion Headquarters came the main line of resistance, Posts " D," " E," " H," and " J," small redoubts organized for all-round resistance ; while the counter-attack party of two platoons was considerably farther back at Vee Bend. After about an hour's march back along the duck-boards you came to the reserve company at Gruytezeele, Craonne, and Montmirail Farms ; while " C " Company were even more distant, at Lapin Farm. As regards the latter, who were in rear of Brigade Headquarters, it was only after great difficulty that any accommodation could be found for them at all, the fact being that we were much stronger than the 7th Buffs, whom we were relieving.

The relief march up to Battalion Headquarters passed without incident, except for a sudden burst of " whizz-bangs " at Les Cinque Chemins, where, but for the extreme muddiness of the surrounding country, we might have sustained serious casualties. In point of fact, no one was hit with anything worse than lumps of thick mud. The front line company, having now to quit the duck-boards, found their task far from easy. The only key to the situation was a tape line to the various posts, and the going in the Houthulst Forest for those destined for that point was extremely trying. In spite of the heavy shell fire, this was still a large forest ; but the number of fallen trees and branches, together with deep pools of mud and water, not to mention miscellaneous stretches of unexpected barbed wire, presented in the dark obstacles to progress of no mean order. At midnight the relief was finally complete, and the 7th Buffs made their way out.

With the exception of the two days in the line in front of Langemarck, the conditions for the men in the front line were probably as unpleasant as at any time in France. The shell-hole posts were literally shell-holes, with the very minimum done to improve them as habitations for six or seven men. The exact locality of the respective British and German front lines was to either side somewhat vague, and we were anxious that the men should not give away their positions by elaborating their shell-holes to such an extent that they would be obviously artificial when examined on an aeroplane photograph. The comfort of this form of abode will be better appreciated when one realizes that the best pattern had been deepened to allow of a sump pit in the centre, across which duck-boards had been fixed to keep the inhabitants above water level. No movement was possible in daylight even in the vicinity of Battalion Headquarters. "Tommy cookers" were allowed in the front line by day, and one man at a time was allowed to smoke.

In the forest itself conditions were slightly better, though the wretched breastworks erected for the protection of the posts were only hurdles of the flimsiest description. The proximity, or the reverse, of the enemy was quite uncertain, and the surrounding mass of gloomy trees and undergrowth was calculated to produce a feeling of considerable uneasiness in the minds of the occupants, which was hardly to be wondered at.

Colombo House was a small pill-box with a large door facing the enemy. The atmosphere within baffles all description. So bad, indeed, was it that the Regimental Sergeant-Major, immediately after entering it, had hastily to withdraw for the purpose of being violently sick. Ajax, on the other hand, never reached quite such a condition. It was a large concrete erection, with walls and roof of reinforced concrete about eight feet thick, much scarred with direct hits, but quite sound. It was square, with a doorway at the side which was protected by a sand-bag wall. In the centre was a huge concrete pillar supporting the roof, and round this the occupants sat on forms. On this occasion the party consisted of the Commanding Officer, Adjutant, and the Intelligence Officer, the Regimental Sergeant-Major, a cook and a servant, six signallers, three gunner signallers, two wireless operators, and some runners. Here we sat from 8 a.m. to 4 p.m. There were two bunks in the corner which we shared in turn, and we had two Primus stoves for cooking purposes. The Company Headquarters next door was also a strong pill-box, but owing to the door facing the enemy it had to be entered and quitted after dark with great caution, for fear the light should shine towards the Germans.

In the early hours of the morning, after relief, it began to freeze. In a short while everything was as hard as iron, and remained so all the time we were in. Except for the acute cold, frost was perhaps not an unmixed evil; one could move about with comparative ease, and everything was hard and dry, instead of soft and sodden. Dry cold is always less insidious than damp cold, and that there was so little sickness caused by this tour was due to the frost. However, it seriously interfered with the wiring programme and the elaborate arrangements made for the improvement of the positions by the addition of small elephants, etc., which we arranged to be sent up. Salvage was abundant, thousands of pounds' worth of Lewis gun drums, machine guns, and other material being scattered in every direction, but it was frozen so hard that only a small quantity was eventually retrieved. Hot tea and stew were brought up nightly on mules to Battalion Headquarters. It was carried in petrol-tins placed in haversacks and packed round with hay. In spite of the four hours which the party took coming from the Quartermaster's stores, the system of packing stood the test, and gave the men in the line the great benefit of warm drinks and warm food. During the night everyone took the maximum amount of exercise possible to restore

152

the circulation. Even the stuffy atmosphere of a pill-box did not keep one warm, and by day it was necessary to wear two sand-bags over each foot to prevent them being reduced to a frozen condition. Each morning, as so often happens during a sharp frost, there was a heavy white mist till the sun got well up. During this time movement about the sector was comparatively safe, though very slippery, and tours of the line by Brigade and Battalion Staffs generally took place about this time. On one occasion the Commanding Officer and Lieutenant Huntley, going round, made so much noise through merriment over the sudden fall of Captain Patteson on a frozen shell-hole, that the Germans opened rapid fire with " minnies," fortunately without any damage being done. They shelled certain spots regularly—Les Cinque Chemins, " J " Post, Battalion Headquarters, and a few other localities.

Egypt House, the 2/5th K.L.R. Headquarters, dropped in for frequent bursts; and the efforts of a siege gunner to range on the White Chateau from our Headquarters produced such violent retaliation on Egypt House that we had in common decency to request him to desist.

On December 19th " C " Company relieved " D " Company in the front line, and " B " Company relieved " A " Company in support. This movement was completed at 9.25 p.m. " A " Company had some gas casualties on the way back, the track being twice shelled; and Captain Bowring, having to put on his small box-respirator for the second time, was disgusted to find that the valve was frozen solid. He tore it off and pulled on his " P.H. " helmet, only to find that he had got it back to front. Next moment he fell into a shell-hole, so, pulling off the helmet, he ran for all he was worth down the duck-boards, and escaped anything worse than a slight touch of sickness. The next afternoon a carrying party of " C " Company near Koekuit was caught in a " crash," and six men killed. The destructive area of a shell striking frozen ground is, as may be supposed, very considerable.

Lieutenant Freeman, the Transport Officer, and his mules had several experiences in their nightly visit to the line, the most amusing being the short cut over the Broembeek which he attempted one night. The mules were got over the single plank bridge without difficulty, but after the bridge had been duly crossed it was found that the party was on an island from which there was no other exit. Time had been wasted during this operation, and when the party once more reached the plank bridge dawn was not very far distant. Gladly, however, as the mules had crossed the bridge in the first instance, now they one and all refused to venture on it. Everything was tried, but without success, and Lieutenant Freeman began to see himself revealed to the attentive gunner when daylight should disclose his unlucky situation. Eventually recourse was had to one of our own batteries, and after long and arduous efforts on the part of all concerned the mules were persuaded to cross the bridge.

On December 21st the battalion was relieved by the 2/7th K.L.R. " D " Company completed their relief at twelve noon, but the handing over of the line was not effected till 9.30 p.m. The 2/7th K.L.R. took over with a new scheme of defence, the main principle of which was that the strength of the front line garrison was increased to six platoons.

It was a long and weary march back to Canal Bank, but the enemy left Clarges Street alone, confining his attention to Hunter Street, the next track, which he shelled persistently.

The next day, about 4 p.m., the Germans carried out a raid on Turenne Crossing, in the right battalion area. We were suddenly startled by the sight of the S.O.S. signals going up—two reds and a white—and next moment our guns opened. The number of S.O.S. signals covered such a front that a stand-to was ordered, but before long we discovered that it was only a raid. However, the 2/5th K.L.R. had to send up two companies, and our luck in having taken Canal Bank instead of Baboon Camp stood us in good stead.

"THE KING'S" (LIVERPOOL REGIMENT)

Our stay at Canal Bank was a short one, for which no one was particularly sorry, for, if better than Baboon Camp, it was still a miserable spot. On Christmas Day we were relieved by the 2/9th K.L.R., and moved to Emile Camp, near Elverdinghe, where we found some really comfortable huts in which we happily installed ourselves. Christmas Day, from the weather point of view, proved a model of all that it should have been. Everything was covered with snow, and the sun shone in a brilliant blue sky. Owing to our anticipation that we should be in the line on Christmas Day, little preparation had been made for dinners till the very last minute, when Captain Smith, the newly arrived Quartermaster, by almost superhuman energy, succeeded at last in buying a pig. This made on Boxing Day a pleasant, if somewhat limited, addition to the rations, which, together with plum puddings, and a large quantity of cigarettes and toffee sent by the generous donors to our Comforts Fund, made quite a good Christmas dinner. Huts were decorated, and good humour abounded.

We now discovered that we were leaving Flanders again and returning to Armentières, a very unexpected piece of news. We also discovered that we were to go by road, which, in fine cold weather, appeared quite a pleasant prospect. However, a thaw, followed by a frost, rather altered our opinion, and when we moved off at 8.30 a.m. on December 29th from Canada area, close to Proven, we found it almost impossible to stand, and even more impossible to march. We moved off, therefore, with many a slip and fall; but the only serious disaster was an accident to the officers' mess-cart, resulting in a broken shaft and a very long delay to that most valuable portion, from the officers' point of view, of the transport. Our camps, which we did not find without considerable difficulty, were called Poodle and Pitchett, and were both most wretched affairs, with indifferent tents set amid a wilderness of snow. The Medical Officer, Lieutenant Gordon, a newly arrived American, reached the camp in a state of considerable exhaustion. Imagining that he was to ride, he had donned an immense fleece-lined overcoat which reached to his ankles. Riding, of course, was an impossibility, and being somewhat new to marching, he had suffered considerably, but he bore his affliction with the utmost good humour.

The next day (December 30th) we moved on again. The weather, from being bright and frosty, was now raw and damp, with a partial thaw. As our road lay over the Mont des Cats and past Meteren, the conditions were particularly trying, and everyone was thoroughly tired when we reached billets at Berthen. Here companies were widely scattered, and the billets of a very varying quality.

The next day we resumed our march, and this was the most trying of all. The road was frozen again and intensely slippery. We moved as a Brigade, and, owing to a misunderstanding, no proper halts occurred for the first two hours, which was a thoroughly bad arrangement, especially under the existing conditions. After passing through Bailleul we eventually arrived at 1.45 p.m., at Hollebeque Camp, near Steenwerck, just vacated by the Australians. It is worth recording that throughout these three trying days not a single man fell out and not a single vehicle failed to complete the journey. Hollebeque Camp, for a summer camp, would have been quite pleasant. In winter it was very far from comfortable. It was composed of one big block of Nissen huts for the men, while on the other side of the field stood a row of similar huts for the officers. A large number of the huts had been stripped of their wooden linings for firewood; they were badly put together and draughty beyond words; and there was an almost complete absence of any of the normal furniture of camps, such as lamps, tables, etc., nor were these readily procurable. However, beyond finding it extremely cold, we had little time to worry, as next evening we relieved the 36th Battalion A.I.F. in our old Houplines sector. As far as Erquinghem the route was more or less new, but from then onward it was very familar both to officers and men. It was a queer sensation picking up the old landmarks and noting the changes. Armentières looked very strange and

156

ghostly in the moonlight, and the silence of absolute desolation was accentuated by the deep snow. Silently we passed through the deserted streets; everything seemed uncannily quiet after the noise and excitement that had been everyday features of our last spell in this city. Not a shot was fired as we moved along that " unhealthy " stretch from Barbed Wire Square to Tissage Dump, and we felt that the enemy must be saving up for some tremendous show, as he was at the moment so inactive.

The moonlight and our knowledge of the ground together made short work of the relief, which was complete at 8.30 p.m. The company sectors were allotted as follows : " A " on the right from London Road to fifty yards beyond Timaru, " B " from there to Edmeads Avenue, inclusive. " D " Company occupied the left, and " C " was in the subsidiary line.

We found the sector in its essential features very much as we had left it, except that considerable work had been expended on the subsidiary line, which now formed a very fine trench, with really good traverses. Except for that improvement, however, the sector generally had greatly deteriorated. The principle of gaps and localities, which had always tended to the neglect of the rest of the trenches, had now reduced the latter to a lamentable state of disrepair. The number of posts in the front line was only seven, and these of a very miserable description from the defensive point of view. Such lateral connecting trenches as had existed had been allowed to fall in, and in the case of the two left posts communication even from the rear was difficult at night and precarious by day. No wire worth speaking of had been erected to defend these isolated spots, and altogether the sector presented no very satisfactory appearance. The left area between No. 7 Post and the River Lys, being frozen hard, presented a perfectly good concealed approach for the enemy, and nothing had been done to deal with this exposed flank.

The garrison of the subsidiary line consisted of three companies, two being found by the battalion in support.

HISTORY OF THE 2/6TH (RIFLE) BATTALION

Our first tour in the line proved of the quietest. A few "pine-apples" from the enemy, a few 6-inch mortars from us, and an occasional shell, made up the daily round. On January 6th we received urgent demands from the authorities for an identification, and two patrols were sent out to try and effect this. Of these, Lieutenant Burton's party got right into the German wire opposite Hobbs Farm before they were spotted, when they had to beat a hasty retreat under considerable fire from machine guns and "pineapples." The other patrol was equally unlucky. In the meantime a deserter had very considerately given himself up to No. 1 Post ("A" Company). He was a Prussian, but recently transferred to the division opposite us. He was understood to have complained that he had considerable difficulty in finding anyone in the sector to whom he might surrender. As he had brought the whole of his kit with him, his solitary peregrination of our sector may well have been tiring. However, Division sent a car to take him down, which rather tactlessly ran into a ditch, nearly killing our valuable "find" and his escort as well.

On January 7th we were relieved by the 2/7th K.L.R., and the battalion, after a somewhat complicated shuffle, found them-selves holding the subsidiary line—"A" and "C" in Epinette, and "B" and "D" in Houplines sectors respectively. Bat-talion Headquarters moved out to billets by the Armentières Level Crossing on the Erquinghem road. One interesting in-novation that may be mentioned here was the Pioneer Platoon, recently started under Lieutenant J. R. Paul, and then taken over by Lieutenant Jones. This consisted of about twenty men, and included the original pioneers and a number of other skilled men. It was their business to attend to all the minor construc-tion work that promoted the comfort of the battalion, such as improving billets, making ovens, drying rooms, etc.; and in the line to carry out any special defensive work which required some-thing more than ordinary care and skill. They were rather a drain

158

on our fighting strength, but they more than justified their existence in a hundred different ways.

One or two changes had recently occurred also in officers. Lieutenant Gordon had been relieved by Captain Kidston as Medical Officer ; Captain Eccles had returned from England and taken over " B " Company from Acting-Captain Broad ; Acting-Captain Fell had now command of " D " Company ; Lieutenant Burton was Battalion Scout Officer, Lieutenant Hazell Intelligence Officer, 2nd-Lieutenant Novelle Signalling Officer ; 2nd-Lieutenant Brighouse had been wounded ; and Lieutenant Adam returned to the 1/6th K.L.R., in exchange for Captain Eccles.

The period spent in the subsidiary line was very quiet, except for the large wiring parties on the left, for which men were drawn from all the reserve companies. Parties were also withdrawn from the trenches for Lewis gun instruction, and others for baths. The Commanding Officer proceeded on leave on January 8th, which left Captain C. W. Wilson in command.

An amusing incident occurred while Headquarters was in billets by the level-crossing. A guard was posted there to stop anyone not in possession of a pass, and it so happened that they had red flashes behind the cap badge not dissimilar to ours. One day we received from Brigade a letter from Division complaining that the sentry at the level-crossing had not turned out the guard to the G.O.C., but merely sloped arms and tapped the sling. This amused us not a little, and we respectfully replied, first, that we had no guard at the level-crossing, and, secondly, that under no circumstances would a rifleman slope arms !

A draft consisting of 2nd-Lieutenant Hicks and twenty men arrived while we were here, most of the men being returned casualties. On January 13th the battalion was relieved by the 2/10th K.L.R., and moved back to Hollebeque Camp. The first three days in camp saw the whole battalion out |on wiring and working parties, day and night, in the Houplines sector. This meant at least an hour and a half's march each way, and it simply streamed with rain. The men were required to complete an elaborate system of wiring in rear of the subsidiary line and in front of some pill-boxes, and also to finish other defences which were being constructed in Nouvel Houplines itself. The nights were of the blackest, and the organization the most inefficient; with the result that six hours were wasted nightly in the most torrential rain. Fuel was indented for and drying-rooms hastily instituted, but the men got so soaked that it was impossible to dry their garments. Fortunately, after our share of working parties was finished, we had three quiet days in which to get dry. We should have had more, only the Lys proceeded to flood the trenches, and the Liverpool Scottish had a bad time. The Scots were nearly drowned, and we were ordered in early to relieve them.

The relief was to take place on January 21st, and that morning Captain Wilson, who had been unwell for some days, was at last removed to hospital seriously ill, and the Adjutant assumed command. The route to the line was viâ Nieppe and Pont de Nieppe, as the Erquinghem Bridge was under water. The battalion moved off at 2 p.m. and proceeded on their long trek to the line. Passing up the road to Pont de Nieppe, it was rather amusing to see some " silent " 6-inch batteries lying like little islands in the sea, with their camouflage showing up beyond any possible hope of concealment. Companies halted one by one in Armentières to put on gum-boots, and an elaborate system of dumps had been arranged in the vicinity of Tissage Dump. The latter, like most complicated systems, proved a failure. Relief was complete at 8.30 p.m., and then one had an opportunity to appreciate the state of the sector. The subsidiary line was dry in the main, but immediately forward of it you got into water, which as you went forward got well over the knees, and in places where the duck-boards were not nailed down you sank up to the top of your thighs. The whole of the support line was knee-deep in water, and so was a great part of the front line ; while the last stretch of communication trench in front of the front line was flooded to a considerable

160

THE TRAIL TO PASSCHENDAELE.

**THE BATTLE OF FLANDERS. GERMAN SHELLS SEARCHING THE
NEWLY CAPTURED GROUND NEAR LANGEMARCK.**

depth. Posts Nos. 6 and 7 were completely flooded out and had to be abandoned. The " cricket field " in front of the left company support line was converted into a very fine lake, and it was impossible to see where the Lys began and ended. Movement throughout the sector was most difficult. Many of the duck boards were floating about, and the mud at the bottom of the water in the trenches was very difficult to negotiate.

Active steps were taken to cope with the situation. Stringent orders were issued as to care of feet, and a place for foot washing was arranged at Tissage Dump. Each man came down daily, changed his gum-boots and socks, washed his feet, and had some hot soup. Men in the front line were, as far as possible, changed daily. Extra duck-boards were taken up, so that raised platforms could be erected clear of the water ; and hot food was sent up as often as feasible. So successful were our efforts, and so effective the support given to our schemes by all ranks, that only two men were affected by foot trouble. The position of companies in the line was " C," "A," " B " from the right ; " D " Company was in the subsidiary line. Work on drainage was commenced with great activity, and snipers, who had been warned to be especially on the alert, claimed several hits on Germans climbing over collapsed portions of their trenches. On January 22nd the Divisional Commander visited the sector to examine conditions for himself.

The only anxiety felt in regard to the enemy arose from our temporary abandonment of our left company front. This was on the near side of a plateau of which the enemy held the farther side ; and it would have seriously affected our hold on our sector if he had taken it into his head to occupy our old posts. Patrols visited their locality almost continuously at night and fired Véry lights and occasional rounds. By day our absence was more conspicuous, as No. 7 Post at this time was a regular rendezvous for wild duck, who used to swim in and out of it with great nonchalance.

HISTORY OF THE 2/6TH (RIFLE) BATTALION

One problem that was raised during this tour was the question of the holding of the brigade front when the forthcoming reduction of a brigade to three battalions took effect; and the possibility of holding the front with two companies instead of three had to be carefully investigated.

On the 24th the battalion was relieved by the 2/7th K.L.R., and moved into billets in Armentières, with Battalion Headquarters at the Convent. Colonel Fletcher, having returned from leave, resumed command of the battalion.

On February 1st the long-expected dissolution of the 2/5th K.L.R. took place simultaneously with the reduction of the number of battalions on the Western Front. A large number were posted to the 13th Battalion K.L.R., but the 2/7th K.L.R. and ourselves shared the balance, our share consisting of seven officers and 180 other ranks. This was a considerable accession of strength, though a large portion of it was paper strength and not actual. But at any rate Captain Williams, 2nd-Lieutenants Wilson, Hooper, Jacobs, and a little later Thomas, actually materialized, together with a considerable number of men, including certain specialists, in which, owing to the loss of our Headquarters Staff at Armentières, we had long been deficient. Amongst them were a sergeant-bootmaker, Sergeant Cox, of the 1st King's, and a sergeant-cook, Sergeant Austin, from the London District School of Cookery.

The presence of these two men was of very great value to the battalion, because, though an army is said to "march on its stomach," it is equally true that it marches on its boots, and both stomachs and boots were now amply provided for. Wilson, Hooper, and Jacobs were posted to " C " Company. The arrangements for the acclimatization and fitting out of the draft had to be done quickly, as the next day we once more relieved the Scottish in the front line.

This relief was duly carried out by 8.35 p.m. Two companies only were to hold the front and support lines, " C " on the right,

"D" on the left; while "A" and "B" manned the subsidiary line. The sector, though still very wet, had much improved since we were last in. All the trenches forward of the subsidiary line were, it is true, to some extent under water, but not to any depth, and dry standings were available in every post.

The tour was quiet in all respects, with just the normal amount of casual shelling on either side, but nothing more. A visit from seven R.F.C. officers afforded a slight comic relief. Only one had ever been in the trenches before, and most of them were unprovided with either respirators or tin hats. One tall officer caused considerable amusement by walking the whole length of the subsidiary line doubled up, till he realized at last that inflicting such discomfort on himself was entirely unnecessary. His fears, however, were probably mild compared with those of an infantryman making a trial trip in an aeroplane over German territory.

We were relieved on February 5th by the 2/7th K.L.R., and took over new dispositions as reserve battalion to the Brigade. Two companies remained in the subsidiary line of the 2/7th and 8th K.L.R., a third being in Nouvel Houplines itself, and another at the Jute Factory in Armentières. Headquarters were at the Convent as before. On February 7th "B" Company were relieved in the subsidiary line by a company of the 2/7th K.L.R., who had just completed a successful raid on our old spot at Centaur Trench, and moved to the Jute Factory. This was a fine large building close to the wooden bridge over the Lys, with massive walls and concrete floors. In the cellars tiers of bunks had been erected, and there was excellent shellproof cover for a whole battalion.

The next day the 2/7th K.L.R. relieved us in reserve, and we went to Pont de Nieppe in Divisional Reserve.

The main attraction at the time was a "demonstration platoon" of another regiment which was on tour. All the officers and N.C.Os. were required to go and see this performance, but the distance was great and the display not above the average. However, it fired the Commanding Officer with enthusiasm to produce something better, in order that the battalion might have ocular proof how admirably drill and similar things can be carried out if the requisite trouble is taken.

The billets in Pont de Nieppe were indescribably dirty, and a great deal of work had to be done in cleaning and improving them. The Pioneer Platoon were invaluable in making ovens and other even more necessary conveniences; and their services were also required to repair and adapt some dilapidated rifle ranges. Units of the 38th Division, too, were in Pont de Nieppe, and the band of one of the battalions used to play daily in the streets, whence it was quite audible in the front line. However, the enemy was very good to us, and never put a shell into the place, which, considering that most of the houses were cellarless, was on the whole, perhaps, as well for us. An attempt was made at this time to force us to change our green diamond for the green square previously used by the 2/5th K.L.R., but happily we were able to prevent this.

On February 11th we relieved the 8th K.L.R. in Houplines, and occupied those trenches, so rich in memories for the battalion, for the last time. " B " Company occupied the right sector, " A " the left sector, and " C " and " D " the subsidiary line. We found the trenches much improved as regards water, but still in need of most urgent attention to prevent a complete collapse of all breastworks. Except for one or two angry bursts on Tissage Dump, the enemy was exceedingly quiet ; and at 8.45 p.m. on February 14th, the first anniversary of our departure for France, we handed over to the 13th Welch and said good-bye to Houplines. Of the many men who served with the battalion, few, if any, will look back on Houplines without some feeling akin to affection. Tissage Dump, the Cemetery, Edmeads or Hobbs Farm, Cambridge, Irish or Spain Avenues—what memories these names conjure up ! Some happy, some tragic, but all happily tempered now by the softening touch of years.

" THE KING'S " (LIVERPOOL REGIMENT)

We spent from February 15th to March 1st in reserve at Pont
de Nieppe, engaged in strengthening the defences of Armentières
and the River Lys. This work the 38th Division had already
commenced, and we took it up where they left off. About 260
men per day were employed in digging and wiring, and a great
deal was achieved against the day when the great German offensive
should commence. Unfortunately, we learnt afterwards that no
men were available to hold our trenches, which in the end caused
little, if any, inconvenience to the enemy, as perhaps was not
unnatural. These great working parties did not end without a
certain amount of friction developing with the R.E., and a
memorable meeting took place at Headquarters between the
Commanding Officer, the C.R.E., and the G.S.O.1. So warm grew
the discussion that a considerable quantity of Benedictine had
eventually to be consumed in order to restore that feeling of
harmonious co-operation on which the textbooks dwell so persistently.

The demonstration platoon composed of riflemen was trained
during this period, and really reached a very high pitch of
efficiency by the time it was called upon to exhibit its powers
to the battalion.

On February 27th, about 9.30 p.m., we received a message
from the 38th Division, warning us that it was understood that a
German offensive was to start up north at dawn, and that a barrage
was to be put down on Pont de Nieppe as a feint. This encouraging
piece of information caused a considerable stir. Arrangements, of
course, had to be made for the speedy evacuation of billets,
should it be found necessary ; and also for providing some cover
for Battalion Headquarters, which would have to remain in
position, bombardment or no bombardment. Fortunately,
nothing happened, and the night proved as quiet as any other.

Captain Ormrod left us on the 20th for six months' home
service in England, whither Lieutenant Goulding had already
preceded him, and Lieutenant Royle was soon to follow. Everyone

thought the war would be over before they were due to return. As a matter of fact, Royle, the last to go and the only one to return, did rejoin before the Armistice.

About 1.30 p.m., on a fine cold day, we embussed for St. Hilaire, arriving there about 4.30 p.m. All were glad to find themselves back in this pleasant area again after a good spell of trench warfare and our fair share of digging. No one anticipated much of a rest ; in point of fact, everyone expected lots of work, as we were to be polished up and trained in view of the impending German offensive. The Commanding Officer was full of zeal for modern methods of training. His enthusiasm had been fired by the training theories of the Inspector-General of Training. The principle was to sustain interest by constant variety, and also to sharpen the intellect by lightning changes from (say) close order drill to bombing, or from rifle exercises to physical drill. With really efficient instructors in sufficient numbers the scheme might have had obvious advantages. For the average battalion, however, it was hardly practicable, though it certainly did inspire our men with a brisk and business-like air which they had been in danger of losing. St. Hilaire presented very reasonable training areas and ranges. Moreover, the Corps Staff Officer responsible for training combined enthusiasm with efficiency, both qualities of some rarity. Things moved apace under the personal supervision of the Commanding Officer, who spared no one, least of all himself, in his efforts to increase the efficiency of the battalion.

On March 8th General Harper, the Corps Commander, inspected the Brigade and presented decorations. Luckily, it was a very fine day, and the march past of the battalion in column of fours after the ceremony was warmly praised by the General, who was good enough to say that " he had never seen a regular battalion march better." Two days later a select party of officers and N.C.Os. were conveyed a great distance by motor lorry to Enguinegatte to see a tank demonstration, which was quite instructive, and ended in a more amusing performance in the shape of joy rides. It was arranged that the Brigade should participate the following week in a counter-attack scheme in co-operation with tanks, and a G.O.C.'s inspection was also scheduled for that week.

However, late on Sunday night—or, more accurately, early on Monday morning—March 10th, a warning "chit" arrived from Brigade intimating an early move by motor bus. Sudden moves are always tiresome; indeed, when out in "rest" that adjective is hardly strong enough. Everything conceivable had been unpacked, and in anticipation of a G.O.C.'s inspection nine-tenths of the transport was dismantled and covered with wet paint. Accordingly, word was sent round at once, and by a stroke of luck orders for an emergency move had been drawn up and circulated only the previous day, so in a short time everyone was astir. Transport men with candles in their hands were hurrying about the transport lines collecting nuts and screws; parties were streaming into the Quartermaster's stores with blankets and other gear; while others were carrying articles of various kinds to the Town Major's office.

Further orders were received during the early hours that we were to move at 8 a.m. by motor buses, the transport to proceed by road at 8.30 a.m. Looking back, one can but feel that we accomplished a very creditable performance. Everything went like clockwork; the Medical Officer, an American but recently arrived, and unused to sudden changes, alone proving not ready at the appointed time. He had forgotten to alter his watch to summer time, which started that day, and was accordingly an hour late in his movements. He was pushed into his clothes and helped into the last lorry just as the column moved off. The Brigadier then appeared on the scene, and seized upon lorries like a gentleman hailing taxis in London, with the result that all our baggage went with us, though it is to be feared that the 2/7th K.L.R. were in consequence grievously short of mechanical transport legitimately theirs.

167

At 11.45 a.m. the battalion debussed at Arrewage, a small hamlet in rear of Merville. The companies were widely scattered, but the billets were not bad, and the weather fine and warm. We at once received orders to be ready to move at two hours' notice. The 33⅓ per cent. battle reserve were told off, evacuation parties for civilians detailed, and we really felt that the day of the great battle was actually at hand.

The next day the G.O.C. inspected the battalion, which made a very creditable turn-out, albeit the transport was entirely coated in thick dust well embedded in what had been wet paint. In conversation with the General Staff, one learnt that a German attack was reckoned to be imminent; and arrangements for reinforcing the Portuguese, who were holding the Laventie area, were pushed forward with even more than the usual zeal. Additional Lewis guns had been issued, making the total twenty per battalion, and Major C. W. Wilson had returned from hospital.

Heavy shelling of Merville was now a daily occurrence, and the countryside, not to mention the billets, was thronged with unfortunate civilians flying for safety, surely one of the saddest sights of war. Meanwhile reconnoitring parties hurried round the Portuguese area, usually to be arrested as spies, while others went off to examine the Sailly bridgehead defences.

In spite of the prospect of early hostilities, an inter-battalion rifle competition was commenced on the miniature range in a corner of the great Forêt de Nieppe, and was finally won by No. 14 Platoon of " D " Company. A Brigade inter-platoon football competition was also started.

An amusing incident of this rather trying period occurred at XI Corps Headquarters, where our guard of riflemen relieved the old guard, which had been formed from a Line Battalion. The Corps Sergeant-Major expended considerable effort in trying to effect a formal relief between the two, but got so involved over sloping arms and fixing bayonets that he finally left the two guard commanders to come to some natural and more satisfactory arrangement.

Meanwhile officers and N.C.Os. proceeded daily to Sailly area, not only to explore the defences, but to seek out a suitable place for a training ground for a raiding party, to be composed of " A " and " C " Companies, under Captains Bowring and Williams.

On March 20th Regimental Sergeant-Major Smith left the battalion to join an Officers' Cadet Battalion, and in due course Regimental Quartermaster-Sergeant Heyworth took over the appointment.

The move to the Sailly area took place on the famous March 21st. We were quite unaware of the stirring events taking place farther south, though trouble was manifestly in the air. The route was viâ Neuf Berquin and Estaires, and our main interest was whether the enemy would or would not shell the road. Fortunately, he did not. We left at 8.15 a.m., and arrived in time for dinner. The 7th Royal Sussex Regiment marched out as we marched in.

Immediately on arrival companies proceeded to occupy for instruction their various defensive positions. In addition to this, the Brigade might, as an alternative, be called upon to occupy a defensive position in rear of the 2nd Portuguese Division, or the line Cockshy House—Laventie Post, etc. Officers had to be despatched to these to learn the emergency routes.

These posts, like the Sailly bridgehead defences, were mostly incomplete, and much work would have been required from the occupants in the short time that would have elapsed before an advancing enemy had come to grips with them. The Sailly defences had a fair reserve of ammunition, but no rations or water.

The next day a working party of 100 men was digging feverishly in the neighbourhood of Fleurbaix, while " A " and " C " Companies were marking out the trace of the practice trenches for their raid.

HISTORY OF THE 2/6TH (RIFLE) BATTALION

On March 23rd we received orders that we were to take over our old Fleurbaix sector, and officers proceeded thither accordingly. In the afternoon the final of the Inter-Battalion Football Competition took place between No. 5 Platoon of " B " Company and a platoon of the 2/7th K.L.R., which the former won by three goals to nil.

On March 25th " all leave and courses cancelled " was received, and rumours of doings in the south became more persistent. The local civilians were also becoming frightened, and carts full of refugees streamed along the roads leading to the rear. The Germans shelled Sailly at night occasionally, but did no real damage.

Word now came that the 12th Division, which had taken our place in reserve, had been rushed south, and we found ourselves with the possibility before us of not only reinforcing the Portuguese, but of holding Sailly bridgehead at the same time. Nothing however, happened, and on the evening of March 26th we relieved the 1/5th Loyal North Lancashire Regiment in our old Fleurbaix sector. All maps and schemes, we found, had been destroyed, and the imminence of an attack, though less acute than a day or so previously, still appeared a matter for serious consideration. Wye Farm we found transformed into a magnificent and palatial pillbox, while others were dotted about the country. The sector also extended farther north than it had done when we previously held it.

It was arranged that " A " and " C " Companies should be in front and support on the right, to enable their men to reconnoitre the area to be raided; and that we should only hold the line for three days to begin with, so as to enable the raiding party to get sufficient training. The tour was not marked by anything of particular moment. " A " Company's Headquarters were subjected to a very considerable bombardment, but luckily without casualties. The efforts of a 6-inch howitzer battery to cut our wire cost us our proposed raid headquarters, and very nearly the lives of the Forward Observation Officer and Lieutenant Hazell, our Intelligence Officer, as well. The enemy wore an air of quiet-

170

ness of a suspicious character, although Intelligence said that the divisions recently concentrated opposite this front had all gone down to the Somme. We had no casualties.

On March 29th the Irish took over from us, and our battalion moved out—Headquarters and " B " Company to Fleurbaix, " D " Company to Canteen Farm in reserve to the front line, and " A " and " C " to Sailly to continue their training. A special telephone was laid to the latter in case of emergency.

Battalion Headquarters and " B " Company were all congregated in a set of farm buildings, which, had the enemy attacked, would certainly have been blown to pieces at the very outset. In the absence, on leave, of Major Charles Wilson, Captain Eccles, the next senior excepting the Adjutant, was appointed O.C. Fleurbaix Defences, and included in his command certain machine guns and trench mortars.

On March 29th the raiding party was reduced from two companies to one, and the date was advanced to the 31st; and the next evening the remaining company were also told they would not be required. Two fighting patrols, under Lieutenant Burton and Corporal Corkill respectively, were sent out to try and obtain identification, but the enemy was evidently expecting a raid, as his front line was quite unoccupied. It was probably, therefore, as well that the raid had been cancelled, though we should have liked to carry it out.

Meantime all surplus stores were ordered to be sent to Estaires, and we found ourselves ready to move without the great mass of transport usually required on such occasions.

On March 31st the Second-in-Command of the 20th Middlesex Regiment arrived to look round, and told us great stories of the retreat. The next day (April 1st) they relieved us, and the battalion moved out at 10.30 p.m. on a long and weary march to Neuf Berquin. There we were joined by the men who had formed the Brigade Pioneer Company, and the battalion presented an appearance of unusual strength.

CHAPTER VII

MERVILLE—PERIOD IN RESERVE—GOMMECOURT—FAMPOUX

ON April 2nd, as we had expected, we entrained for the south, but not till our orders had been cancelled about three times. In fact, if rumour is to be believed, we were very nearly dispatched post haste to Ypres. At any rate, at 5 p.m. we received orders for one company to entrain at Merville at once, and the remainder at 8.5 p.m. The enemy very considerately refrained from shelling the station while we entrained, though he was more attentive to some of the other units of the Division.

At 5.30 a.m. we arrived at Doullens Station, which looked somewhat dilapidated in consequence of an air raid. The station presented a scene of the greatest activity, and it was not till 7.30 a.m. that we were allowed to detrain and move out of the station. " C " Company formed the unloading party. After moving clear of the town we fell out by the roadside for breakfasts, for which, in the case of one company, a dear old lady provided a large quantity of beautiful vegetables gratis. She also gave the officers coffee and rolls, and was most indignant when offered payment. All honour be to her !

The day was warming up when we set off to march to our destination, Ivergny, and after a night in the train no one felt very energetic. We arrived there for dinner after climbing some fairly steep hills, which, coupled with the soft spring air, made everyone feel somewhat tired. The men's billets were good, the officers' poor. In striking contrast to our good lady of Doullens, we found the inhabitants very inhospitable, and many of the

172

houses were crammed with refugees. The Commanding Officer was locked out by his occupier, and the Adjutant was calmly informed that he could not enter his house. The services of De Chauny, the Brigade Interpreter, were soon in request, and everything was settled, though not very amicably. "C" Company were very late, and it was long after dark before they rejoined us after their arduous duties at the station.

We were told that the Division was in General Headquarters Reserve, and likely to be called upon suddenly. The next day all were busied, accordingly, with checking stores and ammunition, and generally seeing that everything was up to concert pitch. The Adjutant seized the occasion of a short spell of leisure to ride over to Bouque Maison, where Colonel Harrison, our first Brigade Commander, was performing nobly the duties of Town Major, and very pleased he seemed to have news of his old Brigade.

At 5 p.m. we received orders to move at an hour's notice, and half an hour later to move at 6.30 p.m. to Grenas viâ Lucheux. As the light failed it began to rain, and at length down it came in a steady torrent, and the night was as black as pitch. The road was hilly, and, to add to our troubles, we got behind a pontoon section, which kept on blocking us; and after we had passed that we got on the heels of the Pioneer Battalion's transport, which was blessed with a jibbing team, and caused various vexatious halts. Despite these, the greatest cheerfulness and good humour prevailed, and the men sang lustily, as, indeed, they always did in the rain. We reached Grenas, which was just across the Arras—Doullens road, at 11.30 p.m., and eventually got the men, wet and tired, into quite fair billets.

The Brigadier, with his usual kindness, invited several of the officers in to supper about 1 a.m.; and it was on that occasion that the Commanding Officer perpetrated on the Brigade Gas Officer his famous joke about the new green container for the small box-respirator. It was briefly this: Seeing the Brigade

Gas Officer come in, the Commanding Officer asked him when the new green container was being issued, for, as he argued, no other container was proof against the new gas. The Gas Officer, suspecting nothing, replied that it was due shortly, and proceeded the next day to make inquiries from his senior at Division. It is rumoured that the inquiry spread thence to the Corps and Army Chemical Advisers, and from there to the highest authorities. It need hardly be added that the quest was in vain !

Before we retired to rest we were told that we must always be ready to move at one hour's notice between 6 a.m. and 12 noon, and at two hours' notice at other times. At 8 a.m. on April 5th the Commanding Officer and the four Company Commanders, exclusive of the two who were to be left out with the surplus " battle personnel "—or " those in the lifeboat " as the saying went—proceeded by motor lorry to reconnoitre the Purple Line in the vicinity of Monchy au Bois, Ransart, and Ficheux, south of Arras.

The battalion meantime was engaged in such training as could be done in the immediate vicinity of billets, with everything kept constantly packed for an immediate departure. On April 7th sixty men arrived as a draft, and N.C.Os. were hastily told off to instruct them in the way they should go ; and on the following day Lieutenant Reed, M.O.R.C., U.S.A., relieved Lieutenant Sullo as Medical Officer. At 10 a.m. that day we resumed our journey, passing through the outskirts of Doullens, and going into billets at Beauval.

As usual, the next morning at 8 a.m. the Commanding Officer and Company Commanders were sent off to reconnoitre the Red Line near Authie; and while they were away the battalion was ordered to proceed to Beauquesne, but this was cancelled. Next morning, at 8 a.m., a lorry arrived once more to carry the Commanding Officer and his Company Commanders, this time to the Purple Line, near Gommecourt and Fonquevillers. All that day the Battalion was waiting to move off, but nothing came of it.

"THE KING'S" (LIVERPOOL REGIMENT)

April 11th was spent in schemes for the defence of a village, which those in authority thought we should be more than likely to have to put into real practice before very much longer. We heard this day, to our wrath, that the Divisional Dump at Estaires had been captured by the enemy. This included many of our records, innumerable gramophones, including one expensive instrument received by Captain Eccles the day we were ordered to send in our surplus stores, and many other articles of priceless value. However, there was little time for lamentation, as we were ordered back to Grenas once more. It was a bright, fine day, and we had quite a pleasant march.

As we passed through Doullens for the third time, a German aeroplane passed over very high up, and a rifleman was heard to remark that all our marching and counter-marching must be intended to bluff the enemy. Really it almost seemed like it at the time. Ever since we left Fleurbaix we had been more or less continuously on the move, often retraversing old ground, and seldom staying more than a night or two in one place. The real explanation was that another great German offensive was thought to be imminent, and our Division, who were the counter-attacking force, had to be placed where the situation, which varied daily, demanded our presence. That kind of life very soon becomes tedious, as everything you want is always packed up on a waggon, and no one is allowed to go any distance from his billet.

The following day (April 13th) we moved off once more, this time nearer the line, our destination being Authie. As we drew near the rain began to descend, and on arrival we found, to our consternation, that French troops were in possession, and that there were no billets for us. After a considerable halt, during which time Lieutenant Freeman, the Transport Officer, most prudently watered his horses, we were informed that we were to bivouac in Authie Wood, a cheerless prospect, as the rain continued to descend steadily. We passed through Authie and turned up a steep hill on our right, and off that into a large forest of small trees, clogged with undergrowth. Here we found the remainder of our Brigade, and as night fell everyone was making elaborate efforts with branches and bracken to form shelters for the night.

About 11 p.m. word was received that some tents had arrived, and parties were collected with difficulty from the companies. The wood was situated on the slope of a very steep hill, intersected by small but precipitous gorges. Movement in the dark was therefore a matter of considerable difficulty. The scene on the road at this time was extraordinary. Three battalions, one field ambulance, and the Brigade Headquarter transports were parked alongside a road of no great width to begin with. In addition, the transport of the Machine Gun Battalion—equal in volume to the whole of a Brigade transport—had just arrived, and were trying to find room to park. Droves of animals were proceeding up and down the hill for watering. Several lorries containing the tents, and others passing through, not to mention motor ambulances and dispatch riders, added considerably to the congestion ; while ration parties, fatigue parties, and miscellaneous details of every description filled what little space was left, which was not much. The babel of shouts and cries was almost deafening. One moment you found yourself in the midst of a drove of kicking mules, the next you were in imminent peril of destruction from a motor lorry, and all this in inky darkness and a steady torrent of rain. Eventually the situation cleared, and soon after midnight, except for a thousand dots of light all over the countryside, you might have imagined that not a man was about. Luckily, no inquisitive enemy airman came round.

The next day the Commanding Officer, Adjutant, and Company Commanders visited the section of the Red Line for which the battalion was to be responsible in the event of a hostile attack. The trenches were only just on the far side of the road, and appeared well situated. Gangs of Chinese were busy—after the leisurely

Photo by
Gale & Polden, Ltd., Aldershot.

LIEUT.-COL. HON. N. C. GATHORNE HARDY, D.S.O.

fashion of British workmen—deepening and continuing the trench system.

Time was, in the old Armentières days, when we thought the scheme for occupying the enemy trenches, if he should retire, complicated and changeable. Compared with the multifarious schemes that now began to pour in on us in connection with the Red Line, that old operation order, with all its amendments and cancellations, faded into complete insignificance. Between this date and our going into the line at Gommecourt on May 6th there were not only four distinct schemes, one of which was a counter-attack in conjunction with tanks, but amendments were issued almost daily, altering the original scheme in the most drastic way. By way of encouragement, each set of orders was prefaced by the words, " The enemy is expected to attack at an early date "; and, indeed, the " powers that were " certainly had made up their minds that a general offensive was to open against us at any moment on that part of the front. However, that is rather a matter for the future.

After two damp and uncomfortable days at Authie we retraced our steps for some distance, and then marched off to Pas. Our route lay for the first part through villages packed with French soldiers—fine, big, upstanding men in the prime of life—who gave us and our bugles a rousing reception as we marched through.

Our billets—or rather bivouacs—we found were situated in Pas Wood, and once more on the top of a precipitous hill, the transport being in a field at the foot. The 2/7th K.L.R. and ourselves shared a section of the wood on a narrow strip of the crest-line of the hill. A sandy lane ran along the edge of the wood, giving access to our " bivvies," which were strung out in twos and threes for a considerable distance, as the wood descended below this strip very suddenly to the valley beneath us. On the other side of the lane was an open field, but there were considerable restrictions as to the erection of any tents, etc., in the field, as our presence in the wood was supposed to be a secret.

Fortunately, the weather was fine and sunny when we took over our bivouacs, and we were able to settle into our tents and ground-sheet shelters pretty comfortably. In fine weather it was not bad, but on cold wet days, of which we had a fair proportion, it was damp and chilly beyond description; and the difficulties of obtaining exercise apart from working parties—for we were still under the one hour's notice to move—proved very disastrous to the health of the battalion; and this was made worse by the quantity of vermin, occasioned by the bad conditions of living and the lack of facilities for bathing for a long period.

Our new situation brought out a fresh scheme for holding the Red Line, but this did not cancel the old one, being merely an alternative. Reconnoitring became the order of the day, and in addition the battalion marched out daily *en masse* to work on the defences in the vicinity of Coigneux and Couin, where we were busy digging and wiring.

The addition of four more Lewis guns to the battalion about this time, bringing the total up to twenty-four guns, meant the creation of large classes for gunners, of which all companies had been getting short. The packing of these guns was also a difficulty. An emergency transport scheme was in existence, which limited the battalion transport considerably, and worked out at half a limber per company. These special vehicles with the battalion's essential battle equipment, were kept loaded night and day. In addition, dumps of preserved rations were formed, and water-bottles always had to be kept full.

On April 20th Captain Fell, who had been injured at St. Hilaire, returned from England and resumed command of " D " Company. which had temporarily been commanded by 2nd-Lieutenant Carr.

Some interesting tests as to the comparative merits in point of speed of Lewis guns and rifle fire were carried out. A Lewis gun, with a second gun to carry on if it had a stoppage, was matched against eight rifles for five minutes' rapid fire, and it was found that, unless a really good man was firing the gun, the total number

178

of hits for the riflemen exceeded the total for the Lewis gun. If the gunner was good, the gun beat the rifle, but only by a small margin.

Each company was now organized into three ordinary platoons and a Lewis gun platoon, the latter under a Company Lewis Gun Officer, and the whole more or less under the supervision of the Battalion Lewis Gun Officer. From the training point of view this plan has many advantages, but whether these would be as great in action is open to question.

The working parties were now employed in the vicinity of Rossignol Farm; and later, on a new switch line, which was the outcome of a suggestion from the Commanding Officer, who had a very remarkable eye for weakness in a trench system. Some of the ground was chalk and flint, other parts consisted of excellent soft soil, with the result that the work which composed the daily task varied exceedingly. Never since the Margate days had the battalion been so good at digging as they became at this time. Lieutenant Jones, our Pioneer Officer, being an expert, proved invaluable in instructing the inexperienced.

A sudden outbreak of influenza, or some kindred ailment, swept over the battalion at this time to a very alarming degree. We had a sick parade daily of over 100, and admissions to hospital amounted to about 250 in a few days. Lieutenant Reed, our invaluable American Medical Officer, did everything he could to check the disease. Rest stations were established in Pas village to take the milder cases, isolation was practised, changes of diet prescribed—everything, in short, was done that was possible—but the complaint ran through the battalion like wildfire. The consequence was that we lost a very serious proportion of our best N.C.Os. and men, for those who go to hospital very seldom rejoin their old battalion. The field ambulance tried to save what they could, but, with the imminence of a battle, they dared not have their dressing-stations full of sick. That the lice, coupled with the bad conditions of living, were responsible there can be little doubt ; nor that, granted reasonable facilities for bathing and disinfecting simultaneously, and not piecemeal, we might have stamped out the lice. However, the Higher Command refused the special facilities, and our losses were consequently great. It made things very difficult, as N.C.Os. and warrant officers had to be replaced almost daily ; and the protective barrage that fell for an hour at dawn each day was a sufficient reminder of possibilities ahead. So loud and emphatic was this on some mornings that we were almost convinced that the threatened offensive had opened, but on each occasion the barrage died away again as suddenly as it had commenced.

During the period in Pas Wood we learnt that Colonel Fletcher had been awarded the Legion of Honour. We were glad to think that he had received this recognition of the splendid work he was doing.

On April 29th our manifold defence schemes were further complicated by the issue of a counter-attack scheme, in conjunction with tanks, for the recovery of Beer Trench, the old British front line in front of Gommecourt, in the event of the German attack succeeding to that extent. This necessitated the pegging-out of assembly positions in due course in the vicinity of the Chateau de la Haie. Meanwhile the old scheme for the manning of the Red Line was put into force on April 28th, the whole Brigade turning out for this practice, which was carried out without incident.

Our early return to front line work was now indicated by instructions to send an advance party into the Gommecourt sector for twenty-four hours' attachment to the 8th Battalion Manchester Regiment. This was done on May 1st, the party returning on May 2nd, but, unfortunately, less Sergeant Roberts, of " C " Company, a most popular N.C.O., who was shot through the head while going round the sector.

The actual relief was fixed for May 6th, and the interval was fully occupied by practice attacks, first of the 8th K.L.R., and

"THE KING'S" (LIVERPOOL REGIMENT)

later by the 172nd Infantry Brigade, assisted by contact aeroplanes.

The time had now arrived for us to leave our peaceful bivouacs and take a more active part in the war. The lengthened stay and the improvement in the weather had enabled us to make our temporary homes a little less primitive than when we took them over, and we were quite sorry to leave them. The surrounding country consisted of fine undulating downs, rolling in long sweeps for miles in every direction. The villages were mostly rustic and pretty, and the woods dotted about in all directions were showing the first signs of young spring green.

May 6th proved fine and warm. The morning was busy with the final preparations for the line and in sorting out the party which formed the "lifeboat," which was destined for the Divisional Camp at Marieux. Strict instructions had been issued that the full 33⅓ per cent. were to be left out, and the party included Captains Eccles and Fell, Lieutenants James and Burton, 2nd-Lieutenants Carr and Upward, and eighty-two other ranks. These marched off at 2 p.m. Rear headquarters were also arranged for at Couin, and consisted of Major C. W. Wilson, the Adjutant (sick), and 2nd-Lieutenant Harris, who was in charge of the Brigade relay stretcher-bearers—also kept out of the line for use in the event of the "push."

The battalion moved off at 3 p.m. to Souastre, where teas were served, and after dark the march into the line commenced. Souastre itself was fairly intact, though the Germans occasionally shelled it with a heavy gun, as certain houses mutely testified. After leaving Souastre the road proceeded almost straight into Fonquevillers, cutting right across open rolling country, and passing through most formidable lines of guns. Endless shell-holes in all directions, both on the road and on either side of it, revealed the fondness of the enemy for "crashing" this main approach to the line, a practice which our gunners had taught him to realize by bitter experience could be very effective. Just before

181

reaching Fonquevillers the road entered a wood, and that point was particularly favoured by the attentions of the Germans.

After passing through this stretch of wood the miserable remains of Fonquevillers village were reached—another very " unhealthy " spot—on the far side of which the tramway to the trenches began. This most important adjunct to trench life was a very favourite target of the enemy. At the place where the tram-line started waggons and fatigue parties used to congregate after dark, to deliver and collect those various items of food and equipment which did so much to make life tolerable. Knowing this full well, the enemy used to open at intervals a concentrated fire on this spot, and woe betide the men that were gathered there at the moment. A series of blinding flashes and terrific explosions was the first warning that you got, and if the shelling was accurate it was at once the beginning and the end. As a matter of fact, however, we were extremely lucky. Not once did our rations get caught at this danger point.

The track led along a glade through Gommecourt Park, once a fine wood of noble trees, now a shattered skeleton of blackened stumps and splintered branches looking gaunt and spectral. A wonderful place this wood had been when the Germans held it. Huge dug-outs were concealed beneath it, with many an underground passage and machine-gun posts cunningly concealed in steel trees which counterfeited most cleverly the surrounding trunks. No wonder the opening attack in 1916 found this place wellnigh impregnable. No wonder the French Government had put up huge notices that the park was preserved as a national memorial, albeit the notices that no work was to be undertaken here without permission of the French Government were now riddled with bullets and splintered with shrapnel. The tide of war had flowed up to Gommecourt Park once more.

On either side of the track were endless pieces of trench and dug-outs, a very handy refuge in time of trouble; and it was with some slight sense of loneliness that you left the protection of these

182

on the far side for a longish walk across the barest of bare open ground, heading for a lone bush which marked the line of direction to the British trenches. The frequent "whizz-bang" holes, some of very recent date, showed that the track was well known to the enemy.

In every direction were compact woods of varying size and geometrical pattern. Biez, Pigeon, the more famous Rossignol Wood, were all distinctive features in the landscape; and by day one expected to see those fleecy white puffs suddenly appearing above them and gradually dissipating again into the air which marked the British shrapnel, or, again, the blacker and more ominous clouds of the German fire.

It was dark when the battalion wound its way along the Souastre—Fonquevillers road, and not only dark but raining. As the night drew on it got blacker and blacker, while the rain increased to a torrential downpour. The Commanding Officer of the Lancashire Fusiliers had suffered severely during his own relief by the ignorance of the guides supplied to him. To prevent a recurrence of this, because a late relief hits both parties, his guides had been over the track nightly, to make certain of the road; but this night the elements were against them. They lost their way, and two companies were piloted into the right battalion sector, and only achieved the relief of their opposite numbers after wanderings comparable with those of the Lost Tribes of Israel. On a drenching night, with an active enemy opposite you, and with dawn approaching, such a trudge in the dark, stumbling over obstacles and wading through mud and water, is no small task, and the men's language, if free, was hardly to be criticized.

The relief was complete at 5 a.m., which left the remnants of the Lancashire Fusiliers the minimum of time to get out of sight before daylight broke—a·proceeding that was most necessary where the enemy had excellent observation, and usually considered a party exceeding three or four a fair target. " C " and

183

" D " Companies were in the front line, which may roughly be described as running from Biez to Rossignol Woods. " B " Company was in support, and " A " Company in reserve.

On the day after relief Captain Oliphant, of the United States Army, and two N.C.Os. were attached to the battalion for two days' instruction.

That night Colonel Fletcher, who had long been overworking, broke down and came to the rear for a rest, and Major C. W. Wilson took over command in the line. Colonel Fletcher was accommodated at Divisional Headquarters at Couin. Captain Broad and 2nd-Lieutenant Waln also retired to hospital, sick, the same day.

The next night (May 8th, 1918) a very determined effort was made by Sergeant Corkill and three other scouts (Hill, Whelan, and Bradley) to obtain identification. Leaving our line from our left post in Oak Trench, they made their way across to a supposed enemy post at the junction of the road and the German front-line trench; this they rushed, killing two of its occupants. Before they had time to do anything more, they were attacked by another post from the left flank. Seizing the machine gun in the post, they made off; but owing to two of the party being immediately wounded, and the check to their movements caused by the weight of the gun, they had to abandon it, and made the best of their way back to our line. For this very gallant little enterprise Corkill received the Military Medal.

The question of the defence of the sector, which had been exercising Colonel Fletcher's mind, and which, owing to his incessant reconnaissances, had given the finishing touch to his weariness, was now settled; and on the night of May 9th–10th the 6th Battalion of the Bedfordshires, who belonged to the Division on our left, took over two left posts of our " D " Company in Oak and Waac Trench, and established, in addition, a joint post. This secured our left far more adequately than before, and also enabled " D " Company to relieve two posts of " C " Company and thus strengthen the line generally.

"THE KING'S" (LIVERPOOL REGIMENT)

This scheme was further perfected on May 11th by the 2/7th
K.L.R. taking over a Lewis gun post of " C " Company, which
was more properly in their area ; and on May 12th the defence line
was based on Herring Trench instead of Bass Trench, which involved some shifting of posts and the taking over from the 9th
K.L.R. of a small portion of their line.

On the night of May 12th–13th the enemy put down a gas shell
barrage for two and a half hours on Fonquevillers, causing very
heavy casualties to the Division on our left. Most unfortunately,
our rations were coming through the village when the barrage
opened, and we were lucky to escape with only seven men wounded
and gassed. The transport stood the proceeding with the greatest
fortitude, and after it was over delivered the rations as if nothing
had happened.

That night the Adjutant was evacuated to hospital, sick, and
Captain F. C. Bowring shortly after took over the duties.

The 1/5th Loyal North Lancashire Regiment relieved us on
May 13th, relief being complete at 1.30 a.m., and the battalion
moved out to the Chateau de la Haie switch, taking over the
trenches occupied by the 2/5th King's Own Royal Lancaster
Regiment.

The time, on the whole, had been moderately quiet, though parts
of the line, more especially High Street, had dropped in for a good
deal of fairly heavy shelling. The trenches had been poor and
wet, and, owing to the extent of the front, only limited improvement had been possible. By 5.30 a.m. the battalion had settled
down in Chateau de la Haie. The same afternoon officers were
examining the trenches on the Sailly au Bois—Fonquevillers road,
and in the evening two and a half companies were up in Beer and
Rum Trenches, working on the defences. " B " Company, on the
way back, were unluckily shelled, and four men were wounded.

We also lost a valuable member of the battalion, Sergeant
Lloyd, who was injured by his horse falling on him. He had done
excellent work as Transport Sergeant.

At 9 p.m. on May 15th the battalion proceeded another stage from the line, and relieved the 2/4th Loyal North Lancashire Regiment in Rossignol Farm, the Brigade being now in Divisional Reserve. The men were accommodated in barns, and the officers in a range of pigstyes, which had concrete floors capable of being sluiced out with water; this was necessary, as the styes were none too free of vermin. The farm buildings were situated on the top of a steep hill, at the bottom of which ran a road and a railway. Up this railway nearly every night a 15-inch railway gun was brought, named "Coppernob" by the troops, and fired several rounds from a position just behind the farm, which was shaken to its foundations at every discharge. This was not conducive to rest, but a further annoyance was added when on two occasions flights of German aeroplanes came over all night long, dropping their "eggs" in the vicinity of the farm in their endeavours to destroy "Coppernob." Ultimately success rewarded their efforts, but in the meantime a number of bombs fell unpleasantly close to our "rest" billets. The time at Rossignol Farm, like most other periods in reserve, was spent mainly in working parties in the forward area. Apart from meaning practically no sleep, and nothing but hard work throughout the hours of darkness, these parties possess the added joy of long marches along roads not infrequently shelled. That this work is necessary is beyond question; that it was unpleasant is hardly less certain. Beer and Rum Trenches, which might be considered the main line of resistance if the front-line battalion were rushed, received most of our attention.

On May 17th Colonel Fletcher proceeded to Paris Plage Officers' Rest Station, in the hope that a few days of quiet recreation would compensate for the strain due to months of overwork, though the hope was not fulfilled.

On May 18th the defence scheme for the reserve brigade of the centre divisional front of the IV Corps was issued, and we plunged once more into the perplexing variety of the probable and possible actions the battalion could be called upon to undertake. From the very start these were sufficiently multifarious, and were finally grouped under three headings—first, to reinforce the right or left brigade in the line; secondly, to counter-attack in one of four directions; or, third and lastly, to form a defensive flank in one of two totally different places. We also learnt that on the message, "Take precautions," the battalion was to assemble at a given spot in "fighting order," and there await news as to the particular part it was to play. This elastic set of orders plunged everyone into a perfect fever of reconnaissance. Before long, amendments and appendices began to arrive, which contained reference to disposal of prisoners, extra stretcher-bearers, and so forth, which certainly gave one the impression that the attack was due shortly. Most people hoped devoutly that it would develop before we entered the front line again, as the battalion holding the line when an offensive starts has a poor time at the best.

On the 20th "C" and "D" Companies moved up to the trenches at the Chateau de la Haie, taking with them the Lewis guns of "A" and "B" Companies in addition, and relieved two companies of the 2/7th K.L.R., who were to occupy Beer Trench, previously not held.

Further orders then arrived, detailing the action if the battalion had to occupy Beer Trench; but on May 21st, before any more of these orders arrived, the battalion proceeded up the line, taking over this time the right sector, and relieving the 2/4th South Lancashire Regiment.

The period behind the line, if not exactly restful, what with incessant working parties and a general feeling of excitement produced by the endless preparations to foil the Germans when they attacked, had yet been distinctly refreshing after the wet and miserable trenches which we had occupied in the line. The weather had been fine and warm, and all the countryside was pleasant with the fresh smell and bright colours of advancing spring. Baths and clean underclothing, better food, the Divisional Band, together with practice on the range and normal routine, had all helped to send the battalion back to the line in splendid fettle once more.

The relief was complete at 2 a.m., but this time one cannot add " without incident." The ration dump was heavily shelled, and, to the great loss of the battalion, Regimental Quartermaster-Sergeant Cousins, but recently appointed to that important post, was killed, and another man wounded. Cousins had been with the battalion from very early days, and had risen steadily. It was indeed a tragedy that, on reaching a post which one may call comparatively safe, he should then have been killed.

The sector in which the battalion now found itself was an awkward one to hold, owing to inadequate lateral communications, and to the fact that the front line companies were not in touch with each other. The former defect was mainly due to the lie of the land, which sloped down from the high ground occupied by the enemy towards our support line in Gommecourt Trench, thus giving the enemy supervision of any movement in that trench. Two companies occupied the front line for four days, and were then relieved by the other two companies—one company in support in Nameless Trench and Gommecourt Trench, and one company in reserve in Rum Trench and in dug-outs in Gommecourt Park, in which latter place Battalion Headquarters also was established. The right front company was in rather a maze of trenches and saps off Welcome and Warrior Streets, and held positions in which it was very inadvisable to have any movement during the hours of daylight, else the enemy artillery, owing to their excellent observation, quickly located the movement, with unpleasant consequences. On our right were the New Zealanders, based on Hebuterne, with whom we held a joint post in front of Minnie Trench. In order to reach the right front company from Battalion Headquarters, it was necessary to go a short distance along Rum Trench, then climb out and dash across the road in

188

full view of the enemy, and drop again into Rum Trench. This dash across the road was quite a sporting proceeding, because the enemy kept a machine gun trained on the spot ; the great activity of all whose duty took them across the road was very noticeable. However, this dangerous place was remedied by driving a tunnel under the road. Continuing the journey to the right company, you proceeded along Rum Trench until you came to Nameless Trench on your left, which you turned down and followed until you struck Gommecourt Trench on your right. This trench, located at the bottom of a valley, was necessarily rather shallow and wet ; but it was a long trench, and being for the greater part of its length under enemy observation, was consequently unhealthy unless you negotiated it at speed. Arrived at the far end, you turned up Richmond Trench, at the head of which Company Head-quarters was found in a deep dug-out. The left front company occupied positions in saps leading off Nameless Trench and Name-less Support, and were responsible for the front from Nameless to the road which ran from Gommecourt Park to the enemy lines. On their left was the 8th Battalion K.L.R. There was no com-munication between the right and left companies during daylight, owing to the fact that west of Nameless Trench the trench called Welcome Street had been blown in for about sixty yards. The slope between Welcome Street and Gommecourt Trench was well pocked with shell-holes, and examination of an aeroplane photo-graph through a magnifying glass showed one curiously shaped mark, which caused some speculation as to what it might be. It was thought that it might be an old gunpit, but when examined by a patrol at night proved to be a bed of ox-eyed daisies in full bloom, evidently a relic of a garden which had been there in the long ago. The reserve company always had to find carrying parties at night to carry water and rations up to the front line companies.

The tour opened quietly enough ; the first two days the enemy devoted considerable attention to back areas, but little to the trenches. The night of May 25th–26th was made distinctly lively by a highly successful raid carried out by a party of four officers and 112 men of the 2/4th South Lancashire Regiment from our left company's front line. The South Lancashires brought in twelve prisoners and one machine gun. During the barrage we had two men killed and six wounded, while 2nd-Lieutenant Thomas was also slightly wounded by a sniper on this day.

On May 25th Colonel Fletcher rejoined rear headquarters.

The rest of the tour was quiet enough—the usual amount of miscellaneous shelling, and the usual two or three casualties daily. 2nd-Lieutenant Thomas was evacuated sick on May 28th to No. 3 Canadian Casualty Clearing Station, which was heavily bombed shortly after his arrival, and caused him to retire to the United Kingdom wounded.

A draft of 126 men was posted to the battalion from the Divisional Wing on May 29th, but remained at Marieux with the nucleus party.

Relief of the battalion took place by the 2/7th K.L.R. on May 29th, but this only constituted the occupation of the reserve trenches instead of the front line, and made very little difference to conditions of existence.

The Transport Officer and Quartermaster, who were both suffering from the effects of gas, had to be sent to the rear, the former to a Casualty Clearing Station and the latter to Marieux. 2nd-Lieutenant Harper took over the duties of Transport Officer. Lieutenant Burton, the Scout Officer, also came up from Marieux, as a raid was looming ahead, and he had to commence preliminary reconnaissances.

The end of the month found our effective strength 43 officers and 860 men. Captain Wurtzburg and 2nd-Lieutenant Jones had been evacuated to England sick, and 2nd-Lieutenant A. E. Sutton for a transfer to the Royal Air Force. 2nd-Lieutenants Jacobs and Anderson had rejoined from a wild-goose chase to No. 2 Entrenching Battalion, whither they had been dispatched some time previously, after a heated argument over our paper strength, when we absorbed half the 2/5th K.L.R. Lieutenant Tebbutt, previously with the 2/5th K.L.R., joined us also ; and 2nd-Lieutenant Lever, M.C., who was wounded at Langemarck, now reappeared. Our casualties had been five men killed and forty-five wounded.

June opened somewhat noisily in comparison with the peace and quiet of the last few days of May. The enemy celebrated the " glorious First of June " by attempting to raid a post of the 2/7th K.L.R., the attempt being preceded by a violent barrage on a broad front, and resulting in the capture by the 2/7th K.L.R. of one prisoner, who was understood to make some very disparaging comments on the officers who were to have accompanied the raiding party. The failure of the enterprise was evidently vexatious to the Germans, who shelled the whole sector vigorously all that day, and early the next morning treated us to two hours' solid gas shelling. The small box-respirator, admirable as it is as a protection, is not an ideal form of headgear, and two hours' continual gassing is apt to provoke considerable resentment on the part of the wearer. Luckily, the storm ceased at 4.20 a.m., when a local relief of 95 men by a party of 121 from Marieux had been arranged for, and was in fact achieved without loss, though at 5.40 a.m. a good number of 4·2's were flung on to Rum Trench. That afternoon 25 more men arrived from the rear, reinforcements from the Base, and were posted to the various companies.

The night of June 3rd our artillery put down a heavy barrage for a raid by the 1/5th Loyal North Lancashire Regiment, but at the eleventh hour the raid itself was postponed till the next night. The enemy took little notice of it, probably imagining that it was retaliation for the previous day's " strafe." Later in the day, however, he shelled Battalion Headquarters with more zeal than was pleasant.

On June 5th and 6th more small reliefs of men were effected, and Captain Eccles came up from rear headquarters and relieved Major Wilson, who went back to Couin for a rest ; while Colonel

Fletcher proceeded to England for fourteen days' leave as a last effort to recover his former vitality.

On June 7th we were relieved by the 1/5th Loyal North Lancashire Regiment, and divided our forces. " C " Company with " D " Company's Lewis guns and Headquarters moved to Chateau de la Haie, where Major Charles Wilson resumed command. " A," " B," and " D " Companies, with Headquarters and Lewis guns, occupied Beer Trench and the defences of Fonquevillers, under the command of Captain Eccles.

We remained doing working parties and some musketry and bathing till June 9th, when we were relieved by the 8th K.L.R. and withdrew to Couin, which we reached at 7.15 p.m.

After a short three days' rest in Couin Wood, we found ourselves once more in the line, this time as left battalion of left brigade, the sector being north-east of Gommecourt, the original sector first occupied by the battalion. " D " Company, who were to carry out a raid in the immediate future, were left out for training, and " B " Company, 8th K.L.R., were attached in their place. The dispositions in the line were " C," " B," " A " in the front line, with " B " Company, 8th K.L.R., in reserve.

The battalion left Couin at 7.30 p.m., and the relief of the 9th K.L.R. was not completed till 2.40 a.m. on June 12th. Unluckily, the take-over was harassed by considerable hostile artillery fire, causing two killed and two wounded. We were fortunate indeed to escape so lightly. The rest of the day was quiet enough, except for some light shelling. Lieutenant Burton, Battalion Scout Officer, arrived the same evening from rear headquarters to commence a reconnaissance of the area to be raided.

On the night of June 16th Lieutenant Burton, accompanied by Riflemen Pennington and Leigh, proceeded into the German trenches. Coming suddenly and unexpectedly on a German post, they found themselves under a fierce fire at close range. Lieutenant Burton fell at once, badly wounded in the chest, and in

GOMMECOURT PARK.

GENERAL VIEW OF FAMPOUX.

spite of the efforts of his two companions to bring him back, they eventually had to leave him, being both seriously wounded themselves. There can be little doubt that Burton was mortally wounded, and could at the best have survived but a short while. By his death the battalion lost one of its most devoted and gallant officers. Entirely devoid of self-interest, he possessed a striking sense of duty, and worked whole-heartedly for the common weal. He was keenly mourned by all ranks. Pennington was awarded the Military Medal.

That night the enemy shelled us pretty heavily, and we sustained fourteen casualties. The next day, June 17th, on the other hand, was exceptionally quiet. The patrolling was continued by Acting-Captain Robinson and two more scouts sent up for the purpose.

On June 18th the enemy, no doubt encouraged by a previous success, sent over another raiding patrol. This one, however, met with a warm reception, and the patrol was forced to beat a hasty retreat, though not till one of its members had been taken prisoner.

. Our raid had been fixed for June 19th, but owing to torrential rain it was decided to postpone it. At 11.30 p.m., however, on June 20th it was duly carried out. The raiding party, under Captain Fell, 2nd-Lieutenants R. E. Noon and L. T. Profit, had been training for six days at Rossignol Farm, where a set of dummy trenches had been constructed from aeroplane photos. The raiders were divided into three parties : Noon's party, fourteen N.C.Os. and men, were on the right ; Profit's party, about thirty N.C.Os. and men, on the left ; and, lastly, there were eight stretcher-bearers under a sergeant.

The plan of operations was as follows : The right party were to strike across No Man's Land up from our No. 2 Post, using the old German support line post " H " Trench, and up to a grave marked by a conspicuous white cross. On arrival there they were to rush the two German posts just beyond it in the present

German front line, then turn left handed to meet the left party. The latter, leaving our No. 3 Post, were to proceed along the old German front line—*i.e.*, parallel with the right party—past the northern end of " H " Trench, after which they were to extend and rush two posts in the German front line, and then move to the right to join the right party.

It will be observed from the sketch map that the old system of trenches during the confusion of the offensive had become, as it were, twisted sideways, and instead of each side holding the original front and support lines, these were now communication trenches, and the old communication trenches had been fashioned into the fire trenches.

At 3 p.m., June 20th, the raiding party left Rossignol Farm for Chateau de la Haie, where they arrived at 3.45 p.m. After tea and dinner the party set off for the line with blackened faces, white armlets, and plenty of bombs.

At 10.25 p.m. raid headquarters were reached, tin helmets were abandoned, and the move to assembly positions carried out. Meanwhile Robinson and the scouts were busy laying tapes and fixing sticks with metal discs to guide the party, and all was ready at 11.15 p.m.

At 11.30 p.m. the 4·5 howitzers, 18-pounders, and machine guns opened the barrage on the enemy front line, and the parties moved forward up their respective saps.

The right party, having reached the white cross, remained in their trench, which they shared with some thirty very dead Germans till 11.34 p.m., when they proceeded to extend and rush the enemy posts. However, some recently erected wire and a volley of bombs somewhat disorganized the movement ; but Noon quickly collected four or five men and made a second rush with great bravery and determination, this time successfully, into the trench.

Two of the post showed fight and were killed ; one bolted for a dug-out, but was taken prisoner. The rest of the post were

killed or escaped over the top.   Two of the raiders worked along
to the right, the remainder to the left towards the other party.
Just at that moment the recall signal went up, two green Véry
lights, and the party only just had time to evacuate the trench
before our protective barrage returned once more to the front
line, whence it had temporarily lifted to the support.

The left party, after reaching " H " Trench, extended and tried
to rush the enemy.   They were met by steady machine-gun and
rifle fire and a large number of bombs, and could make no progress.
Lieutenant Profit and one or two others, with great determination, managed to reach the parapet, but all were wounded and
could do nought.   After one or two further efforts the raiders
withdrew.   On this occasion Rifleman Donaldson and Rifleman
Robert Smith showed the utmost gallantry.   Having penetrated
with Lieutenant Profit as far as the German parapet, they saw
him fall wounded, and in spite of very heavy fire proceeded to
carry him back.   By doing so they missed the gap in the wire.
Nothing daunted, they made their way back to the enemy post,
took their bearings again, and this time brought their casualty
safely through.   The performance was one of great coolness and
courage, and the heavy rain which had begun to fall, coupled with
the fact that Donaldson himself was wounded, did not make their
task any easier.   They were both awarded the Military Medal.

Others who for distinguished conduct during the raid received
the Military Medal were Lance-Corporal Winstanley, who worked
with great devotion in charge of the stretcher-bearers ; Lance-
Corporal Heyes, Riflemen H. E. Harrison and A. Mellor for
gallantry and initiative with Noon's party ; and Riflemen B.
Clarke and W. Whelan, Battalion Scouts, for continuous bold
patrolling before the raid and disregard of danger during its
progress, while laying tapes in No Man's Land and leading
the raiding parties to and from their positions.

Captain Robinson and 2nd-Lieutenant Noon were both awarded
the Military Cross for their respective shares in the success of the

operations. Everything that could have been found out about the enemy's position Robinson had, by persistent patrolling, discovered. Noon's action on the night of the raid has already been described. The casualties were twenty-one wounded, of whom 2nd-Lieutenant Profit subsequently died of his wounds. This had been the first real chance this young officer had had of showing of what stuff he was made. His performance on this night was most gallant, and it was with universal regret that we heard that he had succumbed to his wounds.

One prisoner and a machine gun were the trophies of the raid.

The party returned to the Chateau de la Haie for their breakfast, and thence to Rossignol Farm for twenty-four hours' rest. Congratulations from the B.G.C. and G.O.C. were received on the success of the raid.

On the evening of June 21st " D " Company came into the line, and " B " Company, 8th K.L.R., was relieved after some local rearrangement of the line. Subsequently " D " Company moved into the front line, changing places with " A " Company.

On June 22nd the 62nd Division, on our left, put over a raid with tanks, and we got well shelled in consequence, five men being wounded.

On June 24th there was a thick fog in the evening, and a German wireless message was picked up : " Tell storm troops to stand-by till 6 a.m. opposite Hebuterne." As a result three heavy counter-shoots were carried out by our artillery, though nothing more happened. We had been reinforced by sixty-three men that day from rear headquarters.

On June 25th Colonel Fletcher, who had recently resumed command of the battalion, while going round the right company front with Lieutenant J. R. Paul, had a very narrow escape from a 5·9 which landed full on the parados. Lieutenant Paul was seriously wounded in the back, and two or three men of the post were also wounded. Beyond a few bits of metal in his face and hands, Colonel Fletcher escaped injury. Paul was evacuated, and never rejoined us—to our lasting regret.

Next day a twelve-hour continuous shoot of all available artillery was delivered on to Rossignol Wood. To this the enemy retaliated on us to some purpose, and we had two men killed and thirteen wounded. On this occasion Rifleman P. Walsh, a stretcher-bearer, proved himself so efficient and so regardless of danger that he was recommended for, and was duly awarded, the Military Medal.

Advance parties from the 1/5th Loyal North Lancashire Regiment, and also a liaison party from the New Zealand Division, now began to appear; and by 12.50 a.m. on June 30th the relief was over and we were making our way back to Rossignol Farm, where we took over, as "B" Battalion, Reserve Brigade, from the 2/4th Loyal North Lancashire Regiment. By 4 a.m. all were in their "bivvies."

The casualties for June amounted to 1 officer killed and 2 wounded, 12 men killed and 83 wounded. During the month we had received 211 men as reinforcements, and our ration strength was now 24 officers and 695 men.

The month of July was one of quiet and peace. We were still, it is true, under the shadow of a coming German offensive. We wired and dug unceasingly. We received orders of every description to meet every emergency. We were also kept in a state of perpetual readiness to move, and were liable to test movements at most inconvenient times. Corps and Divisional Commanders revelled in staff rides to tactical features of the ground; and the undoing of the foe, should he be bold enough to attack, was our constant thought and care.

Notwithstanding all this, quiet training, baths, competitions, Brigade and Divisional sports, went on almost as at home in England.

On July 1st Major Wilson, recently returned from Paris Plage Rest-house, took over the command from Colonel Fletcher, who proceeded to the Third Army School after presenting ribbons to those recently decorated. Captain Eccles also left this day for the Senior Officers' Course at Aldershot.

On July 2nd the 2nd Otago Regiment, New Zealand Division, relieved us at Rossignol Farm, and we moved into Corps Reserve in the Bois de Warnimont, between Authie and Bus Les Artois. Here we were on notice of one hour between 9 p.m. and 9 a.m., and two hours for the remainder of the day.

To test our readiness we received word at 7.50 a.m. on July 5th to move to our battle position in the Bus Loop, a phrase reminiscent of, but unconnected with, " strap hanging." We moved off at 8.10 a.m., and were in position at 9.22 a.m.—quite a creditable performance.

On July 6th Major Charles Wilson attended a Corps Commander's Staff ride, which involved hard riding over a good part of France with some sixty or seventy other officers, during which most contingencies were discussed and counter-measures devised. The possibilities of the situation seemed endless. However, we somehow managed to keep pace with Defence Schemes A, B, C, D, E, and F, with their various amendments and appendices ; and as the enemy never attacked, we may perhaps omit further reference to them, in spite of the important part they played in our lives at this time.

A more interesting event, perhaps, was the winning of the Light Heavies in the Brigade Boxing Competition by Sergeant Cox, our Sergeant-Bootmaker.

On July 15th we moved to a camp at Hénu, where Colonel Fletcher resumed command. We were still under the same emergency orders.

On July 21st and 22nd the Divisional Sports were held at Couin. Owing to the distance we had to come, we marched there and back in fighting order. The sports were a great success, and a pleasant variation in the usual routine.

"THE KING'S" (LIVERPOOL REGIMENT)

On July 23rd Colonel Fletcher relinquished command of the battalion at his own request, and Lieutenant-Colonel Hon. N. C. Gathorne-Hardy, Rifle Brigade, took over. Since his breakdown during the first tour in Gommecourt Colonel Fletcher had never been able fully to recover his old vitality, and, ever mindful of his battalion, chose to give up command rather than risk disaster to his " boys " by his breaking down during active operations. Few beyond his intimate friends know what it cost him to ask to be relieved, not from any sense of personal pride, but from his intense love for his battalion. His whole heart and soul were wrapped up in the 2/6th, and leaving it must have been painful to him indeed. The loss to the battalion was very great, and Colonel Fletcher's departure was keenly regretted by all ranks.

Colonel Gathorne-Hardy had for some time been commanding a battalion of the Rifle Brigade in Salonika, and had volunteered, with other Commanding Officers, to come to the Western Front after March 21st. He had not been long with the battalion before he became highly popular with all ranks, different as was his style of command from that to which we had been accustomed. We were lucky to get a Rifleman for a Commanding Officer, which was more than we had dared to hope.

On July 28th our spare kit was taken into store, and at 6.30 a.m. on July 29th we moved to our old billets at Ivergny, and thence at 9 a.m. the next morning to the Etrun area, which we reached at 5.15 p.m. after one hour's halt *en route* at Lattre St. Quentin for dinner. We spent the night in a hutted camp. Here we entrained at 10.30 p.m. at Artillery Corner, and moved up by light railway to the point where the Arras—Lens railway joins the River Scarpe. Here we detrained, and proceeded to the support trenches of the Fampoux South sector, relieving the 72nd Canadian Infantry Battalion. The relief proceeded without any interruption, and was completed by 1.30 a.m.

199

HISTORY OF THE 2/6TH (RIFLE) BATTALION

Before proceeding further, it will not be out of place to give a general description of the area in which the battalion now found itself situated.

Leaving Arras to the south, the River Scarpe takes its course westwards along a plateau as far as the village of Athies, at which point it enters a valley proper, with high ground on either side.

Slightly south-east from Athies a large re-entrant ran south from the river ; in the mouth of this re-entrant was the village of Feuchy.

Farther east down the stream, on the northern bank, the village of Fampoux covered the lower slopes of the high ground which here turned abruptly north. At this point a small triangular island, about 2,500 square yards in area, divided the Scarpe.

The British line, travelling south from Lens, followed the high ground overlooking Douai to Fampoux. Here it bent sharply to the west along the north slope of the valley, crossed the river at Feuchy, and took the line of the re-entrant already referred to— a direction roughly south-west.

The Brigade whilst on duty in this part of the line were responsible for the portion of it immediately north of the river, an area generally spoken of as the Fampoux sector.

The three battalions of the Brigade were disposed as follows : one in the line, one in close support, and the third in reserve at Ste. Catherine, north of Arras. The left flank of the battalion in the line was marked by a communication trench, Camel Avenue, which travelled straight from our rear through the sector over to No Man's Land to the German rear. From Camel Avenue to Fampoux the front line, known as Stoke Trench, with the exception of a very slight bulge towards the enemy, ran north to south, crossing the Arras road ; the front line entered Fampoux, and, passing through it, reached the river bank at the apex of the island.

200

"THE KING'S" (LIVERPOOL REGIMENT)

Fampoux, a village of fair size, was held by both sides, and as a result had few houses left standing, those to the south-west and on the island appearing to have fared the best.

The main road coming from Arras passed in succession through St. Nicolas, St. Laurent-Blangy, Athies, and Fampoux; at this point it became sunken, and then carried on eastwards through the German lines into Roeux.

From Fampoux a sunken road ran north to Gavrelle. Along this road, heavily protected by wire, ran the German front line.

Two kilometres behind, and parallel to, this portion of the German line ran the Roeux—Gavrelle road.

On the left of the sector behind this road rose Greenland Hill, flanked on its left rear by the spires and roofs of Douai.

The island originally carried the Pelves and Monchy—Le Preux roads over the Scarpe, but all the bridges being demolished, it was of little importance, and was merely held by our patrols at night.

From Feuchy to the island was a belt of marshland, bounded on the south by the Arras—Douai railway line, which roughly defined the German positions. Over these we maintained a strict watch from the hill north of the Scarpe.

The right flank of the battalion rested on Feuchy.

Several systems of support trenches ran from north to south down the sector, the most important one, Stoke Support, running parallel to the front line, and commanding it from an average distance of 400 yards.

The two main communication trenches were Camel Avenue in the north and Cam Avenue in the south.

Battalion Headquarters were situated in Cam Valley, a small depression about 400 yards long and 80 yards in width on the north side of the Arras road, north-east of Athies.

Athies, in the hands of support troops, was the ration dump for the sector, and also maintained communication over the river with Feuchy.

HISTORY OF THE 2/6TH (RIFLE) BATTALION

A battalion in reserve manned the Arras—Lens railway embankment between the Scarpe and the Arras road, finding ample and comfortable accommodation in the numerous " bivvies " and dug-outs covering its western slope.

From the top of the embankment a fire trench had an excellent command of the approach from Athies.

Between the embankment and St. Laurent Blangy, two kilometres farther west, intervened the woods, lakes, and grounds of Blangy Park, giving cover to our field batteries.

Brigade Headquarters was on the main road St. Laurent—Blangy; while Quartermaster's Stores and Transport were at Ste. Catherine, north of Arras.

Relieving troops, rations, and supplies were brought up to the sector by means of a light narrow-gauge trench railway, which, leaving the dump and railhead at Anzin St. Aubin, three kilometres north-west of Arras, struck the Scarpe at St. Nicolas, and, travelling along its north bank under the cover afforded by the trees with which it was lined, came to an end just short of Feuchy.

The dispositions of the battalion were—" A " and " C " Companies in Athies, " B " and " D " in Cam Valley. After being at first in the railway cutting, Battalion Headquarters moved on the evening of August 1st to the railway embankment, handing over their old Headquarters to the Munsters, and taking over from the 85th Canadian Infantry Battalion. The tour was very quiet, the only incident being some heavy bursts carried out from 11 a.m. to 7 p.m. on August 6th by our " heavies " on the enemy front line.

The same day a slight readjustment of the line took place between ourselves, the Munsters, and the 8th K.L.R. 2nd-Lieutenant Paterson and Rev. S. J. Hughes joined while we were here, and the Medical Officer was temporarily relieved by Lieutenant Gherman, M.O.R.C., U.S.A.

On August 8th we were relieved by the 2/7th K.L.R., and then proceeded to relieve the 8th K.L.R. in the front line. The operation was finally completed by 1.10 a.m. " D " and " C " Companies held the front line, " A " and " B " were in support.

The tour in the front line was hardly more eventful than when in support. The Corps Commander visited us on two occasions; the battalion on our right was unsuccessfully raided; " A " Company took a prisoner after a patrol encounter; and on August 13th sixteen officers and thirty-two other ranks of the American Army were attached for instruction.

There is no doubt that this was the most " cushy " sector the battalion ever occupied. The weather was fine and warm, the country pleasant, and but for a little artillery and one or two active trench mortars the enemy harmless. On August 15th we were relieved by the 2/7th K.L.R., with the exception of " D " Company, and moved back into reserve at Victory Camp. Here we spent a quiet two days cleaning and training, being joined by " D " Company on August 17th. On August 18th we moved to Ste. Catherine Camp at Anzin, where 2nd-Lieutenant D. J. Williams reported for duty.

CHAPTER VIII

BATTLE OF CAMBRAI

THE move from the line to Ste. Catherine Camp was the beginning of a series of movements, some leisurely, some hasty, which eventually brought the battalion into position to take its part in the Battle of Bapaume and the second Battle of Cambrai. The breaking of the famous " Hindenburg Line," on which the enemy had lavished such skill and pains, and on which it was evident he placed such firm reliance, finally altered the method of warfare from the concentrated attack on an organized trench system to the battle of movement in unfortified areas.

But before briefly describing the systems of the Hindenburg Line, and the general trend of the battle, the preceding movements of our battalion must be sketched.

On the evening of August 18th we moved back from Ste. Catherine Camp to the village of Anzin, two or three miles north-west of Arras, with instructions to move again very early next morning. This we certainly did, as we rose about 2 a.m., and had finished breakfast by 3 a.m. About 6 a.m. we moved down to the railway line between Anzin and St. Aubin—Artillery Point was the name of the spot—and entrained. A pleasant journey in open trucks on the light railway, which twisted and turned amid green woods and cornfields smiling in the lovely summer weather, brought us to Monchy Breton, about twenty miles west-north-west of Arras and some five miles north-east of St. Pol. Here we detrained and marched on about three miles to Magnicourt, another delightful little French village, which had escaped the destroying hand of war and nestled peacefully amid pleasant rural surroundings. Instead of the ordinary hutted camp that had formed our home at Anzin, we were billeted in comfortable farmhouses. We remained here for two days, doing a little quiet training; while some of the more privileged attended, on August 21st, a Tank lecture and demonstration at Monchy Breton. After settling down comfortably for the night, we were suddenly roused up again and told to be ready to move forthwith.

At 2.15 a.m. we were again on the march, and after passing through Chelers and Tinques, arrived about 3.45 a.m. at Penin, some nine miles due south of our starting-point. After breakfast all ranks turned into bed for a good sleep, "Reveillé" being at noon. It was a gorgeous day, but terribly hot, and the effect of the morning's sleep, coupled with the heat, made everyone feel very lethargic. At 9.25 the same night we set off once more, this time due south, passing Givenchy, Lignereuil, Grand Rullecourt, and Sus St. Leger, and reaching Ivergny at 2.45 a.m. on August 23rd. The march had been somewhat complicated by our having to cut across a Canadian Division moving west-north-west. We expected to renew our nocturnal rambles that night, but we were left in peace for twenty-four hours, resuming our march at 2.15 p.m. on August 24th in a north-easterly direction through Sombrin to Barly, some ten miles away, which we reached at 6.45 p.m.

At Barly we remained two days, making final preparations for the offensive. Seven officers and sixty men were detailed for the "nucleus party," and Major C. W. Wilson was appointed to command the Brigade "nucleus." At 11.30 p.m. we left Barly for Ficheux area, arriving at Le Chat Maigre at 2.45 a.m. on August 27th. Here we made a halt, and lay down to rest in the open fields. The march had been made in a fine, clear night and under ideal conditions, and the bivouac was really delightful.

The proximity of active hostilities was evidenced by (among other things) a number of tanks, both large and small, which waddled up the road near us. But the conditions were very different from those at Passchendaele the previous year. There you saw only an interminable stretch of mud and water, with never a living thing to vary the monotony of the scene except soaked and muddy soldiers. Here, on the contrary, we had fine rolling country, dry and firm, which even a spell of wet weather did not convert into a muddy swamp. Ripe corn stood ready for the cutting, birds sang, and save for the distant rumble of the guns all was peaceful and still. The villages, it is true, were razed to the ground and often half overgrown with grass and weeds—sad reminders of the first Battle of Cambrai ; the ground was scarred and pocked with shell-holes, and the ravages of war were only too obvious in many other ways. Yet even in the war zone itself the open, rolling country was always pleasant to the eye, and the ground dry and firm except during actual rain.

At 11 p.m. we moved off to another field a few miles away at Mercatel, arriving soon after midnight. What might be described as our " circular tour of France " was now drawing to a close. These night marches, with all the comic incidents connected with night bivouacs, the confusion of settling down or setting off in the profound darkness, which the restless bombing 'planes made imperative, were soon to be but pleasing memories. One march more was to bring us to the Hindenburg Line.

At 11.30 a.m. we moved off, and in due course arrived at St. Martin, just in front of the redoubtable Line, and the Commanding Officer proceeded to the place forthwith. Meanwhile the men settled down in shell-holes amid the ruins, while Battalion Headquarters was established deep down in a dug-out under the remains of the church. Walking wounded and German prisoners were much in evidence. After a short delay the battalion moved in for the night into the Hindenburg front line, with all its mass of trenches, wire, and dug-outs—a truly magnificent work, but looking somewhat forlorn now that the tide of war had rolled eastward.

"THE KING'S" (LIVERPOOL REGIMENT)

At 7 p.m. on August 29th we moved a little farther along the line, which here bent back in an easterly direction. This brought us to a point nearly due east of Fontaine Lez Croisilles, which was some 2,500 yards away and in close vicinity to the other two Brigades of our Division, which were already in action.

At 10 a.m. the battalion was ordered to take up its position as Brigade Reserve, the 2/7th and 8th Battalions K.L.R having moved up to form a defensive flank during the attack of the Canadian Division on Upton Wood, which was about a mile and a half west of Fontaine.

The companies took up ground positions on the south-west and south-east of Fontaine respectively.

At 6.30 a.m. on August 30th the Brigade took over the front line from the 170th Brigade, of our Division, and the battalion concentrated west of Fontaine. We had now come into the fringe of the battle zone, and had three men killed and four wounded. We remained in this area till the next day, August 31st, when we received orders at 9.30 p.m. that we were to attack on September 1st at 6.5 p.m.

Before describing the attack it should be stated that it was the final stage of the Battle of Bapaume, which had opened on August 21st on the whole front of the Third Army and the left wing of the Fourth Army. It finally resulted in the capture of 3,400 prisoners and 270 guns, and the advance of the line Roye (on the Amiens—Noyon road) to Arleux, ten miles north-west of Arras, up to a line which ran west of Nesle, Peronne, and Bullecourt. In other words, the enemy had been driven right across the old Somme battlefield, and the northern portion of the Hindenburg Line had been pierced. The action in which the battalion, in conjunction with other troops, took part was intended to complete the success which the previous day's fighting had won, and prepare the way for the next great assault. The following extract from the *Morning Post* dated September 3rd, 1918, is worth quoting at this point.

207

HISTORY OF THE 2/6TH (RIFLE) BATTALION

"THE LANCASHIRES' ACHIEVEMENT.

"The breaking of this line was an intricate operation, and a detailed account of its accomplishment would be too technical for the average reader. It is sufficient to say that the Drocourt Line is a series of parallel trenches in two groups, known as the front and support systems, running northward out of the Hindenburg system near Quéant, and in front of the villages of Cagnicourt, Dury, and Etaing to the River Scarpe. Against the greater part of the line—that is, from Etaing on the Scarpe down to Cagnicourt—the English troops and Canadians had only simple front and support trenches to cross. On the right, however, the great triangle of closely woven ditches and tunnels was a much harder obstacle, and our progress in this region has been much slower in the preliminary stages of the advance. You know the trouble caused by Bullecourt and Hendecourt, even more by Riencourt, all of them lying fast in the meshes of the joined defensive systems —Hindenburg and Drocourt—a solid mass of earthworks over three miles deep, riddled with secret refuges and machine-gun emplacements.

"Before the main attack could be made it was essential that we held Hendecourt and Riencourt. That was effected yesterday evening by Lancashire troops. Bullecourt had already been prized loose from the Hindenburg Line by Londoners after several sanguinary efforts and severe counter-attacks. Riencourt had withstood all blows by reason of its commanding position, a group of village walls on a slight crest encircled by trench protected by outlying redoubts. The Lancashires facing it knew its worth. Hendecourt, besides Riencourt, was hardly less difficult a nut to crack. They had been fighting without rest in their conquered portion of the maze. Two days running they delivered attacks at noon, followed by one at four o'clock the next morning. The same night—the night of Sunday—they went out to storm these citadels of the Hun that the victory of to-day might be complete.

MŒUVRES, INCHY, AND CANAL DU NORD
Oblique Aeroplane Photograph.

"THE KING'S" (LIVERPOOL REGIMENT)

They found both village ruins full of Germans and machine guns. It was the usual mixed experience, surrender in the open and resistance in the cellars. Some of the Germans ran away, others rallied under their officers.

" Riencourt and Hendecourt contained many German bodies when they were left quiet, deserted by the forward surge of the battle front, the survivors of grim hand-to-hand encounters with the Lancashire men and their bayonets. All night long the ' mopping up' continued. Hardly had the secret places been declared clear when the Lancashires had to attack again and take up their share of the greater advance at dawn. The Canadians and their brother Britishers on their left know the debt they owe these stout lads of the North, whose unflagging efforts enabled them to attack with easy minds, knowing their flank would be secure.

" Riencourt captured, the striking troops were within easy reach of the Drocourt Line. At Riencourt itself the distance was not over half a mile. Higher up the Canadians on both sides of the Cambrai road were closer at some places. Their front was nearly straight. Before them were unobstructed fields, little scarred by shell, with dull red banks of tangled wire stretched taut in front of the white band of trenches, the ground behind rising gently with the tips of broken roofs and the Church towers of the villages laid against the rain-swept sky of grey.

*   *   *   *   *

" It is now necessary to return to the Lancashire men who were on the Canadian right. They had to attack and pass through the triangle I have described, east of Riencourt. Some of them followed behind the Canadians, then slipped south-east into the trenches and mopped them up. By last accounts they were working satisfactorily down the line of the triangle, and clearing out nests of machine guns. The drive through to Buissy was a phase of the attack following this operation of the Lancashire men.

HISTORY OF THE 2/6TH (RIFLE) BATTALION

" This despatch is necessarily very incomplete, for the battle is still going on and news comes back slowly. Fresh German divisions are no doubt coming up. The Canadians on Mont Dury at eight o'clock could see masses of grey moving westwards at several places ; and although some of the German artillery had begun to drop back, the bombardment was still very heavy. The intermixture of enemy troops is extraordinary. In one narrow Canadian sector prisoners have been taken from seven different divisions. Lancashires on the right have taken them from six divisions. There are Saxons, fresh 1st Guards Reserve, battered 2nd Guards Reserve, bits of the 30th from Bapaume, and the 12th Reserve from Bullecourt ; 7th Cavalry Division, fighting dismounted, and badly at that, and apparently other relics of the fighting of the past three weeks served up with fresh dressing, in the shape of a few rested divisions from ' the back of beyond.' It is a most disorderly order of battle. Something appears to have cracked besides the Drocourt Line."

To return to actual details. At 4.40 a.m. on September 1st the 2/7th and 8th K.L.R. attacked and captured Hendecourt, and advanced to a line running from Terrier Alley (about 1,000 yards due west of Riencourt) up Greyhound Trench to Hendecourt Chateau, about 1,000 yards due north of Riencourt.

The 2/6th K.L.R., in conjunction with two companies of 2/7th K.L.R. on our left and the 52nd Division on our right, were now to attack in the evening and capture Riencourt Lez Cagnicourt, and consolidate a line 500 yards east of the village. The formation was two companies in front—" C " Company (Captain Williams) on the right and " B " Company (Captain Robinson) on the left ; " D " Company (Lieutenant Noon) was in support, with " A " Company (Lieutenant Sage) in reserve.

After spending the night of August 31st–September 1st in an area just west of Fontaine, the battalion moved forward by Crux Trench at 3.15 p.m. in the order " B," " C," " D," " A."

210

The trench at this point was extremely shallow, and there can be little doubt that the movement of the battalion was observed.

The forming-up positions were as follows : The front line companies moved on a line running along the lower part of Terrier Alley, and thence in a northerly direction across to Greyhound Avenue, on the southern edge of Hendecourt, which positions had been captured by the 2/7th K.L.R. in the morning. " D " Company were some 300 yards in rear in Morden Trench ; " A " Company were some 1,200 yards farther back.

The orders were that the Hendecourt—Bullecourt road was not to be crossed till 5.15 p.m. Just at this moment as the companies were moving to cross this road an aeroplane came over, flying very low, and immediately afterwards the enemy artillery opened out on Crux Trench and the road with 5·9's and gas shells, causing many casualties to both " B " and " C " Companies, including many N.C.Os. The aeroplane also fired several belts of ammunition at the men as they lined up.

In spite of this bombardment, the companies moved steadily to their appointed positions, and were ready at 6 p.m., and great credit is due for this to their platoon commanders. Just before zero (6.5 p.m.) the barrage of the right Division (52nd) opened, which caused the enemy to drop a protective barrage on our front also. Luckily, this fell about 100 yards in rear of our companies, and no harm was done. At 6.5 p.m. our artillery opened on the barrage line for three minutes, during which period the two leading companies (with two platoons in front and two in support) advanced through the 8th K.L.R. and moved forward with sections in " worms " up to the barrage. This at zero plus three minutes moved forward at the rate of 200 yards in eight minutes, settling down finally for ninety minutes on the German side of our objective, Emu Alley and Wolf Trench, the far side of Riencourt.

The moment the barrage lifted the enemy opened on our forming-up line, shortening from time to time .but so well did our men keep up to our own barrage that the enemy's was always behind us.

The first opposition was encountered by the right platoon of " C " Company, who were held up by heavy machine-gun fire. The supporting platoon at once commenced an enveloping movement, which apparently disheartened the foe, as the post retired into a dug-out, out of which they were bombed, and the survivors made prisoners. " B " Company then advanced again with three platoons in front, though as progress was made sections darted off to deal with individual posts. " C " Company encountered little opposition till they approached the west edge of the village, when our own barrage, unfortunately, came back 200 yards, causing considerable casualties. A third platoon was accordingly sent forward to reinforce, and just at this moment heavy machine-gun fire was opened from the sunken road. No. 6 Section promptly dashed forward and successfully dealt with this nest of machine guns, when the company proceeded to deploy and move through the village, " B " Company continuing the line from the southern part of the village to the Brigade boundary.

The enemy now concentrated his artillery fire on the village, and both companies sustained somewhat serious casualties. Moreover, some of the enemy had gone to ground, and, reappearing after the leading wave had passed through, came up and opened fire on them from behind. A section was consequently detached to put a stop to this, and successfully drove the enemy back into the arms of " D " Company, who were " mopping up," twenty-one Germans being taken prisoners.

During the passage of the village 2nd-Lieutenant Anderson (No. 5 Platoon) became a casualty, and Sergeant Adlington took over command ; while in " C " Company 2nd-Lieutenants Upward and Paterson were both wounded. Corporal Stevenson, finding both his platoon officer and sergeant out of action, assumed command of his platoon and led them successfully to their final objective in a masterly fashion.

"THE KING'S" (LIVERPOOL REGIMENT)

After passing through the village, where numerous prisoners had been taken, the companies advanced steadily over difficult country to their final objectives. These were reached by " B " and " C " Companies at 7.10 p.m. and 7.15 p.m. respectively.

Shortly before this 2nd-Lieutenant T. L. Williams (No. 11 Platoon) was most unfortunately killed by a shell, and his place was taken by Sergeant Warren, who took the men over to their objective, which he consolidated with marked ability.

The enemy still held out with one very determined machine-gun party at Wolf Alley, and the advance was slightly checked. Rifleman Dury, with the utmost coolness, scored a direct hit on the gun at point-blank range with a rifle grenade, and the whole gun team were taken prisoners.

At 7.25 p.m. the contact aeroplane passed over as prearranged, and the flares were lit. By 9 p.m. both companies had completed the consolidation of their objectives, and on the right were in touch with the Scots Fusiliers. The left company, however, had not succeeded in getting touch with the 2/7th K.L.R., so Captain Robinson and Corporal Lee set out at 9.45 p.m. to try and find the right post of the left battalion. Soon after starting they ran into a party of the enemy, consisting of one officer and twenty-one men, which was apparently working round our left flank. The enemy proceeded to get his machine gun into action, but the officer and N.C.O. who were attending to it were promptly shot dead by Robinson and Lee, while five men of the party were killed as they tried to take cover, whereupon the remainder at once surrendered. For this fine performance and his general conduct throughout the operations, of which too much cannot be said, Captain Robinson received a bar to his Military Cross, while Corporal Lee was awarded the Military Medal.

The left battalion was located about 10 p.m., but being 500 yards away two sections were moved up from " D " Company to fill the gap, the rest of that company forming supporting posts.

213

They had done their " mopping up " well, and took fifty prisoners in Riencourt itself.

Such is a brief and bald account of the taking of Riencourt, a feat of which the battalion may well be proud. The barrage that fell on them as they were moving forward to their assembly positions might well have disorganized the attack. As it was, the N.C.Os. and riflemen rose to the occasion as their seniors became casualties, and carried on admirably. Some names have already been mentioned, but some additions must be made. Rifleman Lewis, after his Company Sergeant-Major and the other N.C.O. at Company Headquarters were knocked out, took charge of the Headquarters personnel and kept up communication with all concerned. Rifleman Prior on liaison patrol tackled a German party of eight men with such determination that two were killed and the rest captured. Sergeant Haigh proved a skilful and bold platoon commander ; Rifleman Dodd an equally dashing section commander. Riflemen Hatton, Fairclough, and Atkin ran backwards and forwards unceasingly throughout the action, keeping up communication ; while Rifleman Mount, as stretcher-bearer, was untiring in his efforts, and entirely regardless of danger. He organized enemy stretcher parties, and many of the battalion wounded undoubtedly owe their lives to his energy and resource.

The resistance offered varied. Generally speaking, from covered positions it was determined. One or two groups certainly gave in rather too readily. One party in particular of the 66th (Würtemberg) Regiment, sixteen strong, issued from a dug-out, pushing in front of them the usual Red Cross man. This fellow came along holding his medicine chest at arm's length, with an expression on his face of " I am touching wood " which was really comical.

The total prisoners captured by us that day amounted to 170, with 13 machine guns and a trench mortar. As against this, we had 1 officer killed and 3 wounded, 19 men killed and 95 wounded.

"THE KING'S" (LIVERPOOL REGIMENT)

The following criticism of a German Sergeant-Major, made to the Divisional Intelligence Officer, may be quoted here in the form in which it was passed on to us.

"57TH DIVISION P. OF W. CAGE,
"2—9—1918.

"A.D.C. FOR G.O.C. 57TH DIVISION.

"In the course of a conversation with a Sergeant-Major of the 7th Cavalry Division, this N.C.O. expressed warm admiration for the British as soldiers, and particularly for the way in which the attack was carried out when he was captured. He said he had not seen a finer attack, and knew how an attack should be carried out, because he had formerly belonged to a 'Sturm' Battalion.

"He said that the infantry were into the trenches the moment the barrage ' lifted,' and this was confirmed by an artillery Observation Officer, who also mentioned that the attack had been very smartly carried out.

"The N.C.O., when asked what badges the attacking troops wore, said they were green diamonds.

(Sgd.)   " S. A. SPALL, *Lieutenant,*
" *Intelligence Officer,*
" *57th Division.*

" *September 2nd,* 1918."

Hearty congratulations on our success were received both from the Commander-in-Chief and from our more immediate Commanders.

In this action, in addition to the rewards already mentioned, Captain Williams and Lieutenant Harris were awarded the Military Cross, and twelve men the Military Medal.

The next morning the Battle of Cambrai and the Hindenburg Line opened with a general attack by the Third Army; and before nightfall we were three miles behind the front line, the 172nd Brigade of our Division and the 63rd Division having passed

215

through us. We had a magnificent view of the battle, and the sight of our artillery galloping up and opening fire was a most welcome reminder of the new type of warfare which was now taking the place of the old. After one peaceful day we were ordered, on September 3rd, to concentrate in the vicinity of Hendecourt, where the rear headquarters, transport, and " nucleus party " joined us.

Here we remained quietly, cleaning up and training, till September 6th, the only excitement being a high velocity gun which shelled us on that day, wounding two men.

This day we received orders to move into the line in the vicinity of Inchy the next day (September 7th), in order to relieve the 190th Brigade, of the 63rd Division. Accordingly, at 10 a.m. our advance party set off to the trenches, followed in the evening by the rest of the battalion.

The Royal Fusiliers, from whom we took over, were in support, and the relief was complete at 2 a.m. on September 9th. The rear headquarters and transport meantime moved to Quéant. Nothing of any moment happened this day in the line. We were issued with a defence scheme, from which we learnt that the Guards Division were on our right and the 2nd Canadian Division on our left ; while we were to be responsible for the main line of resistance, a section of the Hindenburg Support Line about 1,200 yards in extent running round the south-west outskirts of Inchy. " A," " D," and " C " Companies were in front, and " B " in support. The other two battalions were responsible for the temporary main line of resistance, east of Inchy.

Later on during the day these orders were altered, but only in the matter of exact frontages. At " stand-to " on September 10th " D" Company dropped in for some attention, 2nd-Lieutenant Green, who had but recently joined, being wounded, along with one or two others. Otherwise little happened. On September 11th the 2/7th and 8th K.L.R. attempted, at 6.15 p.m., to establish posts on the Canal du Nord. This great canal stands roughly north and south about 1,000 yards east of Inchy and about 500 yards east of Mœuvres, the latter place being just over a mile south-south-east of Inchy. The ground had been excavated to a great depth, and very large banks constructed, but the canal had never been finished and contained no water (*see* photo.). It was, notwithstanding, a formidable obstacle, being 20 feet deep in places, though the embankment had been pierced in places for roads and tram-lines. Opposite Mœuvres the canal banks were in some places quite low.

The attempt of the other two battalions to establish posts proved unsuccessful, and at 10.15 p.m. our " C " Company was pushed forward to replace " A " Company of the 8th K.L.R. in the Hindenburg Line.

At 12.55 a.m. on September 12th orders were received for our Battalion Headquarters to join Headquarters of the 8th K.L.R. ; and we were warned that as many as three companies might be required to form a defensive flank north-east of Mœuvres. At 3.30 a.m. " A " Company was ordered forward for this purpose, with instructions to form platoon posts in Cemetery Trench, just north of Mœuvres, and to gain touch with the 170th Brigade on the right. It was now nearly daylight, and the company experienced the greatest difficulty in gaining its position, as there was no cover, and touch was not obtained with the 170th Brigade. At 6 p.m. the enemy counter-attacked on the Inchy—Mœuvres line, and " A " Company, finding itself being outflanked, after hard fighting was obliged to withdraw. In the course of this movement Lieutenant Sage, the Company Commander and a very gallant officer, and seven men were killed, and twenty-one men wounded.

That night the battalion was relieved by the 2/4th South Lancashire Regiment and one company of the Munster Fusiliers. This was completed at 5.30 a.m. on September 13th. Our new dispositions were two companies in the Buissy Switch and two in the Hindenburg Support north-east of Pronville. After remaining here for two days we learnt, on September 15th, that we were to be relieved by the 52nd Division and go back for a short rest. Taking everything into consideration, we had had a pretty strenuous time since we left Anzin on our preliminary marches, and after our first arrival in the battle area had had our share of fighting and shelling. There was, of course, no cover from the weather except in trenches. Villages had for the most part long since ceased to exist, and were but grass-grown mounds with notice boards to indicate what places they had once been. Our casualties had been fairly heavy, and the reduction in officers and N.C.Os., of course, threw extra work on the remainder, whose opportunities for sleep and rest, small as they were likely to be in any case, were thus further curtailed. A few days' rest and all would be well again, so we greeted the news that we were going back for a while with no little pleasure.

The relief by the 7th Cameronians commenced at 1.30 p.m. on September 16th with Battalion Headquarters, " A " and " D " Companies. This was finished by 4.30 p.m. " C " and " B " Companies could not be relieved till after dark, but had finished by 11.30 p.m. There was very little hostile activity during the relief, only two men being wounded, and the companies made their way back to Croisilles for the night in their own time.

Next day, September 17th, we moved to Boyelles, and entrained there at 4 p.m. for Saulty. Here we detrained and marched to Barly, arriving there at 7.10 p.m. Our rest at Barly will live long in the memory of the battalion. We had enjoyed periods out of the line before, but never was any place so acceptable as Barly. Everyone arrived full of that comfortable feeling which only hard work well done can produce. All were pleasantly tired, but quite ready to make the most of the golden hours so long as they should last. Even the senior officers of the battalion became light-hearted and youthful. Were not the Commanding Officer and the Padre seen hurrying up the main street with pockets and arms filled with bottles of " bubbly," and in no way disconcerted on reaching the Mess to find that a supply had already been obtained ? Our stay lasted till September 25th, and during that time we rested and trained, cleared up and repaired, and generally made ready for the resumption of the offensive.

The second instalment of " Cheerio," published by the " Whizz-bang Press," and edited by Rifleman Wheway, of " B " Company, duly made its appearance, and was acclaimed as a great journalistic success. The "Cheerios" Concert Party made its début here, and produced a really first-class entertainment in the Cinema on September 22nd. As to the doings of these artistes more will be said hereafter.

A number of officers joined us at Barly—2nd-Lieutenant Alty, D.C.M., and 2nd-Lieutenant Shirt on the 18th, 2nd-Lieutenant Hardy on the 21st, 2nd-Lieutenant D. R. Williams on the 22nd, and Lieutenant Kissan on September 23rd. As against this, more than one officer was now suffering from dysentery brought on by shell gas, and Lieutenant Penrice, Captain Robinson, and 2nd-Lieutenant Lever had to be evacuated.

Captain Robinson in particular was a great loss. His command of men was truly remarkable. Forceful and brave in the extreme, he had at Riencourt the opportunity to show the stuff he was made of, and proved himself a fine officer. Lieutenant Kissan took over command of " B " Company.

On September 25th we learnt that our rest was over and that work was before us once more. At 8.40 a.m. on September 26th we entrained at Saulty and proceeded to Vaux Vraucourt, which was reached at 3 p.m. A march took us thence to our concentration area near Quéant, which we reached at 5 p.m. At 2.50 a.m. on September 27th the battalion moved forward from the concentration area to the first assembly position, which was in the Hindenburg front line about 500 yards south-west of Pronville. This was reached at 4.30 a.m. At zero (5.20 a.m.) the battalion moved forward to the second assembly position, which was about 600 yards west of Mœuvres, arriving there at 12.30 p.m.

219

HISTORY OF THE 2/6TH (RIFLE) BATTALION

The battalion now opened up into artillery formation and advanced across the Canal du Nord, through an arm of the Hindenburg Support Line, and on to some high ground about a mile east of Mœuvres. Here we settled down and waited for the attack to develop.

The scheme of operations was on a large scale. The 52nd and 63rd Divisions were to capture the first objective (Red Line), which ran north and south just beyond the main system of the Hindenburg Support Line; and then the second objective (Brown Line), which ran through Anneux Chapel round Anneux to east of Graincourt. After this, the 171st and 172nd Brigades of the 57th Division were to pass through and capture the third objective (Blue Line), which ran round the east side of Fontaine, west of La Folie and east of Cantaing. The 170th Brigade were then to seize the crossings of the Canal de L'Escaut if not already taken, and carry the attack farther. The Canadians on the left and the Guards on the right were continuing the line of attack north and south with the same relative objectives. The 6th Dragoon Guards and Corps cyclists were in reserve; and orders were issued to make a swift advance possible if the conditions should prove favourable. In consequence of these movements, the accumulation of troops behind the front line was very considerable. The country was similar to what had been covered in the previous attacks, though perhaps some of the rolling slopes were bolder and the sunken roads deeper.

Everywhere you looked were groups of men dotted about, and the enemy proceeded to shell vigorously, as the force opposite his front was only too conspicuous. At about 1.30 p.m. a message was received from the 8th K.L.R. that the Sugar Factory beyond the Red Line on the Cambrai—Bapaume road had not been captured, and that in consequence the attack of the 57th Division could not take place.

There was nothing, therefore, to do but for the battalion to dig in, which they proceeded to do under heavy machine-gun and artillery fire, a none too pleasant task.

At 4.30 p.m. news was received that the 63rd Division had captured the Sugar Factory; and at 5.30 p.m. General Long-bourne, our Brigadier, arrived at Battalion Headquarters. It now appeared that the attacking divisions had made progress towards their second objective, and that it was our turn to continue the operation.

Our instructions were to capture Cantaing Trench and Support. This was a double line of trenches which ran in a south-south-easterly direction from the south side of Bourlon Wood round the south-east side of Anneux down to Cantaing. To reach this line we were to move down to our objective from the north, using the section of Cantaing Trench and Support that ran along the west and south sides of Bourlon Wood, and obtaining cover from the vood itself.

It was decided to attack on a two company front—" D " on the right, " C " on the left, with " B " in support and " A " in reserve. " C " Company was responsible for the clearance of Cantaing Trench. Zero was 6.20 p.m., at which hour a twenty minutes' barrage was to begin. The companies moved over at 6 p.m., but the barrage never came off. However, at about 9.30 p.m. word was received from Captain Fell that, as neither Cantaing Trench nor Support was half dug or continuous, he thought it inadvisable to continue before daylight. This was approved.

At 4.30 a.m. on September 28th Captain Patteson, the Brigade Major, arrived with fresh orders. The battalion were now to capture a trench just west of Fontaine and round the southern edge of that place to the east end of Cantaing, the attack to commence at 6.20 a.m.

The formation for the attack was the same as had already been detailed, except that " B " and " A " Companies were given objectives on the left of the attack.

221

HISTORY OF THE 2/6TH (RIFLE) BATTALION

Companies moved off at 6.15 a.m. and at 9.30 a.m. Captain Fell and Captain Williams reported that they had gained their objectives and were moving through Fontaine—where a Divisional Headquarters, complete with maps and papers, was occupied—to take up positions on the east side.

While proceeding to attack Anneux, Lieutenant James, commanding " A " Company, was severely wounded. Notwithstanding, he carried on for eighteen hours, and was only evacuated at length by the direct orders of the Commanding Officer. For his gallantry on this occasion he was awarded the Military Cross.

Platoon posts were established by the three companies, " B," " C " and " D," east of Fontaine, " A " Company being on the western outskirts of the village. The casualties were 2nd-Lieutenant Shirt and ten men wounded. The same morning the 170th Infantry Brigade passed through us to capture the Marcoing Line, which runs north and south about 1,400 yards east of Fontaine, but, having failed to do so, were withdrawn through us early in the morning of September 29th. At 7.30 a.m. on September 29th information was received that the Canadians had captured the Marcoing Line as far south as the trenches just north of the railway embankment which cuts the Cambrai—Bapaume road. Two patrols from " D " and " B " companies were despatched in consequence at 9.30 a.m. to " mop up " the balance of this line north of the Canal De l'Escaut. " D " Company's patrol reached the sunken road which runs from the north end of La Folie Wood towards Cambrai, but were there held up by machine-gun fire. 2nd-Lieutenant Waln and " B " Company's patrol worked along the north side of the railway embankment, which runs from about 100 yards north of Fontaine due east, till they got in touch with the southernmost post of the Canadians in the Marcoing Line. Turning south, he proceeded to clear the Marcoing Line, fighting his way with the utmost coolness and gallantry. At the very outset several of his men were knocked

222

out by artillery and machine-gun fire, but he worked his way doggedly along. Being presently reinforced by another platoon, he completed the clearing of this section of the line, joining hands finally with " D " Company's patrol at the southern end of this section of the line. He finished his task at 6.30 p.m., and brought in one machine gun and sixteen prisoners. For this very gallant performance, which was highly complimented by the Canadians, 2nd-Lieutenant Waln was recommended for the Military Cross, but was awarded a Divisional Commander's Card of Congratulations only. Lance-Corporal Chambers was awarded the Military Medal in the same connection.

At 3 p.m. news was received that the enemy was falling back, and an attack on Proville Trench, on the east side of the Canal De l'Escaut, was ordered. The same formation was prescribed as before, and the advance began at 6.30 p.m. About 7.10 p.m. Captain Fell reported that his company (" D ") were across the Canal de l'Escaut, little opposition being encountered. Shortly afterwards " C " and " B " Companies reported to the same effect. " A " Company were remaining in reserve on our side of the canal and La Folie Wood. But at this point our difficulties began. " C " Company, as darkness fell, found themselves floundering in a swamp, and could make no headway. " D " Company's left platoon reached Proville Trench, but came under heavy machine-gun fire and were forced back to the lock. The rest of that company were similarly checked by the fusilade, and the company established itself in the vicinity of the lock, about 400 yards west of Proville. Reference was made to Battalion Headquarters, and instructions were issued to wait for the dawn to renew the attack.

At 10 p.m. Battalion Headquarters moved up into La Folie Wood and occupied some huts close to the canal, where they were shelled continuously throughout the night with the utmost vigour. At 12.20 a.m. " A " Company was sent over the canal, and a further attack by the leading companies was attempted. However, the enemy machine guns, which had a perfect field of fire, were too much for the attackers, and caused severe casualties. All that could be done was done, Sergeant Bibby in particular distinguishing himself on this occasion, but it became evident that a mere frontal attack was useless. It was accordingly decided that " D " Company should renew the frontal attack while " A " Company supported by " C " Company was to work round the sunken road which ran from our right towards Proville. However, before this order could take effect we were informed that the 2/7th K.L.R. would take over and carry out this attack, which they did successfully, our battalion being concentrated west of the canal by 4 p.m.

At 6 p.m. the 2/5th King's Own Royal Lancaster Regiment relieved us, and the battalion withdrew to bivouac in an open field just west of Fontaine and on the south side of the Cambrai—Bapaume road. This completed an awkward period of desultory but difficult fighting. We took twenty-one prisoners, with one machine gun and one trench mortar, but had two officers killed and two wounded, while among the men there were fifty-nine casualties. The officers killed were 2nd-Lieutenant Purdie, a most popular and gallant Scotsman who had been with us for a long while, and had seen active service during the greater part of the war ; and 2nd-Lieutenant Alty, D.C.M., who had only joined us at Barly, but whose worth we knew, as he won his D.C.M. when serving at Houplines in the ranks of the 2/7th K.L.R. Of the officers wounded, Lieutenant James has been already mentioned ; the other was 2nd-Lieutenant Shirt, who, like Alty, had joined us at Barly, and we regretted his swift departure to " Blighty." Among the men the loss of Company Sergeant-Major Woodward, of " C " Company, who was wounded during the concentration in front of the Canal du Nord, was the most serious. He was one of the very old members of the battalion who had risen steadily to warrant rank. He was badly wounded and his subsequent death in hospital was universally deplored.

PRONVILLE.

INCHY.

QUÉANT.

The Imperial War Museum.

Official Photograph by permission of

Company Quartermaster-Sergeant G. Lane was promoted to fill the vacancy that had occurred.

For the whole of September, during a good part of which the battalion had been engaged in active operations, our casualties had totalled as follows :—Four officers killed and 10 wounded ; 47 men killed and 188 wounded ; 13 men missing. Our "effective strength" was 34 officers and 708 men, as against 42 officers and 919 men on September 1st. Our "trench strength" was, as always, considerably lower than our "effective strength," as the latter included everyone detached, whether on duty or leave, who was not counted in the war establishment of another unit. Moreover, the Transport, rear headquarters, and the $33\frac{1}{3}$ per cent. forming the "nucleus party" have to be further deducted to show the number of "rifles" available for fighting purposes.

The battalion remained in its present position till October 4th. Our habitation consisted of the remnants of old enemy trenches and shell-holes in an open field. To the west of this, at a distance of some 200 yards from the nearest "bivvies," was a line of six 6-inch howitzers, which was continued by six 60-pounders. These two batteries were almost continuously in action, and were frequently engaged in firing salvos for barrages, and the effects of their presence had to be experienced to be properly appreciated. Except for these—and it is a very big exception — we were quiet enough. On October 1st some shells fell among our most eastern "bivvies" and wounded three men. Apart from this we were not troubled ; but the hum of aeroplanes filled the air all night, while the detonations from bombs were sufficiently close to remind one of the unpleasant possibility of our turn coming next.

The weather was fine and mild, but beyond cleaning up and repairing the damage of war very little training was attempted, except some useful demonstrations of the best method of coping with hostile machine guns. On October 1st 2nd-Lieutenant Simpson and a draft of sixty men arrived, which was a welcome reinforcement. The Adjutant had also returned from the United Kingdom and resumed his duties, Captain Bowring departing shortly after to England for a well-earned leave.

Rear headquarters and the transport remained in the field on the north side of the Cambrai—Bapaume road close up to the south-west edge of Bourlon Wood, where they had moved on the evening of September 29th.

Bourlon Wood showed little signs outwardly of the hurricane fire to which it had been treated both in 1917 and again recently. It covers a large area, but is chiefly composed of small bushy trees with but few of the large and stately boles which show the effect of shell fire so markedly. Inside the wood the scent of gas was still fairly strong; while derelict tanks and endless fragments of foreign and British equipment served to show what hard fighting had taken place in its green glades. Forward of Fontaine the country to our immediate front was far less bold in its hills and valleys than the ground that we had traversed. It still consisted of rolling downs, but the slopes were gradual and less pronounced ; and whole areas, especially in the vicinity of the canal, were dead flat right up to Cambrai itself, of which one could obtain a good view from the high ground on which Bourlon Wood itself stands. Columns of smoke could be seen rising from the town, and not infrequent explosions showed that the enemy was preparing for his departure.

An unpleasant incident had occurred with a " booby trap " at Riencourt, which caused the death of a rifleman and hurled Quartermaster Smith to a considerable distance. Consequently, when the fire by the Battalion Headquarters tent suddenly blew up, lodging a considerable quantity of hot potato in the eyes of the cook, we were somewhat alarmed. It turned out, however, to be only a small bomb detonator that the heat had exploded.

While we were in bivouac here word came that the Commanding Officer had been awarded the D.S.O. Although he modestly referred to it as being a recognition of the merit of the battalion, all ranks felt that it was richly deserved. His unofficial exploits in rallying and taking forward stragglers from other units had been noted with approval by the men, and throughout the operations he had been conspicuous by his total disregard of personal safety.

On October 4th we moved up from reserve into support with two companies (" A " and " B ") in the Marcoing Line and " C " and " D " Company in support. Battalion Headquarters were to have occupied the Chateau Pill-box at the corner of La Folie Wood, but this was already in occupation, and eventually they were accommodated for the night in a deep dug-out in the sunken road some two or three hundred yards farther back and next door to Brigade Headquarters.

Next morning (October 5th), most unfortunately, Brigadier General Longbourne was wounded while patrolling in front of the advanced posts. Though his wounds were not at first thought serious, they proved worse than had been suspected, and we saw him no more. He was a fine leader of men, a most gallant gentleman, and as popular with the men as with the officers. No one could wish for a better Brigadier.

The Commanding Officer assumed command of the Brigade, and Major C. W. Wilson of the battalion.

The same morning Battalion Headquarters moved up to the Chateau Pill-box. This was a small concrete erection, of no strength, and the inside was literally covered with flies. Besides this there were various wooden " bivvies" and slit trenches for the men, into which all soon settled. A large number of demolition charges littered the ground in wooden cases about the size of a box that would contain a dozen bottles of beer. These charges seemed to have an unholy attraction for some people. A pioneer was found hacking the casing off one for firewood ; the cooks made a screen round their fire with others ; while a signaller was found carrying one into the pill-box to put his candle on. They may have been safe enough, but you can never tell.

HISTORY OF THE 2/6TH (RIFLE) BATTALION

It was certainly a most unpleasant corner that we were in. There were 8-inch howitzers just behind us which fired at frequent intervals, while the enemy kept us pretty occupied with shells. We had several wounded, two cooks in one instance, bending over their fire, being simultaneously disabled by a " whizz-bang," and the breakfast spoilt. All night long revised orders as to defensive positions to be maintained along the canal bank kept coming in, which kept the companies always on the move.

At 6.45 p.m. on October 6th we relieved the 8th K.L.R. in the front line—" D," " A," " B " Companies in front and from the right, and " C " Company in support. The line ran from a point in the Marcoing Line about 300 yards north-north-east of Proville across the Canal de l'Escaut, and right across an old German aerodrome almost to the Cambrai—Bapaume road, where the Canadians carried on the line. " D " Company were south of the canal, " B " and " A " Companies north of it. Posts were for the most part in old houses and cellars. " A " Company had an enormous covered concrete rifle range (*see* aeroplane photo) on their front. Their posts were at one end, and Company Headquarters at the other—a most convenient arrangement, affording protection from weather or hostilities for the Company Commander when visiting his posts.

During this night rear headquarters and transport lines by Bourlon Wood, to which the Padre and Lieutenant Hazell had been sent sick, and Captain Bowring for a rest prior to going on leave, were visited by an aeroplane and heavily bombed. The destruction caused by these terrific explosions was very considerable. One man was killed and seven wounded ; while among the transport itself, which received the brunt of the bombing, eighteen animals were either blown to pieces or so maimed that they had to be shot. It was a horrible business digging out the wounded men and putting the mutilated and screaming animals out of their pain, and in the morning the place looked like a shambles.

" THE KING'S " (LIVERPOOL REGIMENT)

October 7th passed off quietly with only intermittent shelling; but next day there was a general attack by the Third Army on limited objectives, which was connected with the turning of Cambrai from the flanks, though but mild retaliation occurred on our front.

It was now expected that the enemy might fall back at any moment. Active patrolling for the night of October 7th–8th was arranged by the battalion scouts working in relief. As had been anticipated, no enemy were located in the area bounded by the Cambrai—Bapaume road, the Cambrai embankment, and the canal; but up to 4 a.m. machine guns were still firing across the open country from the south bank of the canal. By this time the general attack of the Canadians, which had commenced at 1.30 a.m., had carried them up to the canal bridgeheads without serious opposition. Accordingly all companies in the front line were instructed to push forward small patrols, to be followed by strong fighting patrols, to keep abreast with the Canadians. At 7.30 a.m. a general advance was ordered, and, after consultation with the 8th K.L.R., who had relieved the 2/7th K.L.R. on our right, we made the following moves : " D " Company worked along the south of the canal up to the railway embankment in front of Cambrai ; " B " Company worked along south of the Cambrai—Bapaume road, crossed the canal in front of Cambrai by a foot-bridge; " A " followed " B " Company, to form the left of our front line, which was now the railway embankment ; while "D" Company occupied "B" Company's old position as support.

By twelve o'clock our new line was established with three companies on the line of the railway embankment running along the western outskirts of the town, and piquets placed over all entrances to Cambrai. Battalion Headquarters had moved from the canal bank up to the rifle range.

At 2 p.m., the pursuit having swept through and past Cambrai, we were concentrated for the night with " A " and " B " Companies in the rifle range, " C," " D," and Headquarters in houses some few hundred yards nearer the town itself. Our casualties from shell and machine-gun fire for three days were three killed and twenty-eight wounded.

The capture of Cambrai was the end of our share in the battles of Bapaume and Cambrai. The month of September and the early days of October saw the final initiation of the battalion, and, in fact, of the whole Division, into the mysteries of a great offensive. Looking back, we have reason to feel that we acquitted ourselves with credit. The following letter from General Sir Julian Byng, commanding Third Army, to our Divisional Commander, is reproduced here by special permission :—

"I cannot allow the 57th Division to leave the Third Army without expressing my sincerest appreciation of its services during the Battle of Cambrai.

"The success that has crowned its efforts has been brought about by careful preparation by the Staff, by skilful tactical handling by all leaders, and by determined resolve of all ranks to beat the enemy.

"The Third Army's record of ground gained, of prisoners and guns captured, is a fine one, and I owe my deepest thanks to all ranks of the 57th Division for their fine share in the achievement."

CHAPTER IX

RUITZ—LILLE—FROYENNES

ON the evening of October 9th orders were received from Brigade that the Division was to " pull out of the line " the next day for a rest. This had been anticipated by all ranks, and the wildest speculations had been rife. " Three weeks at Calais," " A fortnight in the South of France," and other even more ridiculous prophecies had been uttered, each, of course, based on " inside information." After all, when the war really seemed to be nearing its end, any rumours, whether of a " rest " or of a fallen Monarchy, met with ready acceptance.

At 10.30 a.m. on October 10th we commenced our move, so as to strike the Brigade starting-point at Anneux Chapel at 11.15 a.m. Considerable difficulty was experienced in collecting the companies, owing to the barrier produced by the canal. The battalion, however, eventually was joined together, and we tramped along the Bapaume—Cambrai road in high spirits, albeit the recent battle was still in evidence by reason of the dead Germans and slain horses seen lying about.

As we reached Fontaine we met a Scottish Division marching up, and throughout its length the road was very congested. Our Divisional Commander watched us pass, and we picked up our rear headquarters by Bourlon Wood *en route*. As we marched along the switchback road H.R.H. the Prince of Wales and General Byng passed us, motoring up to Cambrai.

The battle area, now that the struggle had gone ahead, looked forlorn and desolate; and we were not sorry when, about two o'clock, we reached the bare hillside at Boursies, where we were to spend the night. Bivouacs were soon constructed, and though it threatened to rain, and in fact did so at intervals, our spirits were in no way damped.

Soon after our arrival we were conscious of a terrific detonation —it would be untrue to say we " heard " it—and, looking back towards Cambrai, we saw a tall pillar of smoke, with a large mushroom top, rising from the town. We wondered whether our Army Commander and the Prince of Wales had left the town in time to avoid the explosion. The next day Brigadier-General Meynell, C.M.G., arrived to take over command of our Brigade, and Colonel Gathorne-Hardy returned to our Headquarters once more. The same day a proportion of our transport moved off to Ruitz, near Bethune, our ultimate destination.

The morning of October 12th proved wet and chilly. As the balance of the transport had to entrain at 7.30 a.m. at Fremicourt, early breakfasts and earlier rising were essential; and by 7 a.m. we found ourselves standing about with nothing to do and nowhere to sit and two hours to pass before we could move. However, in due course the time arrived, and the battalion moved off, the new Brigadier taking the salute.

It took us two and a quarter hours to reach Slag Heap Station, Hermies, and when we did arrive there was no apparent prospect of a train. We sat down accordingly in a field and had some food, and about 12.30 p.m. a train meandered into the station and we set off. There seemed to be more than the usual doubt as to where and when we should arrive, but by the time we had passed Bapaume, Arras, and St. Pol we had a fair inkling that the journey would not be a very short one. Eventually at 4.30 a.m. on October 14th we arrived at Fouquereuil, where we were told to get out. A tiring march of two and a half hours on wet and slippery roads, and with empty stomachs, brought us at last to the little mining town of Ruitz. " A," "C," and " D " Companies were in billets in the village, while Headquarters and " B "

THE FINEST OF FINE TRENCH JOURNALS

CHEERIO! ½ FR.

No 1 — AUGUST 18TH 1918 — 12 PAGES

EDITED BY JOHN W WHEWAY

ILLUSTRATED BY A.R.INGHAM AND A RUNNER

THE JOURNAL OF "B" COY LIVERPOOL RIFLES

EDITORIAL ADDRESS' "CHEERIO" · 7 MINE SHAFT AVE FIFTEEN INCH LANE DUG OUT CITY

A SOUVENIR FOR FRITZ

H.R.INGHAM FRANCE 6·18·

Company had to climb a precipitous hill to a small hutted camp in a wood. This spot had been a Corps Headquarters, and consequently had an unusually pleasant aspect. The rest of that day was spent mainly in sleep; the next day mainly in washing.

Our idea of a long " rest " had become suddenly dispelled by the news that in a day or two at the latest we were to go into the line somewhere north of Bethune. To be frank, no one was particularly elated by this intelligence. If we were to be in the line, we preferred the clear, open country of the Cambrai area. It was impossible to be very enthusiastic at the prospect of floundering once again through mud and water in the dismal country of Northern France, with which we were already only too familiar and had no wish to renew our acquaintance. A conference for Commanding Officers at Barlin the next day revealed our new destination as Fromelles, and on the morning of October 15th the Quartermaster and other details proceeded thither at an early hour.

The battalion followed in busses at 6.45 a.m., and the transport set off at 10 a.m. Our route lay through the outskirts of Bethune and Locon—the former badly damaged, the latter, once a part of Corps Headquarters, the most completely demolished place it is possible to imagine. The mass of shell-holes in every direction testified to the severity of the shelling to which the country had been subjected during the recent push and counter-push.

At 11.30 a.m. the column halted at Pont du Hem; the men debussed and the vehicles drove off. Hardly had they gone when the Corps Commander, General Haking, drove up in a car and informed us that we were now to make for Laventie. This was some way off, and meanwhile our Quartermaster and billeting party were at Fromelles with the " cookers," while the transport were somewhere on the road between there and Ruitz. Needless to say, our bicycles were with the transport—an error never committed again—and two luckless runners had to be dispatched on foot with maps and hosts of directions to collect our details.

HISTORY OF THE 2/6TH (RIFLE) BATTALION

We in the meantime set off for Laventie, where we arrived at 12.15. Few houses, if any, we found had any roofs worth speaking of; billeting, therefore, was not easy. The Irish and 2/7th K.L.R. were each given streets, and ourselves another; and into the forlorn and draughty houses we settled as best we could, waiting hungrily for our dinners, while the rain steadily descended. At 4.15 p.m., when hope had nearly been abandoned, the " cookers " were sighted, and the prospect of a hot meal soon restored us to our normal spirits.

After a very damp night—the orderly-room staff, who were installed in an old caravan, were the only people who kept really dry—we set off soon after 9 a.m. to march to Le Maisnil. The road wound along through the usual scenery of these parts, the beauty of which was by no means enhanced by the fact that our route lay through the old British and German trenches and across No Man's Land. As we climbed the hill which led to our destination, the thoroughness of the enemy was made very apparent by the remains of great pill-boxes, which he had blown to pieces in a most efficient fashion before his departure.

Our Headquarters were some old wooden huts, standing adjacent to what must have been a magnificent pill-box, to judge by the huge masses of concrete that lay about, some of these hurled to a considerable distance from the original site. The companies were a few hundred yards away in some old trenches, which possessed one pill-box still intact. As we moved in, the Munsters moved out.

At 2 p.m. the Commanding Officer, Adjutant, and Company Commanders rode up to the Headquarters of the Brigade in the line at Le Chateau de la Flandre, near Radinghem. After a short discussion the party proceeded on foot, accompanied by the Major-General commanding 47th Division, the Brigadier, and an Intelligence Officer. The route lay across open fields to the railway line by Erquinghem le Sec Railway Station, till recently the front line, and thence up a road to a small group of houses at a

234

place prophetically called (from the war of 1870) Le Fin de la Guerre. Here a conference took place in a somewhat crowded cellar, the Headquarters of the 22nd Londons, while the enemy shelled the place with gas. It was arranged that we should arrive the next day, so as to begin the advance from the present front line at 9.30 a.m., those on the spot to supply us with the local position by means of fighting patrols to be sent out just before dawn.

We then retraced our steps to the Chateau, but did not delay there, as the enemy was using 5·9's freely, one of which shortly afterwards came within an ace of annihilating the Commanding Officer and Adjutant, and their groom.

On our return the arrangements for the morrow were completed. "C" and "D" Companies were to lead the advance, with "A" in support and "B" in reserve. Captain Eccles rejoined this day and took over "B" Company from Captain Kissan, who now assumed the duties of Intelligence Officer. This post had been vacant since Lieutenant Hazell had been sent to hospital with dysentery during the last days of the Battle of Cambrai, though his place had been temporarily filled by Lieutenant Lever.

At 7.30 a.m. on October 17th the battalion began to move off by platoons at 100-yard intervals. The 22nd Londons had nothing of particular interest to tell us on our arrival, except that all was quiet. The 47th Division were expecting to go to Italy, and the thought of that fair country loomed large on their horizon.

At 10.45 a.m. the Commanding Officer, with the Brigade Major, visited the front line, where they found that the companies had successfully grasped the situation, and were in touch on their flanks. Scouts had been sent forward to ascertain how things were going in front. Nothing could be seen of the Germans, so the line proceeded cautiously forward in the direction of Lille. On went the scouts, and on went the battalion. It was a queer, uncanny sensation, and not a few expected a sudden crash of shells or the rattle of machine guns. Soon, however, the pace became so fast that, from extended order, the leading companies formed into lines of sections in column, while the support and reserve companies assumed ordinary column of fours. Battalion Headquarters kept incessantly moving, and had hardly time to report their new location before they were on the move again. All this while the Commanding Officer was marching ahead, steering the battalion with whistle and arm signals after the most approved form of open order drill, as laid down in " Infantry Training." La Petite Coutre was passed, and on the flanks could be seen Fort Englos and Premesques, once the strongholds of German heavy artillery in the old Houplines days. Le Marais, just short of Lille, was reached without incident, though the huge craters in the roads showed that the enemy were determined to make our advance as difficult as possible. Mines were still going up, and the efforts of some sappers to remove a " booby trap " from a house resulted in an explosion which only missed Battalion Headquarters by a few minutes.

Shortly before midday the battalion found itself marching along the tram lines in the suburbs of Lille. As the men tramped down the empty road to Pont de Canteleu, two children appeared, timid and round-eyed. " Where is everybody ? " asked the Commanding Officer, in his best French. Apparently, our noble opponents had spread it abroad that we should kill everyone we saw, and all had been warned to remain in their cellars. The children retired, and shortly after one or two women and one or two old men appeared. Finding us friendly, their relations were summoned in shrill tones, and before long the street was thronged with people. Never was such a scene! Everyone cheered and sang, laughed and wept. Flags of the Allies, sold to the French by the Germans ere their departure, soon adorned every window. " Vivent les Anglais !" went up from hundreds of throats. Everyone embraced everyone else ; officers and men alike were kissed and kissed again by the enthusiastic people; while horses and equipment were soon half smothered in flags and flowers. Progress became very difficult, so dense was the crowd and so anxious to express their joy and gratitude. Of all the sights of the war there were few, if any, half so moving as the picture of this almost miraculous awakening of these unhappy folk from their long and cruel nightmare. How they laughed and cried! With what intense feeling they sang " The Marseillaise " ! Not a man was there who did not feel that here at last was a reward worth all the misery and dangers of our campaigning.

At last we reached the Pont de Canteleu, the entrance to the famous City of Lille. The bridge, like all other bridges, was, of course, in ruins; but there was sufficient of it left standing for civilians to cross one at a time. Guards were posted at all these bridges, and no one crossed into the town, the Corps Commander's orders being very strict on this point. About 5 p.m. the 172nd Brigade, which had been detailed to take charge of Lille, began to arrive, and the men were passed over one at a time. As soon as this long performance was completed our piquets were withdrawn. Billets were now selected for the battalion in the vicinity of the bridgehead, and very good they were. Battalion Headquarters secured a magnificent chateau, where everything looked so suspiciously arranged for our comfort that, in spite of the inspection carried out by the special R.Es., we were quite prepared to discover some large-sized " booby trap." An old French gentleman dug up from the garden two bottles of excellent claret and one of old brandy, which he gave to us, and it need hardly be said that the present was most acceptable.

At 6.30 p.m. the transport and rear headquarters arrived, and Lieutenant Drewsen was dispatched to reconnoitre the bridges to the north. He returned with a full description of the destructive thoroughness of the enemy. About three bridges out of some fourteen could be crossed by one man at a time with difficulty; the rest were beyond hope.

237

HISTORY OF THE 2/6TH (RIFLE) BATTALION

At 7.15 a.m. the next morning orders were issued for the Brigade to support the right and left flanks of the 74th and 59th Divisions, who had moved round Lille from the north and south respectively, and whose inner flanks were not yet in touch. It appeared that the enemy, who had evacuated Lille in the early hours of the previous morning, was retiring on the Scheldt, and fighting a rearguard action as he went.

The 8th K.L.R., who had followed behind the 2/7th K.L.R. and ourselves in our joint march on Lille, were now to lead the Brigade; and about 8 a.m. they crossed the remains of the Pont de Canteleu and set off round the southern outskirts of Lille. Fearing that it might be difficult to recross the moat on the other side of Lille, we moved down towards Haubourdin, where there was rumoured to be a pontoon bridge. The transport was to follow. The route, which lay through endless wrecked factories, derelict railway lines, and narrow back streets, was somewhat confusing, but in the end the bridge was found and the battalion passed over.

After crossing at Haubourdin we moved round towards Ronchin, viâ the Faubourg des Postes, receiving everywhere a most enthusiastic greeting from the populace. From the neighbourhood of Ronchin we proceeded to Hallemes, where we settled down on a German aerodrome for a good halt for dinner. The day was fine and warm, but the quantity of *pavé* made marching hard work.

After a dinner halt we pushed on again towards Flers, there being a distressing lack of either orders or information. On another aerodrome just south of the village we found the Acting Commanding Officer of the Irish, also suffering from the same lack of instructions as ourselves. The Germans took this opportunity to send over some stray " whizz-bangs," but they did no damage, though as a precaution we spread out the battalion into artillery formation. A council of war was held, and the Irish decided to move on to Annappes, and we to billet in Flers, which after a march of thirteen miles we were quite ready to do. We

238

noticed that the enemy shelled the former place quite stiffly as the Irish moved in, but the firing soon subsided. Runners were now sent to collect the transport, which in due course arrived, as also the Brigadier.

The inhabitants of Flers were most friendly, and regaled us with stories of their late masters; and one heard with some misgiving that the bed allotted to " Monsieur le Capitaine " had been occupied by a German as late as 7 a.m. that morning. However, a bed is a bed, when all is said and done, and not a thing to be sneezed at when you are campaigning.

It was here that we first discovered that the German soldiers had used all the beds for themselves and left the inhabitants to sleep on the floor. Our first efforts at billeting, therefore, became rather complicated till the difference in custom was cleared up. There is little doubt that by our novel methods of proceeding we distinctly lost caste among people accustomed to the haughty ways of the Prussian. The local inhabitants were inclined to think, as we did not order them about like dogs, that we were rather poor creatures.

The orders for the next day (October 19th) were a repetition of those of the day before, and at 9.15 a.m. we pushed on to Annappes. Here we found the Irish still in possession, and a joint Headquarters was formed, and the transport was instructed to follow us up. A thriving trade was done by the inhabitants by the sale of paper ten-centime pieces and other relics of the German occupation.

About midday the Irish got orders to move on, and ourselves to follow at 3 p.m., to Willems. The Irish were to throw out an outpost line in front of the place, and we were in support in billets in the town. It was dark and raining when we reached the town, and a brigade of the 74th Division had already got the best billets. The Mayor, we found, was the keeper of the principal public-house, and thither the Commanding Officer, Adjutant, Regimental-Sergeant-Major, and other French scholars repaired to try and arrange for billets. The estaminet was much like any other, and was already full of soldiers and civilians trying to swallow a pale yellow liquid, which had sufficient smell to suggest that it had been poured once (not oftener) into a recently emptied beer bottle. Into this mass of chattering people we pushed our way, and tried to get into conversation with the proprietor. As he appeared to find our French difficult to follow, and was busy serving out the so-called beer, our efforts were productive of very little result. Eventually the situation began to dawn on him, and the entirely fallacious services of a girl reputed to speak English were called into requisition. All the French in the place at once joined in, and not a few of the Tommies. The confusion and din soon became appalling, and all this time the battalion were seated, patiently or impatiently, by the roadside in the rain. The situation really seemed hopeless, but after quieting the friends and supporters of the Mayor, we eventually succeeded, and billets— which our Billeting Officer had wisely been searching for on his own account—were duly approved and the battalion moved in.

At 7.10 the following morning (October 20th) we received orders that the Brigade was to seize the bridgeheads over the Scheldt north of Froyennes—*i.e.*, just above Tournai—the 8th K.L.R., as before, leading the way. We moved off at 9 a.m., and shortly after crossing the Belgian frontier received word from the 8th K.L.R. that they were completely held up in front of Blondain, where they had established their Headquarters. We were ordered not to advance any farther, and were billeted for the night in a little hamlet called Les Empires.

Blondain was shelled freely, and our own vicinity slightly, consequently our arrival in this part of the world was hardly welcome. The inhabitants had seen but little of the actualities of war, and, much as some of them disliked the Germans, they could hardly be expected to watch with much pleasure their houses being shattered. Some 18-pounders arrived about this time and settled down near our transport lines, which resulted in the latter being shelled out soon after.

The Imperial War Museum and Canadian War Memorial Fund.

THE CAMBRAI—BAPAUME ROAD,
NEAR FONTAINE NOTRE DÂME.

CANAL DE L'ESCAUT NEAR
CAMBRAI.

Official Photographs by permission of

THE CANAL DU NORD.

"THE KING'S" (LIVERPOOL REGIMENT)

For the next day (October 21st) we received orders that we were to pass through the 8th K.L.R. at 8.30 a.m., seize the bridgeheads, and, passing the Scheldt, capture the high ground on the other side. To assist us in this somewhat ambitious scheme, we received one battery R.F.A., two sections M.G.C., one mobile medium trench mortar battery, and two bridging sections, R.E.

The action which followed will be described in some detail, as it proved a very interesting operation, and the only one of its kind in which the battalion took part. It was real open warfare, as distinct from the miscellaneous fighting which followed a " set piece " attack during the recent battles.

The country between us and the River Scheldt was flat in the main, dotted with houses and small woods, and rising slightly towards Froyennes, whence it fell away to an open stretch of grassland up to the near bank of the river. It was an excellent position for a rearguard to hold ; and in addition, on the Tournai—Courtrai road, about one mile north of Froyennes, the enemy enjoyed magnificent observation from the Convent, and also for his guns from Mont St. Aubers, a conspicuous eminence on the far side of the river. He had a considerable number of guns, and evidently an ample supply of ammunition.

We, on the other hand, suffered the usual disadvantages of an attacking force in open warfare. We had no knowledge of the strength or location of the enemy, while our own movements could not be concealed. Moreover, the hasty advance and the interruption of communications due to the complete demolition of all bridges, the damage to roads by mines, and the absolute destruction of all railways—every single metal on the lines having had a piece blown out—had effectually prevented the advance of any heavy artillery, and the 18-pounders which we had were but scantily provided with ammunition.

We moved off at 8 a.m. to take over from the Irish—" A " Company on the right, " B " on the left, " C " in support, and " D " in reserve. The front line, which was some 2,000 yards

241   R

in extent, ran north and south about 1,500 yards east of the hamlet of Honnevain. This was taken over by 10 a.m., the 8th K.L.R. being collected into groups near that place, with " C " Company and Battalion Headquarters just in front. The two front line companies now endeavoured to advance.

In this and subsequent similar attempts we were heavily handicapped by being the only battalion of the Division in the line. On our left was the 59th Division, and on our right the 74th Division, which belonged to another Corps. The isolated attempts that resulted from this position of affairs enabled the enemy to concentrate his attention on our unfortunate companies, there being no time for our request for flanking support to reach all the authorities concerned.

" A " Company, moving forward on a four platoon frontage, came at once under intense machine-gun and trench-mortar fire from woods and houses opposite their front, and sustained various casualties. The Lewis gun team of No. 2 Platoon spotted one of the enemy machine-gun posts, and dealt with it successfully. The advance was thereby able to proceed a little farther, but at no point was the amount of ground gained very considerable— about 500 yards in all. About 1 p.m. the advance was compelled to cease, owing to the determined and accurate fire of the enemy and the heavy shelling which had also commenced. The situation was further complicated by the death of the Company Commander, Captain Carr, who was shot through the head while moving forward to make a personal reconnaissance. The death of this able and gallant young officer was felt as a great loss, and the delay in getting hold of Lieutenant Blake, the next senior officer, who, owing to the grave shortage of officers, was with a platoon, for some time made it hard for this company to operate collectively.

In the meantime, on the left, Captain Eccles sent forward patrols to ascertain the position. No. 7 Platoon, hearing from their patrol of certain hostile positions, including a machine gun firing from a window in the Convent, advanced at 11.30 a.m., but after proceeding a short distance came under intense machine-gun fire, 2nd-Lieutenant Waln and one man, unhappily, being killed and eight men wounded. The remainder of the platoon were forced to fall back. Riflemen O'Sullivan and R. O. Jones, who were with the platoon as stretcher-bearers, endeavoured to go forward to bring in the wounded. The enemy, however, opened fire on them, and they were compelled to lie down. As they lay watching they observed some of the wounded sitting up applying field dressings. Seeing that the enemy took no notice of this, they proceeded to bandage each other for imaginary wounds. They then rose to their feet and limped towards the wounded, whom they were able materially to assist in tying up their wounds and eventually crawling to the rear. For their gallantry and initiative they were both awarded the Military Medal.

The loss of 2nd-Lieutenant Waln was very great. He had won the Divisional Commander's Card for his gallantry in the Battle of Cambrai, and on this occasion he proved himself no less regardless of danger. He had gained the respect and admiration of all ranks.

Second-Lieutenant Bardgett and the reserve platoon were sent up and formed a post, the remnant of No. 7 Platoon being sent into reserve. No. 6 Platoon, after waiting for some while for their patrol to return, sent out a further party, which was followed by the platoon itself. Crossing the railway, they forced their way into one of a small group of houses, of one of which the door was barricaded, and were almost immediately fired on from the doorway of an adjoining house. The fire was returned, and two of the enemy were seen to fall ; but further hostile activity developing, they withdrew to the railway and established a post there. Their original patrol joined them at dusk, having been held up by hostile fire and unable to move. No. 5 Platoon could make no move owing to the open nature of the ground in front of them, each attempt being met with heavy fire.

At midday two platoons of " C " Company were sent up to each of the front line companies, as their advance, short as it was, was leaving their flanks in an exposed position. One half company under 2nd-Lieutenant Simpson took up a position in the right rear of " A " Company ; the other half company was located near " B " Company Headquarters as reserve.

At 1.30 p.m. " D " Company was ordered forward from reserve to work down the railway line, which ran through the centre of " B " Company's front, and endeavour to get round the east side of the wood on the south of the railway line. In spite of heavy fire, the company moved up without casualties, cleared the wood, and by 5 p.m. had established posts on the far edge.

About 7 p.m. the advance of both companies was once more attempted. " A " Company, on the right, advanced some 200 yards, which brought it more into line with " B " Company, but could make no farther headway. Captain Eccles then issued orders for the advance to the Tournai—Cambrai road, and No. 8 Platoon managed to get within about 400 yards of the Convent, where they were absolutely stopped. No. 6 Platoon could make no headway at all ; and No. 8 Platoon, which was isolated, was consequently withdrawn for a short distance to preserve the general front. Company Headquarters, which had moved forward, and incidentally were all but demolished by a shell of very large dimensions, withdrew to their previous location, and all posts prepared for the night. " D " Company in the meantime, having been passed by " B " Company, were concentrated at Mont Garnis in reserve. Machine guns were posted at important tactical posts for the night.

Throughout the day, in addition to intense machine-gun fire, the enemy had kept up a heavy and more or less continuous bombardment with every class of shell up to 8-inch. The slightest movement produced great hostile activity, and it was simply owing to the small number of men engaged on a comparatively large front that saved us from heavy casualties. Trench-mortar and artillery support was available, and was employed as far as the conditions of moving warfare and lack of observation permitted.

At 4.30 a.m., October 22nd, patrols from " A " Company reported Froyennes clear of the enemy, but that they were fired on from the east bank of the river after passing through the village. " A " Company accordingly moved forward, occupied the village, and established posts along the Tournai—Cambrai road.

" B " Company's patrols were fired on from the Convent, but after a few rounds the enemy withdrew. The company followed, and continued the line of posts on the Tournai—Cambrai road. Patrols were at once sent forward, in spite of a brisk fire from the far bank of the river, to try and discover a bridge, but without success. Meanwhile touch was gained with the 74th Division on the right and the 170th Brigade (who had relieved the right brigade of the 59th Division) on the left. No enemy were located on our side of the river except on the extreme right, where contact was gained and two enemy prisoners (91st I.R., 2nd Prussian Division) were captured.

The G.S.O.2 of the Corps visited Captain Eccles during the course of the morning, and agreed that any attempt to cross the river would be absurd. The Commanding Officer, after reconnoitring the line, came to the same conclusion, and the general line of the road was consolidated. " B " Company established their headquarters in the Convent, but made a speedy evacuation on being informed that it was mined. " D " Company were moved up to Trieu de Loquet; and Battalion Headquarters would have moved up to Froyennes but for the information that we were to be relieved early next morning. The enemy kept up a continual harassing fire all day, distributed generally over the front, but causing few casualties.

The weather, after being wet and disagreeable, had now cleared, but it was distinctly cold. It was somewhat strange to be living in houses during active operations ; and, indeed, the civilians got rather mixed up with the firing line, as they kept coming along with coffee for the men in the posts. This well-meant but mistaken kindness was very inconvenient, and, in addition, refugees kept coming in from the German line. There were many minor spy scares, some of the civilians, out of friendliness to us or enmity towards their neighbours, being rather inclined to point out people as acting in that capacity. Battalion Headquarters, which was a small isolated house not shown on the map, was in fact destroyed by shell fire the very day after we left it, which rather looked as if the enemy had received information as to its position.

During the night, which was extremely cold, though very fine and with a full moon, an R.E. officer made a complete reconnaissance of the river, but failed to locate any kind of bridge. As a matter of fact, the line on our section of the front remained just as we had established it until the Armistice.

At 8.30 a.m. on October 23rd the 2/7th K.L.R. arrived, and proceeded to take over our line, establishing their headquarters in the house selected by us in Froyennes for the purpose. The battalion moved out to Le Cornet, where an unfortunate incident occurred, owing to the efforts of another Commanding Officer, whose battalion had not been in action, to take forcible possession of our billets, in spite of the presence of our Billeting Officer, who had with full authority taken over from the 2/7th K.L.R. As a result our men had to sit by the roadside, tired and weary after two days' hard fighting, till Divisional Headquarters could be communicated with. The reply from there was as prompt as it was satisfactory, and the offending battalion, who themselves appeared none too pleased with the action of their Commanding Officer, at once withdrew.

The billets were good all round, Headquarters itself being established in a lovely old farm called Hardy Planq, evidently the ancestral residence of some old French family. All were glad of a good rest and a " clean up," as the strain and, for most people, the discomfort of the last two days had been considerable. Our casualties during that time, besides Captain Carr and 2nd-Lieutenant Waln, were seven men killed and twenty-five wounded. In connection with these operations Captain Eccles was shortly after awarded the Military Cross.

Just before we came out of the line Major C. W. Wilson left us for England at his own request. He had not been in good health for some time, and the wound in his foot—a relic of the South African War—bothered him. He was a great loss to the battalion, with which he had served since its formation. His grit and determination, his enthusiasm and energy, were an inspiration to all ranks. His position as Second-in-Command was filled by the Adjutant, Captain Bowring reassuming the latter's duties.

At 2.30 p.m. on October 24th we moved off from our pleasant quarters at Le Cornet and marched back to Willems into Divisional Reserve. We found Willems quite a pleasant little town, and our billets were on the whole good. Battalion Headquarters were situated nearly opposite Divisional Headquarters, and we were thus enabled to renew our acquaintance with the Divisional Staff.

We stayed at Willems till October 30th, and very pleasant it was. We had been on the move almost without a stop since we left Ruitz, and the stay at that place had been no more than a brief pause in our continuous movements which commenced when we left the Scarpe on August 17th, more than two months before. During the two advances—the one on Cambrai, the other on Tournai—dumps had been left at all kinds of places, and we now had to set to work to collect our material and our guards from widely separated spots. This was successfully accomplished in the end, nor was anything of any consequence lost or overlooked in the process.

We spent the first part of our time at Willems resting and cleaning up ; the latter part in training and reorganizing, as it was clear that before long we should be required to follow up the retiring enemy once more. Considerable attention was paid to the bugle band, which practised from morning to night, and sounded the recognized calls throughout the day. It was during the days in reserve on the Somme that attention became centred on our bugles. Extra cornets were purchased, and a pair of cymbals was presented by Lieutenant Huntley. Whenever conditions were favourable the bugles were given every opportunity of practising, and, under the skilful handling of Sergeant Cadman and Lance-Corporal Frost, the cornet soloist, they proved a most efficient and excellent addition to the battalion.

The difficulty of keeping pace with the bewildering rapidity of the Allied advance suggested the advantage of a battle map, and accordingly the necessary sheets of the 1 : 250,000 map were fastened on a board and the situation shown by cotton on pins. This was placed in a prominent position outside Battalion Headquarters; and here, too, were pinned the telegrams announcing the different stages of the advance. The arrangement proved very satisfactory, enabling as it did not only the troops, but also the civilians, to see at a glance how the war was progressing. The crowd around the board at once testified to its popularity.

For (as it proved) the last time in our history we were now ordered to reconnoitre defensive positions and emergency routes in the event of a German counter-attack. This was a most unlikely event, as we were on one side and they on the other of a wide river. It was, however, quite fitting that our active service should end, as it had begun, with this necessary but illusive form of military exercise.

At 10 a.m. on October 30th we left Willems for the Hallemes area, passing our relieving battalion, the 19th Londons, *en route*. The hopes of a trip to Italy, so strongly entertained by the 47th Division, had apparently been dashed to the ground once more.

Owing to a sudden attack of influenza, an ambulance had to be requisitioned to remove Captain Fell, the Quartermaster, Lieutenant F. E. Evans, Captain Noon, now in command of " A " Company, and 2nd-Lieutenant D. R. Williams. The Commanding

APPROACH TO CAMBRAÏ.   RIFLE RANGE IN FOREGROUND.

Photographed by Aeroplane, 1st October, 1918.

Officer was on a course, and the Headquarters Staff now consisted of the Adjutant, the Intelligence Officer, and the Transport Officer. After a short march along the side-roads we came on to the great highway between Lille and Tournai, and at 1.30 p.m. arrived at the Faubourg de Fives, one of the suburbs of Lille, where billets were awaiting us. Battalion Headquarters, including all the details, were accommodated in a house and a series of factory buildings on the main road, Rue Pierre le Grand. The companies were in two or three roads to the rear of Headquarters, and were billeted after the fashion of 1914—two or three men to a house. For the sick officers another house in the main street was taken over, and here they were kept isolated, except Fell and Williams, who had to go to hospital.

Several new officers now began to arrive. Lieutenant Belk had joined us in Willems, and 2nd-Lieutenants Bethell and Forshaw, A.S.C., arrived at Fives on our second day. Captain Bowring returned that day also from United Kingdom leave, and took over the duties of Adjutant, the latter acting as Second-in-Command. The following day 2nd-Lieutenants Cufflin and Woodworth, M.M., reported for duty.

From our arrival at Fives till the Armistice we were busy enough. First of all there were the billets to be seen to, which, good as they were, still required much attention. Then the general question of refitting and training had to be considered. It was still quite uncertain whether the enemy would come to terms or not; and it was understood that if he did not we should certainly be required before long. Meanwhile a sudden passion for lecturing took possession of the Higher Command, including General Haking, our Corps Commander, who addressed us at some length.

On November 5th we had the first of a series of battalion concerts. There was a most convenient little hall not far from our billets, and here " The Cheerios " gave their performance—and an excellent one it was. It was at Barly, during the rest in the

Cambrai Battle, that the concert party were first got together, and now they were to exhibit their powers once more. They worked very hard, under the kindly eye of the Padre, and the resulting success more than justified their efforts. Without wishing to make invidious distinctions, it may be said that Corporal Henderson was the heart and soul of the party, while his singing of Chevalier's songs was absolutely first-rate. The introduction of local talent, in the form of an *enfant prodigue* who played the violin, and a French girl who sang with great vigour proved highly popular.

On November 6th our American Medical Officer, Lieutenant Reed, left us, to our infinite regret. Dour and silent as he was, he had won a very warm place in our hearts ; and it is pleasant to think that he was sorry enough to leave us after more than six months' active campaigning together. Captain Bullock took his place, and proved in his turn a most popular Medical Officer.

Football now began to figure prominently in our lives. The great aerodrome, where we halted outside Flers the day after Lille was taken, had been converted into one vast football field, with some seven or eight pitches. Incidentally, it was also our training ground, and a little friction was occasionally caused when other battalions used to allow their battalion teams to practise all the morning in our vicinity while we were drilling.

The last few days before the Armistice were somewhat trying. It was impossible to keep your thoughts away from the possible termination of hostilities and all that that involved. The authorities, with what seemed a rather unnecessary lack of confidence in their troops, deluged us with advice to maintain our morale. In point of fact, there appeared no shred of evidence that anyone was in danger of losing his morale, or, for the matter of that, any particular reason why he should, even though one might be glad if the war was really over.

When the telegram reached us on November 11th there was no excitement, no wild cheering or parading of the streets. It was too big a thing to treat in that fashion. Men became silent and thoughtful—thankful for their own escape, reminiscent of those less fortunate. Lille itself, unlike London, did not become a scene of rowdy rejoicings. Thankfulness for deliverance from the infernal horrors of the war, with its all too recent and sad memories, was too deep for a form of celebration more properly associated with Boat Race night in Leicester Square or a " rag " in a 'Varsity town.

CHAPTER X

WITH the cessation of hostilities began what was really the most difficult period of the war. Training, always irksome, had now lost its one stimulus—the prospect of battle. No one supposed for a moment that hostilities could ever be resumed. The question of demobilization immediately sprang to the front ; and though most men realized clearly enough that the delay would necessarily be long, yet it was impossible not to chafe a little, and to feel that at the best you were merely killing time. It was evident from the outset that everything possible must be done to prevent boredom and stagnation. Training could clearly be reduced to a minimum, and that only retained which would insure fresh air and exercise. Athletics and amusements could now be freely cultivated, as men could be spared more generously than during hostilities. Education was also likely to be of great assistance in occupying the men's minds and assisting them to restore their thinking powers, which in many cases soldiering had greatly weakened. Unfortunately, no preparations for the commencement of this form of occupation had been possible, and it was not till the battalion reached Arras that our arrangements were sufficiently advanced to commence operations.

In the meantime the daily routine consisted of a march with the " bugles " to the Divisional Football Ground, some battalion drill, physical training, musketry, and rifle bombing. These were varied by an occasional route march to Roubaix, Mons en Baroeuil (an outwork of the defences of Lille, where British prisoners had

252

been confined under appalling conditions), and a weekly field day, often interfered with by a heavy mist. The afternoons were taken up with football and visits to Lille, which, after first being guarded like some sacred shrine, was soon accessible to all.

Considerable attention was devoted to messing arrangements, and before long a fine Central Mess was provided in the covered yard of a large brewery. Here the whole battalion, except Headquarters, sat down together for meals. Cookers and field kitchens were installed in the yard, and the whole staff of cooks worked under the eye of Sergeant Austin, the Sergeant-Cook. Similar quarters were arranged for Battalion Headquarters.

Except for the factories, where millions of pounds' worth of machinery had been stolen or wrecked, Fives had suffered structurally very little damage from the Germans. It is true none of our beds had brass knobs, and similar articles of that metal had been everywhere removed, but that, after all, was not a very serious matter. The treatment of the inhabitants is a very different story, but that is rather beyond the scope of this book. Anyhow, we were most hospitably received, and it is doubtful whether in all the history of the battalion the men had better billets.

The concert party took on their self-appointed tasks with great vigour and success. Costumes of brown canvas, with ruffs of " four by two," made an excellent show; and the party contrived to make their performances regular and varied, which speaks well for their industry. They were composed of Riflemen Brookes (piano), Evans (baritone), Beesley, Frith, and Lance-Corporal Snowden (comedians), and Lance-Corporal Henderson. The latter was the life and soul of the party, and a host in himself. Later Rifleman McConnell (ragtime), Lance-Corporal Hassall (comedian), and Company Sergeant - Major Lane (baritone) were added to the party, Sergeant Stevenson taking over the duties of pianist. Lieutenant Drewsen and the Padre gave active assistance, while Rifleman Cooper proved a great attraction as a Chinese Magician on one occasion, and variety was also introduced in the form of local French talent. There can be no question but that the " Cheerios " were a great success.

In addition, the Divisional Concert Party, " The Dons "—a very efficient and amusing company—established themselves close to us. This was a great convenience, and enabled many, who had had no chance of seeing them during the war, to attend their performances.

The " bugles " improved daily, and proved a great attraction in the streets of Fives during " Retreat " and " First Post." A small party of children became very attached to the drummers, and accompanied the battalion on one route march, which proved so long and so wet that the poor little mites had to be dragged along by the hand, till a passing lorry could be obtained to take them home.

Further additions were made to our strength during this month. Major D. Grant-Dalton, C.M.G., D.S.O., West Yorkshire Regiment, came as Second-in-Command, the Adjutant, who was performing that duty, taking over the work of P.R.I. and O.C. Amusements ; and the following other officers also joined—viz., Lieutenant Lutz, M.C., who had fought for the Boers against us at Spion Kop, Lieutenants Beavan and Fry, 2nd-Lieutenant Bardsley, and Lieutenant Royle, who returned after six months in England. This sudden influx of officers—ten in one month— was rather overwhelming, and was less valuable than it would have been a month previously, when we were very short-handed.

Our stay in Lille was all too short. We felt we were far too comfortable to be left alone, and before the month was out rumours of a move, either forward or back, filled the air. Eventually we found that Arras was to be our destination, and as there were reputed to be only fifty houses or so intact in that ill-used town, the prospect was none of the brightest, especially as there was every indication of a wet winter.

At 8.30 a.m. on December 2nd the battalion moved off to join the Brigade group, Major Grant-Dalton in command. Colonel

" THE KING'S " (LIVERPOOL REGIMENT)

Gathorne-Hardy had proceeded to England on November 24th, whence, to our very great regret, he never returned, having while on leave been transferred to the Home Establishment. He had been a most popular Commanding Officer, and during his command of the battalion during many days of fighting had won the respect and confidence of all ranks.

The route was viâ Lezennes, Ronchin, Lesquin, Templemars, and Seclin. Carvin, our destination, was reached at 1.30 p.m., and we found ourselves accommodated in huts for the night. Most of these were of German construction, and sunk in the ground by the roadside with wonderful skill from the point of view of concealment. Carvin itself is a dismal and depressing spot.

We were off again the next day (December 3rd, 1918) at 7.45 a.m., and in spite of the weather the march was interesting enough, as the route lay past Lens and the Vimy Ridge. The former place is probably the largest ruined town in France. Without being absolutely levelled to the ground, it yet possesses no building that can be described as anything but a ruin. Shattered masonry and woodwork are heaped in the wildest chaos in every direction, mingled with broken machinery and all kinds of interior fittings. There is not one single roof in position, not a wall that is not pierced or shattered. Standing as the place does on the slope of a hill, the effect of the annihilation which has visited the town is very striking. The Vimy Ridge is a bold, up-standing piece of ground, bare as bare can be, and dotted now with graves and monuments. In this part of the country it forms a very marked eminence, though in reality of no great height.

It rained steadily as we tramped along the slippery *pavé*, and the aspect of our billets, with the rain pouring through the rents in roof and wall, was enough to dismay the boldest heart. As may be imagined, after the comforts of Lille these quarters were hardly popular, but the men accepted the situation nobly. It was 4.15 p.m. when we got in, and there was little enough time to make their billets habitable. The next and subsequent days the job was tackled with the utmost energy, while caustic reports were forwarded to the Higher Command.

Company route marches accompanied by limbers—" scrounging parades," we called them—were instituted, and the material was soon collected from derelict huts and trenches to repair the most serious damage. So strong were our protests that we were informed that we were to move to Warlus Camp, a few miles away, at an early date. This was out of the frying-pan into the fire. Warlus Camp had not been used for some time. Most of the fittings had been removed to another camp, and what little was left had been " borrowed " by the civilians. There was not a duck-board or a stove in the camp. All the huts were Nissen, and from these most of the lining had already vanished.

In the meanwhile our houses in Arras were assuming quite a habitable appearance, and the change was viewed with considerable dismay. Fortunately, there was no water at the camp—or, rather, there was no drinking water ; in the huts themselves there was enough and to spare—so the move was postponed till after Christmas; though an advance party, under Lieutenant Beavan, composed mainly of pioneers, moved over there to begin the work of rebuilding the camp.

The question of education now began to excite more attention. Letters from the Higher Command were full of schemes and exhortations, and in view of the eminently desirable results which our educational programme might be hoped to achieve, the problem was carefully considered.

The results hoped for were—first, a new, and therefore to a certain extent an attractive, form of employment for the men during the mornings ; and, secondly, the sharpening of their thinking powers, which, as has been mentioned above, had become somewhat blunted. The difficulties of the task became apparent at the outset. We had to begin in profound ignorance as to the educational standards of the men, who, of course, were drawn from every rank of life. Then we had no qualified teachers,

Official Photograph by permission of

The Imperial War Museum.

HÔTEL DE VILLE, ARRAS.

no educational books, no note-books or paper, no class-rooms, and no syllabus of work. These were the initial difficulties; there were others to follow later.

To overcome the first difficulty, each company in turn was set a simple examination paper, which consisted of a short précis, a short piece of dictation, the interpretation and correct use of half a dozen four-syllable words, and some simple questions in arithmetic. From the results obtained—and it should be stated that but for the cordial co-operation of all ranks the results would have been nil—we were able to grade the battalion into three classes in English and arithmetic, " X," " Y " and "Z." From this, again, we were able to divide the battalion into three main groups: the General Education Group, subdivided into elementary and intermediate classes for English subjects and arithmetic respectively; the Commercial Group, who did book-keeping, commercial correspondence, shorthand, and languages, in addition to a restricted programme of general subjects; and the Preliminary Group, who were instructed in reading and writing.

The organization required to work this rather ambitious scheme was not inconsiderable. Large supplies of note-books and text-books were ordered from England, and many books were sent for by members of the battalion and loaned to the educational staff. Volunteer instructors were called for, and stepped nobly into the breach. Syllabuses for all the subjects were drawn up and time-tables prepared, which had to be reconciled with parades, guards, leave, etc., both as regards teachers and pupils. Our Battalion Comforts Fund in Liverpool and other friends of the battalion subscribed generously to the considerable expense of the venture, which but for the sudden rapidity of demobilization that soon set in would have proved valuable in its results. Regimental Sergeant-Major Heyworth, Company Sergeant-Major Griffiths, Sergeant-Major Lane, and many other N.C.Os. and men, not to mention some of the officers, worked very hard to make the scheme a success.

HISTORY OF THE 2/6TH (RIFLE) BATTALION

It should in passing be noted that, apart from technical classes, which were well organized by the Higher Command, the assistance received from the Army Authorities was negligible. The Director of Education for Liverpool, on the other hand, to whom application was made for advice, proved most helpful in the selection of suitable text-books and in drawing up of syllabuses.

Throughout this last chapter of the battalion's history the work of education was carried on under the most bewildering and irritating difficulties, and the results cannot be really appraised, but it must be admitted that at the worst they cannot have been harmful, and in some cases were distinctly beneficial.

On December 12th Lieutenant-Colonel C. C. Stapledon, of the Manchester Regiment, arrived and took over the command of the battalion.

From this time till Christmas the daily life of the battalion varied but little. A certain number of parades and route marches, frequent football matches, latterly education classes in the Y.M.C.A. hut, an occasional concert in the same place, varied by motor-lorry trips to Lille, Cambrai, Armentières, and other places of interest, made up our daily round. The fact that we were in a town, dilapidated though it might be, helped to relieve the monotony, as there were some shops open, and a certain number of things to be seen. The departure of thirty-five coal-miners for demobilization about this time also stimulated the hope of early dissolution, albeit some feeling was caused by the fact that the total war service of some of these men amounted to about as many days as the war had lasted years.

Preparations for Christmas were an important part of our work at this period. Our unexpected rest at Christmas, 1917, had caught us unprepared, and we could do but little; but this time the funds received from home, which included a handsome contribution from the 5th (Territorial Force) Reserve Battalion Private Fund, made it possible for us to arrange an entertainment almost regardless of expense. The Army provided us with excellent plum-puddings, and we took care to have these delivered early. Enormous quantities of turkeys were ordered from the Expeditionary Force Canteen, and the country was scoured for fruit, vegetables, and beer. The " Cheerios " set to work on a most excellent programme for Christmas night, and the prospect of a really good Christmas seemed assured. But, alas ! for the hopes of the men. The Expeditionary Force Canteen, on whom we had relied, were lavish in their promises, and that was all. Up till 10 p.m. on Christmas Eve they assured us that the turkeys, like John Gilpin's hat and wig, were " upon the road," and, indeed, expected every moment. They never came. A number of pheasants, however, which arrived at the eleventh hour and fifty-ninth minute, were purchased, and the town was scoured in every direction for pork. In the end, two companies only had their Christmas dinner on Christmas Day, the other two on Boxing Day. It was a great disappointment, especially after the valiant exertions of our Quartermaster's staff and others.

However, that Christmas Day was a success few will deny, and the " Cheerios," filled with the good food and (possibly) drinks suitable to the day, produced an excellent programme, which was highly appreciated.

On the following day the Officers played the Sergeants at football ; but the Sergeants were so overcome, apparently, by the proceedings of the previous day that the Officers won by five goals to nil. The rest of the day was occupied with the usual activities connected with a move which had to be made on December 27th to Warlus Camp, a distance of about five miles.

At 10.30 a.m. on December 27th we set off for Warlus Camp. The prospect of our new abode was not enhanced by the cold wind and steady drizzle which we encountered *en route*. We arrived at 12.30 p.m. and proceeded to settle in. All things considered, the camp was far better than we had anticipated in our most sanguine moments a week ago. Lieutenants Beavan and Hooper, with the most able support of Sergeant Patterson and the pioneers and company working parties, had wrought wonders. Duck-board paths were installed nearly everywhere in place of lanes of thick mud ; huts had windows, most had stoves and floor-boards, and generally the camp was now in a state which made one feel considerably less hopeless as to its possible amenities.

The scheme of operations which had to be worked out now fell under three headings—camp improvement, salvage, and education. To this end companies were allotted time during mornings in succession to put their own huts in order, with the assistance of one or two experts from the Pioneer Platoon. As regards salvage, a very large area—covering ground till recently in our close vicinity at Arras, and now several miles away—had been allotted to us, and for this two companies and a great deal of transport was required daily. Their task was to clear ammunition dumps and convey the material either to a central dump or to a light railway siding for removal, or else to clear barbed-wire defences. Education had to be fitted in with these two demands for men, and very difficult was the problem how to arrange for the right instructors to be available for the right classes.

In recreation some ambitious schemes had been formulated at Arras, but the scarcity of suitable ground put a very effective damper on these. We had one football field just behind the camp, but wet weather and frequent use very soon reduced it to a quagmire. There was a fine hospital hut for a general recreation-room, but it had very little flooring, was very draughty, and impossible to keep warm and too big to light with the means at our disposal. However, some flooring was put in and some stoves obtained. The stage which had been removed from Warlus to Dainville, where French troops were billeted, was boldly removed without opposition, and in due course, through the kindness of an Australian Special Works Company, the whole place was lit by acetylene light, including footlights for the stage.

" THE KING'S " (LIVERPOOL REGIMENT)

Thanks again to the great generosity of our Comforts Fund, and also to Mr. A. Percy Eccles, we had a lot of money to spend on newspapers, novels, and games. A good supply of these was put in the recreation hut, in the Sergeants' Mess—two Nissen huts fixed end on with great skill by Sergeant Patterson—and also the Corporals' hut.

The main event of importance at this time was the Divisional Race Meeting, held on the Arras Race Course on January 1st and 2nd. A large and varied programme had been arranged for both these days, and in addition various side-shows to wile away the intervals between the races had been devised. The weather was cold and grey, but there was little rain, and the great crowd of officers and men who assembled pointed clearly to the success of the venture. Lord Derby was present, and many other distinguished people ; but the event that interested us most was the winning of the Divisional Commander's Cup (three furlongs flat race) by Colonel Stapledon on his horse Zloazel. Captain Bowring, on Bean, was third. The Commanding Officer, with a red football jersey over his tunic, looked a fine sight ; but the amusing thing was that neither he nor anyone else had backed him on the Totalizator for a penny. However, he got a silver cup, and everyone in the battalion was highly pleased. The horse in question had been exchanged by Colonel Gathorne-Hardy with the Brigade Signalling Officer for a pack-pony !

For the next two months there is little enough to say. Salvage went on slowly and unenthusiastically ; education, which the arrival of text-books, etc., should have made easier, was made more complicated by departures ; the camp got steadily better, and the weather got steadily colder.

Boxing, cross-country running, and football were the mainstay of those athletically inclined. Once each week our Concert Party, now attired in real costumes, performed with great *éclat*, and an interchange with other units' parties was effected.

HISTORY OF THE 2/6TH (RIFLE) BATTALION

Company whist drives were organized under considerable difficulty in the darkness of the recreation hut before the acetylene arrived; and in every way all ranks tried their best to fill in those rather irksome days which had to be gone through before each man left for civilian life once more. Demobilization was proceeding, in fact, faster than had been expected. Drafts departed two or three times a week, and several officers and men on leave in the United Kingdom had benefited by that unfortunate order allowing of demobilization from leave.

All horses and mules were carefully examined and checked, with the result that Divisional, Corps and Army Orders became full of notices as to animals " found." Spare animals are excellent things on active service, but awkward at official inspections.

Motor-lorry trips were organized to different places, of which Lille was by far the most popular; and once a week a full load of cheery people would drive off from Warlus at 8 a.m. in the morning for several hours' journey through a land covered with frozen snow. The weather was like at our first initiation into active service—bitterly cold with heavy snow and hard frost, but generally a bright sun, though a biting wind.

On January 19th, like a bolt from the blue, Lieutenant-Colonel Macdonald, D.S.O., Manchester Regiment, arrived to take over command. Needless to say, no one had heard any tidings of his impending arrival, but a few days later Colonel Stapledon was ordered off to the 2nd Manchesters, and Colonel Macdonald assumed command. We were sorry to lose Colonel Stapledon. He had been with us but a short while, but he was universally popular, as, indeed, his successor became in a very short time.

During the month of January 7 officers and 148 men were demobilized, and our ration strength was down to 20 officers and 382 men, enabling two company cook-houses to be closed.

The month of February saw even further reduction, as, in addition to demobilization, 1 officer and 96 men were sent on February 26th up to the Army of Occupation. This rapid disintegration of the battalion brought most activities to a standstill. The railway piquets which we had had to maintain at Arras to keep order and stop looting were recalled ; education died for want of instructors ; football teams, concert parties faded in their time away. The battalion was rapidly approaching its cadre strength, and its days as a unit were numbered.

There is one event that occurred during this month that cannot be passed over in silence. On February 14th, the second anniversary of the departure of the battalion to France, our old Commanding Officer, Colonel Fletcher, died from pneumonia following upon a sudden attack of influenza. It is difficult for one who knew him so intimately, and worked in such close touch with him for so many months, to write of him with becoming restraint. As a Commanding Officer many found him hard and exacting, but he was even more exacting and hard on himself. His whole mind and his whole energy were devoted to his battalion to a degree that only those who saw most of him could ever realize. Wonderfully strong himself, he impressed others with his own strength ; lofty in ideals, he led others to a higher plane. Nothing that was mean or selfish, that was not strictly true and honest, would he tolerate for a moment ; and never was a man more outspoken in his condemnation of anything that was not right in the highest sense. By his devotion to his battalion he worked himself beyond the measure of human endurance, and there can be no doubt that his death was due to the havoc wrought on his frame by the endless work, physical and mental, which he accomplished for his battalion even after the gassing at Armentières, the severe physical effects of which he refused to recognize. Colonel Fletcher represented the highest type of British gentleman, and it was with thoughts of pride as well as sorrow that we learnt that in his last hours his mind ran unceasingly on the comfort and safety of " his boys."

The last days of the battalion require but a brief telling. More drafts left for the Army of Occupation ; more officers and men went off to complete the tour of rest camps, " delousing camps," demobilization camps, and finally dispersal camps *en route* for civilian life. From Christmas onwards the melancholy break-up of our old battalion, of which we had been such proud and happy members, had been proceeding apace. Friendships that had seemed the normal part of our existence were now rudely rent asunder. Men whom we had grown to admire and love vanished one by one, perhaps never to be seen again. The memories of the past grew daily more distant and more unreal as the prospect of civilian life came steadily nearer.

On March 18th the fragments of the battalion, now one company strong, moved to the Brigade Concentration Camp at Maroeuil; and here the gradually diminishing force remained till May 11th, ever expecting to move, only to be disappointed again.

At last, after one or two false alarms, the party, having handed over all its animals, proceeded at 9.5 p.m. on May 11th, with all its transport vehicles, by train for the Base.

At 10.45 p.m. the engine did its best still further to delay matters by leaving the train on a downward slope and coming back to meet it when the train had gathered a good speed. Several vehicles of ours were destroyed, and several men of other cadres injured. A bridge party, consisting of the Commanding Officer, Adjutant, Quartermaster, and Lieutenant Wilson, seated on plush chairs in a cattle truck, was indeed slightly disarranged, but beyond the destruction of the whisky bottle only slight injuries were inflicted.

At 2.35 p.m. on May 12th Havre was reached, and Harfleur Reception Camp was the home for the night. Thence next day the cadre joined No. 2 Wing Despatch Division, and after many formalities embarked on May 15th for Southampton in s.s. *Lydia*. From Southampton to Felixstowe, and thence to Prees Heath, took a few days more, and much man-handling of vehicles and stores; but by 12 noon on May 22nd, 1919, the

LT.-COL. C. C. STAPLEDON.

LT.-COL. C. L. MACDONALD, D.S.O.

" THE KING'S " (LIVERPOOL REGIMENT)

2/6th (Rifle) Battalion " The King's " Liverpool Regiment had ceased to exist.

But in the hearts of those who were numbered among its members the memory of it, and of those who lie buried in the cemeteries of France, will live for ever ; and when in years to come, in the different quarters of the world, men meet each other, how gladly will they cast back their minds to the good old days in the " Second Sixth " !

Finis.

APPENDICES

APPENDIX I

1. *Scouts.*—The origin of the Scout Section can be traced from the earliest days at Liverpool, where the provision of civilian bicycles and the varied nature of their duties made that branch of training popular. With the move to Blackpool they came under the direction of 2nd-Lieutenant G. C. T. Giles, who served with us ungazetted for a time, but was subsequently gazetted to the Divisional Cyclist Company.

From then onwards till the Upstreet days they still continued to exist in an unostentatious fashion; but at Upstreet the scouts and snipers were properly organized under Lieutenant F. O. J. Huntley and Sergeant Fenner. From then onwards till the battalion proceeded overseas their efficiency grew apace, the last few weeks of their training being under Lieutenant Alcock, when Lieutenant Huntley joined Brigade Headquarters Staff. Colonel Fletcher always took the greatest interest in their work, buying them all kinds of snipers' rifle sights, telescopic periscopes, and other valuable aids to their special work. Overseas, under the successive leaderships of Lieutenants Alcock and Royle, 2nd-Lieutenants Little, Noon, and Upward, Lieutenant Burton, and Lieutenant Hazell, the scouts, snipers, and observers more than justified their existence. In addition to Sergeant Fenner, there was Lance-Corporal Peterson and seventeen men in the original contingent, while at Brigade were Corporal Stirrup and three more. After the Armentières gas attack reorganization became necessary, and first Corporal Harper, and later Sergeant Corkill and Lance-Corporal Darcy, were the leading scouts. It is invidious to pick out individuals from such a highly trained and enthusiastic party, but there can be no doubt that, taken all round, Sergeant Corkill was the best of a very good collection of men. The duties of these men varied from patrolling, either collectively or individually with company patrols, leading raiding parties, sniping, manning observation posts, and so forth, in the trenches, to blocking side roads during relief nights, exploring emergency routes, or reconnoitring ordinary routes when the battalion was out of the line.

2. *Runners.*—It is doubtful if any collection of individuals had to work so consistently hard and under such trying conditions, and managed withal to be so invariably cheerful, as the Battalion and Company Runners. Organized at Woking, and recruited largely from the buglers, they first really came into active existence at Strazeele. Throughout the history of the battalion there appears to have been no occasion when a runner failed to reach his destination, except through being incapacitated by wounds. Always on the move, they were the first in the line and the last out of it, with endless messages going day and night; one day cycling along the ominous Houplines road, another day leaving the safety of a pill-box to make their way across mud and shell-holes in the blackness of the night; or, again, dashing (not once, but again and again) through a barrage. Such were some of the duties of which a runner's life was composed.

Before the gas bombardment the Battalion Runners had no actual N.C.O. in charge of them, but later Lance-Corporal Brown, one of the originals, was appointed to take charge of them.

3. *Lewis Gunners.*—In training Lewis Gunners at home we were more than fortunate in possessing Lieutenant Bowring and Sergeant Machell, with the result that we went overseas with gunners possessed of an efficiency of which any battalion might be proud. From then onwards was one unceasing struggle to keep up the numbers. Holding as they often did the dangerous posts, the

casualties were not few, and as our numbers dwindled the supply of guns grew steadily greater. The teams generally had to go into the line twenty-four hours before the remainder of the battalion, and, in addition to the ordinary impedimenta of a relief, they had to carry, at any rate along the trenches, their guns and ammunition, which, when conditions were bad, often proved an almost overwhelming burden. Out of the line they had to be cleaning their guns and ammunition unceasingly, while the care of innumerable spare parts was enough to drive anyone crazy. After Lieutenant Bowring, 2nd-Lieutenants Rothwell, Dwyer, Hicks, and Lieutenants Wilson and Drewsen, in turn took charge of their destinies ; while Sergeants Bond, Simpson, and Rowlandson acted in succession as Battalion Lewis Gun Sergeants.

4. *Battalion Orderly-Room.*—After the first days of chaos we soon settled down to a continued period of great efficiency, broken only by one temporary interruption caused by the gas bombardment. At home, the records and administration of the battalion passed successfully through the hands of Colour-Sergeants Robinson, Sutherland, and Evans, and the completeness of their work can be seen at once by anyone who has to deal with the old battalion orders. Overseas we were no less fortunate in our orderly-room sergeants—Ewan, Longridge, Llewellyn, and Myers. It is one thing to keep files complete and records accurate in the comfortable security of a properly organized orderly-room in England. To maintain no less efficiency and accuracy in France is a very different proposition. Space and stationery are limited ; half your records are always packed and inaccessible ; the orderly-room may be represented by a small " bivvy," a tent lit by one guttering candle, a " lean-to " composed of an old ground sheet, or other commodious habitation. Work under such conditions is trying and difficult, but it always went on ; the orders were always issued, the records always kept, no matter what the obstacles. The amount of work which had to be done may be estimated by the fact that two typewriters were fully employed.

5. *Quartermaster's Department.*—The comprehensive activities of the Quartermaster and his staff would, if adequately dealt with, require a volume in themselves. A few notes on some aspects of their work will only be given.

In England the principal task was, first, to obtain equipment, and, secondly, to account for deficiencies. These difficulties rested in the able hands of Lieutenant Barnett and, latterly, Lieutenant Sutherland. Overseas the responsibilities of an efficient Quartermaster widen out indefinitely. The provision of rations and equipment, no small work in itself, is obviously his main concern; but, apart from that, a zealous Quartermaster regards himself as responsible for everything that conduces to the comfort and welfare of his battalion. He arranges for billets and baths; he acts as commission agent for all kinds of purchases for messes and individuals; he looks after the postal arrangements, obtains money from the field cashier, drinks, cigarettes, and so forth from the Expeditionary Force Canteen; he mends your boots and clothes; he " scrounges " tar felting and oil silk—in a word, he represents to the battalion all the resources of a town, with its shops and its general conveniences of civilization. Lieutenant Sutherland's services to the battalion were beyond all reckoning. He literally slaved day and night to ensure that no battalion was better fed, better clothed, better equipped, and generally better looked after than ours. Captain Smith, who later became Quartermaster, followed in the same tradition, and it is doubtful if we were ever in lack of anything that we seriously wanted. In this work it will be realized that the Quartermaster must have received the whole-hearted support of his staff. Wallas, Heyworth, Cousins, and Benson each in their turn proved most able Regimental Quartermaster-Sergeants. They further controlled an expert staff, each in their different periods supremely efficient in their own particular line—Blackburn, rations; Cooper, coal (he could always " win " an extra hundredweight); Yates, ordnance stores; Handley, mobilization stores; Kessen as a cheese-cutter; and

" THE KING'S " (LIVERPOOL REGIMENT)

Corporal Bell as understudy to the Regimental Quartermaster-Sergeant ; and there were many others who at varying times had their place in " Q " Department. For bootmaking, we had first Sergeant Mottram and later Sergeant Cox, a powerful representative of the 1st King's, who was as fine a boxer as bootmaker. For tailoring, we had originally Sergeant Jewers, and then Greenham, under whom worked an efficient band with strange Russian names.

Another most important branch was represented by the cooks, a most hard-working and efficient body of men, who proved their worth again and again, not only in the ordered cook-houses of England and the better billets of France, but still more in the rough and shelled shanties in the line, in the crude trench fires during a battle, or with their field kitchens on the march. Under Sergeant Lane, who had a curious passion for strolling in No Man's Land at night, and later under Sergeant Austin, the cooks attained a high degree of excellence ; and in spite of the dwindling scale of rations and of the curious articles of food which used to be issued " in lieu of " ordinary items which the war had made scarce, they provided, in spite of their predilection for stew, a diet of which no one, however fastidious, could seriously complain. Rifleman Anderson probably enjoys the record for length of service as a cook, while Rifleman Frith earned the title of " Rissole King."

In this connection one cannot pass over without mention the self-sacrificing service of the men who went on the nightly pilgrimage of the trenches, carrying the awkward and weighty burden of " hot food containers." As you met them struggling in the dark along the narrow and tortuous ways, now stopping to pass beneath an overhead traverse, now forcing their way through a trench whose sides were almost closed in, you could not but admire the persistence and energy which these men exhibited, and on which the chances of hot tea or hot soup for the front line posts entirely depended.

273   T

Of the Pioneers mention has already been made in the narrative of the book. Prior to the formation of the Pioneer Platoon the original establishment of battalion pioneers worked as efficiently and energetically for their limited numbers as their more numerous party did under the later organization.

Two other duties connected with " the Stores " are deserving of mention. The Canteen Corporals—Corporal Hobden for the greater period of our service abroad, and at the latter part Corporal Trapnell—carried out a difficult and arduous task with great ability. Long tramps to distant canteens, and uncomfortable quarters in the line in which to exhibit their wares, constituted their life. The difficulty of reconciling the strict rationing enforced by the Expeditionary Force Canteen with the demands of the battalion made their office no sinecure.

The other duty referred to is that of Post Corporal, the leading exponent being Lance-Corporal A. L. Reade. Endless walking to distant Field Post Offices, long waits for the mail, a long trek home, and innumerable letters to sort—all this was merely a preliminary to the nightly journey up to the line. With all the letters to be re-addressed, and all the registered letters to be handed to their recipients, the task of Post Corporal was full of hard work, responsibility, and often danger.

In conclusion, it must be realized that the Quartermaster's Department enjoyed no immunity from shell fire, with which people are only too apt to connect the lives of those not dwelling in the line itself. Their stores and billets were frequently and —in Armentières, for instance—very heavily shelled. The nightly trip to the line was no sinecure, but often enough a most dangerous performance. Apart from this, their labours were unending. The battalion came out from the line for spells in reserve, or even in rest ; the work of the Quartermaster's Department only varied, it did not decrease.

6. *Transport.*—During the early days at Blackpool, when we first received a few horses and some old civilian waggons, and

from the time at Upstreet, when we became possessed of the regulation transport, the tradition of smartness and efficiency never wavered. Lieutenant Hutchinson had a genius for mules and horse management in general, and was able to complete and consolidate the work begun by 2nd-Lieutenant Eccles. After his transfer to the R.F.C. in 1917, Lieutenant Freeman took over, with all the experience he had enjoyed during many years with the A.S.C. Consequently one expected not only well-groomed animals and spotless vehicles, but also a sound and efficient organization. The latter was always in evidence, and the former only varied in degree according to the situation presented by circumstances. In England Sergeant Walker and Sergeant Lloyd, and overseas Lloyd and latterly Sergeant McGowan, were the successive Transport Sergeants; while in France mention should also be made of Corporals Davis, Tweddle, Steele, and Raws.

The task of a regimental transport on active service is hard. The hours of work and mileage covered by the vehicles daily were often almost incredible. The transfer of the A.S.C. waggons to duties for which the pre-war regulations had not provided put an enormous strain on battalion transport. The increase in material and equipment also produced a legitimate quantity of stuff far in excess of the capacity of the vehicles, and on occasions when M.T. or G.S. waggons were not forthcoming meant heavy work for our horses.

The supply of rations and water to the battalion, when in the trenches or in a battle, always presented a problem requiring bravery and initiative. Never did our transport fail us, whether limbers or pack mules, no matter the difficulties, no matter the shelling.

7. *Signallers.*—The first beginning of the Signal Section can be traced to Liverpool; and though there was a section at Blackpool, under 2nd-Lieutenant E. C. Adam, regular training can hardly be said to have begun before the battalion reached Canterbury, when instruction of a very sound nature commenced under Sergeant

Bowman, of the 1/6th K.L.R. 2nd-Lieutenant Rathbone was here made responsible for the section.

When the 43rd Provisional Battalion was formed, Sergeant Haydon became Signal Sergeant, and a large part of the success and efficiency of the section from then up till November, 1917, was due to his efforts. Lieutenant Wyatt had meanwhile followed 2nd-Lieutenant Rathbone as Signalling Officer. Flag wagging had by now been more than mastered; and the intricacies of the " D III " telephone were now being absorbed, and a limited amount of practical work done with this instrument. At Upstreet the first battalion line was laid, connecting Battalion and Brigade Headquarters. A further step in instruction was taken in the systematic and careful schooling of linemen, and the efficiency thereby obtained proved of the utmost value later. Corporal Gillison was particularly conspicuous in this direction.

The Signal Section soon after this came under the command of Lieutenant J. T. Hazell, a really brilliant exponent of the signaller's art. From the time the battalion went to Aldershot till it left for France, the training went on with fewer and fewer interruptions; and the high standard attained may be realized from the fact that at the official tests, held late in 1916, we produced twenty-nine first-class and four second-class signallers out of thirty-three candidates entered, thereby bringing our total up to about fifty first-class signallers, and, further, won easily the signalling in the Aldershot Command Efficiency Competitions, in spite of powerful rivals. The names of the competitors, all of whom received bronze medals, were as follows :—

Officer in charge	...	...	... Lieut. J. T. Hazell.
N.C.O. in charge	...	...	... Sergt. H. J. Haydon.
Visual sender	...	...	... L./Cpl. S. H. Bell.
Visual caller	...	...	... Rfn. A. C. Cowie.
Visual reader	...	...	... Rfn. W. Whitehead.
Visual writer	...	...	... Rfn. G. Potter.
First line layer	...	...	... Rfn. W. A. Tomlinson.

"THE KING'S" (LIVERPOOL REGIMENT)

Second line layer ...	...	...	Rfn. A. W. Hassall.
Third line layer ...	...	...	Rfn. E. Fryer.
Buzzer sender	...	...	Rfn. W. Harrocks.
Buzzer reader	...	...	Rfn. W. O. Copland.
Runner ...	...	...	Rfn. A. Wood.

During the time the battalion was in France the section not only fulfilled all calls upon its activities in a most efficient manner, but it was continually improving on its methods, learning the latest instruments—fullerphones, power buzzers, Lucas lamps, and so forth. Not only was the system of telephones in every sector we occupied improved and simplified, and communication kept up no matter how often the enemy or wandering individuals smashed the wire, but in raids and periods of fighting, the section, both individually and collectively, showed itself as brave as it was resourceful. In Sergeant Payne was found a worthy successor to Sergeant Haydon. 2nd-Lieutenants Novelle and Thomas in turn acted as Signalling Officers, though the inspiration of Lieutenant Hazell, until he was evacuated shortly before the Armistice, was always present.

Esprit de corps, evident though it was in all ranks, was, if possible, more marked in the case of the signallers; and for their work, of which little can be said here, and of which, by reason of their success, much often passed unnoticed, the battalion owes a great debt.

8. *Medical*.—The hygienic and medical side of a battalion, whether at home or abroad, is of first-rate importance. As Medical Officer's Orderly, Corporal Lawton, Corporal Stubbs, and Corporal Henderson, each in their turn proved their worth again and again. On the sanitary side Sergeant Lawton and, latterly, Corporal Barwise were regular wizards in detecting anything wrong and providing the means to set things right.

Stretcher-bearers have been referred to in several places already. The work of self-sacrifice of stretcher-bearers has been testified by every unit of the British Army, and our own lived up to the highest traditions of their calling ; and our Medical Officers one and all set them an example which they might well be proud to follow. Lance-Corporal Winstanley, who during the latter part of the campaign was in charge of all stretcher-bearers, deserves a special mention for his admirable work.

The " water duty men," originally R.A.M.C. and later Riflemen, performed a thankless and arduous task with perseverance, often under conditions of great danger.

9. *Miscellaneous Instructors.*—The branches of knowledge with which the ordinary soldier has to be familiar are so diverse and so manifold that a host of instructors have to be equipped with special knowledge, in order that each may receive at any rate some instruction in special subjects.

In addition, therefore, to Musketry and Physical Instructors—of the latter, Sergeants Taylor, Jones, Hoskyn, and Ashcroft, and of the former Sergeants Beaumont, Griffiths, Kernighan, and Farrington were the principal exponents—we have Gas N.C.Os. (Sergeant Nicholls, Corporals Harvey and Roles) and Bombing Instructors (Corporal Cathrell, Sergeant Kerr, and Sergeant Grahl). The important duties performed by these N.C.Os. and by the officers who were similarly trained—Lieutenant Wyatt (physical drill), 2nd-Lieutenant Clarke and Lieutenant Burton (bombers), and Lieutenant James (Gas Officer)—are often hardly appreciated, and those who hold those special appointments are not infrequently thought to be in " cushy " jobs. That is as it may be ; the fact remains that invaluable work was performed, and efficiency and protection obtained in vital branches of warfare.

10. *Bugles.*—From the earliest days at Blackpool the Bugles commenced to flourish, and throughout our long training in England they were an established part of our unit. In the early days of France they languished, but after the first " rest " their important position was recovered. In England Sergeant Kernighan was Sergeant-Bugler. During the latter part of the time in France Sergeant Cadman filled that office, while Lance-Corporal

Frost proved a splendid cornet-player. The addition of five cornets was a great success, and latterly whenever out of the line the bugles sounded the recognized calls and carried out the normal routine of barrack life in England. In Lille the mere sight of the buglers produced an enthusiastic crowd, and there can be no question that their performance was well worth watching.

11. *Machine Gunners.*—The origin of this section dates from Blackpool in 1914, when the first beginnings were made under 2nd-Lieutenant Royston. After he proceeded overseas it passed under the care of 2nd-Lieutenant Rathbone, and from him again to Lieutenant Bowring. Under the latter, with the able assistance of Sergeant Machell, the section achieved the highest efficiency, and the arrival of a Vickers gun at Margate enabled the men to give practical demonstrations of their skill.

With the formation of the new Machine Gun Corps, instructions came to us, as to other units, for all our trained machine gunners to be transferred. Accordingly, in May, 1916, twenty-two men were discharged from the Territorial Force and were re-enlisted into the Machine Gun Corps, and formed No. 1 Section of " I " Machine Gun Company, at Grantham. After the normal period at Grantham, the major portion of these men proceeded to Mesopotamia in October, 1916, and fought in the principal action connected with the attempted recovery of Kut and the subsequent advance to Baghdad. The following spring they proceeded to Palestine, and took part in the chief operations there, which constituted the final obliteration of the Turk in that country. A further party of five were transferred to the Machine Gun Corps from Bourley Camp in July, 1916. Of these some proceeded to France, and thence to Salonika.

The various experiences of these men would cover many pages, but it is rather beyond the scope of this work. It may, however, be added that the extremely rapid promotion of our drafts speaks not only for their own merit, but also for that of the battalion in which they obtained their training as soldiers. Out of twenty-seven men, eighteen received promotion, including two warrant officers and three sergeants, while two men received commissions.

12. *Light Trench Mortar Battery.*—In July, 1916, the authorities decided that a Light Trench Mortar Battery should be formed in each of our Brigades, and in due course contingents from each battalion assembled in a corner of our camp to commence instruction in the Stokes trench mortar. Our contribution consisted of Lieutenant D. G. Leonard, one sergeant, two corporals, and nine men, with Lieutenant (later Captain) H. E. Barrow to command the Brigade Battery. The majority of the personnel had previously been sent to a preliminary course at Aldershot. Training accordingly proceeded apace, and the battery was soon firing live ammunition at Pirbright, where it subsequently took up its quarters permanently.

During the various vicissitudes of the Brigade our Trench Mortar Battery took its share of our pleasures and sorrows in full measure. At Houplines it proved more than a match for the German " pine-apples." During raids of our own or the enemy's the men proved themselves worthy of the best traditions, while in open warfare they revealed surprising mobility. From time to time many other men were drafted from every battalion to the battery to replace casualties and to form reserves, and several of the men earned distinctions ; while Captain Barrow, shortly before his transfer in 1917 to the W.A.F.F., was awarded the Military Cross.

APPENDIX II

COMMANDING OFFICERS.

Colonel G. A. Wilson, V.D.

Lieutenant-Colonel W. A. L. Fletcher, D.S.O.

Lieutenant-Colonel Hon. N. C. Gathorne-Hardy, D.S.O., Rifle Brigade.

Lieutenant-Colonel C. C. Stapledon, Manchester Regiment.

Lieutenant-Colonel C. L. Macdonald, D.S.O., Manchester Regiment.

SECONDS-IN-COMMAND.

Major J. Howard Temple.

Major H. K. Wilson.

Major C. W. Wilson, M.C.

Major D. Grant-Dalton, C.M.G., D.S.O.

ADJUTANTS.

Captain W. A. L. Fletcher, D.S.O.

Captain J. Barnett.

Captain C. E. Wurtzburg, M.C.

Captain C. W. Wilson, M.C.

Captain F. C. Bowring.

Captain F. E. Evans.

HISTORY OF THE 2/6TH (RIFLE) BATTALION

QUARTERMASTERS.
Lieutenant J. Barnett.
Lieutenant T. Sutherland.
Lieutenant T. Jackson.
Captain F. V. Smith.

COMPANY COMMANDERS (OVERSEAS).

" A " Company.
Captain F. G. Gilling.
Captain C. T. A. Wyatt.
Captain F. C. Bowring.
Captain J. McWilliam, M.C.
Lieutenant S. E. B. Sage.
Lieutenant C. James, M.C.
Captain J. C. Carr.
Captain R. E. Noon, M.C.

" B " Company.
Captain C. T. Steward.
Lieutenant W. Penrice.
Lieutenant E. C. Adam.
Captain A. H. Broad.
Captain A. G. Eccles, M.C.
Captain T. Robinson, M.C.
Captain E. D. Kissan.

" C " Company.
Captain A. G. Eccles, M.C.
Captain H. Ormrod.
Captain T. A. Williams, M.C.

282

" THE KING'S " (LIVERPOOL REGIMENT)

" D " Company.

Captain C. W. Wilson, M.C.
Captain K. H. Burton.
Captain T. K. Fell.
Captain J. Beavan.

WARRANT OFFICERS (OVERSEAS).

Regimental Sergeant-Majors ... ... {R. Smith.
J. L. Heyworth, M.C.

Regimental Quartermaster-Sergeants {T. Wallas.
J. L. Heyworth, M.C.
G. Cousins.
J. A. Benson.

" A " Company.

Company Sergeant-Majors ... ... {W. C. Bowman.
J. A. Benson.
H. Morrall, M.M.

Company Quartermaster-Sergeants ... {N. E. Jenner.
H. M. Griffiths.
A. L. Beaumont.
F. J. Fenner.

" B " Company.

Company Sergeant-Majors ... ... {A. Kelly.
C. J. Pennington.
T. R. Machell.
H. Gedd.

Company Quartermaster-Sergeants ... {C. J. Pennington.
C. W. Walter.
J. L. Tipping.
R. Batson.

HISTORY OF THE 2/6TH (RIFLE) BATTALION

"C" Company.

Company Sergeant-Majors ... ... $\begin{cases} \text{J. L. Heyworth, M.C.} \\ \text{R. J. Woodward.} \\ \text{G. Lane.} \end{cases}$

Company Quartermaster-Sergeants ... $\begin{cases} \text{R. D. Jackson.} \\ \text{G. Cousins.} \\ \text{J. T. Pollitt.} \end{cases}$

"D" Company.

Company Sergeant-Majors ... ... $\begin{cases} \text{R. Barker, D.C.M.} \\ \text{H. M. Griffiths.} \end{cases}$

Company Quartermaster-Sergeants ... $\begin{cases} \text{R. Batson.} \\ \text{G. Lane.} \\ \text{R. F. Farrington.} \end{cases}$

APPENDIX III.

NOMINAL ROLL.

NOTE.—This Roll has been compiled from the battalion's Part II Orders, and though every effort has been taken to make it accurate, the author feels that for various reasons—in particular the somewhat scanty records of the early period of 1914–15—some errors of fact and date may be present. It is hoped that, as some 4,000 names are recorded, those who suffer from inaccuracies will accept in extenuation the magnitude of the task.

It had been intended to give, where applicable, some record of service done with other units, but it has been found impossible to obtain a complete record of this, and the Roll in consequence is confined to details of service, distinctions, etc., in the battalion. This restriction is the more to be regretted as so many members of the battalion gained high rank and honours with other units, among them being Rifleman G. G. Coury, who shortly after obtaining his commission won the Victoria Cross.

A ✠ has been placed against the name of every officer and man who was killed in action or died of wounds or disease.

ROLL OF OFFICERS.

NAME.	PERIOD SERVED WITH BATTALION.	HIGHEST RANK.	APPOINTMENTS.	HONOURS OR AWARDS.
ADAM, E. C. ...	13/11/14—11/5/15, posted 1/6 K.L.R. ...	Lieut. ...	Int. Officer	—
ALCOCK, P. F. ...	11/8/17—9/1/18, posted 1/6 K.L.R.	Lieut. ...	—	—
ALLEN, L. S. ...	5/2/15—30/7/17, wounded ...	2/Lieut. (T./Lieut.)	—	—
✠ALTY, H., D.C.M. ... (9th K.L.R. attached)	28/4/15—14/1/17, trsfd. Tank Corps / 18/9/18—30/9/18, died of wounds	2/Lieut. ...	—	—
ANDERSON, W. R. ... (Liverpool R. attached)	8/11/17—6/9/18, wounded ...	2/Lieut. ...	—	—
BARDGETT, J. V. ...	17/6/18—29/3/19, demobilized ...	2/Lieut. ...	—	—
BARDSLEY, J. P. ... (7th K.L.R. attached)	26/11/18—10/4/19, trsfd. Base ...	2/Lieut. ...	—	—
BARNETT, J. ...	1/11/14—3/11/16, invalided ...	Captain ...	Q.M., Adjutant	—
BARROW, H. E. ...	16/10/14—19/1/18, trsfd. K. African R.	Lieut. (A./Capt.)	Comd. 171 L.T.M.B.	M.C.
BEAVAN, J. ... (14th K.L.R. attached)	29/11/18—24/3/19, demobilized ...	T./Lieut. (A./Capt.)	Company Comdr. ...	—
BELK, W. A. ...	23/10/18—21/3/19, trsfd. A. of O.	2/Lieut. ...	—	—
BISLAND, J. ... (15th K.L.R. attached)	28/5/15—2/3/16, trsfd. R.E. ...	2/Lieut. ...	—	—
BIRKETT, G. ...	1/10/14—11/5/15, posted 1/6 K.L.R.	Lieut. ...	—	—
BLAKE, J. N. ...	25/4/17—24/3/19, demobilized ...	Lieut. ...	—	—
BOULT, R. H. S. ...	13/1/14—16/2/15, posted 1/6 K.L.R.	2/Lieut. ...	—	—
BOWRING, F. C. ...	2/3/15—26/2/19, demobilized ...	Lieut. (A./Capt.)	M.G.O., L.G.O., Coy. Comdr., Adjutant	Twice M. in D.
BRETHEL, I. P. ... (R.A.S.C. attached)	11/11/18—10/4/19, trsfd. Base ...	2/Lieut. ...	—	—
BRIGGS, H. ...	31/3/17—15/4/17, sick ...	2/Lieut. ...	—	—
BRIGHOUSE, T. J. ...	23/8/17—14/1/18, wounded ...	2/Lieut. ...	—	—
BROAD, A. H. ...	5/8/15—8/11/15, posted 1/6 K.L.R. / 5/8/17—10/7/18, sick ...	Lieut. (A./Capt.)	Company Comdr.	—
BROCKLEBANK, R. E. R. ...	27/11/14—17/6/15, posted 3/6 K.L.R.	Lieut. (T./Capt.)	—	—
BUCKLEY, E. K. ...	20/11/14—11/5/15, posted 1/6 K.L.R.	2/Lieut. ...	—	—
BURTON, G. B. ...	12/3/15—11/7/15, posted 1/6 K.L.R.	2/Lieut. ...	—	—
✠BURTON, K. H. ...	14/5/15—16/6/18, killed in action	Lieut. (A./Capt.)	Company Comdr.	—
CAMERON, C. W. ...	18/2/15—23/5/15, posted 3/6 K.L.R.	2/Lieut. ...	Scout Officer	—
✠CARR, J. C. ... (Liverpool R. attached)	15/9/17—21/10/18, killed in action	2/Lieut. (A./Capt.)	Company Comdr.	—
CLARKE, C. W. ...	20/8/15—4/2/18, wounded ...	Lieut. ...	—	M.C.
✠COLLINGE, W. R. ...	21/6/15—7/8/17, died of wounds	Lieut. ...	—	—
CUFFLIN, C. A. ... (Liverpool R. attached)	2/11/18—21/3/19, trsfd. A. of O.	2/Lieut. ...	—	—
DAVIDSON, W. H. H. ...	13/11/14—30/4/15, posted 1/6 K.L.R.	2/Lieut. ...	—	—

Name	Dates and remarks	Rank	Appointment	Honours, etc.
DREWSEN, J. B. R. (Lancs. Hussars attached)	17/6/18—18/2/19, demobilized	2/Lieut.	—	—
DUGDALE, D. (4th K.O.R.L. attached)	4/2/17— —/6/17, sick	Lieut.	—	—
DWYER, W. J. (Liverpool R. attached)	22/10/17—29/4/18, sick	2/Lieut.	L.G. Officer	—
EASTWOOD, D.	19/8/15—8/11/15, posted 1/6 K.L.R.	2/Lieut.	Transport Officer	M.C.
ECCLES, A. G.	5/10/14—30/7/17, wounded	Captain	Company Comdr.	—
EUPEN, C. F. (Liverpool R. attached)	5/1/18—5/1/19, demobilized	2/Lieut.	—	—
EVANS, F. E.	5/9/17—21/1/18, sick; 4/2/17—30/7/17, wounded	Lieut. (A./Capt.)	Assistant Adjutant; Adjutant	—
FELL, T. K.	3/10/18—22/5/19, demobilized	Lieut. (A./Capt.)	Company Comdr.	—
FLETCHER, G. L.	17/3/17—22/11/18, sick; 13/11/14—17/6/15, posted as C.O. 3/6 K.L.R.	Captain	Company Comdr.	—
FLETCHER, W. A. L., D.S.O.	10/11/14—30/7/17, wounded; 10/9/17—23/7/18, resigned command	Major (T./Lt./Col.)	Adjutant, C.O.	Twice M. in D., Brevet Major, Chev. L. d'Honneur
FORSHAW, A. F. (Liverpool R. attached)	1/11/18—9/4/19, demobilized	2/Lieut.	—	—
FREEMAN, C. S.	28/8/17—14/2/19, demobilized	Lieut.	Transport Officer	M. in D.
FRY, A. J. (Liverpool R. attached)	29/11/18—8/4/19, demobilized	Lieut.	—	—
GATHORNE-HARDY, Hon. N. C. (Rifle Bde. attached)	23/7/18—24/11/18, trsfd.	Major (A./Lt./Col.)	C.O.	D.S.O. Twice M. in D.
GRANT-DALTON, D., C.M.G., D.S.O. (W. Yorks R. attd.)	21/11/18—22/2/19, trsfd.	Major	2nd-in-Command	—
GILLING, F. G.	13/11/14—2/6/17, sick	Lieut. (T./Capt.)	Company Comdr.	—
GOFFEY, W.	29/4/15—23/5/15, posted 3/6 K.L.R.	2/Lieut.	—	—
GOULDING, E. A.	14/2/17—6/2/18, tour of duty in Eng.	2/Lieut.	—	—
GREEN, H. G.	17/6/18—13/9/18, wounded	2/Lieut.	—	—
GROOME, A. C. H. (14th K.L.R. attached)	28/5/15—20/7/16, trsfd. R.F.C.	2/Lieut.	—	—
HARDY, F. (Liverpool R. attached)	21/9/18—8/3/19, trsfd. A. of O.	2/Lieut.	—	—
HARPER, C. R. (Liverpool R. attached)	5/9/17—15/9/18, trsfd. R.A.F.	2/Lieut.	—	—
HARRIS, J. K.	23/4/18—13/2/19, demobilized	2/Lieut.	Sig. O., Int. O.	M.C.
HAZELL, J. T.	3/7/15—1/11/18, sick	Lieut.	—	—
HERSCHELL, E.	13/11/14—22/3/15, posted 1/6 K.L.R.	Lieut. (T./Capt.)	Company Comdr.	—
HICKS, J. E.	7/12/17—5/9/18, wounded	2/Lieut.	L.G. Officer	—
HODGKINSON, W.	17/3/17—5/11/17, trsfd. R.F.C.	2/Lieut.	—	—
HOLLAND, L. M.	31/10/14—24/8/16, trsfd.	Lieut. (T./Capt.)	—	—
HOOPER, F.	1/2/18—24/3/19, demobilized	2/Lieut.	Pioneer Officer	—
HOWARD, W. R. (5th K.L.R. attached)	13/11/14—15/8/15, trsfd. 43 Prov. Bn.	Lieut.	—	—

NAME.	PERIOD SERVED WITH BATTALION.	HIGHEST RANK.	APPOINTMENTS.	HONOURS OR AWARDS.
HUGHES, E. V.	23/11/14—11/7/15, posted 1/6 K.L.R.	2/Lieut.		—
HUNTLEY, F. O. J.	26/6/15— —/12/18	Lieut.	Brigade Int. O.	M. in D.
HUTCHINSON, A.	7/6/15—22/7/17, attached R.F.C.	Lieut.	Transport Officer	—
JACKSON, T. R.	9/9/17—4/11/17, sick	Lieut. and Q.M.		—
JACOBS, A.	1/2/18—25/8/18, trsfd. R.A.F.	2/Lieut.	Bn. Gas Officer	—
JAMES, C.	21/5/16—30/9/18, wounded	Lieut.	Company Comdr.	M.C.
JOHNSON, F. J. (15th K.L.R. attached)	5/6/15—1/5/16, trsfd.	2/Lieut.		—
JONES, T. W. (Liverpool R. attached)	5/9/17—28/4/18, sick	2/Lieut.	Pioneer Officer	—
JONES, W. J.	13/11/14—11/5/15, posted 1/6 K.L.R.	Lieut.		—
KELK, A. E. (attached)	14/5/15—18/10/15, relinquished comn.	Lieut. and Q.M.		—
KISSAN, E. D. (14th K.L.R. attached)	16/9/18—29/12/18, demobilized	T./Lieut. (A./Capt.)	Company Comdr., Int. Officer	—
LAWRENCE, E.	13/11/14—14/3/15, T.F.Res.	Captain	Company Comdr.	—
LEONARD, D. G.	27/5/16—17/11/17, attd. 171 L.T.M.B.	Lieut. (A./Capt.)		M.C.
LEVER, T.	5/9/17—25/1/19, demobilized	2/Lieut.		—
LITTLE, J. H. M.	15/10/15—30/7/17, wounded	2/Lieut.	Int. Officer	—
LOUDEN, T. H.	8/7/17—2/4/19, demobilized	Lieut.		—
LUTZ, F., M.C. (Liverpool R. attached)	15/11/18—16/2/19, demobilized	Lieut.		—
McCORMICK, P. C. (6th Lancs. Fus. attached)	15/11/16—14/2/17	Lieut.	Empl. Div. H.Q.	—
MACDONALD, C. L., D.S.O. (Manchester R. attached)	20/1/19—22/5/19, demobilized	T./Lieut./Col.	C.O.	—
McWILLIAM, J.	17/3/17—12/11/17, wounded	2/Lieut. (A./Capt.)	Company Comdr.	M.C.
MATHER, P. D.	4/6/15—23/8/15, posted 1/6 K.L.R.	2/Lieut.		—
MAY, L. G.	22/9/14—15/8/15, trsfd. Home Service unit	2/Lieut. (T./Lieut.)	Transport Officer	—
MILLER, A. T.	13/11/14—16/6/15, posted 3/6 K.L.R.	Captain	Company Comdr.	—
MOON, J.	27/11/14—18/12/16, attd. Portugese E.F.	Lieut. (T./Capt.)	Company Comdr.	—
MOSELEY, O. V. (6th Lancs. Fus. attached)	15/11/16—30/7/17, attd. 57 H.T.M.B.	Lieut.		—
NOON, R. E.	14/4/17—24/3/19, demobilized	Lieut. (A./Capt.)	Company Comdr.	M.C.
NOVELLE, F. (Liverpool R. attached)	5/9/17—6/2/19, demobilized	2/Lieut.	Sig. Officer	—
ORMROD, H. (6th Bn. Lancs. F. attd.)	16/11/16—22/2/18, tour of duty in Eng.	Lieut. (A./Capt.)	Company Comdr.	—
PARKER, P. G. F.	7/11/14—28/6/17, wounded	Lieut. (T./Capt.)	Company Comdr.	—
PARKINSON, J. A. (5th K.O.R.L. attached)	4/2/17—30/7/17, wounded	Lieut.		—
PATERSON, J. (N.F. attached)	3/8/18—5/9/18, wounded	2/Lieut.		—
PAUL, E. E. (6th Bn. Lancs. F. attd.)	15/11/16—24/6/17, wounded; 30/7/17, wounded	2/Lieut.		—

Name	Dates / Remarks	Rank	Appointment	Award
PAUL, J. R.	12/6/15—29/7/17, wounded	Lieut.	—	
PEGGE, W. J.	7/12/17—4/7/18, wounded	2/Lieut.	—	
PENRICE, W.	25/4/17—30/7/17, wounded	Lieut.	—	
✠PROFIT, L. T. (3rd K.L.R. attached)	13/7/17—5/10/18, sick	Lieut.	—	
	5/9/17—3/11/17, wounded	2/Lieut.	—	
✠PURDIE, D. S. (9th K.L.R. attached)	6/4/18—20/6/18, died of wounds		—	
	3/12/17—30/9/18, died of wounds	2/Lieut.	—	
RATHBONE, R. R.	15/10/14—15/8/15, trsfd.	2/Lieut.	—	
REID, W.	24/12/14—6/2/15, posted 1/6 K.L.R.	2/Lieut.	—	
RIGBY, A. W. (9th K.L.R. attached)	23/11/17—23/3/18, sick	2/Lieut.	—	
ROBERTS, H. J. (Liverpool R. attached)	5/9/17—6/6/18, sick	2/Lieut.	Asst. Adjt. Company Comdr.	M.C. & bar
ROBINSON, T. (Liverpool R. attached)	5/9/17—28/9/18, sick	2/Lieut. (A./Capt.)	—	
ROGERS, G. P.	13/11/14—15/8/15, trsfd. 43rd Prov. Bn.	Capt.	—	
ROTHWELL, G.	7/2/17—30/7/17, wounded	2/Lieut.	Int. Officer	
ROYLE, H. H. E.	17/10/17—13/3/18, tour of duty in Eng.	Lieut.	—	
	15/11/18—25/1/19, demobilized			
ROYSTON, J. W.	13/11/14—11/5/15, posted 1/6 K.L.R.	Lieut.	—	
RULE, R. (4th K.O.R.L. attached)	4/2/17—2/7/17, trsfd.	2/Lieut.	—	
RYCROFT, J. A. (Liverpool R. attached)	5/9/17—22/1/18, trsfd.	2/Lieut.	—	
✠SAGE, S. E. B. (4th Bn. Glouc. R. attached)	1/2/18—13/9/18, died of wounds	Lieut.	Company Comdr.	
SHIRT, R.	18/9/18—1/10/18, wounded	2/Lieut.	—	
SIMPSON, H. (9th K.L.R. attached)	1/10/18—24/3/19, demobilized	2/Lieut.	—	
SMITH, F. V. (4th Bn. Ches. R. attd.)	13/12/17—22/5/19, demobilized	Capt. and Q.M.	—	
STAPLEDON, C. C. (Manch. R. attached)	13/12/18—26/1/19, trsfd.	Major (A./Lt./Col.)	C.O.	
STEWARD, C. T.	30/4/15—30/7/17, wounded	Lieut. (A./Capt.)	Company Comdr.	
	14/10/17—-/1/19...		Attd. H.Q. 171 Bde.	
SUTHERLAND, T	20/10/15—14/7/17, wounded	Lieut. and Q.M.	—	M. in D.
SUTTON, A. E. B.	7/12/17—14/5/18, trsfd.	2/Lieut.	—	
TEBBUT, J. L. (5th K.L.R. attached)	19/2/18—25/9/18, sick	Lieut.	—	
TEMPLE, J. H.	8/10/14—31/3/15, trsfd. R.N.V.R.	Major	2nd-in-Command	
THOMAS, I. T. B. (5th K.L.R. attached)	1/2/18—4/6/18, wounded	2/Lieut.	Signalling Officer	
UPWARD, S. P. G. (Liverpool R. attached)	5/9/17—10/9/18, wounded	2/Lieut.	Scout Officer	
✠VAUGHAN, D. (3rd K.L.R. attached)	5/9/17—30/10/17, killed in action	2/Lieut.	—	

NAME.	PERIOD SERVED WITH BATTALION.	HIGHEST RANK.	APPOINTMENTS.	HONOURS OR AWARDS.
✠WALN, E. A.	7/12/17—21/10/18, killed in action	2/Lieut.	—	—
WILLIAMS, D. J. (Liverpool R. attached)	15/8/18—26/2/19, trsfd. A. of O.	2/Lieut.	—	—
WILLIAMS, D. R. (Liverpool R. attached)	22/9/18—27/2/19, demobilized	2/Lieut.	—	—
WILLIAMS, T. A. (5th K.I.R. attached)	1/2/18—5/2/19, demobilized	Lieut (A./Capt.)	Company Commdr.	M.C.
✠WILLIAMS, T. L. (Liverpool R. attached)	5/9/17—1/9/18, killed in action	2/Lieut.	—	—
WILSON, C. W.	31/10/14—21/10/18, trsfd. to U.K.	Capt. (A./Major)	Company Commdr. Adjt., 2nd-in-Comd.	M.C., Belgian C. de G.
WILSON, D. (3rd N.F. attached)	31/8/18—24/1/19, demobilized	2/Lieut.	—	—
WILSON, G. A., V.D.	25/9/14—6/8/15, resigned command	Colonel	C.O.	—
WILSON, H. K.	31/10/14—30/7/17, wounded 27/12/17, sick	Capt. (A./Major)	2nd-in-Command	M. in D.
WILSON, S. M.	1/2/18—22/5/19, demobilized	Lieutenant	Assist. Adjt.	—
WITHERS, H. R. (5th K.I.R. attached)	21/5/15—8/11/15, posted 3/6 K.L.R.	2/Lieut.	—	—
WOODWORTH, T. W., M.M. (Liverpool R. attached)	2/11/18—8/3/19, trsfd. A. of O.	2/Lieut.	—	—
WURTZBURG, C. E.	22/9/14—3/9/17, sick 7/12/17—16/5/18, sick 26/9/18—20/2/19, demobilized	Capt.	Adjt.	M.C.
WYATT, C. T. A.	14/5/15—26/9/17, wounded	Lieut. (A./Capt.)	Sig. Officer Company Commdr.	—

MEDICAL OFFICERS.

UNITED KINGDOM.

LIEUT. T. ATKINS, R.A.M.C.
CAPT. R. J. ROGERS, R.A.M.C.

OVERSEAS.

LIEUT. L. A. WILSON, R.A.M.C.
CAPT. T. McHUGH, R.A.M.C.
CAPT. H. ROBINSON, R.A.M.C.
CAPT. A. G. G. PLUMLEY, R.A.M.C.
CAPT. O. H. BULLOCK, R.A.M.C.

CAPT. J. LIVINGSTON, R.A.M.C.
LIEUT. L. A. WILSON, R.A.M.C.

LIEUT. W. H. GORDON, M.O.R.C., U.S.A.
MAJOR N. W. KIDSTON, R.A.M.C.
LIEUT. N. A. SULLO, M.O.R.C., U.S.A.
LIEUT. N. S. REED, M.O.R.C., U.S.A.

CHAPLAINS—OVERSEAS.

REV. M. J. ELAND.
REV. S. WEAVER.

REV. F. H. SIMMS.
REV. S. J. HUGHES.

ROLL OF WARRANT OFFICERS,
NON-COMMISSIONED OFFICERS, AND MEN.

A † after date of leaving indicates that service in battalion was not continuous.

NAME.	REGTL. NO.	DATE OF JOINING.	DATE OF LEAVING WITH CAUSE.	HIGHEST RANK.	HONOURS OR AWARDS.
Abbey, H. ...	2407	11/9/14	5/8/15, transferred	Rifleman.	
Ackroyd, E. ...	2954	12/11/14	12/1/15, transferred ...	Rifleman.	
Ackroyd, E. ...	1600	23/2/15	26/6/15, transferred ...	Rifleman.	
Acton, E. ...	3037	16/11/14	16/2/16, transferred ...	Rifleman.	
Adams, A. R. ...	241017	11/11/14	3/10/18, wounded	Sergeant.	
Adams, B. C. ...	2097	31/8/14	26/6/15, transferred ...	Rifleman.	
Adams, C. ...	2732	2/11/14	12/1/15, transferred ...	Rifleman.	
Adams, C. ...	243663	6/10/16	21/1/19,† demobilized ...	L./Corpl.	
Adams, E. C. ...	2116	31/8/14	13/11/14, commission ...	Rifleman.	
Adams, H. ...	2481	11/9/14	5/8/15, transferred	Rifleman.	
Adams, J. H. ...	242348	8/3/16	30/11/18, wounded	Rifleman.	
Adams, S. ...	47467	24/2/18	9/7/18, transferred	Rifleman.	
Adamson, J. H. ...	3136	4/12/14	25/2/15, commission	Rifleman.	
Adamson, T. C. ...	1680	23/10/14	26/6/15, transferred ...	L./Corpl.	
Addison, J. ...	2983	12/11/14	26/6/15, transferred ...	Rifleman.	
Adlington, T. ...	17264	6/6/18	30/1/19, demobilized ...	Sergeant.	M.M.
Adshead, R. ...	50703	18/8/17	16/5/18, wounded	Rifleman.	
Agar, W. ...	50179	7/3/18	10/2/19, demobilized ...	Rifleman.	
Ainscough, J. ...	242531	24/5/16	22/1/19, demobilized ...	Rifleman.	
Ainslie, K. ...	1873	23/10/14	12/1/15, transferred ...	A./Corpl.	
Ainsworth, J. ...	16501	27/6/18	11/1/19, sick	L./Corpl.	
Aird, W. ...	5002	18/3/16	18/10/16, transferred ...	Rifleman.	
Aitchison, T. H. G. ...	3185	4/1/15	5/8/15, transferred	Rifleman.	
Albin, D. ...	57386	14/6/18	28/8/18, sick	Rifleman.	
Alcock, E. G. ...	3144	7/12/14	26/6/15, transferred ...	Rifleman.	
Alcock, J. ...	242415	21/3/16	16/4/17, transferred ...	Rifleman.	
Alcock, S. ...	27519	27/6/18	18/1/19, demobilized ...	Rifleman.	
Aldecocea, G. ...	2724	30/10/14	1/12/15, demobilized ...	Rifleman.	
Aldous, S. ...	241274	29/3/15	5/9/18, sick	Sergeant.	
Aldridge, H. ...	105557	12/7/18	26/2/19, demobilized...	Rifleman.	
Alexander, J. H. ...	2763	6/11/14	26/6/15, transferred ...	Rifleman.	
Alexander, L. ...	2281	2/9/14	—/—/15, transferred...	Rifleman.	
Alexander, P. V. ...	2636	7/10/14	16/2/15, commission ...	A./Corpl.	
Alexander, R. E. ...	1627	23/10/14	26/6/15, transferred ...	Rifleman.	
Alldridge, D. ...	1705	23/2/15	26/6/15, transferred ...	Rifleman.	
Allen, J. ...	2759	6/11/14	26/6/15, transferred ...	Rifleman.	
Allen, J. A. ...	2963	12/11/14	12/1/15, transferred ...	Rifleman.	
Allen, R. ...	380275	27/5/18	10/10/18, wounded ...	Rifleman.	
Allen, W. ...	240991	10/11/14	16/9/18, transferred ...	Sergeant.	
Allen, W. ...	88182	8/11/17	9/4/18, transferred ...	Rifleman.	
Allen, W. H. ...	80300	24/8/17	7/9/18, wounded	Rifleman.	
Allen, W. J. ...	202196	14/3/18	26/2/19, posted 25th K.L.R.	Rifleman.	
Allenby, A. G. ...	72508	13/8/17	28/3/19, posted 13th K.L.R.	Rifleman.	
Allenby, C. ...	2676	19/10/14	26/6/15, transferred ...	Rifleman.	
Allford, B. ...	88112	5/10/17	19/11/17, sick	Rifleman.	
Allinson, F. E. ...	3274	18/2/15	26/6/15, transferred	Rifleman.	
Allinson, J. ...	50704	18/8/17	22/3/19, posted 25th K.L.R.	Rifleman.	

HISTORY OF THE 2/6TH (RIFLE) BATTALION

NAME.	REGTL. NO.	DATE OF JOINING.	DATE OF LEAVING WITH CAUSE.	HIGHEST RANK.	HONOURS OR AWARDS.
Allinson, W. ...	202406	22/6/18	—/—/19, demobilized ...	Rifleman.	
Allman, S. ...	88107	5/10/17	14/3/18, transferred ...	Rifleman.	
Allsopp, W. ...	3386	3/7/15	22/7/16,† transferred...	Rifleman.	
Alpine, G. ...	242409	20/3/16	23/10/18, posted 13th K.L.R.	Rifleman.	
Alty, H. ...	30062	1/2/18	5/3/19, demobilized ...	Rifleman.	
Alty, H. ...	243763	10/10/16	17/8/17, transferred ...	Rifleman.	
Amery, E. S.	241265	19/3/15	18/10/17, wounded ...	Rifleman.	
Amos, A. H. ...	241350	3/7/15	6/3/19,† demobilized	Sergeant.	
✠Anderson, J. H.	241275	29/3/15	1/9/18, killed in action	Corporal.	
Anderson, J. W.	5221	14/5/16	18/8/16, transferred ...	Rifleman.	
Anderson, L.	451	23/10/14	26/6/15, transferred ...	Rifleman.	
Anderson, P. ...	240644	10/9/14	10/2/19, demobilized	Rifleman.	
Anderson, R. S.	2252	1/9/14	—/—/15, transferred...	Rifleman.	
Anderton, F. ...	6536	10/10/16	12/11/16, transferred	Rifleman.	
Anderton, W. ...	40114	1/2/18	18/1/19, demobilized	Corporal.	
Andrews, A. G. ...	2423	11/9/14	12/1/15, transferred ...	Rifleman.	
✠Angell, A. ...	241279	28/3/15	12/7/17, killed in action	Rifleman.	
Anglesey, J.	241235	9/2/15	12/9/17, posted 1/6th K.L.R.	L./Corpl.	
Annison, —. ...	2408	11/9/14	12/1/15, transferred ...	Rifleman.	
Anslow, F. P.	241375	27/5/15	17/7/18, commission ...	Sergeant.	
Antrobus, G. H.	3704	6/8/15	6/9/15, transferred ...	Rifleman.	
Applebee, W.	50930	18/8/17	20/8/17, posted 2/8th K.L.R.	Rifleman.	
Appleton, T. ...	331670	27/8/17	19/1/18, sick	Corporal.	
Apsimmon, G. ...	1473	27/2/15	26/6/15, transferred ...	Rifleman.	
Arbery, W. J. ...	2656	13/10/14	10/9/15, transferred ...	L./Corpl.	
Arden, E. ...	88213	8/11/17	26/1/18, sick	Rifleman.	
Arden, T. ...	22003	30/5/18	26/1/19, demobilized	Rifleman.	
Argue, T. C. ...	2233	1/9/14	—/—/15, transferred	Rifleman.	
Arkwright, F. ...	50702	18/8/17	28/3/19, posted 13th K.L.R.	Rifleman.	
Armitage, W. ...	72530	13/8/17	29/8/18, posted 1st K.L.R. ...	Rifleman.	
Armstrong, G. T.	200925	25/11/18	2/3/19, demobilized ...	Corporal.	
Armstrong, T. H.	1282	27/2/15	2/4/15, commission ...	A./Sergt.	
Armstrong, W. ...	243774	10/10/16	24/2/18, sick	L./Corpl.	
Arnold, E. ...	49683	24/2/18	16/1/19, demobilized ...	Rifleman.	M.M.
Arnold, F. J. ...	95737	17/4/18	6/9/18, wounded ...	Rifleman.	
Arnold, T. G. ...	2814	9/11/14	26/6/15, transferred ...	Rifleman.	
Arrowsmith, H. ...	3170	28/12/14	21/8/15, commission... ...	Rifleman.	
Ashall, T. ...	90759	7/3/18	29/8/18, posted 1st K.L.R. ...	Rifleman.	
Ashbridge, J. ...	243826	13/10/16	28/3/19,† posted 13th K.L.R.	Rifleman.	
✠Ashcroft, J. E. ...	240830	5/10/14	23/7/17, killed in action	Rifleman.	
Ashcroft, L. ...	22604	6/6/18	21/2/19, demobilized	Sergeant.	
Ashford, F. ...	5050	21/3/16	31/8/16, discharged ...	Rifleman.	
Ashley, G. A. ...	242261	26/1/16	21/8/17, wounded ...	Rifleman.	
Ashton, T. ...	240760	18/9/14	11/8/17, invalided to England	Rifleman.	
Ashurst, T. R. ...	242125	11/1/18	17/1/18, posted 13th K.L.R.	Rifleman.	
Ashworth, F. ...	108754	28/9/18	20/11/18, transferred	Rifleman.	
Ashworth, R. C.	240496	31/8/14	13/3/17, transferred ...	Rifleman.	
✠Ashworth, T. ...	50705	18/8/17	31/10/17, died of wounds	Rifleman.	
Ashworth, W. ...	243734	9/10/16	20/5/17,† posted 1st K.L.R.	Rifleman.	
Ashworth, W. J.	300464	27/5/18	29/1/19, demobilized	Corporal.	
Ashworth, W. L.	241277	29/3/15	6/7/17, wounded ...	L./Corpl.	
✠Askew, R. ...	202951	22/6/18	1/9/18, killed in action	Rifleman.	
Aspell, S. G. ...	3063	19/11/14	5/8/15, transferred ...	Rifleman.	
Aspinall, A. ...	235424	1/2/18	5/3/19, demobilized ...	Rifleman.	
Astley, H. C. ...	1363	27/2/15	20/11/15, commission ...	A./Sergt.	
Astley, W. ...	88682	11/3/18	7/1/19, demobilized ...	Rifleman.	
Atcheson, W. T.	3193	8/1/15	2/8/17, transferred ...	Rifleman.	
Atherton, J. H. ...	1598	23/2/15	26/6/15, transferred ...	Rifleman.	

"THE KING'S" (LIVERPOOL REGIMENT)

NAME.	REGTL. NO.	DATE OF JOINING.	DATE OF LEAVING WITH CAUSE.	HIGHEST RANK.	HONOURS OR AWARDS.
Atherton, R. ...	202408	1/2/18	7/3/18, sick	Rifleman.	
Atherton, W. H.	242192	21/1/16	21/3/19,† sick	Rifleman.	
Atkin, J.	51742	14/6/18	15/10/18, wounded	Rifleman	M.M.
Atkin, P. M.	241396	3/7/15	29/12/17, wounded ...	Sergeant.	
✠Atkinson, J. ...	243656	6/10/16	8/8/17, died of wounds ...	Rifleman.	
Atkinson, J. ...	56918	13/8/17	28/1/19, demobilized ...	Rifleman.	
Atkinson, J. ...	95735	17/4/18	4/6/18, sick	Rifleman.	
Atkinson, J. P. ...	381190	1/2/18	26/10/18, wounded	Rifleman.	
Atkinson, R. G. ...	3197	8/1/15	9/4/16, transferred	Rifleman.	
✠Atkinson, R. G. ...	243773	10/10/16	4/6/17, killed in action ...	Rifleman.	
Audley, S. ...	240972	9/11/14	4/9/18, transferred	Sergeant.	
Aughton, M. ...	88105	5/10/17	10/5/18, sick	Rifleman.	
Auster. N. C. L. ...	2496	16/9/14	26/6/15, transferred	Rifleman.	
Austin, J. B. ...	240504	31/8/14	13/3/17, transferred	Rifleman.	
Austin R. ...	300579	1/2/18	7/2/19, demobilized	Sergeant	M. in D.
Austin, T. H. ...	2660	13/10/14	17/5/15, transferred	Rifleman.	
Austin, W. H. ...	1571	27/2/15	26/6/15, transferred	Rifleman	
Avery, H. ...	2711	29/10/14	12/1/15, transferred	Rifleman.	
Avery, J. ...	243728	9/10/16	16/5/17, transferred	Rifleman.	
Aynsley, W. H. ...	2551	23/9/14	12/1/15, transferred	Rifleman.	
Axson, H. ...	200579	8/7/17	6/8/17, sick	Rifleman.	
Babut, A. ...	243686	7/10/16	26/2/19, posted 25th K.L.R.	Rifleman.	
Bacon, F. H. ...	2664	14/10/14	2/1/16, commission	A./Sergt.	
Baddley, J. ...	49629	1/2/18	8/9/18, wounded	Rifleman.	
Bagshaw, R. ...	88248	8/11/17	14/2/18, sick	Rifleman.	
Bailey, A. ...	26665	1/2/18	9/12/18, transferred	Rifleman.	
Bailey, A. ...	50901	1/2/18	—/—/19, demobilized	Rifleman.	
Bailey, G. ...	2389	10/9/14	1/5/15, transferred	Rifleman.	
Bailey, G. ...	242258	25/1/16	17/1/19, demobilized	Rifleman.	
Bailey, G. F. ...	240719	14/9/14	18/5/18, wounded	Rifleman.	
Bailey, H. ...	21239	2/7/18	20/1/19, transferred	Rifleman.	
Bailey, J. ...	241469	6/8/15	17/4/18,† transferred ...	Rifleman	M.M.
Bailey, J. ...	243756	10/10/16	15/9/17, posted 1/6th K.L.R.	Rifleman.	
Bailey, W. ...	240135	27/2/15	20/9/18,† commission ...	Rifleman.	
Bain, C. J. ...	2297	10/9/14	5/8/15, transferred	Rifleman.	
✠Bain, R.	29156	27/5/18	1/9/18, killed in action ...	Sergeant.	
Baines, G. ...	88201	8/11/17	26/2/19, posted 13th K.L.R.	Corporal.	
Baines, H. ...	2746	4/11/14	26/6/15, transferred	Rifleman.	
Baines, H. ...	29962	18/3/18	5/3/19, demobilized	Rifleman.	
Baines, — ...	2393	10/9/14	12/1/15, transferred	Rifleman.	
Baker, A. ...	241135	26/11/14	10/8/17, invalided to England	Rifleman.	
Baker, G. ...	88595	1/2/18	29/3/18, transferred	Rifleman.	
Baker, G. H. ...	88683	1/2/18	26/2/19, posted 25th K.L.R.	Rifleman.	
Baker, S. ...	2832	9/11/14	26/6/15, transferred	Rifleman.	
Baker, S. R. ...	2831	9/11/14	17/5/15, transferred	A./L./Corpl.	
Baker, Thos. ...	2921	11/11/14	26/6/15, transferred	Rifleman.	
Baker, T. B. ...	241461	6/8/15	28/7/17, wounded	Rifleman.	
Baker, W. ...	88539	19/9/17	29/8/18, sick	Rifleman.	
Baker, W. S. ...	2392	10/9/14	12/1/15, transferred	Rifleman.	
Baker, W. H. ...	241997	5/5/17	20/5/17, transferred	Rifleman.	
Balfour, A. ...	2796	9/11/14	12/1/15, transferred	Rifleman.	
Ball, E.	243748	9/10/16	9/9/17,† posted 1/9th K.L.R.	Rifleman.	
Ball, R. H. ...	2226	1/9/14	23/12/15, commission ...	Rifleman.	
Ball, R. H. ...	2455	12/9/14	12/1/15, transferred	Rifleman.	
Ball, T. S. ...	3027	16/11/14	5/8/15, transferred	Rifleman.	
Ball, W.	50297	2/7/18	5/3/19, demobilized	Rifleman.	
Ball, W.	241703	11/1/18	17/1/18, posted 13th K.L.R.	Rifleman.	

NAME.	REGTL. NO.	DATE OF JOINING	DATE OF LEAVING WITH CAUSE.	HIGHEST RANK.	HONOURS OR AWARDS
Ball, W. T. ...	4821	26/1/16	6/2/17, commission	Rifleman.	
Balloch, W. T. ...	3219	18/1/15	5/8/15, transferred	A./L./Corpl.	
Ballsdon, H. ...	241083	16/11/14	5/2/19, demobilized	Rifleman.	
Balmforth, C. E. ...	2501	11/9/14	7/10/15, commission	Rifleman.	
Balshaw, T. J. ...	242078	5/5/17	20/5/17, transferred	Rifleman.	
Bamber, C. ...	88243	8/11/17	12/2/19, demobilized ...	L./Corpl.	
Bamber, T.	243838	13/10/16	30/6/17, wounded	Rifleman.	
✠Bamber, T. ...	50718	18/8/17	29/10/17, killed in action ...	Rifleman.	
✠Bandell, H. ...	241547	6/8/15	1/9/18, killed in action or died of wounds ...	Rifleman.	
Banks, A. F. ...	2087	31/8/14	—/—/15, transferred ...	Rifleman.	
Banks, E. ...	202404	1/2/18	—/—/19, transferred ...	Corporal.	
Banks, F. R. ...	241686	5/5/17	20/5/17, transferred	Rifleman.	
Banks, G. ...	63660	13/8/17	31/5/18, sick	Rifleman.	
Banner, J. H. ...	2777	7/11/14	2/5/16, discharged	Rifleman.	
Banning, J. ...	2838	9/11/14	12/1/15, transferred	Rifleman.	
Bannister, J. ...	266779	27/5/18	22/1/19, demobilized ...	Rifleman.	
Barber, E. C. ...	2902	10/11/14	7/3/15, commission	A./Sergt.	
Barclay, W. ...	3502	31/5/15	17/5/16, discharged	Rifleman.	
Barford, V. E. ...	2559	22/9/14	5/8/15, transferred	Rifleman.	
Barker, H. ...	243821	12/10/16	15/5/18, sick	Rifleman.	
Barker, H. A. ...	3177	—/12/14	26/6/15, transferred	Rifleman.	
Barker, J. W. ...	2606	29/9/14	12/1/15, transferred	Rifleman.	
Barker, R. ...	240961	9/11/14	29/9/18, commission	C.S.M.	D.C.M.
Barkley, B. G. ...	242450	24/3/16	15/5/17, transferred	Rifleman.	
Barlow, F. ...	243764	10/10/16	9/7/18, posted 8th K.L.R. ...	Rifleman.	
Barlow, G. ...	381296	10/7/18	10/8/18, posted 1/5th K.L.R.	Rifleman.	
Barlow, W. ...	405976	16/1/18	17/1/19, demobilized ...	Rifleman.	
✠Barned, L. ...	242249	25/1/16	12/9/18, killed in action ...	Rifleman.	
Barnes, F. ...	88246	8/11/17	11/2/19, demobilized ...	Rifleman.	
Barnes, G. ...	2286	2/9/14	—/—/15, transferred ...	Rifleman.	
Barnes, H. ...	50712	18/8/17	21/4/18, wounded	Rifleman.	
Barnes, P. B. ...	597	27/2/15	26/6/15, transferred	Sergeant.	
Barnett, H. ...	202356	1/2/18	18/6/18, wounded	Rifleman.	
Barnett, J. ...	2943	11/11/14	26/6/15, transferred	Rifleman.	
✠Barnham, W. ...	88596	1/2/18	12/9/18, killed in action	Rifleman.	
Baron, G. ...	56411	13/8/17	9/7/18, posted 8th K.L.R. ...	Rifleman.	
Baron, T. ...	108815	28/9/18	11/12/18, demobilized ...	Rifleman.	
Barrett, A. ...	39113	27/5/18	—/3/19, posted 25th K.L.R.	Rifleman.	
Barrett, H. ...	300574	8/11/17	10/12/18, demobilized ...	L./Corpl.	
Barrett, J. W. ...	243747	9/10/16	26/2/19, posted 25th K.L.R.	Rifleman.	
Barrow, W. T. ...	2699	27/10/14	3/8/17,† invalided to England	Rifleman.	
Bartle, F. B. ...	50711	18/8/17	26/2/19, posted 25th K.L.R.	Rifleman.	
Barton, A. C. ...	2756	5/11/14	26/6/15, transferred	Rifleman.	
Barton, E. ...	267306	27/5/18	22/10/18, posted 13th K.L.R.	Rifleman.	
Barton, G. A. ...	3106	26/11/14	22/8/16, transferred	Rifleman.	
Barton, P. ...	204169	27/5/18	30/9/18, wounded	Rifleman.	
Barton, W. ...	243765	10/10/16	28/3/19, transferred	Rifleman.	
Barwise, W. ...	84587	1/2/18	26/4/19, transferred	A./Corpl.	
Basnett, W. A. ...	242544	29/5/16	12/9/18, prisoner of war ...	Rifleman.	
Baster, F. E. ...	241287	9/4/15	28/11/17,† sick	Rifleman.	
Batchelor, F. ...	25603	27/5/18	28/10/18, wounded	Rifleman.	
Batchelor, W. ...	51252	2/7/18	12/11/18, sick	Rifleman.	
Bate, R. ...	241408	3/7/15	22/7/17, wounded	Rifleman.	
Bateman, H. ...	53037	24/2/18	12/9/18, wounded	L./Corpl.	
Batson, R. ...	240057	23/10/14	11/2/19, demobilized ...	C.Q.M.S.	M. in D.
Batson, F. S. ...	1447	27/2/15	16/8/15, transferred	A./L./Corpl.	
Batty, J. H. ...	2195	1/9/14	—/—/15, transferred	Rifleman.	

NAME.	REGTL. NO.	DATE OF JOINING.	DATE OF LEAVING WITH CAUSE.	HIGHEST RANK.	HONOURS OR AWARDS.
Batty, J. S. ...	2271	1/9/14	16/9/15, commission	Rifleman.	
Baxendale, J. ...	265903	27/6/18	—/—/19, disembodied ...	Rifleman.	
Baxter, R. ...	50721	18/8/17	9/11/17, wounded ...	Rifleman.	
Bean, A. G. ...	3151	8/12/14	12/1/15, transferred ...	Rifleman.	
Bear, G. A. ...	88118	5/10/17	16/4/18, sick ...	Rifleman.	
Beatham, J. ...	88540	19/9/17	5/6/18, wounded ...	Rifleman.	
Beaumont, A. L.	241079	14/11/14	3/6/18, wounded ...	C.Q.M.S.	
Beaumont, H. J.	242447	24/3/16	6/9/17, sick ...	Rifleman.	
Beausire, P. J. ...	2198	1/9/14	5/11/15, commission ...	Rifleman.	
Becalick, C. W. ...	2828	9/11/14	22/8/16, transferred ...	Rifleman.	
Beckwith, D. ...	1558	23/10/14	26/6/15, transferred ...	Rifleman.	
Beer, L. ...	108757	28/9/18	26/2/19, posted 25th K.L.R.	Rifleman.	
Beesley, A. ...	16286	27/5/18	18/1/19, demobilized	Rifleman.	
Beeston, E. ...	2295	10/9/14	—/—/15, transferred ...	L./Corpl.	
Begley, J. ...	241304	20/4/15	13/8/17, wounded	Rifleman.	
Beisley, F. E. ...	243786	6/10/16	9/8/17, invalided to England	Rifleman.	
Bell, A. ...	1459	27/2/15	1/12/15, transferred ...	Corporal.	
Bell, A. ...	243784	10/10/16	30/4/17, posted 1st K.L.R. ...	Rifleman.	
Bell, C. T. ...	242342	7/3/16	7/8/17, invalided to England	Rifleman.	
Bell, D. H. ...	242185	21/1/16	3/8/17, wounded	Rifleman.	
Bell, G. H. ...	3237	25/1/15	26/6/15, transferred ...	Rifleman.	
Bell, J. H. ...	2703	28/10/14	12/1/15, transferred ...	Rifleman.	
Bell, J. R. ...	241052	12/11/14	6/8/17, sick	Corporal.	
Bell, P. ...	1309	23/2/15	20/1/17, transferred ...	Rifleman.	
Bell, S. ...	3160	21/12/14	9/4/16, transferred ...	Rifleman.	
Bell, S. H. ...	241305	20/4/15	14/4/18, sick	L./Corpl.	
Bell, T. ...	2438	15/9/14	12/1/15, transferred ...	Rifleman.	
Bellion, A. J. ...	240912	6/11/14	18/8/17, wounded ...	Rifleman.	
Bellion, H. ...	331457	22/6/18	20/9/18, sick ...	Rifleman.	
Bellion, H. G. ...	2657	13/10/14	7/9/16, transferred ...	Rifleman.	
Bellis, B. ...	88244	8/11/17	24/6/18, sick	Rifleman.	
Bellringer, E. A.	242318	1/3/16	13/6/18, sick	Sergeant.	
Bellwood, P. R. ...	241048	12/11/14	6/8/17,† invalided to England	Rifleman.	
Benardo, M. ...	90717	7/3/18	27/2/19, demobilized ...	Rifleman.	
Bendle, E. J. ...	204269	16/5/18	22/5/19, demobilized ...	Rifleman.	
Bennett, A. T. ...	3335	19/4/15	10/6/15, commission ...	Rifleman.	
Bennett, J. ...	90751	7/3/18	22/12/18, demobilized	Rifleman.	
Bennett, R. G. ...	3471	6/8/15	5/10/16, commission	Rifleman.	
Benson, J. A. ...	241286	8/4/15	22/5/19, demobilized ...	A./R.Q.M.S.	M.S.M.
Benson, J. B. ...	241062	12/11/14	26/2/19, demobilized	Rifleman.	
Benson, J., ...	2572	24/9/14	17/2/15, discharged ...	Rifleman.	
✠Benson, W. ...	50710	18/8/17	29/9/18, killed in action	Rifleman.	
Bentham, J. ...	2740	3/11/14	23/11/15,† transferred ...	Rifleman.	
Bentley, C. ...	3139	7/12/14	21/5/16, transferred ...	A./Sergt.	
Bentley, E. ...	88106	5/10/17	26/2/19, posted K.L.R. ...	Rifleman.	
Bentley, F. ...	2721	30/10/14	12/1/15, transferred ...	Rifleman.	
Bentley, T. ...	242220	22/1/16	17/10/18, wounded ...	Rifleman.	
Benzie, J. ...	243817	12/10/16	12/8/17, wounded ...	Rifleman.	
Beresford, P. ...	241095	16/11/14	10/10/18, wounded ...	Rifleman.	
Bernstein, J. ...	3271	18/2/15	16/8/15, transferred ...	Rifleman.	
Bernstein, J. ...	51679	1/2/18	7/2/19, demobilized ...	Rifleman.	
Bernstein, R. ...	16507	28/2/18	3/3/19, demobilized ...	Rifleman.	
Berry, F. P. ...	109001	28/9/18	14/12/18, demobilized	Rifleman.	
✠Betham, H. ...	265241	8/7/17	20/7/17, died of wounds	Rifleman.	
Beveridge, W. J.	242381	18/3/16	26/3/18, sick	Rifleman.	
Bewley, E. R. ...	3141	7/12/14	28/6/15, commission ...	Rifleman.	
Bibby, A. ...	59521	27/5/18	25/1/19, demobilized ...	Sergeant	M.M.
Bibby, T. ...	242148	20/1/16	5/8/17, invalided to England	Rifleman.	

NAME.	REGTL. NO.	DATE OF JOINING.	DATE OF LEAVING WITH CAUSE.	HIGHEST RANK.	HONOURS OR AWARDS.
Bickerton, A. J.	242190	21/1/16	19/5/17, wounded	Rifleman.	
Biggs, J. ...	242448	24/3/16	9/8/17, invalided to England	Rifleman.	
Bill, H. ...	267864	27/8/17	9/7/18, posted 1/6th K.L.R.	Rifleman.	
Billington, W. ...	203988	1/2/18	8/3/19, posted 13th K.L.R.	Rifleman.	
Bingham, P. R. ...	2146	31/8/14	—/—/15, transferred ...	Rifleman.	
Birch, H. ...	200628	8/7/17	10/8/17, invalided to England	Rifleman.	
Birch, H. ...	200700	14/9/18	3/2/19, demobilized ...	Rifleman.	
Birch, F. ...	2183	31/8/14	—/—/15, transferred ...	Rifleman.	
Birchall, H. ...	2966	12/11/14	26/6/15, transferred	Rifleman.	
Birchall, S. ...	406269	16/1/18	16/1/19, demobilized ...	Rifleman.	
Bird, A. A. ...	3046	17/11/14	5/8/15, transferred	Rifleman.	
Bird, W. H. ...	1866	23/10/14	26/6/15, transferred	Rifleman.	
Birkett, G. R. ...	2249	1/9/14	—/—/15, transferred ...	Rifleman.	
Biss, G. A. ...	235563	14/4/18	20/5/18, sick	Rifleman.	
✠Bissell, T. J. ...	241395	3/7/15	1/7/17, killed in action ...	Rifleman.	
Black, D. S. ...	2167	31/8/14	—/—/15, transferred ...	Rifleman.	
Black, J. H. ...	59412	1/2/18	11/7/18, posted 1/6th K.L.R.	Rifleman.	
Black, T. ...	241487	6/8/15	3/8/17, invalided to England	Sergeant.	
Black, W. ...	241442	6/8/15	5/3/19,† demobilized ...	Sergeant.	
✠Blackburn, A. ...	2836	9/11/14	19/3/15, died	Rifleman.	
Blackburn, C. ...	1289	23/2/15	26/6/15, transferred	Rifleman.	
Blackburn, F. G.	242398	20/3/16	—/—/19, transferred ...	A./L./Corpl.	
Blackburn, G. ...	2083	31/8/14	25/9/15, commission ...	Rifleman.	
✠Blackburn, J. W.	235598	12/7/18	4/10/18, killed in action ...	Rifleman.	
Blackburn, J. ...	241011	10/11/14	4/7/17, transferred ...	Rifleman.	
Blackburn, W. H.	242378	18/3/16	28/3/19, posted 13th K.L.R.	Corporal.	
Blackburn, —. ...	10	—/—/14	31/3/15, discharged	Col./Sergt.	
Blackey, J. W. ...	4692	20/1/16	18/10/16, transferred ...	Rifleman.	
Blackham, C. H.	242257	25/1/16	14/2/19, demobilized ...	Rifleman.	
Blackley, H. ...	201260	1/2/18	19/3/18, sick	Rifleman.	
Blain, R. ...	3739	6/8/15	28/10/15, transferred ...	Rifleman.	
✠Blakely, G. ...	243684	7/10/16	7/9/17, killed in action ...	Rifleman.	
Blakemore, J. M.	88315	27/6/18	6/10/18, wounded	Rifleman.	
Blakey, J. W. ...	241121	23/11/14	11/7/17, commission	A./Corpl.	
Bland, A. ...	1423	23/2/15	26/6/15, transferred	Rifleman.	
Bleakley, G. ...	50713	18/8/17	14/10/18, wounded	Rifleman.	
Blenkhorn, A. ...	88503	19/9/17	28/3/19, posted 13th K.L.R.	Rifleman.	
Blenkinsop, A. ...	202350	1/2/18	22/1/19, demobilized ...	Rifleman.	
Blount, C. ...	88226	8/11/17	28/2/19, transferred ...	Rifleman.	
Blower, F. D. ...	1646	23/2/15	1/12/15, transferred ...	Corporal.	
Blower, J. A. ...	2922	11/11/14	26/6/15, transferred	Rifleman.	
Blundell, E. ...	240913	6/11/14	23/5/17, invalided to England	Rifleman.	
Blundell, G. ...	52336	27/5/18	9/9/18, wounded	Rifleman.	
Blundell, J. ...	58587	27/6/18	3/2/19, demobilized ...	Rifleman.	
Blundell, J. W. ...	2947	11/11/14	5/8/15, transferred	Rifleman.	
Blyde, J. ...	2375	10/9/14	12/1/15, transferred	Rifleman.	
Blythe, F. J. ...	2548	23/9/14	5/8/15, transferred	A./L./Corpl.	
Boardman, B. ...	266461	8/7/17	8/10/17, posted 2/9th K.L.R.	Rifleman.	
Boardman, H. ...	50722	18/8/17	17/9/18, wounded	Rifleman.	
Boardman, R. ...	14919	13/8/17	5/7/18, wounded	Rifleman.	
Boast, J. H. ...	243711	9/10/16	26/2/19, posted 25th K.L.R.	Corporal.	
Boddy, T. ...	3163	21/12/14	26/6/15, transferred	Rifleman.	
Boileau, R. ...	242368	15/3/16	26/2/19, posted 25th K.L.R.	Rifleman.	
Bolshaw, A. ...	242149	20/1/16	14/2/18, sick	Corporal.	
Bolton, E. ...	88144	11/10/17	26/2/19, posted 25th K.L.R.	Rifleman.	
Bolton, F. C. ...	1380	27/2/15	23/9/16,† transferred ...	Corporal.	
Bolton, H. G. ...	1173	23/2/15	26/6/15, transferred	Rifleman.	
Bolton, W. ...	2390	10/9/14	5/8/15, transferred	A./Sergt.	
Bond, D. ...	2583	25/9/14	11/3/15, commission	A./L./Corpl.	

"THE KING'S" (LIVERPOOL REGIMENT)

NAME.	REGTL. NO.	DATE OF JOINING.	DATE OF LEAVING WITH CAUSE.	HIGHEST RANK.	HONOURS OR AWARDS.
Bond, G. ...	241327	3/7/15	30/8/17, wounded	Corporal	M.M.
Bond, J. ...	202171	15/2/18	—/—/19, transferred...	Sergeant.	
Bond, R. ...	242353	13/3/16	27/2/19, demobilized	Rifleman.	
Booth, J. ...	88532	19/9/17	9/11/17, wounded	Rifleman.	
Booth, W. H. ...	88279	27/6/18	26/2/19, posted 13th K.L.R.	Rifleman.	
Bordessa, G. ...	17279	27/5/18	30/1/19, demobilized	Rifleman.	
Boschen, R. T. ...	240981	10/11/14	19/5/18, wounded	Rifleman.	
Bosomworth, E.	1214	23/10/14	1/6/15, transferred	Rifleman.	
Bott, C. H. ...	243730	9/10/16	24/4/17, sick	Rifleman.	
Bott, G. G. R. ...	2391	10/9/14	12/1/15, transferred	A./L./Corpl.	
Botting, O. ...	380347	26/9/18	26/1/19, demobilized	L./Corpl.	
Bottom, J. ...	48613	24/2/18	26/2/19, posted 25th K.L.R.	Rifleman.	
Bottrill, S. N. ...	2115	31/8/14	—/—/15, transferred	Rifleman.	
Boullin, R. G. ...	260230	20/9/17	29/3/19, transferred	Rifleman.	
Boumphrey, N. R.	240869	22/10/14	22/8/17,† commission	Rifleman.	
Bourne, W. H. J.	3310	22/3/15	19/8/16,† transferred	Rifleman.	
✠Bowen, A. ...	380792	3/4/18	7/10/18, died of wounds	Rifleman.	
Bowen, R. ...	6646	16/10/16	7/11/16, transferred	Rifleman.	
Bower, F. H. ...	242552	30/5/16	17/1/19,† demobilized	Rifleman.	
Bowes, T. ...	50931	18/8/17	20/8/17, posted 2/8th K.L.R.	Rifleman.	
Bowker, J. R. ...	88093	29/9/17	—/—/19, transferred...	Rifleman.	
Bowler, F. ...	241102	17/11/14	9/7/18,† posted 1/6th K.L.R.	Rifleman.	
Bowman, H. R. ...	14	27/2/15	28/6/15, transferred	Sergeant.	
Bowman, C. ...	240692	11/9/14	15/7/18, transferred	C.S.M.	
Bowman, F. H. ...	242402	20/3/16	4/9/18, transferred	Sergeant.	
Bowsher, A. ...	242468	19/10/16	15/3/19, demobilized	Rifleman.	
Boyd, G. S. ...	2739	2/11/14	29/1/18, transferred	Rifleman.	
✠Boyd, W. ...	57395	27/5/18	12/9/18, killed in action or died of wounds ...	Rifleman.	
Boyd, W. ...	242361	15/3/16	1/8/17, invalided to England	Rifleman.	
✠Boyd, W. A. ...	241307	22/4/15	22/6/17, killed in action	Rifleman.	
Boydell, E. ...	2680	20/10/14	5/8/15, transferred	A./L./Cpl.	
Boyden, W. H. ...	50716	18/8/17	26/2/19, posted 13th K.L.R.	Rifleman.	
Boyland, J. ...	201576	1/2/18	22/5/19, demobilized	Rifleman.	
Boynton, H. ...	60992	27/6/18	16/1/19, demobilized	Rifleman.	
Bracegirdle, J. ...	269404	27/8/17	26/2/19, posted 25th K.L.R.	Rifleman.	
Bradbury, H. ...	88541	19/9/17	26/2/19, posted 25th K.L.R.	Rifleman.	
Bradbury, W. ...	300468	6/6/18	24/6/18, wounded	Rifleman.	
Brade, H. ...	242335	2/3/16	—/—/19, demobilized	Rifleman.	
Brading, C. F. ...	26710	27/6/18	12/9/18, wounded	Rifleman.	
✠Bradley, B. V. ...	240801	25/9/14	15/7/17, killed in action	Rifleman.	
Bradley, F. ...	27341	1/2/18	28/5/18, wounded	Rifleman.	
Bradley, G. H. ...	2446	14/9/14	12/1/15, transferred	Rifleman.	
Bradley, H. ...	88185	8/11/17	26/2/19, posted 25th K.L.R.	Rifleman.	
Bradshaw, C. H.	2126	31/8/14	—/—/15, transferred	Rifleman.	
Bradshaw, E. ...	243723	9/10/16	11/11/18, sick	Rifleman.	
Bradshaw, H. ...	88542	19/9/17	14/6/18, posted 1/5th K.L.R.	Rifleman.	
Bradshaw, J. E. ...	50706	18/8/17	—/—/19, transferred	Rifleman.	
Braithwaite, H. ...	202361	1/2/18	28/3/19, posted 13th K.L.R.	A./Corpl.	
Braithwaite, J. N.	2144	31/8/14	27/11/16, discharged	Rifleman.	
Brakell, G. V. ...	1337	23/10/14	28/7/15, discharged	Rifleman.	
Bramwell, W. M.	241133	24/11/14	19/11/17, commission	Rifleman.	
Branagan, R. ...	88247	8/11/17	19/4/18, sick	Rifleman.	
Brand, H. ...	1584	23/2/15	26/6/15, transferred	Rifleman.	
Brandon, P. T. ...	260181	20/9/17	15/1/18, wounded	L./Sgt.	
Brebner, J. ...	50932	18/8/17	20/8/17, posted 2/8th K.L.R.	Rifleman.	
Breese, T. ...	2315	10/9/14	16/8/15,† transferred	Rifleman.	
Breeze, F. W. ...	2650	10/10/14	26/6/15, transferred	Rifleman.	
Brennan, M. ...	8328	7/3/18	14/3/18, posted 4th K.L.R.	Sergeant.	

NAME.	REGTL. NO.	DATE OF JOINING.	DATE OF LEAVING WITH CAUSE.	HIGHEST RANK.	HONOURS OR AWARDS.
Brennan, P. C. ...	242523	22/5/16	16/10/17,† posted 2/5th K.L.R.	Rifleman.	
Brenton, R. A. ...	243796	11/10/16	22/9/17, sick	Rifleman.	
Brereton, A. ...	202391	1/2/18	3/10/18, wounded	Rifleman.	
Bretherton, R. ...	242705	11/1/18	17/1/18, posted 13th K.L.R.	Rifleman.	
Bretherwick, H.	2686	20/10/14	12/1/15, transferred	Rifleman.	
Brew, L. S. ...	2610	26/9/14	8/5/16, transferred	A./C.S.M.	
Brewerton, R. H.	3635	6/8/15	23/9/16,† transferred	Rifleman.	
Brice, H. ...	240910	5/11/14	3/8/17, invalided to England	Rifleman.	
Bricknell, J. R. ...	242363	15/3/16	26/2/19, posted 25th K.L.R.	Rifleman.	
Bride, F. ...	12799	13/8/17	7/11/17, wounded	Rifleman.	
Brides, T.	25947	22/6/18	2/3/19, demobilized	Rifleman.	
Bridge, A. ...	88543	19/9/17	14/3/18, transferred	Rifleman.	
Brierley, A. ...	203942	1/2/18	26/2/19, posted 25th K.L.R.	Rifleman.	
Brierley, H. ...	406068	16/1/18	11/7/18, transferred	Rifleman.	
Brierley, J. H. ...	242267	26/1/16	26/12/17, wounded	Rifleman.	
Brierley, T. ...	203915	1/2/18	—/—/19, discharged ...	Rifleman.	
Briers, J. ...	108947	28/9/18	17/2/19, demobilized ...	Rifleman.	
Briggs, A. A. ...	50709	18/8/17	6/5/18, sick	Rifleman.	
Briggs, L. ...	242210	21/1/16	9/8/17, wounded	Rifleman.	
Brindle, W. ...	50720	18/8/17	13/11/17, wounded ...	Rifleman.	
✠Brindley, T. W. ...	242214	22/1/16	22/6/17, killed in action	L./Corpl.	
Brindley, W. C. ...	88245	8/11/17	16/6/18, sick	Rifleman.	
Briscoe, W. J. ...	240112	27/2/15	15/7/18,† transferred ...	Rifleman.	
Broadbent, F. ...	95742	17/4/18	—/3/19, posted 25th K.L.R.	Rifleman.	
Broadbent, G. E.	2161	31/8/14	1/12/15, discharged ...	Rifleman.	
Broadbent, G. R.	3095	24/11/14	23/9/16,† transferred ...	Rifleman.	
Brockless, H. ...	88043	28/9/17	4/5/18, sick	L./Corpl.	
Brodrick, H. ...	50714	18/8/17	24/8/18, posted 13th K.L.R.	Rifleman.	
Bromilow, T. ...	202310	1/2/18	14/5/18, sick	Rifleman.	
Brook, G. ...	202185	1/2/18	29/8/18, posted 1st K.L.R. ...	L./Corpl.	
Brook, H. ...	36351	27/5/18	29/8/18, posted 1st K.L.R. ...	Rifleman.	
Brooke, W. ...	241271	25/3/15	7/8/17,† invalided to England	Rifleman.	
Brookhouse, E. F.	50708	18/8/17	25/8/17, sick	Rifleman.	
Brooks, G. C. ...	242199	21/1/16	2/8/17, sick	Rifleman.	
Brooks, R. H. ...	50719	18/8/17	26/1/19, demobilized ...	Rifleman.	
Broom, J. ...	2459	11/9/14	12/1/15, transferred	Rifleman.	
Broster, W. C. ...	2061	31/8/14	—/—/14, posted 1/6th K.L.R.	Rifleman.	
Browitt, J. ...	48667	1/2/18	5/2/19, demobilized	L./Corpl.	
Brown, A. ...	405920	16/1/18	22/10/18, posted 13th K.L.R.	Rifleman.	
Brown, A. S. ...	242344	8/3/16	14/5/18, sick	L./Corpl.	
Brown, A. ...	2785	7/11/14	12/1/15, transferred	Rifleman.	
Brown, E. ...	240271	23/2/15	3/2/19, demobilized	Corporal.	
Brown, E. H. ...	200714	1/2/18	18/10/18, wounded ...	Sergeant.	
Brown, F. ...	243732	9/10/16	—/—/19, transferred	Rifleman.	
Brown, F. J. ...	241242	16/2/15	1/2/19, demobilized ...	A./Sergt.	
Brown, G. ...	2430	12/9/14	20/4/17, transferred	Rifleman.	
Brown, H. R. ...	2804	9/11/14	26/6/15, transferred	Rifleman.	
Brown, J. ...	88241	8/11/17	22/12/18, demobilized ...	Rifleman.	
Brown, J. ...	243719	9/10/16	30/6/17, transferred	Rifleman.	
Brown, J. F. ...	3120	30/11/14	4/5/16, transferred	Rifleman.	
Brown, R. ...	241118	20/11/14	1/8/18,† posted 12th K.L.R.	Rifleman.	
Brown, S. J. ...	240518	31/8/14	13/2/19, discharged	Rifleman.	
Brown, W. ...	26312	27/6/18	5/9/18, wounded	Rifleman.	
✠Brown, W. D. ...	50715	18/8/17	18/12/17, killed in action ...	L./Corpl.	
Brown, W. E. ...	2545	22/9/14	22/8/16, transferred	Rifleman.	
Brown, W. G. ...	201403	1/2/18	5/3/19, demobilized	Rifleman.	
Brownhill, H. ...	50717	18/8/17	7/9/18, wounded	Rifleman.	
Brownhill, R. ...	308470	8/7/17	10/2/19, demobilized ...	L./Sergt.	

NAME.	REGTL. NO.	DATE OF JOINING.	DATE OF LEAVING WITH CAUSE.	HIGHEST RANK.	HONOURS OR AWARDS.
Brownrigg, A. T.	2558	22/9/14	5/8/15, transferred	Rifleman.	
Brundrett, F. ...	235425	1/2/18	15/4/18, sick	Rifleman.	
Brunner, E. W. D.	2416	11/9/14	—/—/15, transferred ...	Rifleman.	
Bryning, A. C. ...	1641	23/10/14	5/8/15, transferred	Rifleman.	
Bryson, T. W. ...	2410	11/9/14	12/1/15, transferred	Rifleman.	
Buck, S. G. ...	3707	6/8/15	9/12/15, transferred	Rifleman.	
Buck, R.	3350	21/4/15	4/5/16, transferred	Rifleman.	
Buckley, A.	269633	10/10/17	18/2/19, sick	Rifleman.	
Buckley, W. S. ...	242345	8/3/16	5/8/17, invalided to England	L./Corpl.	
Bucknall, A. W.	240632	10/9/14	6/8/17, invalided to England	L./Corpl.	
Buffel, J. R. ...	242181	21/1/16	13/8/17, wounded	Rifleman.	
Bullen, F. R. ...	5871	27/2/15	10/5/15, transferred	Sgt./Instr.	
Bulmer, W. ...	269339	22/6/18	26/2/19, posted 25th K.L.R.	Rifleman.	
Burbage, —. ...	2413	11/9/14	12/1/15, transferred	Rifleman.	
Burch, G. ...	2778	7/11/14	19/8/16, transferred	A./Sergt.	
Burden, A. ...	240863	20/10/14	24/2/19, sick	Rifleman.	
✠ Burden, J. E. ...	241216	19/1/15	28/10/17, missing, assumed dead	Corporal.	
Burge, A. ...	2850	9/11/14	5/8/15, transferred	Rifleman.	
Burgess, J.	52529	1/2/18	18/5/18, sick	Rifleman.	
Burgess, J. ...	268051	27/8/17	4/3/18, sick	Rifleman.	
Burgess, R. ...	46628	13/8/17	5/2/19, demobilized	Rifleman.	
Burgess, S. ...	29668	7/3/18	5/9/18, wounded	Rifleman.	
Burke, J. ...	3647	6/8/15	28/10/15, transferred	Rifleman.	
Burke, J. ...	50707	18/8/17	29/12/18, demobilized ...	L./Corpl.	
Burke, J. E. ...	2378	10/9/14	5/8/15, transferred	Rifleman.	
Burke, W. ...	266803	27/8/17	21/11/17, posted 2/7th K.L.R.	Rifleman.	
Burke, W. H. D.	241045	12/11/14	27/6/17, commission ...	Corporal.	
Burl, G.	405914	16/1/18	29/11/18, transferred ...	Rifleman.	
Burn, G. H. ...	201419	1/2/18	29/3/19, demobilized ...	Rifleman.	
Burn, G. J. ...	240775	23/9/14	1/7/18, commission	Sergeant.	
Burn, P. J. ...	3490	3/7/15	22/11/15, discharged	Rifleman.	
Burns, J. ...	26214	13/8/17	27/7/18, transferred	Rifleman.	
Burns, J. T. ...	242696	25/5/18	28/3/19, demobilized ...	Rifleman.	
Burrell, L. ...	88544	19/9/17	26/8/18, transferred	Rifleman.	
✠ Burrow, J. ...	243809	12/10/16	2/5/17, killed in action ...	Rifleman.	
✠ Burrows, A. ...	243725	9/10/16	22/6/17, killed in action ...	Rifleman.	
Burstall, L. G. ...	242164	20/1/16	14/10/17, commission ...	Corporal.	
Burtinshaw, J. A.	2535	22/9/14	5/8/15, transferred	A./L./Corpl.	
Burton, F. ...	6454	6/10/16	12/11/16, transferred ...	Rifleman.	
Burton, G. B. ...	1856	23/10/14	11/3/15, commission ...	Rifleman.	
Burton, J. ...	53050	13/8/17	14/10/18, sick	Rifleman.	
Burton, K. H. ...	3365	3/5/15	13/5/15, commission ...	Rifleman.	
Bury, E. D. ...	88528	19/9/17	31/10/18, wounded	Rifleman.	
Busby, E. F. ...	31548	27/6/18	27/10/18, wounded	Rifleman.	
Butler, H. A. ...	4979	14/3/16	22/7/16, transferred ...	Rifleman.	
Butler, N. ...	50847	1/2/18	26/2/19, posted 25th K.L.R.	Rifleman.	
Butler, R. W. ...	2132	31/8/14	18/1/16, discharged	Rifleman.	
Butler, W. ...	242606	2/4/18	19/4/18, posted 1/6th K.L.R.	Rifleman.	
Butler, W. G. ...	1508	27/2/15	26/6/15, transferred	Rifleman.	
Butterfield, W. ...	243692	7/10/16	5/8/17, invalided to England	Rifleman.	
Bygrove, C. E. ...	241553	6/8/15	9/7/18, posted 1/6th K.L.R.	Rifleman.	
Byng, W. ...	243837	13/10/16	7/8/17, invalided to England	L./Corpl.	
Byrn, E.... ...	243827	13/10/16	—/—/19, discharged ...	Rifleman.	
Caddy, W. J. ...	3293	8/3/15	26/6/15, transferred	Rifleman.	
Cadman, B. ...	17562	14/6/18	21/2/19, demobilized ...	Sergeant.	
Cain, G. H. ...	241570	6/8/15	9/4/18, transferred	Rifleman.	
Cain, J.	268035	27/8/17	29/8/18, posted 1st K.L.R. ...	Rifleman.	

NAME.	REGTL. NO.	DATE OF JOINING.	DATE OF LEAVING WITH CAUSE.	HIGHEST RANK.	HONOURS OR AWARDS.
Cain, J. S. ...	241561	6/8/15	31/5/18, transferred	Rifleman.	
Cairns, J.... ...	51116	27/5/18	22/9/18, transferred ...	Rifleman.	
Cairns, —. ...	2159	31/8/14	—/—/15, transferred ...	Rifleman.	
Caldecott, A. ...	1568	23/10/14	2/3/16, discharged	Rifleman.	
Calderley, J. A. ...	50835	18/8/17	14/1/18, sick	Rifleman.	
Caldwell, J. ...	47218	1/2/18	22/4/18, transferred	Rifleman.	
Callaghan, D. ...	2837	9/11/14	26/6/15, transferred	Rifleman.	
Calvey, G. ...	267921	27/8/17	10/11/17, sick	Rifleman.	
Calvey, T. ...	1162	23/2/15	26/6/15, transferred	Corporal.	
Calvey, W. R. ...	1385	23/2/15	26/6/15, transferred	Rifleman.	
Cama, V. ...	2692	23/10/14	12/1/15, transferred	Rifleman.	
Campbell, A. ...	330920	28/9/18	31/10/18, posted 9th K.L.R.	Rifleman.	
Campbell, D. ...	2674	17/10/14	5/8/15, transferred	Rifleman.	
Campbell, J. ...	50859	1/2/18	26/2/19, posted 25th K.L.R.	Rifleman.	
Campbell, V. ...	241172	28/12/14	12/7/18,† transferred ...	Rifleman.	
Campey, —. ...	2474	10/9/14	26/6/15, transferred	Rifleman.	
Candy, G. ...	50306	27/5/18	18/1/19, demobilized ...	Rifleman.	
Canham, W. ...	50607	24/2/18	5/2/19, demobilized	Rifleman.	
Cann, J. ...	88545	19/9/17	27/5/18, sick	Rifleman.	
Cannon, R. ...	22340	22/6/18	29/1/19, demobilized ...	Rifleman.	
Cantrell, H. G. ...	2600	28/9/14	—/—/15, transferred ...	A./Sergt.	
Cardwell, R. ...	306142	27/8/17	22/11/17, posted 2/8th K.L.R.	Corporal.	
Carefull, H. ...	1932	23/10/14	5/6/17, commission	A./Corpl.	
Carnegie, C. ...	17559	27/6/18	10/2/19, demobilized ...	Rifleman.	
Carney, E. ...	241495	6/8/15	2/8/17,† wounded	Rifleman.	
✠Carney, J. W. ...	72494	2/7/18	30/9/18, killed in action	Rifleman.	
Carr, J. H. ...	2882	10/11/14	26/6/15, transferred	Rifleman.	
Carr, W. H. ...	50727	18/8/17	28/5/18, sick	Rifleman.	
Carr, W. J. ...	243860	16/10/16	26/6/18, transferred ...	Rifleman.	
Carradus, A. D. ...	243818	12/10/16	9/2/19, demobilized	Rifleman	M. in D.
Carrick, J. G. W. ...	243701	9/10/16	3/11/17, wounded	Rifleman.	
Carroll, A. G. ...	3175	—/12/14	26/6/15, transferred	Rifleman.	
Carter, E. C. ...	242351	9/3/16	11/4/18, sick	L./Sergt.	
Carter, F. H. ...	3661	6/8/15	15/11/16, transferred ...	L./Corpl.	
Carter, H. ...	243789	10/10/16	21/11/17, wounded	Rifleman.	
Carter, J. H. ...	243795	11/10/16	7/3/17, invalided to England	Rifleman.	
Carter, S. ...	241643	8/7/17	12/9/17, wounded	Rifleman.	
Carter, W. ...	110538	27/11/18	26/2/19, posted 25th K.L.R.	Rifleman.	
Cartledge, G. ...	88534	19/9/17	27/5/18, sick	Rifleman.	
Cartmell, G. ...	305655	27/8/17	21/2/19, demobilized	Rifleman.	
Carver, H. ...	88116	5/10/17	26/12/17, sick	Rifleman.	
Carvey, L. G. ...	50726	18/8/17	25/3/18, sick	Rifleman.	
Case, W. ...	202924	27/5/18	—/—/19, transferred ...	Rifleman.	
Cass, E. ...	88546	19/9/17	26/2/19, posted 13th K.L.R.	L./Corpl.	
Cassidy, W. H. ...	241153	3/12/14	4/12/18, sick	Rifleman.	
Cassofski, J. ...	203268	1/2/18	12/2/19, demobilized ...	Rifleman.	
Casson, J. ...	5020	18/3/16	31/1/17, transferred ...	Rifleman.	
Casson, T. L. B. ...	243830	13/10/16	25/10/17, transferred ...	Rifleman.	
Castle, W. ...	88417	2/7/18	22/12/18, demobilized ...	Rifleman.	
Cathels, H. ...	242175	20/1/16	11/3/18, sick	L./Corpl.	
Catherall, R. ...	3278	22/2/15	5/8/15, transferred	Rifleman.	
Cathrell, T. ...	241434	6/8/15	5/8/17, invalided to England	Corporal.	
✠Catterall, W. ...	50728	18/8/17	30/10/17, died	Rifleman.	
Cazes, H. ...	2550	23/9/14	3/12/15, transferred ...	Rifleman.	
Cederberg, E. H. ...	2859	10/11/14	12/1/15, transferred	Rifleman.	
Chadwick, A. ...	243726	9/10/16	9/8/17, invalided to England	Rifleman.	
Chadwick, G. ...	88179	8/11/17	26/2/19, posted 25th K.L.R.	Rifleman.	
Chadwick, H. ...	40133	13/8/17	13/6/18, sick	Corporal.	

NAME.	REGTL. NO.	DATE OF JOINING.	DATE OF LEAVING WITH CAUSE.	HIGHEST RANK.	HONOURS OR AWARDS.
Chadwick, H. ...	40366	13/8/17	25/5/18, transferred	Rifleman.	
Chadwick, W. H.	243841	13/10/16	23/4/18, sick	Corporal.	
Chambers, J. W.	330677	27/5/18	20/1/19, transferred	L./Sergt.	M.M.
Chant, F.	88549	19/9/17	24/1/18, sick	Rifleman.	
Chappell, C. ...	2238	1/9/14	—/—/14, posted 1/6th K.L.R.	Rifleman.	
Charles, G. T. ...	2896	10/11/14	5/8/15, transferred	Rifleman.	
Charlton, T. H. ...	2298	10/9/14	27/1/17, released for munitions	A./Sergt.	
Charters, J.	242336	2/3/16	30/6/17, transferred	Rifleman.	
Checkland, F. J.	3042	17/11/14	26/6/15, transferred	Rifleman.	
Cheney, J. ...	52063	22/6/18	14/2/19, demobilized ...	Sergeant.	
Chevaux, A. E. ...	242174	20/1/16	8/3/19, posted 13th K.L.R.	Rifleman.	
✠Child, W. J. ...	43780	30/5/18	30/9/18, killed in action ...	Rifleman.	
Chisholm, G. O. ...	241044	12/11/14	9/8/17,† invalided to England	Rifleman.	
Chisholm, R. G.	241348	3/7/15	11/1/18, commission	Rifleman.	
Christall, J. R. ...	200067	13/3/18	18/5/18, sick	Sergeant.	
Christian, J.	241496	6/8/15	9/10/17, transferred	Rifleman.	
Christian, J. A. ...	202313	11/3/18	26/1/19, demobilized ...	Corporal.	
Christian, P. E. ...	241552	6/8/15	30/6/18, sick	Rifleman.	
Church, A. E. V.	241370	3/7/15	29/3/19, demobilized ...	A./Sergt.	M. in D.
Clague, A. T. ...	2377	10/9/14	26/6/15, transferred	Rifleman.	
Clague, H.	108745	28/9/18	25/10/18, wounded	Rifleman.	
Clague, W. H. ...	203304	6/6/18	28/3/19, posted 13th K.L.R.	L./Corpl.	
Clampitt, A. ...	267285	27/5/18	5/3/19, demobilized	Rifleman.	
Clancey, J. S. ...	242377	18/3/16	28/3/19, posted 13th K.L.R.	Rifleman.	
Clare, J.	52880	14/6/18	6/9/18, wounded	Sergeant.	
Clark, A.	57637	30/5/18	11/2/19, demobilized ...	Rifleman.	
Clark, A. G.	235287	27/5/18	18/10/18, wounded ...	Rifleman.	
Clark, E.	4882	25/2/16	2/12/16, commission	Rifleman.	
Clark, F.	3210	13/1/15	6/9/15, transferred	Rifleman.	
✠Clark, J.	243777	10/10/16	16/6/18, killed in action ...	Rifleman.	
Clark, N. ...	72444	13/8/17	5/6/18, sick	Rifleman.	
Clark, R. ...	3041	17/11/14	26/6/15, transferred	Rifleman.	
Clark, T. ...	241572	6/8/15	26/2/19, demobilized ...	Sergeant.	
Clark, T. C. ...	243819	12/10/16	5/10/18, wounded	Rifleman.	
Clark, W. E. ...	240482	23/10/14	8/3/18, transferred	Rifleman.	
Clarke, A. E. ...	265359	8/7/17	1/8/18,† sick	Rifleman.	
Clarke, A. H. ...	2820	9/11/14	12/1/15, transferred	Rifleman.	
Clarke, A. J. ...	2021	23/10/14	5/8/15, transferred	Rifleman.	
Clarke, B. ...	50731	18/8/17	14/2/19, demobilized ...	Sergeant	M.M.
Clarke, E. ...	2470	15/9/14	26/6/15, transferred	Rifleman.	
✠Clarke, F. ...	12892	14/9/18	30/9/18, killed in action ...	Rifleman.	
Clarke, F. ...	88547	19/9/17	—/—/19, demobilized ...	Rifleman.	
Clarke, G. W. ...	50736	18/8/17	—/—/19, demobilized ...	L./Corpl.	
Clarke, J. A. ...	243713	9/10/16	1/9/17, transferred	Rifleman.	
Clarke, J. W. ...	108833	28/9/18	26/2/19, posted 25th K.L.R.	Rifleman.	
Clarke, R. ...	88129	27/6/18	30/8/18, sick	Rifleman.	
Clarke, T. A. ...	2157	31/8/14	—/—/15, transferred	Rifleman.	
Clarkson, J. A. ...	2203	1/9/14	—/—/15, transferred	Rifleman.	
Clausen, H. J. ...	3236	25/1/15	23/8/15, transferred	Rifleman.	
Clawley, C. ...	242556	19/10/16	11/4/19, demobilized ...	Rifleman.	
Clawson, A. ...	242206	21/1/16	23/3/19, sick	L./Sergt.	
Clayton, A. H. ...	1291	23/2/15	26/6/15, transferred	Rifleman.	
Clayton, J. E. ...	241384	3/7/15	4/9/17, wounded	A./Corpl.	
Cleasby, T. W. ...	242460	25/3/16	24/11/17, sick	L./Corpl.	
Cleaver, E. ...	3073	20/11/14	5/8/15, transferred	Rifleman.	
Clegg, H. ...	241546	6/8/15	9/8/17,† invalided to England	Rifleman.	
Clegg, J. J. ...	243722	9/10/16	7/8/17, invalided to England	Rifleman.	
Clemenson, J. ...	380328	10/7/18	26/7/18, posted 12th K.L.R.	Rifleman.	

NAME.	REGTL. NO.	DATE OF JOINING.	DATE OF LEAVING WITH CAUSE.	HIGHEST RANK.	HONOURS OR AWARDS.
Clements, G. ...	200717	1/2/18	21/1/19, demobilized ...	Corporal.	
Clements, W. J.	88969	17/12/17	5/9/18, wounded ...	Rifleman.	
Cliffe, A. H. ...	3049	17/11/14	26/6/15, transferred ...	Rifleman.	
Clift, J. ...	200508	1/2/18	27/3/18, sick ...	Rifleman.	
Clifton, F.	88535	19/9/17	5/1/18, wounded ...	Rifleman.	
Clinch, E. ...	2085	31/8/14	—/—/15, transferred ...	Rifleman.	
Clough, F. ...	50897	14/9/18	17/2/19, demobilized	Rifleman.	
Clough, H. ...	110854	27/11/18	26/2/19, posted 25th K.L.R.	Rifleman.	
Clough, J. ...	50918	14/9/18	25/10/18, wounded ...	Rifleman.	
Clough, J. ...	88180	8/11/17	1/11/18, injured ...	Rifleman.	
Clough, S. ...	88143	11/10/17	14/11/17, sick ...	Rifleman.	
Clowes, E. ...	3128	1/12/14	16/8/15, transferred ...	Rifleman.	
Clydesdale, C. ...	240970	9/11/14	29/3/19, demobilized ...	Rifleman.	
Coates, J. J. ...	269313	27/8/17	2/12/17, sick ...	Rifleman.	
Cobbledick, J. D.	12316	14/9/18	3/10/18, wounded ...	Rifleman.	
Cocker, A. ...	29422	6/11/18	7/2/19, sick ...	Rifleman.	
Cocker, F. ...	50730	18/8/17	—/—/19, demobilized ...	Rifleman.	
Cockerill, J. ...	241494	6/8/15	5/10/18, wounded ...	Rifleman.	
Cockersol, W. J.	201346	1/2/18	11/8/18, sick ...	Rifleman.	
Cody, E. ...	64812	13/8/17	4/2/19, demobilized ...	Rifleman.	
Coggin, G.	49223	27/6/18	18/1/19, demobilized ...	Rifleman.	
Coghill, A. ...	110848	27/11/18	—/—/19, demobilized ...	Rifleman.	
Cohen, J. ...	240790	22/9/14	10/2/19, demobilized ...	L./Corpl.	
Coker, G. A.	88609	1/2/18	5/9/18, wounded ...	Rifleman.	
Colclough, J. ...	40371	13/8/17	26/2/19, posted 13th K.L.R.	Rifleman.	
Coleman, G. M. ...	240249	23/10/14	17/6/17,† transferred ...	Rifleman.	
Coleman, J. F. ...	50723	18/8/17	9/7/18, posted 1/6th K.L.R.	Rifleman.	
Coles, C. ...	50733	18/8/17	18/1/18, sick ...	Rifleman.	
Coley, G. H. ...	88611	1/2/18	26/3/18, transferred ...	Rifleman.	
Colley, H.	95763	17/4/18	—/3/19, posted 25th K.L.R.	Rifleman.	
Collier, H. ...	19199	13/8/17	19/11/17, sick ...	Corporal	
Colligan, R. J. ...	1761	23/10/14	12/1/15, transferred ...	Rifleman.	
Collin, K. G.	1744	27/2/15	1/4/15, commission ...	Rifleman.	
Collins, F. G. ...	242559	2/6/16	12/10/17,† transferred ...	Rifleman.	
Collins, W. ...	12301	27/6/18	10/12/18, transferred ...	A./Sergt	M.M.
Collins, — ...	2417	11/9/14	12/1/15, transferred ...	Rifleman.	
Collison, O. J. ...	240842	25/9/14	31/7/17, commission ...	Rifleman.	
Collister, T. J. ...	202413	1/2/18	23/6/18, sick ...	Rifleman.	
Colquhoun, A. S.	2094	31/8/14	—/—/15, transferred ...	Rifleman.	
Commons, P. J. E.	242527	22/5/16	30/4/17,† posted 1st K.L.R.	Rifleman.	
Connerton, H. ...	88231	8/11/17	14/7/18, posted 2/7th K.L.R.	Rifleman.	
Connolly, F. E. ...	241383	3/7/15	9/11/17,† wounded ...	Rifleman.	
Connor, J. F. ...	16645	27/5/18	21/6/18, wounded ...	Rifleman.	
Conway, B. ...	5224	19/5/16	18/8/16, transferred ...	Rifleman.	
Conway, C. ...	2387	10/9/14	16/8/15, transferred ...	Rifleman.	
Cook, J. ...	242816	25/6/18	29/8/18, sick ...	Rifleman.	
Cook, J. J. G. ...	50920	2/7/18	—/—/19, transferred	Rifleman.	
Cook, W. ...	242565	6/6/16	12/1/18, sick ...	Rifleman.	
Cook, G. W. ...	2090	31/8/14	—/—/15, posted 1/6th K.L.R.	Rifleman.	
Cooke, H. ...	1421	27/4/15	26/7/15, transferred ...	L./Corpl.	
✠Cooke, J. A. ...	235270	6/6/18	21/10/18, killed in action ...	L./Corpl.	
Cooke, S. ...	235428	10/3/18	8/9/18, wounded ...	Rifleman.	
Cookson, T. M. ...	172	23/2/15	28/6/15, transferred ...	Sergeant.	
Coope, R. ...	85753	7/3/18	15/7/18, transferred ...	Rifleman.	
Cooper, A. ...	241501	6/8/15	30/8/17, wounded ...	Sergeant.	
Cooper, A. E. ...	242256	25/1/16	—/—/19, demobilized ...	Rifleman.	
Cooper, E. ...	88551	19/9/17	12/1/18, sick ...	Rifleman.	
Cooper, E. ...	110504	27/11/18	26/2/19, posted 13th K.L.R.	Rifleman.	

NAME.	REGTL. NO.	DATE OF JOINING.	DATE OF LEAVING WITH CAUSE.	HIGHEST RANK.	HONOURS OR AWARDS.
Cooper, F. ...	88550	19/9/17	8/7/18, transferred	Rifleman.	
Cooper, J.	240481	5/5/17	20/5/17, posted 1st K.L.R. ...	Rifleman.	
✠Cooper, J.	381131	27/5/18	30/8/18, died of wounds ...	Rifleman.	
Cooper, R. E.	88552	19/9/17	22/5/19, demobilized ...	Rifleman.	
Cooper, T. E. ...	2944	11/11/14	26/6/15, transferred ...	Rifleman.	
Cooper, W.	1917	23/10/14	1/6/15, transferred ...	Rifleman.	
Cooper, W.	50729	18/8/17	—/—/19, transferred ...	Rifleman.	
Copland, W. O. ...	241123	23/11/14	18/9/18, wounded ...	Rifleman.	
Corcoran, J.	202321	1/2/18	5/9/18, wounded ...	Rifleman.	
Cordon, W. J. ...	300211	30/5/18	5/3/19, demobilized ...	Rifleman.	
Cordon, R.	2228	1/9/14	—/—/14, transferred ...	Rifleman.	
Corfe, A.	2456	12/9/14	14/7/15, discharged ...	Rifleman.	
Cork, J.	17300	7/3/18	23/1/19, demobilized ...	Sergeant.	
Corkill, N. L.	241259	11/3/15	24/10/18, commission ...	Sergeant	M.M., M.S.M.
Corkill, W. A.	2528	19/9/14	4/5/16, transferred ...	Rifleman.	
Corkish, R. N.	110535	27/11/18	26/2/19, posted 25th K.L.R.	Rifleman.	
Corlett, A. G.	50724	18/8/17	26/2/19, posted 25th K.L.R.	Rifleman.	
Corlett, J. A.	241321	3/7/15	21/8/17, wounded	A./Corpl.	
Corlett, W.	108829	28/9/18	3/11/18, wounded ...	Rifleman.	
Cormack, F. J. ...	9	—/—/14	26/6/15, transferred ...	Sergeant.	
Cornes, W.	2399	11/9/14	12/1/15, transferred ...	Rifleman.	
Cornish, H. R. ...	5227	23/5/16	16/6/16, commission ...	Rifleman.	
Cornock, J. N. ...	50735	18/8/17	—/—/19, transferred...	Rifleman.	
Cornwell W. ...	88553	19/9/17	22/12/18, demobilized	Rifleman.	
Corran, R. D. ...	2289	2/9/14	—/—/15, transferred ...	Rifleman.	
Corrigall, J.	2182	31/8/14	—/—/14, transferred ...	Rifleman.	
Corrigall, J.	2527	10/9/14	26/6/15, transferred ...	Rifleman.	
Corrigan, J.	204017	1/2/18	26/2/19, posted 25th K.L.R.	Rifleman.	
Corrin, C.	242235	22/1/16	29/8/18, posted 1st K.L.R. ...	L./Corpl.	
Corry, T. W. ...	243814	12/10/16	14/2/19, demobilized ...	Rifleman.	
Costello, R.	242225	22/1/16	15/10/18, sick	Corporal.	
Costello, T.	17113	14/6/18	15/2/19, demobilized ...	Rifleman.	
Cottam, J.	243864	17/10/16	15/7/17, invalided to England	Rifleman.	
Cottle, T.	1960	23/10/14	26/6/15, transferred ...	Rifleman.	
Cotton, C.	2405	11/9/14	21/9/15, commission ...	L./Corpl.	
Cottrell, H.	240934	9/11/14	7/7/18,† sick	L./Corpl.	
Cottrell, H. A. ...	381100	1/2/18	23/7/18, transferred ...	Rifleman.	
Coulthard, A.	39035	27/6/18	2/10/18, sick	Rifleman.	
Courtney, J.	110740	27/11/18	26/2/19, posted 25th K.L.R.	Rifleman.	
Coury, G. G.	2482	12/9/14	24/4/15, commission ...	Rifleman.	
Coury, —.	2662	13/10/14	9/11/14, medically unfit ...	Rifleman.	
✠Cousins, G. H.	240779	23/9/14	21/5/18, killed in action ...	A./R.Q.M.S.	
Cowan, H.	2066	31/8/14	—/—/14, transferred ...	Rifleman.	
Coward, H.	50933	18/8/17	20/8/17, posted 2/8th K.L.R.	Rifleman.	
Cowdroy, E. G. J. B.	235480	1/2/18	28/4/18, sick	Corporal.	
Cowell, A.	88194	8/11/17	8/12/17, sick	Rifleman.	
Cowie, A. B. ...	241115	19/11/14	15/2/19, demobilized ...	Rifleman.	
Cowley, F. H. ...	3617	6/8/15	27/3/16, discharged ...	Rifleman.	
Cowley, G.	202490	14/3/18	26/2/19, posted 25th K.L.R.	Rifleman.	
Cowley, T.	241089	16/11/14	29/11/17,† wounded ...	Rifleman.	
Cowman, F. G. ...	2908	10/11/14	26/6/15, transferred ...	Rifleman.	
Cowpe, F.	88208	8/11/17	14/1/18, sick	Rifleman.	
Cox, A.	2374	10/9/14	28/8/15, civil employment ...	Rifleman.	
Cox, A. H. ...	2386	10/9/14	20/8/15, commission ...	Rifleman.	
Cox, H. B. ...	2073	31/8/14	20/2/15, commission ...	Riflemen.	
Cox, J.	8482	1/2/18	12/1/19, sick	Sergeant.	
Cox, L. H. ...	1050	23/2/15	29/7/15, commission ...	Rifleman.	
Cox, R. F. ...	2815	9/11/14	12/1/15, transferred ...	Rifleman.	

NAME.	REGTL. NO.	DATE OF JOINING.	DATE OF LEAVING WITH CAUSE.	HIGHEST RANK.	HONOURS OR AWARDS.
Crabb, A. F.	53471	19/9/17	28/9/17, posted 2/5th K.L.R.	Rifleman.	
Cracknell, A. F.	88612	1/2/18	27/6/18, wounded	Rifleman.	
Crafter, H.	2521	18/9/14	12/1/15, transferred	A./Col./Sgt.	
Craig, J.	242456	25/3/16	9/8/17, invalided to England	Rifleman.	
Craig, T. R.	2934	11/11/14	5/8/15, transferred	Rifleman.	
Craine, J.	48878	1/2/18	—/—/19, demobilized	Rifleman.	
Craine, W.	242147	20/1/16	5/8/17, invalided to England	Rifleman.	
Crane, C.	3729	6/8/15	6/9/15, transferred	Rifleman.	
Crank, T. S.	110543	27/11/18	23/12/18, sick	Rifleman.	
Crawford, J. H.	242299	17/2/16	24/5/17, sick	Rifleman.	
Crean, —.	2278	2/9/14	—/—/14, transferred	Rifleman.	
Cregeen, A. H.	241190	8/1/15	7/8/17, invalided to England	Rifleman.	
Cribb, J.	3240	29/1/15	4/5/16, transferred	Rifleman.	
Crippin, W.	2806	9/11/14	26/6/15, transferred	Rifleman.	
Crisp, J.	242162	20/1/16	21/7/17, wounded	Rifleman.	
Crocker, L. N.	2089	31/8/14	20/6/15, transferred	Rifleman.	
Crone, A. A.	956	27/2/15	9/3/15, medically unfit	Sergeant.	
Crockford, W.	88195	8/11/17	14/3/18, transferred	Rifleman.	
Crompton, T. P.	306590	30/5/18	26/2/19, demobilized	Rifleman.	
Crook, J.	58582	7/3/18	11/6/18, wounded	Rifleman.	
Crook, W.	40568	13/8/17	26/2/19, posted 25th K.L.R.	Rifleman.	
Crookall, J.	203903	1/2/18	18/5/18, wounded	Rifleman.	
Cropper, R.	202710	8/7/17	5/2/19, demobilized	Rifleman.	
Crosby, F. C.	268053	27/8/17	11/6/18, wounded	Rifleman.	
Crosby, H. E.	2705	28/10/14	26/6/15, transferred	Rifleman.	
Crosby, J. C.	3107	26/11/14	26/6/15, transferred	Rifleman.	
Crosby, R. S.	16509	30/5/18	17/1/19, demobilized	Rifleman.	
Cross, C.	2388	10/9/14	12/1/15, transferred	Rifleman.	
Cross, C.	3035	16/11/14	26/6/15, transferred	Rifleman.	
Cross, G. R.	268041	27/8/17	14/5/18, sick	Rifleman.	
Cross, J. A.	50889	2/7/18	28/3/19, posted 25th K.L.R.	Rifleman.	
Cross, P.	3682	6/8/15	21/8/15, discharged	Rifleman.	
Crouchley, J.	2483	16/9/14	12/1/15, transferred	Rifleman.	
Crow, H.	57781	6/6/18	10/7/18, transferred	Rifleman.	
Crowley, W. J.	50904	1/2/18	13/12/18, demobilized	Rifleman.	
Croxton, D. S.	2591	1/10/14	9/12/15, transferred	Rifleman.	
Crugman, S.	242306	25/2/16	3/8/17, invalided to England	Rifleman.	
Cruise, W. J.	49348	13/9/18	22/5/19, demobilized	Rifleman.	
Crumbie, J.	34505	13/8/17	2/12/17, transferred	Rifleman.	
Cuddy, F.	50734	—/8/17	11/11/17, wounded	Rifleman.	
Cuddy, —.	2428	11/9/14	20/10/14, medically unfit	Rifleman.	
Culcannon, H.	50725	18/8/17	26/2/19, posted 13th K.L.R.	Rifleman.	
✠Cullen, F.	88230	8/11/17	11/9/18, killed in action	Rifleman.	
Cummings, H.	3277	22/2/15	4/5/16, transferred	Rifleman	
Cummins, F.	240786	22/9/14	4/9/17, commission	Sergeant.	
Cummins, R.	242414	21/3/16	10/8/17, invalided to England	Rifleman.	
Cunane, J. T.	243687	7/10/16	10/8/17, wounded	Rifleman.	
Cunliffe, G.	2961	12/11/14	1/12/15, demobilized	Rifleman.	
Cunningham, J.	108949	28/9/18	28/3/19, posted 13th K.L.R.	Rifleman.	
Cunningham, J. J.	59055	1/2/18	5/3/19, demobilized	Rifleman.	
Cunnington, J.	202706	8/7/17	26/2/19, posted 25th K.L.R.	Rifleman.	
Curnock, C.	91882	27/6/18	26/2/19, posted 25th K.L..R.	Rifleman.	
Curran, F.	88113	5/10/17	16/4/18, sick	Rifleman.	
Curran, R.	2898	10/11/14	26/6/15, transferred	Rifleman.	
Currie, J.	2441	15/9/14	26/6/15, transferred	Rifleman.	
Currie, T.	2202	1/9/14	—/—/14, transferred	Rifleman.	
Cursi, F.	241021	11/11/14	7/2/19,† demobilized	L./Corpl.	
Curtis, W. H.	3260	11/2/15	26/6/15, transferred	Rifleman.	

NAME.	REGTL. NO.	DATE OF JOINING.	DATE OF LEAVING WITH CAUSE.	HIGHEST RANK.	HONOURS OR AWARDS.
Curwen, C. W. ...	241539	6/8/15	7/2/19, demobilized ...	Corporal.	
Curwen, R. ...	2063	31/8/14	—/—/15, posted 1/6th K.L.R.	Rifleman.	
Curwen, W. H. ...	2937	11/11/14	12/1/15, transferred	Rifleman.	
Cuthbert, G. ...	3147	7/12/14	4/5/16, transferred ...	Rifleman.	
Cuthbert, R. ...	240879	28/10/14	9/10/18,† wounded	Rifleman.	
Cuthbertson, W. A.	241040	11/11/14	15/9/17, posted 1/6th K.L.R.	Rifleman.	
Cutts, E.	50732	18/8/17	29/12/17, transferred ...	Rifleman.	
Dagnall, W. J. ...	242201	21/1/16	19/7/17, wounded	Rifleman.	
Dale, T.	22971	13/8/17	9/7/18, posted 8th K.L.R. ...	Rifleman.	
Daley, M. ...	12933	14/9/18	15/10/18, sick	Rifleman.	
Daley, W. E. ...	2652	12/10/14	12/1/15, transferred	Rifleman.	
✠Dalrymple, J. ...	57372	6/6/18	17/9/18, died of wounds ...	Sergeant	M.M.
Dalrymple, W. ...	242168	20/1/16	12/2/19, demobilized ...	Rifleman.	
Daniels, A.	57918	1/2/18	1/8/18, posted 12th K.L.R.	Rifleman.	
Daniels, F. C. ...	3209	12/1/15	5/8/15, transferred	A./Corpl.	
Daniels, G. L. ...	240844	10/10/14	30/6/17, wounded	Rifleman.	
Danily, J. ...	2166	31/8/14	—/—/15, transferred... ...	Rifleman.	
Darcy, H. ...	241376	3/7/15	12/8/18, prisoner of war ...	Corporal.	
Darcy, J. ...	204009	1/2/18	8/3/19, posted 13th K.L.R.	Rifleman.	
Davey, A. E. ...	2109	31/8/14	—/—/15, transferred ...	Rifleman.	
Davey, H. ...	240939	9/11/14	13/8/17, wounded	Rifleman.	
Davey, S. F. ...	242561	31/5/16	6/8/17, invalided to England	A./Corpl.	
✠Davidson, A. E.	242446	24/3/16	29/4/17, killed in action ...	A./Corpl.	
Davidson, W. H. H.	2084	31/8/14	13/11/14, commission ...	Rifleman.	
Davie, W. L. ...	1538	23/2/15	26/6/15, transferred ...	Rifleman.	
Davies, A. ...	3026	16/11/14	5/8/15, transferred	Rifleman.	
Davies, A. ...	20183	24/2/18	5/10/18, wounded	Rifleman.	
Davies, B. ...	241355	3/7/15	12/8/17, wounded	Rifleman.	
Davies C. H. ...	2383	10/9/14	12/1/15, transferred	Rifleman.	
Davies, E. R. ...	242297	17/2/16	27/6/17, wounded	Rifleman.	
✠Davies, F. ...	242195	21/1/16	4/9/18, died of wounds ...	Rifleman.	
Davies, F. A. ...	2092	31/8/14	20/1/16, commission ...	Rifleman.	
Davies, G. ...	2956	12/11/14	26/6/15, transferred	Rifleman.	
Davies, G. A. ...	50743	18/8/17	26/2/19, posted 25th K.L.R.	Rifleman.	
Davies, G. J. ...	2086	31/8/14	11/7/16, commission ...	Rifleman.	
Davies, G. N. ...	381003	21/11/17	29/8/18, posted 1st K.L.R.	L./Corpl.	
Davies, H. ...	241421	8/7/17	19/8/17, wounded	Rifleman.	
Davies, H. ...	50740	18/8/17	20/1/19, demobilized ...	Rifleman.	
Davies, H. L. ...	2125	31/8/14	24/10/16, commission ...	Rifleman.	
✠Davies, H. S. ...	240688	10/9/14	30/10/17, killed in action ...	Rifleman.	
Davies, J. ...	2651	12/10/14	5/8/15, transferred	Rifleman.	
Davies, J. ...	2914	10/11/14	26/6/15, transferred	Rifleman.	
Davies, J. ...	57783	27/6/18	22/5/19, demobilized ...	Rifleman.	
Davies, J. ...	240794	24/9/14	7/8/17, invalided to England	L./Corpl.	
Davies, J. E.	108951	28/9/18	28/3/19, posted 13th K.L.R.	Rifleman.	
Davies, J. H. ...	1310	23/2/15	4/5/16, transferred	Rifleman.	
Davies, J. P. ...	242150	20/1/16	17/1/18,† posted 13th K.L.R.	Rifleman.	
Davies, N. ...	2138	31/8/14	—/—/15, transferred ...	Rifleman.	
Davies, R. ...	51900	22/6/18	22/5/19, demobilized ...	Rifleman.	
Davies, R. E. ...	2057	31/8/14	—/—/15, posted 1/6th K.L.R.	Rifleman.	
Davies, T. ...	22360	24/2/18	29/5/18, sick	L./Corpl.	
Davies, T. ...	88554	19/9/17	7/2/19, demobilized ...	Rifleman.	
Davies, T. G. ...	242437	23/3/16	28/9/17, discharged ...	Rifleman.	
Davies, T. J. ...	241136	26/11/14	10/2/19,† demobilized. ...	Rifleman.	
Davies, T. J. ...	242397	20/3/16	11/5/18, sick	L./Corpl.	
Davies, W. ...	200695	1/2/18	3/2/19, demobilized ...	Rifleman.	
Davies, W. E. ...	3145	7/12/14	4/10/15, transferred ...	Rifleman.	

x

NAME.	REGTL. NO.	DATE OF JOINING.	DATE OF LEAVING WITH CAUSE.	HIGHEST RANK.	HONOURS OR AWARDS.
Davies, W. H. ...	2642	9/10/14	26/6/15, transferred	Rifleman.	
Davies, W. S. ...	2104	31/8/14	—/—/15, transferred ...	Rifleman.	
Davis, F. ...	88676	1/2/18	15/7/18, wounded	Rifleman.	
Davis, H. ...	53095	30/5/18	29/8/18, posted 1st K.L.R. ...	Rifleman.	
Davis, H. ...	201183	1/2/18	9/1/19, sick	Rifleman.	
Dawes, A. W. ...	53099	30/5/18	20/9/18, wounded	Rifleman.	
Dawson, A. B. ...	40149	1/2/18	26/2/19, posted 25th K.L.R.	Rifleman.	
Dawson, E. ...	243657	6/10/16	18/7/17,† transferred ...	Rifleman.	
Dawson, F. ...	242430	22/3/16	5/8/17, invalided to England	L./Corpl.	
Dawson, G. ...	22361	13/8/17	1/7/18, wounded	Rifleman.	
Dawson, J. ...	2621	5/10/14	23/8/15,† transferred ...	Rifleman.	
Dawson, W. J. ...	241202	13/1/15	17/8/17, wounded	Rifleman.	
Day, J. D. ...	243770	10/10/16	25/12/17, sick	Rifleman.	
Deacon, G. ...	241752	1/2/18	12/9/18, sick	Rifleman.	
Deakin, W. ...	9087	27/6/18	7/1/19, demobilized	Rifleman.	
Dean, C. H. ...	50742	18/8/17	17/11/17, commission ...	Rifleman.	
Dean, E. ...	88555	19/9/17	14/1/18, sick	Rifleman.	
Dean, E. V. ...	2869	10/11/14	12/1/15, transferred ...	Rifleman.	
Dearing, P. ...	2833	9/11/14	26/6/15, transferred ...	Rifleman.	
Dean, H. E. ...	2928	11/11/14	12/1/15, transferred ...	Rifleman.	
Dean, L. ...	3031	16/11/14	9/8/15, transferred ...	Rifleman.	
Deane, E. N. ...	1487	23/10/14	12/1/15, transferred ...	Rifleman.	
Deans, E. D. ...	242186	21/1/16	5/8/17, invalided to England	Rifleman.	
Deans, R. H. ...	243876	28/1/17	7/8/17, invalided to England	Rifleman.	
Dearden, H. ...	6441	6/10/16	7/1/17, transferred ...	Rifleman.	
De Courcy, H. ...	2946	11/11/14	28/7/15, discharged	Rifleman.	
De Courcy, H. ...	2242	1/9/14	29/7/15, discharged	Rifleman.	
Dee, A.	225	23/2/15	26/6/15, transferred	L./Corpl.	
Delan, V. S. ...	1975	23/10/14	28/6/15, medically unfit ...	Rifleman.	
Delaney, T. B. ...	243815	12/10/16	10/8/17, wounded	Rifleman.	
Dempsey, T. E. ...	2924	11/11/14	26/6/15, transferred	Rifleman.	
Denholme, E. F.	235429	25/2/18	14/6/18, posted 1/5th K.L.R.	Rifleman.	
Dennett, F. G. ...	2114	31/8/14	—/—/15, transferred ...	Rifleman.	
Dennett, W. ...	5093	25/3/16	15/7/16, discharged	Rifleman.	
Dennison, J. R. ...	72489	13/8/17	26/1/19,† demobilized ...	L./Corpl.	M.M.
Depattie, W. ...	30310	13/8/17	9/6/18, wounded	Rifleman.	
Derbyshire, T. S.	22670	27/6/18	21/2/19, demobilized ...	Rifleman.	
Devereux, T. ...	242166	20/1/16	28/9/17, sick	Rifleman.	
✠Devoy, J. ...	13036	27/6/18	1/9/18, killed in action ...	Corporal.	
Dewar, J. ...	3443	6/8/15	23/8/15, transferred ...	Rifleman.	
Dewett, F. ...	50741	18/8/17	26/12/17, wounded ...	Rifleman.	
Dexter, R. H. ...	2515	15/9/14	26/6/15, transferred ...	Rifleman.	
Deyes, T. G. ...	241176	31/12/14	2/3/17, wounded	Rifleman.	
Dick, J. ...	3043	17/11/14	5/8/15, transferred ...	Rifleman.	
Dick, —	2385	10/9/14	12/1/15, transferred	L./Corpl.	
Dickenson, C. V.	57791	30/5/18	1/10/18, wounded	Rifleman	
Dickenson, E. ...	202868	27/5/18	3/3/19, demobilized	Rifleman.	
Dickenson, H. ...	51757	30/5/18	14/2/19, demobilized ...	Corporal.	
Dickenson, J. ...	6503	9/10/16	2/2/17, sick	Rifleman.	
Diggle, J. H. ...	2510	17/9/14	12/1/15, transferred ...	Rifleman.	
Disley, H. ...	242571	8/6/16	11/2/19, demobilized ...	Corporal.	
Ditchfield, C. P.	2993	12/11/14	26/6/15, transferred	Rifleman.	
Dixon, A. ...	2299	10/9/14	12/1/15, transferred ...	Rifleman.	
Dixon, C. L. ...	2156	31/8/14	—/—/15, transferred ...	Rifleman.	
Dixon, G. ...	265346	8/7/17	8/8/17, invalided to England	Rifleman.	
Dixon, G. F. ...	1290	23/2/15	26/6/15, transferred	A./Corpl.	
Dixon, G. H. K. ...	241157	5/12/14	21/8/17, wounded	Rifleman.	
Dixon, H. ...	2900	10/11/14	26/6/15, transferred	Rifleman.	

NAME.	REGTL. NO.	DATE OF JOINING.	DATE OF LEAVING WITH CAUSE.	HIGHEST RANK.	HONOURS OR AWARDS.
Dixon, H. S.	2382	10/9/14	12/1/15, transferred	Rifleman.	
Dixon, R.	72477	13/8/17	28/6/18, sick	Rifleman.	
Dixon, T.	242156	20/1/16	27/12/17, wounded.	Rifleman.	
Dixon, R. D.	2731	2/11/14	26/6/15, transferred	Rifleman.	
Dobbie, T.	2505	12/9/14	26/6/15, transferred	Rifleman.	
Dobson, C.	35476	22/6/18	22/5/19, demobilized	Corporal.	
Dobson, J. G.	2858	10/11/14	12/1/15, transferred	Rifleman.	
Dodd, E.	242387	18/3/16	21/8/17, wounded	Rifleman.	
Dodd, H. E.	3024	16/11/14	26/6/15, transferred	Rifleman.	
Dodd, H. S.	22673	30/5/18	26/2/19, demobilized	Rifleman.	M.M.
Dodd, R.	241491	6/8/15	1/9/17,† posted 1/7th K.L.R.	Rifleman.	
Dodd, T. S.	5250	29/5/16	18/8/16, transferred	Rifleman.	
Dodd, W. A.	3084	23/11/14	17/12/15, commission	Rifleman.	
Dolby, C. N.	2280	1/9/14	13/10/14, discharged	Rifleman.	
Doleman, G. S.	241195	11/1/15	25/5/17,† wounded (accid.)	Rifleman.	
Donaldson, T.	300573	8/11/17	24/8/18, posted 13th K.L.R.	Rifleman	M.M.
Donkin, V.	241403	3/7/15	7/3/17,† transferred	Rifleman.	
Doodson, G.	242275	28/1/16	3/11/17, wounded	Rifleman.	
Doonan, T.	300240	6/6/18	6/3/19, demobilized	Rifleman.	
Dosser, —	2414	11/9/14	12/1/15, transferred	Rifleman.	
Dossett, D.	50745	18/8/17	29/3/18, transferred	Rifleman.	
Douglas, W.	2475	11/9/14	26/6/15, transferred	Rifleman.	
Doughty, G. C.	202349	1/2/18	5/9/18, wounded	Rifleman.	
Dow, H. V.	242600	8/7/16	6/8/17, invalided to England	Rifleman.	
Doward, S.	2757	5/11/14	26/6/15, transferred	Rifleman.	
Dowd, F.	50738	18/8/17	30/6/18, sick	Rifleman.	
Dowell, S.	3341	19/4/15	29/4/16, discharged	Rifleman.	
Dowling, J.	204069	1/2/18	25/1/19, demobilized	Rifleman.	
Downer, A. C.	51384	27/5/18	30/1/19, demobilized	Sergeant.	
Downes, F.	243727	9/10/16	4/5/17, transferred	Rifleman.	
Downey, J.	16964	6/6/18	19/6/18, wounded	Rifleman.	
Downey, T. J.	202251	8/7/17	5/3/19, demobilized	L./Corpl.	
Downing, W.	242145	5/5/17	20/5/17, transferred	Rifleman.	
Dowsett, F. H.	242522	17/5/16	15/7/18†, posted 1/6th K.L.R.	Rifleman.	
Dowson, F. J.	243862	16/10/16	15/9/17,† sick	Rifleman.	
Doyle, H. P.	2596	2/10/14	26/6/15, transferred	Rifleman.	
Doyle, J.	88556	19/9/17	29/8/18, posted 1st K.L.R.	Rifleman.	
Doyle, J. S.	2679	19/10/14	12/1/15, transferred	Rifleman.	
Doyle, S. P.	1396	23/2/15	26/6/15, transferred	Rifleman.	
Dransfield, J.	241061	13/11/14	28/5/17, wounded	Rifleman.	
Draper, J.	88242	8/11/17	5/5/18, sick	Corporal.	
Draper, R. E.	241453	14/4/17	30/4/17, posted 1st K.L.R.	Rifleman.	
Draycott, J. N.	2234	1/9/14	7/1/17, transferred	Rifleman.	
Drew, W. R.	242558	19/10/16	24/2/19, demobilized	Rifleman.	
Drewitt, E. C.	242417	21/3/16	30/6/17, transferred	Rifleman.	
Drinkwater, H. O.	50744	18/8/17	14/6/18, posted 1/5th K.L.R.	Rifleman.	
Dron, G. M.	242405	20/3/16	31/8/17, sick	Rifleman.	
Druce, P. C.	88615	1/2/18	16/2/18, sick	Rifleman.	
Drury, J.	331939	27/8/17	11/6/18, sick	Rifleman.	
Drury, J. W.	266664	22/6/18	7/2/19, demobilized	Corporal	M.M.
Dubois, T. B.	2012	23/2/15	6/3/16, transferred	Rifleman.	
Ducker, W.	22061	22/6/18	14/12/18, transferred	Rifleman.	
Duckett, —	2170	31/8/14	12/1/15, transferred	Rifleman.	
Duddy, J. M.	8816	27/6/18	21/9/18, wounded	Rifleman.	
Dudson, J. A.	240714	15/9/14	12/9/17, posted 1/6th K.L.R.	L./Corpl.	
Duerden, E. F.	241284	6/4/15	17/8/17, wounded	A./Corpl.	
Duffell, A. W.	53094	30/5/18	20/2/19, demobilized	Rifleman.	
Duffy, C.	1520	23/10/14	5/8/15, transferred	Rifleman.	

NAME.	REGTL. NO.	DATE OF JOINING.	DATE OF LEAVING WITH CAUSE.	HIGHEST RANK.	HONOURS OR AWARDS.
Dugdale, W. F. ...	50739	18/8/17	31/12/17, wounded	Rifleman.	
Dunbar, A. J. ...	990	23/2/15	26/6/15, transferred	Rifleman.	
Dunbar, J. ...	57511	30/5/18	18/1/19, demobilized ...	Rifleman.	
Duncan, J. ...	3671	6/8/15	11/9/15, discharged	Rifleman.	
Dunkerley, H. ...	52577	30/5/18	17/1/19, demobilized ...	Rifleman.	
Dunn, A. H. ...	4828	27/1/16	5/8/17, invalided to England	L./Corpl.	
Dunn, J. ...	3015	14/11/14	5/8/15, transferred	Rifleman.	
✠Dunn, S. ...	4992	16/3/16	10/2/17, died	Rifleman.	
Dunn, W. ...	243752	10/10/16	2/8/17, wounded ...	Rifleman.	
Dunning, T. ...	2133	31/8/14	7/12/15, discharged	Rifleman.	
Dunwell, G. ...	2216	1/9/14	—/—/15, posted 1/6th K.L.R.	Rifleman.	
Durham, T. ...	50737	18/8/17	15/7/18, wounded	Rifleman.	
Durrance, S. W. W.	1234	23/2/15	26/6/15, transferred	Rifleman.	
Dutton, G. ...	241313	3/7/15	30/9/17, sick	L./Corpl.	
Dutton, H. ...	88256	17/12/17	15/4/18, sick	Rifleman.	
Dutton, T. ...	95705	17/4/18	6/2/19, demobilized ...	Rifleman.	
Dutton, — ...	2661	13/10/14	12/1/15, transferred ...	Rifleman.	
Dwyer, E. J. ...	3324	6/4/15	20/1/17, transferred	Rifleman	
Dyson, W. H. ...	266722	8/7/17	9/8/17, invalided to England	Rifleman.	
Earle, C. H. ...	241393	3/7/15	28/12/17, sick	Rifleman.	
Earle, J. ...	2178	31/8/14	—/—/15, transferred ...	Rifleman.	
Earle, W. ...	1541	23/10/14	23/9/16,† transferred ...	Rifleman.	
Eastman, R. H. ...	1851	23/10/14	28/6/15, transferred ...	Rifleman.	
✠Eastwood, H. ...	243685	7/10/16	3/8/17, died of wounds ...	Rifleman.	
Eastwood, R. C....	2145	31/8/14	31/1/15, transferred ...	Rifleman.	
Eaton, R. ...	240693	11/9/14	22/2/19,† demobilized ...	Rifleman.	
Ebbels, E. ...	241538	6/8/15	9/9/17,† posted 1/9th K.L.R.	Rifleman.	
✠Eccles, J. ...	6437	6/10/16	28/10/16, died ...	Rifleman.	
✠Eccles, R. ...	241510	6/8/15	8/6/17,† killed in action ...	Rifleman.	
Eccles, W. ...	50747	18/8/17	22/4/18, transferred	Rifleman.	
Eccleston, H. ...	202318	1/2/18	15/4/18, sick	Rifleman.	
Eccleston, R. D.	2102	31/8/14	27/5/15, commission ...	Rifleman.	
Eckett, H. S. ...	241484	6/8/15	27/2/17, commission ...	Rifleman.	
Eckersall, E. ...	88150	14/10/17	26/9/18, wounded	Rifleman.	
Edgar, J. ...	243778	9/10/16	30/4/17, posted 1st K.L.R. ...	Rifleman.	
Egerton, N. ...	243761	10/10/16	30/4/17,† posted 1st K.L.R.	Rifleman.	
Edge, T. H. ...	240213	23/10/14	15/7/18,† transferred ...	Rifleman.	
✠Edgeley, S. ...	88874	2/7/18	30/9/18, killed in action ...	Rifleman.	
Edinborough, G.	58568	30/5/18	25/6/18, wounded	Rifleman.	
✠Edmonds, J. P. ...	47460	5/10/17	1/9/18, killed in action ...	Rifleman.	
Edmondson, A. ...	242423	21/3/16	9/8/17, wounded	Rifleman.	
Edmondson, C. ...	300572	8/11/17	17/4/18, transferred	Rifleman.	
Edwards, A. ...	88102	29/9/17	10/7/18, transferred	Rifleman.	
Edwards, A. M. ...	2775	6/11/14	12/1/15, transferred	Rifleman.	
Edwards, E. S. ...	3068	19/11/14	26/6/15, transferred	Rifleman.	
✠Edwards, F. ...	242524	23/5/16	2/11/17, died of wounds ...	L./Corpl.	
Edwards, J. ...	241092	16/11/14	11/8/17,† invalided to England	L./Corpl.	
Edwards, J. ...	241489	6/8/15	30/8/15, transferred	Rifleman.	
Edwards, P. ...	241351	6/8/15	5/3/19,† demobilized ...	Rifleman.	
Edwards, R. ...	31568	27/5/18	12/9/18, prisoner of war ...	Rifleman.	
Edwards, S. ...	88110	5/10/17	7/9/18, wounded	Rifleman.	
Edwards, V. S. ...	240854	14/10/14	29/3/19,† demobilized ...	Rifleman.	
Egerton, A. ...	241152	2/12/14	22/5/19, demobilized ...	Rifleman.	
Eglin, T. ...	200727	1/2/18	19/10/18, wounded	Rifleman.	
Eilbeck, C. F. ...	2485	16/9/14	20/5/16, transferred	Rifleman.	
Elder, W. ...	92021	7/3/18	12/1/19, demobilized ...	A./Sergt.	
Eldridge, E. J. ...	2300	10/9/14	12/1/15, transferred	A./L./Cpl.	
Eley, J. ...	243769	9/10/16	17/8/17, transferred	Rifleman.	

NAME.	REGTL. NO.	DATE OF JOINING.	DATE OF LEAVING WITH CAUSE.	HIGHEST RANK.	HONOURS OR AWARDS.
Elias, C. V. ...	242906	21/9/14	6/3/18,† sick	Rifleman.	
Elleray, F. R. ...	3156	11/12/14	26/6/15, transferred	Rifleman.	
Ellicott, A. S. ...	242365	15/3/16	26/2/19, posted 25th K.L.R.	Rifleman.	
Elliott, P. ...	241571	6/8/15	22/5/19, demobilized ...	Rifleman.	
Elliott, J. ...	2529	19/9/14	26/6/15, transferred	Rifleman.	
Ellis, C. S. ...	241168	21/12/14	17/6/17,† transferred ...	Rifleman.	
✠ Ellis, F. G. ...	27184	27/5/18	21/10/18, died of wounds ...	Corporal.	
Ellis, J. ...	50746	18/8/17	17/12/17, wounded	Rifleman.	
Ellis, R. ...	235552	14/3/18	29/8/18, posted 1st K.L.R. ...	Rifleman.	
Ellis, T. E. ...	2123	31/8/14	—/—/15, transferred ...	Rifleman.	
Ellison, A. ...	15762	27/6/18	11/2/19, demobilized ...	L./Corpl.	
✠ Ellison, J. ...	53248	24/8/17	25/10/17, died of wounds ...	Rifleman.	
Ellison, J. ...	202807	30/5/18	30/1/19, demobilized ...	Rifleman.	
Ellwand, R. H. ...	200439	8/7/17	10/8/17, invalided to England	Rifleman.	
Elms, S. ...	47387	30/5/18	25/10/18, wounded ...	A./Sergt.	
Elsworth, F. J. ...	240189	27/2/15	16/5/17, commission	A./Sergt.	
Elsworth, F. L. ...	2758	5/11/14	26/6/15, transferred	A./L./Cpl.	
Elsworth, W. E. ...	2991	12/11/14	23/8/15, transferred	Rifleman.	
Elvin, T. E. ...	3238	26/1/15	27/3/15, discharged	Rifleman.	
Emmett, A. ...	240708	11/9/14	3/8/17, invalided to England	L./Corpl.	
Entwistle, W. ...	108729	28/9/18	17/2/19, demobilized ...	Rifleman.	
Epstein, J. ...	2231	1/9/14	—/—/15, transferred ...	Rifleman.	
Ervine, W. ...	202717	27/5/18	28/3/19, posted 13th K.L.R.	L./Corpl.	
Essery, J. H. ...	2128	31/8/14	—/—/15, transferred ...	Rifleman.	
Etheridge, E. ...	50934	18/8/17	30/1/19,† demobilized ...	Rifleman.	
Evans, C. L. ...	201949	1/3/18	23/4/18, transferred	Rifleman.	
Evans, D. S. ...	242183	21/1/16	30/1/19, demobilized ...	Rifleman.	
Evans, E. H. ...	2784	7/11/14	20/11/15, commission ...	A./L./Cpl.	
Evans, F. A. ...	3206	11/1/15	9/1/17, commission	Rifleman.	
Evans, F. M. ...	2554	23/9/14	28/6/15, transferred	Rifleman.	
Evans, F. W. ...	240803	26/9/14	31/1/18, sick	A./L./Cpl.	
Evans, H. ...	3619	6/8/15	7/12/15, discharged	Rifleman.	
Evans, H. ...	50748	18/8/17	23/12/17, wounded	Rifleman.	
Evans, J. A. ...	39217	1/2/18	29/9/18, sick	Rifleman.	
Evans, J. G. ...	241316	3/7/15	2/11/17, wounded	L./Sergt.	
Evans, J. H. ...	17769	27/6/18	24/2/19, transferred	Rifleman.	
✠ Evans, J. H. ...	306190	16/4/18	20/10/18, died	Sergeant.	
✠ Evans, T. ...	88050	28/9/17	10/9/18, died of wounds ...	L./Sergt.	
Evans, R. E. ...	242540	29/5/16	6/7/17, wounded	Rifleman.	
Evans, T. ...	241155	7/12/14	10/8/17, wounded	Rifleman.	
Evans, T. F. ...	240684	10/9/14	3/3/19, demobilized	Col./Sergt.	
Evans, W. ...	242560	3/6/16	12/9/17, posted 1/6th K.L.R.	L./Corpl.	
Evans, W. ...	331315	28/9/18	29/3/19, demobilized ...	Rifleman.	
Evans, W. D. ...	2782	7/11/14	12/1/15, transferred	Rifleman.	
Evans, W. ...	2449	14/9/14	28/7/15, transferred	Rifleman.	
Evening, H. ...	94899	2/4/18	28/5/18, sick	Rifleman.	
Ewan, W. M. ...	240897	2/11/14	5/8/17, invalided to England	Sergeant.	
Ewen, W. ...	50935	18/8/17	20/8/17, posted 2/8th K.L.R.	Rifleman.	
Exton, F. A. ...	240956	9/11/14	9/8/17, wounded	Rifleman.	
Fagan, J.	30351	7/3/18	3/2/19, demobilized	A./Corpl.	
Fairbairn, D. ...	22373	27/5/18	18/1/19, demobilized ...	Rifleman.	
Fairbridge, C. M. F.	3263	15/2/15	26/6/15, transferred	Rifleman.	
Fairclough, H. ...	16450	30/5/18	3/3/19, demobilized	Rifleman.	
Fairclough, H. ...	38277	14/6/18	29/3/19, demobilized	Rifleman.	
✠ Fairclough, R. ...	50751	18/8/17	29/10/17, killed in action ...	Rifleman.	
Fairclough, R. ...	204079	1/2/18	28/3/19, posted 13th K.L.R.	Rifleman	M.M.
Fairclough, W. ...	2220	1/9/14	15/12/16, commission ...	Rifleman	

NAME.	REGTL. NO.	DATE OF JOINING.	DATE OF LEAVING WITH CAUSE.	HIGHEST RANK.	HONOURS OR AWARDS.
Fairhurst, J. D.	3181	4/1/15	26/6/15, transferred	Rifleman.	
Fallows, H. W. ...	2760	6/11/14	26/6/15, transferred ...	Rifleman.	
Falls, W. W.	2873	10/11/14	16/8/15, transferred ...	Rifleman.	
Fargher, J. E. ...	269787	3/8/17	26/1/19, demobilized ...	Rifleman.	
Farmer, J. B. ...	2667	15/10/14	26/6/15, transferred ...	Rifleman.	
Farmer, W. ...	31649	14/6/18	3/1/19, transferred ...	Sergeant.	
✠Farmeroy, G. E.	53467	28/9/17	18/12/17, killed in action ...	Rifleman.	
Farnham, H. C. ...	2768	6/11/14	5/8/15,† transferred ...	Rifleman.	
Farquhar, J. ...	57352	2/7/18	7/2/19, demobilized ...	Rifleman.	
Farragher, D. ...	240783	23/9/14	9/8/17, wounded ...	Rifleman.	
Farrant, T. E. J.	72561	13/8/17	14/12/18, demobilized ...	Rifleman.	
Farrell, J. ...	86649	25/4/18	26/3/19, demobilized ...	Rifleman.	
Farrell, P.	2646	10/10/14	12/1/15, transferred ...	Rifleman.	
Farrell, W. G. ...	2139	31/8/14	—/—/15, transferred	Rifleman.	
Farrington, R. ...	48645	24/8/17	12/2/19, demobilized	A./C.Q.M.S.	
Farrington, T. ...	84866	1/2/18	11/12/18, demobilized ...	Rifleman.	
Fawcett, J. H. ...	2118	31/8/14	—/—/15, transferred ...	Rifleman.	
Fawkes, T. ...	3717	6/8/15	9/12/15, transferred ...	Rifleman.	
Fazakerley, H. D.	2218	1/9/14	18/5/16, transferred ...	Rifleman.	
Fazakerley, J. P.	5032	20/3/16	22/7/16, transferred ...	Rifleman.	
Fearon, T. ...	3028	16/11/14	1/5/15, transferred ...	Rifleman.	
Fell, W. R. ...	2134	31/8/14	24/10/16, commission ...	Rifleman.	
Fellows, J. A. ...	22074	22/6/18	5/10/18, sick	Rifleman.	
Felstead, A. ...	242343	7/3/16	9/8/17, invalided to England	Rifleman.	
✠Felton, H. ...	90721	7/3/18	30/9/18, killed in action ...	Rifleman.	
Fenner, F. J. ...	241175	—/12/14	8/3/19, posted 13th K.L.R.	C.Q.M.S.	
Fenton, H. M. ...	243848	16/10/16	20/9/17, sick	Rifleman.	
Fenton, R. ...	88235	8/11/17	2/6/18, sick	Rifleman.	
Ferguson, C. H. ...	2189	1/9/14	—/—/14, posted 1/6th K.L.R.	Rifleman.	
Ferguson, C. ...	2802	9/11/14	12/1/15, transferred ...	Rifleman.	
Ferguson, M. ...	2317	10/9/14	12/1/15, transferred ...	Rifleman.	
Ferguson, P. ...	2864	10/11/14	5/8/15, transferred ...	Rifleman.	
Ferguson, S. R. ...	242337	3/3/16	16/10/19, demobilized ...	Rifleman.	
Ferguson, T. J. ...	241132	24/11/14	17/6/17,† transferred ...	Rifleman.	
Ferley, J. E. ...	64822	24/8/17	13/6/18, wounded	Rifleman.	
Ferrick, J. ...	24729	27/6/18	29/3/19, demobilized ...	L./Corpl.	
Ferro, H. F. ...	241229	8/2/15	5/11/17, sick	Rifleman.	
Ffoulkes, J. ...	50936	18/8/17	20/8/17, posted 2/8th K.L.R.	Rifleman.	
Filkin, G. ...	72517	13/8/17	16/5/18, sick	Rifleman.	
Findley, A. ...	242157	20/1/16	13/12/17, sick	L./Corpl.	
Findlow, T. G. ...	2381	10/9/14	12/1/15, transferred ...	A./L./Cpl.	
Fineberg, M. ...	3340	15/4/15	18/8/16, transferred ...	Rifleman.	
Finigan, A. L. ...	2519	18/9/14	—/—/15, transferred ...	Rifleman.	
✠Finney, A. H. ...	3390	3/7/15	25/2/17, killed in action ...	Rifleman.	
Firth, F. ...	88100	29/9/17	—/4/19, transferred ...	Rifleman.	
Firth, J. ...	153	—/—/15	26/6/15, transferred ...	A./C.Q.M.S.	
Fisher, B. ...	59288	24/8/17	2/10/18, wounded ...	Rifleman.	
Fisher, G. L. H.	2190	1/9/14	23/2/15, commission ...	Rifleman.	
Fisher, M. ...	1314	27/2/15	26/6/15, transferred ...	Rifleman.	
Fisher, R. H. ...	2121	31/8/14	—/—/15, posted 1/6th K.L.R.	Rifleman.	
Fisher, W. H. ...	94900	2/4/18	23/7/18, transferred ...	Rifleman.	
Fitzgerald, J. ...	88625	1/2/18	24/3/20, demobilized ...	Rifleman.	
Fitzpatrick, P. ...	241568	6/8/15	22/5/19, demobilized ...	Rifleman.	
Fitzsimons, J. ...	3290	5/3/15	15/2/16, physically unfit ...	Rifleman.	
Flahety, — ...	94905	2/4/18	4/9/18, wounded	Rifleman.	
Flannery, J. J. ...	201319	1/2/18	27/2/19, demobilized ...	Rifleman.	
Fleming, R. G. ...	1612	27/2/15	26/6/15, transferred ...	Rifleman.	
Fletcher, G. ...	2578	25/9/14	12/1/15, transferred ...	Rifleman.	

NAME.	REGTL. NO.	DATE OF JOINING.	DATE OF LEAVING WITH CAUSE.	HIGHEST RANK.	HONOURS OR AWARDS.
Fletcher, H.	242373	16/3/16	26/2/19, posted 25th K.L.R.	Rifleman.	
✠Fletcher, R.	88209	8/11/17	17/5/18, died of wounds	Rifleman.	
Fletcher, W. H.	110516	27/11/18	21/2/19, demobilized	Rifleman.	
Fletcher, W. T.	16812	27/5/18	10/9/18, wounded	Rifleman.	
Flynn, F.	2004	23/10/14	26/6/15, transferred	Rifleman.	
Flitcroft, R.	307890	8/7/17	7/7/18, wounded	Rifleman.	
Flood, J. L.	164	27/2/15	26/6/15, transferred	A./L./Cpl.	
Foden, H. H.	2201	1/9/14	—/—/14, transferred	Rifleman.	
Foggett, W.	242240	22/1/16	23/6/17, wounded	Rifleman.	
✠Foley, T.	242383	18/3/16	21/6/18, died of wounds	L./Corpl.	
Fontenay, A. E.	2282	2/9/14	27/12/15, commission	Rifleman.	
Forber, W. T.	2440	15/9/14	—/—/15, transferred	Rifleman.	
Ford, G. W.	16452	30/5/18	11/1/19, demobilized	Rifleman.	
Ford, J. E.	266314	27/8/17	22/5/19, demobilized	Corporal.	
Ford, L.	242233	22/1/16	10/8/17, invalided to England	Rifleman.	
✠Ford, S. T.	88530	19/9/17	30/10/17, killed in action	Rifleman.	
Ford, W. F.	2598	26/9/14	12/1/15, transferred	Rifleman.	
Forfar, G.	242193	21/1/16	21/1/18, sick	Rifleman.	
Forrester, T.	200782	5/4/18	22/6/18, sick	Corporal.	
Forryan, A. F.	88056	27/5/18	20/1/19, demobilized	Rifleman.	
Forshaw, C.	201048	1/2/18	31/3/18, sick	Rifleman.	
Forshaw, H.	243737	9/10/16	26/4/17, transferred	Rifleman.	
Forster, A.	2597	2/10/14	26/6/15, transferred	Rifleman.	
Forster, F.	57861	30/5/18	1/10/18, wounded	Rifleman.	
Forster, S.	242401	20/3/16	2/11/17, wounded	Rifleman.	
Forster, S.	94904	2/4/18	13/11/19, demobilized	Rifleman.	
Fortune, J.	241124	23/11/14	6/8/17, invalided to England	Rifleman.	
Fosbrooke, E. L.	1640	23/10/14	12/1/15, transferred	Rifleman.	
Foster, A. E.	203262	23/9/17	27/5/18, wounded	Rifleman.	
Foster, D.	241105	17/11/14	5/8/17, invalided to England	Rifleman.	
✠Foster, J.	243798	11/10/16	9/4/18, killed in action	Rifleman.	
Foster, J.	64858	24/2/18	18/1/19, demobilized	Rifleman.	
Foster, R.	94903	2/4/18	30/12/18, sick	Rifleman.	
Foster, T.	241507	6/8/15	9/8/17,† invalided to England	Rifleman.	
Foster, W.	243772	10/10/16	—/—/19, transferred...	Rifleman.	
Foulds, T.	88206	8/11/17	26/2/19, posted 25th K.L.R.	Rifleman.	
Foulkes, C. H.	2380	10/9/14	3/12/15, transferred	A./L./Cpl.	
Foulkes, H.	241057	13/11/14	29/7/17, wounded	Rifleman.	
Foulkes, J.	1458	27/2/15	26/6/15, transferred	A./L./Cpl.	
Foulkes, W. F.	110568	27/11/18	26/2/19, posted 13th K.L.R.	Rifleman.	
Fowler, A.	2316	10/9/14	12/1/15, transferred	Rifleman.	
Fowler, H. R.	3217	18/1/15	26/6/15, transferred	Rifleman.	
Fowler, J.	242517	18/5/16	1/9/17,† posted 1/7th K.L.R.	Rifleman.	
Fowler, W.	2881	10/11/14	26/6/15, transferred	Rifleman.	
Fox, J.	1721	27/2/15	26/6/15, transferred	Rifleman.	
Fox, J. S.	240870	26/10/14	29/3/19,† demobilized	Rifleman.	
Fox, L.	3358	26/4/15	1/5/15, transferred	Rifleman.	
Fox, W.	108907	28/9/18	12/2/19, demobilized	Rifleman.	
Foxe, V. J.	1521	23/10/14	26/6/15, transferred	Corporal.	
Foxley, F.	240751	16/9/14	19/6/18, wounded	Corporal.	
✠Foy, J. H.	50750	18/8/17	1/9/18, killed in action	Rifleman.	
Francis, J. R.	5218	19/5/16	28/12/16, transferred	Rifleman.	
Frankland, H. J.	260182	20/9/17	3/3/18, commission	Sergeant.	
✠Fraser, F. J.	241219	25/1/15	7/1/18, killed in action	Rifleman.	
Fraser, F.	2268	1/9/14	2/5/17, transferred	Rifleman.	
Fraser, J.	50937	18/8/17	20/8/17, posted 2/8th K.L.R.	Rifleman.	
Frazer, W. M.	2629	5/10/14	26/6/15, transferred	Rifleman.	
Freedman, J.	242284	17/2/16	26/8/17, wounded	Rifleman.	

NAME.	REGTL. NO.	DATE OF JOINING.	DATE OF LEAVING WITH CAUSE.	HIGHEST RANK.	HONOURS OR AWARDS.
Freegard, A. B. ...	201117	12/4/18	30/11/18, transferred ...	Rifleman.	
Freeman, W. ...	2728	2/11/14	16/8/15, transferred ...	Rifleman.	
Freeman, W. ...	260205	20/9/17	22/5/19, demobilized ...	Rifleman.	
Freeney, A. ...	94902	2/4/18	6/5/18, sick	Rifleman.	
Frith, D. ...	240885	29/10/14	2/2/19, demobilized ...	Rifleman.	
Frost, F. ...	57646	30/5/18	28/3/19, posted 13th K.L.R.	Rifleman.	
Frost, R. H. ...	200012	1/2/18	30/1/19, demobilized	L./Corpl.	
✠Fry, F. W. ...	88164	16/10/17	18/12/17, died of wounds ...	Rifleman.	
Fry, J. ...	2152	31/8/14	—/—/15, transferred ...	Rifleman.	
Fryer, E. ...	240856	16/10/14	3/8/17, invalided to England	Rifleman.	
Fullagar, F. H. ...	3022	16/11/14	4/5/16, transferred ...	Rifleman.	
Fullalove, J. H. ...	50749	18/8/17	7/10/18, wounded ...	Corporal.	
✠Fuller, J. B. ...	240100	27/2/15	20/9/17,† died ...	Rifleman.	
Fuller, T. ...	240947	9/11/14	7/8/17, invalided to England	Rifleman.	
Furber, G. ...	242292	17/2/16	6/3/18, sick	Rifleman.	
Furniss, T. M. ...	2127	31/8/14	—/—/15, transferred ...	Rifleman.	
Gabie, H. ...	2320	10/9/14	12/1/15, transferred ...	Rifleman.	
Gabriel, W O. ...	241100	17/11/14	10/8/17, invalided to England	Rifleman.	
Gadsden, G. C. ...	241357	23/5/15	15/9/17,† posted 1/6th K.L.R.	Rifleman.	
Gagg, C. ...	88225	8/11/17	30/8/18, transferred ...	Rifleman.	
Gallagher, W. ...	406734	10/7/18	26/7/18, posted 12th K.L.R.	Rifleman.	
Galloway, W. T.	1847	23/2/15	5/8/15, transferred ...	L./Corpl.	
Galvin, J. ...	88557	19/9/17	22/12/18, demobilized ...	Rifleman.	
Galway, S. J. ...	240821	28/9/14	11/5/18, sick	Sergeant.	
Gamble, R. H. ...	242303	25/2/16	25/8/17, wounded ...	Rifleman.	
Gandy H. ...	52269	30/5/18	22/5/19, demobilized ...	Rifleman.	
Gardiner, C. ...	57536	1/2/18	4/3/19, demobilized ...	Rifleman.	
Gardiner, D. ...	50938	18/8/17	20/8/17, posted 2/8th K.L.R.	Rifleman.	
✠Gardner, A. H. ...	300252	30/5/18	27/6/18, killed in action ...	Rifleman.	
Gardner, A. J. ...	72497	13/8/17	12/6/18, sick	Rifleman.	
Gardner, R. ...	88211	8/11/17	12/2/18, sick	Rifleman.	
Gardner, W. ...	241548	6/8/15	9/8/17,† invalided to England	L./Corpl.	
Garland, W. J. ...	42838	13/8/17	26/2/19, posted 13th K.L.R.	Corporal.	
Garrod, E. A. ...	242449	24/3/16	7/8/17, invalided to England	Rifleman.	
Garrod, G. W. ...	2812	9/11/14	22/8/16, transferred ...	A./L./Sgt.	
Garside, L. ...	243673	6/10/16	9/4/18, transferred ...	Rifleman.	
Garton, W. N. ...	2734	2/11/14	10/4/15, medically unfit ...	Rifleman.	
Garvin, M. ...	94911	16/5/18	26/2/19, transferred ...	Rifleman.	
Gaskin, H. ...	242177	20/1/16	4/8/17, invalided to England	Rifleman.	
Gates, A. ...	201255	1/2/18	28/3/18, sick	Rifleman.	
Gattrell, A. W. ...	2465	14/9/14	26/6/15, transferred ...	Rifleman.	
Gaunt, W. ...	5217	18/5/16	18/8/16, transferred ...	Rifleman.	
Gedd, H. ...	24546	27/5/18	20/1/19, transferred ...	C.S.M.	M. in D.
Geddes, J. T. ...	109879	24/12/18	5/3/19, demobilized ...	Rifleman.	
Geelan, F. ...	94920	2/4/18	13/9/18, wounded ...	Rifleman.	
Geldart, F. J. ...	2862	10/11/14	26/6/15, transferred ...	L./Corpl.	
Geoghegan, J. ...	242151	20/1/16	18/4/17, wounded ...	L./Corpl.	
George, C. H. ...	2967	12/11/14	10/9/16, transferred ...	Rifleman.	
George, R. ...	99512	27/6/18	28/3/19, posted 13th K.L.R.	Rifleman.	
George, T. ...	242255	25/1/16	—/3/19, posted 25th K.L.R.	Rifleman.	
Georgeson, W. ...	331943	27/8/17	27/3/18, sick	Rifleman.	
Gerken, E. ...	241335	3/7/15	13/11/17,† sick	Rifleman.	
Gerrard, H. ...	242445	23/3/16	9/8/17, invalided to England	Rifleman.	
Gerrard, H. ...	30524	13/9/18	17/1/19, demobilized ...	L./Corpl.	
Gerrard, W. ...	65237	13/8/17	26/2/19, posted 25th K.L.R.	Rifleman.	
Getty, — ...	2180	31/8/14	21/9/14, commission	Rifleman.	
Gibbings, W. C. ...	2225	1/9/14	4/2/15, commission	Rifleman	

NAME.	REGTL. NO.	DATE OF JOINING.	DATE OF LEAVING WITH CAUSE.	HIGHEST RANK.	HONOURS OR AWARDS.
Gibbons, A. P. ...	50755	18/8/17	26/2/19, posted 13th K.L.R.	Rifleman.	
✠Gibbons, J.	94915	2/4/18	29/9/18, killed in action ...	Rifleman.	
Gibbons, R. E. ...	88629	1/2/18	26/2/19, posted 25th K.L.R.	Rifleman.	
Gibbs, J.	88558	19/9/17	11/10/18, injured	L./Corpl.	
Gibson, A. A. ...	2212	1/9/14	28/5/15, discharged	Rifleman	
Gibson, A. M.	2524	15/9/14	1/5/15, transferred ...	Rifleman	
Gibson, A. N. ...	2981	14/11/14	26/6/15, transferred ...	Rifleman.	
Gibson, F. G. ...	1582	23/10/14	14/8/16, transferred ...	Rifleman.	
Gibson, G. H. ...	2112	31/8/14	—/—/15, transferred ...	Rifleman.	
Gibson, H. ...	61017	24/8/17	3/5/18, transferred ...	Rifleman.	
Gibson, S. ...	88115	5/10/17	—/3/19, sick	Rifleman.	
Gibson, W. H.	1435	23/2/15	26/6/15, transferred ...	Rifleman.	
Gifford, J. W. ...	94912	2/4/18	—/—/19, demobilized ...	Rifleman.	
Gilbert, A. ...	242557	19/10/16	15/7/18, transferred ...	Rifleman.	
Gilbert, T. ...	94916	2/4/18	9/7/18, sick	Rifleman.	
✠Gilbertson, R. ...	241425	1/2/18	11/10/18, died of wounds ...	Sergeant.	
Gill, C. H. E. ...	3590	6/8/15	9/4/16, transferred ...	Rifleman.	
Gill, C. S. ...	3261	11/2/15	21/7/15, discharged ...	Rifleman.	
Gill, J. C. ...	2488	16/9/14	30/8/15,† transferred ...	Rifleman.	
Gill, S.	1496	27/2/15	23/11/15,† transferred ...	Rifleman.	
Gill, V.	94913	2/4/18	21/5/18, sick	Rifleman.	
Gillespie, J. ...	57413	24/8/17	18/1/18, sick	Rifleman.	
Gillibrand, J. ...	88255	17/12/17	26/2/19, posted 25th K.L.R.	Rifleman.	
Gillison, W. J. ...	240864	20/10/14	10/8/17, wounded ...	Corporal.	
Gilmore, A. V. ...	242528	24/5/16	30/3/19, demobilized ...	Rifleman.	
Girdlestone, W. C.	2395	10/9/14	26/6/15, transferred ...	Rifleman.	
Gladwinfield, C.	2129	31/8/14	—/—/15, posted 1/6th K.L.R.	Rifleman.	
Glendinning, P. R.	243771	10/10/16	28/3/19, posted 13th K.L.R.	Rifleman.	
Glickman, D. ...	269497	22/6/18	17/10/19, wounded ...	Rifleman.	
Glover, J. V. ...	2404	11/9/14	12/1/15, transferred ...	Rifleman.	
Glover, J. ...	108928	28/9/18	11/12/18, demobilized ...	Rifleman.	
Glover, W. C. ...	2265	1/9/14	8/1/15, commission ...	Rifleman.	
Glynn, T. ...	88146	11/10/17	26/2/19, posted 25th K.L.R.	Rifleman.	
Goadby, L. H. ...	2433	15/9/14	5/8/15, transferred ...	L./Corpl.	
Goddard, A. ...	95038	2/4/18	8/10/18, wounded ...	Sergeant.	
Godfrey, R. J. ...	3227	19/1/15	5/8/15, transferred ...	Rifleman.	
Godfrey, S. ...	3189	5/1/15	5/8/15, transferred ...	Rifleman.	
Golder, C. G.	3025	16/11/14	26/6/15, transferred ...	Rifleman.	
Golding, A. ...	88237	8/11/17	7/2/19, demobilized ...	Rifleman.	
✠Golds, F. ...	26342	30/5/18	17/6/18, killed in action ...	Rifleman.	
Goldstone, L. ...	242176	20/1/16	6/8/17, invalided to England	Rifleman.	
Goodall, H. A. ...	4706	20/1/16	3/6/16, transferred ...	Rifleman.	
✠Goodger, E. ...	243832	13/10/16	19/5/17, killed in action ...	Rifleman.	
Goodier, F. ...	3080	19/11/14	26/6/15, transferred ...	Rifleman.	
Goodier, P. ...	88559	19/9/17	18/1/19, demobilized ...	Rifleman.	
Goodman, L. ...	1905	3/4/15	26/7/15, transferred ...	Rifleman.	
Goodrich, G. ...	405279	22/6/18	1/2/19, demobilized ...	Sergeant.	
Goodwin, G. ...	2793	7/11/14	26/6/15, transferred ...	Rifleman.	
Goodwin, — ...	1630	23/10/14	9/3/15, medically unfit ...	Rifleman.	
Gordon, T. ...	56375	24/8/17	10/9/18, wounded ...	L./Corpl.	
Gore, C.	2561	22/9/14	26/6/15, transferred ...	Rifleman.	
Gore, S.	88527	19/9/17	27/7/18, transferred ...	Rifleman.	
Gorst, T. ...	243836	13/10/16	6/8/17, invalided to England	Rifleman.	
Gough, C. B. ...	242563	5/6/16	4/9/18, transferred ...	Rifleman.	
Gough, T. ...	5049	21/3/16	18/10/16, transferred ...	Rifleman.	
Goulding, P. G. ...	300257	30/5/18	10/12/18, demobilized ...	Rifleman.	
Grace, A. E. ...	5064	22/3/16	5/6/16, transferred ...	Rifleman.	
Grace, J. ...	1404	27/2/15	26/6/15, transferred ...	Rifleman.	

HISTORY OF THE 2/6TH (RIFLE) BATTALION

NAME.	REGTL. NO.	DATE OF JOINING.	DATE OF LEAVING WITH CAUSE.	HIGHEST RANK.	HONOURS OR AWARDS.
Grace, S. F.	21504	14/6/18	9/7/18, wounded	L./Corpl.	
Graham, C.	243704	9/10/16	30/4/17, posted 1st K.L.R.	Rifleman.	
Graham, G. G.	72480	13/8/17	24/7/18, wounded	Rifleman.	
Graham, J.	243717	5/10/16	17/9/17, transferred	Rifleman.	
Graham, J.	243812	12/10/16	16/10/17,† transferred	Rifleman.	
Graham, J. H.	240964	9/11/14	3/11/17, wounded	Rifleman.	
Graham, N. R.	2318	10/9/14	30/9/15, commission	Rifleman.	
Graham, W.	4722	20/1/16	22/2/16, transferred	Rifleman.	
Graham, W.	6615	13/10/16	31/1/17, transferred	Rifleman.	
Grahl, F. W.	380995	13/9/18	21/2/19, demobilized	Sergeant.	
Grainger, J. H.	88560	19/9/17	7/11/17, wounded	Rifleman.	
Grantham, H. C.	2910	10/11/14	26/6/15, transferred	Rifleman.	
Grassby, T. H.	3697	6/8/15	6/9/15, transferred	Rifleman.	
Grattan, C. E.	241303	20/4/15	22/3/19,† disembodied	Rifleman.	
Gratton, J. W.	2321	10/9/14	12/1/15, transferred	Rifleman.	
Graves, H.	242266	26/1/16	9/8/17, wounded	Rifleman.	
Gray, A.	242237	22/1/16	7/10/17, transferred	Rifleman.	
Gray, C.	243715	9/10/16	19/6/17, invalided to England	Rifleman.	
Gray, H. J.	50753	18/8/17	29/8/18, posted 1st K.L.R.	Rifleman.	
Gray, W. H.	2257	1/9/14	—/—/15, transferred	Rifleman.	
Greaves, A.	94919	2/4/18	17/2/19, demobilized	Rifleman.	
Greaves, A. E.	243681	6/10/16	19/8/17, transferred	Rifleman.	
Green, A.	50754	18/8/17	2/1/18, sick	Rifleman.	
Green, E.	3239	29/1/15	15/12/15, transferred	Rifleman.	
Green, G.	16177	30/5/18	3/11/18, transferred	Rifleman.	
Green, H.	8679	24/2/18	14/7/18, sick	Rifleman.	
Green, H. G.	88470	19/9/17	10/11/17, wounded	Rifleman.	
Green, J.	200641	1/2/18	13/5/18, transferred	Sergeant.	
Green, J. E.	94917	2/4/18	19/11/19, demobilized	Rifleman.	
Green, P. C.	2319	10/9/14	12/1/15, transferred	Rifleman.	
Green, R.	50939	18/8/17	20/8/17, posted 2/8th K.L.R.	Rifleman.	
Green, S.	53649	24/8/17	11/6/18, sick	Rifleman.	
Green, T.	242424	21/3/16	28/6/17, wounded	Rifleman.	
Green, T. H.	88060	27/5/18	18/1/19, demobilized	Rifleman.	
Greene, C. T. F.	1537	23/10/14	5/12/14, medically unfit	Rifleman.	
Greenhalgh, A.	94908	2/4/18	15/6/18, sick	Rifleman.	
Greenhalgh, G.	94907	2/4/18	5/9/18, wounded	Rifleman.	
Greenhalgh, H.	267886	24/8/17	28/3/19, posted 13th K.L.R.	Rifleman.	
Greenhalgh, J.	94906	2/4/18	29/8/18, posted 1st K.L.R.	Rifleman.	
Greenhall, J.	86832	13/9/18	10/12/18, demobilized	Rifleman.	
Greenham, C. G.	240886	29/10/14	21/2/19, demobilized	L./Sergt.	
Greenland, R.	2110	31/8/14	22/11/16, commission	Rifleman.	
Greenlee, W.	203024	27/6/18	29/3/19, demobilized	Rifleman.	
Greenlees, F. H.	243859	16/10/16	3/4/18, sick	Rifleman.	
Greenwood, H.	94909	2/4/18	16/5/18, sick	Rifleman.	
Greenwood, T.	6511	9/10/16	12/11/16, transferred	Rifleman.	
Gregory, J.	110557	27/11/18	14/12/18, demobilized	Rifleman.	
Gregory, T. C.	2603	29/9/14	26/6/15, transferred	Rifleman.	
Gregory, W.	243658	5/10/16	14/9/18,† wounded	Rifleman.	
Gregory, W.	2245	1/9/14	14/3/15, transferred	Rifleman.	
Gregory, J.	2638	7/10/14	1/6/15, transferred	Rifleman.	
Gregson, A. G.	88228	8/11/17	4/9/18, wounded	Rifleman.	
Gregson, J. W.	50242	27/5/18	—/—/19, transferred	Rifleman.	
Gregson, R.	204046	1/2/18	—/—/19, transferred	Rifleman.	
Grew, A.	109007	28/9/18	28/3/19, posted 13th K.L.R.	Rifleman.	
Gribbon, H. V.	240244	27/2/15	15/3/19,† demobilized	Rifleman.	
Grierson, W. B.	2613	28/9/14	26/6/15, transferred	Rifleman.	
Griffen, A.	300033	30/5/18	29/8/18, posted 1st K.L.R.	Rifleman.	

"THE KING'S" (LIVERPOOL REGIMENT)

NAME.	REGTL. NO.	DATE OF JOINING.	DATE OF LEAVING WITH CAUSE.	HIGHEST RANK.	HONOURS OR AWARDS
Griffies, F. V. K.	2929	11/11/14	12/1/15, transferred	Rifleman.	
Griffin, E. S.	2411	11/9/14	12/1/15, transferred	Rifleman.	
Griffiths, A.	202210	18/2/18	23/4/18, sick	Rifleman.	
Griffiths, E.	2753	5/11/14	12/1/15, transferred	Rifleman.	
✠Griffiths, G.	241238	11/2/15	8/7/17, killed in action	A./Corpl.	
Griffiths, G. L.	4972	13/3/16	17/1/17, transferred	Rifleman.	
Griffiths, H.	6468	7/10/16	8/12/16, physically unfit	Rifleman.	
Griffiths, H.	41086	24/8/17	5/9/18, wounded	Rifleman.	
Griffiths, H.	308583	27/8/17	22/11/17, posted 2/8th K.L.R.	Rifleman.	
Griffiths, H. M.	241573	6/8/15	10/2/19, demobilized	C.S.M.	
Griffiths, J. M.	64939	24/8/17	26/2/19, posted 25th K.L.R.	Rifleman.	
✠Griffiths, M.	381387	13/9/18	27/9/18, killed in action	Rifleman.	
Griffiths, R.	3002	14/11/14	5/8/15, transferred	Rifleman.	
Griffiths, R.	23023	6/6/18	29/1/19, demobilized	L./Corpl.	
Griffiths, R.	88258	17/12/17	26/2/19, posted 25th K.L.R.	Rifleman.	
Griffiths, R. O.	202316	1/2/18	29/8/18, posted 1st K.L.R.	L./Corpl.	
Griffiths, T.	306066	27/8/17	22/11/17, posted 2/8th K.L.R.	Rifleman.	
Griffiths, W.	80105	1/5/19	11/6/19, disembodied	Rifleman.	
Griffiths, W.	242137	1/2/18	20/10/18, sick	Rifleman.	
Griffiths, W.	2276	1/9/14	22/8/16,† transferred	A./Corpl.	
Grimes, T.	269546	10/10/17	26/2/19, posted 25th K.L.R.	Rifleman.	
Grimes, T. A.	15653	27/6/18	24/8/18, commission	Sergeant	
Grinton, J.	2322	10/9/14	12/1/15, transferred	Rifleman.	
Gripton, S.	88561	19/9/17	12/11/17, wounded	Rifleman.	
Grisdale, T. H.	94918	2/4/18	—/3/19, posted 25th K.L.R.	Rifleman.	
Grogan, J.	50752	18/8/17	25/3/18, sick	Rifleman.	
Grossmith, H.	242461	27/3/16	25/1/18, transferred	Rifleman.	
Grundill, J. C.	94910	2/4/18	—/3/19, posted 25th K.L.R.	Rifleman.	
Guest, A.	110651	6/11/18	11/12/18, demobilized	Rifleman.	
Gunderson, F. J.	1968	27/2/15	5/6/15, discharged	Rifleman.	
Gyte, A. D.	2422	11/9/14	5/3/15, medically unfit	Rifleman.	
Hackett, E.	94934	2/4/18	—/3/19, posted 25th K.L.R.	Rifleman.	
Hadden, J.	269684	27/8/17	8/3/19, posted 13th K.L.R.	Rifleman.	
Haddock, T. E.	94926	2/4/18	27/6/19, demobilized	Rifleman.	
Haddrill, C. M.	242239	22/1/16	29/8/18, posted 1st K.L.R.	Rifleman.	
Hadley, T.	50849	1/2/18	2/10/18, wounded	Rifleman.	
Hague, C. H.	6458	6/10/16	30/10/16, transferred	Rifleman.	
Haigh, J. E.	2776	7/11/14	26/6/15, transferred	Rifleman.	
Hale, G.	202447	14/3/18	8/5/18, sick	Rifleman.	
Halewood, G.	242586	4/8/17	15/7/18, transferred	L./Corpl.	
Halford, S.	11961	24/2/18	11/1/19, demobilized	Rifleman.	
Halfpenny, W. H.	3059	18/11/14	11/5/15, commission	Rifleman.	
Hall, A.	88203	8/11/17	26/2/19, posted 25th K.L.R.	Rifleman.	
Hall, A. B.	2518	18/9/14	19/10/14, medically unfit	Rifleman.	
Hall, E.	2292	3/9/14	2/3/15, commission	Rifleman.	
Hall, F.	243759	10/10/16	30/4/17,† posted 1st K.L.R.	Rifleman.	
Hall, F. R.	17844	27/5/18	5/3/19, demobilized	Rifleman.	M.M.
Hall, G.	1703	23/10/14	26/6/15, transferred	Rifleman.	
Hall, G. C.	308324	8/7/17	29/8/18, posted 1st K.L.R.	Rifleman.	
Hall, H.	84850	1/2/18	6/9/18, wounded	Rifleman.	
Hall, H. C.	1387	27/2/15	26/6/15, transferred	Rifleman.	
Hall, J.	94924	2/4/18	18/5/18, sick	Rifleman.	
Hall, J. A.	3052	17/11/14	26/6/15, transferred	Rifleman.	
Hall, J. H.	94922	2/4/18	15/7/18, wounded	Rifleman.	
Hall, N.	94921	2/4/18	6/11/18, sick	Rifleman.	
Hall, R.	270021	27/8/17	26/2/19, posted 25th K.L.R.	Rifleman.	
✠Hall, W.	241273	29/3/15	3/5/17, killed in action	Rifleman.	

NAME.	REGTL. NO.	DATE OF JOINING.	DATE OF LEAVING WITH CAUSE.	HIGHEST RANK.	HONOURS OR AWARDS.
Hall, W. G. ...	406625	13/9/18	3/10/18, wounded	Rifleman.	
Hallam, J. ...	2301	10/9/14	23/2/15, transferred	A./Corpl.	
Hallam, W. ...	88471	19/9/17	10/2/19, demobilized ...	Rifleman.	
Halligan, R. ...	50940	18/8/17	20/8/17, posted 2/8th K.L.R.	Rifleman.	
Halliwell, H. ...	110510	27/11/18	28/3/19, posted 25th K.L.R.	Rifleman.	
Halsall, A. R. ...	2508	17/9/14	12/1/15, transferred	A./Corpl.	
Halsall, H. ...	72506	24/8/17	29/8/18, posted 1st K.L.R. ...	Rifleman.	
Ham, F. J. ...	88568	19/9/17	29/8/18, posted 1st K.L.R. ...	Rifleman.	
Hamer, J. H. ...	300435	27/5/18	18/1/19, demobilized ...	L./Corpl.	
Hamer, P. ...	243767	10/10/16	22/1/19, demobilized ...	Rifleman.	
Hamill, H. ...	241344	3/7/15	9/8/17,† invalided to England	Rifleman.	
Hamill, P. ...	88119	5/10/17	12/2/19, demobilized ...	Rifleman.	
Hamilton, B. ...	31514	13/8/17	27/2/19, demobilized ...	Rifleman.	M.M.
Hammond, G. ...	50764	18/8/17	20/2/18, sick	Rifleman.	
Hamnett, T. H. ...	2327	10/9/14	12/1/15, transferred	Rifleman.	
Hampson, R. ...	2707	28/10/14	12/1/15, transferred	Rifleman.	
✠Hampson, W. H. ...	88562	19/9/17	30/10/17, killed in action ...	Rifleman.	
Hancock, H. D. ...	241156	7/12/14	22/6/17, invalided to England	L./Corpl.	
Handley, J. ...	2445	14/9/14	12/1/15, transferred	L./Corpl.	
Handley, J. A. ...	242454	24/3/16	—/—/19, demobilized ...	Rifleman.	
Hands, J. ...	88563	19/9/17	4/10/18, transferred	Rifleman.	
Hankey, J. R. ...	170	23/2/15	26/6/15, transferred	Corporal.	
Hannah, S. B. ...	1994	23/10/14	26/6/15, transferred	L./Corpl.	
Harbour, H. G. ...	88474	19/9/17	15/11/17, sick	Rifleman.	
Harcourt, J. D. ...	240837	7/10/14	5/12/17, sick	Rifleman.	
Hardacre, J. ...	243787	9/10/16	8/8/17, invalided to England	Rifleman.	
Hardacre, R. ...	59470	13/8/17	24/5/18, prisoner of war ...	Rifleman.	
Harding, A. ...	50941	18/8/17	20/8/17, posted 2/8th K.L.R.	Rifleman.	
Harding, H. G. ...	3728	6/8/15	7/9/15, commission	Rifleman.	
Harding, L. ...	2107	31/8/14	—/—/15, transferred ...	Rifleman.	
Hardman, H. ...	243678	6/10/16	14/1/19, demobilized ...	Rifleman.	
Hardman, H. ...	243688	7/10/16	22/4/17, wounded ...	Rifleman.	
Hare, R. K. ...	2894	10/11/14	26/6/15, transferred	Rifleman.	
Hargreaves, A. ...	50758	18/8/17	26/12/17, wounded	Rifleman.	
Hargreaves, E. ...	88101	29/9/17	1/2/18, sick	Rifleman.	
Hargreaves, J. ...	36705	7/3/18	29/8/18, posted 1st K.L.R. ...	Rifleman.	
Hargreaves, J. D.	6634	16/10/16	3/2/17, sick	Rifleman.	
Hargreaves, R. ...	240186	23/10/14	16/10/17,† posted 2/5th K.L.R.	A./Corpl.	
Hargreaves, W. ...	39486	27/5/18	1/11/18, sick	Rifleman.	
Hargrove, H. ...	242316	1/3/16	3/2/19, demobilized ...	Rifleman.	
Harold, J. ...	110526	27/11/18	26/2/19, posted 25th K.L.R.	Rifleman.	
Harper, C. ...	3311	22/3/15	28/10/15, transferred ...	Rifleman.	
Harper, H. ...	50765	18/8/17	26/2/19, posted 25th K.L.R.	Rifleman.	
Harper, T. ...	2148	31/8/14	—/—/15, transferred ...	Rifleman.	
Harper, W. ...	57710	24/8/17	11/5/18, sick	Sergeant.	
Harrall, H. V. ...	242372	16/3/16	2/1/18, transferred	Rifleman.	
Harries, S. ...	241502	6/8/15	12/6/17, wounded	Rifleman.	
Harris, F. D. ...	2607	29/9/14	5/8/15, transferred	Rifleman.	
Harris, G. ...	305745	8/7/17	22/1/19, demobilized ...	Rifleman.	
Harris, H. ...	3362	26/4/15	1/5/15, transferred	Rifleman.	
Harris, J. ...	203039	27/6/18	28/3/19, posted 13th K.L.R.	Rifleman.	
Harris, J. E. ...	50768	18/8/17	23/7/18, commission ...	Corporal.	
Harris, J. ...	3044	17/11/14	26/6/15, transferred	Rifleman.	
✠Harris, S. ...	26735	1/2/18	15/5/18, died of wounds ...	Corporal.	
Harris, W. ...	241463	6/8/15	10/11/17,† wounded	Corporal.	
Harrison, A. G. ...	241268	20/3/15	15/5/17, discharged ...	Rifleman.	
Harrison, C. C. ...	1841	23/2/15	26/6/15, transferred	Rifleman.	
Harrison, H. E. ...	241269	20/3/15	29/8/18, posted 1st K.L.R. ...	Rifleman	M.M.

"THE KING'S" (LIVERPOOL REGIMENT)

NAME.	REGTL. NO.	DATE OF JOINING.	DATE OF LEAVING WITH CAUSE.	HIGHEST RANK.	HONOURS OR AWARDS.
Harrison, S. ...	242410	21/3/16	14/2/19, demobilized ...	Sergeant.	
Harrison, T. ...	242230	22/1/16	15/5/18, sick	Corporal.	
Harrison, W. ...	3718	6/8/15	8/12/15, transferred ...	Rifleman.	
Harrison, W. ...	405116	1/2/18	18/3/18, sick	Rifleman.	
Harrison, W. H....	2403	11/9/14	12/1/15, transferred ...	Rifleman.	
Harrocks, W. ...	241005	10/11/14	5/8/17, invalided to England	Rifleman.	
Harrop, E. B. ...	2168	31/8/14	18/12/16, commission	Rifleman.	
✠Harrop, J. E. ...	88564	19/9/17	27/1/18, died of wounds ...	Rifleman.	
Hart, C. E. ...	240892	30/10/14	7/8/17, invalided to England	Rifleman.	
Hart, D. C. ...	5096	25/3/16	15/11/16, transferred ...	Rifleman.	
Hart, F. E. ...	88472	19/9/17	26/2/18, sick	Rifleman.	
Hart, J. J. ...	2722	30/10/14	16/8/15, transferred ...	Rifleman.	
Hart, W. M. ...	240812	28/9/14	9/8/17, invalided to England	Rifleman.	
Hartley, A. ...	88473	19/9/17	1/4/18, posted 13th K.L.R.	Rifleman.	
Hartley, R. H. ...	2211	1/9/14	—/—/14, transferred ...	Rifleman.	
Harton, A. ...	3425	6/8/15	11/11/16,† transferred ...	Rifleman.	
Harton, J. C. ...	240734	14/9/14	5/3/19,† demobilized ...	Rifleman.	
Harvey, E. ...	242362	15/3/16	3/2/19, demobilized ...	Sergeant.	
Harvey, J. H. ...	264	5/8/14	13/8/14, transferred ...	Rifleman.	
Harvey, J. ...	88631	1/2/18	25/7/18, transferred ...	Rifleman.	
Harvey, R. A. ...	2805	9/11/14	26/6/15, transferred ...	Rifleman.	
Harwood, P. H.	2250	1/9/14	—/—/14, posted 1/6th K.L.R.	Rifleman.	
Haslam, E. ...	243845	16/10/16	27/8/17, wounded	Rifleman.	
Haslam, F. ...	243733	9/10/16	30/4/17,† posted 1st K.L.R.	Rifleman.	
Haslam, J. B. ...	242315	1/3/16	27/10/17, wounded	Rifleman.	
Haslam, J. T. ...	50763	18/8/17	26/2/19, posted 13th K.L.R.	Rifleman.	
Hassall, A. W. ...	241251	25/2/15	5/3/19, demobilized	L./Corpl.	
Haswell, C. ...	2710	29/10/14	12/1/15, transferred ...	Rifleman.	
Hatch, C. J. ...	2328	10/9/14	12/1/15, transferred.	Rifleman.	
Hatch, J. F. ...	2330	10/9/14	12/1/15, transferred ...	Rifleman.	
✠Hatch, M. ...	201386	14/9/18	21/10/18, killed in action ...	Rifleman.	
Hatte, F. S. ...	2149	31/8/14	—/—/15, transferred ...	Rifleman.	
Hatton, E. ...	50767	18/8/17	28/3/19, posted 13th K.L.R.	Rifleman.	M.M.
Hawitt, T. H. ...	2323	10/9/14	12/1/15, transferred ...	Rifleman.	
Hawitt, A. ...	2787	7/11/14	12/1/15, transferred ...	Rifleman.	
Hawkes, R. ...	241120	21/11/14	26/8/17, wounded	L./Corpl.	
Hawkins, W. G. ...	242187	21/1/16	6/4/17, wounded	Rifleman.	
Hawkins, W. H. P.	2113	31/8/14	—/—/15, transferred ...	Rifleman.	
Hawksley, H. ...	2187	1/9/14	—/—/14, transferred ...	Rifleman.	
Hawksworth, M.	2593	1/10/14	12/1/15, transferred ...	Rifleman.	
Hawksworth, S....	2970	12/11/14	26/6/15, transferred ...	Rifleman.	
Haworth, R. S. ...	3083	23/11/14	5/8/15, transferred ...	Rifleman.	
Haworth, R. ...	2174	31/8/14	30/5/15, commission ...	Rifleman.	
Hay, D.	200692	25/6/18	27/9/18, wounded ...	Rifleman.	
Hay, J. B. ...	243699	9/10/16	28/2/17, commission ...	Rifleman.	
Haydon, H. J. ...	240029	23/2/15	15/12/17, sick	Sergeant.	
Hayes, A. ...	17590	7/3/18	18/1/19, demobilized ...	Corporal.	M.M.
Hayes, J.... ...	2920	11/11/14	26/6/15, transferred ...	Rifleman.	
Hayes, R. W. ...	110842	27/11/18	26/2/19, posted 13th K.L.R.	Rifleman.	
Hayhurst, H. ...	243800	11/10/16	21/8/17, wounded ...	Rifleman.	
Hayhurst, J. ...	1733	23/10/14	16/8/15, transferred ...	L./Corpl.	
Hayhurst, R. ...	243670	6/10/16	17/8/17, transferred ...	Rifleman.	
Haynes, F. A. ...	242115	1/2/18	29/3/19, demobilized ...	Rifleman.	
Hayston, H. ...	260020	25/5/18	19/6/18, wounded ...	Rifleman.	
Head, J. G. ...	4698	20/1/16	6/8/17, invalided to England	Rifleman.	
Heald, V. ...	52123	7/3/18	29/5/18, sick	Rifleman.	
✠Healing, A. ...	242290	17/2/16	30/10/17, killed in action ...	Rifleman.	
✠Healy, W. ...	64836	13/8/17	6/1/18, killed in action ...	Rifleman.	

817

NAME.	REGTL. NO.	DATE OF JOINING.	DATE OF LEAVING WITH CAUSE.	HIGHEST RANK.	HONOURS OR AWARDS.
Heap, G. ...	267357	27/8/17	7/7/18, sick	Rifleman.	
Heap, H. ...	88097	29/9/17	30/3/18, transferred ...	Rifleman.	
Heap, J. B. ...	129	23/2/15	26/6/15, transferred ...	Rifleman.	
Heaps, J....	50760	18/8/17	13/5/18, sick	Rifleman.	
Hearn, H. ...	268073	27/8/17	8/3/19, posted 13th K.L.R.	Rifleman.	
Heath, J....	240728	12/9/14	18/2/19,† demobilized ...	Rifleman.	
Heath, T. ...	4968	8/3/16	11/7/16, discharged	Rifleman.	
Heathcote, F. ...	50942	18/8/17	20/8/17, posted 2/8th K.L.R.	Rifleman.	
Heathcote, J. ...	88565	19/9/17	10/11/17, wounded	Rifleman.	
Heathcote, T. ...	243738	9/10/16	10/8/17, wounded	Rifleman.	
Heaton, G. ...	32637	7/3/18	11/1/19, sick	Rifleman.	
Heaton, G. A. ...	84811	1/2/18	28/3/19, posted 13th K.L.R.	Rifleman.	
Heaton, J. ...	108748	28/9/18	17/11/18, transferred ...	Rifleman.	
Heaton, J. R. ...	108834	28/9/18	13/12/18, demobilized ...	Rifleman.	
Heaton, T. ...	3103	23/11/14	21/5/15, commission	Rifleman.	
Hedgecock, T. ...	268077	27/8/17	8/3/19, posted 13th K.L.R.	Rifleman.	
Hedgecock, W. ...	2290	2/9/14	6/9/16, transferred	Rifleman.	
Heilbron, G. ...	2755	5/11/14	26/6/15, transferred	Rifleman.	
Hemmings, F. H. ...	2227	1/9/14	22/8/16, transferred	Rifleman.	
Henderson, A. N. ...	2895	10/11/14	30/8/15, transferred	Rifleman.	
Henderson, J. ...	72459	13/8/17	3/2/19, demobilized	Corporal.	
Henderson, J. L. ...	3001	12/11/14	12/1/15, transferred	Rifleman.	
Henderson, W. F. ...	2893	10/11/14	5/8/15, transferred	Rifleman.	
Hendry, J. ...	242406	20/3/16	8/8/17, invalided to England	Rifleman.	
Henry, H. S. ...	108002	16/12/18	23/3/19, demobilized ...	Rifleman.	
Henshaw, A. ...	201389	27/6/18	18/2/19, demobilized ...	Rifleman.	
✠Henshaw, B. ...	241482	6/8/15	12/7/17, killed in action ...	L./Corpl.	
Henshaw, E. R. ...	240709	11/9/14	8/1/19, sick	Rifleman.	
Hepworth, W. ...	243660	6/10/16	21/4/17, transferred	Rifleman.	
Herbert, J. B. ...	24995	27/6/18	5/3/19, demobilized	Corporal.	
Hesketh, F. O. ...	1839	23/2/15	4/5/16, transferred	Rifleman.	
Hesketh, J. ...	84588	1/2/18	14/3/18, transferred	Rifleman.	
✠Hesmondhalgh, R. ...	50766	18/8/17	29/5/18, killed in action ...	Rifleman.	
Hetherington, J. ...	39107	2/7/18	29/3/19, demobilized ...	Rifleman.	
Hetherington, T. ...	2618	6/10/14	12/1/15, transferred	Rifleman.	
Hetherington, W. S.	241250	25/2/15	24/5/17, transferred	Rifleman.	
Hewitt, F. ...	50942	18/8/17	20/8/17, posted 2/8th K.L.R.	Rifleman.	
Hewitt, J. ...	2700	27/10/14	12/1/15, transferred	Rifleman.	
Hewitt, J. E. ...	64782	13/8/17	21/7/19, transferred	Rifleman.	
Hewlett, T. C. ...	242428	22/3/16	20/7/17, invalided to England	Rifleman.	
Hey, W.	80867	24/8/17	5/5/18, sick	Rifleman.	
Heyes, G. ...	203995	1/2/18	18/5/18, wounded	Rifleman.	
Heyes, W. ...	50769	18/8/17	10/11/17, wounded	Rifleman.	
Heys, J.	88198	8/11/17	24/8/18, posted 13th K.L.R.	Rifleman.	
Heys, T. H. ...	6477	7/10/16	4/12/16, transferred	Rifleman.	
Heywood, J. ...	109644	6/11/18	24/2/19, demobilized ...	Rifleman.	
Heyworth, J. L. ...	240749	16/9/14	31/1/19, demobilized ...	A./R.S.M.	M.C., M.S.M.
Hibbert, J. ...	2799	9/11/14	26/6/15, transferred	Rifleman.	
Hickey, A. ...	2876	10/11/14	26/6/15, transferred	Rifleman.	
Hickey, F. H. ...	2717	29/10/14	26/6/15, transferred	Rifleman.	
✠Hickey, P. B. ...	24125	13/9/18	30/9/18, killed in action ...	Rifleman.	
✠Hicks, H. W. ...	88476	19/9/17	28/10/17, killed in action ...	Rifleman.	
Hicky, J. J. ...	22113	22/6/18	26/1/19, demobilized ...	Rifleman.	
Higginbottom, C. ...	1671	23/10/14	11/9/15, commission	A./Sergt.	
Higgins, A. ...	47356	27/6/18	29/3/18, demobilized ...	Rifleman.	
Higgins, G. ...	5072	23/3/16	15/3/17, transferred	Rifleman.	
Higgins, J. ...	88177	8/11/17	24/11/19, demobilized ...	Rifleman.	
Higgins, J. P. ...	2076	31/8/14	—/—/15, transferred ...	Rifleman.	

NAME.	REGTL. NO.	DATE OF JOINING.	DATE OF LEAVING WITH CAUSE.	HIGHEST RANK.	HONOURS OR AWARDS.
Higgins, W. ...	46022	13/8/17	13/4/18, sick	Rifleman.	
Higgins, W. S. ...	2067	31/8/14	2/11/16, transferred ...	Rifleman.	
✠Higginson, W. J.	242350	8/3/16	1/7/17, killed in action	Rifleman.	
✠Highfield, A. ...	88475	19/9/17	30/10/17, killed in action ...	Rifleman.	
Highton, J. H. ...	5087	24/3/16	10/12/16, discharged ...	Rifleman.	
Higson, P. J. ...	2497	16/9/14	26/6/15, transferred ...	Rifleman.	
Higson, G. J. ...	2500	16/9/14	20/7/15, transferred ...	Rifleman.	
Hildred, F. C. ...	241226	1/2/15	17/8/17, wounded	Corporal.	
✠Hill, C. R. ...	241518	6/8/15	28/10/17, killed in action ...	Corporal.	
Hill, E. B. ...	1770	23/10/14	26/6/15, transferred ...	L./Corpl.	
Hill, E. W. ...	88566	19/9/17	22/12/18, demobilized ...	Rifleman.	
Hill, F. ...	50756	18/8/17	19/12/19, demobilized ...	Rifleman.	
Hill, F. ...	50944	18/8/17	20/8/17, posted 2/8th K.L.R.	Rifleman.	
✠Hill, G. ...	88217	8/11/17	12/9/18, killed in action ...	Rifleman.	
Hill, G. E. ...	2324	10/9/14	22/8/16, transferred ...	A./Sergt.	
Hill, H. ...	88477	19/9/17	22/1/19, demobilized ...	Rifleman.	
Hill, H. T. ...	241480	6/8/15	11/8/17, invalided to England	Rifleman.	
Hill, R. ...	242180	21/1/16	17/1/19, demobilized ...	Corporal.	
Hill, R. W. ...	13347	24/8/17	15/11/17, wounded ...	Rifleman.	
Hill, T. J. ...	57789	24/8/17	15/1/19, demobilized ...	Rifleman.	
Hill, T. R. ...	2421	11/9/14	12/1/15, transferred ...	A./Sergt.	
Hill, R. ...	240171	27/2/15	17/6/17,† transferred ...	Rifleman.	
Hill, W. ...	11558	27/6/18	10/12/18, demobilized ...	L./Corpl.	
Hill, W. ...	241385	3/7/15	21/8/17, wounded ...	Rifleman.	
✠Hillman, L. ...	41202	27/5/18	29/9/18, killed in action ...	Rifleman.	
Hills, S. ...	240495	23/10/14	5/8/17, invalided to England	Rifleman.	
Hilton, J. ...	41310	13/8/17	26/12/17, commission ...	Rifleman.	
Hinchcliffe, S. ...	109008	28/9/18	24/2/19, demobilized ...	Rifleman.	
Hinchcliffe, W. ...	6643	16/10/16	8/1/17, physically unfit ...	Rifleman.	
✠Hind, C. E. ...	260216	20/9/17	1/9/18, killed in action ...	Corporal.	
Hind, J. ...	242229	22/1/16	18/4/18, transferred ...	A./Corpl.	
Hinde, A. S. ...	2205	1/9/14	21/1/15, commission ...	Rifleman.	
Hinde, H. E. ...	2397	10/9/14	26/6/15, transferred ...	A./Sergt.	
✠Hindley, J. ...	41299	27/5/18	4/10/18, died of wounds ...	Rifleman.	
Hinds, W. ...	201730	27/5/18	3/7/18, wounded ...	Rifleman	
Hinks, L. H. ...	241173	28/12/14	22/5/19,† demobilized ...	Rifleman.	
Hinmars, C. E. ...	241500	5/5/17	20/5/17, posted 1st K.L.R. ...	Rifleman.	
Hipkins, T. A. ...	242314	1/3/16	14/6/18, posted 1/5th K.L.R. ...	Rifleman.	
Hirons, G. ...	49944	27/5/18	28/3/19, posted 13th K.L.R. ...	L./Sergt.	
Hirst, R. ...	3264	15/2/15	28/7/15, discharged	Rifleman.	
Hitchin, H. ...	269378	10/10/17	9/11/18, sick	Rifleman.	
✠Hitchmough, W.	65076	13/8/17	29/10/17, killed in action ...	Rifleman.	
Hoare, E. ...	3200	11/1/15	5/8/15, transferred	Rifleman.	
Hoare, F. ...	242360	14/3/16	20/4/17, wounded	L./Corporal.	
Hoare, R. ...	1510	27/2/15	26/6/15, transferred ...	Rifleman.	
Hobden, C. R. ...	240941	9/11/14	7/2/19, demobilized ...	Corporal.	
Hockenhull, W. ...	2473	10/9/14	17/6/15, transferred ...	A./C.S.M.	
Hodge, A. ...	94925	2/4/18	19/6/18, wounded ...	Rifleman.	
Hodgett, W. ...	94930	2/4/18	29/8/18, posted 1st K.L.R. ...	Rifleman.	
Hodgkins, W. ...	16909	27/6/18	6/9/18, wounded ...	Rifleman.	
Hodgkinson, J. ...	88147	11/10/17	3/2/19, demobilized ...	Rifleman.	
Hodgman, S. ...	307803	8/7/17	21/10/18, wounded ...	Rifleman.	
Hodgson, F. ...	88181	8/11/17	14/1/18, sick	Rifleman.	
Hodgson, J. ...	240053	23/2/15	2/4/19,† demobilized ...	Sergeant.	
Hodgson, J. J. ...	243779	10/10/16	15/5/17, transferred ...	Rifleman.	
Hodson, E. W. ...	2262	1/9/14	18/12/16, commission ...	Rifleman.	
✠Hogarth, T. ...	94923	2/4/18	1/9/18, killed in action ...	Rifleman.	
Hogg, A. ...	241300	20/4/15	15/8/17,† sick	Rifleman.	

NAME.	REGTL. NO.	DATE OF JOINING.	DATE OF LEAVING WITH CAUSE.	HIGHEST RANK.	HONOURS OR AWARDS.
Hogg, F. A. ...	3298	15/3/15	31/5/15, transferred	Rifleman.	
Holbrook, F. ...	88478	19/9/17	9/11/17, wounded	Rifleman.	
Holding, B. ...	32850	13/8/17	9/11/17, sick	Rifleman.	
Holden, W. ...	110509	27/11/18	28/3/19, posted 13th K.L.R.	Rifleman.	
Holding, R. ...	242534	24/5/16	9/8/17, invalided to England	Rifleman.	
Holford, J. ...	260114	20/9/17	21/2/18, sick	Rifleman.	
Holgate, T. ...	243822	12/10/16	15/5/18, sick	Rifleman.	
Holgate, G. ...	2096	31/8/14	—/—/15, transferred	Rifleman.	
Holland, A. M. ...	3338	13/4/15	10/12/15, physically unfit ...	Rifleman.	
Holland, J. ...	20968	1/2/18	28/6/18, wounded	Rifleman.	
Holland, J. E. ...	243846	16/10/16	23/11/17, sick	Rifleman.	
Holland, W. L. ...	241576	6/8/15	7/8/17. invalided to England	Rifleman.	
Hollinghurst. H.	240580	1/9/14	12/7/18,† transferred ...	L./Corpl.	
Holmes, H. ...	110717	6/11/18	16/1/19, demobilized	Rifleman.	
Holmes, J. S. ...	243707	9/10/16	17/1/18,† posted 13th K.L.R.	Rifleman.	
Holmes, M. ...	35705	24/8/17	7/11/17, wounded	Rifleman.	
Holmes, P. ...	242247	25/1/16	8/8/17, wounded	Rifleman.	
Holmes, W. ...	2530	19/9/14	26/6/15, transferred	A./Sergt.	
Holmes, W. ...	6444	6/10/16	30/10/16, transferred ...	Rifleman.	
Holmes, W. ...	200321	8/7/17	29/3/19,† demobilized ...	Rifleman.	
✠ Holt, B. ...	50759	18/8/17	20/2/18, died of wounds ...	Rifleman.	
Holt, C. N. ...	240736	15/9/14	30/7/18, transferred	Rifleman.	
Holt, E. ...	6457	6/10/16	12/11/16, transferred ...	Rifleman.	
Holt, E. T. ...	5080	24/3/16	18/8/16, transferred	Rifleman.	
Holt, J. ...	6459	6/10/16	25/1/17, sick	Rifleman.	
Holt, L. ...	2029	23/2/15	26/6/15, transferred	Rifleman.	
✠ Holt, N. ...	94927	2/4/18	11/9/18, killed in action ...	Rifleman.	
Homer, H. G. ...	3013	14/11/14	26/6/15, transferred	Rifleman.	
Honderwood, R. S.	2490	16/9/14	12/1/15, transferred	A./Corpl.	
Honeybourne, E. H.	242393	18/3/16	17/6/17, transferred	Rifleman.	
Hooper, E. J. ...	2098	31/8/14	28/10/16, commission ...	Rifleman.	
Hope, A. J. ...	74367	24/8/17	27/2/18, sick	Rifleman.	
✠ Hopkins, J. W. ...	88479	19/9/17	1/9/18, killed in action ...	Rifleman.	
Hopkins, W. E. ...	241185	6/1/15	6/8/17, wounded	Rifleman.	
Hopley, — ...	2332	10/9/14	12/1/15, transferred	Rifleman.	
Horabin, L. J. ...	88172	28/10/17	26/1/19, demobilized ...	Rifleman.	
Horan, J. ...	2326	10/9/14	12/1/15, transferred	Rifleman.	
Horgan, M. ...	72473	13/8/17	14/2/19, demobilized ...	Rifleman.	
Hornby, A. ...	3006	14/11/14	5/8/15, transferred	Rifleman.	
Hornby, D. ...	1688	23/2/15	10/3/15, commission	Rifleman.	
Hornby, J. E. ...	111240	27/11/18	21/12/19, demobilized ...	Rifleman.	
Horner, A. O. ...	2171	31/8/14	31/12/15, commission ...	Rifleman.	
Horniblow, G. E.	5014	18/3/16	5/6/16, transferred	Rifleman.	
Horrocks, J. C. ...	2478	11/9/14	23/9/16, transferred	L./Corpl.	
Horsfall, J. ...	241212	18/1/15	15/5/17, transferred	Rifleman.	
Horton, J. ...	202939	27/5/18	29/8/18, posted 1st K.L.R. ...	Rifleman.	
Hosker, F. ...	204052	1/2/18	1/11/18, sick	Rifleman.	
Hoskinson, F. ...	268056	27/8/17	28/6/18, wounded	Rifleman.	
Hoskyn, J. H. ...	2325	10/9/14	12/2/17, commission	A./C.S.M.	
Hotchkiss, E. G. ...	77	23/2/15	26/6/15, transferred	L./Corpl.	
Hough, J. H. ...	6520	9/10/16	30/10/16, transferred ...	Rifleman.	
Hough, R. S. ...	300278	6/6/18	24/10/18, wounded	Sergeant.	M.M.
Houghton, B. R. ...	2887	10/11/14	12/1/15, transferred	Rifleman.	
Houghton, A. ...	2940	11/11/14	26/6/15, transferred	Rifleman.	
Houghton, F. ...	2200	1/9/14	6/5/16, discharged	Rifleman.	
Houghton, J. R. ...	241231	8/2/15	5/9/17,† posted 1/6th K.L.R.	Rifleman.	
Houghton, W. ...	3254	8/2/15	20/9/15, transferred	Rifleman.	
Houghton, W. ...	3499	3/7/15	2/8/16, discharged	Rifleman.	

"THE KING'S" (LIVERPOOL REGIMENT)

NAME.	REGTL. NO.	DATE OF JOINING.	DATE OF LEAVING WITH CAUSE.	HIGHEST RANK.	HONOURS OR AWARDS.
Houghton, W. G.	243691	7/10/16	31/7/17, commission ...	Rifleman.	
Houston, J. ...	2741	3/11/14	12/1/15, transferred	Rifleman.	
✠Howard, A. ...	94935	2/4/18	4/9/18, died of wounds ...	Rifleman.	
Howard, H. ...	243689	7/10/16	28/7/17, wounded	Rifleman.	
Howard, J. ...	242184	21/1/16	26/2/19, posted 25th K.L.R.	L./Corpl.	
Howard, J. ...	307529	22/6/18	21/9/18, wounded	Rifleman.	
Howard, J. W.	47141	13/8/17	12/2/19, demobilized ...	Rifleman.	
Howard, P. ...	88632	1/2/18	28/3/19, posted 13th K.L.R.	Rifleman.	
✠Howard, T. ...	41592	13/8/17	18/12/17, killed in action ...	Rifleman.	
Howard, W. ..,	88215	8/11/17	26/2/19, posted 25th K.L.R.	L./Corpl.	
Howard, W. ...	94929	2/4/18	—/3/19, posted 25th K.L.R.	Rifleman.	
Howarth, A. ...	50757	18/8/17	9/11/18, sick	Rifleman.	
✠Howarth, E. ...	243749	9/10/16	31/7/17, missing, assumed dead	Rifleman.	
Howarth, H. ...	94932	2/4/18	8/2/19, sick	Rifleman.	
Howarth, J. ...	243755	10/10/16	20/5/17,† transferred ...	Rifleman.	
✠Howarth, R. ...	243762	10/10/16	22/7/17, killed in action ...	Rifleman.	
Howarth, T. ...	3218	18/1/15	14/8/16, transferred ...	L./Corpl.	
Howarth, T. ...	88219	8/11/17	23/7/18, transferred ...	Rifleman.	
Howarth, V. ...	307746	8/7/17	17/4/18, sick	Rifleman.	
Howarth, W. ...	243766	10/10/16	15/3/17, transferred ...	Rifleman.	
Howat, R. H. ...	1580	23/2/15	23/12/17, sick	Rifleman.	
Howcroft, A. ...	50762	18/8/17	21/12/18, demobilized ...	Rifleman.	
Howe, G. ...	241041	12/11/14	5/7/18, sick	Rifleman.	
Howell, H. L. ...	88480	19/9/17	23/11/17, wounded ...	Rifleman.	
Howell, W. ...	50761	18/8/17	26/2/19, posted 13th K.L.R.	Rifleman.	
Howson, R. N. ...	240080	23/2/15	15/3/19,† demobilized ...	L./Corpl.	
Hoyle, J. ...	90763	7/3/18	30/5/18, sick	Rifleman.	
Hubbard, C. W. ...	260180	20/9/17	28/5/18, sick	Rifleman.	
Hubbard, H. ...	2821	9/11/14	12/1/15, transferred ...	Rifleman.	
Hudson, A. ...	2798	9/11/14	10/11/14, transferred ...	Rifleman.	
Hudson, A. M. ...	5256	1/6/16	18/8/16, transferred ...	Rifleman.	
Hudson, D. ...	52396	24/8/17	5/3/19, demobilized ...	L./Corpl.	
Hudson, E. ...	3355	22/4/15	3/12/15, transferred ...	Rifleman.	
✠Hudson, F. G. ...	88567	19/9/17	1/11/17, died of wounds ...	Rifleman.	
✠Huggett, T. E. ...	260218	20/9/17	15/6/18, died of wounds ...	Rifleman.	
Hughes, A. ...	2827	9/11/14	26/6/15, transferred ...	Rifleman.	
Hughes, A. ...	88481	19/9/17	25/10/18, wounded ...	Rifleman.	
Hughes, C. W. ...	2942	11/11/14	5/8/15, transferred ...	Rifleman.	
Hughes, D. J. ...	1699	23/2/15	26/6/15, transferred ...	Rifleman.	
Hughes, D. L. ...	2331	10/9/14	18/8/15, commission ...	A./Sergt.	
Hughes, E. C. ...	241530	6/8/45	5/8/17,† invalided to England	Rifleman.	
Hughes, E. F. ...	53468	28/9/17	18/11/17, wounded ...	Rifleman.	
Hughes, F. ...	241207	18/1/15	18/2/19,† discharged ...	Rifleman.	
Hughes, G. S. ...	242525	23/5/16	15/9/17, posted 1/6th K.L.R.	Rifleman.	
Hughes, H. ...	241066	13/11/14	27/2/19, demobilized ...	Rifleman.	
Hughes, H. D. ...	1400	27/2/15	26/6/15, transferred ...	Rifleman.	
Hughes, J. ...	4784	22/1/16	13/5/16, discharged ...	Rifleman.	
Hughes, J. ...	20285	1/2/18	6/11/18, sick	L./Corpl.	
Hughes, J. ...	241208	18/1/15	15/9/17,† posted 1/6th K.L.R.	Rifleman.	
Hughes, J. ...	243870	19/10/16	2/8/17, wounded	Rifleman.	
Hughes, J. T. ...	200993	1/2/18	22/5/19, demobilized ...	Rifleman.	
✠Hughes, R. ...	16819	27/6/18	12/9/18, killed in action ...	L./Corpl.	
Hughes, R. A. ...	93	23/2/15	26/6/15, transferred ...	Sergeant.	
Hughes, R. E. ...	1833	23/10/14	26/6/15, transferred ...	Rifleman.	
Hughes, R. J. ...	5067	22/3/16	22/6/16, transferred ...	Rifleman.	
Hughes, T. ...	108818	28/9/18	14/12/18, demobilized ...	Rifleman.	
Hughes, T. A. ...	2751	5/11/14	12/1/15, transferred ...	Rifleman.	
Hughes, W. ...	241294	12/4/15	11/2/19, demobilized ...	Rifleman.	

NAME.	REGTL. NO.	DATE OF JOINING.	DATE OF LEAVING WITH CAUSE.	HIGHEST RANK.	HONOURS OR AWARDS.
Hughes, W. ...	53061	13/8/17	4/11/18, wounded	L./Corpl.	
Hulatt, J. B. ...	200516	1/2/18	10/2/19, demobilized ...	Sergeant.	
Hulbert, H. F. ...	241317	3/7/15	16/10/17,† transferred ...	Rifleman.	
Hulme, J. ...	242416	21/3/16	6/3/18, sick	Rifleman.	
Hulme, J. ...	306739	27/6/18	27/2/19, demobilized ...	Rifleman.	
Hulme, J. A. ...	1766	23/10/14	5/8/15, transferred	Rifleman.	
Hulme, J. A. ...	240929	7/11/14	5/8/17, invalided to England	L./Corpl.	
Hulme, W. ...	240994	10/11/14	17/6/17,† transferred ...	Rifleman.	
Humphrey, J. B. ...	2412	11/9/14	3/12/14, commission ...	Rifleman.	
Hunt, D. C. ...	331921	27/8/17	22/11/17, posted 2/8th K.L.R.	Rifleman.	
Hunt, G. ...	50664	27/5/18	3/7/18, sick	Rifleman.	
Hunt, G. ...	52633	24/8/17	14/3/18, transferred ...	Rifleman.	
Hunt, R. W. F. ...	2409	11/9/14	12/1/15, transferred ...	Rifleman.	
Hunt, W. ...	94931	2/4/18	28/6/18, sick	Rifleman.	
Hunter, T. ...	1972	23/10/14	21/11/14, transferred ...	Rifleman.	
Hurst, B....	94933	2/4/18	27/9/18, wounded ...	Rifleman.	
Hurstfield, J. ...	94928	2/4/18	19/5/18, sick	Rifleman.	
Huston, F. ...	2406	11/9/14	12/1/15, transferred ...	Rifleman.	
Hutchinson, B. ...	72454	13/8/17	22/6/18, transferred ...	Rifleman.	
Hutchinson, J. ...	108811	28/9/18	21/7/19, transferred ...	Rifleman.	
Hutchinson, J. E.	243696	7/10/16	11/11/17, sick	Rifleman.	
Hutchinson, J. T.	243866	18/10/16	5/8/17, invalided to England	Rifleman.	
Huxham, J. ...	241161	8/12/14	30/6/17,† wounded ...	Rifleman.	
Hyde, E. C. ...	2001	23/10/14	26/6/15, transferred ...	Rifleman.	
Hyde, H. E. ...	2813	9/11/14	12/1/15, transferred ...	Rifleman.	
Hyde, H. K. ...	2916	10/11/14	15/6/16, transferred ...	Rifleman.	
Hyde, J. W. ...	6652	16/10/16	7/11/16, transferred ...	Rifleman.	
Hyde, S. ...	22735	27/5/18	12/9/18, prisoner of war ...	Rifleman.	
Hydes, W. ...	2329	10/9/14	26/6/15, transferred ...	Rifleman.	
Hyland, J. ...	72528	1/2/18	14/2/19, demobilized ...	Rifleman.	
Hyndman, R. ...	241551	6/8/15	8/8/17, invalided to England	Rifleman.	
Ingham, H. ...	407033	30/5/18	11/1/19, demobilized ...	Rifleman.	
Ingleby, E. ...	241291	12/4/15	17/4/18,† posted 9th K.L.R.	Rifleman.	
Ingledew, L. ...	50141	27/6/18	19/10/18, wounded ...	Rifleman.	
Inglis, D. ...	241091	16/11/14	9/8/17, invalided to England	Rifleman.	
Ion, J.	3279	25/2/15	28/12/15, transferred ...	Rifleman.	
Ion, J. E. ...	3257	11/2/15	26/6/15, transferred ...	Rifleman.	
Ireland, A. P. ...	242443	23/3/16	28/7/17, invalided to England	Rifleman.	
Irving, S.... ...	200256	28/3/18	29/3/18, transferred ...	Rifleman.	
Isaacs, A. ...	240849	13/10/14	28/5/18, sick	Sergeant.	
Isherwood, A. ...	50770	18/8/17	29/8/18, posted 1st K.L.R. ...	Rifleman.	
Isherwood, H. ...	240718	14/9/14	16/4/17, wounded ...	Rifleman.	
Jack, R.	50945	18/8/17	20/8/17, posted 2/8th K.L.R.	Rifleman.	
✠Jack, W. ...	3058	18/11/14	25/2/17, killed in action ...	Rifleman.	
Jackson, C. ...	2334	10/9/14	12/1/15, transferred ...	Rifleman.	
Jackson, C. ...	260235	19/9/17	6/9/18, wounded ...	Sergeant.	
Jackson, F. ...	50774	18/8/17	17/4/18, sick	Rifleman.	
Jackson, G. ...	4834	28/1/16	30/6/16, transferred ...	Rifleman.	
Jackson, G. ...	243851	16/10/16	22/1/19, demobilized ...	Rifleman.	
Jackson, H. ...	4835	28/1/16	20/6/16, transferred ...	Rifleman.	
Jackson, J. ...	1604	23/2/15	22/12/16, transferred ...	L./Corpl.	
Jackson, J. ...	2861	10/11/14	5/8/15, transferred ...	Rifleman.	
Jackson, J. ...	202187	1/2/18	27/9/18, wounded ...	Rifleman.	
Jackson, J. B. ...	240568	1/9/14	—/—/15, transferred ...	Rifleman.	
Jackson, R. D. ...	240872	26/10/14	22/8/17, wounded	A./C.Q.M.S.	
Jackson, L. ...	95041	2/4/18	8/10/18, injured	Corporal.	

NAME.	REGTL. NO.	DATE OF JOINING.	DATE OF LEAVING WITH CAUSE.	HIGHEST RANK.	HONOURS OR AWARDS.
Jackson, T. W. ...	72434	13/8/17	6/5/18, sick	Rifleman.	
Jackson, W. A. ...	240724	14/9/14	8/6/19, discharged ...	Rifleman.	
✠ Jackson, W. E. ...	240569	1/9/14	26/7/17, killed in action ...	Rifleman.	
Jackson, W. H. ...	1504	23/2/15	26/6/15, transferred ...	Rifleman.	
Jacobs, A. ...	2738	2/11/14	26/6/15, transferred ...	Rifleman.	
Jaeger, J. K. ...	241237	11/2/15	9/7/18, posted 1/6th K.L.R.	Rifleman.	
James, A. H. ...	72471	13/8/17	29/1/18, sick	Rifleman.	
James, E. ...	2817	9/11/14	12/1/15, transferred ...	Rifleman.	
James, E. G. ...	2702	28/10/14	22/1/15, commission	A./Sergt.	
James, G. W. ...	242668	14/10/17	1/10/18,† sick	Rifleman.	
James, J.... ...	94937	2/4/18	30/1/19, demobilized ...	Rifleman.	
James, J. H. ...	50772	18/8/17	2/5/18, sick	Rifleman.	
James, R. R. C. ...	2269	1/9/14	—/—/15, transferred ...	Rifleman.	
Jarrett, T. W. ...	50771	18/8/17	28/10/17, sick	L./Corpl.	
Jarvis, J. ...	243735	9/10/16	24/8/18, transferred ...	Rifleman.	
Jeffs, H. C. ...	241233	8/2/15	29/5/18,† transferred ...	Rifleman.	
Jenion, C. ...	242294	17/2/16	7/8/17, invalided to England	Rifleman.	
Jenkins, J. ...	242458	25/3/16	7/8/17, invalided to England	Rifleman.	
Jenkins, J. A. ...	242535	24/5/16	9/8/17, invalided to England	Rifleman.	
Jenkins, W. ...	200605	8/7/17	9/8/17, wounded	Rifleman.	
Jenkins, W. T. ...	406591	1/2/18	30/5/18, wounded	Rifleman.	
Jenkinson, B. ...	88193	8/11/17	29/8/18, posted 1st K.L.R. ...	Rifleman.	
Jenkinson, R. ...	243825	13/10/16	12/9/18, discharged ...	Rifleman.	
Jenner, N. E. ...	240654	10/9/14	7/8/17, invalided to England	A./C.Q.M.S.	
Jennings, E. T. ...	491	23/2/15	26/6/15, transferred ...	Rifleman.	
Jennings, H. ...	201358	14/3/18	14/9/18, wounded	Corporal.	
Jennings, T. L. ...	3351	21/4/15	30/8/15, transferred ...	Rifleman.	
Jennings, W. ...	49950	7/3/18	22/12/18, demobilized ...	Rifleman.	
✠ Jenvey, J. A. ...	235548	14/3/18	21/10/18, killed in action ...	Rifleman.	
Jepson, E. ...	24508	27/6/18	24/2/19, demobilized ...	Corporal.	
Jepson, W. ...	88233	8/11/17	13/2/18, sick	Rifleman.	
Jervis, J. ...	88117	5/10/17	28/3/19, posted 13th K.L.R.	Rifleman.	
Jervis, R. J. ...	64907	24/8/17	3/11/17, sick	Rifleman.	
Jevons, L. B. S.	268067	27/8/17	8/3/19, posted 13th K.L.R.	Rifleman.	
Jewers, W. ...	240949	9/11/14	6/8/17, invalided to England	A./Sergt.	
Johns, D. ...	202480	10/3/18	3/2/19, demobilized ...	Rifleman.	
Johnson, A. ...	241633	5/5/17	20/5/17, posted 1st K.L.R. ...	Rifleman.	
Johnson, A. J. ...	241127	23/11/14	29/3/17, invalided to England	Rifleman.	
Johnson, C. ...	2009	23/2/15	26/6/15, transferred ...	Rifleman.	
Johnson, F. ...	94939	2/4/18	28/3/19, posted 13th K.L.R.	Rifleman.	
Johnson, H. ...	268046	27/8/17	11/7/18, posted 1/6th K.L.R.	Rifleman.	
Johnson, H. G. ...	241543	6/8/15	3/6/17, wounded	Rifleman.	
Johnson, J. ...	3077	20/11/14	18/3/16, transferred ...	Rifleman.	
Johnson, J. ...	94938	2/4/18	29/8/18, posted 1st K.L.R. ...	Rifleman.	
Johnson, J. W. ...	42	23/10/14	2/11/16, transferred ...	Sergeant.	
Johnson, R. A. ...	110567	27/11/18	26/2/19, posted 25th K.L.R.	Rifleman.	
Johnson, R. H. ...	2729	2/11/14	12/1/15, transferred	Rifleman.	
Johnson, S. ...	380171	27/6/18	22/1/19, demobilized ...	Rifleman.	
Johnson, T. ...	95168	27/6/18	10/12/18, demobilized ...	Rifleman.	
Johnson, W. ...	23069	24/10/18	1/1/19, demobilized ...	Sergeant.	
Johnson, W. ...	64914	13/8/17	4/8/18, transferred	Rifleman.	
Johnston, H. E.	52045	27/5/18	26/2/19, posted 25th K.L.R.	Rifleman.	
Johnston, H. J. ...	6581	11/10/16	1/12/16, transferred ...	Rifleman.	
Johnston, J. G. ...	241525	6/8/15	14/3/19, demobilized ...	Rifleman.	
Johnston, L. ...	5280	12/6/16	27/7/16, transferred ...	Rifleman.	
Johnstone, F. ...	243829	13/10/16	16/5/18, sick	Rifleman.	
Johnstone, H. H.	241246	18/2/15	5/4/17,† wounded	Rifleman.	
Johnstone, J. F....	1603	23/2/15	23/1/18,† sick	Rifleman.	

NAME.	REGTL. NO.	DATE OF JOINING.	DATE OF LEAVING WITH CAUSE.	HIGHEST RANK.	HONOURS OR AWARDS.
Jolley, R. ...	21743	27/5/18	17/1/19, demobilized ...	Rifleman.	
Jolly, T. ...	2477	11/9/14	26/6/15, transferred ...	Rifleman.	
Jones, A. ...	2162	31/8/14	—/—/15, posted 1/6th K.L.R.	Rifleman.	
Jones, A. ...	3056	18/11/14	23/2/15, discharged ...	Rifleman.	
Jones, A. ...	240272	23/2/15	4/8/17, wounded ...	Rifleman.	
Jones, A. ...	242442	23/3/16	5/8/17, invalided to England	Rifleman.	
Jones, A. E. ...	3245	2/2/15	4/5/16, transferred ...	Rifleman.	
Jones, A. G. ...	2957	11/11/14	26/6/15, transferred ...	Rifleman.	
Jones, A. W. ...	1410	27/2/15	26/6/15, transferred ...	Rifleman.	
Jones, B. S. ...	1419	23/2/15	12/2/17, commission ...	Rifleman.	
Jones, C. ...	1957	23/10/14	24/2/16, transferred ...	Rifleman.	
Jones, C. ...	4778	22/1/16	22/2/16, transferred ...	Rifleman.	
Jones, D. G. ...	94936	2/4/18	13/5/18, sick ...	Rifleman.	
Jones, D. L. ...	2907	10/11/14	26/6/15, transferred ...	Rifleman.	
Jones, D. T. ...	240796	24/9/14	5/8/17, invalided to England	Rifleman.	
Jones, E. ...	88265	4/1/18	21/9/18, sick ...	Rifleman.	
✠ Jones, E. ...	242198	21/1/16	1/6/17, killed in action ...	Rifleman.	
Jones, E. A. ...	1882	23/10/14	23/2/15, transferred ...	Rifleman.	
Jones, E. C. ...	200513	1/2/18	27/2/19, demobilized ...	Sergeant.	
Jones, E. H. ...	2236	1/9/14	—/—/14, transferred ...	Rifleman.	
Jones, E. L. ...	2247	1/9/14	—/—/14, transferred ...	Rifleman.	
Jones, E. L. ...	242539	25/5/16	30/1/19, demobilized ...	Rifleman.	
Jones, E. O. ...	22744	27/5/18	30/7/18, commission ...	Corporal.	
✠ Jones, F. ...	87952	7/3/18	30/9/18, killed in action ...	Rifleman.	
Jones, F. E. ...	2644	9/10/14	12/1/15, transferred ...	Rifleman.	
Jones, F. H. ...	88569	19/9/17	3/9/18, transferred ...	Rifleman.	
Jones, G. ...	2192	1/9/14	—/—/14, posted 1/6th K.L.R.	Rifleman.	
Jones, G. D. ...	2716	29/10/14	17/5/15, transferred ...	A./Corpl.	
Jones, G. E. ...	2333	10/9/14	4/5/16, transferred ...	Rifleman.	
Jones, G. F. ...	268036	27/8/17	2/9/18, wounded ...	Rifleman.	
Jones, G. M. ...	2955	12/11/14	12/1/15, transferred ...	Rifleman.	
Jones, G. R. ...	241191	11/1/15	13/8/17, wounded ...	Corporal.	
Jones, H. ...	4792	22/1/16	13/3/16, transferred ...	Rifleman.	
Jones, H. ...	240817	26/9/14	26/6/17, commission ...	A./Sergt.	
Jones, H. A. ...	2587	26/9/14	26/6/15, transferred ...	Rifleman.	
Jones, H. G. ...	48424	27/5/18	9/1/19, demobilized ...	Rifleman.	
Jones, H. G. ...	242152	20/1/16	10/8/17, invalided to England	Rifleman.	
Jones, H. S. ...	241280	30/3/15	16/3/17, sick ...	Rifleman.	
Jones, H. W. ...	88089	29/9/17	21/5/18, sick ...	Rifleman.	
Jones, H. W. ...	242465	11/1/18	17/1/18, posted 13th K.L.R.	Rifleman.	
Jones, I. H. ...	49514	27/5/18	12/11/18, wounded ...	Rifleman.	
Jones, J. ...	1509	27/2/15	26/6/15, transferred ...	Rifleman.	
Jones, J. ...	2062	31/8/14	12/5/16, discharged ...	Rifleman.	
✠ Jones, J. ...	50773	18/8/17	30/10/17, killed in action	Rifleman.	
Jones, J. ...	51910	1/2/18	29/3/19, demobilized ...	Rifleman.	
Jones, J. ...	241278	29/3/15	7/8/17, invalided to England	A./Sergt.	
Jones, J. A. G. ...	2619	5/10/14	12/1/15, transferred ...	Rifleman.	
Jones, J. L. ...	2665	14/10/14	1/12/15, transferred ...	Rifleman.	
Jones, J. R. ...	2853	9/11/14	12/1/15, transferred ...	Rifleman.	
Jones, J. S. ...	332043	22/6/18	5/9/18, wounded ...	Rifleman.	
Jones, L. ...	242313	1/3/16	10/2/19, demobilized ...	Rifleman.	
Jones, L. ...	241822	1/2/18	30/1/19, demobilized ...	Rifleman.	
Jones, L. ...	243760	10/10/16	9/8/17, invalided to England	Rifleman.	
Jones, M. ...	20434	24/2/18	27/4/18, sick ...	Rifleman.	
Jones, O. ...	108825	28/9/18	13/12/18, demobilized ...	Rifleman.	
Jones, O. J. ...	240084	27/2/15	17/6/17,† transferred ...	Corporal.	
Jones, O. Y. ...	3283	25/2/15	22/6/17,† sick... ...	Rifleman.	
Jones P. ...	2056	31/8/14	31/3/16, discharged ...	Rifleman.	

NAME.	REGTL. NO.	DATE OF JOINING.	DATE OF LEAVING WITH CAUSE.	HIGHEST RANK.	HONOURS OR AWARDS.
✠ Jones, P. G. ...	240833	5/10/14	22/6/17, killed in action	Rifleman.	
Jones, P. N.	1133	23/2/15	18/2/16, physically unfit	Rifleman.	
Jones, R. ...	88570	19/9/17	2/11/17, wounded	Rifleman.	
Jones, R. H.	2533	21/9/14	12/1/15, transferred	Rifleman.	
Jones, R. H. ...	2825	9/11/14	9/4/16, transferred	Rifleman.	
Jones, R. O.	380205	1/2/18	11/12/18, demobilized	Rifleman	M.M.
Jones, S. ...	2165	31/8/14	—/—/15, posted 1/6th K.L.R.	Rifleman.	
Jones, S. ...	242433	22/3/16	26/7/17, wounded	Rifleman.	
✠ Jones, S. ...	65024	13/8/17	27/6/18, died of wounds	Rifleman.	
Jones, S. ...	300486	27/5/18	25/6/18, wounded	Rifleman.	
Jones, S. N.	2273	1/9/14	10/12/14, discharged	Rifleman.	
Jones, S. W.	2079	31/8/14	29/7/15, commission	Rifleman.	
Jones, T.	2532	21/9/14	14/8/16, transferred	Rifleman.	
Jones, T. ...	2860	10/11/14	28/6/15, transferred	A./L./Sergt.	
Jones, T. E.	2489	16/9/14	12/1/15, transferred	Rifleman.	
Jones, T. H.	50839	1/2/18	26/2/19, posted 25th K.L.R.	Rifleman.	
Jones, V. H.	1926	23/2/15	26/6/15, transferred	Rifleman.	
Jones, W. ...	242155	20/1/16	17/9/17, posted 12th K.L.R.	Rifleman.	
Jones, W. F.	242400	20/3/16	18/10/17, wounded	Rifleman.	
Jones, W. G.	105558	12/7/18	13/12/18, demobilized	Rifleman.	
Jones, W. H.	3491	3/7/15	18/1/17, sick	Rifleman.	
✠ Jones, W. H. ...	242269	25/1/16	4/8/17, died of wounds	Rifleman.	
Jones, W. H.	405125	1/2/18	29/8/18, posted 1st K.L.R.	Rifleman.	
Jones, W. J.	2176	31/8/14	13/11/14, commission	Rifleman.	
Jones, W. J.	2469	14/9/14	15/3/17, transferred	Rifleman.	
✠ Jones, W. M.	242236	22/1/16	28/4/17, killed in action	Rifleman.	
Jones, W. R.	2210	1/9/14	8/8/16, commission	Rifleman.	
Jory, H. ...	88571	19/9/17	18/1/19, demobilized	Rifleman.	
Joughin, H. J.	2960	12/11/14	12/1/15, transferred	Rifleman.	
Jowett, R. H.	2745	4/11/14	16/8/15, transferred	Rifleman.	
✠ Joyce, A. N.	21732	22/6/18	1/9/18, killed in action	Corporal.	
Joyce, J. J.	72446	13/8/17	30/1/19, demobilized	Rifleman.	
Joynson, A. J.	2863	10/11/14	12/1/17, sick	L./Corpl.	
Joynson, H.	17395	13/8/17	5/6/19, demobilized	Corporal.	
Joynson, J. R.	240492	27/2/15	5/8/17, invalided to England	A./Sergt.	
Judd, A. ...	35915	27/5/18	5/9/18, wounded	Rifleman.	
Kadansky, K. V.	243868	18/10/16	17/6/17, transferred	Rifleman.	
Kane, F. P.	3435	3/7/15	4/5/16, transferred	Rifleman.	
Kay, E. ...	200644	1/2/18	21/5/18, sick	Sergeant.	
Kay, J. ...	241574	6/8/15	28/9/17,† transferred	Rifleman.	
Kay, R. ...	241166	14/12/14	6/8/17, invalided to England	Rifleman.	
Kay, T. ...	2135	31/8/14	—/—/15, posted 1/6th K.L.R.	Rifleman.	
Kay, W. ...	109004	28/9/18	11/12/18, demobilized	Rifleman.	
Kaye, H. N.	242389	18/3/16	7/8/17, invalided to England	Rifleman.	
Kearns, M.	242234	22/1/16	18/5/18, wounded	Rifleman.	
Keates, G. H.	3004	13/11/14	5/8/15, transferred	Rifleman.	
✠ Keedwell, G.	24780	24/8/17	16/5/18, died of wounds	Rifleman.	
Keefe, J.	88197	8/11/17	17/4/18, sick	Corporal.	
Keegan, H. R.	2091	31/8/14	—/—/15, transferred	Rifleman.	
Keeling, F. G.	88572	19/9/17	22/12/18,† demobilized	Rifleman.	
Keepence, H.	1631	23/10/14	25/2/15, transferred	Rifleman.	
Keggan, J.	46600	27/5/18	4/10/18, wounded	Rifleman.	
Kehoe, J. M.	2336	10/9/14	5/8/15, transferred	Rifleman.	
Keill, A. W.	3248	5/2/15	2/1/17,† sick	Rifleman.	
Kellett, R.	88224	8/11/17	25/5/18, sick	Rifleman.	
Kelly, A.	10564	31/8/14	28/2/18, sick	R.S.M.	
Kelly, C. ...	2436	15/9/14	26/7/15, commission	Rifleman.	

HISTORY OF THE 2/6TH (RIFLE) BATTALION

NAME.	REGTL. NO.	DATE OF JOINING.	DATE OF LEAVING WITH CAUSE.	HIGHEST RANK.	HONOURS OR AWARDS.
✠Kelly, C. ...	88573	19/9/17	12/9/18, killed in action or died of wounds...	Rifleman.	
Kelly, J. H. ...	3715	6/8/15	4/5/16, transferred ...	Rifleman.	
Kelly, J. H. ...	268042	27/8/17	13/1/19, demobilized ...	Rifleman.	
Kelly, L. ...	2761	6/11/14	6/9/15, transferred ...	L./Corpl.	
Kelly, R. D. ...	94940	2/4/18	28/6/18, sick ...	Rifleman.	
Kelly, T. ...	2562	22/9/14	18/3/16, transferred ...	Rifleman.	
Kelly, W. ...	56915	27/5/18	5/9/18, wounded ...	Rifleman.	
Kempe, R. A. S.	2070	31/8/14	25/7/16, discharged ...	Rifleman.	
Kempsey, E. ...	242197	21/1/16	6/8/17, invalided to England	Rifleman.	
✠Kendal, J. ...	242741	1/2/18	26/10/18, died ...	L./Corpl.	
Kendrick, G. F.	242189	21/1/16	4/8/17, invalided to England	Rifleman.	
Kendrick, S. ...	3149	8/12/14	27/5/16, transferred ...	Rifleman.	
Kennedy, A. ...	242161	20/1/16	5/8/17, invalided to England	Rifleman.	
Kennedy, J. ...	94941	2/4/18	—/3/19, posted 25th K.L.R.	Rifleman.	
Kennedy, J. ...	243783	10/10/16	19/5/18,† sick ...	Rifleman.	
Kent, J. ...	2337	10/9/14	12/1/15, transferred ...	Rifleman.	
Kenyon, J. ...	242499	19/10/16	26/3/19, transferred ...	Rifleman.	
Kenyon, J. A. ...	242457	25/3/16	28/6/17, wounded ...	Rifleman.	
Kenyon, T. W. ...	2620	5/10/14	12/1/15, transferred ...	Rifleman.	
Ker, W. E. ...	2534	21/9/14	2/7/15, commission ...	Rifleman.	
Kerfoot, E. ...	204039	1/2/18	7/9/18, wounded ...	Sergeant.	
Kermack, W. ...	50946	18/8/17	20/8/17, posted 2/8th K.L.R.	Rifleman.	
Kermode, J. H. ...	3123	27/11/14	26/6/15, transferred ...	Rifleman.	
Kermode, W. H.	72526	13/8/17	29/8/18, posted 1st K.L.R. ...	Rifleman.	
Kernighan, A. E.	240986	10/11/14	5/6/18, commission ...	Sergeant.	
Kerr, J. H. ...	3114	30/11/14	26/6/15, transferred ...	Rifleman.	
Kerr, G. ...	240851	13/10/14	30/4/17,† posted 1st K.L.R.	Rifleman.	
Kerr, H. S. ...	17403	27/5/18	5/2/19, demobilized ...	Rifleman.	
Kerr, J. B. ...	200781	1/2/18	11/7/18, transferred ...	Sergeant.	
Kerr, N. M. ...	3003	14/11/14	3/12/15, transferred ...	Rifleman.	
Kerr, R. ...	332375	27/5/18	26/6/18, posted 9th K.L.R.	Rifleman.	
Kersey, W. ...	241429	6/8/15	9/8/17,† invalided to England	Rifleman.	
Kershaw, J. ...	243669	6/10/16	17/9/17, posted 12th K.L.R.	Rifleman.	
Kershaw, J. A. ...	332832	22/6/18	15/12/18, sick ...	Rifleman.	
Kessen, H. E. ...	242399	20/3/16	5/8/17, invalided to England	Rifleman.	
Kewish, E. ...	240546	31/8/14	—/—/15, transferred ...	Rifleman.	
✠Kewley, J. ...	240304	27/2/15	9/6/17, died of wounds ...	L./Sergt.	
Key, T. ...	49318	13/8/17	15/2/19, demobilized ...	Rifleman.	
Key, J. L. ...	2287	2/9/14	24/10/16, commission ...	Rifleman.	
Keyworth, W. ...	6504	9/10/16	1/1/17, sick ...	Rifleman.	
Kidd, M. ...	88094	29/9/17	26/7/18, posted 25th K.L.R.	Rifleman.	
✠Kiggins, T. E. ...	242223	22/1/16	12/7/17, killed in action ...	Rifleman.	
Killard, J. ...	266986	22/6/18	—/—/19, disembodied ...	Rifleman.	
Killey, S. B. G. ...	72461	24/8/17	17/2/18, sick ...	Rifleman.	
King, B. ...	200861	1/2/18	19/3/19, sick ...	Rifleman.	
King, E. ...	57652	27/5/18	31/12/18, demobilized ...	Rifleman.	
King, E. S. ...	88640	1/2/18	26/2/19, posted 25th K.L.R.	Rifleman.	
King, J. H. ...	3130	1/12/14	12/1/15, transferred ...	Rifleman.	
King, M. ...	88204	8/11/17	7/1/18, sick ...	Rifleman.	
King, R. H. ...	3129	1/12/14	12/1/15, transferred ...	Rifleman.	
King, W. ...	242455	25/3/16	3/8/17, invalided to England	Rifleman.	
Kinghorn, W. A.	240866	20/10/14	17/8/17, wounded ...	Corporal.	
Kinsella, T. A. ...	265364	27/8/17	29/3/19, demobilized ...	Rifleman.	
Kinsey, F. O. B.	240820	28/9/14	12/2/19,† demobilized ...	L./Corpl.	
Kipping, S. W. ...	242312	1/3/16	9/9/18, wounded ...	Rifleman.	
Kirby, R. J. ...	270022	27/8/17	1/4/18, transferred ...	Rifleman.	
✠Kirkby, J. ...	34596	24/8/17	28/10/17, died ...	Corporal.	

" THE KING'S " (LIVERPOOL REGIMENT)

NAME.	REGTL. NO.	DATE OF JOINING.	DATE OF LEAVING WITH CAUSE.	HIGHEST RANK.	HONOURS OR AWARDS.
Kirkland, T. ...	50947	18/8/17	20/8/17, posted 2/8th K.L.R.	Rifleman.	
Kirkwood, W. L.	241349	3/7/15	19/12/17,† commission ...	A./Corpl.	
Kissack, E. J. ...	2302	10/9/14	22/9/16, transferred ...	Rifleman.	
Kitchen, J. S. ...	240342	23/10/14	8/8/17, invalided to England	Sergeant.	
✠Kitchener, P. ...	88574	19/9/17	30/10/17, killed in action ...	Rifleman.	
Kitofsky, S. ...	269455	22/6/18	17/1/19, demobilized ...	Rifleman.	
Kitson, G. W. ...	242307	25/2/16	7/8/17, wounded	Rifleman.	
Knapp, A. ...	56916	24/2/18	15/10/18, wounded	Rifleman.	
Kneale, J. F. ...	3062	19/11/14	5/8/15, transferred	Rifleman.	
Kneale, S. J. ..	3061	10/11/14	5/8/15, transferred	Rifleman.	
Kneen, T. M. ...	242566	6/6/16	4/3/17, invalided to England	Rifleman.	
Kneen, V. J. ...	2634	7/10/14	22/8/16, transferred ...	Rifleman.	
Knight, A. J. ...	241225	1/2/15	30/6/17, transferred	L./Corpl.	
Knowles, A. F. ...	88482	19/9/17	9/2/18, sick	Rifleman.	
Knowles, C. S. ...	308165	27/5/18	5/9/18, wounded	Rifleman.	
Knowles, W. ...	202352	1/2/18	9/2/19, transferred	Rifleman.	
Knowlson, E. ...	2780	7/11/14	5/8/15, transferred	Rifleman.	
✠Laing, F. W. ...	331295	22/6/18	1/9/18, killed in action ...	Rifleman.	
Laing, J. ...	50948	18/8/17	20/8/17, posted 2/8th K.L.R.	Rifleman.	
Laing, S. ...	243775	10/10/16	16/10/17,† posted 2/5th K.L.R.	Rifleman.	
Lamb, J. ...	81	27/2/15	14/2/17, transferred	A./Sergt.	
Lamb, J. ...	64956	27/5/18	24/8/18, posted 13th K.L.R.	Rifleman.	
Lambert, H. ...	90328	23/2/18	26/2/18, transferred	Rifleman.	
Lambert, S. ...	240287	23/10/14	1/6/17,† wounded	Rifleman.	
Lambert, W. ...	200784	25/2/18	28/6/18, posted 12th K.L.R.	Rifleman.	
Lane, A. E. ...	88216	8/11/17	11/10/18, injured	Rifleman.	
Lane, A. E. ...	241296	14/4/15	26/6/18,† wounded	Sergeant.	
Lane, A. G. ...	242568	7/6/16	9/8/17, invalided to England	Rifleman.	
Lane, E. ...	88483	19/9/17	13/4/18, sick	Rifleman.	
Lane, G. ...	240932	7/11/14	6/8/17, invalided to England	A./Corpl.	
Lane, G. ...	242403	20/3/16	30/9/19, demobilized ...	A./C.S.M.	
Lane, H. J. ...	240578	1/9/14	—/—/14, transferred	Rifleman.	
Langhorne, C. ...	2526	15/9/14	26/6/15, transferred	Rifleman.	
Langhorne, G. H.	242289	17/2/16	19/5/17, invalided to England	Rifleman.	
Langley, R. ...	50878	1/2/18	18/1/19, demobilized ...	Rifleman.	
Langridge, V. ...	57947	27/6/18	6/3/19, demobilized	Rifleman.	
Langtry, W. ...	243674	6/10/16	8/9/17, wounded	Rifleman.	
Lanoue, A. ...	241550	6/8/15	10/8/17, invalided to England	Rifleman.	
Lardner, W. G. ...	88484	19/9/17	26/2/19, posted 25th K.L.R.	Rifleman.	
Larkin, P. ...	203117	11/10/17	29/8/18, posted 1st K.L.R. ...	Rifleman.	
Latham, A. ...	201278	1/2/18	4/9/18, transferred	Sergeant.	
Latham, H. J. ...	242268	26/1/16	25/1/19, demobilized ...	Rifleman.	
Latham, T. B. ...	2742	3/11/14	12/1/15, transferred	Rifleman.	
Latham, P. ...	240763	15/9/14	15/7/17, wounded	L./Corpl.	
Lathwood, G. ...	94947	2/4/18	29/8/18, posted 1st K.L.R. ...	Rifleman.	
Laville, T. ...	57426	24/8/17	1/8/18, posted 12th K.L.R.	L./Corpl.	
Lavin, C. C. ...	2255	1/9/14	—/—/14, transferred	Rifleman.	
Law, J. ...	202353	1/2/18	26/2/19, posted 25th K.L.R.	Sergeant.	
Law, J. C. ...	48254	1/2/18	12/2/19, demobilized ...	Rifleman.	
Law, T. ...	53056	1/2/18	7/7/18, sick	L./Corpl.	
✠Laws, A. F. ...	88485	19/9/17	30/10/17, killed in action ...	Rifleman.	
Lawson, W. ...	84911	24/2/18	26/2/18, posted 25th K.L.R.	Rifleman.	
Lawson, W. H. ...	201563	1/2/18	14/6/18, posted 1/5th K.L.R.	Rifleman.	
Lawton, A. ...	88486	19/9/17	21/12/17, sick	Rifleman.	
Lawton, A. S. ...	240730	12/9/14	30/5/18, commission	L./Sergt.	
Lawton, B. ...	241356	6/8/15	5/9/17,† posted 1/6th K.L.R.	Rifleman.	
Lawton, F. ...	94944	2/4/18	1/8/18, posted 12th K.L.R.	Rifleman.	
Lawton, H. ...	47799	13/8/17	27/7/18, transferred	Rifleman.	

NAME.	REGTL. NO.	DATE OF JOINING.	DATE OF LEAVING WITH CAUSE.	HIGHEST RANK.	HONOURS OR AWARDS.
Lawton, J. ...	88487	19/9/17	27/11/17, sick	Rifleman.	
Lawton, J. ...	300307	27/5/18	8/9/18, wounded	Rifleman.	
Lawton, W. ...	88488	19/9/17	30/6/18, sick ...	Rifleman.	
Lazarus, I. ...	2727	2/11/14	26/6/15, transferred ...	Rifleman.	
Lea, A. ...	3169	28/12/14	28/10/15, commission ...	Rifleman.	
Lea, A. ...	3306	22/3/15	4/5/16, transferred ...	Rifleman.	
Leach, H. ...	4887	1/3/16	12/7/16, transferred ...	Rifleman.	
Leach, W. ...	58376	13/9/18	11/1/19, demobilized	Rifleman.	
Leadbetter, L. C.	32502	1/2/18	22/5/19, demobilized	Rifleman.	
✠Leader, J. ...	39126	7/3/18	26/5/18, killed in action	Rifleman.	
✠Lear, A. ...	88575	19/9/17	30/10/17, killed in action	Rifleman.	
✠Leary, W. ...	88579	19/9/17	30/10/17, killed in action	Rifleman.	
Leask, J. R. ...	26	14/11/14	28/6/15, transferred ...	A./C.Q.M.S.	
Leatham, E. S. ...	240928	7/11/14	28/6/17, wounded ...	Rifleman.	
Leather, S. C. ...	242367	15/3/16	6/8/17, invalided to England	Corporal.	
Leaver, — ...	2472	11/9/14	12/1/15, transferred ...	Rifleman.	
✠Ledson, C. ...	50667	22/6/18	1/9/18, killed in action ...	Rifleman.	
Lee, A. ...	2962	12/11/14	12/1/15, transferred ...	Rifleman.	
Lee, A. V. ...	2163	31/8/14	21/6/15, commission	Rifleman.	
Lee, F. ...	243750	9/10/16	31/10/18, discharged ...	Rifleman.	
Lee, G. H. ...	50865	7/5/18	29/11/18, injured ...	Rifleman.	
Lee, G. W. ...	3203	11/1/15	11/12/15, transferred ...	Rifleman.	
Lee, H. ...	2766	6/11/14	12/1/15, transferred ...	Rifleman.	
Lee, J. ...	249	—/—/16	5/4/16, discharged ...	Sergeant.	
Lee, M. ...	32379	13/8/17	29/3/19, demobilized ...	Rifleman.	
Lee, R. J. ...	3029	16/11/14	5/8/15, transferred ...	Rifleman.	
Lee, S. ...	94942	2/4/18	27/1/19, demobilized	Rifleman.	
Lee, S. ...	260183	20/9/17	8/12/17, sick	Sergeant.	
Lee, T. H. ...	1693	27/2/15	26/6/15, transferred ...	Rifleman.	
Lee, V. ...	240998	10/11/14	30/4/18, commission ...	A./Corpl.	
Lee, W. ...	240963	9/11/14	21/2/19, demobilized ...	Sergeant.	M.M.
Leedham, H. ...	94943	2/4/18	14/3/19, transferred ...	Rifleman.	
✠Leese, A. E. ...	88576	19/9/17	19/12/17, killed in action	Rifleman.	
Legge, W. S. ...	240905	4/11/14	16/8/17, wounded ...	Rifleman.	
Leigh, A. W. ...	88577	19/9/17	21/6/18, wounded ...	Rifleman.	
Leigh, G. H. ...	200030	1/2/18	10/2/19, demobilized	Rifleman.	
Leigh, J. ...	94946	2/4/18	23/9/18, transferred ...	Rifleman.	
Leigh, R. ...	2905	10/11/14	12/1/15, transferred ...	Rifleman.	
Leighfield, J. ...	53442	7/3/18	21/5/18, sick	Rifleman.	
Leighton, G. W.	1690	23/10/14	7/1/16, discharged ...	Rifleman.	
Leighton, W. ...	59581	13/8/17	2/2/19, demobilized ...	Rifleman.	
Leith, W. ...	50949	18/8/17	20/8/17, posted 2/8th K.L.R.	Rifleman.	
Lennie, G. H. ...	2563	22/9/14	12/1/15, transferred ...	Rifleman.	
✠Leonard, E. ...	50777	18/8/17	28/10/17, killed in action ...	Rifleman.	
Lewin, H. ...	242286	17/2/16	5/8/17, invalided to England	Rifleman.	
Lewin, R. ...	241074	14/11/14	16/8/17, wounded ...	Rifleman.	
Lewis, D.... ...	110845	27/11/18	28/3/19, posted 13th K.L.R.	Rifleman.	
Lewis, D. W. ...	79884	24/8/17	30/1/19, demobilized	Rifleman.	
Lewis, E. E. ...	240656	10/9/14	24/2/19, demobilized	L./Corpl.	
Lewis, H. ...	2437	15/9/14	14/9/15, commission ...	A./Sergt.	
Lewis, H. L. ...	380851	10/7/18	26/7/18, posted 12th K.L.R.	Rifleman.	
Lewis, J. ...	11439	28/9/18	24/2/19, transferred ...	Rifleman.	
Lewis, J.... ...	51672	1/2/18	12/2/19, demobilized	Rifleman.	M.M.
Lewis, M. ...	49357	13/8/17	22/1/19, demobilized	Rifleman.	
✠Lewis, R.... ...	88489	19/9/17	29/10/17, died ...	Rifleman.	
Lewis, R. G. ...	50775	18/8/17	26/1/19, demobilized	Rifleman.	
Lewis, T. ...	60812	13/8/17	3/2/19, demobilized ...	Rifleman.	
✠Lewis, T. ...	88578	19/9/17	21/10/18, killed in action ...	Rifleman.	

"THE KING'S" (LIVERPOOL REGIMENT)

NAME.	REGTL. NO.	DATE OF JOINING.	DATE OF LEAVING WITH CAUSE.	HIGHEST RANK.	HONOURS OR AWARDS.
Lewis, W. J. ...	2466	14/9/14	1/6/15, transferred	A./Col./Sgt.	
Lewis, H.	2241	1/9/14	—/—/14, transferred ...	Rifleman.	
Ley, C. ...	241209	18/1/15	9/8/17, invalided to England	Rifleman.	
Liderth, H.	241528	6/8/15	3/3/19,† demobilized ...	Sergeant.	
Liggett, H. W. ...	2199	1/9/14	—/—/14, transferred ...	Rifleman.	
Lightfoot, H. ...	67136	24/8/17	19/5/18, sick	Corporal.	
Lightfoot, T. H.	300305	27/5/18	30/9/18, sick	Rifleman.	
Lilley, W. ...	240944	9/11/14	24/5/17,† wounded ...	Rifleman.	
Linaker, J. L. ...	3204	11/1/15	20/9/15, transferred ...	Rifleman.	
Lindop, H.	88490	19/9/17	28/3/19, posted 13th K.L.R.	Rifleman.	
✠Lindsay, A. H. ...	235310	14/6/18	5/10/18, killed in action ...	Rifleman.	
Lindsey, A. W. ...	88491	19/9/17	20/5/18, sick	L./Corpl.	
Linton, J. E. ...	3720	6/8/15	4/5/16, transferred ...	Rifleman.	
Litchfield, J. R.	240534	31/8/14	—/—/15, posted 1/6th K.L.R.	Rifleman.	
Litherland, N. ...	241082	12/11/14	15/3/19, demobilized ...	Rifleman.	
Little, J. H. M. ...	3195	8/1/15	14/10/15, commission ...	Rifleman.	
Little, R. ...	2935	11/11/14	23/11/15,† transferred ...	Rifleman.	
Little, W. ...	243804	12/10/16	10/8/17, invalided to England	Rifleman.	
Littler, G. ...	242207	21/1/16	10/2/19, demobilized ...	L./Corpl.	
Livesey, A.	406255	6/6/18	26/7/18, posted 25th K.L.R.	Rifleman.	
Llewellyn, J. S. ...	241302	20/4/15	8/12/18, sick	Sergeant.	M.S.M.
Lloyd, A. V. ...	2556	23/9/14	26/6/15, transferred ...	Rifleman.	
Lloyd, C. ...	2213	1/9/14	4/8/16, commission ...	Rifleman.	
Lloyd, C. R. ...	241527	6/8/15	3/11/17,† wounded ...	Rifleman.	
Lloyd, G....	23088	6/6/18	25/1/19, demobilized ...	Corporal.	
Lloyd, H. D. ...	240940	9/11/14	20/5/18, sick	A./Sergt.	M. in D.
Lloyd, P. ...	240245	23/2/15	7/8/17, invalided to England	A./Corpl.	
Lloyd, T. H. ...	5052	21/3/16	6/5/16, commission ...	Rifleman.	
Lloyd, S. ...	2208	1/9/14	—/—/14, transferred ...	Rifleman.	
Lobley, — ...	2514	17/9/14	19/10/14, medically unfit ...	Rifleman.	
Lock, T. W. ...	91233	26/2/18	2/6/19, transferred ...	Rifleman.	
Lockett, J. A. ...	110505	27/11/18	2/4/19, sick	Rifleman.	
Lockhart, A. ...	2570	23/9/14	26/6/15, transferred ...	A./L./Corpl.	
Loftus, T. ...	243802	11/10/16	15/8/17, wounded ...	Rifleman.	
Logan, A. C. ...	201482	1/2/18	29/8/18, posted 1st K.L.R. ...	Rifleman.	
Lomas, C. L. ...	2467	14/9/14	25/8/15, commission ...	Rifleman.	
Lomax, F. ...	243675	6/10/16	5/8/17, wounded ...	Rifleman.	
Lomax, M. ...	57274	26/9/18	26/2/19, posted 25th K.L.R.	Rifleman.	
Long, E. ...	85420	1/2/18	14/3/18, sick	Rifleman.	
Long, J. ...	240657	10/9/14	30/6/17, transferred ...	Rifleman.	
Long, T. ...	240787	22/9/14	10/8/17, invalided to England	Rifleman.	
Long, W. G.	1874	27/2/15	26/6/15, transferred ...	Rifleman.	
Longden, J. L. ...	50776	18/8/17	1/11/17, wounded ...	Rifleman.	
Longley, F. S. ...	202936	27/5/18	22/1/19, demobilized ...	Rifleman.	
Longridge, J. ...	241144	30/11/14	11/6/18, commission ...	Sergeant.	
Lonsdale, F. ...	243758	10/10/16	26/2/19, posted 25th K.L.R.	Rifleman.	
Lonsdale, J. ...	94945	2/4/18	—/3/19, posted 25th K.L.R.	Rifleman.	
Looney, W. ...	240715	15/9/14	16/8/17, wounded ...	A./Sergt.	
Lord, S. ...	243668	6/10/16	8/8/17, wounded ...	Rifleman.	
Lord, W. ...	88582	19/9/17	20/4/18, sick	Rifleman.	
Lovatt, F. ...	50779	18/8/17	26/2/19, posted 25th K.L.R.	Corporal.	
Lovegreen, T. J.	187	23/2/15	26/6/15, transferred ...	Corporal.	
Loveland, W. J.	50860	14/3/18	29/8/18, posted 1st K.L.R.	Rifleman.	
Lowe, A. ...	1344	23/10/14	23/11/15,† transferred ...	Rifleman.	
Lowe, T. ...	2939	11/11/14	26/6/15, transferred ...	Rifleman.	
Lowes, J. M. ...	241197	11/1/15	22/5/19, demobilized ...	Rifleman.	
Lowey, J. ...	59245	13/8/17	10/12/17, sick ...	Rifleman.	
Lowry, S. ...	242317	1/3/16	26/1/19, demobilized ...	Rifleman.	

NAME.	REGTL. NO.	DATE OF JOINING.	DATE OF LEAVING WITH CAUSE.	HIGHEST RANK.	HONOURS OR AWARDS.
Lucas, L. J. ...	201112	1/2/18	29/8/18, posted 1st K.L.R. ...	Rifleman.	
Lucas, R. ...	242546	22/5/16	12/2/19, demobilized ...	Rifleman.	
Luce, A. J. ...	241247	19/2/15	13/8/17, transferred ...	Rifleman.	
Lucock, C. ...	240379	27/6/18	1/10/18, wounded ...	L./Corpl.	
Lumb, C. ...	50778	18/8/17	6/1/18, sick ...	Rifleman.	
Lundbeck, F. ...	242407	20/3/16	20/5/18, sick ...	Rifleman.	
Lupton, R. B. ...	2723	30/10/14	12/1/15, transferred ...	Rifleman.	
Lutas, T. S. ...	242564	2/6/16	17/4/17, commission ...	Rifleman.	
Luya, F. H. ...	2891	10/11/14	4/5/16, transferred ...	Rifleman.	
Lymn, C. ...	2926	11/11/14	12/1/15, transferred ...	Rifleman.	
Lynan, J. ...	268066	27/8/17	30/1/18, sick ...	Rifleman.	
Lynch, — ...	2425	11/9/14	12/1/15, transferred ...	Rifleman.	
Lynch, E. F. ...	2743	3/11/14	16/8/15, transferred ...	Rifleman.	
Lynch, J. ...	241457	6/8/15	22/5/19, demobilized ...	L./Corpl.	
Lynch, J. ...	241949	25/2/16	21/2/19, demobilized ...	L./Corpl.	
Lynch, P. P. ...	241544	6/8/15	10/7/17, wounded ...	Rifleman.	
Lynch, W. ...	331853	28/9/18	28/11/18, sick ...	Rifleman.	
Lyon, J. A. ...	241532	6/8/15	18/8/17,† wounded ...	Rifleman.	
Lyons, R. M. ...	2240	1/9/14	—/—/14, transferred ...	Rifleman.	
Lyon, T. ...	1451	23/2/15	26/6/15, transferred ...	Rifleman.	
Lyons, A. E. ...	88492	19/9/17	22/12/18, demobilized ...	Rifleman.	
Lyth, E. ...	2950	11/11/14	12/1/15, transferred ...	Rifleman.	
Lyth, J. ...	72474	13/8/17	14/6/18, posted 1/5th K.L.R.	Rifleman.	
McAdam, J. H. ...	3007	14/11/14	4/5/16, transferred ...	Rifleman.	
McAllister, F. ...	241165	10/12/14	1/10/17,† commission ...	Sergeant.	
McAllister, H. ...	3082	23/11/14	11/12/15, transferred ...	Rifleman.	
McAllister, K. ...	241312	26/4/15	21/8/17,† wounded ...	L./Sergt.	
McArdle, D. ...	266107	27/8/17	14/3/18, transferred ...	Rifleman.	
✠McCabe, F. ...	72533	13/8/17	30/9/18, killed in action ...	Rifleman.	
McCabe, W. ...	405150	1/2/18	9/7/18, sick ...	Rifleman.	
✠McCartney, R. W.	23104	22/6/18	26/6/18, killed in action ...	Rifleman.	
McClelland, W. J.	3299	15/3/15	31/5/15, transferred ...	Rifleman.	
McConnell, A. E....	3480	3/7/15	15/6/16, physically unfit ...	Rifleman.	
McConnell, H. ...	242359	14/3/16	12/3/19, sick ...	L./Corpl.	
McConville, H. ...	26203	27/6/18	21/2/19, demobilized ...	Rifleman.	
McCormack, W. ...	67516	24/8/17	13/11/17, sick ...	Rifleman.	
McCormick, J. J.	110500	27/11/18	26/2/19, posted 25th K.L.R.	Rifleman.	
McCoy, J. ...	2479	11/9/14	26/6/15, transferred ...	A./Corpl.	
McCoy, W. ...	242408	20/3/16	5/3/19, demobilized ...	Rifleman.	
McCrainer, W. ...	30889	13/8/17	10/11/17, wounded ...	Rifleman.	
✠McCutcheon, J. ...	4703	20/1/16	25/2/17, killed in action ...	Rifleman.	
McDiarmid, A. ...	17892	24/2/18	24/8/18, posted 13th K.L.R.	L./Corpl.	
McDonald, J. ...	48856	24/8/17	2/7/18, posted 8th K.L.R. ...	Rifleman.	
McDonald, R. ...	42645	13/8/17	3/3/19, demobilized ...	Rifleman.	
McDonnell, F. ...	2709	29/10/14	12/1/15, transferred ...	Rifleman.	
McDonnell, W. ...	3086	23/11/14	5/8/15, transferred ...	Rifleman.	
McDonough, B. ...	203958	1/2/18	10/4/19, posted 4th K.L.R.	Rifleman.	
McDougall, C. ...	242371	16/3/16	5/8/17, invalided to England	Rifleman.	
McDougall, E. A.	241106	18/11/14	12/8/17, wounded ...	Rifleman.	
McDougall, T. ...	57505	27/6/18	30/1/19, demobilized ...	Sergeant.	
McElhinney, G. ...	2345	10/9/14	12/1/15, transferred ...	Rifleman.	
McEvinney, T. ...	240828	6/10/14	10/8/17, invalided to England	Rifleman.	
McEvoy, H. ...	268069	27/8/17	22/11/17, posted 2/8th K.L.R.	Rifleman.	
McEvoy, J. ...	88239	8/11/17	24/4/18, sick ...	Rifleman.	
McFee, W. L. ...	242173	20/1/16	5/8/17, invalided to England	Rifleman.	
McFeeley, F. A. ...	240200	27/2/15	12/2/18,† sick ...	Rifleman.	
McFeeley, J. J. C.	1358	27/2/15	14/8/15, commission ...	Rifleman.	

NAME.	REGTL. NO.	DATE OF JOINING.	DATE OF LEAVING WITH CAUSE.	HIGHEST RANK.	HONOURS OR AWARDS.
McGeachen, C. ...	240054	23/2/15	9/7/17,† discharged	L./Corpl.	
McGee, J. ...	110503	27/11/18	23/3/19, demobilized ...	Rifleman.	
McGeorge, T. S.	2274	1/9/14	—/—/14, transferred ...	Rifleman.	
McGibbon, F. ...	241232	8/2/15	17/1/18,† posted 13th K.L.R.	Rifleman.	
McGill, W. ...	240920	6/11/14	20/3/17, invalided to England	Rifleman.	
✠McGinn, J. P. ...	50783	18/8/17	29/10/17, died	Rifleman.	
McGinn, S. P. V. G.	59195	24/8/17	8/2/18, sick	Rifleman.	M.M.
McGinty, F. ...	333012	22/6/18	5/10/18, wounded ...	Rifleman.	
McGivering, D. ...	2119	31/8/14	—/—/14, transferred ...	Rifleman.	
✠McGlone, E. F. ...	203150	25/2/18	22/10/18, killed in action ...	Rifleman.	
McGorian, R. J.	3038	16/11/14	26/6/15, transferred ...	Rifleman.	
McGowan, J. A.	240946	9/11/14	22/5/19, demobilized ...	Sergeant.	
McGowan, R. ...	242396	18/3/16	15/5/17, transferred ...	Rifleman.	
McGrath, J. ...	44852	24/8/17	14/2/19, demobilized ...	A./Sergt.	M.M.
McGrath, J. J. ...	2137	31/8/14	—/—/15, posted 1/6th K.L.R.	Rifleman.	
McGrath, L. ...	50613	27/5/18	23/7/18, transferred ...	Rifleman.	
McGreavey, B. ...	3070	18/11/14	23/11/15,† transferred ...	Rifleman.	
Machell, T. R. ...	240993	10/11/14	25/5/18, sick	C.S.M.	
Machin, W. ...	240103	23/2/15	17/6/17,† transferred ...	Rifleman.	
Machray, C. ...	87971	29/9/17	25/3/18, sick	Rifleman.	
McIntosh, O. C. ...	4883	25/2/16	23/9/16, transferred ...	Rifleman.	
McIntyre, W. ...	242412	21/3/16	12/4/18, wounded ...	Rifleman.	
McKay, J. C. ...	2537	21/9/14	14/7/15, commission	A./Corpl.	
Mackenzie, W. A.	240554	31/8/14	—/—/15, transferred ...	Rifleman.	
MacKenzie, — ...	2304	10/9/14	12/1/15, transferred ...	A./Corpl.	
McKeon, G. ...	3356	22/4/15	5/9/16,† transferred ...	Rifleman.	
McKeown, E. ...	36937	13/8/17	11/11/17, sick ...	Rifleman.	
McKerrow, E. W.	2538	21/9/14	16/4/15, commission	Rifleman.	
McKim, T. B. ...	57438	27/6/18	5/2/19, demobilized ...	Rifleman.	
McKinn, E. ...	242421	21/3/16	21/8/17, wounded	Rifleman.	
McKinnerley, J.	42384	13/8/17	28/5/18, transferred ...	Rifleman.	
Maclaren, J. A. ...	2418	11/9/14	23/9/16,† transferred ...	A./C.S.M.	
McLean, A. ...	3498	3/7/15	16/8/15, transferred ...	Rifleman.	
McLean, H. ...	242301	17/2/16	8/6/18, sick	Rifleman.	
McLean, J. R. ...	240769	21/9/14	27/7/17,† invalided to England	L./Corpl.	
McLean, N. A. ...	241217	22/1/15	6/10/18,† sick	L./Sergt.	
McLean, T. ...	202205	1/2/18	4/3/18, posted 2/7th K.L.R.	Rifleman.	
McLeary, T. D. ...	241394	3/7/15	5/6/18,† sick	Rifleman.	
McLellan, W. ...	88234	8/11/17	27/4/18, sick	Rifleman.	
McLoughlin, J. ...	32411	13/8/17	15/2/19, demobilized ...	Rifleman.	
McLoughlin, T. ...	305615	27/6/18	14/8/18, wounded ...	Rifleman.	
McMahon, W. M.	2696	26/10/14	26/6/15, transferred ...	Rifleman.	
McMeakin, T. J....	240629	2/9/14	14/3/18,† transferred ...	Rifleman.	
McMillan, J. ...	2953	10/11/14	26/6/15, transferred ...	Rifleman.	
McMullin, J. ...	14048	27/2/18	4/9/18, wounded ...	Rifleman.	M.M
McMurray, T. ...	243808	12/10/16	2/8/17, wounded ...	Rifleman.	
McNair, R. ...	2305	10/9/14	12/1/15, transferred ...	Rifleman.	
McNally, G. V. ...	242549	1/6/16	10/6/17, wounded ...	Rifleman.	
McNally, M. ...	267631	27/8/17	6/9/18, wounded ...	Corporal.	
McWean, T. ...	22	27/4/15	26/7/15, transferred ...	C.S.M.	
McWilliam, F. ...	243698	6/10/16	29/5/18, wounded ...	Rifleman.	
McWilliam, P. ...	268040	27/8/17	11/4/18, sick	Rifleman.	
Maddock, T. S. ...	240894	2/11/14	30/5/18,† wounded ...	Corporal.	
Maddocks, W. ...	64930	13/8/17	3/10/17, sick	Rifleman.	
Maddox, J. ...	265155	27/5/18	28/8/18, sick	Corporal.	
Mahon, T. ...	88191	8/11/17	26/2/19, posted 25th K.L.R.	Rifleman.	
Mair, E. D. ...	240999	10/11/14	9/7/17, wounded	Rifleman.	
✠Makin, A. ...	50780	18/8/17	18/12/17, killed in action ...	Rifleman.	

NAME.	REGTL. NO.	DATE OF JOINING.	DATE OF LEAVING WITH CAUSE.	HIGHEST RANK.	HONOURS OR AWARDS.
Makin, J. W.	50603	14/6/18	5/3/19, demobilized	Rifleman.	
Maleady, J.	12186	7/3/18	6/5/18, sick	Rifleman.	
Malone, J.	242153	20/1/16	20/5/17,† transferred	Rifleman.	
✠Malone, A.	240658	10/9/14	9/7/17, killed in action	L./Corpl.	
Maloney, W. J.	88493	19/9/17	20/1/18, wounded	Rifleman.	
Mander, A.	88531	19/9/17	25/4/18, sick	Rifleman.	
✠Manders, F. W.	88581	19/9/17	1/11/17, died of wounds	Rifleman.	
Manick, J. P.	242352	9/3/16	29/8/18,† posted 1st K.L.R.	Rifleman.	
Mann, G. B.	2750	4/11/14	26/6/15, transferred	Rifleman.	
Mann, J.	241389	6/8/15	9/7/18, posted 1/6th K.L.R.	Corporal.	
Mann, R.	2736	2/11/14	1/6/15, transferred	Rifleman.	
Mannion, T.	72516	13/8/17	29/8/18, posted 1st K.L.R.	Rifleman.	
Mansell, H. L.	240585	31/8/14	—/—/15, posted 1/6th K.L.R.	Rifleman.	
✠Marc, E.	242194	21/1/16	22/6/17, died	Rifleman.	
Marland, S.	1574	23/10/14	4/5/16, transferred	Rifleman.	
Marriott, C.	31659	13/8/17	29/3/18, demobilized	Rifleman.	
Marsden, C.	48487	6/6/18	26/2/19, posted 25th K.L.R.	Rifleman.	
Marsden, H. E.	2579	25/9/14	12/1/15, transferred	Rifleman.	
Marsden, J. E.	58515	13/8/17	26/2/19, posted 13th K.L.R.	Rifleman	M. in D.
Marsden, T. J.	2865	10/11/14	5/8/15, transferred	Rifleman.	
Marsh, C. F.	242341	6/3/16	5/9/17, posted 1/6th K.L.R.	Rifleman.	
Marsh, D. C.	240788	22/9/14	5/8/17, invalided to England	Rifleman.	
Marsh, R.	243803	10/10/16	7/8/17, invalided to England	Rifleman.	
Marshall, B.	308639	27/6/18	23/1/19, sick	Rifleman.	
Marshall, P.	4950	2/3/16	3/3/17, transferred	Rifleman.	
Marshall, R.	88548	19/9/17	2/12/17, transferred	Rifleman.	
Marshall, W.	50950	18/8/17	20/8/17, posted 2/8th K.L.R.	Rifleman.	
Marsland, J. C.	268050	27/8/17	8/12/18, sick	Rifleman.	
Marten, C.	3178	—/12/14	5/8/15, transferred	Rifleman.	
Marten, R.	3455	6/8/15	9/4/16, transferred	Rifleman.	
Martin, C. A.	242196	21/1/16	11/2/19, demobilized	Rifleman.	
Martin, E.	88091	29/9/17	19/11/17, sick	Rifleman.	
Martin, H.	2653	12/10/14	7/12/14, medically unfit	Rifleman.	
Martin, J.	2809	9/11/14	21/5/16, transferred	Rifleman.	
Martin, S. D.	1912	23/10/14	23/2/15, transferred	Rifleman.	
Martin, W.	50951	18/8/17	20/8/17, posted 2/8th K.L.R.	Rifleman.	
Mason, A. E.	2767	6/11/14	5/8/15, transferred	Rifleman.	
Mason, E.	64992	24/2/18	29/8/18, posted 1st K.L.R.	Rifleman.	
Mason, E. A.	241414	6/8/15	23/4/17,† wounded	Rifleman.	
Mason, G. E.	5016	18/3/16	24/2/17, discharged	Rifleman.	
Mason, H.	88580	19/9/17	19/5/18, wounded	Rifleman.	
Mason, H. C.	2461	12/9/14	26/6/15, transferred	A./Sergt.	
Mason, W.	88642	5/4/18	10/8/18, transferred	Rifleman.	
Mason, W. J.	2536	21/9/14	12/1/15, transferred	Rifleman.	
Massey, H. T.	2343	10/9/14	12/1/15, transferred	Rifleman.	
Massey, T. H.	3295	9/3/15	6/7/15, discharged	Rifleman.	
Massey, J.	2246	1/9/14	—/—/14, transferred	Rifleman.	
Matchett, H.	241260	11/3/15	22/5/19,† demobilized	L./Corpl.	
Mather, P. D.	2341	10/9/14	3/6/15, commission	A./Corpl.	
Mathers, J.	3294	8/3/15	26/6/15, transferred	Rifleman.	
Mathews, C.	26604	7/3/18	6/9/18, wounded	Rifleman.	
Matthews, G.	50952	18/8/17	20/8/17, posted 2/8th K.L.R.	Rifleman.	
Matthie, E.	4827	27/1/16	22/7/16, transferred	Rifleman.	
Maude, T.	241529	6/8/14	20/1/19, demobilized	Rifleman.	
Maudsley, J.	2131	31/8/14	—/—/15, posted 1/6th K.L.R.	Rifleman.	
Maudsley, J.	242419	21/3/16	15/5/17, discharged	Rifleman.	
Maudsley, T.	2460	12/9/14	4/5/16, transferred	Rifleman.	
Mawdsley, C.	39428	14/6/18	22/1/19, demobilized	Rifleman.	

NAME.	REGTL. NO.	DATE OF JOINING.	DATE OF LEAVING WITH CAUSE.	HIGHEST RANK.	HONOURS OR AWARDS.
Maxfield, H. ...	2555	23/9/14	5/8/15, transferred	Rifleman.	
Maxwell, J. ...	2493	16/9/14	5/8/15, transferred	Rifleman.	
Maxwell, J. E. ...	241446	6/8/15	4/4/18,† transferred	Rifleman.	
Maxwell, L. R. ...	2855	9/11/14	18/1/17,† sick	Rifleman.	
✠Maxwell, W. S. ...	241224	29/1/15	12/7/17, killed in action ...	A./L./Corpl.	
May, L. ...	3005	13/11/14	26/6/15, transferred ...	Rifleman.	
Maynard, S.	88220	8/11/17	30/9/18, sick	Rifleman.	
✠Mayo, E. D. ...	88494	19/9/17	3/9/18, died of wounds ...	Rifleman.	
Mayoh, H. ...	50782	18/8/17	9/1/18, sick	Rifleman.	
Mayor, H. ...	241012	10/11/14	7/3/18,† posted 1/5th K.L.R.	Rifleman.	
✠Mayor, J. W.	42473	24/2/18	22/6/18, died	Rifleman.	
Mayor, T. E. ...	243714	9/10/16	30/3/18, transferred ...	Rifleman.	
✠Maziere, A.	241272	26/3/15	7/6/17, killed in action ...	Rifleman.	
Meadows, R. W.	242404	20/3/16	9/8/17, invalided to England	Rifleman.	
Meek, F. ...	59053	16/8/17	20/8/17, posted 2/8th K.L.R.	Rifleman.	
Meers, A. F. ...	2972	12/11/14	12/1/15, transferred ...	Rifleman.	
Melbourne, J. ...	110825	27/11/18	14/2/19, sick	Rifleman.	
✠Melia, J. ...	267083	6/6/18	1/9/18, killed in action ...	Rifleman.	
Mellalieu, L. ...	243861	16/10/16	31/8/17, sick	Rifleman.	
Mellor, A. ...	2580	25/9/14	16/8/15, transferred ...	Rifleman.	
Mellor, A. ...	380988	21/11/17	29/8/18, posted 1st K.L.R. ...	L./Corpl.	M.M.
Mellor, F. ...	88263	30/12/17	26/2/19, posted 13th K.L.R.	Rifleman.	
Meloney, H. ...	110830	27/11/18	13/2/19, sick	Rifleman.	
Melville, J. ...	50784	18/8/17	29/10/17, prisoner of war ...	Rifleman.	
Menage, B. E. ...	260184	20/9/17	23/7/18, transferred ...	Corporal.	
Mercer, W. W. ...	243855	12/10/16	6/7/17, wounded	Rifleman.	
Merrigan, J. ...	2976	12/11/14	5/8/15, transferred ...	Rifleman.	
Merrigan, P. ...	266530	22/6/18	2/10/18, wounded	Rifleman.	
Merritt, E. ...	88210	8/11/17	4/6/18, sick	L./Corpl.	
Mesloff, S. ...	243872	19/10/16	7/8/17, invalided to England	Rifleman.	
Metcalf, G. ...	330369	27/8/17	5/3/19, demobilized	L./Sergt.	
Metcalfe, C. A. ...	1114	23/2/15	26/6/15, transferred ...	A./Corpl.	
Metcalfe, F. ...	92202	7/3/18	31/5/18, wounded	Rifleman.	
Mew, F. ...	3090	23/11/14	26/6/15, transferred ...	Rifleman.	
Mezgar, R. ...	3215	13/1/15	26/6/15, transferred	Rifleman.	
Middleton, A. F.	202371	1/2/18	26/2/19, posted 25th K.L.R.	Rifleman.	
Middleton, A. J....	3234	25/1/15	23/9/16, transferred	Rifleman.	
Milbourne, C. H.	2654	12/10/14	11/6/15,† transferred ...	Rifleman.	
Miles, W. J. ...	3360	26/4/15	1/5/15, transferred	Rifleman.	
✠Millard, W. ...	88538	19/9/17	31/10/17, died of wounds ...	L./Corpl.	
Miller, A. ...	405935	26/9/18	—/4/19, transferred ...	Rifleman.	
Miller, A. E. ...	2720	30/10/14	12/1/15, transferred ...	Rifleman.	
Miller, C. W. ...	94096	27/6/18	—/3/19, posted 25th K.L.R.	Rifleman.	
Miller, J. C. ...	200629	1/2/18	21/4/18, sick	Sergeant.	
Miller, J. J. ...	64791	13/8/17	30/1/19, demobilized ...	L./Corpl.	
Miller, S. J. ...	242438	23/3/16	17/6/17, wounded	A./Corpl.	
Miller, W. D. ...	2877	10/11/14	5/8/15, transferred ...	Rifleman.	
Millman, M. ...	300314	28/9/18	22/12/18, transferred ...	L./Corpl.	
Mills, T. ...	243697	7/10/16	10/4/18, sick	Rifleman	M.M.
Mills, W. ...	6535	9/10/16	10/2/17, transferred ...	Rifleman.	
Milns, F. H. ...	4864	17/2/16	5/8/16, discharged	Rifleman.	
Milton, C. L. ...	50785	18/8/17	24/4/18, sick	Rifleman.	
✠Mingham, E. ...	40196	24/8/17	4/11/17, killed in action ...	Rifleman.	
Mitchell, C. L. ...	243852	16/10/16	11/6/19, demobilized ...	Rifleman.	
Mitchell, G. ...	235438	1/2/18	8/3/19, posted 13th K.L.R.	Rifleman.	
Mitchell, J. W. ...	72435	13/8/17	6/5/18, posted 1/6th K.L.R.	Rifleman.	
Mitchell, P. ...	242219	22/1/16	6/9/18, wounded	Corporal.	
✠Moffat, A. ...	300316	6/6/18	30/8/18, killed in action ...	Rifleman.	

NAME.	REGTL. NO.	DATE OF JOINING.	DATE OF LEAVING WITH CAUSE.	HIGHEST RANK.	HONOURS OR AWARDS.
Moir, J. S. ...	2794	7/11/14	26/6/15, transferred	Rifleman.	
Molyneaux, J. ...	72501	24/8/17	1/8/18, posted 12th K.L.R.	Rifleman.	
Molyneux, B. ...	2303	10/9/14	5/8/15, transferred ...	Rifleman.	
Molyneux, F. T.	2663	13/10/14	24/9/15, commission ...	Rifleman.	
Molyneux, J. ...	88188	8/11/17	5/9/18, wounded	Rifleman.	
Molyneux, R. ...	2117	31/8/14	—/—/15, transferred	Rifleman.	
Molyneux, T. ...	15757	1/2/18	29/7/18, sick	Rifleman.	
Moody, C. ...	242228	22/1/16	14/2/19, demobilized ...	Rifleman.	
Moon, W. ...	202430	1/2/18	22/2/19, demobilized ...	Rifleman.	
Moore, A. ...	242538	25/5/16	29/8/18, posted 1st K.L.R. ...	Rifleman.	
Moore, F. ...	85817	7/3/18	9/1/19, injured	Rifleman.	
Moore, G. ...	5003	18/3/16	2/5/18, sick	Rifleman.	
Moore, H. ...	2747	4/11/14	26/2/15, transferred ...	Rifleman.	
Moore, H. ...	243703	9/10/16	26/5/17, wounded ...	Rifleman.	
Moore, J. ...	242202	21/1/16	3/1/18, transferred ...	Rifleman.	
Moore, J. H. ...	241891	5/5/17	20/5/17, transferred ...	Rifleman.	
Moore, W. ...	88190	8/11/17	25/1/18, sick	Rifleman.	
Moore, W. C. ...	88497	19/9/17	14/3/18, sick	Rifleman.	
Moore, W. D. ...	242338	3/3/16	9/8/17, invalided to England	Corporal.	
✠Morgan, A. ...	88495	19/9/17	30/8/18, killed in action ...	Rifleman.	
Morgan, C. ...	88496	19/9/17	20/1/19, demobilized ...	Rifleman.	
Morgan, J. B. ...	63974	24/8/17	27/10/18, wounded	L./Corpl.	
Morgan, J. S. ...	64898	13/8/17	25/1/19, demobilized ...	Rifleman.	
Morgan, L. F. ...	72529	24/8/17	7/7/18, transferred ...	Rifleman.	
Morgan, M. ...	57865	22/6/18	15/1/19, demobilized ...	Rifleman.	
Morland, H. ...	242224	22/1/16	21/10/17, commission ...	L./Corpl.	
Morrall, H. ...	241129	24/11/14	7/2/19, demobilized	C.S.M.	M.M.
Morris, A. O. ...	162	23/2/15	28/6/15, transferred ...	C.Q.M.S.	
✠Morris, G. ...	241578	6/8/15	28/7/17, killed in action ...	Rifleman.	
✠Morris, G. ...	242574	12/6/16	23/7/17, died of wounds ...	Corporal.	
✠Morris, J. H. ...	241194	11/1/15	15/7/17, killed in action ...	Rifleman.	
Morris, S. C. ...	202192	1/2/18	8/3/19, posted 13th K.L.R.	Rifleman.	
Morris, S. S. ...	65	23/2/15	26/6/15, transferred ...	Corporal.	
Morris, T. ...	3119	30/11/14	26/6/15, transferred ...	Rifleman.	
Morris, W. ...	200920	1/2/18	19/1/19, demobilized ...	Rifleman.	
Morrison, R. ...	242536	24/5/16	6/8/17, invalided to England	Rifleman.	
Mortenson, A. ...	4716	20/1/16	18/4/17, commission	L./Corpl.	
Mossop, G. H. ...	242459	25/3/16	7/8/17, invalided to England	Rifleman.	
Mostyn, T. ...	88051	28/9/17	28/12/17, wounded	Rifleman.	
Mottershead, G. R.	242576	14/6/16	2/9/19, demobilized	Rifleman.	
Mottram, B. W.	241345	3/6/15	5/8/17, invalided to England	Sergeant.	
Moulsdale, F. ...	241171	28/12/14	8/3/19, demobilized	Rifleman.	
Moulton, S. J. ...	242231	22/1/16	—/3/19, posted 25th K.L.R.	Rifleman.	
✠Mount, H. J. ...	201604	22/6/18	29/9/18, killed in action ...	Rifleman.	M.M.
✠Mountford, F. G.	243724	9/10/16	28/6/17, died of wounds ...	Rifleman.	
Mountford, J. W.	2781	7/11/14	12/1/15, transferred ...	Rifleman.	
Muckelt, E. ...	88189	8/11/17	12/5/18, transferred ...	Rifleman.	
Muir, F. W. ...	2229	1/9/14	27/12/15, commission ...	Rifleman.	
Mulgrew, F. ...	3138	4/12/14	21/7/15, commission	Rifleman.	
Mullen, F. ...	450	23/2/15	26/6/15, transferred ...	L./Corpl.	
Mullen, P. ...	6658	18/10/16	17/11/16, sick	Rifleman.	
Mulligan, J. ...	13133	27/6/18	31/12/18, demobilized ...	Rifleman.	
Mullineaux, A. ...	108812	28/9/18	11/12/18, demobilized ...	Rifleman.	
Mullock, J. R. ...	50781	18/8/17	19/11/18, sick	L./Corpl.	
Murdo, W. B. ...	241310	26/4/15	17/8/17,† wounded	Rifleman.	
Murdoch, E. G. ...	242434	22/3/16	24/7/18, transferred ...	Rifleman.	
Murdoch, H. ...	2344	10/9/14	12/1/15, transferred ...	Rifleman.	
Murphy, A. ...	242260	26/1/16	25/1/18,† posted 1/6th K.L.R.	Rifleman.	

NAME.	REGTL. NO.	DATE OF JOINING.	DATE OF LEAVING WITH CAUSE.	HIGHEST RANK.	HONOURS OR AWARDS.
Murphy, B. ...	48319	13/8/17	7/12/18, transferred	Rifleman.	
Murphy, F. ...	2209	1/9/14	—/—/14, transferred ...	Rifleman.	
Murphy, J. F. ...	241341	3/7/15	10/10/18, wounded	L./Corpl.	
Murphy, L. ...	16258	27/5/18	18/7/18, posted 13th K.L.R.	Rifleman.	
Murphy, T. ...	50926	7/3/18	16/5/18, wounded	Rifleman.	
Murray, G. H. B.	1819	27/2/15	26/6/15, transferred	Rifleman.	
Murray, R. J. ...	241577	8/7/17	13/8/17, wounded	Corporal.	
Murray, W. ...	46662	13/8/17	28/3/19, posted 13th K.L.R.	Rifleman.	
Murray, W. D. ...	243854	12/10/16	8/8/17, invalided to England	Rifleman.	
Muscovitch, J. ...	47264	24/8/17	26/2/19, posted 13th K.L.R.	Rifleman.	
Mutch, A. H. ...	241290	12/4/15	23/7/17, wounded	Rifleman.	
Mutch, J. ...	241336	3/7/15	5/3/19, demobilized	Rifleman.	
Myers, J. A. ...	241288	9/4/15	22/5/19, demobilized ...	A./Sergt.	
Myers, W. T. ...	1540	23/2/15	26/6/15, transferred	Rifleman.	
Myerscough, L. ...	2342	10/9/14	—/—/15, transferred	Rifleman.	
✠Myerscough, S. ...	241285	8/4/15	15/7/17, killed in action ...	Rifleman.	
Mylchreest, G. ...	242167	20/1/16	10/8/17, wounded	Rifleman.	
Mylrea, J. L. ...	2635	8/10/14	12/1/15, transferred	Rifleman.	
Mynard, H. ...	242160	20/1/16	8/8/17, invalided to England	Rifleman.	
Nadin, G. ...	2577	24/9/14	12/1/15, transferred	Rifleman.	
Naginton, T. C. ...	241567	6/8/15	31/10/17, transferred ...	Rifleman.	
Nall, J.	57816	7/3/18	15/12/18, sick	Rifleman.	
Nancollis, R. T.	16546	27/5/18	4/1/19, demobilized	L./Corpl.	
Nash, G. ...	243710	9/10/16	23/2/17, transferred ...	Rifleman.	
Nava, P. ...	6645	16/10/16	28/12/16, transferred ...	Rifleman.	
Neale, C. H. ...	2788	7/11/14	12/1/15, transferred	Rifleman.	
Neale, R. J. ...	2517	18/9/14	5/8/15, transferred	Rifleman.	
Neale, R. T. ...	88498	19/9/17	6/11/17, commission ...	L./Corpl.	
Neave, P. ...	243853	16/10/16	22/11/18, discharged ...	Rifleman.	
Nelson, P. ...	241465	6/8/15	22/4/18,† transferred ...	Rifleman.	
Nelson, T. H. ...	240957	9/11/14	2/8/17, invalided to England	Rifleman.	
Nelson, W. ...	108746	28/9/18	11/12/18, demobilized ...	Rifleman.	
Newbert, C. ...	88049	28/9/17	26/2/19, posted 25th K.L.R.	Rifleman.	
Newbold, S. G. ...	87753	27/6/18	2/10/18, sick	Rifleman.	
Newbolt, G. H. ...	241119	20/11/14	24/5/17,† wounded	Rifleman.	
Newbolt, J. J. ...	241117	20/11/14	14/1/19, injured	Rifleman.	
Newhouse, H. ...	88238	8/11/17	12/1/18, sick	Rifleman.	
Newman, A. J. ...	242420	21/3/16	26/1/19, demobilized ...	Rifleman.	
Newnes, J. ...	242253	25/1/16	25/5/17, wounded	Rifleman.	
Newport, C. ...	240056	23/2/15	17/6/17,† transferred ...	Rifleman.	
✠Newsome, R. ...	243790	11/10/16	31/7/17, killed in action ...	Rifleman.	
Newton, P. ...	331832	28/9/18	5/3/19, demobilized	Rifleman.	
Nicholas, A. ...	242385	18/3/16	9/8/17, invalided to England	Rifleman.	
Nicholas, C. E. ...	3670	6/8/15	22/7/16, transferred	Rifleman.	
Nicholl, C. ...	242422	21/3/16	8/7/17, wounded	Rifleman.	
Nicholl, S. V. ...	2346	10/9/14	12/1/15, transferred	Rifleman.	
Nicholls, E. ...	94207	13/9/18	17/10/18, transferred ...	Rifleman.	
Nicholls, E. B. ...	109115	28/9/18	—/4/19, posted 13th K.L.R.	Rifleman.	
Nicholls, H. B. ...	240428	23/10/14	24/8/17, wounded	Sergeant.	
Nicholls, H. T. ...	242347	8/3/16	5/6/18,† sick	Rifleman.	
Nicholls, K. ...	242386	18/3/16	30/5/17, discharged ...	Rifleman.	
Nicholson, C. ...	50787	18/8/17	11/11/17, wounded	Rifleman.	
Nicholson, R. ...	2553	23/9/14	27/10/14, medically unfit ...	Rifleman.	
Nickels, T. A. ...	2769	6/11/14	5/12/14, medically unfit ...	Rifleman.	
Nicoll, D. ...	50954	18/8/17	20/8/17, posted 2/8th K.L.R.	Rifleman.	
Nightingale, R. J.	2142	31/8/14	1/5/16, transferred	Rifleman.	
Nimmo, T. ...	242208	21/1/16	13/8/17, wounded	Rifleman.	

NAME.	REGTL. NO.	DATE OF JOINING.	DATE OF LEAVING WITH CAUSE.	HIGHEST RANK.	HONOURS OR AWARDS.
Niven, H. ...	242418	21/3/16	30/7/17, invalided to England	Rifleman.	
Nixon, D. J. ...	2464	14/9/14	16/8/15,† transferred ...	Rifleman.	
Nixon, W. J. ...	16983	27/6/18	22/1/19, demobilized	L./Corpl.	
Noakes, A. ...	39260	24/8/17	26/3/19, demobilized ...	Rifleman.	
✠Noble, F. ...	86185	27/5/18	17/9/18, died of wounds ...	Rifleman.	
Noble, H. ...	50955	18/8/17	20/8/17, posted 2/8th K.L.R.	Rifleman.	
Noble, J. ...	201741	8/7/17	3/11/17, wounded	Rifleman.	
Nolan, J. ...	12687	27/6/18	5/2/19, demobilized	Rifleman.	
Norman, G. ...	2936	11/11/14	12/1/15, transferred ...	Rifleman.	
Norman, E. G. R. ...	241322	3/7/15	11/12/17, commission ...	Sergeant.	
Norman, S. ...	50786	18/8/17	27/9/18, transferred ...	L./Corpl.	
Norman, W. H. ...	2484	16/9/14	23/8/15, transferred ...	Rifleman.	
Norris, T. ...	3057	18/11/14	5/8/15, transferred ...	Rifleman.	
Norris, W. ...	242376	17/3/16	7/11/19, demobilized ...	Rifleman.	
✠Nunns, G. ...	51109	27/5/18	1/9/18, killed in action ...	Rifleman.	
Nuttall, J. W. ...	242251	25/1/16	29/8/18, posted 1st K.L.R. ...	L./Corpl.	
Nuttall, R. ...	204751	14/6/18	26/10/18, wounded	Rifleman.	
Nye, W. E. H. ...	243840	13/10/16	25/10/18, wounded	L./Corpl.	
Oakley, A. ...	108731	28/9/18	2/11/18, sick	Rifleman.	
O'Brien, R. J. ...	241239	15/2/15	29/10/17,† sick	Rifleman.	
O'Brien, S. ...	72544	13/8/17	31/10/17, wounded ...	Rifleman.	
O'Brien, W. ...	204072	3/3/18	5/6/18, sick	Rifleman.	
O'Callaghan, T. ...	242172	20/1/16	24/8/17, wounded ...	Rifleman.	
O'Connor, T. J. ...	1535	27/2/15	26/6/15, transferred ...	Rifleman.	
Oddie, J. A. ...	406046	26/9/18	26/2/19, posted 25th K.L.R.	Rifleman.	
Oddy, C. ...	2261	1/9/14	—/—/14, posted 1/6th K.L.R.	Rifleman.	
✠O'Donnell, C. ...	240942	9/11/14	26/5/18, killed in action ...	L./Corpl.	
O'Donnell, W. ...	240516	31/8/14	—/—/15, transferred ...	Rifleman.	
Ogden, C. ...	36164	24/8/17	26/2/19, posted 13th K.L.R.	Rifleman.	
Ogden, F. ...	88042	28/9/17	27/1/18, sick	Rifleman.	
Ogden, W. ...	82034	24/8/17	28/12/17, sick	Rifleman.	
Ogg, F. G. ...	2695	26/10/14	30/8/15, transferred ...	Rifleman.	
✠Ogilvy, J. ...	57562	13/8/17	1/11/18, died	Rifleman.	
Ogley, H. F. ...	300324	27/5/18	26/1/19, demobilized ...	L./Corpl.	
O'Hara, T. J. ...	53461	28/9/17	26/2/19, posted 25th K.L.R.	Rifleman.	
O'Kane, C. ...	242384	18/3/16	21/7/17, wounded ...	L./Corpl.	
O'Kane, J. H. ...	242227	22/1/16	26/2/19,† posted 25th K.L.R.	L./Corpl.	
Old, A. ...	47756	24/8/17	28/4/18, transferred ...	Rifleman.	
Oldfield, F. ...	21966	22/6/18	22/1/19, demobilized ...	Rifleman.	
Oldfield, J. ...	5232	22/5/16	20/6/18, discharged ...	Rifleman.	
Oliver, J. ...	200997	14/9/18	29/3/19, demobilized ...	Rifleman.	
Ollive, T. R. ...	242391	18/3/16	3/11/17, wounded	Rifleman.	
O'Meara, H. V. ...	3034	16/11/14	10/6/15, commission ...	Rifleman.	
Orchard, G. H. ...	84570	1/2/18	6/7/18, sick	Rifleman.	
Ormandy, S. ...	16234	27/5/18	12/9/18, prisoner of war	Rifleman.	
Orme, A. ...	50788	18/8/17	19/11/17, wounded ...	Rifleman.	
Orme, W. ...	241473	6/8/15	29/3/19, demobilized ...	Rifleman.	
Ormerod, F. ...	243666	6/10/16	6/8/17, invalided to England	Rifleman.	
Orr, T. ...	50956	18/8/17	20/8/17, posted 2/8th K.L.R.	Rifleman.	
Orrell, T. W. ...	241147	30/11/14	8/12/18, sick	L./Corpl.	
Osborne, A. ...	242226	22/1/16	31/7/17, wounded ...	Rifleman.	
Osborne, A. W. ...	241542	6/8/15	10/8/17, invalided to England	Rifleman.	
O'Shea, S. M. ...	242191	21/1/16	—/3/19, posted 25th K.L.R.	A./L./Corpl.	
O'Sullivan, J. ...	48243	24/2/18	24/12/18, sick	Rifleman.	M.M.
Ovenden, C. ...	3208	12/1/15	5/8/15, transferred ...	Rifleman.	
Owen, G. ...	2933	11/11/14	26/6/15, transferred ...	Rifleman.	
Owen, G. E. ...	265950	8/7/17	3/3/19,† demobilized ...	L./Corpl.	

" THE KING'S " (LIVERPOOL REGIMENT)

NAME.	REGTL. NO.	DATE OF JOINING.	DATE OF LEAVING WITH CAUSE.	HIGHEST RANK.	HONOURS OR AWARDS.
Owen, J. ...	3137	4/12/14	26/6/15, transferred ...	Rifleman.	
Owen, J. G.	240502	31/8/14	5/8/17,† invalided to England	Rifleman.	
Owen, O.	4868	17/2/16	5/6/16, transferred ...	Rifleman.	
Owen, W. E.	3117	30/11/14	26/6/15, transferred ...	Rifleman.	
Owens, E. E.	241164	11/12/14	7/8/17, invalided to England	Rifleman.	
Owens, H. O.	240838	8/10/14	30/10/18,† commission	L./Corpl.	
Owens, H. W.	3303	18/3/15	1/5/15, transferred ...	Rifleman.	
Owens, R.	241064	13/11/14	5/8/15, transferred ...	Rifleman.	
Owens, S. N.	3000	13/11/14	5/8/15, transferred ...	L./Corpl.	
Owens, W. E.	2823	9/11/14	23/8/15, transferred ...	Rifleman.	
Owens, W. H.	2347	10/9/14	12/1/15, transferred ...	Rifleman.	
Packwood, W. A.	88259	17/12/17	18/3/18, sick ...	Rifleman.	
Padley, J. S. L. ...	2770	6/11/14	26/6/15, transferred ...	Rifleman.	
Page, G. T.	48339	28/9/18	3/2/19, demobilized ...	Rifleman.	
Paisley, J.	5257	1/6/16	28/2/17, commission	Rifleman	
✠Palmer, H. F. ...	241406	3/7/15	12/8/17,† died of wounds	Rifleman.	
Palmer, W.	50957	18/8/17	20/8/17, posted 2/8th K.L.R.	Rifleman.	
Palmer, W.	51745	14/6/18	22/1/19, demobilized	Rifleman.	
Paris, G. ...	53462	28/9/17	15/1/19, demobilized	Rifleman.	
Park, B. ...	243702	9/10/16	—/—/19, transferred...	Rifleman.	
Park, G. ...	17083	27/5/18	20/9/18, wounded ...	Rifleman.	
Park, J. ...	241169	22/12/14	2/3/19, demobilized ...	L./Corpl.	
Parke, J. J.	242425	21/3/16	23/3/18, transferred ...	Rifleman.	
✠Parker, A. ...	241163	11/12/14	1/6/17, killed in action	Rifleman.	
Parker, J.	241033	11/11/14	15/7/17, invalided to England	Rifleman.	
Parker, J.	3700	6/8/15	18/3/16, transferred ...	Rifleman.	
Parker, J. H.	2307	10/9/14	12/1/15, transferred ...	A./Sergt.	
Parker, T. P.	3167	26/12/14	26/6/15, transferred ...	Rifleman.	
Parker, W. L.	2352	10/9/14	12/1/15, transferred ...	Rifleman.	
Parkes, J.	240199	23/2/15	8/12/17,† transferred	Rifleman.	
Parkes, J. B.	1441	23/2/15	5/8/15, transferred ...	Rifleman.	
Parkins, J. E.	243716	3/10/16	5/8/17, invalided to England	Rifleman.	
Parkins, J. H.	2879	10/11/14	5/8/15, transferred ...	Rifleman.	
Parkins, R. W. ...	242567	7/6/16	11/7/18, posted 1/6th K.L.R.	Rifleman.	
Parkinson, F. H.	241340	3/7/15	26/8/17, wounded ...	Rifleman.	
Parkinson, H. ...	50797	18/8/17	16/1/18, sick ...	Rifleman.	
Parrington, E. ...	3093	23/11/14	5/8/15, transferred ...	Rifleman.	
Parrington, E. R.	2520	18/9/14	12/1/15, transferred ...	A./Corpl.	
✠Parry, A. V. ...	405855	22/6/18	27/9/18, died of wounds	Rifleman.	
Parry, C. J.	2093	31/8/14	—/—/15, transferred	Rifleman.	
Parry, E.	2348	10/9/14	12/1/15, transferred ...	Rifleman.	
Parry, E.	60972	13/8/17	25/10/17, sick	Rifleman.	
Parry, G.	242431	22/3/16	26/2/18, discharged ...	Rifleman.	
Parry, G. V. E. ...	2625	6/10/14	26/6/15, transferred ...	Rifleman.	
Parry, H.	242200	21/1/16	15/8/17, wounded ...	Rifleman.	
Parry, H. E.	241868	5/5/17	20/5/17, transferred ...	Rifleman.	
Parry, H. L.	2566	22/9/14	18/10/16,† transferred	Rifleman.	
Parry, H. V.	2645	9/10/14	13/9/15, transferred ...	Rifleman.	
Parry, J. H.	2615	30/9/14	12/1/15, transferred ...	Rifleman.	
Parry, R. A.	242432	22/3/16	27/8/17, wounded ...	Rifleman.	
Parry, S.	49172	24/8/17	26/2/19, posted 25th K.L.R.	Rifleman.	
Parry, T.	1206	27/2/15	28/6/15, transferred ...	A./Corpl.	
Parry, T. L.	241027	11/11/14	1/10/17,† wounded ...	Rifleman.	
Parry, T. S.	2069	31/8/14	—/—/15, transferred	Rifleman.	
Parry, W.	50958	18/8/17	20/8/18, posted 2/8th K.L.R.	Rifleman.	
Parry, W. H.	241178	4/1/15	8/2/18, wounded ...	Rifleman.	
Parslow, C.	2906	10/11/14	12/1/15 transferred ...	Rifleman.	

z

NAME.	REGTL. NO.	DATE OF JOINING.	DATE OF LEAVING WITH CAUSE.	HIGHEST RANK.	HONOURS OR AWARDS.
Parsons, D. ...	50959	18/8/17	20/8/17, posted 2/8th K.L.R.	Rifleman.	
Parsons, L. A. ...	3216	15/1/14	16/8/18,† sick	Rifleman.	
Partington, R. T.	241499	6/8/15	25/10/17,† sick	Rifleman.	
Partridge, H. H.	2649	10/10/14	27/10/14, medically unfit ...	Rifleman.	
Partridge, S. V. ...	2912	10/11/14	26/6/15, transferred ...	Rifleman.	
Pasquill, H. ...	203966	1/2/18	7/6/18, sick	Rifleman.	
Passmore, W. C.	3213	13/1/15	5/8/15, transferred ...	Rifleman.	
Patching, F. N. ...	88499	19/9/17	29/1/19, demobilized ...	Rifleman.	
Paterson, F. W.	2984	13/11/14	26/6/15, transferred	Rifleman.	
Paterson, G. ...	241179	4/1/15	22/5/17, transferred	Rifleman.	
Paterson, R. A. ...	240374	23/2/15	13/8/17,† invalided to England	Rifleman.	
Patterson, A. C.	21596	14/6/18	20/7/18, wounded	Rifleman.	
Patterson, G. ...	241535	6/8/15	16/8/17, wounded	Rifleman.	
Patterson, E. H.	241130	24/11/14	11/2/19, demobilized ...	Sergeant.	M.S.M.
Payne, A. S. ...	3101	24/11/14	26/6/15, transferred ...	Rifleman.	
Paynter, W. ...	3067	18/11/14	5/8/15, transferred ...	Rifleman.	
Payne, J. ...	241080	14/11/14	10/2/19, demobilized ...	Sergeant.	M.S.M., Belg. C. de G.
Peach, G. B. ...	50792	18/8/17	21/10/17, sick	Rifleman.	
Pearce, J. ...	57617	7/3/18	21/2/19, demobilized ...	A./L./Cpl.	
Pearce, R. G. ...	2174	31/8/14	30/5/15, commission ...	Rifleman.	
Pearson, E. ...	241364	6/8/15	2/11/17,† wounded	Rifleman.	
Pearson, F. ...	88099	29/9/17	15/2/19, sick	Corporal	M.M.
Pearson, F. J. ...	241255	2/3/15	16/5/18, wounded ...	Rifleman.	
Pearson, J. ...	242513	20/11/17	9/2/18, sick	Rifleman.	
✠Pearson, J. L. ...	57821	27/5/18	23/6/18, killed in action ...	Rifleman.	
✠Pearson, J. M. ...	241262	15/3/15	30/10/17, killed in action ...	Rifleman.	
Pearson, W. ...	49779	27/6/18	12/2/19, demobilized ...	Rifleman.	
Pearson, W. ...	242304	25/2/16	17/7/17, wounded	Rifleman.	
Peck, C. E. ...	2420	11/9/14	28/6/15,† commission ...	A./Corpl.	
Peck, S.	2068	31/8/14	—/—/15, transferred ...	Rifleman.	
Pedon, D. ...	2035	23/2/15	26/6/15, transferred ...	Rifleman.	
Peel, W. ...	242213	22/1/16	5/8/17, invalided to England	Rifleman.	
Peers, H. A. ...	202315	1/2/18	27/6/18, wounded	Rifleman.	
Peet, G. ...	51918	27/6/18	16/8/18, transferred	Rifleman.	
Peet, H. ...	243708	9/10/16	12/7/17, transferred	Rifleman.	
Pegg, J. ...	88500	19/9/17	25/4/18, sick	Rifleman.	
Penborthy, T. ...	72441	24/8/17	16/9/18, wounded	Rifleman.	
Pender, —. ...	15	14/11/14	9/3/15, medically unfit ...	A./Col./Sgt.	
Pendleton, H. ...	269790	27/8/17	20/5/18, transferred	Rifleman.	
Pendleton, J. ...	202869	1/2/18	18/1/19, demobilized ...	Rifleman.	
Penketh, J. ...	3211	13/1/15	4/5/16, transferred	Rifleman.	
Pennington, C. F.	241306	22/4/15	21/1/18, commission	C.S.M.	
Pennington, N. ...	72478	13/8/17	19/6/18, wounded	Rifleman	M.M.
Percy, W. H. ...	3009	14/11/14	5/8/15, transferred	Rifleman.	
Perry, T. C. ...	242288	17/2/16	8/8/17, invalided to England	Rifleman.	
Peters, J. H. ...	2867	10/11/14	16/6/15, transferred	L./Corpl.	
Peters, W. ...	29754	24/2/18	2/10/18, wounded	Rifleman.	
✠Peterson, C. W. ...	88096	29/9/17	29/10/18, killed in action ...	Rifleman.	
Peterson, E. ...	240424	23/10/14	10/8/17, wounded	L./Corpl.	
Petherbridge, A. T.	1674	23/10/14	26/6/15, transferred	A./Sergt.	
Petrie, J. L. ...	3449	3/7/15	16/8/16, transferred	Rifleman.	
Philips, T. H. ...	240615	1/9/14	—/—/15, transferred ...	Rifleman.	
Phillingham, J. ...	2633	6/10/14	12/1/15, transferred	Rifleman.	
Phillips, F. A. ...	50796	18/8/17	26/2/19, posted 13th K.L.R.	Rifleman.	
Phillips, H. ...	2617	2/10/14	12/1/15, transferred	Rifleman.	
Phillips, J. E. ...	5269	3/6/16	18/10/16, transferred ...	Rifleman.	
Phillips, T. ...	2350	10/9/14	—/—/15, posted 1/6th K.L.R.	Rifleman.	

NAME.	REGTL. NO.	DATE OF JOINING.	DATE OF LEAVING WITH CAUSE.	HIGHEST RANK.	HONOURS OR AWARDS.
Phillips, W. ...	54493	13/8/17	15/2/18, sick	Rifleman.	
Phillips, W. R. ...	2306	10/9/14	—/—/15, posted 1/6th K.L.R.	Rifleman.	
Phipps, G. ...	241140	30/11/14	24/9/17,† commission ...	Sergeant.	
Pickavance, T. ...	88257	17/12/17	7/9/18, wounded	Rifleman.	
Pickering, G. ...	16838	7/3/18	3/2/19, demobilized	Corporal.	
Pickering, H. ...	242570	8/6/16	17/6/17, wounded	Rifleman.	
Pickering, R. J.	3016	14/11/14	26/6/15, transferred	Rifleman.	
Pickup, G. W. ...	242262	26/1/16	3/10/18, wounded	Rifleman.	
Pickup, H. ...	88145	11/10/17	8/2/18, sick	Rifleman.	
Pickup, H. T. ...	241227	3/2/15	26/2/18,† sick	Rifleman.	
Pidgeon, J. G. ...	2263	1/9/14	23/10/14, commission ...	Rifleman.	
Pierce, C. H. ...	1270	27/2/15	26/6/15, transferred	Rifleman.	
Pierce, F. C. ...	3256	9/2/15	16/8/15,† transferred ...	Rifleman.	
Pierpoint, W. ...	61052	13/8/17	17/4/18, transferred ...	Rifleman.	
Pighills, W. A. ...	241512	6/8/15	2/8/17, wounded	Rifleman.	
Pilkington, E. ...	241059	13/11/14	29/8/18, posted 1st K.L.R.	Rifleman.	
✠Pilkington, E. ...	269975	27/5/18	21/10/18, killed in action ...	Rifleman.	
Pilkington, F. W.	203926	1/2/18	14/3/18, transferred ...	Rifleman.	
Pilkington, J. ...	5252	30/5/16	18/10/16, transferred ...	Rifleman.	
Pilkington, J. ...	204021	1/2/18	11/2/19, demobilized ...	Rifleman.	
Pilkington, W. M.	3111	26/11/14	4/11/16,† medically unfit ...	Rifleman.	
Pilling, J. F. ...	3292	8/3/15	23/9/16,† transferred ...	Rifleman.	
✠Pimlott, C. E. ...	50798	18/8/17	1/9/18, killed in action ...	Rifleman.	
Pinches, J. ...	2678	19/10/14	12/1/15, transferred	Rifleman.	
Pinder, W. ...	32881	1/2/18	3/4/19, transferred	Sergeant.	
Pinder, H. ...	50960	18/8/17	20/8/17, posted 2/8th K.L.R.	Rifleman.	
Piper, J. ...	405320	27/6/18	5/9/18, wounded	Rifleman.	
Pitchford, F. ...	50793	18/8/17	26/2/19, posted 25th K.L.R.	Rifleman.	
Plant, W. G. ...	240221	8/7/17	8/1/18, sick	L./Sergt.	
Platt, R. ...	1742	23/10/14	12/1/15, transferred	Rifleman.	
Platt, R. ...	300583	27/5/18	6/9/18, wounded	Rifleman.	
Platten, D. E. ...	2196	1/9/14	6/5/17, medically unfit ...	Rifleman.	
Plummer, J. ...	15385	27/6/18	17/2/19, demobilized ...	Rifleman.	
Pollard, — ...	2594	1/10/14	16/6/15, transferred ...	Rifleman.	
Pollitt, J. T. ...	201109	5/4/18	22/5/19, demobilized ...	C.Q.M.S.	
Pomford, E. ...	203215	6/6/18	28/3/19, posted 13th K.L.R.	Rifleman.	
Pomfret, W. ...	50794	18/8/17	26/2/19, posted 25th K.L.R.	Rifleman.	
Poole, H. ...	88108	5/10/17	28/5/18,† sick	Rifleman.	
Poole, T. ...	201217	1/2/18	15/7/18, sick	Rifleman.	
Poole, W. ...	50961	18/8/17	20/8/17, posted 2/8th K.L.R.	Rifleman.	
Pope, W. ...	50962	18/8/17	20/8/17, posted 2/8th K.L.R.	Rifleman.	
Pope, W. H. ...	1607	23/10/14	26/6/15, transferred	Rifleman.	
Porritt, J. E. ...	63733	13/8/17	29/3/18, sick	Rifleman.	
Portener, W. ...	12150	28/9/18	17/11/18, transferred ...	Rifleman.	
Porter, N. ...	2997	13/11/14	26/6/15, transferred ...	Rifleman.	
Porter, P. F. ...	260137	20/9/17	5/2/18, sick	Rifleman.	
Porter, T. ...	307974	28/9/18	22/5/19, demobilized ...	L./Corpl.	
Porter, T. B. ...	2221	1/9/14	—/—/14, posted 1/6th K.L.R.	Rifleman.	
Potter, A. ...	240754	11/9/14	29/6/17, wounded ...	A./Corpl.	
Potter, F. ...	95659	17/4/18	3/2/19, demobilized	Rifleman.	
Potter, G. A. ...	240663	10/9/14	2/11/17, wounded	Rifleman.	
Potter, H. ...	88501	19/9/17	26/2/19, posted 25th K.L.R.	Rifleman.	
Potter, J. ...	33063	24/8/17	14/6/18, posted 1/5th K.L.R.	Rifleman.	
Potter, J. C. ...	2353	10/9/14	12/1/15, transferred	Rifleman.	
Poulson, W. H. ...	2684	20/10/14	23/8/15, commission ...	Rifleman.	
✠Pounder, J. ...	50799	18/8/17	29/10/17, killed in action ...	Rifleman.	
Povey, A. ...	80970	24/8/17	25/12/17, sick	Rifleman.	
Powell, A. H. ...	50789	18/8/17	26/2/19, posted 25th K.L.R.	Rifleman.	

NAME.		REGTL. NO.	DATE OF JOINING.	DATE OF LEAVING WITH CAUSE.		HIGHEST RANK.	HONOURS OR AWARDS.
Powell, C.	...	50790	18/8/17	9/11/17, wounded	... ...	Rifleman.	
Powell, F. W.		242429	22/3/16	1/1/17, wounded	... ...	Sergeant.	M.M.
Power, W.	...	242264	26/1/16	10/8/17, invalided to England		Rifleman.	
Pownall, J.		240026	23/2/15	2/6/17, transferred	... ...	Q.M.S.	
Pownall, E.		2511	17/9/14	21/7/15, commission	...	Rifleman.	
Pragnell, R.	...	88044	28/9/17	19/10/17, sick	... ...	Rifleman.	
Preece, H.		50791	18/8/17	26/2/19, posted 13th K.L.R.		Rifleman.	
Prendergast, F.	...	241343	5/5/17	23/7/17, posted 1/6th K.L.R.		Rifleman.	
Prendeville, F.	...	2006	23/2/15	26/6/15, transferred	...	Rifleman.	
Prescott, N.	...	265969	27/6/18	11/1/19, demobilized		Rifleman.	
Preston, B.	...	88111	5/10/17	13/12/18, demobilized	...	Rifleman.	
Preston, B. F.	...	2911	10/11/14	26/6/15, transferred	...	Rifleman.	
Preston, F.		240997	10/11/14	15/3/17, invalided to England		L./Corpl.	
Price, A.	...	240918	6/11/14	22/1/19, demobilized	...	Sergeant.	
Price, C. E.	...	240662	10/9/14	30/6/17,† transferred	...	Rifleman.	
Price, F.	...	240826	5/10/14	1/8/17, wounded	...	Rifleman.	
Prince, F. J.		2688	20/10/14	12/1/15, transferred	...	Rifleman.	
✠Prior, H.	...	25623	27/6/18	29/9/18, killed in action	...	Rifleman	Chevalier de l'Ordre de Leopold II.
Pritchard, A. B.		240776	23/9/14	30/6/17,† invalided to England		Rifleman.	
Pritchard, C. T.		201806	8/7/17	10/8/17, invalided to England		Rifleman.	
Pritchard, P. G.		2675	17/10/14	5/8/15, transferred	...	Rifleman.	
Pritchard, R.	...	3064	19/11/14	26/6/15, transferred	...	Rifleman.	
✠Probert, W.	...	45472	13/8/17	12/3/18, killed in action	...	L./Corpl.	
Procter, E.		50881	14/3/18	28/6/18, posted 12th K.L.R.		Rifleman.	
Prosser, A. G.		88502	19/9/17	8/11/18, sick	... ...	Rifleman.	
Proudfoot, J.		243776	10/10/16	9/9/17, posted 1/9th K.L.R.		Rifleman.	
Pryce, C.	...	2516	17/9/14	12/1/15, transferred	...	A./Sergt.	
Pughe, W. C.	...	50795	18/8/17	26/2/19, posted 25th K.L.R.		Rifleman.	
Pulford, G. E.	...	241540	6/8/15	3/3/19, demobilized	...	L./Corpl.	
Pullen, R. H.	...	240147	23/2/15	30/6/17,† transferred	...	Rifleman.	
Purdon, C. H.	...	240550	31/8/14	—/—/15, transferred	...	Rifleman.	
Purdon, H. R.	...	240548	31/8/14	31/7/17, commission	...	Rifleman.	
Pye, J. E.	...	242547	30/5/16	7/8/17, wounded	...	Rifleman.	
Pye, T.	...	72495	13/8/17	19/11/18, sick	... ...	Rifleman.	
Pyke, H.	...	2701	27/10/14	5/8/15, transferred	...	Rifleman.	
Quarrie, R. H.	...	2354	10/9/14	12/1/15, transferred	...	Rifleman.	
Quayle, A. E.	...	13186	14/9/18	22/1/19, demobilized		Rifleman.	
Quilliam, R. P.	...	2284	2/9/15	—/—/15, transferred	...	Rifleman.	
Quinlan, E.		35832	7/3/18	29/3/19, demobilized		Rifleman.	
Quinn, J.	...	88504	19/9/17	9/5/18, sick	... ...	Rifleman.	
Quirk, S.	...	241036	12/11/14	9/6/17, wounded	...	L./Corpl.	
Rabbitt, T.	...	5019	18/3/16	18/10/16, transferred	...	Rifleman.	
Radley, A.		242285	17/2/16	18/7/17, commission	...	Rifleman.	
Rae, W.	...	242346	8/3/16	25/5/17, wounded	...	Rifleman.	
Rafferty, B.	...	242188	1/2/16	5/8/17, invalided to England		Rifleman.	
Raglan, C.		1635	27/2/15	5/2/16, transferred	...	Rifleman.	
Railton, S. C.		241329	3/7/15	15/4/18, transferred	...	Rifleman.	
Raine, T. W.		53470	28/9/17	14/2/19, demobilized	...	Rifleman.	
Rainsford, J.		270088	27/5/18	11/1/19, demobilized		Rifleman.	
Raisman, L.		242444	23/3/16	25/4/18, sick	... ...	Rifleman.	
Raley, C.		2839	9/11/14	12/1/15, transferred	...	Rifleman.	
Ramage, A. W.	...	50800	18/8/17	13/5/18, sick	... ...	Rifleman.	
Ramsay, W.	...	105525	12/7/18	20/8/18, sick	... ...	Rifleman.	
Ramsden, J.	...	27090	27/5/18	5/3/19, demobilized	...	Rifleman.	

NAME.	REGTL. NO.	DATE OF JOINING.	DATE OF LEAVING WITH CAUSE.	HIGHEST RANK.	HONOURS OR AWARDS.
Ramsden, J. ...	50833	18/8/17	19/5/18, sick	Rifleman.	
Rance, F. ...	24773	7/3/18	15/7/18, transferred	L./Corpl.	
Randall, H. T. ...	242572	9/6/16	2/7/17, wounded	Rifleman.	
Randell, R. ...	12144	24/2/18	26/5/18, sick	Rifleman.	
Rankin, A. ...	240048	27/2/15	15/3/19,† demobilized ...	Rifleman.	
Rankin, S. ...	1915	23/2/15	18/3/16, transferred ...	Rifleman.	
Rashbrook, A. R. ...	2540	21/9/14	12/1/15, transferred ...	Rifleman.	
Rashbrooke, W. E.	241365	3/7/15	21/5/18, sick	Corporal.	
Ratchford, T. B.	6565	10/10/16	30/10/16, transferred ...	Rifleman.	
Ratchford, W. ...	46709	11/3/18	21/5/18, sick	Rifleman.	
Ratcliffe, P. J. ...	241162	10/12/14	21/8/17,† wounded	Rifleman.	
Rawlinson, J. W.	160	23/10/14	26/6/15, transferred ...	A./Corpl.	
Raws, H. G. ...	240955	9/11/14	7/1/19, demobilized	L./Corpl.	
Raws, W. ...	2235	1/9/14	—/—/14, transferred ...	Rifleman.	
Rawstron, L. V.	59053	1/2/18	26/2/19, posted 13th K.L.R.	Rifleman.	
Ray, H. C. ...	5223	22/5/16	18/8/16, transferred ...	Rifleman.	
Raymond, W. D.	2080	31/8/14	5/2/16, commission ...	Rifleman.	
Raynor, J. A. ...	243850	16/10/16	9/8/17, wounded	Rifleman.	
Raynsford, F. ...	50802	18/8/17	28/3/19, posted 13th K.L.R.	Rifleman.	
Read, W. H. ...	2616	2/10/14	26/6/15, transferred ...	Rifleman.	
✠Read, W. O. ...	53615	24/8/17	27/6/18, killed in action	Rifleman.	
Readdie, W. ...	240753	11/9/14	2/7/17,† wounded	L./Corpl.	
Reade, A. L. ...	242451	24/3/16	3/2/19, demobilized	Corporal.	
Readman, E. ...	63735	1/2/18	4/3/19, demobilized	Rifleman.	
Reamsbottom, N. S.	2258	1/9/14	30/12/15, commission ...	Rifleman.	
Redfern, J. A. ...	332960	27/8/17	21/7/19, transferred ...	Rifleman.	
Redmayne, R. ...	50963	18/8/17	20/8/17, posted 2/8th K.L.R.	Rifleman.	
Redmond, S. E. B.	3127	1/12/14	15/5/17, transferred	A./Sergt.	
Redmond, J. D.	2424	11/9/14	12/1/15, transferred ...	Rifleman.	
Reed, T.	243757	10/10/16	15/5/17, transferred	Rifleman.	
Reed, W. ...	241210	18/1/15	2/8/17, invalided to England	L./Corpl.	
Rees, A. J. ...	2355	10/9/14	4/5/16, transferred	Rifleman.	
Rees, L. J. ...	1807	23/10/14	5/8/15, transferred	Rifleman.	
Reeve, J. ...	50964	18/8/17	20/8/17, posted 2/8th K.L.R.	Rifleman.	
Reeve, R. ...	88048	28/9/17	29/3/18, transferred ...	Rifleman.	
Reeves, A. ...	22229	7/3/18	29/8/18, posted 1st K.L.R. ...	Rifleman.	
Reeves, D. ...	64778	13/8/17	25/10/18, wounded	Rifleman.	
Reeve, J. ...	53469	28/9/17	21/7/19, transferred ...	Rifleman.	
Reeves, J. ...	91235	26/2/18	29/5/18, transferred ...	Rifleman.	
Reeves, W. H. ...	3012	14/11/14	26/6/15, transferred ...	Rifleman.	
Regan, A. ...	637	23/2/15	26/6/15, transferred ...	Rifleman.	
Regan, F. ...	240106	23/2/15	15/3/19,† demobilized ...	Rifleman.	
Regan, W. A. ...	200103	8/7/17	10/7/18, commission	Corporal.	
Reid, A.	49093	27/6/18	11/2/19, demobilized ...	Rifleman.	
Reid, J. D. ...	240992	10/11/14	28/12/17,† wounded	Rifleman.	
Reid, P.	2492	16/9/14	26/6/15, transferred ...	Rifleman.	
Reilly, H. ...	25484	27/5/18	5/9/18, wounded	Rifleman.	
Relton, J. ...	16869	27/6/18	12/1/19, sick	Rifleman.	
Rennison, H. W.	2476	11/9/14	20/7/15, transferred ...	A./Sergt.	
Renshaw, J. ...	405900	10/7/18	18/7/18, transferred ...	Rifleman.	
Resnik, J. ...	242305	25/2/16	5/8/17, invalided to England	Rifleman.	
Rettie, C. ...	156	23/2/15	26/6/15, transferred	Rifleman.	
Revill, M. ...	2291	4/9/14	13/4/16, discharged	Rifleman.	
Reynolds, H. R....	1806	23/10/14	26/6/15, transferred ...	Rifleman.	
Rhodes, A. ...	88222	8/11/17	26/2/19, posted 25th K.L.R.	Rifleman.	
Rhodes, L. ...	5030	20/3/16	15/12/16, transferred ...	Rifleman.	
Richards, D. ...	2971	12/11/14	5/8/15, transferred	Rifleman.	
Richards, J. B. ...	2918	10/11/14	26/6/15, transferred ...	Rifleman.	

HISTORY OF THE 2/6TH (RIFLE) BATTALION

NAME.	REGTL. NO.	DATE OF JOINING.	DATE OF LEAVING WITH CAUSE.	HIGHEST RANK.	HONOURS OR AWARDS.
Richards, F. P. ...	2994	12/11/14	26/6/15, transferred	Rifleman.	
Richards, J. E. ...	241281	1/4/15	5/8/17, invalided to England	A./Sergt.	
Richards, R. ...	6456	6/10/16	12/11/16, transferred ...	Rifleman.	
Richards, T. ...	240930	7/11/14	26/2/19, sick	Rifleman.	
✠Richards, T. A. ...	242246	25/1/16	15/10/18, died of wounds ...	Corporal.	
Richards, W. ...	240952	9/11/14	29/8/18,† posted 1st K.L.R.	Rifleman.	
Richardson, L. T. ...	88169	20/10/17	—/3/19, posted 25th K.L.R.	Rifleman.	
Richardson, R. ...	380880	14/3/18	27/5/18, sick	Rifleman.	
Richardson, S. ...	243700	9/10/16	7/8/17, invalided to England	Rifleman.	
Riches, J. ...	50269	27/5/18	28/3/19, posted 13th K.L.R.	Rifleman.	
Richmond, H. R. ...	2567	22/9/14	12/1/15, transferred	Rifleman.	
Rickard, — ...	2357	10/9/14	12/1/15, transferred	Rifleman.	
Riddell, J. ...	2737	2/11/14	26/6/15, transferred	Rifleman.	
Riddick, R. ...	2376	10/9/14	23/3/16, transferred	Rifleman.	
Riddick, T. ...	2105	31/8/14	8/11/15, discharged	Rifleman.	
Ridgeway, G. H. ...	90442	23/2/18	26/2/18, transferred	Rifleman.	
Riding, J. ...	242529	24/5/16	26/1/19, demobilized ...	Rifleman.	
Rigby, G. ...	2360	10/9/14	12/1/15, transferred	Rifleman.	
Rigby, S. ...	243793	10/10/16	9/7/17, wounded	Rifleman.	
Rigby, W. ...	2592	1/10/14	16/8/15, transferred	Rifleman.	
Rigby, W. ...	1440	23/2/15	23/11/15, transferred ...	Rifleman.	
✠Rigby, W. ...	109003	28/9/18	24/10/18, died of wounds ...	Rifleman.	
Riley, A. ...	243709	9/10/16	20/1/19, demobilized ...	Rifleman.	
Riley, F. ...	203031	1/2/18	13/4/19, demobilized ...	Rifleman.	
Riley, F. ...	242211	22/1/16	8/8/17, invalided to England	Rifleman.	
Riley, J. A. ...	109099	28/9/18	17/11/18, transferred ...	Rifleman.	
Riley, R. ...	88505	19/9/17	28/11/17, sick	Rifleman.	
Riley, S. A. ...	88506	19/9/17	5/12/18, demobilized ...	Rifleman.	
Riley, T. A. ...	2986	13/11/14	5/8/15, transferred	Rifleman.	
Riley, W. ...	50270	14/6/18	17/2/19, demobilized ...	Rifleman.	
Rimmer, A. ...	58675	14/6/18	26/1/19, demobilized ...	Rifleman.	
Rimmer, C. ...	241541	6/8/15	21/7/17,† wounded	Rifleman.	
Rimmer, E. ...	64848	13/8/17	30/1/19, demobilized ...	Rifleman.	
Rimmer, E. J. ...	242320	1/3/16	21/3/17, discharged	Rifleman.	
Rimmer, E. ...	88251	12/11/17	26/2/19, posted 25th K.L.R.	Rifleman.	
Rimmer, G. ...	308599	27/5/18	28/3/19, posted 13th K.L.R.	Rifleman.	
Rimmer, H. ...	2689	20/10/14	22/8/16, transferred	Rifleman.	
Rimmer, H. ...	84853	1/3/18	26/1/19, sick	Rifleman.	
Rimmer, J. ...	332120	22/6/18	14/2/19, demobilized ...	Rifleman.	
Rimmer, L. ...	2979	14/11/14	26/6/15, transferred	Rifleman.	
Rimmer, P. ...	242411	21/3/16	5/8/17, invalided to England	Rifleman.	
Rimmer, W. H. ...	1624	27/2/15	26/6/15, transferred	Rifleman.	
Rishton, C. ...	242241	22/1/16	1/3/18, wounded	Rifleman.	
Rivett, W. E. ...	88507	19/9/17	29/8/18, posted 1st K.L.R. ...	Rifleman.	
Roach, G. F. ...	88104	29/9/17	26/6/19, transferred	Rifleman.	
✠Roache, D. ...	24458	24/8/17	7/9/17, died of wounds ...	Rifleman.	
Robb, W. J. ...	241515	6/8/15	9/8/17, wounded	Rifleman.	
Robbins, H. J. ...	241298	19/4/15	30/6/17, transferred	Rifleman.	
Roberts, A. ...	17455	14/6/18	7/11/18, sick	Rifleman.	
Roberts, A. ...	241483	6/8/15	12/9/17,† posted 1/6th K.L.R.	Rifleman.	
Roberts, A. S. ...	2783	7/11/14	28/6/15,† medically unfit ...	Rifleman.	
✠Roberts, C. ...	242542	26/5/16	1/5/18, killed in action ...	Sergeant.	
Roberts, C. H. ...	242216	22/1/16	14/9/17, transferred	Rifleman.	
Roberts, D. ...	1613	27/2/15	23/11/15,† transferred ...	Rifleman.	
Roberts, D. E. ...	381215	27/2/18	26/2/19, posted 25th K.L.R.	Rifleman.	
Roberts, D. G. ...	2605	29/9/14	25/7/17, commission	A./Sergt.	
Roberts, E. ...	2169	31/8/14	—/—/15, transferred	Rifleman.	
Roberts, E. ...	201070	14/3/18	9/6/18, sick	Corporal.	

" THE KING'S " (LIVERPOOL REGIMENT)

NAME.	REGTL. NO.	DATE OF JOINING.	DATE OF LEAVING WITH CAUSE.	HIGHEST RANK.	HONOURS OR AWARDS.
Roberts, F. G. ...	240639	10/9/14	10/9/17, commission ...	Sergeant.	
Roberts, G. ...	241060	12/11/14	28/7/17,† wounded	Rifleman.	
Roberts, G. H. ...	242248	25/1/16	12/5/18, sick	Rifleman.	
Roberts, H. ...	1474	27/2/15	26/6/15, transferred ...	Rifleman.	
Roberts, H. ...	240669	10/9/14	3/3/19, demobilized	Rifleman.	
Roberts, H. ...	52450	14/6/18	7/9/18, wounded	Rifleman.	
Roberts, H. ...	242390	18/3/16	5/3/17, invalided to England	Rifleman.	
Roberts, H. B. ...	2058	31/8/14	8/4/15, discharged	Rifleman.	
Roberts, J. ...	243679	6/10/16	10/8/17, wounded	Rifleman.	
Roberts, J. G. ...	2704	28/10/14	12/1/15, transferred ...	Rifleman.	
Roberts, J. T. ...	1804	23/2/15	26/6/15, transferred ...	Rifleman.	
Roberts, J. W. ...	88508	19/9/17	12/1/19, sick	Rifleman.	
Roberts, N. P. ...	2698	26/10/14	16/6/15, transferred ...	Rifleman.	
Roberts, O. E. ...	240996	10/11/14	29/8/18, posted 1/6th K.L.R.	L./Corpl.	
Roberts, P. ...	24261	27/5/18	22/10/18, posted 13th K.L.R.	Rifleman.	
Roberts, P. J. E.	2415	11/9/14	12/1/15, transferred ...	Rifleman.	
Roberts, R. F. ...	202896	14/6/18	20/9/18, wounded	Rifleman.	
Roberts, R. L. ...	2486	16/9/14	12/1/15, transferred	A./Sergt.	
Roberts, R. N. ...	242453	24/3/16	31/1/19, demobilized ...	L./Corpl.	
Roberts, T. ...	1438	23/2/15	2/6/15, medically unfit ...	Rifleman.	
✠ Roberts, T. ...	242298	17/2/16	30/3/17, died of wounds ...	Rifleman.	
Roberts, T. ...	203949	5/2/18	29/8/18, posted 1st K.L.R. ...	Rifleman.	
Roberts, T. A. ...	2111	31/8/14	20/9/15, commission ...	Rifleman.	
Roberts, T. C. ...	2677	19/10/14	23/2/15, transferred ...	Rifleman.	
Roberts, T. E. ...	2604	29/9/14	12/1/15, transferred	Rifleman.	
Roberts, T. M. ...	240834	6/10/14	1/9/17,† posted 1/7th K.L.R.	Sergeant.	
Roberts, W. ...	2150	31/8/14	29/11/15, commission ...	Rifleman.	
✠ Roberts, W. E. ...	240819	28/9/14	30/10/17, killed in action ...	A./Sergt.	
Roberts, W. H. ...	2277	1/9/14	25/9/15, commission ...	Rifleman.	
Roberts, W. N. ...	2458	12/9/14	12/1/15, transferred ...	Rifleman.	
Roberts, W. R. ...	241584	8/7/17	13/9/17, sick	Rifleman.	
Robertson, A. H.	2251	1/9/14	—/—/15, transferred ...	Rifleman.	
Robertson, G. ...	3244	2/2/15	23/8/15, transferred ...	Rifleman.	
Robertson, J. ...	2359	10/9/14	29/11/15, transferred ...	L./Corpl.	
✠ Robertson, J. B.	17937	13/9/18	1/10/18, died of wounds ...	L./Sergt.	
Robertson, W. ...	2124	31/8/14	—/—/15, transferred ...	Rifleman.	
Robinson, A. ...	2172	31/8/14	—/—/15, transferred ...	Rifleman.	
Robinson, B. ...	112719	27/11/18	24/2/19, demobilized ...	Rifleman.	
Robinson, B. W. ...	242245	25/1/16	28/8/17, commission ...	L./Corpl.	
Robinson, C. L. ...	1501	27/2/15	26/6/15, transferred ...	Rifleman.	
Robinson, E. D. ...	1712	23/2/15	26/6/15, transferred ...	Rifleman.	
Robinson, E. R. ...	2400	11/9/14	15/1/15, transferred ...	A./Sergt.	
Robinson, G. E. ...	1567	23/2/15	26/6/15, transferred ...	Rifleman.	
Robinson, H. ...	2595	2/10/14	16/8/15, transferred ...	Rifleman.	
Robinson, H. ...	242374	16/3/16	1/3/17, transferred ...	Rifleman.	
Robinson, H. W. ...	50965	18/8/17	20/8/17, posted 2/8th K.L.R.	Rifleman.	
Robinson, J. ...	2429	11/9/14	5/8/15, transferred ...	Rifleman.	
Robinson, J. ...	50162	24/2/18	18/7/18, sick	Rifleman.	
Robinson, J. ...	241493	6/8/15	28/5/17,† wounded ...	Rifleman.	
Robinson, J. B. ...	241206	18/1/15	1/6/17,† wounded ...	Rifleman.	
Robinson, P. ...	85719	28/9/18	28/3/19, posted 13th K.L.R.	Corporal.	
Robinson, R. ...	269283	27/8/17	3/2/19, demobilized	Rifleman.	
Robinson, R. J. ...	2310	10/9/14	26/6/15, transferred ...	Rifleman.	
Robinson, R. ...	241081	16/11/14	18/6/17, invalided to England	Rifleman.	
Robinson, V. ...	1489	23/2/15	26/6/15, transferred ...	Rifleman.	
Robinson, V. ...	242354	13/3/16	1/3/17, transferred ...	Rifleman.	
Robinson, W. ...	2081	31/8/14	11/8/16, discharged	Rifleman.	
Robinson, W. ...	5220	9/5/16	1/8/16, discharged	Rifleman.	

NAME.	REGTL. NO!	DATE OF JOINING.	DATE OF LEAVING WITH CAUSE.	HIGHEST RANK.	HONOURS OR AWARDS.
Robinson, W. J.	89132	1/6/18	—/4/19, transferred	Rifleman.	
Robinson, W. S.	50801	18/8/17	28/3/19, posted 13th K.L.R.	Rifleman.	
Robson, H.	2581	25/9/14	12/1/15, transferred	Rifleman.	
✠Roby, M. G.	242215	22/1/16	22/6/17, killed in action	Rifleman.	
Roby, W.	242274	28/1/16	14/2/19, demobilized	Rifleman.	
Roche, M.	29651	14/6/18	17/9/18, wounded	Corporal.	
Rodgers, —	2356	10/9/14	5/8/15, transferred	Rifleman.	
Rodwell, G. H.	243785	6/10/16	9/8/17, wounded	Rifleman.	
Roe, T.	240255	23/10/14	29/3/18, transferred	Rifleman.	
Rogers, G.	330914	22/6/18	4/9/18, wounded	Rifleman.	
Rogers, J.	715	23/2/15	26/6/15, transferred	Rifleman.	
Rogers, J.	243834	13/10/16	11/2/19, demobilized	Rifleman.	
✠Rogers, J. E.	90809	7/3/18	17/6/18, killed in action	Rifleman.	
Rogers, W.	1802	23/10/14	26/6/15, transferred	Rifleman.	
Rogers, W. B.	3363	26/4/15	1/5/15, transferred	Rifleman.	
Rogerson, A.	243745	9/10/16	7/8/17, invalided to England	Rifleman.	
Roles, F. G.	242452	24/3/16	30/10/17, commission	Corporal.	
Rome, E. T.	2309	10/9/14	27/10/14, commission	Rifleman.	
Rook, W. H.	51674	27/6/18	11/7/18, commission	Rifleman.	
Roscoe, J. J.	241104	17/11/14	5/2/19, demobilized	A./Sergt.	
✠Rose, W.	88090	29/9/17	1/9/18, killed in action	Rifleman.	
Ross, J.	108955	28/9/18	29/3/19, demobilized	Rifleman.	
Ross, L.	269033	27/8/17	10/10/18, wounded	Rifleman.	
Ross, N. D.	2075	31/8/14	—/—/15, transferred	Rifleman.	
Rossall, J.	243797	11/10/16	15/3/17, transferred	Rifleman.	
Rossiter, J.	725	23/2/15	10/6/15, transferred	L./Sergt.	
Rostron, T. H.	108819	28/9/18	17/2/19, demobilized	Rifleman.	
Rothwell, W. J.	2752	5/11/14	12/1/15, transferred	Rifleman.	
Roughsedge, A.	240962	9/11/14	29/1/19, demobilized	A./C.Q.M.S.	
Roughley, M.	1526	23/2/15	26/6/15, transferred	Rifleman.	
Rowbottom, E.	240365	23/2/15	19/8/17, wounded	Sergeant.	
Rowe, B.	108838	28/9/18	21/7/19, transferred	Rifleman.	
Rowe, C. H.	2726	2/11/14	22/9/15, commission	Rifleman.	
Rowe, J.	3472	6/8/15	9/4/16, transferred	Rifleman.	
Rowe, T.	84595	1/2/18	30/1/19, demobilized	Rifleman.	
Rowlandson, H. C.	241531	6/8/15	18/4/19, transferred	Sergeant.	
Rowlandson, J. H.	2749	4/11/14	17/6/15, transferred	Rifleman.	
Royal, G.	88205	8/11/17	7/2/19, demobilized	Rifleman.	
Royal, J.	88509	19/9/17	6/9/18, wounded	Rifleman.	
✠Royle, J.	50608	14/6/18	13/9/18, died of wounds	Rifleman.	
Royle, —	2398	11/9/14	12/1/15, transferred	Rifleman.	
Royston, J. H.	241004	10/11/14	15/3/19,† demobilized	Rifleman.	
Ruane, J. T.	2945	11/11/14	5/8/15, transferred	Rifleman.	
Ruckley, A.	2868	10/11/14	26/6/15, transferred	Rifleman.	
Rudd, F.	2267	1/9/14	—/—/14, transferred	Rifleman.	
Ruddle, —	2541	21/9/14	12/1/15, transferred	Rifleman.	
Rudkin, —	1969	23/10/14	26/6/15, transferred	Rifleman.	
Rule, W. H.	240184	23/2/15	9/8/17, invalided to England	Corporal.	
Rule, W. S.	2975	12/11/14	26/6/15, transferred	Rifleman.	
Rushton, H. A.	49208	24/2/18	30/9/18, wounded	Rifleman.	
Rushton, W. F.	2878	10/11/14	7/12/14, medically unfit	Rifleman.	
Russell, D.	1301	23/10/14	25/1/15, medically unfit	Rifleman.	
Russell, E. A.	240270	5/5/17	20/5/17, posted 1st K.L.R.	Rifleman.	
Russell, E. F. L.	2232	1/9/14	21/10/15, commission	Rifleman.	
Russell, G.	88510	19/9/17	4/11/17, wounded	Rifleman.	
Russell, J.	6451	6/10/16	3/1/17, sick	Rifleman.	
Russell, J. G.	53463	28/9/17	19/11/17, sick	Rifleman.	
Russell, T.	57581	24/8/17	18/9/18, wounded	Rifleman.	

" THE KING'S " (LIVERPOOL REGIMENT)

NAME.	REGTL. NO.	DATE OF JOINING.	DATE OF LEAVING WITH CAUSE.	HIGHEST RANK.	HONOURS OR AWARDS.
Ryan, J.	38932	24/8/17	12/9/18, wounded	Rifleman.	
Rylands, F. ...	332679	28/9/18	13/1/19, demobilized ...	Rifleman.	
Sachs, R. D. ...	243890	4/8/17	19/8/17, transferred	Rifleman.	
Sadler, W. ...	241215	19/1/15	28/7/17,† wounded	Rifleman.	
Sage, F.	50966	18/8/17	20/8/17, posted 2/8th K.L.R.	Rifleman.	
Salisbury, D. ...	1527	27/2/15	26/6/15, transferred	Rifleman.	
Salt, A.	88266	4/1/18	—/—/19, transferred ...	Rifleman.	
Samways, H. ...	88047	28/9/17	9/4/18, transferred	Rifleman.	
Sanderson, J. ...	50810	18/8/17	26/1/19, demobilized ...	A./L./Corpl.	
✠Sandham, J. B. ...	16940	27/5/18	1/9/18, killed in action ...	Rifleman.	
Sandon, R. ...	240080	23/2/15	15/3/19,† demobilized ...	Rifleman.	
Sankey, J. ...	50967	18/8/17	20/8/17, posted 2/8th K.L.R.	Rifleman.	
Sargeant, E. J. ...	201211	1/2/18	16/10/18, wounded	Rifleman.	
Saunders, H. V.	2363	10/9/14	26/6/15, transferred	Rifleman.	
Saunders, L. ...	50968	18/8/17	20/8/17, posted 2/8th K.L.R.	Rifleman.	
Savage, A. ...	243667	6/10/16	26/2/19, posted 25th K.L.R.	Rifleman.	
Savage, E. D. ...	2270	1/9/14	—/—/14, posted 1/6th K.L.R.	Rifleman.	
Savage, W. ...	241150	2/12/14	10/2/19, demobilized ...	A./Q.M.S.	M.S.M., M. in D.
Saxon, H. ...	49178	4/3/18	5/3/19, demobilized	Rifleman.	
Scaife, J. J. ...	243801	11/10/16	30/9/17, wounded	Rifleman.	
Scanlon, J. ...	331960	22/6/18	25/8/18, transferred	Rifleman.	
Scantlebury, A. ...	2691	22/10/14	12/1/15, transferred	Rifleman.	
Schofield, W. ...	405498	14/5/18	16/10/19, demobilized ...	Rifleman.	
Scholefield, H. W.	2773	6/11/14	12/1/15, transferred	Rifleman.	
Scholes, A. ...	50836	18/8/17	29/8/18, posted 1st K.L.R. ...	Rifleman.	
Scholfield, S. H.	243695	7/10/16	26/5/17, transferred	Rifleman.	
Scoins, A. J. ...	2078	31/8/14	—/—/15, transferred ...	Rifleman.	
Scorgie, C. G. ...	2082	31/8/14	—/—/15, posted 1/6th K.L.R.	Rifleman.	
Scott, C.	50988	18/8/17	20/8/17, posted 2/8th K.L.R.	Rifleman.	
Scott, H. ...	243806	12/10/16	25/8/17, wounded	Rifleman.	
✠Scott, J.	243824	13/10/16	28/9/17, died of wounds ...	Rifleman.	
Scott, J. H. ...	243781	10/10/16	23/10/18,† posted 13th K.L.R.	Rifleman.	
Scott, P. W. ...	2480	11/9/14	12/1/15, transferred	Rifleman.	
Scowcroft, W. H.	65054	13/8/17	21/10/17, sick	Rifleman.	
Scroggie, D. ...	242691	25/5/18	28/3/19, posted 13th K.L.R.	Rifleman.	
Scruby, J. ...	88046	28/9/17	16/4/18, transferred	Rifleman.	
Seafield, T. W. H.	3323	6/4/15	3/12/15, transferred	Rifleman.	
Seaton, H. ...	50969	18/8/17	20/8/17, posted 2/8th K.L.R.	Rifleman.	
Seddon, G. ...	241221	25/1/15	16/5/18, wounded	Rifleman.	
Seddon, T. ...	50805	18/8/17	26/2/19, posted 25th K.L.R.	Rifleman.	
Seery, J. P. ...	241218	22/1/15	21/3/18, transferred	Rifleman.	
Sefton, H. ...	2122	31/8/14	—/—/15, transferred ...	Rifleman.	
✠Sergeant, N. ...	300366	27/5/18	16/6/18, died of wounds ...	Rifleman.	
Serjeant, J. E. ...	241266	22/3/15	14/3/18,† transferred ...	Rifleman.	
Sesson, A. ...	110529	27/11/18	29/3/19, demobilized ...	Rifleman.	
Sexton, W. ...	53464	19/9/17	19/11/17, wounded	Rifleman.	
Shails, A.... ...	50970	18/8/17	20/8/17, posted 2/8th K.L.R.	Rifleman.	
Shakeshaft, T. ...	242357	14/3/16	16/10/18, wounded	Rifleman.	
Shallcross, C. ...	241380	3/7/15	13/5/17,† wounded	L./Corpl.	
Shallcross, T. ...	2673	16/10/14	12/1/15, transferred	Rifleman.	
Shannock, L. ...	2829	9/11/14	26/6/15, transferred	Rifleman.	
Shannon, G. ...	240280	23/2/15	25/5/17, posted 1/6th K.L.R.	Rifleman.	
Sharkey, J. ...	200792	14/9/18	22/5/19, demobilized ...	Rifleman.	
Sharp, C. A. ...	260148	20/9/17	4/3/19, demobilized	L./Corpl.	
Sharp, H. ...	108946	28/9/18	25/10/18, wounded	Rifleman.	
Sharpe, T. ...	201047	1/2/18	1/4/18, transferred	Rifleman.	

NAME.	REGTL. NO.	DATE OF JOINING	DATE OF LEAVING WITH CAUSE.	HIGHEST RANK.	HONOURS OR AWARDS.
Sharpe, W. ...	53597	24/8/17	4/10/18, transferred	Rifleman.	
Sharples, R. ...	77937	24/8/17	9/7/18, transferred ...	Rifleman.	
Sharples, S. E. ...	2179	31/8/14	6/3/15, transferred ...	Rifleman.	
Sharples, W. ...	19636	14/6/18	18/1/19, demobilized ...	Rifleman.	
✠Sharrock, J. ...	88254	5/12/17	18/12/17, died of wounds ...	Rifleman.	
Shaw, A. N. ...	2365	10/9/14	20/12/15, commission ...	Rifleman.	
Shaw, B. ...	53465	28/9/17	26/3/19, transferred ...	Rifleman.	
Shaw, C. C. ...	2735	2/11/14	23/9/16, commission ...	Rifleman.	
Shaw, E. C. ...	72510	13/8/17	30/1/19, demobilized ...	Rifleman.	
Shaw, G. ...	242632	5/5/17	20/5/17, transferred ...	Rifleman.	
Shaw, J.	204071	1/2/18	11/2/19, demobilized ...	Rifleman.	
Shaw, J. ...	240855	16/10/14	15/10/18, sick ...	Rifleman.	
Shaw, J. H. ...	243842	14/10/16	3/8/17, wounded ...	Rifleman.	
Shaw, T.	243849	16/10/16	15/8/17, posted 2/5th K.L.R.	Rifleman.	
Shaw, T. W. ...	240985	10/11/14	20/8/18, sick	Sergeant.	
Shaw, W. ...	203270	25/2/18	3/12/18, transferred ...	Rifleman.	
Shearer, W. ...	50834	18/8/17	10/11/19, demobilized ...	Rifleman.	
Sheen, J. ...	2487	15/9/14	18/3/16, transferred	Rifleman.	
Shepherd, F. ...	1620	23/2/15	26/6/15, transferred	Rifleman.	
Shepherd, R. B. ...	2285	2/9/14	—/—/15, transferred ...	Rifleman.	
Shepherd, W. N. ...	241170	23/12/14	26/3/17, invalided to England	Rifleman.	
Sheridan, A. P. ...	2120	31/8/14	—/—/15, posted 1/6th K.L.R.	Rifleman.	
Sherrard, T. ...	243831	13/10/16	28/6/18, posted 12th K.L.R.	Rifleman.	M.S.M.
Sherwood, C. E. ...	269751	10/10/17	13/9/18, wounded	Rifleman.	
Shields, J. ...	22833	24/2/18	25/10/18, wounded ...	Rifleman.	
Shimmin, T. ...	72519	24/8/17	14/1/18, sick	Rifleman.	
Shipham, —. ...	2623	6/10/14	12/1/15, transferred	Rifleman.	
Shone, F. ...	22830	27/5/18	6/9/18, wounded ...	Rifleman.	
Shore, F. R. ...	4875	25/2/16	18/10/16, transferred ...	Rifleman.	
Shore, G. T. ...	3288	4/3/15	5/8/15, transferred	Rifleman.	
Short, S.	50808	18/8/17	12/2/19, demobilized ...	Rifleman.	
Shorter, L. B. ...	3161	21/12/14	26/6/15, transferred	Rifleman.	
Shuter, E. ...	240214	23/10/14	27/5/18,† posted 4th K.L.R.	C.S.M.	
Sidebotham, —. ...	2643	9/10/14	12/1/15, transferred	Rifleman.	
Sides, A.	241714	25/5/18	9/7/18, posted 1/6th K.L.R.	Rifleman.	
Sidney, R. J. H. ...	2191	1/9/14	30/11/14, commission ...	Rifleman.	
Silberbach, B. H. ...	2462	12/9/14	17/6/15, transferred	A./C.Q.M.S.	
Sill, G.	88187	8/11/17	18/5/18, sick	Rifleman.	
Silver, F. M. ...	241950	14/10/17	16/10/17, transferred ...	Rifleman.	
Simm, W. ...	50971	18/8/17	20/8/17, posted 2/8th K.L.R.	Rifleman.	
Simmons, W. ...	242250	25/1/16	5/8/17, invalided to England	Rifleman.	
Simpson, T. ...	52402	24/8/17	10/2/19, demobilized ...	Sergeant.	
Sinclair, G. R. ...	105562	12/7/18	26/3/19, demobilized ...	Rifleman.	
Singles, H. ...	241257	4/3/15	29/3/19,† demobilized ...	A./Sergt.	
Singleton, C. H. ...	50059	27/5/18	3/2/19, demobilized ...	Rifleman.	
Singleton, J. ...	201043	14/9/18	20/1/19, demobilized ...	Rifleman.	
Singleton, J. ...	243839	13/10/16	29/8/18, posted 1st K.L.R.	Rifleman.	
Singleton, R. ...	243794	11/10/16	16/9/18, wounded ...	Rifleman.	
Sinnott, P. ...	266472	22/6/18	3/3/19, demobilized ...	Rifleman.	
Sipek, J. F. ...	3734	6/8/15	4/5/16, transferred ...	Rifleman.	
Skelhorne, G. F. ...	242441	23/3/16	3/8/17, invalided to England	Rifleman.	
Skewes, C. ...	241299	19/4/15	7/8/17,† wounded	Rifleman.	
Skinner, B. ...	1796	23/2/15	11/12/15, transferred ...	Rifleman.	
Skinner, C. ...	240936	9/11/14	16/8/15, transferred ...	Rifleman.	
Slack, H. ...	2260	1/8/14	22/7/15, transferred	Rifleman.	
Slade, — ...	2361	10/9/14	12/1/15, transferred	Rifleman	
Slee, W. R. ...	1608	27/2/15	24/11/15,† transferred ...	Rifleman.	
Sleigh, J. A. B. ...	243754	10/10/16	30/4/17,† posted 1st K.L.R.	Rifleman.	

NAME.	REGTL. NO.	DATE OF JOINING.	DATE OF LEAVING WITH CAUSE.	HIGHEST RANK.	HONOURS OR AWARDS.
Slocombe, C. J. ...	68	23/2/15	26/6/15, transferred	Sergeant.	
Slocombe, P. W.	1698	27/2/15	26/6/15, transferred	Rifleman.	
Smalley, H. ...	1514	27/2/15	26/6/15, transferred	Rifleman.	
Smaridge, L. B. ...	2671	16/10/14	23/9/16, transferred	Rifleman.	
Smart, E. ...	88511	19/9/17	22/4/18, sick	L./Corpl.	
Smart, H. ...	88533	19/9/17	5/10/18, sick	Rifleman.	
Smart, P. H	3159	14/12/14	5/8/15, transferred	Rifleman.	
Smethurst, C. J....	88095	29/9/17	29/12/17, sick	Rifleman.	
Smith, A. ...	241174	—/12/14	20/8/17, commission	Corporal.	
Smith, A. ...	39163	24/8/17	16/5/18, transferred	Rifleman.	
✠Smith, A. ...	10156	13/8/17	30/10/17, killed in action or died of wounds	Rifleman.	
✠Smith, A. ...	50806	18/8/17	30/9/18, killed in action ...	Rifleman.	
Smith, A. ...	243816	12/10/16	30/8/17, wounded	Rifleman.	
Smith, A. E. ...	3122	30/11/14	12/1/15, transferred	Rifleman.	
Smith, A. H. ...	2568	22/9/14	26/6/15, transferred	Rifleman.	
Smith, C. ...	6526	9/10/16	8/2/17, transferred	Rifleman.	
Smith, C. ...	50972	18/8/17	20/8/17, posted 2/8th K.L.R.	Rifleman.	
Smith, C. A. ...	242302	25/2/16	20/3/17, commission	Rifleman.	
Smith, C. C. ...	242435	22/3/16	12/4/18, sick	Rifleman.	M.M.
Smith, C. J. ...	241337	3/7/15	12/5/18, sick	Sergeant.	
Smith, E. ...	18835	27/6/18	16/1/19, demobilized ...	Rifleman.	
Smith, E. ...	202287	8/7/17	21/11/19, demobilized ...	L./Sergt.	
Smith, E. B. ...	4724	20/1/16	28/1/16, transferred	Rifleman.	
Smith, E. G. ...	3115	30/11/14	7/9/15, commission	Rifleman.	
Smith, E. P. ...	53308	24/2/18	9/5/18, sick	Rifleman.	
Smith, F.... ...	50973	18/8/17	20/8/17, posted 2/8th K.L.R.	Rifleman.	
Smith, F.... ...	406041	27/6/18	26/2/19, posted 25th K.L.R.	Rifleman.	
Smith, G. O. ...	241264	17/3/15	15/7/18, transferred	A./C.Q.M.S.	
Smith, G. W. ...	88512	19/9/17	14/6/18, posted 1/5th K.L.R.	Rifleman.	
Smith, H. ...	1562	23/10/14	5/8/15, transferred	Rifleman.	
Smith, H. G. ...	260150	20/9/17	14/6/18, posted 1/5th K.L.R.	Rifleman.	
✠Smith, H. H. ...	241292	12/4/15	5/11/18, died	Rifleman.	
Smith, H. P. ...	3275	19/2/15	26/6/15, transferred	Rifleman.	
Smith, J. ...	1554	23/2/15	16/8/15, transferred	Rifleman.	
Smith, J. ...	2108	31/8/14	30/6/15, transferred	Rifleman.	
Smith, J. ...	2451	14/9/14	—/—/15, transferred ...	Rifleman.	
Smith, J. ...	18377	14/6/18	6/9/18, wounded	Rifleman.	
Smith, J. ...	25553	27/6/18	3/2/19, demobilized ...	Rifleman.	
✠Smith, J. ...	243813	12/10/16	30/10/17, killed in action ...	Rifleman.	
Smith, J. ...	265395	27/6/18	22/5/19, demobilized ...	Rifleman.	
Smith, J. A. E.. ...	2880	10/11/14	26/6/15, transferred	Rifleman.	
Smith, J. E. ...	307079	27/8/17	9/11/17, wounded	Rifleman.	
Smith, J. M. ...	241244	17/2/15	21/8/17, wounded	L./Corpl.	
Smith, J. R. ...	3357	26/4/15	1/5/15, transferred	Rifleman.	
✠Smith, J. R. ...	88148	11/10/17	12/1/18, died of wounds ...	Rifleman.	
Smith, J. R. C. ...	243683	6/10/16	21/8/17, transferred	Rifleman.	
Smith, J. V. ...	3228	19/1/15	11/12/15, transferred ...	Rifleman.	
Smith, L.... ...	2631	5/10/14	27/3/15, discharged ...	Rifleman.	
✠Smith, M. ...	235116	27/6/18	12/9/18, killed in action ...	Rifleman.	
Smith, P.... ...	88098	29/9/17	9/3/19, transferred	Rifleman.	
Smith, R. ...	1432	23/2/15	26/6/15, transferred	Rifleman.	
✠Smith, R. ...	50809	18/8/17	30/8/18, killed in action ...	L./Corpl.	M.M.
Smith, R. ...	2177	31/8/14	—/—/15, transferred ...	Rifleman.	
Smith, R. ...	240642	10/9/14	22/3/18, commission	T./R.S.M.	
✠Smith, R. ...	243693	7/10/16	9/7/17, killed in action ...	Rifleman.	
Smith, R. C. ...	242562	3/6/16	9/5/17, commission	A./Corpl.	
Smith, S. A. ...	241137	26/11/14	7/8/17, invalided to England	Rifleman.	

HISTORY OF THE 2/6TH (RIFLE) BATTALION

NAME.	REGTL. NO.	DATE OF JOINING.	DATE OF LEAVING WITH CAUSE.	HIGHEST RANK.	HONOURS OR AWARDS.
Smith, S. G. ...	4810	25/1/16	18/10/16, transferred ...	Rifleman.	
Smith, S. T. H. ...	2230	1/9/14	—/—/15, transferred ...	Rifleman.	
Smith, T.... ...	17471	27/5/18	21/1/19, demobilized ...	Rifleman.	
Smith, T.... ...	29654	24/2/18	26/2/19, demobilized ...	Rifleman.	
Smith, T. A. ...	240795	24/9/14	1/10/18, wounded	L./Sergt.	
Smith, T. A. ...	241149	1/12/14	5/8/17,† invalided to England	Rifleman.	
Smith, W. ...	4989	15/3/16	6/1/17, transferred ...	L./Corpl.	
✠Smith, W. E. ...	241522	6/8/15	17/6/17, died of wounds ...	Rifleman.	
Smith, W. E. ...	2217	1/9/14	—/—/14, transferred ...	Rifleman.	
Smith, W. F. ...	242310	1/3/16	13/3/18, commission	A./Corpl.	
Smythe, H. W. ...	240515	31/8/14	—/—/15, transferred ...	Rifleman.	
Snow, G. B. ...	240951	9/11/14	5/8/17, wounded	Rifleman.	
Snowden, H. ...	57664	27/5/18	21/2/19, demobilized ...	L./Corpl.	
Sorfleet, E. ...	1275	23/2/15	26/6/15, transferred ...	Rifleman.	
Southers, T. ...	10842	13/8/17	1/11/17, wounded	Rifleman.	
Sowerby, G. ...	241253	28/2/15	10/2/19, demobilized ...	Corporal.	
Sowerby, G. ...	72500	13/8/17	15/2/18, sick	Rifleman.	
Spalding, F. ...	241016	11/11/14	5/8/17, invalided to England	Rifleman.	
Sparks, T. ...	85062	14/3/18	30/1/19, demobilized ...	Rifleman.	
Speakman, J. ...	40208	13/8/17	2/1/18, sick	Rifleman.	
Spear, J. H. ...	2283	2/9/14	—/—/15, transferred ...	Rifleman.	
Spears, J. ...	50974	18/8/17	20/8/17, posted 2/8th K.L.R.	Rifleman.	
Spence, A. M. ...	2219	1/9/14	5/8/15,† transferred ...	Rifleman.	
Spence, J. ...	3258	11/2/15	5/8/15, transferred ...	Rifleman.	
Spence, W. J. ...	88513	19/9/17	26/2/19, posted 25th K.L.R.	Rifleman.	
Spencer, E. ...	242158	20/1/16	—/—/19, discharged ...	Rifleman.	
Spencer, J. ...	2184	31/8/14	22/7/16, discharged ...	Rifleman.	
Spencer, J. W. ...	32681	30/5/18	2/7/18, wounded	Rifleman.	
Spencer, J. W. ...	243661	6/10/16	3/8/17, invalided to England	Rifleman.	
Spencer, W. ...	267964	27/5/18	7/7/18, sick	Rifleman.	
Sprainger, W. ...	240722	14/9/14	21/8/17, wounded	Sergeant.	
Spratt, H. F. ...	2715	29/10/14	26/6/15, transferred ...	Rifleman.	
✠Springer, E. ...	241192	11/1/15	4/6/17, killed in action ...	Rifleman.	
Staley, E. P. ...	95042	2/4/18	21/5/18, sick	Corporal.	
Stalford, J. C. ...	3124	10/11/14	7/8/16, discharged	A./Sergt.	
Stamp, W. E. ...	6524	9/10/16	13/2/17, transferred ...	Rifleman.	
Standring, J. ...	243664	6/10/16	13/8/17, invalided to England	Rifleman.	
Stapleton, E. ...	241581	6/8/15	9/8/17, invalided to England	Rifleman.	
Starbuck, J. T. ...	2973	12/11/14	—/—/15, transferred ...	Rifleman.	
Statton, E. ...	73039	24/8/17	4/2/18, sick	Rifleman.	
Steadman, E. ...	55	23/2/15	26/6/15, transferred ...	Rifleman.	
Stedman, H. J. ...	2542	21/9/14	12/1/15, transferred ...	Rifleman.	
Steele, J. S. ...	240831	5/10/14	31/12/18, sick	L./Corpl.	M. in D.
Steele, S. ...	16400	27/5/18	24/3/19, demobilized ...	Rifleman.	
✠Steen, A. ...	50807	18/8/17	30/10/17, killed in action ...	Rifleman.	
Steen, J. D. ...	241517	6/8/15	23/7/17, wounded	Rifleman.	
Steer, E. ...	241158	7/12/14	26/3/19, demobilized ...	Sergeant.	
Stephen, A. ...	88214	8/11/17	7/2/19, demobilized ...	Corporal.	
Stephens, F. G. ...	88514	19/9/17	26/2/19, posted 25th K.L.R.	Rifleman.	
✠Stephenson, R. ...	243835	13/10/16	12/7/17, killed in action ...	Rifleman.	
Sterne, C. ...	268919	10/10/17	28/3/19, posted 13th K.L.R.	Rifleman.	
Stevenette, F. H.	3065	19/11/14	29/1/16, discharged ...	Rifleman.	
Stevens, T. ...	2571	24/9/14	9/12/15, transferred ...	Rifleman.	
Stevenson, H. ...	2362	10/9/14	12/1/15, transferred ...	Rifleman.	
Stevenson, K. V.	242182	21/1/16	14/2/19, demobilized ...	Sergeant.	M.M.
Stewart, C. G. ...	200831	14/9/18	22/1/19, demobilized ...	Rifleman.	
Stewart, D. ...	17483	27/5/18	25/1/19, demobilized ...	Rifleman.	
Stewart, E. ...	50975	18/8/17	20/8/17, posted 2/8th K.L.R.	Rifleman.	

NAME.	REGTL. NO.	DATE OF JOINING.	DATE OF LEAVING WITH CAUSE.	HIGHEST RANK.	HONOURS OR AWARDS.
Stewart, I. A. ...	2849	9/11/14	12/2/17,† commission ...	Rifleman.	
Stewart, J. N. ...	3317	29/3/15	23/9/16,† commission	Rifleman.	
Stewart, L. A. ...	2801	9/11/14	26/6/15, transferred ...	Rifleman.	
Stewart, R. ...	243811	12/10/16	30/4/17, posted 1st K.L.R. ...	Rifleman.	
Stewart, S. C. ...	3112	26/11/14	26/6/15, transferred ...	Rifleman.	
Stinton, R. ...	50803	18/8/17	22/4/18, sick	Rifleman.	
Stirrup, W. ...	241097	17/11/14	21/1/19, demobilized ...	A./Corpl.	
Stoba, R.... ...	12269	27/5/18	29/1/19, demobilized	L./Corpl.	
Stockdale, C. R.	241241	15/2/15	19/6/17,† wounded ...	Rifleman.	
Stockdale, W. ...	2072	31/8/14	29/12/15, commission	Rifleman.	
Stockwell, J. P. ...	242349	8/3/16	7/5/18, sick	Rifleman.	
Stokes, T. ...	200933	14/9/18	10/2/19, demobilized ...	Rifleman.	
Stone, P. B. ...	268047	27/8/17	8/11/17, wounded ...	Rifleman.	
Stopforth, W. ...	72532	13/8/17	22/1/19, demobilized	Rifleman.	
Storey, A. ...	240096	23/2/15	10/5/17, discharged ...	Rifleman.	
✠Stothard, N. ...	53569	24/8/17	31/8/18, died of wounds	Rifleman.	
Stott, C. G. ...	3113	26/11/14	14/5/15, commission	Rifleman.	
Stott, E.	243746	9/10/16	8/3/19, posted 13th K.L.R.	Rifleman.	
Stott, J.	243718	9/10/16	17/4/18, sick	Rifleman.	
Stott, R.	37412	24/8/17	3/5/18, transferred ...	Rifleman.	
Strickland, H. T.	202299	14/9/18	7/7/19, demobilized ...	Rifleman.	
Stringfellow, J. H.	50804	18/8/17	21/6/18, transferred ...	L./Corpl.	
Strong, W. W. ...	2708	29/10/14	16/8/15, transferred ...	Rifleman.	
Stubbs, H. ...	88218	8/11/17	26/2/19, posted 25th K.L.R.	Rifleman.	
Stubbs, H. A. ...	241186	7/1/15	12/11/17, wounded ...	L./Corpl.	
Stubbs, J. J. ...	241022	11/11/14	7/1/18,† wounded ...	L./Sergt.	M.M.
Studholme, H. A.	243712	9/10/16	10/4/18, sick	Rifleman.	
Styles, T.... ...	305177	8/7/17	27/2/19, demobilized ...	Rifleman.	
Sullivan, J. W. ...	24269	14/6/18	3/3/19, demobilized ...	Rifleman.	
✠Sullivan, M. M. ...	241419	6/8/15	17/6/17, died of wounds	Rifleman.	
Sumner, G. ...	2364	10/9/14	12/1/15, transferred ...	Rifleman.	
Sunderland, F. ...	243671	6/10/16	7/8/17, invalided to England	Rifleman.	
Sutcliffe, R. ...	88186	8/11/17	22/4/18, transferred ...	Rifleman.	
Sutcliffe, S. ...	2599	28/9/14	5/8/15, transferred ...	A./Sergt.	
Sutherland, T. ...	2586	26/9/14	19/10/15, commission ...	A./R.Q.M.S.	
Sutton, E. ...	19934	24/2/18	31/8/18, sick	L./Sergt.	
Sutton, J. W. ...	242232	22/1/16	16/10/17,† transferred ...	Rifleman.	
Sutton, R. ...	63639	24/8/17	1/2/19, demobilized ...	Rifleman.	
Swain, T.... ...	88178	8/11/17	26/2/18, sick	Rifleman.	
✠Swain, T. H. ...	243662	6/10/16	8/6/17, killed in action ...	Rifleman.	
Swainbank, W. ...	72456	24/8/17	11/7/18, posted 1/6th K.L.R.	Rifleman.	
Swan, A.	243810	12/10/16	4/11/17, sick	Rifleman.	
Swan, E. W. ...	87828	27/6/18	7/2/19, demobilized ...	Rifleman.	
Swan, P. S. ...	2141	31/8/14	—/—/15, transferred ...	Rifleman.	
Swanton, W. ...	94466	27/6/18	16/10/19, demobilized ...	Rifleman.	
Swarbrick, J. ...	109124	28/9/18	28/3/19, posted 13th K.L.R.	Rifleman.	
Swede, H. ...	242575	13/6/16	11/2/19, demobilized ...	Rifleman.	
Swetman, A. E. ...	49026	24/2/18	8/5/18, sick	Rifleman.	
Swift, C. W. ...	260152	20/9/17	11/2/19, demobilized ...	Rifleman.	
Swift, H. ...	72523	13/8/17	23/9/17, sick	Rifleman.	
Swindells, W. ...	95675	17/4/18	—/3/19, posted 25th K.L.R.	Rifleman.	
Swindlehurst, W.	72475	13/8/17	26/1/19, demobilized ...	Rifleman.	
Syddall, J. W. ...	40423	24/8/17	4/4/18, sick	Rifleman.	
Sykes, A. J. ...	1998	23/2/15	26/6/15, transferred ...	Rifleman.	
Symonds, J. E. ...	5230	22/5/16	18/8/16, transferred ...	Rifleman.	
Symonds, S. K. ...	1446	23/10/14	26/6/15, transferred ...	Rifleman.	

NAME.	REGTL. NO.	DATE OF JOINING.	DATE OF LEAVING WITH CAUSE.	HIGHEST RANK.	HONOURS OR AWARDS.
Taft, G.	88664	14/9/18	16/1/19, demobilized ...	Rifleman.	
Taggart, H. ...	17	—/11/14	9/2/16, transferred ...	R.Q.M.S.	
Tague, J. H. ...	72502	27/5/18	5/9/18, wounded ...	Rifleman.	
Tallon, W. ...	201844	27/5/18	5/3/19, demobilized ...	L./Corpl.	
Tankard, C. ...	2852	9/11/14	12/1/15, transferred ...	Rifleman.	
Tarbet, C. E. ...	2367	10/9/19	12/1/15, transferred ...	Rifleman.	
Tate, W.	242436	22/3/16	1/2/18, sick	Corporal.	
Taylor, A. ...	243744	9/10/16	3/3/17, transferred ...	Rifleman.	
Taylor, A. ...	42408	13/8/17	29/5/18, sick ...	Corporal.	
Taylor, A. ...	63740	24/8/17	28/3/19, demobilized ...	Rifleman.	
Taylor, B. D. ...	243792	11/10/16	2/10/18, wounded ...	Rifleman.	
Taylor, C. ...	50870	22/6/18	28/3/19, posted 13th K.L.R.	Rifleman.	
Taylor, C. A. ...	6644	16/10/16	7/11/16, transferred ...	Rifleman.	
Taylor, C. T. ...	241063	13/11/14	12/5/17,† wounded ...	Rifleman.	
Taylor, E. ...	241791	5/5/17	20/5/17, posted 1st K.L.R. ...	Rifleman.	
✠Taylor, F. ...	241249	25/2/15	7/7/17, killed in action ...	Rifleman.	
Taylor, F. H. ...	240966	9/11/14	12/8/17,† invalided to England	Rifleman.	
Taylor, G. ...	3102	23/11/14	26/6/15, transferred ...	Rifleman.	
Taylor, G. ...	3378	3/7/15	14/8/16, transferred ...	Rifleman.	
Taylor, G. A. ...	266829	10/10/17	21/9/18, wounded ...	Rifleman.	
Taylor, H. ...	240501	31/8/14	5/9/17,† posted 1/6th K.L.R.	Rifleman.	
Taylor, H. ...	243782	10/10/16	28/3/19, posted 13th K.L.R.	Rifleman.	
Taylor, H. J. ...	3094	24/11/14	12/1/15, transferred ...	Rifleman.	
Taylor, J. ...	23510	7/3/18	29/5/18, sick ...	Rifleman.	
Taylor, J. ...	41091	24/8/17	26/3/18, transferred ...	Rifleman.	
✠Taylor, J. ...	50816	18/8/17	21/10/18, killed in action ...	Rifleman.	
Taylor, J. ...	80104	24/8/17	5/4/19, demobilized ...	Corporal.	
Taylor, J. ...	80434	24/8/17	11/2/18, sick ...	Rifleman.	
Taylor, J. ...	243741	9/10/16	30/7/17, wounded ...	Rifleman.	
✠Taylor, J. ...	243844	12/10/16	30/10/17, missing, assumed dead	Corporal.	
Taylor, J. A. ...	3536	6/8/15	15/9/16,† transferred ...	Rifleman.	
Taylor, J. D. ...	42943	24/8/17	9/7/18, wounded ...	Rifleman.	
Taylor, J. H. ...	242375	17/3/16	30/8/17, wounded ...	Rifleman.	
Taylor, J. R. ...	241318	6/8/15	9/6/18, sick ...	Rifleman.	
Taylor, N. ...	241055	12/11/14	7/2/19, demobilized ...	A./Sergt.	
Taylor, O. A. ...	2499	16/9/14	30/3/15, transferred ...	Rifleman.	
Taylor, R. B. L. ...	2639	7/10/14	4/8/16, commission ...	Rifleman.	
Taylor, T. ...	52359	24/8/17	10/2/19, demobilized ...	Rifleman.	
Taylor, W.	2668	15/10/14	26/6/15, transferred ...	Rifleman.	
Taylor, W. ...	110517	27/11/18	26/2/19, posted 25th K.L.R.	Rifleman.	
Taylor, W. D. ...	52200	24/8/17	5/3/19, demobilized ...	Rifleman.	
Taylor, W. R. ...	63847	13/8/17	9/7/18, posted 1/6th K.L.R.	Rifleman.	
Taylor, — ...	2509	17/9/14	12/1/15, transferred ...	Rifleman.	
Teare, E. ...	24794	13/8/17	2/10/18, wounded ...	Rifleman.	
Teasdale, J. ...	12006	14/9/18	1/10/18, wounded ...	Rifleman.	
Teasdale, V. W. ...	2502	12/9/14	26/6/15, transferred ...	Rifleman.	
Telfer, R. J. ...	240965	9/11/14	17/4/18, sick ...	Rifleman.	
Telfer, W. ...	2904	10/11/14	26/6/15, transferred ...	Rifleman.	
Tennion, H. ...	243833	13/10/16	3/3/17, transferred ...	Rifleman.	
Terry, A. N. ...	241112	19/11/14	26/9/18, commission ...	L./Sergt.	M. in D
Terry, F. R. ...	241332	3/7/15	8/6/17, wounded ...	Rifleman.	
Terry, H. M. ...	2272	1/9/14	—/—/15, transferred ...	Rifleman.	
Theobald, A. ...	72484	13/8/17	22/10/18, posted 13th K.L.R.	Rifleman.	
✠Thom, W. N. ...	241099	17/11/14	1/8/17, died of wounds ...	Rifleman.	
Thomas, A. ...	241131	24/11/14	9/8/17, invalided to England	Rifleman.	
Thomas, A. H. ...	240716	15/9/14	18/2/19, demobilized ...	Rifleman.	
Thomas, D. H. ...	2584	25/9/14	9/12/15, transferred ...	Rifleman.	
Thomas, E. J. ...	242427	22/3/16	27/8/17, wounded ...	Rifleman.	

" THE KING'S " (LIVERPOOL REGIMENT)

NAME.	REGTL. NO.	DATE OF JOINING.	DATE OF LEAVING WITH CAUSE.	HIGHEST RANK.	HONOURS OR AWARDS.
Thomas, E. J. ...	268076	27/8/17	22/1/19, demobilized ...	A./Corpl.	
Thomas, H. A. ...	242291	17/2/16	9/8/17, wounded	Rifleman.	
Thomas, J. E. W.	40213	24/8/17	14/5/18, sick ...	Rifleman.	
Thomas, R. H. ...	242212	22/1/16	21/8/17, wounded ...	Rifleman.	
Thomas, R. J. E.	240871	26/10/14	17/5/18, sick	Rifleman.	
Thomas, R. L. ...	2444	14/9/14	25/8/15, commission ...	Rifleman.	
Thomas, R. W. ...	201702	8/7/17	5/2/19, demobilized ...	L./Corpl.	
Thomas, S. ...	241896	8/7/17	3/2/19, demobilized ...	Corporal.	
Thomas, W. ...	50812	18/8/17	17/2/19, demobilized	L./Corpl.	
Thomas, W. ...	88529	19/9/17	23/11/17, wounded ...	Rifleman.	
Thomas, W. H. ...	2239	1/9/14	—/—/14, posted 1/6th K.L.R.	Rifleman.	
Thompson, C. ...	88515	19/9/17	5/2/18, sick	Rifleman.	
Thompson, D. ...	19973	1/2/18	9/11/18, posted Home Depot	Rifleman.	
Thompson, E. M.	242633	4/8/17	—/—/19, demobilized ...	Rifleman.	
Thompson, F. C.	241301	20/4/15	9/9/17, posted 1/9th K.L.R.	Rifleman.	
Thompson, H. ...	56691	27/5/18	2/3/19, demobilized ...	Rifleman.	
Thompson, J. ...	3695	6/8/15	20/1/17, transferred ...	Rifleman.	
Thompson, J. ...	64920	24/8/17	26/9/18, wounded ...	Rifleman.	
Thompson, J. W.	242532	23/5/16	14/2/19, demobilized	Rifleman.	
Thompson, R. A.	242388	18/3/16	11/9/18, discharged ...	Rifleman.	
Thompson, R. E.	242480	25/5/18	23/6/18, sick	Rifleman.	
Thompson, S. M.	3085	23/11/14	26/6/15, transferred ...	Rifleman.	
Thompson, S. M.	203173	21/11/17	3/3/19, demobilized ...	Rifleman.	
Thompson, T. A. W.	2396	10/9/14	26/6/15, transferred ...	Sergeant.	
Thompson, W. ...	2874	10/11/14	12/1/15, transferred ...	Rifleman.	
Thompson, W. ...	49403	5/4/18	14/6/19, disembodied ...	Sergeant.	
Thompson, W. ...	64764	14/6/18	7/11/18, sick	Rifleman.	
Thompson, W. E.	241360	6/8/15	22/5/19, demobilized	Rifleman.	
Thompson, W. L.	5260	2/6/16	2/12/16, commission ...	Rifleman.	
Thomson, K. ...	50974	18/8/17	20/8/17, posted 2/8th K.L.R.	Rifleman.	
Thomson, T. ...	242218	22/1/16	26/2/19,† posted 25th K.L.R.	Rifleman.	
Thorley, R. ...	50815	18/8/17	21/7/19, transferred ...	Rifleman.	
Thorley, W. ...	88516	19/9/17	26/2/19, posted 25th K.L.R.	Corporal.	
Thorne, H. ...	2431	12/9/14	5/1/17,† sick	Rifleman.	
Thornton, R. ...	72491	13/8/17	26/2/19, posted 25th K.L.R.	Rifleman	
Thorp, F. E. ...	2546	23/9/14	16/8/15, transferred ...	Rifleman.	
Thorpe, J. ...	6462	6/10/16	2/2/17, sick	Rifleman.	
Thorpe, J. W. ...	64883	14/9/18	22/1/19, demobilized ...	Rifleman.	
Threadgold, R. ...	2432	15/9/14	16/8/15, transferred ...	Rifleman.	
Thwaite, H. ...	243706	9/10/16	4/3/19, transferred ...	Rifleman.	
Tickle, F. W. ...	241533	6/8/15	5/8/17,† invalided to England	Rifleman.	
Till, G.	88517	19/9/17	22/12/18, demobilized ...	Rifleman.	
Till, R. J. C. ...	260236	19/9/17	29/10/17, prisoner of war ...	Corporal.	
Tilling, R. ...	241047	11/11/14	12/5/18, sick	Rifleman.	
✠Timewell, A. H. ...	59528	13/8/17	2/12/17, died	Rifleman.	
Timothy, H. ...	2744	4/11/14	12/1/15, transferred ...	Rifleman.	
Timson, F. ...	242369	16/3/16	—/—/19, transferred	Rifleman.	
Tipping, J. ...	240772	21/9/14	31/1/18, commission ...	A./C.S.M.	
Titherington, T.	5238	23/5/16	1/2/17, transferred ...	Rifleman.	
Titherington, W.	242366	15/3/16	21/8/17, wounded ...	Rifleman.	
Todd, A.	50814	18/8/17	3/11/17, wounded ...	Rifleman.	
Todd, F.	2917	10/11/14	28/6/15, transferred ...	Rifleman.	
Todd, G.	2848	9/11/14	26/6/15, transferred ...	Rifleman.	
Todd, W.	2366	10/9/14	5/8/15, transferred ...	Rifleman.	
Todhunter, J. ...	243805	12/10/16	16/7/17, wounded ...	Rifleman.	
Todhunter, W. H.	2143	31/8/14	—/—/15, transferred ...	Rifleman.	
Tollet, W. ...	242203	21/1/16	24/6/18, wounded ...	Rifleman.	
Tomkinson, S. E.	2254	1/9/14	26/6/15, transferred ...	Rifleman.	

351

NAME.	REGTL. NO.	DATE OF JOINING.	DATE OF LEAVING WITH CAUSE.	HIGHEST RANK.	HONOURS OR AWARDS.
Tomlinson, J. ...	50813	18/8/17	30/1/19, demobilized ...	L./Corpl.	
Tomlinson, W. A.	241181	4/1/15	29/8/18, posted 1st K.L.R. ...	Rifleman.	
Tommins, W. ...	88223	8/11/17	29/4/18, transferred	Rifleman.	
Tonks, G. W. E.	241333	3/7/15	9/8/17, wounded	A./Corpl.	
Tooby, A. ...	243739	9/10/16	17/8/17, wounded ...	Rifleman.	
Toot, L.	85694	7/3/18	31/5/18, sick	Rifleman.	
Toovey, J. ...	88518	19/9/17	12/11/18, sick ...	Rifleman.	
Totten, R. ...	12737	13/9/18	17/1/19, demobilized ...	Rifleman.	
Toumine, J. ...	5056	22/3/16	29/7/16, discharged ...	Rifleman.	
Towler, J. W. ...	88519	19/9/17	1/12/17, sick	Rifleman.	
Townsend, H. ...	201012	12/4/18	12/10/18, wounded ...	Rifleman.	
Townsend, J. W.	2982	12/11/14	26/6/15, transferred ...	Rifleman.	
Townsend, W. J.	240960	9/11/14	18/5/17, wounded ...	Rifleman.	
Trafford, T. ...	241109	18/11/14	30/8/17, wounded ...	Rifleman.	
Trainor, L. C. ...	2589	28/9/14	28/7/15, discharged ...	Rifleman.	
Tranton, F. ...	242541	29/5/16	14/1/18, wounded ...	Corporal.	
Trapnell, F. J. B.	242178	20/1/16	11/2/19, demobilized ...	Corporal.	
Travill, R. ...	2136	31/8/14	—/—/15, transferred	Rifleman.	
Traynor, M. ...	202163	25/2/18	12/2/19, demobilized	Rifleman.	
Treacy, E. H. ...	2681	20/10/14	5/8/15, transferred ...	Rifleman.	
Trench, J. K. ...	1788	23/10/14	28/10/15, commission ...	Rifleman.	
Trigg, W. W. ...	88520	19/9/17	25/5/18, wounded ...	Rifleman.	
Trinder, C. ...	91234	26/2/18	20/5/18, sick	Rifleman.	
Troillett, W. H.	243768	9/10/16	5/8/17, invalided to England	Rifleman.	
Trott, W. ...	240461	23/10/14	1/9/17,† posted 1/7th K.L.R.	A./Corpl.	
Troughton, G. ...	72472	13/8/17	23/12/17, wounded ...	Rifleman.	
Troughton, T. ...	6570	9/10/16	12/11/16, transferred ...	Rifleman.	
Tudor, J. ...	108809	28/9/18	14/12/18, demobilized ...	Rifleman.	
Tudor, R. ...	24397	13/8/17	26/3/19, demobilized ...	Rifleman.	
Tunna, S. ...	241245	18/2/15	5/8/17, wounded ...	Rifleman.	
Tunstall, T. R. ...	2641	9/10/14	12/1/15, transferred ...	Rifleman.	
Turnbull, A. ...	50977	18/8/17	20/8/17, posted 2/8th K.L.R.	Rifleman.	
Turnbull, H. ...	64823	13/8/17	30/1/19, demobilized ...	Rifleman.	
Turner, A. ...	2903	10/11/14	26/6/15, transferred ...	Rifleman.	
Turner, C. ...	50811	18/8/17	8/9/18, wounded ...	Rifleman.	
Turner, C. J. ...	240888	29/10/14	9/7/18,† posted 1/6th K.L.R.	Rifleman.	
Turner, E. ...	88202	8/11/17	17/1/19, demobilized ...	Rifleman.	
Turner, E. ...	242222	22/1/16	26/2/19, posted 25th K.L.R.	Rifleman.	
Turner, F. ...	2147	31/8/14	26/6/15, transferred ...	Rifleman.	
Turner, H. ...	204003	10/2/18	9/11/18, wounded ...	Rifleman.	
Turner, J. ...	268460	22/6/18	7/2/19, demobilized ...	Rifleman.	
Turner, R. ...	241486	6/8/15	6/8/17,† invalided to England	Rifleman.	
Turnock, W. ...	242165	20/1/16	9/8/17, invalided to England	Rifleman.	
Tweddle, T. ...	240804	30/9/14	30/1/19, demobilized ...	Corporal.	
Twentyman, P. ...	2765	6/11/14	5/8/15, transferred ...	Rifleman.	
Twiss, W. N. ...	2064	31/8/14	4/10/16, discharged ...	Rifleman.	
✠Twist, R. ...	64850	13/8/17	21/6/18, killed in action ...	Rifleman.	
Tyrer, C. F. ...	2256	1/9/14	—/—/14, transferred	Rifleman.	
Tyrer, F. ...	3118	30/11/14	26/6/15, transferred ...	Rifleman.	
Tyson, C. ...	2194	1/9/14	27/10/14, commission ...	Rifleman.	
Tyson, R. ...	88240	8/11/17	13/6/18, sick	Rifleman.	
Tyson, R. B. ...	204006	14/9/18	12/2/19, demobilized ...	Rifleman.	
Tyson, S. H. ...	1959	23/10/14	31/10/15, commission ...	A./Sergt.	
Tyson, W. J. ...	2103	31/8/14	8/1/15, commission ...	Rifleman.	
Tytler, E. ...	240513	31/8/14	—/—/15, transferred	Rifleman.	
✠Ullyott, F. ...	57602	27/5/18	15/6/18, killed in action ...	Rifleman.	
Underwood, G. D.	242205	21/1/16	28/3/19, posted 13th K.L.R.	Rifleman.	

"THE KING'S" (LIVERPOOL REGIMENT)

NAME.	REGTL. NO.	DATE OF JOINING.	DATE OF LEAVING WITH CAUSE.	HIGHEST RANK.	HONOURS OR AWARDS.
Unsworth, H. ...	50817	18/8/17	28/3/19, posted 25th K.L.R.	Rifleman.	
Unsworth, W. ...	110850	27/11/18	3/3/19, demobilized	Rifleman.	
Upton, J. ...	3266	15/2/15	26/6/15, transferred	Rifleman.	
Uren, R. H. ...	242170	20/1/16	17/2/19, demobilized	Rifleman.	
Usher, R. ...	235269	27/6/18	12/9/18, prisoner of war ...	Rifleman.	
Valentine, J. ...	242244	25/1/16	—/3/19, posted 25th K.L.R.	Rifleman.	
Valentine, O. H. S.	300398	22/6/18	22/5/19, demobilized ...	Corporal.	
Vance, R. B. ...	94027	27/6/18	—/3/19, posted 25th K.L.R.	Rifleman.	
Vaughan, H. ...	59457	24/8/17	1/11/17, wounded	Rifleman.	
Vaughan, J. ...	3071	19/11/14	26/6/15, transferred	Rifleman.	
✠Vaughan, J. ...	26293	24/2/18	6/10/18, died of wounds ...	Rifleman.	
Venables, N. ...	241067	13/11/14	24/2/18, sick	Sergeant.	
✠Verso, F. S. ...	242204	21/1/16	1/6/17, killed in action ...	Rifleman.	
Vickerman, F. ...	54329	27/5/18	12/9/18, prisoner of war ...	L./Corpl.	
Vickers, L. ...	243823	13/10/16	30/6/17, transferred	Rifleman.	
Vickers, L. ...	115055	7/3/18	14/4/18, sick	Rifleman.	
Vipond, A. ...	88045	28/9/17	21/2/18, sick	Rifleman.	
Vlasto, T. ...	2294	7/9/14	23/5/15,† discharged ...	Rifleman.	
Waddington, J. ...	88200	8/11/17	1/4/18, posted 13th K.L.R.	Rifleman.	
Wade, W. V. ...	6586	11/10/16	7/11/16, transferred	Rifleman.	
Wain, R. ...	63747	13/8/17	21/2/19, demobilized ...	Rifleman.	
Wait, W. E. ...	50822	18/8/17	18/1/19, demobilized ...	Corporal.	
✠Waiting, H. ...	72493	13/8/17	30/10/17, died	Rifleman.	
Wakefield, W. ...	1437	23/2/15	26/6/15, transferred	Rifleman.	
Wakeham, A. R.	3140	7/12/14	26/6/15, transferred	Rifleman.	
Waldemar, W. ...	243788	10/10/16	19/8/17, wounded	Rifleman.	
Walkden, C. ...	243659	27/9/16	16/4/17, transferred	Rifleman.	
Walker, B. ...	88199	8/11/17	—/3/19, posted 25th K.L.R.	Rifleman.	
Walker, E. N. ...	2419	11/9/14	12/1/15, transferred	Rifleman.	
Walker, F. T. ...	46	7/12/14	20/9/15, transferred	Sergeant.	
Walker, G. F. ...	2453	12/9/14	11/12/15, transferred ...	Corporal.	
Walker, G. O. ...	241713	5/5/17	1/11/17, transferred	Rifleman.	
Walker, H. ...	61073	13/8/17	25/5/18, sick	Rifleman.	
Walker, H. C. ...	2312	10/9/14	12/1/15, transferred	Rifleman.	
Walker, J. ...	50978	18/8/17	20/8/17, posted 2/8th K.L.R.	Rifleman.	
Walker, J. ...	88521	19/9/17	12/1/18, wounded	Rifleman.	
Walker, J. ...	242339	3/3/16	5/8/17, invalided to England	Rifleman.	
Walker, J. ...	267590	27/6/18	26/2/19, posted 25th K.L.R.	Rifleman.	
Walker, J. W. ...	241346	3/7/15	8/8/17, invalided to England	Corporal.	M. in D.
Walker, L. E. ...	2927	11/11/14	26/6/15, transferred	Rifleman.	
Walker, R. W. ...	2214	1/9/14	—/—/14, posted 1/6th K.L.R.	Rifleman.	
Wallace, S. ...	50282	27/5/18	16/1/19, demobilized ...	Rifleman.	
Wallace, W. A. ...	201089	14/3/18	17/10/18, transferred ...	Rifleman.	
Wallas, T. ...	240922	7/11/14	17/8/17, wounded	R.Q.M.S.	
Waller, S. ...	34306	7/3/18	29/8/18, posted 1st K.L.R. ...	Rifleman.	
Walls, A. C. ...	88227	8/11/17	11/7/18, posted 1/6th K.L.R.	Rifleman.	
Walls, H. E. ...	242358	14/3/16	11/2/18, transferred	Rifleman.	
Wallwork, W. ...	88522	19/9/17	10/12/18, demobilized ...	Rifleman.	
Walmesley, H. ...	88103	29/9/17	26/2/19, posted 13th K.L.R.	Rifleman.	
Walmesley, H. ...	269312	27/8/17	23/9/17, wounded	Rifleman.	
Walmsley, C. H.	3180	1/1/15	16/2/15, medically unfit ...	Rifleman.	
Walmsley, L. ...	241182	5/1/15	26/2/19, demobilized ...	Corporal.	
Walpole, E. ...	3168	26/12/14	26/6/15, transferred	Rifleman.	
Walsh, A. ...	243690	7/10/16	5/10/17, transferred	Rifleman.	
Walsh, P. ...	88229	8/11/17	26/2/19, posted 13th K.L.R.	Rifleman.	
Walsh, P. ...	88236	8/11/17	28/3/19, posted 13th K.L.R.	L./Corpl.	M.M.

NAME.	REGTL. NO.	DATE OF JOINING.	DATE OF LEAVING WITH CAUSE.	HIGHEST RANK.	HONOURS OR AWARDS.
Walshaw, A. B. ...	201417	14/9/18	22/1/19, transferred	Rifleman.	
Walter, C. W. ...	240726	12/9/14	5/8/17, invalided to England	C.Q.M.S.	
Walters, H. ...	88523	19/9/17	14/3/18, transferred	Rifleman.	
✠Walton, B. ...	38770	13/8/17	30/9/18, killed in action ...	Rifleman.	
Walton, H. ...	50825	18/8/17	10/11/17, wounded	Rifleman.	
Walton, R. ...	30981	24/8/17	29/8/18, posted 1st K.L.R. ...	Rifleman.	
Walton, T. ...	204028	18/2/18	26/2/19, posted 25th K.L.R.	L./Corpl.	
Walton, W. ...	243753	10/10/16	17/5/17, wounded	Rifleman.	
Warbrick, J. H.	242321	1/3/16	12/6/17, sick	Rifleman.	
Warburton, C. ...	50827	18/8/17	26/2/19, posted 25th K.L.R.	L./Corpl.	
Warburton, H. ...	90726	7/3/18	26/2/19, posted 25th K.L.R.	Rifleman.	
Warburton, J. E. D.	50818	18/8/17	31/10/17, wounded	Rifleman.	
Warburton, — ...	2507	17/9/14	12/1/15, transferred	A./Sergt.	
Ward, A. ...	57663	27/5/18	—/—/19, transferred... ...	Rifleman.	
Ward, A. B. ...	240360	23/10/14	5/1/19, demobilized	Rifleman.	
Ward, C. F. ...	53317	27/5/18	1/1/19, demobilized	Corporal.	
Ward, F. ...	3419	3/7/15	9/4/16, transferred	Rifleman.	
Ward, H. ...	2952	12/11/14	26/6/15, transferred	Rifleman.	
Ward, J. ...	50821	18/8/17	26/2/19, posted 13th K.L.R.	Rifleman.	
Ward, J. ...	88668	4/3/18	27/7/18, transferred	Rifleman.	
Ward, L. H. ...	2275	1/9/14	—/—/14, transferred ...	Rifleman.	
Ward, M. J. ...	242379	18/3/16	30/5/18, wounded	Rifleman.	
Ward, W. M. J. ...	2648	10/10/14	25/8/15, transferred	Rifleman.	
Wardle, G. ...	88524	19/9/17	14/1/18, wounded	Rifleman.	
✠Wardman, G. ...	42276	24/8/17	12/9/18, killed in action ...	Corporal.	
Wareham, F. A. ...	2259	1/9/14	—/—/14, transferred ...	Rifleman.	
Warhurst, J. ...	243729	9/10/16	3/8/17, transferred	Rifleman.	
Waring, R. ...	1970	23/10/14	26/6/15, transferred	Rifleman.	
Warins, J. ...	25305	27/5/18	24/2/19, demobilized ...	Rifleman.	
Warner, G. ...	50978	18/8/17	20/8/17, posted 2/8th K.L.R. ...	Rifleman.	
Warren, C. ...	242221	22/1/16	25/1/19, demobilized	Sergeant.	M.M.
Warrington, H. M.	240553	31/8/14	—/—/15, transferred ...	Rifleman.	
Warwick, R. ...	241556	6/8/15	25/2/18,† sick	Rifleman.	
Waters, E. ...	50826	18/8/17	1/11/17, wounded	Rifleman.	
✠Wathall, S. M. ...	50829	18/8/17	2/6/18, killed in action ...	Rifleman.	
Watkins, A. W. ...	1583	27/2/15	8/12/15, commission	Rifleman.	
Watkins, B. I. ...	241126	23/11/14	24/4/18, transferred	Rifleman.	
Watkinson, G. ...	241445	6/8/15	29/7/17,† wounded	Rifleman.	
Watkinson, J. ...	2980	14/11/14	26/6/15, transferred	Rifleman.	
Watkinson, T. J.	242394	18/3/16	20/12/17,† sick	Rifleman.	
Watkinson, W. ...	200240	8/10/18	7/2/19, demobilized	Sergeant.	
Watkinson, W. R.	2244	1/9/14	31/3/15, transferred	Rifleman.	
Watson, A. H. ...	2491	16/9/14	12/1/15, transferred	Rifleman.	
Watson, E. J. ...	3246	3/2/15	31/12/15, commission	A./Corpl.	
Watson, H. ...	241028	11/11/14	10/2/19,† demobilized ...	Rifleman.	
Watson, S. H. ...	2293	4/9/14	24/9/15, commission	Rifleman.	
Watt, D. ...	50980	18/8/17	20/8/17, posted 2/8th K.L.R.	Rifleman.	
Watt, W. ...	3126	1/12/14	12/1/15, transferred	Sergeant.	
Watts, F. C. ...	241014	10/11/14	19/5/18, wounded	Rifleman.	
Weaitt, W. ...	84969	27/5/18	29/1/19, demobilized ...	Rifleman.	
Wearing, J. ...	242490	20/4/16	25/2/18, commission	L./Sergt.	
Wearing, R. T. ...	242555	19/10/16	17/6/17, transferred	Rifleman.	
Weatherley, G. H.	1523	27/2/15	26/6/15, transferred	Rifleman.	
Weaver, J. ...	3361	26/4/15	1/5/15, transferred	Rifleman.	
Webb, A. W. ...	2602	28/9/14	1/8/16, transferred	Rifleman.	
Webb, T. ...	241093	16/11/14	9/8/17, invalided to England	Corporal.	
Webster, E. ...	53466	28/9/17	2/2/18, sick	L./Corpl.	
Webster, F. M. ...	2714	29/10/14	6/12/15, transferred	Rifleman.	

"THE KING'S" (LIVERPOOL REGIMENT)

NAME.	REGTL. NO.	DATE OF JOINING.	DATE OF LEAVING WITH CAUSE.	HIGHEST RANK.	HONOURS OR AWARDS.
Webster, H. ...	240677	10/9/14	24/2/19, demobilized ...	Sergeant.	
Webster, H. ...	50828	18/8/17	30/1/19, demobilized ...	Rifleman.	
Webster, J. ...	50981	18/8/17	20/8/17, posted 2/8th K.L.R.	Rifleman.	
✠Webster, T. ...	53596	24/8/17	30/10/17, died	Rifleman.	
Wedgewood, E. W.	5074	23/3/16	17/1/17, transferred	Rifleman.	
Weinstein, P. ...	4877	25/2/16	18/10/16, transferred ...	Rifleman.	
Weir, J. E. ...	240616	1/9/14	—/—/14, transferred ...	Rifleman.	
Weissenberg, H. E.	241688	8/7/17	21/8/17, wounded ...	Rifleman.	
✠Wells, E. O. ...	242537	24/5/16	4/9/18, died of wounds ...	Corporal.	
✠Welsby, W. ...	84963	27/5/18	17/9/18, died of wounds ...	Rifleman.	
✠Welsby, W. G. ...	241382	3/7/15	1/7/17, died	Rifleman.	
Wensley, A. ...	16849	27/5/18	8/6/18, prisoner of war ...	Rifleman.	
Wensley, C. W. ...	2463	12/9/14	23/8/15, transferred ...	Rifleman.	
West, G.	243682	6/10/16	17/6/17, transferred ...	Rifleman.	
West, H. ...	2215	1/9/14	—/—/14, transferred ...	Rifleman.	
West, J. C. ...	241002	10/11/14	17/6/17,† transferred ...	Rifleman.	
Westbrook, W. ...	203912	14/3/18	—/4/19, transferred ...	A./Sergt.	
Westrup, A. I. ...	3285	1/3/15	2/12/16, commission ...	Rifleman.	
Westrup, E. ...	3286	1/3/15	23/9/16,† transferred ...	Rifleman.	
Wharmby, R. G. ...	3162	21/12/14	9/3/15, medically unfit ...	Rifleman.	
Wharmby, T. ...	53052	7/3/18	6/9/18, wounded ...	Rifleman.	
Wharton, H. E. ...	241549	6/8/15	19/8/17, wounded ...	Rifleman.	
Wharton, J. ...	90419	7/3/18	24/5/18, sick	Rifleman.	
✠Wharton, T. ...	72514	13/8/17	21/6/18, killed in action	Rifleman.	
Wheelan, J. ...	84711	24/8/17	3/1/18, sick	Rifleman.	
Whelan, W. ...	35879	24/8/17	5/3/19, demobilized ...	Rifleman	M.M.
Wheway, J. W. ...	27061	27/5/18	15/1/19, demobilized	Rifleman.	
✠Whipp, J. ...	63883	24/8/17	30/10/17, killed in action ...	Rifleman.	
Whiston, D. ...	13861	24/8/17	25/1/19, demobilized ...	Rifleman.	
Whitaker, J. M. ...	4819	26/1/16	12/2/17, commission ...	Rifleman.	
Whitby, L. ...	240599	1/9/14	12/7/17, transferred ...	Rifleman.	
Whitby, W. N. ...	2789	7/11/14	12/1/15, transferred ...	Rifleman.	
White, A. ...	50982	18/8/17	20/8/17, posted 2/8th K.L.R.	Rifleman.	
White, A. E. ...	242364	15/3/16	4/11/17, wounded ...	Rifleman	M.M.
White, G. H. ...	241263	16/3/15	21/8/17, wounded ...	Corporal.	
White, T. L. ...	2248	1/9/14	25/2/16, discharged ...	Rifleman.	
Whitehead, F. ...	48832	13/8/17	30/10/18, wounded ...	Rifleman.	
Whitehead, J. E. ...	241521	6/8/15	22/8/17, sick	Rifleman.	
Whitehead, W. ...	241289	9/4/15	3/8/17, invalided to England	Rifleman.	
Whitehouse, E. ...	88537	19/9/17	4/1/18, sick	Rifleman.	
Whitehouse, G. ...	2575	24/9/14	12/1/15, transferred ...	Rifleman.	
Whitehurst, J. G.	2448	14/9/14	5/8/15, transferred ...	Rifleman.	
Whitelaw, P. ...	4978	14/3/16	5/6/16, transferred ...	Rifleman.	
Whitfield, R. ...	240602	1/9/14	—/—/14, transferred ...	Rifleman.	
Whitley, H. ...	25723	27/6/18	22/5/19, demobilized ...	Corporal.	
Whittaker, A. ...	50830	18/8/17	5/10/18, wounded ...	Rifleman.	
Whittaker, E. N. ...	3072	20/11/14	16/9/15, commission ...	Rifleman.	
Whittaker, J. ...	2925	11/11/14	5/8/15, transferred ...	Rifleman.	
Whittaker, R. F. ...	110857	27/11/18	1/2/20, demobilized ...	Rifleman.	
Whittaker, S. ...	88212	8/11/17	9/9/18, transferred ...	Rifleman.	
Whittaker, — ...	2608	26/9/14	14/8/15, transferred ...	Rifleman.	
Whittall, H. N. ...	3105	25/11/14	26/6/15, transferred ...	Rifleman.	
Whittingham, R. ...	242462	27/3/16	28/3/19, posted 13th K.L.R.	Rifleman.	
✠Whittingham, T. ...	242530	24/5/16	1/11/17, died of wounds ...	Rifleman.	
Whittle, J. ...	90760	7/3/18	26/2/19, posted 25th K.L.R.	Rifleman.	
Whittle, W. ...	331606	27/5/18	4/9/18, wounded	Rifleman.	
Whitworth, A. ...	50831	18/8/17	11/7/18, posted 1/6th K.L.R.	Rifleman.	
Whitworth, C. ...	1585	23/2/15	26/6/15, transferred ...	Rifleman.	

AA 2

NAME.	REGTL. NO.	DATE OF JOINING.	DATE OF LEAVING WITH CAUSE.	HIGHEST RANK.	HONOURS OR AWARDS.
Whitworth, H. ...	243820	12/10/16	20/5/17,† transferred ...	Rifleman.	
Whyte, A. ...	31652	24/8/17	16/6/18, prisoner of war ...	Rifleman.	
Wicks, G. T. ...	9101	24/8/17	19/1/18, sick	Rifleman.	Belgian Croix de Guerre.
✠Wiggins, W. ...	241258	8/3/15	28/4/17, killed in action ...	Rifleman.	
Wightman, — ...	9174	27/2/15	5/4/15, transferred	Sergt./Instr.	
Wilcock, G. ...	243858	16/10/16	25/10/17,† transferred ...	Rifleman.	
Wilcox, F. W. ...	1499	27/2/15	26/6/15, transferred	Rifleman.	
Wild, G. H. ...	3669	6/8/15	18/3/16, transferred	Rifleman.	
Wild, V.	88114	5/10/17	19/2/18, transferred	Rifleman.	
Wilding, F. K. ...	2803	9/11/14	26/6/15, transferred	Rifleman.	
✠Wilding, J. C. ...	265818	27/5/18	12/9/18, killed in action ...	Rifleman.	
Wildman, A. ...	50819	18/8/17	13/11/17, wounded	L./Corpl.	
Wilkes, H. ...	88183	8/11/17	17/2/19, demobilized	Rifleman.	
Wilkinson, A. G. ...	2932	11/11/14	12/1/15, transferred	Rifleman.	
Wilkinson, F. ...	3736	6/8/15	23/9/16,† transferred ...	Rifleman.	
Wilkinson, J. ...	51947	13/8/17	22/1/19, demobilized	Rifleman.	
Wilkinson, P. ...	3104	25/11/14	26/6/15, transferred	Rifleman.	
Willett, D. E. ...	260176	20/9/17	30/5/18, wounded	Rifleman.	
Williams, A. ...	2253	1/9/14	13/3/17, discharged	Rifleman.	
Williams, A. E. ...	240274	23/2/15	10/8/17,† invalided to England	Rifleman.	
Williams, A. L. ...	2659	13/10/14	5/8/15, transferred	Rifleman.	
Williams, A. R. ...	3040	17/11/14	26/6/15, transferred	Rifleman.	
Williams, A. W. ...	2977	12/11/14	12/1/15, transferred	Rifleman.	
Williams, D. ...	2175	31/8/14	—/—/15, transferred	Rifleman.	
Williams, D. ...	242169	20/1/16	10/8/17, invalided to England	Rifleman.	
Williams, D. C. ...	2154	31/8/14	5/8/15, transferred	Rifleman.	
Williams, D. T. ...	2494	16/9/14	23/2/15, transferred	L./Corpl.	
Williams, E. ...	242355	13/3/16	15/9/17, posted 1/6th K.L.R.	Rifleman.	
Williams, E. H. ...	58054	27/6/18	17/1/19, demobilized ...	Rifleman.	
Williams, F. ...	2188	1/9/14	8/3/17, transferred	Rifleman.	
Williams, F. ...	3701	6/8/15	28/10/15, transferred ...	Rifleman.	
Williams, F. ...	3735	6/8/15	5/10/15, discharged	Rifleman.	
Williams, F. ...	242296	17/2/16	6/8/17, invalided to England	Rifleman.	
Williams, F. R. ...	242569	8/6/16	21/5/17, sick	Rifleman.	
Williams, G. ...	22290	13/8/17	11/5/18, sick	Rifleman.	
Williams, G. ...	36810	27/5/18	26/1/19, demobilized ...	Rifleman.	
Williams, G. ...	242295	17/2/16	22/8/17, wounded	Rifleman.	
Williams, G. H. ...	2669	7/10/14	10/6/15, transferred	Rifleman.	
Williams, H. ...	2055	31/8/14	30/1/15, commission	Rifleman.	
Williams, H. ...	22899	27/6/18	17/1/19, demobilized ...	Rifleman.	
Williams, H. ...	88196	8/11/17	8/3/19, demobilized	Rifleman.	
Williams, H. K. ...	3011	14/11/14	5/8/15, transferred	Rifleman.	
✠Williams, H. S. ...	241537	6/8/15	26/10/17, killed in action ...	Rifleman.	
Williams, H. V. ...	3307	22/3/15	8/12/15, transferred	Rifleman.	
Williams, I. L. ...	242238	22/1/16	1/11/17, wounded	Rifleman.	
Williams, J. ...	202439	23/2/18	30/9/18, sick	Rifleman.	
Williams, J. ...	241354	3/7/15	5/8/17,† invalided to England	Rifleman.	
Williams, J. ...	1179	23/2/15	26/6/15, transferred	Rifleman.	
Williams, J. E. ...	240474	23/10/14	15/3/19,† demobilized ...	Rifleman.	
Williams, J. G. ...	241189	8/1/15	5/8/17, wounded	Rifleman.	
Williams, J. H. ...	3225	18/1/15	15/3/17, transferred	Rifleman.	
Williams, J. L. ...	2841	9/11/14	5/8/15, transferred	Rifleman.	
Williams, L. ...	85069	1/2/18	13/3/18, sick	Rifleman.	
Williams, N. J. ...	2164	31/8/14	24/10/16, commission ...	Rifleman.	
Williams, O. ...	1599	27/2/15	26/6/15, transferred	Rifleman.	
Williams, R. ...	56843	13/8/17	1/12/17, sick	Rifleman.	
Williams, R. ...	88525	19/9/17	5/2/19, demobilized	Rifleman.	

"THE KING'S" (LIVERPOOL REGIMENT)

NAME.	REGTL. NO.	DATE OF JOINING.	DATE OF LEAVING WITH CAUSE.	HIGHEST RANK.	HONOURS OR AWARDS.
Williams, R. G. ...	242497	5/5/17	20/5/17, transferred	Rifleman.	
Williams, R. J. ...	350084	22/6/18	4/10/18, wounded	Rifleman.	
Williams, R. S. ...	1392	27/2/15	26/6/15, transferred ...	Rifleman.	
Williams, R. S. ...	241848	5/5/17	20/5/17, transferred ...	Rifleman.	
Williams, S. ...	240572	1/9/14	17/7/18, transferred ...	Rifleman.	
✠Williams, S. ...	50823	18/8/17	1/9/18, killed in action ...	Rifleman.	
Williams, S. ...	201342	1/2/18	4/3/18, posted 2/7th K.L.R.	Rifleman.	
Williams, T. A. ...	2394	10/9/14	29/11/15, commission ...	A./Sergt.	
Williams, T. H. ...	1588	23/10/14	30/8/15, transferred ...	Rifleman.	
Williams, T. J. ...	242254	25/1/16	4/9/18, transferred	Rifleman.	
Williams, W. E.	1267	27/2/15	1/6/17,† transferred	Rifleman.	
Williams, W. L. ...	2871	10/11/14	12/1/15, transferred ...	Rifleman.	
Williams, W. R. ...	2279	2/9/14	—/—/15, posted 1/6th K.L.R.	Rifleman.	
Williams, W. T. ...	2513	17/9/14	26/6/15, transferred ...	Rifleman.	
Williams, W. T. ...	3020	16/11/14	26/6/15, transferred ...	Rifleman.	
Williamson, J. ...	243705	9/10/16	20/5/17,† transferred	Rifleman.	
✠Williamson, R. ...	72518	24/8/17	30/10/17, killed in action	Rifleman.	
Williamson, R. ...	241077	14/11/14	5/8/17, invalided to England	Rifleman.	
Williamson, T. ...	36651	1/2/18	14/3/18, transferred	Rifleman.	
Willimas, T. ...	88526	19/9/17	29/8/18, posted 1st K.L.R. ...	Rifleman.	
Willimott, R. E. ...	2875	10/11/14	26/6/15, transferred ...	Rifleman.	
Willmott, J. R. ...	242319	1/3/16	17/1/18,† posted 13th K.L.R.	Rifleman.	
✠Willnow, A. J. ...	242440	23/3/16	23/10/18, died	Corporal.	
Willis, E. ...	29770	27/6/18	19/2/19, sick	Rifleman.	
Wilson, A. ...	2373	10/9/14	12/1/15, transferred ...	Rifleman.	
Wilson, A. ...	2771	6/11/14	12/1/15, transferred ...	Rifleman.	
Wilson, C. ...	88671	1/2/18	23/7/18, transferred ...	Rifleman.	
Wilson, C. L. ...	2197	1/9/14	5/2/16, commission ...	Rifleman.	
Wilson, D. ...	265400	10/10/17	14/6/18, sick	Rifleman.	
Wilson, E. ...	41264	13/8/17	26/2/19, posted 25th K.L.R.	Rifleman.	
Wilson, E. J. ...	2368	10/9/14	4/1/17, commission ...	Corporal.	
Wilson, F. M. ...	2224	1/9/14	—/—/14, transferred	Rifleman.	
Wilson, F. T. ...	50832	18/8/17	5/9/18, wounded	Rifleman.	
Wilson, H. W. ...	3188	5/1/15	16/8/15, transferred ...	Rifleman.	
Wilson, H. W. V. ...	6594	12/10/16	30/10/16, transferred ...	Rifleman.	
Wilson, J. ...	3050	17/11/14	26/6/15, transferred ...	Rifleman.	
Wilson, J. ...	28787	7/3/18	3/3/19, demobilized ...	Rifleman.	
✠Wilson, J. ...	243843	14/10/16	11/5/17, died of wounds ...	Rifleman.	
✠Wilson, J. ...	243865	18/10/16	30/9/18, killed in action ...	Rifleman.	
Wilson, J. E. ...	2223	1/9/14	—/—/15, transferred ...	Rifleman.	
Wilson, J. W. ...	2369	10/9/14	26/6/15, transferred ...	Rifleman.	
Wilson, L. ...	240678	10/9/14	3/8/17, invalided to England	L./Sergt.	
Wilson, P. ...	202687	22/6/18	19/10/18, posted 1/5th K.L.R.	Rifleman.	
Wilson, P. T. ...	260186	20/9/17	15/2/18, sick	Sergeant.	
Wilson, S. ...	406184	30/5/18	11/1/19, demobilized ...	Rifleman.	
Wilson, S. M. ...	2626	5/10/14	26/6/15, transferred ...	Rifleman.	
Wilson, T. ...	241187	8/1/15	22/1/19, demobilized ...	Rifleman.	
✠Wilson, W. ...	17739	24/8/17	16/5/18, died of wounds ...	L./Corpl.	
Wilson, W. C. ...	57852	27/5/18	8/7/18, sick	Rifleman.	
Wilson, W. E. ...	240113	27/2/15	15/7/18,† transferred	Rifleman.	
Windsor, C. ...	240758	17/9/14	5/8/17,† invalided to England	Rifleman.	
Windsor, W. ...	53497	27/6/18	22/1/19, demobilized ...	Rifleman.	
Wingrave, E. C. ...	242413	21/3/16	28/1/18, transferred ...	Rifleman.	
Winrow, J. ...	109101	28/9/18	14/12/18, demobilized ...	Rifleman.	
Winrow, T. ...	242293	17/2/16	7/8/17, wounded ...	Rifleman.	
Winspear, W. ...	3325	6/4/15	20/1/17, transferred ...	Rifleman.	
Winstanley, C. B. ...	241072	14/11/14	27/2/19, demobilized ...	L./Corpl.	M.M.
Winstanley, E. ...	88184	8/11/17	1/5/18, sick	Rifleman.	

357

NAME.	REGTL. NO.	DATE OF JOINING.	DATE OF LEAVING WITH CAUSE.	HIGHEST RANK.	HONOURS OR AWARDS.
Winstanley, J. R.	72414	1/2/18	11/12/18, demobilized ...	Rifleman.	
Winstanley, L. ...	2060	31/8/14	—/—/15, transferred ...	Rifleman.	
Winstanley, S. W.	2088	31/8/14	—/—/15, transferred ...	Rifleman.	
Winter, R.	243867	18/10/16	21/2/19, demobilized ...	Rifleman.	
Winters, W. ...	48039	27/5/18	26/2/19, posted 25th K.L.R.	Rifleman.	
Wisdell, A. J. ...	42927	24/8/17	5/3/19, demobilized	L./Corpl.	M.M.
Withers, H. R. ...	2313	10/9/14	20/5/15, commission	Rifleman.	
Wivell, J. ...	241065	13/11/14	1/3/19, demobilized	Sergeant.	
Wolfenden, J. T.	50824	18/8/17	8/9/18, wounded	Rifleman.	
Wolfson, J.	242209	21/1/16	24/6/17, wounded	L./Corpl.	
Wolstenholme, J. W.	88232	8/11/17	24/1/18, sick	Rifleman.	
Woltenscroft, T. N.	243743	9/10/16	17/9/17, posted 12th K.L.R.	Rifleman.	
Wood, A....	241295	12/4/15	10/8/17, invalided to England	Rifleman.	
Wood, A. H. ...	52125	27/5/18	26/3/19, demobilized ...	Rifleman.	
Wood, A. L. ...	1461	23/10/14	30/6/15, commission	Rifleman.	
Wood, B....	240679	10/9/14	17/9/17, commission	Rifleman.	
Wood, H. ...	50983	18/8/17	20/8/17, posted 2/8th K.L.R.	Rifleman.	
Wood, H. ...	8686	1/2/18	22/12/18, demobilized ...	Sergeant.	
Wood, W. H. ...	242340	6/3/16	9/8/17, invalided to England	Rifleman.	
Wood, W. ...	50984	18/8/17	20/8/17, posted 2/8th K.L.R.	Rifleman.	
Woodall, W. ...	88260	17/12/17	7/9/18, wounded	Rifleman.	
Woodcock, T. ...	50965	18/8/17	20/8/17, posted 2/8th K.L.R.	Rifleman.	
✠Wooding, F. ...	2857	10/11/14	19/6/15, died	Rifleman.	
Woodley, J. M. ...	242543	27/5/16	31/3/17, invalided to England	Rifleman.	
Woods, E. ...	241366	3/7/15	29/8/18,† posted 1st K.L.R.	Rifleman.	
Woods, J. J. ...	2222	1/9/14	—/—/14, posted 1/6th K.L.R.	Rifleman.	
Woods, R. A. ...	240498	31/8/14	30/6/17, transferred ...	Rifleman.	
Woods, T. ...	22890	22/6/18	11/2/19, demobilized ...	Corporal.	
Woods, W. F. ...	241198	12/1/15	18/8/17, wounded	Rifleman.	
Woodward, A. ...	22891	22/6/18	22/1/19, demobilized ...	Rifleman.	
Woodward, R. J.	241159	8/12/14	11/10/18, wounded	C.S.M.	M.S.M.
Woodworth, A. ...	1431	27/2/15	26/6/15, transferred ...	Rifleman.	
Woodworth, J. ...	240761	10/9/14	12/8/17, wounded	Rifleman.	
Wooley, J. ...	1928	23/10/14	5/8/15, transferred ...	Rifleman.	
Woollam, F. ...	201104	27/6/18	29/9/18, sick	Rifleman.	
Woolrich, A. V. ...	242426	22/3/16	6/9/18, wounded	Rifleman.	
Woosey, J. H. ...	243875	14/4/17	30/4/17, posted 1st K.L.R. ...	Rifleman.	
Woosey, J. M. ...	331069	26/1/19	29/3/19, demobilized ...	Sergeant.	
Woosey, J. S. ...	2856	9/11/14	26/6/15, transferred ...	Rifleman.	
Wooten, H. W. ...	88536	19/9/17	7/4/18, sick	Rifleman.	
Worden, J. ...	28214	27/6/18	25/10/18, wounded	L./Corpl.	
Worrall, B. ...	51886	13/8/17	30/3/19, demobilized ...	Rifleman.	
Worsley, H. W. ...	50820	18/8/17	29/3/18, transferred ...	Rifleman.	
Worsley, W. ...	49254	24/2/18	11/2/19, demobilized ...	Rifleman.	
Worsley, W. ...	88221	8/11/17	25/4/18, sick	Rifleman.	
Worthington, J.	108853	28/9/18	21/7/19, transferred ...	Rifleman.	
Worthington, J. H.	4754	21/1/16	5/6/16, transferred	Rifleman.	
Worthington, S.	242775	8/7/17	28/3/19, posted 13th K.L.R.	Rifleman.	
Worthington, W. H.	330106	28/9/18	4/1/19, sick	Rifleman.	
Wragg, T. E. H.	241243	16/2/15	9/8/17,† invalided to England	Rifleman.	
Wren, W. J. ...	1981	23/10/14	26/6/15, transferred ...	Rifleman.	
Wright, A. E. ...	2949	11/11/14	5/8/15, transferred ...	Rifleman.	
Wright, A. L. ...	84818	1/2/18	17/1/19, sick	Rifleman.	
Wright, E. ...	88207	8/11/17	29/8/18, posted 1st K.L.R. ...	Rifleman.	
Wright, G. ...	57966	27/5/18	21/6/18, sick	Rifleman.	
Wright, G. ...	235032	22/6/18	12/2/19, demobilized ...	Rifleman.	
Wright, H. ...	242163	20/1/16	26/6/17, commission	Rifleman.	
Wright, H. A. ...	57854	22/6/18	20/1/19, demobilized ...	L./Corpl.	

NAME.	REGTL. NO.	DATE OF JOINING.	DATE OF LEAVING WITH CAUSE.	HIGHEST RANK.	HONOURS OR AWARDS.
Wright, J.	50986	18/8/17	20/8/17, posted 2/8th K.L.R.	Rifleman.	
Wright, J.	242356	13/3/16	28/3/19, posted 13th K.L.R.	Rifleman.	
Wright, J. C.	241151	2/12/14	5/8/17,† invalided to England	B.Q.M.S.	
Wright, J. H.	241122	23/11/14	13/2/19,† sick	Sergeant.	
Wright, R. H.	23872	22/6/18	16/9/18, wounded	Rifleman.	
Wright, S.	2683	20/10/14	25/10/15, discharged	Rifleman.	
✠Wright, W.	243791	11/10/16	29/9/18, died of wounds	Rifleman.	
Wright, W. W.	2786	7/11/14	5/8/15, transferred	Rifleman.	
Wrigley, E. J.	2544	21/9/14	26/6/15, transferred	Rifleman.	
Wyatt, C. T. A.	3182	4/1/14	13/5/15, commission	A./Sergt.	
Wylde-Brown, H.	260178	20/9/17	17/11/17, commission	Rifleman.	
Wynn, A.	242252	25/1/16	21/10/19, demobilized	L./Corpl.	
Wynne, W.	242382	18/3/16	5/11/17, wounded	L./Corpl.	
Yarrington, T. E.	2206	1/9/14	—/—/14, transferred	Rifleman.	
Yates, F. S.	241125	23/11/14	1/1/19, sick	Corporal.	
Yates, J.	243731	9/10/16	24/6/17, sick	Rifleman.	
Yates, J.	306321	8/7/17	5/6/18, sick	Corporal.	
Yates, W.	88192	8/11/17	1/8/18, posted 12th K.L.R.	Rifleman.	
Yeates, J. S.	201016	14/9/18	3/3/19, demobilized	Rifleman.	
Yeo, S.	35836	13/8/17	12/6/18, sick	Rifleman.	
York, S.	22904	22/6/18	29/3/19, demobilized	Rifleman.	
Young, A.	50987	18/8/17	20/8/17, posted 2/8th K.L.R.	Rifleman.	
Young, C. C.	1372	27/2/15	26/6/15, transferred	Rifleman.	
Young, H.	2140	31/8/14	—/—/15, transferred	Rifleman.	
✠Young, J.	204022	1/2/18	1/9/18, killed in action	Rifleman.	
Young, J. G.	57744	27/5/18	8/1/19, demobilized	L./Sergt.	
Young, W. R.	241200	13/1/15	4/8/17, invalided to England	Rifleman.	

INDEX

OF PERSONS AND PRINCIPAL PLACES

Only leading references are given.

INDEX

Bowring, Capt. F. C., 102, 123, 127, 138, 169, 185, 270, 279
Boyelles, 218
Bradley, Rfmn. F., 184
Bray, Brig.-Gen. R. N., C.M.G., D.S.O., 64, 128, 133
Brettell, 2/Lieut. I. P., 249
Bridge Camp, 145
Brigade—Reserve Liverpool Inf., 6; 170th Inf., *passim*; 171st Inf., *passim*; 172nd Inf., *passim*; 190th Inf., 216
Brighouse, 2/Lieut. J. W., 159
Broad, Capt. A. H., 129, 159, 184
Broad, Capt. W. H., 2, 5
Broadwood, Lieut.-Gen. R. G., C.B., 23, 104
Brookes, Major W. H., M.C., 59, 80, 103
Brookes, Rfmn., 253
Brookwood, 28, 31
Brown, L./Cpl. A. S., 270
Brunner, L./Cpl. E. W. D., 3
Buckley, L./Cpl. W. S., 93
Buffs, The, 7th Bn., 150
Buissy, 209, 217
Bullecourt, 208, 211
Bullock, Capt. O. H., 250
Burden, Rfmn. A., 93
Burton, Lieut. K. H., 115, 159, 192, 269, 278
Bus Les Artois, 198
Busnes, 131
Byng, Gen. Lord, G.C.B., 230, 231

C.

Cadman, Sergt. B., 248, 278
Cagnicourt, 208
Calais, 146
Calonne, 131
Cambrai, 226, 229; second Battle of, 215
Cameronians, 7th Bn., 218
Canadian E.F., 205, 220; 2nd Division, 216; 72nd Bn., 199; 85th Bn., 202
Canal Bank Camp, 148
Canal de L'Escaut, 220, 223
Canal du Nord, 216, 220
Cantaing, 220
Canterbury, 8, 13
Carr, Capt. J. C., 129, 242
Carvin, 255
Cathels, L./Cpl. H., 67
Cathrell, Cpl. T., 278

Chambers, L./Cpl. J. W., M.M., 223
Chapelle D'Armentières, 60
Chateau de la Haie, 180, 185
Chat Maigre, Le, 205
" Cheerio," 219
" Cheerios," The, 219, 249, 253
Chelers, 205
Chertsey, 25
Cinq Chemins, Les, 149
Clarke, Rfmn. B., M.M., 195
Clarke, Lieut. C. W., M.C., 101, 123, 141, 278
Clarke, Capt. W. R., 5, 10
Cohen, Lieut.-Col. J. B., 64
Coigneux, 178
Collinge, Lieut. W. R., 123
Collins, Rfmn., 93
Comforts Fund, Battalion, 155, 257
Connaught, H.R.H. Duke of, 28
Cooper, Rfmn. W., 253, 272
Copland, L./Cpl. W. O., 277
Cordonnerie, 128
Corkill, Sergt. N. L., M.M., 82, 114, 184, 270
Cormack, Sergt. F. J., 3
Couin, 178, 192, 198
Cousins, R.Q.M.S. G., 188, 272
Cowie, Rfmn. A. C., 276
Cox, Sergt. J., 162, 198, 273
Croisilles, 218
Croix du Bac, 101
Cufflin, 2/Lieut. C. A., 249

D.

Dainville, 260
Darcy, L./Cpl. H., 270
Davies, Rfmn. J. N. C., 8
Davis, Cpl., 275
De Chauny, Mons., 173
Derby, Earl of, K.G., 261
Derry, Major A., D.S.O., 64
Director of Education, Liverpool, 258
Division—Guards, 216, 220; Home Counties, 20; 12th, 170; 38th, 164; 47th, 234; 52nd, 210, 218, 220; 57th, *passim*; 58th, 143; 59th, 238; 62nd, 196; 3rd, 216, 220; 74th, 238
Dixon, Rfmn. G., 114
Dobell, Lieut. R. L., 10
Dodd, Rfmn. H. S., M.M., 214
Donaldson, Rfmn. T., M.M., 195
" Dons," The, 55, 254
Douai, 200
Doullens, 172, 174, 175

362

INDEX

INDEX

INDEX

INDEX

INDEX

INDEX

Lightning Source UK Ltd.
Milton Keynes UK
UKHW050626080620
364539UK00002B/21